Foreign Affairs Federalism

Foreign Affairs Federalism

The Myth of National Exclusivity

MICHAEL J. GLENNON

ROBERT D. SLOANE

OXFORD
UNIVERSITY PRESS

OXFORD
UNIVERSITY PRESS

Oxford University Press is a department of the University of Oxford. It furthers the University's objective of excellence in research, scholarship, and education by publishing worldwide.

Oxford New York
Auckland Cape Town Dar es Salaam Hong Kong Karachi Kuala Lumpur Madrid Melbourne Mexico City Nairobi New Delhi Shanghai Taipei Toronto

With offices in
Argentina Austria Brazil Chile Czech Republic France Greece Guatemala Hungary Italy Japan Poland Portugal Singapore South Korea Switzerland Thailand Turkey Ukraine Vietnam

Oxford is a registered trademark of Oxford University Press in the UK and certain other countries.

Published in the United States of America by
Oxford University Press
198 Madison Avenue, New York, NY 10016

Library of Congress Cataloging-in-Publication Data

Names: Glennon, Michael J., 1947- author. | Sloane, Robert D., author.
Title: Foreign affairs federalism : the myth of national exclusivity /
Michael J. Glennon, Robert D. Sloane.
Description: New York : Oxford University Press, 2016. |
Includes bibliographical references and index.
Identifiers: LCCN 2015039708 | ISBN 9780199941490 (hardback)
Subjects: LCSH: United States—Foreign relations—Law and legislation. |
International relations—United States—States. | Federal
government—United States. | Constitutional law—United States—States. |
Treaty-making power—United States—States.
Classification: LCC KF4651 .G595 2016 | DDC 342.73/0412—dc23 LC record available at
http://lccn.loc.gov/2015039708

Note to Readers

This publication is designed to provide accurate and authoritative information in regard to the subject matter covered. It is based upon sources believed to be accurate and reliable and is intended to be current as of the time it was written. It is sold with the understanding that the publisher is not engaged in rendering legal, accounting, or other professional services. If legal advice or other expert assistance is required, the services of a competent professional person should be sought. Also, to confirm that the information has not been affected or changed by recent developments, traditional legal research techniques should be used, including checking primary sources where appropriate.

(Based on the Declaration of Principles jointly adopted by a Committee of the American Bar Association and a Committee of Publishers and Associations.)

For Joanna, William, Fiona, Miranda, and Alice

Summary Table of Contents

Detailed Table of Contents

Preface

FOREIGN AFFAIRS FEDERALISM refers to the constitutional allocation of foreign affairs powers between the federal government and the states. The purpose of this book is twofold. The first is to explain the current law clearly and accessibly. We identify those areas where the law can be ascertained with confidence, and, where it cannot be, we suggest what we regard as the most plausible or compelling perspectives on existing doctrine. The second is to appraise existing doctrine against the background of the diverse and at times incompatible goals of—as well as challenges facing—the United States in the twenty-first century.

One objective of this book is to highlight three pervasive myths about foreign affairs federalism. The first myth afflicts federalism in constitutional discourse generally but has special force in the realm of foreign affairs: that federalism has a particular political valence. It is commonly thought that more state power means more conservative policies and that less state power (or more federal power) means more liberal policies. The second myth is that a meaningful distinction can be drawn between domestic and foreign affairs. The third myth, related to the second, is that the realm of foreign affairs is, and should be, exclusively federal.

Whatever kernel of truth these myths may have held in the past, they do not accurately describe the state of affairs in the United States in the twenty-first century. Nor, we suggest, is this cause for regret.

The idea that "states' rights" means conservative politics originated in the mid-nineteenth century. The Civil War took place within the context of a quintessential liberal-conservative divide over slavery. The federal government sought to preserve national political union in the face of the alleged right to secede on which the eleven states constituting the Confederacy insisted. A century later, especially in the 1950s and 1960s, a similar federal-state divide not only persisted but took on a reinvigorated prominence in the politics of the era. Governmental opposition to the civil rights movement emanated largely from states, cities, school boards, and other local government institutions. Battles over issues such as school desegregation and integrated public transportation, housing, and dining facilities were waged primarily by state against federal authorities, although of course recalcitrant states also sought to influence these battles through a small but vocal group of congressional representatives. Today, the myth that state control equates with conservative—and federal with liberal—political causes is reinforced by state efforts to curtail illegal immigration, deny homosexuals the right to marry, limit abortion rights, and implement similar policies.

Reality, however, is far more complex. State governments span the liberal-conservative spectrum. Many recent state initiatives, particularly in the realm of foreign affairs, have been more liberal than anything emerging from inside the beltway. States have limited greenhouse gas emissions consistent with the Kyoto Protocol,[1] despite the Senate's refusal to approve the Protocol. Cities have declared themselves nuclear free zones or sanctuaries for illegal immigrants. Years before the federal government passed the 1986 Comprehensive Anti-Apartheid Act,[2] California and various localities nationwide stopped investing money from state pension funds in apartheid South Africa.[3] Massachusetts limited the authority of its agencies to purchase goods and services from companies doing business with the autocratic government of Myanmar (Burma) several months before Congress enacted a federal law to similar effect. As discussed in Chapter 9, the Supreme Court later found the Massachusetts statute preempted by federal law under the Supremacy Clause.[4]

Other state and local actions that may touch upon foreign affairs have no obvious conservative or liberal implications. One example is a California law that required insurers doing business in that state to disclose information about policies sold in Europe between 1920 and 1945. The Supreme Court struck down this statute,[5] too, although on far more questionable grounds, as discussed in

---

1. Kyoto Protocol to the United Nations Framework Convention on Climate Change, Dec. 11, 1997, 37 I.L.M. 32 (1998) (entered into force Feb. 16, 2005). In 2006, for example, California entered into a memorandum of understanding with the United Kingdom to limit emissions. *See Blair Signs Climate Pact with Schwarzenegger*, THE GUARDIAN, Aug. 1, 2006, http://www.theguardian.com/environment/2006/aug/01/greenpolitics.usnews. In 2015, eleven U.S. states and foreign subnational governments, including California, Vermont, Oregon, and Washington, and local governments in Canada, Germany, Brazil, and Mexico, agreed to limit their emissions by 80 to 95 percent by 2050. *See California, International Leaders Sign Climate Change Agreement*, REUTERS, May 19, 2015, http://uk.reuters.com/article/2015/05/19/us-climate-change-agreements-idUKKBN0O42IV20150519.

2. Comprehensive Anti-Apartheid Act of 1986, Pub. L. No. 99-440, 100 Stat. 1086 (1986).

3. *See* Bd. of Trustees of the Emps. Retirement Sys. v. Mayor of Baltimore City, 562 A.2d 720 (Md. 1989); Constitutionality of South African Divestment Statutes Enacted by State and Local Governments, 10 U.S. Op. Off. Legal Counsel 49 (1986).

4. Crosby v. Nat'l Foreign Trade Council, 530 U.S. 363 (2000).

5. Am. Ins. Ass'n v. Garamendi, 539 U.S. 396 (2003).

Chapter 4. Beyond those cases involving state or local action in the realm of foreign affairs that have reached the courts, Chapter 2 canvasses a broad range of state and local actions in foreign affairs and, in the process, refutes the claim that states pursue *either* conservative *or* liberal policies in foreign affairs.

The second myth—that we can readily distinguish domestic and foreign affairs—also originated early in U.S. constitutional history. From the outset, federal practice under the new Constitution reflected this supposed distinction. President George Washington appointed Thomas Jefferson as his secretary of state and assigned him the task of handling international issues, and early in the nineteenth century, the Senate established the Committee on Foreign Relations, and the House of Representatives the Committee on Foreign Affairs. The supposition that there exists a neat distinction between domestic and foreign affairs, although more defensible and doubtless expedient in 1789 and the early nineteenth century, regrettably persists today in the academy, politics, and government. Dedicated specialist journals such as *Foreign Affairs* and *International Security* inform the international cognoscenti of pioneering thought in the many and diverse fields subsumed by the label "foreign affairs." Leading academic institutions establish departments in the equally broad field of international relations, which overlaps substantially with political science, law, economics, and numerous other disciplines. Departments of international relations offer a wide variety of popular courses to students captivated by the significance and seeming romance of foreign studies and by the excitement of travel and study abroad programs. The idea that international and domestic affairs are easily differentiated continues to exercise a firm grip on intellectual and political life in the United States.

Here again, however, this assumption is a fiction. As early as 1974, long before the emergence of "globalization" (a term we analyze in greater depth later), the estimable former chairman of the Senate Foreign Relations Committee, J. William Fulbright, noted the avalanche of commentary celebrating (or bemoaning) the blurring of national boundaries. He remarked that "[i]t has ceased to be useful, if it ever was, to deal with foreign policy as a category distinct from domestic policy."[6] A moment's reflection shows why. Consider the issue of economic assistance to developing countries. Contrary to popular belief, most such assistance is spent *within* the United States and measurably stimulates the U.S. economy. Or consider arms sales to foreign countries. What may at first blush seem like a paradigmatic foreign policy issue turns out to be much more complex. Arms sales abroad fuel a massive domestic industry that provides skilled jobs to thousands of Americans and exerts a nontrivial influence on the U.S. economy.

---

6. J. William Fulbright, *What Is the National Interest?*, THE CTR. MAG. 40, 41 (Jan.–Feb. 1974).

Conversely, consider several putative local issues. Suppose that state or local legislators decide that all students must pass a course in calculus to graduate from high school. This requirement would directly affect the comparative prospects for the American labor force in an intensely competitive global economy. Or consider state healthcare requirements, which, notwithstanding the federal Patient Protection and Affordable Care Act,[7] remain robust and, so it would seem, fall squarely within the province of traditional state laws governing domestic matters such as the health, safety, and welfare of a state's population. But state healthcare requirements also add to the cost of products competing within global markets and influence decisions by multinational businesses on where to establish their headquarters or local offices. Or consider state privacy laws, which typically govern official authority to secretly record the telephone conversations (and, today, also the emails and other forms of communication) of state residents. Increasingly, many of those communications involve persons not only in other states but in foreign nations.

Finally, consider the weighty legal questions that vex the formulation of counterterrorism strategy, which is surely, at first glance, a classic topic of foreign rather than domestic policy. Flying an airplane into a building and killing three thousand people is of course criminal. But by and large, it is criminal because of *state* laws, which criminalize, among other conduct, murder and property destruction. And those crimes were perpetrated against not only the U.S. citizens killed or injured in the terrorist attacks of September 11, 2001, but also against nearly four hundred foreign nationals from about eighty foreign countries.[8] It is not for nothing that the cabinet officer charged with principal responsibility for counterterrorism policy is called the Secretary of *Homeland* Security. Nor is it coincidental that a focal point of the debate on how to fight terrorism is whether it is properly conceptualized as crime or war, as a responsibility of the military or of law enforcement. International and domestic security turn out, in the end, to be not all that different.

The third myth is related: that foreign policy is or should be, with a few minor and inconsequential exceptions, exclusively federal. American lawyers internalize this fiction first in law school. Law courses often draw an artificial distinction between state and federal law, even though the law in particular areas—such as corporate regulations and criminal prohibitions—frequently overlaps and

7. Patient Protection and Affordable Care Act, Pub. L. No. 111-148, 124 Stat. 119-1025 (2010).

8. Gaby Leslie, *Facts You Probably Didn't Know about 9/11*, Yahoo News, Sept. 5, 2011, https://uk.news.yahoo.com/ten-interesting-facts-you-probably-didn%E2%80%99t-know-about-9-11.html#AULg0J2.

interacts. Relative to foreign affairs, in particular, few fictions become more firmly implanted in the psyches of American lawyers, inculcated over the years by scores of familiar *ipse dixit*s of the Supreme Court and the popular media. Unexamined dicta are repeated—often acontextually—from decisions dating back to the nineteenth century and continuing to the present. "It was one of the main objects of the Constitution to make us, so far as regarded our foreign relations, one people, one nation," as the Court said in 1840.[9] "For local interests the several states of the union exist," it said in 1889, but "for national purposes, embracing our relations with foreign nations, we are but one nation, one people, one power."[10] "[I]n respect of our foreign relations generally, state lines disappear," it said in 1937. "As to such purposes the state . . . does not exist."[11] "Power over external affairs is not shared with the States," it said in 1942; "it is vested in the national government exclusively."[12] And again, in 2012, the Court announced that "where foreign affairs is at issue, the practical need for the United States to speak 'with one voice and ac[t] as one,' is particularly important."[13] The popular media have absorbed and often reiterate this myth. A 2012 *New York Times* editorial attacking Arizona's immigration law, for example, captured the popular understanding of state competence in the constitutional scheme. "By the framers' intent, foreign-policy making is entrusted to the federal government through presidential and Congressional powers," the *Times* opined. "That authority is exclusive, barring any state intrusion."[14]

These and other sweeping, absolutist pronouncements have only the flimsiest connection with what modern state and local governments actually *do*.[15] The Constitution empowers the federal government to exercise *potentially plenary*

---

9. Holmes v. Jennison, 39 U.S. (14 Pet.) 540, 575–76 (1840).

10. The Chinese Exclusion Case, 130 U.S. 581, 606 (1889); *cf.* THE FEDERALIST NO. 42, at 279 (James Madison) (Jacob E. Cooke ed., 1961) ("If we are to be one nation in any respect, it clearly ought to be in respect to other nations.").

11. United States v. Belmont, 301 U.S. 324, 331 (1937).

12. United States v. Pink, 315 U.S. 203, 233 (1942); *see also* Zschernig v. Miller, 389 U.S. 429, 442 (1968) (Stewart, J., concurring) (finding that provisions of Oregon law "launch the state upon a prohibited voyage into a domain of exclusively federal competence").

13. Zivotofsky *ex rel.* Zivotofsky v. Clinton, 132 S. Ct. 1421, 1438 (2012); *see also* Zivotofsky *ex rel.* Zivotofsky v. Kerry, 135 S. Ct. 2076 (2015).

14. *An Invitation to Abuse and Chaos*, N.Y. TIMES, Apr. 21, 2012, http://www.nytimes.com/2012/04/22/opinion/sunday/an-invitation-to-abuse-and-chaos.html?_r=0.

15. *See* Edward T. Swaine, *Negotiating Federalism: State Bargaining and the Dormant Treaty Power*, 49 DUKE L.J. 1127, 1134 (2000) (noting the "profound dissonance between theory and practice").

authority in foreign relations, but it does not contemplate *exclusive* authority in this realm by *default*—nor, as a practical matter, could it.[16] The distinction is crucial. The text of the Constitution often leaves decisions about the allocation of foreign relations authority between the state and federal governments to the latter's discretion. But in the exercise of that discretion, the federal government often does *not*, in fact, choose to exclude the states; concurrent authority is relatively common. It is, of course, a truism that the Constitution vastly increased the federal government's powers in foreign relations as compared to the Articles of Confederation, and as we discuss in Chapter 1, these changes were indispensable to the resolution of some of the most serious defects in the Articles.[17] But neither the Framers nor the Constitution they painstakingly drafted proposed a rigid division between the respective foreign affairs roles of the state and national governments. Equally significant, categorical pronouncements such as those quoted above ignore the real-life day-to-day conduct of state and local governments. In fact, state activities in the realm of foreign affairs have become so common as to call to mind the old story of the preacher asked whether he believed in baptism by immersion. "Believe in it?" he responded, "Hell, I've seen it!"

A survey of what states and cities actually do in the international realm will be left to Chapter 2. Suffice it to say here that their foreign affairs initiatives are frequent in number, broad in scope, and extensive in effect. To cite just a few examples, states and cities have implemented unratified treaties (including the Kyoto Protocol[18] and the Convention on the Elimination of All Forms of Discrimination Against Women[19]), taken stands on myriad foreign policy questions (from Vietnam to Nicaragua to the proposed nuclear weapons freeze), concluded oil import agreements with foreign countries, established local offices to represent them abroad,[20] demanded that foreign corporations come up with

16. Jack Goldsmith, *Federal Courts, Foreign Affairs, and Federalism*, 83 VA. L. REV. 1617, 1619 (1997).

17. Indeed, despite the Confederacy's emphasis on the rights of its constituent states, "[e]ven the Constitution of the Confederate States continued virtually the same limitations on the states in regard to foreign relations as are in the United States Constitution." LOUIS HENKIN, FOREIGN AFFAIRS AND THE US CONSTITUTION 422 n.2 (2d ed. 1996). *Compare* U.S. CONST. art. I, § 10, *with* CONFED. CONST. art. I, § 10.

18. Judith Resnick et al., *Ratifying Kyoto at the Local Level: Sovereigntism, Federalism, and Translocal Organizations of Government Actors*, 50 ARIZ. L. REV. 709, 719 (2008).

19. Andrew Stelzer, *Gender: For U.S., Lessons in CEDAW from San Francisco*, INTER PRESS SERV., Nov. 25, 2009, http://www.ipsnews.net/2009/11/gender-for-us-lessons-in-cedaw-from-san-francisco/.

20. *See generally* EARL FRY, THE EXPANDING ROLE OF STATE AND LOCAL GOVERNMENTS IN U.S. FOREIGN AFFAIRS (2d ed. 1998).

comprehensive written plans to protect the personal data of state residents, and used sister-city relationships to advance human rights agendas abroad.[21]

At first blush, one might think state and city officials responsible for such actions simply lack sufficient regard for the Constitution or knowledge of the Supreme Court's interpretation of it. But another—and, we suggest, more accurate—interpretation would be that we are witnessing institutional gravity in action as political water seeks its lowest point: these officials have been doing what seems to them to be necessary or prudent for their localities, what their constituents want—and what Congress, after all, has seldom demanded that they stop doing.

To be clear, we do not suggest that the states either do or should have carte blanche to act in the realm of foreign policy—even were this realm capable of more precise demarcation. No one questions, for example, Congress's authority to preempt state initiatives by legislating within the scope of its Article I powers, including those foreign affairs powers it shares with the president. Nor does anyone question executive authority to preempt state measures by the exercise of those constitutional powers vested exclusively in the president by Article II.[22] Similarly, valid treaties made by the president with the advice and consent of the Senate may preempt state laws.[23] And finally, all the familiar constitutional limits on governmental power generally, including but not limited to those enumerated in the Bill of Rights,[24] limit what state governments may do internationally. We discuss these limits in Chapter 9 and elsewhere as they arise.

---

21. As the book went to press, Tumwater, Washington, was considering whether to end a sister-city relationship because of anti-homosexual laws in Uganda. Andy Hobbs, *Tumwater Might End Sister-City Relationship with Ugandan Town*, SEATTLE TIMES, May 17, 2014, http://seattletimes.com/html/localnews/2023610754_tumwatersistercityxml.html. *See also* Brandon Howell, *Lansing Council Votes to End St. Petersburg, Russia Sister City Relationship over Gay Rights Violations*, MICH. LIVE, Aug. 12, 2013, lansing_council_votes_to_end_st_petersburg_russia_sister_city_ties_over_gay_rights_violations.

22. The scope of the "executive power," U.S. CONST. art. II, § 1, remains a source of continuing controversy. *Compare* Saikrishna B. Prakash & Michael D. Ramsay, *The Executive Power over Foreign Affairs*, 111 YALE L.J. 231 (2001), *with* Curtis A. Bradley & Martin S. Flaherty, *Executive Power Essentialism and Foreign Affairs*, 102 MICH. L. REV. 545 (2004).

23. *See* U.S. CONST. art. II, § 2, cl. 2.; *id.* art. VI, cl. 2. That said, renewed controversy over the scope of the treaty power in the context of federalism, culminating in the Supreme Court's recent decision in *Bond v. United States*, 134 S. Ct. 2077 (2014), persists. We discuss *Bond* in Chapter 6. The extent to which the president may validly preempt state law by entering into a sole executive agreement—or indeed, perhaps even by merely expressing a federal policy or preference on a particular issue, *see American Insurance Ass'n v. Garamendi*, 539 U.S. 396 (2003), also remains the subject of vigorous debate. See Chapter 4.

24. *Cf.* Reid v. Covert, 354 U.S. 1 (1957).

Yet in recent years, the Supreme Court has not honored the long-standing presumption *against* preemption. We will suggest that preemption ought to be applied more narrowly than it has been in recent foreign-affairs federalism cases. We will also suggest that the Court ought not overturn what states do within the international realm—as it has recently—under the guise of enforcing an ill-conceived dormant foreign-affairs doctrine. Nor should it routinely invoke a broad conception of the dormant Foreign Commerce Clause to preempt state commercial regulations. We discuss these issues in Chapters 4 and 5, respectively.

Perhaps, at the extreme margins, the Court should properly police these judgments in unusual cases that arise in unforeseeable circumstances and in the face of congressional and presidential silence. But as a rule, settled constitutional principles allocate such decisions to the political branches of the federal and state governments. We should be leery of giving the judiciary power to adjudicate the allocation of foreign affairs authority as between the federal and state governments under indeterminate or vague standards, because in so doing, even with the best of intentions, courts too often wander out of their lane. The difficulty in distinguishing foreign from domestic affairs, as others have pointed out, could subject virtually any state law to judicial invalidation, resulting in a massive transfer of lawmaking power to the federal courts at the expense of the states.[25] The Court ought to decide these and other foreign affairs questions, not by giving controlling force to factitious distinctions—such as the notion that state activities can be classified as inherently international or domestic—but by considering, at the outset, whether as a practical matter the activity can and should be judicially controlled in a consistent and principled fashion.[26] A paramount objective, we suggest, should be to simplify constitutional analysis—to provide greater predictability, giving everyone who cares as much notice as possible about what's permissible and what's not.

It may sound as though this book will be yet another conceit that the Supreme Court would do a better job if only the courts heeded the advice of law professors. We hope it will not be. Much of the book is devoted simply to exposition of existing legal doctrine. It is an effort, above all, to explore and clarify what the law of foreign affairs federalism *is* in the early twenty-first century. Only then do we offer, we hope with due modesty, arguments and tentative suggestions about how the law might be refined for the better. But understanding the law—its origins, limits, evolution, and rationales—is a necessary first step in any informed

25. *See* Jack Goldsmith, *Statutory Foreign Affairs Preemption*, 2001 Sup. Ct. Rev. 175 (2001).

26. *Cf.* United States v. Lopez, 514 U.S. 549, 615 (Breyer, J., dissenting).

critique of where it arguably went wrong or how it might be improved. At any rate, we expect that many readers seek, first and foremost, not a polemical blueprint for how the law should be changed, but a clear understanding of what the law currently permits and prohibits—and what remains unclear. It is chiefly for these readers—including state and federal legislators and their staffs, city council members, state and federal lawyers, corporate counsel facing regulatory issues, judges, and students of the Constitution trying to sort it all out—that this book is written.

Acknowledgments

WE ARE INDEBTED to a number of individuals and organizations for help in preparing this book. Matthew Hoisington, Julie Krosnicki, Angela Linhardt, Robert Konkel, Margot Marston, Seth Pate, Emma Wright, Jonathan Hempton, Shea Miller, Ashley Novak, Jaclyn Reinhart, and Christopher Walczyszyn gave unstintingly of time and talent in providing research assistance. Thanks also to Gary Lawson and Mike Dorf for helpful comments on Chapter 6. Chapter 10 is reprinted with the permission of the *Policy Review*, in which an earlier version appeared as "State-Level Cybersecurity" in February/March 2012. That article was supported by a grant from the Hitachi Foundation. Chapter 6 is reprinted with the permission of the *Yale Journal of International Law*, in which an earlier version appeared as "The Sad, Quiet Death of *Missouri v. Holland*: How *Bond* Hobbled the Treaty Power," Originally published by *The Yale Journal of International Law*, Vol. 41 (2016).

Mostly, we are indebted to our families, whose support and understanding made this book possible, and to whom it is dedicated.

I

Why Empower States?

WHY HAVE STATES? Most nations don't. Chile, the People's Republic of China, France, Greece, Israel, Japan, the Netherlands, Spain, Sweden, and Turkey, among others, do not. Their national authorities govern their respective nations as a unit. Those nations generally manage just fine; to the extent they don't, the fault seldom lies with their unitary models of governance. In contrast, the United States is one of a handful of federal nations. Others include Australia, Brazil, Canada, Germany, India, Mexico, Russia, and Switzerland. Federal nations comprise a federation of states,[1] local polities within the nation differentiated by territorial boundaries within which they exercise a degree of political autonomy from the national government.

Some of the Framers of the Constitution and their countrymen apparently believed that they were the first free agents to design a new government. John Adams, for example, captured this shared sense of good fortune when he remarked, "You and I, my dear friend, have been sent into life at a time when the greatest lawgivers of antiquity would have wished to live."[2] "In no age before," wrote one American historian in 1789, "in no other country, did man ever possess an election of the kind of government under which he would choose to live."[3] Earlier free governments, he wrote, had been "thrown together by accident."[4] In

---

1. The nomenclature differs among countries. Local polities within a nation may be called provinces, cantons, Länders, oblasts, or otherwise. Even within the United States, some states—Massachusetts, Kentucky, Virginia, and Pennsylvania—choose to self-identify as "commonwealths."

2. John Adams, *Thoughts on Government*, The John Harvard Library (Pamphlet No. 65) 27 (1776), *quoted in* BERNARD BAILYN, THE IDEOLOGICAL ORIGINS OF THE AMERICAN REVOLUTION 273 n.39 (1967).

3. 1 DAVID RAMSAY, HISTORY OF THE AMERICAN REVOLUTION 356 (1789).

4. *Id.* at 31.

the United States alone would free men, guided by the lodestars of reason, history, and experience, self-consciously design the architecture of their government. Whatever kernel of truth these sentiments may contain, the reality is that both pre- and post-Revolutionary political history limited the potential forms that the government could take. No one seriously believed that the new nation, the "united States," could establish a national government that did not share political power with the states. The reason is obvious: states had existed for decades, some for more than a century. They were hardly inclined to relinquish all of their authority to a national government. To ask whether the United States would have been better off as a unitary nation is academic. A United States without states is almost as implausible today as it was to the Framers.

The policy rationales for states must therefore be understood largely as post hoc justifications. The Framers and their countrymen did not choose to create a federal nation comprised of thirteen states; it could hardly have been otherwise. Still, the rationales for federalism matter. The Framers, the judiciary, political theorists, and others have suggested various rationales for a nation constituted by states, often extolling federalism's political virtues. The real questions, today as in the past, concern how much and what kind of authority the states should exercise. Should twenty-first century states become little more than geographic subdivisions of the United States, primarily of interest to Google Maps? Presumably not. These are the questions that make it worthwhile, indeed necessary, to consider the rationales for federalism today—in foreign, no less than domestic, affairs. If the rationales for federalism remain compelling, if the benefits of states outweigh their costs, then a stronger state role in general, and in the realm of foreign affairs in particular, may be warranted. If federalism's rationales now seem dubious or anachronistic, if few reasons beyond historical sentimentality exist for federalism, then it may make more sense to lodge broader foreign-affairs powers in the federal government.

This chapter thus begins by exploring federalism's origins in the United States. It analyzes how the Constitution's text reflects principles of federalism. And it applies those principles to assess the cogency of federalism's policy rationales in the context of foreign affairs.

I. The Origins of American Federalism

Many Americans do not know it, but the Constitution is the second foundational charter of the United States. The first, the Articles of Confederation, didn't work. For eight years (1781–1789), the Articles technically[5] constituted the national

5. "Technically"—because the operation of both the national and state governments during these years hardly conformed to the blueprint established by the Articles.

government of the newly independent "united States." The Articles failed for several reasons but, above all, because of a defect widely acknowledged by scholars: the national government had too little power and the states too much.

The problem with the Articles, however, ran deeper. The states not only enjoyed too much power; they also abused it. The Framers convened the Philadelphia Convention that culminated in the Constitution not simply because of widespread dissatisfaction with the performance of the national government under the Articles of Confederation; increasingly, they also found themselves disillusioned with how the states conducted their political affairs under *their own* constitutions, which most states had reconstituted or revised after the Declaration of Independence. Jack Rakove emphasizes that

> [b]y far the greatest influence that the experience of the states exerted on the deliberations of 1787 lay . . . in the area of constitutional theory itself. For when the framers set about designing the new national government, the crucial lessons they applied were drawn from their observations of the state constitutions written since independence. It was in the drafting of these charters, rather than the Articles of Confederation, that the revolutionaries had expressed their original notions of republican government most clearly . . . . How the framers at the Federal Convention thought about such major theoretical issues as representation and the separation of powers was largely a response to their assessment of the relevant provisions and practices of the state constitutions. The states had served, in effect, as the great political laboratory upon whose experiments the framers of 1787 drew to revise the theory of republican government.[6]

This attitudinal shift of the Framers is as unfamiliar as it is indispensable to understanding the context in which they drafted the Constitution, which is by no stretch a revision of the Articles. It reflects and embodies a distinct political philosophy that had evolved in response to what the Framers personally witnessed between 1776 and 1787.[7] In the course of drafting, debating, and ultimately ratifying the Constitution, the Framers combined that new political philosophy with earlier Revolutionary ideals, Enlightenment political thought, and, despite the recent separation from Great Britain based on the Declaration's litany of grievances against the Crown, lessons drawn from Britain's own political history and experience.

---

6. Jack N. Rakove, Original Meanings: Politics and Ideas in the Making of the Constitution 30–31 (1996).

7. *See generally* Forrest McDonald, *Novus Ordo Seclorum*: The Intellectual Origins of the Constitution 143–83 (1985).

The Constitution is not, of course, a perfect document.[8] But it is not accidental that the Constitution of the United States is the world's oldest continually operating written constitution. The approach adopted by the Framers in 1787 began with a pragmatic, clear-eyed appreciation of human nature and motivation. It adapted innovative political theories supplied by Enlightenment thinkers to post-Revolutionary circumstances in the United States. And it reflected the recent real-world experiences of the framing generation under several forms of government, with the virtues and the defects of each informing the final document.

The conduct of the states, both under their own constitutions and the Articles, provided much of that experience. It led many of the most influential Framers to re-evaluate some of their earlier assumptions. It is well known that the Framers inherited ideas from Enlightenment luminaries such as Locke, Hobbes, Montesquieu, and Rousseau; from earlier transformational theorists such as Grotius and Pufendorf; and from the great thinkers of the Scottish Enlightenment, including Hume. But their ideas supplied only a theoretical framework, "a general context within which the Constitution can be located."[9] The Framers did not adopt their ideas without modification. They instead adapted the insights of the great European political theorists in view of the manifest failure of both the Articles and republican state constitutions. Other features of the Constitution were shaped by the abuses of British imperial rule, which the Framers had witnessed firsthand. But even though the grievances culminating in the Declaration of Independence and Revolutionary War remained fresh in their minds, still other political insights incorporated into the Constitution reflected Great Britain's *own* political history, culminating in the Glorious Revolution of 1689.[10]

Throughout the period during which the Articles were in force, the states occupied center stage. For even more than the failures of the Articles, the infirm political structures and troubling experiences under post-Revolutionary state

8. *See, e.g.*, SANFORD LEVINSON, OUR UNDEMOCRATIC CONSTITUTION: WHERE THE CONSTITUTION GOES WRONG (AND HOW WE THE PEOPLE CAN CORRECT IT) (2006); ROBERT A. DAHL, HOW DEMOCRATIC IS THE AMERICAN CONSTITUTION? (2002). Despite the Constitution's defects, there is, and has long been, a tendency to treat the document with a dogmatic, uncritical, and at times almost theological reverence: "The practice of 'constitution worship' has been quite solidly ingrained in our political culture from the beginning of our constitutional history." Henry P. Monaghan, *Our Perfect Constitution*, 56 N.Y.U. L. REV. 353, 356 (1981). Selective invocations of the Constitution or snippets of its text can serve a transparent rhetorical purpose, arrogating the authority of the document in the service of particular political ideologies. It is precisely because many Americans dogmatically revere the Constitution that this strategy can be effective.

9. *See* RAKOVE, *supra* note 6, at 18-20.

10. *Id.* at 20.

constitutions were the paramount influence on the new Constitution.[11] State sovereignty, during this period, remained undiluted. It is commonly thought that "*the* United States" declared independence in 1776. It did not. Rather, "thirteen united States of America" proclaimed in the Declaration of July 4, 1776, their status as "Free and Independent States" with "full Power . . . to do all . . . Acts and Things which independent States may of right do."[12] Each of the former colonies initially regarded itself, not foremost as part of a new nation, a single, unitary sovereign, but as an autonomous, distinct, and self-governing country. "When people in 1776 talked about their 'country' or even their 'nation,'' Gordon Wood observes, "they usually meant Virginia or Massachusetts or Pennsylvania."[13]

In 1776 and for many years after, the states regarded *sovereignty*, as the law of nations understood this legal concept at the time,[14] to reside in each of them as a distinct polity.[15] Justice George Sutherland's (in)famous thesis[16] about the existence of extraconstitutional foreign-affairs powers is mistaken in, among many other respects, its insistence that "[t]he Framers' Convention was called and exerted its powers upon the irrefutable postulate that though the states were several[,] their people in respect of foreign affairs were one."[17] The former British overseers of the American colonies had regarded sovereignty as indivisible; in the realm of foreign relations, at least, they operated on the assumption that each

---

11. RAKOVE, *supra* note 6, at 21–22, 30–31.

12. THE DECLARATION OF INDEPENDENCE (U.S. 1776).

13. GORDON S. WOOD, THE AMERICAN REVOLUTION: A HISTORY 70–71 (2002).

14. For convenience, and in conformity with the terminology of earlier judicial decisions, unless otherwise indicated, we use the phrases "law of nations" and "international law" synonymously.

15. *See* AKHIL REED AMAR, AMERICA'S CONSTITUTION: A BIOGRAPHY 27–28 (2005) [hereinafter "AMERICA'S CONSTITUTION"]; BAILYN, *supra* note 2, 198–200; MCDONALD, *supra* note 7, at 150; GORDON S. WOOD, THE CREATION OF THE AMERICAN REPUBLIC, 1776–1787, at 345–54 (1969).

16. *See* United States v. Curtiss-Wright Export Co., 299 U.S. 304, 316 (1936) ("By the Declaration of Independence, the Representatives of the United States of America declared the United (not the several) Colonies to be free and independent states, and as such to have full Power to levy War, conclude Peace, contract Alliances, establish Commerce and to do all other Acts and Things which Independent States may of right do.") (internal quotation marks omitted). Sutherland developed this thesis well before he joined the Court. *See* GEORGE SUTHERLAND, CONSTITUTIONAL POWER AND WORLD AFFAIRS (1918); George Sutherland, *The Internal and External Powers of the National Government*, 191 N. AM. REV. 373 (1909).

17. *Curtiss-Wright Export Co.*, 299 U.S. at 317. Sutherland's historical account in *Curtiss-Wright* has long been critiqued and, most would say, debunked. *See, e.g.*, David M. Levitan, *The Foreign Relations Power: An Analysis of Mr. Justice Sutherland's Theory*, 55 YALE L.J. 467 (1946); Charles A. Lofgren, United States v. Curtiss-Wright Export Corp.: *An Historical Reassessment*, 83 YALE L.J. 1 (1973); *see also* Michael D. Ramsay, *The Myth of Extraconstitutional Foreign Affairs Power*, 42

nation could have one and only one seat of ultimate authority. But the states recognized that this conception of sovereignty precluded shared political authority and, in the Articles, rejected it.[18]

Indeed, the conception of sovereignty as indivisible had ranked among the rationales for parliamentary supremacy during the colonial era. Faced with repeated usurpations of colonial authority, often effected without regard for local interests, the colonists gradually came to question this rationale, leading to many of the heated differences and disputes that culminated in the eruption of the American Revolution and the ultimate dissolution of Britain's North American colonies (excepting the territories that would become Canada).[19] The sheer distance, geographic and psychological, from which the Crown and Parliament managed colonial affairs exacerbated those differences. Consequently, after the Revolution, a bloody, eight-year conflict fought to free themselves from a remote sovereign in London, the former colonists were not about to reestablish a Leviathan with complete and centralized sovereignty governing from a remote region of North America. Rejecting the British premise of indivisible sovereignty, the states instead carefully and closely guarded their sovereignty by reposing it in Albany, Boston, Philadelphia, and elsewhere. For this reason, perhaps the most pressing political necessity after the Revolution consisted in the efforts of states to replace their old colonial charters with new, constitutive legal and political frameworks that would both reflect and instantiate the core values animating the Revolution.

Those values can be captured in a single, but ambiguous, word: *republican*.[20] Since its inception in antiquity during the Greco-Roman era, the meaning of republican government has evolved significantly.[21] But its evolution in

---

WM. & MARY L. REV. 379 (2000). *But see* LOUIS HENKIN, FOREIGN AFFAIRS AND THE US CONSTITUTION 19, 329 n.10 (2d ed. 1996) (citing scholarship defending Sutherland's history). At any rate, after the Constitution entered into force, the locus of sovereignty clearly resided in the Union rather than the several states. To the extent any residual doubts remained, early Supreme Court decisions under Chief Justice Marshall, such as *Martin v. Hunter's Lessee*, 14 U.S. 304 (1816), clarified matters. The Civil War put such doubts to rest once and for all.

18. The Articles of Confederation thus lodged "sovereignty" in the several states, emphasizing that "[e]ach state retains its sovereignty, freedom, and independence, and every power, jurisdiction, and right, which is not by this Confederation expressly delegated to the United States, in Congress assembled." ARTICLES OF CONFEDERATION art. II (U.S. 1781).

19. Britain retained full control of the region of North America that now constitutes Canada until 1867 and partial control until 1931 (and, to a far more trivial extent, 1982). Canada Act, 1982, c. 11 (U.K.), *reprinted in* R.S.C. 1985, app II, no 44 (Can.); Statute of Westminster, 1931, Geo. 5 c. 4; JACKSON J. SPIELVOGEL, WESTERN CIVILIZATION 535, 637–38 (6th ed. 2006).

20. WOOD, *supra* note 13, at 48.

21. *See* Knud Haakonssen, *Republicanism*, *in* A COMPANION TO CONTEMPORARY POLITICAL PHILOSOPHY 729 (Robert E. Goodin & Philip Pettit eds., 1993); THOMAS PAINE, POLITICAL WRITINGS 177–83 (Bruce Kuklick ed., 2000).

the minds of the Framers, during the intensive decade of experience with the Articles and state constitutions between 1776 and 1787, culminated in perhaps the most durable and profound transformation of republican theory in political history.[22] In Europe, beginning with Renaissance thinkers such as Machiavelli,[23] political theorists had typically contrasted republicanism with monarchism.[24] Republicanism, as conceptualized by Rousseau, Montesquieu, Locke, and others, infused Enlightenment political thought. Yet with the exception of a few Dutch and Italian city-states and some Swiss cantons, notably the (Calvinist) Republic of Geneva that inspired Rousseau's *On the Social Contract*,[25] few actual republics existed at the time. Early historical precedents from ancient Greece and Rome were, instead, the principal source of inspiration. But those precedents were intellectually far less accessible than they are today because of the comparatively undeveloped state of historical research at the time.[26] The Framers were nonetheless well aware of the ultimate failures of republicanism in antiquity; it was lost on no one present in Philadelphia in 1787 that the Roman Republic ended in a bloodbath. Still, in 1776 and the years leading up to the Articles of Confederation, classical republican theory increasingly appealed to cosmopolitan intellectuals despondent about corruption, arbitrary government, and incestuous, hereditary monarchies that oppressed most countries. In taverns, coffeehouses, and salons in North America, as in Europe, the Enlightenment ideas of John Locke,

---

22. *See* AMERICA'S CONSTITUION, *supra* note 15, at 276–80; BAILYN, *supra* note 2, at 281–301; MCDONALD, *supra* note 7, at 143–83.

23. Popular opinion (reflected in the adjective "Machiavellian") situates Nicolló Machiavelli within the political realist tradition, largely on account of his most well-known work, *The Prince* (1513). Both in *The Prince* and other works, especially *The Discourses on the Ten Books of Titus Livy*, however, Machiavelli can be seen as one of the earliest proponents of republicanism, which he deemed more stable than the more authoritarian princedom or city-state that took center stage in *The Prince*. NICOLLO MACHIAVELLI, DISCOURSES ON LIVY (Harvey Mansfield & Nathan Tarcov trans., University of Chicago Press 1996). Rakove notes that "few books have contributed more to our understanding of the larger world of ideas within which American constitutionalism took shape that J.G.A. Pocock's *The Machiavellian Moment*," in which Pocock identified the preoccupation of the Framers with Machiavelli's focus on "the life cycle of republican polities," in particular, the problem of how a republic could "remain morally and politically stable in a stream of irrational events conceived as eventually destructive of all systems of secular stability." RAKOVE, *supra* note 6, at 35–36 (internal quotation marks omitted); *see also* WOOD, *supra* note 13, at 66.

24. *See* MCDONALD, *supra* note 7, at 66; PAINE, *supra* note 21, at 171–83; Nathan Perl-Rosenthal, *The "Divine Right of Republics": Hebraic Republicanism and the Debate over Kingless Government in Revolutionary America*, 66 WM. & MARY Q. 535 (2009).

25. JEAN-JACQUES ROUSSEAU, *On the Social Contract*, *in* THE BASIC POLITICAL WRITINGS OF JEAN-JACQUES ROUSSEAU 141 (Donald A. Cress ed., 1987) (1762).

26. After the Revolution, Americans at first focused considerable, but "selective," attention on the Greek and Roman republicanism of antiquity. WOOD, *supra* note 13, at 50–51.

Jean-Jacques Rousseau, Baron de Montesquieu, James Harrington, Agernon Sidney, John Milton, and the luminaries of the Scottish Enlightenment (David Hume, Francis Hutcheson, Adam Smith, John Millar, and others) permeated discourse among educated political elites.[27] The ideas of republicanism gradually took hold among the people as well. Faced with what increasingly appeared to be rank incompetence and inequity on the part of the monarch's representatives, they saw no reason that they could not or should not govern themselves.

People *could* govern themselves because, in the opinion of many, the middle class of the day, including, for example, shopkeepers, artisans, and merchants, possessed the civic virtues deemed indispensable to republican government—foremost among them, a genuine devotion to the public good and self-identification as responsible, engaged citizens. It required neither wealth nor education nor social status to appreciate what constituted the good life, which, in republican theory, is government's task to promote. An influential 1776 pamphlet, probably published in New England, made the republican case succinctly: "The people know best their own wants and necessities," it argued, "and therefore are best able to rule themselves."[28] In 1775, John Adams proclaimed that "democratic despotism is a contradiction in terms."[29]

People *should* govern themselves because republicanism deemed self-government a moral entitlement. In the prevailing intellectual atmosphere, Americans saw no tension between the prospect that good citizens might prosper financially (as had everyone's republican ideal, George Washington) and the assumption that everyone could nonetheless cultivate or maintain the simplicity, ingenuousness, civic virtue, and sound moral compass that the patriots had found lacking among the English aristocracy.

But the republicanism embodied in state constitutions during the period of the Articles of Confederation suffered from fundamental defects in both theory and practice. The Framers gradually perceived the causes of these defects in the years culminating in the Philadelphia Convention. As a form of government, republicanism for early Americans could not be separated from the presumptive virtues of its constituents: "restraint, temperance, fortitude, dignity, and independence."[30] Many believed that the republicanism of antiquity, of ancient Athens and Rome, had failed largely because of a decline in the "character and spirit of

---

27. *See* BAILYN, *supra* note 2, at 24–25; MCDONALD, *supra* note 7, at 66, 144; WOOD, *supra* note 13, at 50.

28. BAILYN, *supra* note 2, at 294.

29. JOHN DUNN, DEMOCRACY: A HISTORY 80 (2005).

30. WOOD, *supra* note 13, at 50; MCDONALD, *supra* note 7, at 70–71, 87–88.

their people. Frugality, industry, temperance, and simplicity—the rustic traits of the sturdy yeoman—were the stuff that made society strong," in combination with the "virile martial qualities—the scorn of ease, the contempt of danger, [and] the love of valor[.]"[31] This conception of republicanism, which Machiavelli, Rousseau, and others revived and further developed during the Renaissance and Enlightenment, relied on civic virtue. From 1776 to 1787, the same conception prevailed among Americans: "sacrifice of individual interests to the greater good of the whole formed the essence of republicanism and comprehended for Americans the idealistic goal of their Revolution."[32]

This vision of republicanism, however, as Rousseau's *Social Contract* made clear, could not work in the absence of a relatively homogenous and small polity.[33] For civic virtue to flourish in any polity, citizens must share common values and interests, and their personal desires must remain consistent with the general will. That is only feasible in a sufficiently small and homogenous polity. Only in such a polity can citizens appreciate the need to sacrifice self-regard for the good of the polity, for in the view of Rousseau and similar thinkers, citizens of a republic presumptively *identify* the latter with their own long-term or overarching interests even when particular political decisions appear contrary to it. Early republicans in the United States shared a conception of the common good required for a genuine republic to be *associative* (the general will) rather than *aggregative* (the aggregate of everyone's self-interests).[34] That is why, in the immediate aftermath of the Revolution, "the solution to the problems of American politics seemed to rest not so much in emphasizing the private rights of individuals against the general will as it did in stressing the public rights of the collective people against the supposed privileged interests of their rulers."[35]

The new state constitutions enacted after 1776 embraced these optimistic, if not quixotic, republican premises despite the relatively large size and heterogeneity of the U.S. population. For that reason, they naturally chose to vest paramount political power in state legislatures, which, they presumed, instantiated local rule by the people, with the remote national government relegated to a comparatively minimal, secondary role. But state constitutions took plenary, often exclusive, legislative power to an extreme. Legislatures could make treaties and alliances. They

---

31. WOOD, *supra* note 13, at 52.

32. *Id.* at 53, 68.

33. *See* ROUSSEAU, *supra* note 25, at 141, 147–48, 155–56, 165–70; *see also* WOOD, *supra* note 13, at 57–58.

34. *See* WOOD, *supra* note 13, at 58–61, 69.

35. *Id.* at 61.

could issue pardons. They could check the appointment power of governors. State constitutions made the office of governor much weaker than it had been in colonial state governments. Indeed, Pennsylvania eliminated the office of governor altogether.[36] Not until the late stages of this project of, often radical, revision of state constitutions, and not until the major Revolutionary battles were all but concluded (the Battle of Yorktown took place in October 1781), did the states, in March 1781, finally approve a national charter, the Articles of Confederation. The Continental Congress had submitted it to them some four years earlier.

The balance struck in the Articles between state and national authority established a confederation of the states, which, recall, understood themselves as *sovereign* in the international legal sense. Under the Articles of Confederation, the nation thus resembled, in certain respects, the modern European Union. The balance between state and national political power—and, in particular, the extraordinary weakness of the national government relative to the states—proved deficient and dysfunctional in five key areas.

First, the states retained exclusive taxation power. Congress lacked authority even to impose import taxes. It could borrow money abroad only at stiff interest rates, which rose as the Confederacy's reputation and creditworthiness rapidly declined. Second, the states retained all power to regulate commerce, both among themselves and with foreign nations. They freely taxed foreign commerce to and from other states that passed through their borders. Naturally, each sought to secure a comparative economic advantage over the others; and for the same reason, they retaliated against one another, culminating in a mutually disadvantageous downward cycle that is a paradigm of modern game theory. Third, the Confederacy lacked a national judiciary. States alone had judicial systems, and each had its own. State judiciaries did not always treat out-of-state litigants equally or respect foreign state judgments. Fourth, a single state could veto any proposed amendment to the Articles. In practice, this prevented even the most sensible reforms. Three efforts to amend the Articles to give Congress taxation power, for example, failed for this reason. Fifth, the Articles gave the national government no power to enforce the Articles. Compliance by the states with the Articles depended entirely on their political whim, rendering the Articles little more than a "treaty of amity," as James Madison put it.[37]

For these and other reasons, the framework established by the Articles, both as a blueprint for a national government and in the popular perception of states and their constituents, rapidly disintegrated. Increasingly, the Articles came to be

---

36. *Id.* at 137.

37. James Madison, Vices of the Political System of the United States 351 (1787).

regarded less as binding constitutive law for a unified nation and more as mere guidelines for autonomous members.

Meanwhile, as their newly empowered legislatures ran amuck, state governments themselves began to deteriorate. The quality of citizen-legislators fell. Demagoguery and corruption rose. Parochial interests distorted the legislative process. Legislators took on executive, including military, functions. They granted special privileges and exemptions. They flouted contribution allotments decreed by Congress. And they sought constantly to secure an economic advantage over neighboring states through stiff levies on goods passing through their territory. With civic republican virtue thin and earlier optimistic Enlightenment presuppositions about rationality and public-spiritedness increasingly and obviously dubious, the euphoria of the framing generation, with its belief in the impossibility of legislative despotism, yielded to intense concern about the future of the nation—even among the most ardent republicans. Jefferson rued the "elective despotism" that had descended over the states, manifest in abuses "so frequent and so flagrant," as Madison wrote, "as to alarm the most steadfast friends of Republicanism"; and for Madison, the prevalence of these abuses and of despotic state legislatures, even more than the failures of the Articles, contributed to the disquiet that led to the Philadelphia Convention.[38] For "while the manifest defects of the Confederation were few and conspicuous, the problems of state government were more complex and difficult to diagnose."[39]

Meeting in Philadelphia, the Framers were sobered by the failure of the grand experiments with classical republican theory and disappointed by the lamentable want of civic virtue exhibited by their countrymen.

> A bitter lesson emerged from the disruptions in New England [i.e., Shays' Rebellion], one that was reinforced elsewhere by corruption, demagoguery, and the refusal or inability of Congress and the several states to honor their obligations. The lesson, as some were candid enough to put it, was that the American public did not possess a sufficient stock of virtue to sustain a republic, as republics had traditionally been conceived. Man did not have such virtue naturally, nor did he obtain it by laboring in the earth, nor did many men acquire it through religious instruction.[40]

---

38. Wood, *supra* note 13, at 152.

39. Rakove, *supra* note 6, at 29.

40. McDonald, *supra* note 7, at 179.

The Framers sought to establish a more nuanced and realistic republican system, one that would rely less on the problematic assumption of a morally impartial, virtuous citizenry—the principal danger discounted by the drafters of the earlier, and, in retrospect, naïve state constitutions. The new system would be founded upon a different and more candid understanding of human nature. It would acknowledge people's natural tendency toward self-regard and the corrosive effect of state competition on the nation as a whole. The Framers also recognized the risks of civic vice. They sought to develop political mechanisms, not only to control it, but ideally to harness and redeploy it in the service of the nation's common good. In Madison's well-known words, "[a]mbition must be made to counteract ambition" among governmental officials, with multiple and diverse checks and counterchecks intended to establish and maintain political equilibrium.[41] To do so would connect the "interest of man" with the "constitutional rights of the place" to "control the abuses of government."[42]

Of course, as Louis Henkin wrote, despite the manifest failures of the Articles and republican state constitutions, "the Framers were hardly ready to replace the representative inefficiency of many with an efficient monarchy, and unhappy memories of royal prerogative, fear of tyranny, and reluctance to repose trust in any one person" persisted.[43] The people would retain ultimate power. But the institutions of government to which that power would be delegated would be a step or two removed from the people and restructured to avoid the defects of both the Articles and early state constitutions.

The new political atmosphere contrasted classical *republicanism*—insofar as it meant either the models from antiquity or the Enlightenment paradigm of Rousseau[44]—with *republican* as revised by the Framers to render it less *directly* democratic in a simple majoritarian sense.[45] The Senate would now be chosen

---

41. The Federalist No. 51, at 349 (James Madison) (Jacob E. Cooke ed., 1961).

42. *Id.*

43. Henkin, *supra* note 17, at 27–28.

44. Rousseau, *supra* note 25.

45. *See generally* Rakove, *supra* note 6, at 46–56; Wood, *supra* note 13. Madison set forth the general contours of this new conception of republicanism in *The Federalist*. *See* The Federalist No. 10 (James Madison). *But see* America's Constitution, *supra* note 15, at 276–80 (arguing that Madison's contrast of republic with democracy did not represent "eighteenth-century usage" or "sway large numbers of would-be ratifiers"). The Guarantee Clause of the Constitution requires the federal government to "guarantee to every state in this union a republican form of government." U.S. Const. art. IV, § 4. It does not, however, define "a republican form of government." The Supreme Court has held that the Guarantee Clause generally presents a non-justiciable political question, meaning that it delegates responsibility for its application and enforcement to Congress rather than the judiciary, for which the

by state legislators, not directly by the people.[46] The president would be chosen by electors, themselves selected by state legislators, not directly by the people.[47] Treaties and presidential appointments would be approved by the Senate rather than the new House of Representatives, the popular body of the Constitution's bicameral legislature. Property requirements would ensure that only people of independent judgment would vote in elections and participate in decisions of state.[48] Powerful federal courts would now enforce federal law and preserve the national legal and political order. Although the Constitution did not expressly set forth the power of judicial review in its text (in fact, some of the Framers, notably Madison, considered it anathema),[49] the Framers created a Supreme Court—composed of appointed, not popularly elected, justices—who soon claimed power to invalidate acts of the national legislative and executive branches.[50] And perhaps most significant, the Constitution created a powerful new national government and executive branch, presided over by a president, that would be literally and figuratively removed from most of the country's population. In these and other ways, by 1787, many of the Framers had reconsidered and redefined the kind of republic they sought to establish. The new constitutional institutions and mechanisms were contrasted with those dominated by the hoi polloi, "democratic" mobs to whom governmental power could not be directly entrusted.

What then of the elusive situs of sovereignty in the new governmental blueprint created by the Constitution? The issue naturally generated considerable debate and discourse throughout the founding era. Yet the most revealing evidence of its resolution and ultimate disposition in Philadelphia lies in

---

question is said to be ill-suited. *See* Pacific States Tel. & Tel. Co. v. Oregon, 223 U.S. 118 (1912); Luther v. Borden, 48 U.S. (7 How.) 1 (1849).

46. In 1913, the Seventeenth Amendment provided for the direct election of senators. U.S. CONST. amend. XVII.

47. U.S. CONST. amend. XII.

48. The Constitution itself does not specify voting qualifications, leaving them to be determined by the states. *See* U.S. CONST. art. I, § 4; *id.* art. II, § 3. Before the Fourteenth Amendment, the states imposed a variety of requirements restricting the right to vote based on, most prominently, identity as a property-owning Caucasian male, as well as, for example, poll taxes or other qualifications. *See generally* ALEXANDER KEYSSAR, THE RIGHT TO VOTE: THE CONTESTED HISTORY OF DEMOCRACY IN THE UNITED STATES 26–52 (2000).

49. *See* THE FEDERALIST NO. 48, at 332 (James Madison) (Jacob E. Cooke ed., 1961) ("It is agreed on all sides, that the powers properly belonging to one of the departments, ought not to be directly and completely administered by either of the other departments. It is equally evident, that neither of them ought to possess directly or indirectly, an overruling influence over the others in the administration of their respective powers.").

50. Marbury v. Madison, 5 U.S. (1 Cranch) 137 (1803).

the number of times the word appears in the Constitution: *zero.* The Framers shared a commitment, above all and despite their sometimes sharply divergent views on particular issues, to pragmatism. They knew that no abstract theorem could resolve the concrete controversies that would inevitably arise in the fledgling nation's future evolution,[51] especially controversies about political power and its allocation. Who, or what institution, at which level or branch, of which government, is competent to do what? Such questions were left to be worked out in political struggle, as history unfolded. For the Framers, it would have been both naïve and unhelpful to expect questions about, say, the permissibility of a national bank,[52] or the power to regulate interstate steamboat traffic,[53] or for that matter, the validity of a national healthcare program,[54] to be settled by reference to the supposed locus of sovereignty. The very meaning of sovereignty, then as now, was unclear and controversial. Consequently, the text's sole arguable reference to the locus and nature of sovereignty resides in the Constitution's opening words, "We the People."[55] The text thereby identifies the ultimate source of authority for the new governmental institutions as the national populace; *people*, not the several states or Congress, would henceforth be the font of political authority. The Constitution, accordingly, would be approved (or not) by popular ratifying conventions to be convened apart from the tainted state legislatures.

This monumental revision of the concept of republicanism in Philadelphia in 1787, and its bold rejection (or reconceptualization) of the oft-abused concept of sovereignty, helps explain why the U.S. Constitution is the world's oldest, continuously operating written constitution. The Framers'[56] stroke of genius that hot summer resided in large part in their rejection of utopian notions of

---

51. The Framers would surely have agreed in this regard with future-Justice Oliver Wendell Holmes Jr.'s well-known dictum: "General propositions do not decide concrete cases." Lochner v. New York, 198 U.S. 45, 76 (1905) (Holmes, J., dissenting).

52. McCulloch v. Maryland, 17 U.S. (4 Wheat.) 316 (1819).

53. Gibbons v. Ogden, 22 U.S. (9 Wheat.) 1 (1824).

54. Nat'l Fed'n of Indep. Bus. v. Sebelius, 132 S. Ct. 2566 (2012).

55. U.S. CONST. pmbl.

56. We do not suggest that the views of the Framers control the resolution of questions of constitutional interpretation. Subsequent practice, text, structure, history, and experience, for example, matter at least as much to any practical student of the political and legal framework for resolving issues of constitutional law. Nor do we suggest that the views of the Framers may readily be discerned; it would be naïve to assume that the Framers invariably shared a monolithic view on the diverse issues involved in drafting the new Constitution and then putting it into practice. Often, their intentions, as Justice Robert H. Jackson memorably put it, "must be divined from materials almost as enigmatic as the dreams Joseph was called upon to interpret

egalitarianism predicated on the assumption that every citizen possessed equal civic virtue and skill in the arts of government. They rather created a system in which the locus and nature of sovereignty would not be the decisive element; the allocation of sovereign authority would be neither sharp nor fixed. That is, perhaps above all, why the Constitution has been able to endure and adapt to new circumstances for centuries. The Framers, wrote Walter Bagehot, "shrank from placing sovereign power anywhere. They feared that it generated tyranny . . . ."[57]

Hence, as some of them contemplated, adjustments would be made continually (for more than 230 years as of this writing), through, among other means, constitutional amendment, judicial interpretation, tradition, historical practice, institutional adaptation, and even civil war. The continuous effort to allocate governmental authorities sensibly against a constantly shifting political backdrop has been the paramount enduring drama of American constitutionalism. Yet the basic formula has persisted: the states would be neither mere geographic subdivisions nor autonomous, independent nations; rather, they would be authentic, distinct polities with powers and responsibilities adaptable to changed times and circumstances—always subject, however, to the sovereignty of the people and to categorical limits that no government could lawfully transgress. The Framers thereby remedied the disequilibrium in federal-state power that had doomed the Articles of Confederation. Their solutions were not, of course (and as they anticipated), universally embraced. The arguments of the Anti-Federalists against the new Constitution were motivated and informed largely by their belief that the power of the states had been dangerously curtailed. But their new approach, the Framers hoped, would remedy the excesses of popular democracy and the earlier conceptions of republicanism that had doomed state governments.

---

for Pharoh." Youngstown Sheet & Tube v. Sawyer (The Steel Seizure Case), 343 U.S. 579, 634 (1952) (Jackson, J., concurring). Still, and notwithstanding the flaws and prejudices of the era, the Framers were of course both remarkably erudite and politically astute. They brought to bear a combination of insights from ancient and Enlightenment political philosophy, historical jurisprudence, and the practical wisdom cultivated by their experience with, first, abusive government of the colonies under the Crown, and second, inept government under the several states and the Articles of Confederation. Despite the dramatic differences between the agrarian, seaboard nation of some 3 million people in 1789 and the contemporary, industrialized, tweeting, videoconferencing, suburbanite America of some 330 million people, it would be remiss and imprudent to neglect their insights. For elaboration, see MICHAEL J. GLENNON, CONSTITUTIONAL DIPLOMACY 44–46 (1990).

57. WALTER BAGEHOT, THE ENGLISH CONSTITUTION 218 (1867).

II. *Federalism in the New Constitution*

At the outset, the Framers faced a critical decision: whether to amend the Articles or discard them altogether and start anew. They chose to start anew.[58] The document they produced on September 17, 1787, addressed the principal deficiencies of the Articles. Among other changes, it sharply curtailed the power of the states under the Articles and, conversely, empowered the federal government, to cite one critical example, "[t]o regulate commerce with foreign nations, and among the several states . . . ."[59] It created a national judiciary.[60] It established a process for amending the Constitution, which, although still a formidable task,[61] rendered the adoption of amendments a far more manageable task than it had been under the Articles. And a key provision, the Supremacy Clause, supplied the cornerstone of the Constitution's revised conception of federalism:

> This Constitution, and the Laws of the United States which shall be made in Pursuance thereof; and all Treaties made, or which shall be made, under the Authority of the United States, shall be the supreme Law of the Land; and the Judges in every State shall be bound thereby, any Thing in the Constitution or Laws of any State to the Contrary notwithstanding.[62]

---

58. To amend the Articles of Confederation would have required that every alteration proposed by Congress "be afterwards confirmed by the legislatures of every State." ARTICLES OF CONFEDERATION art. XIII (U.S. 1781). Quite apart from the host of substantive defects in the Articles that required attention, the futility of this amendment process doubtless contributed to the decision of the Framers to begin anew rather than amend the Articles. At any rate, had they framed the Constitution as a series of amendments to the Articles, it is highly improbable that it would have been adopted. The Framers also chose to meet behind closed doors, lest the enterprise be sidetracked by public opposition before a final, defensible instrument could be worked out and made public. *See* 13 THE RECORDS OF THE FEDERAL CONVENTION 44–65 (Max Farrand ed., 1907).

59. U.S. CONST. art. I, § 1, cl. 3.

60. Technically, the Constitution requires only the establishment of the Supreme Court of the United States, while leaving it to congressional discretion to establish "such inferior courts as the Congress may from time to time ordain and establish." *Id.* art. III, § 1. But from the outset, Congress established lower federal courts, and today, if not in 1789, it is inconceivable that a federal judiciary could function without them.

61. *See id.* art. V.

62. *Id.* art. VI, cl. 2.

Other provisions in the new Constitution expressly limited the foreign affairs powers of the states. Article I, section 10, expressly sets forth three clauses of restrictions. Clauses 1, 2, and 3, respectively, provide:

> No State shall enter into any Treaty, Alliance, or Confederation; grant letters of Marque and Reprisal; coin Money; emit Bills of Credit; make any Thing but gold and silver Coin a Tender in Payment of Debts; pass any Bill of Attainder, ex post facto Law, or Law impairing the Obligation of Contracts, or grant any Title of Nobility.
>
> No State shall, without the Consent of the Congress, lay any Imposts or Duties on Imports or Exports, except what may be absolutely necessary for executing it's [sic] inspection Laws: and the net Produce of all Duties and Imposts, laid by any State on Imports or Exports, shall be for the Use of the Treasury of the United States; and all such Laws shall be subject to the Revision and Controul of the Congress.
>
> No State shall, without the Consent of Congress, lay any Duty of Tonnage, keep Troops, or Ships of War in time of Peace, enter into any Agreement or Compact with another State, or with a foreign Power, or engage in War, unless actually invaded, or in such imminent Danger as will not admit of delay.

Many of these restrictions on state power were modeled on similar limits in the Articles of Confederation, concerning, for example, prohibitions against engaging in war[63] and entering into international agreements without congressional approval.[64] Yet the Framers recognized that merely adapting the language of these provisions in the new Constitution could not cure a chief defect of the Articles, viz., the utter inability of the federal government to enforce limits on state power. Under the Articles, the states had, for example, even in the face of explicit textual prohibitions, waged war against Indian tribes, made agreements among themselves, and maintained standing armies—all without congressional approval.[65]

The states had also refused to carry out treaties approved by Congress, including the vitally important 1783 Treaty of Paris by which Britain recognized the former colonies' independence[66]—subject to provisions, which, if breached,

---

63. Articles of Confederation art. VI, cl. 1 (U.S. 1781).

64. *Id.*

65. America's Constitution, *supra* note 15, at 27–29.

66. Andrew C. McLaughlin, A Constitutional History of the United States 125–46 (1935).

could supply Britain with a new casus belli. The Treaty of Paris required, for example, that "creditors on either side shall meet with no lawful impediment to the recovery of the full value in sterling money of all bona fide debts heretofore contracted."[67] Under the Articles, the states notoriously failed to honor this obligation. And as Madison emphasized, the Articles suffered generally from the failure to provide the national government with an element necessary to effective law and government, the capacity for coercion. "A sanction is as essential to the idea of law," Madison wrote, "as coercion is to that of government."[68] The new Constitution would not make the same mistake.

The Constitution also discarded the most important guarantee of what many now refer to as "states' rights," a provision that appeared prominently in the Articles. The first substantive provision of the Articles, immediately following the denomination of the new nation as the "United States of America,"[69] proclaimed: "Each state retains its sovereignty, freedom, and independence, and every power, jurisdiction, and right, which is not by this Confederation expressly delegated to the United States, in Congress assembled."[70] The Framers' rationale for omitting a similar guarantee from the new Constitution mirrored their rationale for (initially) omitting a bill of rights—a feature of constitutions with which they were surely familiar, for all state constitutions contained one. Relative to the new federal government, the Framers regarded both a guarantee of state sovereignty and a bill of rights as superfluous. Article I, section 8, of the new Constitution spelled out the national government's authority precisely, vesting it with power to regulate commerce, coin money, establish post offices, and so forth. The Framers saw no need to deny the national government authority it lacked in the first place, which might, ironically, imply the existence of other national powers that the states were presumably to retain. The Constitution implicitly prohibited anything not enumerated in its text as a power of the national government; to have enumerated state or individual rights risked implying that those rights *not* enumerated did not exist.

But the Anti-Federalist camp regarded this scheme of implicit prohibition as too risky and inadequate to guarantee either individual or states' rights. They insisted that the Constitution be amended upon its adoption to add what we now refer to as the Bill of Rights, consisting of the first ten amendments to the

---

67. *See* Definitive Treaty of Peace, U.S.-Gr. Brit. art. IV, Sept. 3, 1783, 8 Stat. 80; *see also id.* arts. V–VI.

68. MADISON, *supra* note 37.

69. ARTICLES OF CONFEDERATION art. I (U.S. 1781).

70. *Id.* art. II.

Constitution. Led by Madison, the First Congress proposed twelve amendments in September 1789. Ten of them were subsequently ratified by three-fourths of the states and entered into force in December 1791. The Bill of Rights concludes with a narrower formulation of the states' rights that constituted Article II of the Articles of Confederation. The Tenth Amendment provides: "The powers not delegated to the United States by the Constitution, nor prohibited by it to the States, are reserved to the States respectively, or to the people."

These words of the Tenth Amendment were to be the font of states' rights. But the precise contours of that font were unclear from the outset and remain a major source of contention among constitutional lawyers and others. For nowhere does the Constitution say precisely *which* rights the states reserve.[71] The Tenth Amendment seems to imply that Congress and the president may exercise only those powers vested by Articles I and II, respectively,[72] while the states (or the people) retain the residuum. But the Tenth Amendment does not reserve to the states in so many words all powers not *expressly* granted to the three branches of the federal government. Were it to emerge, as it since has in practice, precedent, and doctrine, that Congress and the president may exercise *implied* powers under the Constitution—powers identified in the main by federal, not state, courts—the Tenth Amendment font could go dry. Three decades after the Constitution's enactment, in the seminal 1819 opinion in *McCulloch v. Maryland*,[73] the Court decided just that. It held that Article I and the Necessary and Proper Clause implicitly vest the national government with the power to establish the Bank of the United States, even though the text does not expressly enumerate that power among those delegated to Congress. Ninety-eight years later, the Court held that the president, too, enjoys implied powers beyond those expressly specified in Article II.[74] What powers the Tenth Amendment in fact reserves to the states

71. Nor does it make clear which rights the people retain. The notoriously opaque Ninth Amendment says that "[t]he enumeration in the Constitution, of certain rights, shall not be construed to deny or disparage others retained by the people." U.S. CONST. amend. IX. The Tenth Amendment's disjunctive, and equally unclear, reference to rights reserved by "the people" further complicates the task of discerning its meaning. *Id.* amend. X.

72. Article III, which defines the jurisdiction and competence of the federal judiciary, also carves out some authority theretofore exercised by the several states. But controversies under the Tenth Amendment, and the principal constitutional domain in which it arguably operates, generally concern federal executive or legislative power. *See id.* art. III.

73. McCulloch v. Maryland, 17 U.S. (4 Wheat.) 415 (1819).

74. Marshall v. Gordon, 243 U.S. 521 (1917); *see also In re* Neagle, 135 U.S. 1 (1890); *cf.* Brig Amy Warwick (The Prize Cases), 67 U.S. (2 Black) 635 (1863). The multiple separate opinions in *Youngstown Sheet & Tube Co. v. Sawyer (The Steel Seizure Case)*, 343 U.S. 579 (1952), also suggest that the president enjoys unenumerated, inherent or implicit, executive power,

therefore became a question of far greater complexity and controversy than it may have seemed upon its adoption in 1791.

One thing that was true in 1791, however, remains so today: whereas the constitutional text tells the states only what they may *not* do in the realm of foreign affairs, the text tells the president and Congress what they *may* do. And their powers—the textual grants of foreign affairs powers to the federal government—are, as one would expect, significant.

The Constitution is popularly believed to confer "the foreign affairs power" explicitly and exclusively upon the president. It does not. No such provision exists. The Constitution divides foreign affairs powers between the president and Congress. And contrary to popular belief, *Congress*, not the president, enjoys the clearest, most numerous, and apparently the most expansive textual grants of foreign affairs powers. Those vested in the president seem paltry in comparison. Article II says that the president "shall be Commander in Chief of the Army and Navy of the United States, and of the militia of the several States, when called into the actual service of the United States"; it empowers him to "to make treaties, provided two thirds of the Senators present concur"; it gives him power to "nominate, and by and with the advice and consent of the Senate, . . . appoint ambassadors, other public ministers and consuls," as well as to "receive ambassadors, and other public ministers"; and it directs him to "take care that the laws," including, of course, those bearing upon foreign affairs, "be faithfully executed."[75]

In contrast, Article I, section 8, gives Congress power "[t]o lay and collect taxes, duties, imposts and excises, to pay the debts and provide for the common defence and general welfare of the United States"; to "regulate commerce with foreign nations"; to "establish a uniform rule of naturalization"; to "define and punish piracies and felonies committed on the high seas, and offences against the law of

---

although the concurring and dissenting justices in *Youngstown* disagreed significantly on its nature, source, and scope. The Supreme Court has also found non-enumerated national powers in the alleged incidents of the mere existence of the United States as an independent nation, quite apart from anything specified expressly in the Constitution. *See* Jones v. United States, 137 U.S. 202 (1890); Chai Chan Ping v. United States (The Chinese Exclusion Case), 130 U.S. 581 (1889).

75. U.S. CONST. art. II, §§ 2–3. Some jurists embrace the so-called Unitary Executive thesis, which regards Article II's Vesting Clause, the grant to the president of "*the* Executive power," U.S. CONST. art. II, § 1 (emphasis added), as conferring upon the president many robust foreign affairs powers that the text does not expressly enumerate. *See, e.g.*, Saikrishna B. Prakash & Michael D. Ramsay, *The Executive Power over Foreign Affairs*, 111 YALE L.J. 231 (2001). *But see* Curtis A. Bradley & Martin S. Flaherty, *Executive Power Essentialism and Foreign Affairs*, 102 MICH. L. REV. 545 (2004). The express language of the constitutional text, however, vests Congress, not the president, with the bulk of foreign affairs powers.

nations"; to "declare war, grant letters of marque and reprisal, and make rules concerning captures on land and water"; to "raise and support armies"; to "provide and maintain a navy"; to "make rules for the government and regulation of the land and naval forces"; to "provide for calling forth the militia to execute the laws of the union, suppress insurrections and repel invasions"; to "provide for organizing, arming and disciplining the militia, and for governing such part of them as may be employed in the service of the United States, reserving to the states respectively, the appointment of the officers, and the authority of training the militia according to the discipline prescribed by Congress"; and to "make all laws which shall be necessary and proper for carrying into execution the foregoing powers, and all other powers vested by this constitution in the government of the United States, or in any department or officer thereof."

This, in broad outline, is the textual foundation for exploring issues of foreign affairs federalism—a compendium of powers allocated between, and sometimes shared by, the president and Congress; a handful of express limits on state activities in foreign affairs; and the Tenth Amendment's assurance that the states nonetheless retain certain unenumerated powers.

But the Constitution's text does not exhaust its meaning.[76] History must be consulted if for no other reason than to understand what the text meant to those who framed, ratified, or read it (or what it would have meant to a reasonably intelligent and literate citizen in 1789). Most constitutional scholars would add that practice, precedent, tradition, political theory, structure, and other methodological tools may properly be used to discern the meaning of the Constitution or adjudicate issues on this basis. Justice Hugo Black often liked to suggest that the answer to constitutional questions could be found merely by consulting the pocket copy of the Constitution that he carried faithfully in his vest pocket. But the hundreds of volumes of Supreme Court cases interpreting the Constitution and an honest look at history and practice under it, belie any suggestion that its words alone are, or could be, dispositive. Further sources of authority must be consulted to resolve interpretive disputes. For this reason, judges and commentators, no less than the Framers, have recognized the need to identify the *functions* that institutions created or presupposed by the Constitution, including the several states, were intended to serve—and to consider whether and how particular interpretations of the text either advance or undermine those functions.

---

76. For a famous argument to that effect, see Thomas C. Grey, *Do We Have an Unwritten Constitution?*, 27 Stan. L. Rev. 703 (1975); *see also* Akhil Reed Amar, America's Unwritten Constitution: The Precedents and Principles We Live By (2012).

The laudable functions of states within the context of the sociopolitical and legal structure of the United States, often referred to as the "values of federalism,"[77] supply its chief policy rationales, the received answers to the question: Why have states? These functions and values also provide a metric for gauging whether the states should be permitted to do the sorts of things that they have come to do more frequently in the international realm, as described in Chapter 2. At the same time, certain countervailing functions and values—implying certain limits on state power—may be inferred from the Constitution's express grants of various foreign-affairs powers to the federal government. These, too, should be scrutinized to identify the scope and limits of state foreign-affairs powers.

III. The Functional Rationale for Federalism

The benefits of federalism—the reasons to have states—reside principally in its potential to promote three values: freedom, efficiency, and innovation. The costs of federalism—the reasons to limit state power, as relevant here, in foreign affairs—reside principally in the value of uniformity in foreign relations.[78] These costs tend to be associated with two core arguments: The first is that the federalism values of freedom, efficiency, and innovation, although forceful in the domestic context, bear little relevance to foreign affairs and, indeed, may even tend to undercut national foreign-affairs interests. The second is the idea that the nation must speak with "one voice" internationally, and presumably, entrusting foreign affairs to the federal government best guarantees this.[79] The tension between these competing values lies at the heart of virtually every dispute about foreign affairs federalism.

A. The Case for the States

The existence of states in the constitutional blueprint has long been thought to promote at least three values: first, preventing tyranny and promoting liberty by diffusing governmental authority; second, making government more

77. *See generally* ERWIN CHEMERINSKY, ENHANCING GOVERNMENT: FEDERALISM FOR THE 21ST CENTURY 98–144 (2008).

78. *Cf.* THE FEDERALIST NO. 70, at 472 (Alexander Hamilton) (Jacob E. Cooke ed., 1961).

79. Am. Ins. Ass'n v. Garamendi, 539 U.S. 396, 415 (2003); Crosby v. Nat'l Foreign Trade Council, 530 U.S. 363 (2000); Japan Line, Ltd. v. County of Los Angeles, 441 U.S. 434, 452–53 (1979). We argue in Chapters 4 and 5 that the "one voice" principle is problematic and has often been misapplied. *See* Sarah H. Cleveland, Crosby *and the "One Voice" Myth in U.S. Foreign Relations*, 46 VILL. L. REV. 975 (2001); David H. Moore, *Beyond One Voice*, 98 MINN. L. REV. 953 (2014).

efficient and democratically responsive by virtue of the greater proximity of states to local communities; and third, serving as laboratories of policy experimentation, to paraphrase Justice Brandeis's famous dictum.[80] To appraise these contentions in the context of foreign affairs, it is helpful to consider both how forceful they prove in general and whether that force extends to the realm of foreign relations.

1. Freedom

The first critical check established by the Framers to secure the nation against a slide toward tyranny owes its intellectual origins primarily to the French Enlightenment luminary Baron de Montesquieu. His seminal treatise *The Spirit of the Laws*,[81] well known to the Framers, offered the most developed theory and defense at that time of the idea of separation of powers.[82] This check, the *horizontal* division of power at the federal level, establishes a general—though, notably, *not* hermetic—separation of executive, judicial, and legislative powers. The Constitution thus divides and sequentially describes the powers of Congress (Article I), the president (Article II), and the federal judiciary (Article III). James Madison offered one of the most compelling and well-known defenses of the separation of powers in the *Federalist*: "[T]he great security against a gradual concentration of the several powers in the same department," he wrote, "consists in giving to those who administer each department, the necessary constitutional means, and personal motives, to resist encroachments by the others . . . Ambition must be made to counteract ambition."[83] This dynamic would establish an equilibrium antithetical to tyranny by impeding the aggregation of power in any one branch of government. In part for the same reason, the Framers also divided power *vertically*, between the federal and state governments. The "utility and necessity of local administrations, for local purposes," Hamilton aptly observed, "would be a complete barrier against the oppressive use of such power,"[84] albeit this overstates the case.

---

80. New State Ice Co. v. Liebmann, 285 U.S. 262, 311 (1932) (Brandeis, J., dissenting) ("It is one of the happy incidents of the federal system that a single courageous state may, if its citizens choose, serve as a laboratory; and try novel social and economic experiments without risk to the rest of the country.").

81. Baron de Montesquieu, The Spirit of the Laws (1748).

82. Montesquieu expanded upon John Locke's arguments in this regard, *see* John Locke, *The Second Treatise of Civil Government* ¶¶ 143–48, *in* Political Writings 261, 335–37 (David Wooton ed., 1993), emphasizing the need for an independent judicial power, as well as the separation of executive and legislative powers.

83. The Federalist No. 51, at 349 (James Madison) (Jacob E. Cooke ed., 1961).

84. *Id.* No. 32, at 199 (Alexander Hamilton).

The Supreme Court has relied upon this rationale in a number of recent federalism cases. In 1991, for example, the Court said that "a healthy balance of power between the States and the Federal Government will reduce the risk of tyranny and abuse from either front."[85] Justice Blackmun, dissenting in *Coleman v. Thompson*, decided the same year, further clarified that "[s]tate sovereignty is not just an end in itself"; "[r]ather, federalism secures to citizens the liberties that derive from the diffusion of sovereign power."[86] More recent federalism decisions have echoed the same theme. In 1995, in *United States v. Lopez*, the first decision since the New Deal era to invalidate an exercise of congressional power as beyond the scope of the Commerce Clause, the majority emphasized that the "constitutionally mandated division of authority was adopted by the Framers to ensure protection of our fundamental liberties."[87] Two years later, in *Printz v. United States*, the Court said that "[t]he separation of the two spheres [federal and state] is one of the Constitution's protections of liberty."[88]

2. *Efficiency*

A second rationale for federalism is that state and local governments, by virtue of their greater proximity and responsiveness to local polities, can handle local issues more efficiently and with greater perceived legitimacy than a national official regulating them from afar. Local problems, the theory goes, vary greatly from place to place. A distant bureaucracy is more likely to apply a misguided one-size-fits-all solution. Local officials, in contrast, will be more directly familiar with the particular difficulties and needs of their respective communities and even, sometimes, the specific people involved. Distance also inhibits efficiency. It is easier for state citizens to travel to their state capitals than to Washington to engage in face-to-face efforts to "petition for a redress of grievances,"[89] in the words of the First Amendment. The efficiency associated with proximity thus dovetails with the freedom protected by dividing power with the states, yielding a more responsive and legitimate form of democratic governance.

---

85. Gregory v. Ashcroft, 501 U.S. 452, 458 (1991).

86. Coleman v. Thompson, 501 U.S. 722, 759 (1991) (Blackmun, J., dissenting).

87. United States v. Lopez, 514 U.S. 549, 552 (1995).

88. Printz v. United States, 521 U.S. 898, 921 (1997).

89. U.S. Const. amend. I.

3. Innovation

Justice Louis Brandeis eloquently expressed the idea that states serve as laboratories of democracy, experimenting with innovative social, political, and economic programs without placing the entire nation at risk:

> Denial of the right to experiment may be fraught with serious consequences to the nation. It is one of the happy incidents of the federal system that a single courageous state may, if its citizens choose, serve as a laboratory; and try novel social and economic experiments without risk to the rest of the country.[90]

Subsequent cases echo Brandeis's insight. In 1982, Justice Sandra Day O'Connor wrote in dissent that "[c]ourts and commentators frequently have recognized that the 50 states serve as laboratories for the development of new social, economic, and political ideas," a phenomenon that she characterized as "one of the most valuable aspects of our federalism."[91] To similar effect, Justice Lewis Powell wrote in 1985 that states have "opportunities to experiment and serve as laboratories."[92] Consider, as a contemporary example, Massachusetts's healthcare law,[93] enacted during the tenure of Governor Mitt Romney, and which, in its essentials, served as the model for federal healthcare reform in the Obama administration.[94] Still another, equally contentious, example lies in the numerous states that have legalized medical marijuana, and more recently, recreational marijuana. These laws have been enacted notwithstanding the persistence of conflicting federal legislation, the Controlled Substances Act, which classifies marijuana (alongside heroin and the like) as a Schedule I drug, meaning it has "a high potential for abuse," "no currently accepted medical use in treatment in the United States," and "a lack of accepted" medical protocols for safe use.[95]

---

90. New State Ice Co. v. Liebmann, 285 U.S. 262, 311 (1932) (Brandeis, J., dissenting).

91. FERC v. Mississippi, 456 U.S. 742, 788 (1982) (O'Connor, J., dissenting).

92. Garcia v. San Antonio Metro Transit Auth., 469 U.S. 528, 567–68, 567 n.13 (1985) (Powell, J., dissenting).

93. An Act Providing Access to Affordable, Quality, Accountable Health Care, ch. 58, 2006 Mass. Acts 77 (codified as amended in scattered sections of the General Laws of Massachusetts).

94. Patient Protection and Affordable Care Act, 42 U.S.C. § 18001 (2012).

95. 21 U.S.C. § 812 (2012).

B. The Case against the States

"[I]f we are to be one nation in any respect," Madison wrote in *The Federalist*, "it clearly ought to be in respect to other nations."[96] Whatever the value of federalism in domestic affairs, in the realm of foreign affairs, the Supreme Court has consistently echoed Madison. It has regularly construed the Constitution to confer plenary foreign-affairs authority upon the federal government. Broad dicta to this effect permeates the Court's jurisprudence. Two seminal cases on the preemptive force of sole executive agreements (see Chapter 9) vis-à-vis state law offer typical examples. Both involved the refusal of New York State to give effect to a claims settlement agreement negotiated by the administration of President Franklin D. Roosevelt with the Soviet Union. New York argued that the deal conflicted with New York law and the claimed rights of New York state citizens under the New York law. In *United States v. Belmont*, the Court struck down New York's policy as unconstitutional and, in the course of its opinion, proclaimed, "Plainly, the external powers of the United States are to be exercised without regard to state laws or policies."[97] "In respect of . . . our foreign relations generally," it continued, "state lines disappear. As to such purposes the state . . . does not exist."[98] In *United States v. Pink*, the Court added that "power over external affairs is not shared by the States; it is vested in the national government exclusively."[99]

In the international realm, the Court has reiterated that the need for a uniform approach outweighs whatever values federalism may promote. The Court has generally declined to engage in any balancing of these values against national uniformity.[100] Time and again, it has embraced the general principle of federal exclusivity, even in cases in which the executive told the Court that the state statute at issue did not "unduly interfere with the United States' conduct of foreign relations."[101] State or local action with more than "some incidental or indirect effect in foreign countries" is invalid.[102]

---

96. The Federalist No. 42, at 279 (James Madison) (Jacob E. Cooke ed., 1961).

97. United States v. Belmont, 301 U.S. 324, 331 (1937).

98. *Id.*

99. United States v. Pink, 315 U.S. 203, 233 (1942).

100. In *Cooley v. Bd. of Wardens*, 53 U.S. (12 How.) 299 (1851), an important, early dormant Commerce Clause decision, the Court applied the sort of balancing test that could readily have been adapted to foreign-affairs federalism questions. The (limited) influence of this approach is evident in *Wardair Canada, Inc. v. Florida. Dep't of Revenue*, 477 U.S. 1 (1986), discussed in Chapter 5.

101. Zschernig v. Miller, 389 U.S. 429, 434 (1968).

102. *Id.* at 432. *See also* Am. Ins. Ass'n v. Garamendi, 539 U.S. 396, 418 (2003); Clark v. Allen, 331 U.S. 503, 517 (1947).

1. The Inapplicability of the Traditional Federalist Rationales

What accounts for this categorical approach? One reason the Court generally declines to countenance more than an incidental role for the states in foreign affairs may be that the three policy arguments for states laid out above apply less forcefully in the realm of foreign affairs.

First, although the diffusion of authority may well safeguard liberty and limit the concentration of power that leads to tyranny, state power to act internationally would pose no self-evident check on the exercise of arbitrary or corrupted national power. Diffusion of authority is neither the object nor the effect of state forays into foreign affairs. True, the states at times, particularly in recent years, have sought to use their voices, political constituencies, and resources to promote freedom, human rights,[103] environmentalism, and other values abroad. But among the putative purposes of federalism has never been its role or ability to enhance the liberty or improve the circumstances of *foreign* peoples in *foreign* countries. Whatever the relative merits of past instances of state efforts to influence foreign countries, it is at best unclear whether such state activities—for example, boycotts, divestment campaigns, ballot initiatives enabling state citizens to embrace hortatory positions on foreign relations issues, and the like—directed abroad have had even a marginal effect on the freedom and flourishing of the states' *own* residents.

Second, the relevance of the efficiency rationale in foreign affairs is equally questionable. It is not at all clear that the geographic proximity of the government to the governed promotes efficiency or any other benefit in foreign relations. Phone, email, videoconferencing, and other technologies often provide ample effective channels for both formal and personal exchanges. It makes little apparent difference whether the relevant official on the computer or phone sits in Washington, DC, rather than Springfield, Albany, or Carson City. Furthermore, specialization and division of labor can promote efficiency. Specialists in foreign affairs generally work for the federal government. Washington has comparatively far greater resources and capacity than the states to undertake the many tasks required for the sound conduct of foreign affairs. The federal government includes, and this is by no means an exhaustive list, the Foreign Affairs, Armed Services, and Intelligence Committees of Congress; the Departments of State, Defense, Treasury, Justice,

103. *See, e.g.*, Act to End Atrocities and Terrorism in the Sudan, 15 ILL. COMP. STAT. 520/22.5; ILL. COMP. STAT. 5/1-11-.5 (2005); MASS. GEN. LAWS ch. 7, § 22G-M (Burma Law) (1996); 15 ILL. COMP. STAT. 520/22.6, repealed by P.A. 95-521 (repealed 2007). In 1986, Ordinance No. 765 amended Baltimore City Code, Art. 22, §§ (7)(a), (35)(a), requiring the divestment of pension funds in banks or financial institutions that make loans to South Africa or Namibia.

and Homeland Security; the Central Intelligence Agency, Federal Bureau of Investigation, and National Security Agency; and many other institutions and bodies devoted in whole or part to foreign affairs. Federal departments, institutions, and agencies of this sort house and benefit from centuries of institutional memory, terabytes of data, and thousands of employees armed with education and experience in virtually every aspect of foreign policy. That they often err does not suggest that states and cities would necessarily do better. The states possess more limited resources and expertise in most relevant respects. And the federal government's remoteness from citizens in comparison to state governments may well be a virtue vis-à-vis foreign relations. Distance, both literally and figuratively, from the local concerns, interests, and at times parochial views and prejudices of particular state constituencies, cultivates greater detachment, balance, and providence—all of which tend to foster a more sensible, long-term foreign policy.

Third, and finally, a federalist system of competitive innovation and experimentation is a two-way street: laboratories, after all, can produce "Frankensteins." The inevitable competition among states and cities, which experiment with tax cuts, subsidies, and other incentives to boost local employment by encouraging businesses to (re)locate within them, may culminate in a catastrophic "race to the bottom."[104] Domestically, it may deprive local governments of critical tax revenues and degrade public safety, transportation, education, and other public goods (see Chapter 2). Even arguably successful state experimentation in the form of, say, generous unemployment support, adjustment assistance, in-state tuition subsidies, or healthcare benefits might attract an influx of immigrants, overwhelming state resources. When states confront a problem that they cannot realistically address on their own, the case for federal action is greater. Erwin Chemerinsky points to the example of child labor. Because of lower labor costs, businesses in states that permitted child labor enjoyed a competitive advantage over businesses in states that prohibited it. The latter were therefore subject to pressure to repeal the prohibition.[105] Many foreign affairs issues resemble child labor insofar as they exceed the capacity of states to act effectively and in conformity with the public

104. Ironically, Justice Brandeis, who coined the famous state-as-laboratory metaphor, *see New State Ice Co. v. Liebmann*, 285 U.S. 262, 311 (1932) (Brandeis, J., dissenting), also appears to have coined the phrase "race to the bottom." Louis K. Ligget Co. v. Lee, 288 U.S. 517, 558–59 (1933). Yet it seems more likely that this reflects, not inconsistency in Justice Brandeis's views on federalism, but rather a sophisticated jurisprudence that appreciates the need for nuance in appraising federalism values, the consequences of which differ by issue and context. Indeed, we suggest throughout this book that the constitutional jurisprudence that shapes the evolving role of states in foreign affairs should be less dogmatic and more sensitive to a searching, evidence-based analysis of federalism's functions, appraising its costs and benefits empirically within the concrete context of the national and international legal orders of the twenty-first century.

105. CHEMERINSKY, *supra* note 77, at 119.

good; the problems at issue therefore require federal attention. Unlike many of the local issues that fall within the rubric of traditional state functions[106]—such as education, crime control, zoning regulations, and public safety—foreign affairs issues ordinarily call for uniformity, not diversity, in approach.

2. *The Danger of Retaliation against the Entire Nation*

Above all, however, the Framers stressed a concern at the outset that continues to be politically relevant today: "that the peace of the WHOLE ought not to be left at the disposal of a PART," for "[t]he union will undoubtedly be answerable to foreign powers for the conduct of its members."[107] State involvement in the international realm risks conflicts with nations that may retaliate—economically, militarily, or otherwise—against the United States as a whole.[108] For the Framers, this was no hypothetical danger. Their experience under the Articles of Confederation underscored the very real threats and concrete retaliatory conduct, including war, that state disregard of national treaty obligations had provoked. Since 1789, the Supreme Court has consistently echoed the same concerns. In 1832, in *Brown v. Maryland*,[109] the Court struck down a Maryland law that required licenses for certain imports, emphasizing that the state law at issue could spark disputes with other nations. "What answer," Chief Justice Marshall asked, "would the United States give to the complaints and just reproaches to which such an extraordinary circumstance would expose them? No apology could be received, or even offered."[110] It is one thing, the Court has suggested, for a state to expose itself to

---

106. Politically, even if (in theory) no longer legally, *see Garcia v. San Antonio Metropolitan Transit Authority*, 469 U.S. 528 (1985), the idea of traditional state functions persists in contemporary Supreme Court case law. *See, e.g.*, Bond v. United States, 134 S. Ct. 2077 (2014); *Garamendi*, 539 U.S. at 396.

107. The Federalist No. 80, at 535–36 (Alexander Hamilton) (Jacob E. Cooke ed., 1961).

108. Today, as in 1789, general international law clearly holds countries as a whole accountable for the conduct of their political subdivisions. *See* The International Law Commission's Articles on State Responsibility: Introduction, Text, and Commentaries 94, art. 4 ¶¶ 1-2 (James Crawford ed., Cambridge University Press 2002). The importance of preventing conflict between the law of nations and state common law has been litigated in the Supreme Court numerous times since the earliest days. *See* Curtis Bradley, International Law in the U.S. Legal System 16 n.82 (2013) (noting the Court's concern that state law would contravene the law of nations in United States v. Smith, 18 U.S. (5 Wheat.) 153 (1820); United States v. Worrall, 2 U.S. (2 Dall.) 384 (1798); and Talbot v. Jansen, 3 U.S. (2 Dall.) 133 (1795)); *see also* Cleveland, *supra* note 79, at 980 (citing Worcester v. Georgia, 31 U.S. (6 Pet.) 515 (1832) (invalidating an act by Georgia regarding relations with the Cherokee, which were still considered issues of an "international" nature at the time)).

109. 25 U.S. (12 Wheat.) 419 (1832).

110. *Id.* at 447.

the risks of conflict with a foreign power, but it is quite another to arrogate to itself the power to expose its fellow states to those risks. Hence, in the same vein, the Court in 1875 struck down a California law that in effect regulated immigration, and by implication, commerce with foreign nations. The injured nation could not direct a claim for redress to California, the Court observed, because California could:

> hold no exterior relations with other nations. It [the foreign claim] would be made upon the government of the United States. If that government should get into a difficulty which would lead to war, or to suspension of intercourse, would California alone suffer, or all the Union?[111]

A century later, in 1979, California imposed an ad valorem property tax on foreign-owned cargo containers. The Court again invalidated the state law, mindful that the "risk of retaliation by Japan . . . [was] acute, and such retaliation of necessity would be felt by the Nation as a whole."[112] The Court's concerns in this regard are now embodied in the so-called "one voice" doctrine—a putative requirement, inferred from the Constitution's text and structure, that the nation speak with one voice in the realm of foreign affairs.

The one-voice doctrine often reflects a reasonable national interest in bolstering the efficacy of American foreign policy. The national interest sometimes benefits from at least the appearance of national unity and popular support. Open conflict between the federal and state governments on key foreign policy questions can undermine national foreign policy objectives. Of course, sometimes the foreign policy of the federal government is less than clear. Yet the federal government's silence with respect to a particular issue of foreign policy does not necessarily imply an absence of a federal policy. Still less does it indicate that the states should feel free to enter the field. Federal silence, inaction, or ambiguity may be calculated. Sometimes the best policy is to do and say nothing, or deliberately to attempt, with nuance, to leave national policy unclear.[113] But the question is whether the doctrine has been expanded beyond the limit of its logic.[114]

---

111. Chy Lung v. Freeman, 92 U.S. 275, 279 (1875).

112. Japan Line, Ltd. v. County of Los Angeles, 441 U.S. 434, 452–53 (1979).

113. *See generally* Richard B. Bilder, *The Role of the States and Cities in Foreign Relations*, *in* Foreign Affairs and the U. S. Constitution 121 (Louis Henkin, Michael J. Glennon & William D. Rogers eds., 1990).

114. *Cf.* Benjamin Cardozo, The Nature of the Judicial Process 52 (1922) ("The tendency of a principle to expand itself to the limit of its logic may be counteracted by the tendency to confine itself within the limits of its history.").

IV. Assessment

Doubtless the United States constitutionally must, at times, speak with one voice. The federal government, for example, is and must remain the sole representative of the United States, as a nation, in its interactions with foreign nations.[115] No state may send an ambassador to a foreign government or purport to negotiate with it on behalf of the United States. As noted earlier, the Constitution expressly denies the states any direct role in making treaties,[116] engaging in war, or making agreements or compacts without the consent of Congress.[117] And it is well settled that under the Supremacy Clause, valid treaties and acts of Congress preclude the states from adopting conflicting legislation.[118]

But the United States does not, in fact, always speak with one voice in foreign relations. And it makes little sense to insist that the United States always *should* speak with one voice in foreign relations. As Sarah Cleveland has observed, "it is clear that the Framers guaranteed, as a matter of constitutional design, that the United States would *not* 'speak with one voice' in foreign relations."[119] The Constitution divides the nation's foreign affairs powers among the three branches of the federal government. Congress and the federal judiciary, not the president alone, constitutionally "speak" and exercise an important role in the realm of foreign affairs. Historically, as Cleveland notes, this has "yielded a number of memorable conflicts."[120]

The United States may be "one nation," in Madison's words,[121] without the entire American people holding or expressing only one opinion, or always acting in unison. The nation consists of different people of different ethnicities, different religions, and different politics, today much more than in Madison's

115. *See generally* Bilder, *supra* note 113.

116. The states may, however, indirectly influence the treaty process by virtue of the requirement that Article II treaties be made by the president "by and with the advice and consent of the Senate, . . . provided two thirds of the Senators present concur." U.S. CONST. art. II, cl. 2. That the states lack a comparable role in congressional-executive and sole executive agreements arguably suggests a constitutional problem with the so-called interchangeability thesis. *See generally* Laurence H. Tribe, *Taking Text and Structure Seriously: Reflections on Free-Form Method in Constitutional Interpretation*, 108 HARV. L. REV. 1221 (1995).

117. We discuss the meaning of Article I, § 10, clause 2, which provides in relevant part that "[n]o state shall, without the consent of Congress, . . . enter into any agreement or compact with another state," in Chapter 8.

118. U.S. CONST. art. VI, cl. 2.; *see, e.g.*, Hines v. Davidowitz, 312 U.S. 52 (1941).

119. Cleveland, *supra* note 79, at 984 (emphasis added); *see also* Moore, *supra* note 79.

120. Cleveland, *supra* note 79, at 985.

121. THE FEDERALIST NO. 39, at 279 (James Madison) (Jacob E. Cooke ed., 1961).

time. Foreign leaders know that. Many citizens find state and local governments more accessible and responsive to their views than the federal government and thus find it easier to participate in politics and to be heard at the local level. It is only natural and healthy that they should seek to express and, where appropriate, vindicate their views through the official channels they may more readily access. In that sense, as Richard Bilder has emphasized, "state and local involvement in foreign relations represents a strengthening, rather than a weakening, of our democratic process."[122]

It is also worth recalling the precarious security of the nation in Madison's day. This made it prudent, but not *always* constitutionally compelled, for the federal government to ensure that it avoided "entanglements," as Washington warned in his farewell address.[123] At the time, state action in the realm of foreign affairs clearly risked such entanglements; that was, after all, one of the principal lessons of the experience under the Articles of Confederation. In the late eighteenth and early nineteenth centuries, France, Spain, and Britain all maintained active colonies on the borders of the fledgling nation. On the north, south, and west, the United States was hemmed in by the world's powers. A single misstep by a single state could imperil the entire country. For all the challenges that the United States confronts today, few would suggest that twenty-first century America must continue to walk on eggshells as did the thirteen newly-free colonies 230 years ago. Sometimes, it makes sense to "let a thousand flowers bloom." This is not an argument against the Supremacy Clause: of course the federal government must retain the power to preempt imprudent or dangerous activities by the states in the realm of foreign affairs that risk damaging retaliation. But such situations clearly will arise less frequently than they did in the early days of the fragile Republic.

As to the supposed complexity of the issues involved, although state and local officials seldom possess the expertise of legions of federal officials who handle foreign policy issues, many such issues do not present questions so intricate as to require that expertise. Sufficient relevant knowledge often can be gleaned from sources readily available on the Internet, and as the United States has too frequently been reminded, the "best and the brightest" do not always devise the wisest policies. The truth is that nearly any American adult with a little common sense and access to the Internet can formulate a reasonably intelligent position on virtually every foreign policy question, which is not, of course, to say they

122. *See* Bilder, *supra* note 113.

123. Farewell Address from President George Washington to The People of the United States of America (Sept. 19, 1796).

will. But it's difficult to point to many recent concrete examples of state or local foreign-policy initiatives that have clearly and significantly damaged the nation as a whole.[124]

Rather than attempting the impossible task of excluding states and cities altogether from the international realm, therefore, a better approach would be to assess whether control, as a practical matter, is possible; to allow states and cities broad discretion when the federal government is silent; and when the federal government has expressed a view, to presume, except in unforeseeable extreme circumstances, that states may still act unless Congress has clearly said otherwise. Such an approach would be more consistent with what states and cities actually do, and will continue to do, whatever abstract formulae the courts, scholars, and the executive branch may proclaim. If the life of law is not logic, but experience, as Holmes famously put it,[125] a glimpse in the next chapter at the nation's modern experience —a survey of what states and cities actually do in the quotidian world of foreign relations—will prove illuminating.

---

124. A prominent counter-example, however, is the saga of state decisions and executions following the International Court of Justice's trio of decisions, *see* Vienna Convention on Consular Relations (Paraguay v. United States), 1998 I.C.J. Rep. 248 (April 9); LaGrand (Germany v. United States), Judgment, 2001 I.C.J. Rep. 466 (June 27); Avena and Other Mexican Nationals (Mexico v. United States), Judgment, 2004 I.C.J. Rep. 2004 12 (March 31), in the cases involving death-row inmates who had been denied their right to consular assistance under the Vienna Convention on Consular Relations, Apr. 24, 1963, 21 U.S.T. 77, 596 U.N.T.S. 261. In each of these cases, the ICJ ordered the United States not to carry out certain executions of foreign nationals, but the states, in general, declined to abide by the orders. *See* Medellin v. Texas, 552 U.S. 491 (2008).

125. Oliver Wendell Holmes, Jr., The Common Law, Lecture I, 5 (Mark DeWolfe Howe ed., Little, Brown 1963) (1881).

2

States, Cities, and Globalization

GIVEN THE ABSOLUTIST shibboleth of federal exclusivity regularly incanted over the years by the Supreme Court, one might expect that states and cities would generally steer clear of foreign affairs and conduct in the international arena. Yet the evidence unambiguously establishes the contrary. Over the last few decades—quietly, with little fanfare—states and cities have emerged as major participants in U.S. foreign affairs. They have entered into compacts and agreements with foreign countries; adopted international standards on matters such as climate change, even when the federal government has declined to do so; established offices in foreign countries; sent representatives to foreign countries; offered economic incentives to attract businesses from those countries; barred purchases from those countries with "Buy American" statutes; established countless "sister city" relationships with foreign cities; adopted statements of policy, often based on local referenda, about international issues; given teeth to some of those policies with, for example, economic sanctions and trade bans; enacted laws and adopted police practices to discourage illegal immigration; acted to protect their citizens' data and privacy on the Internet; and contributed to the effort to keep the country safe from national security threats.

What motivates this new and reinvigorated "local internationalism"? At least three factors account for much of it. First, globalization: the same globalizing forces that perforate state and national boundaries, perhaps paradoxically, lead state and local officials to venture into an international arena that, until comparatively recently, they regarded as forbidden territory. Second, federal inaction or inertia: the federal government has been unable or unwilling to address many of the most serious problems caused by globalization, including, for example, those relating to immigration and cyber-intrusions (see Chapters 9 and 10); sometimes, for example, with immigration reform, federal incapacity is a consequence of political polarization and gridlock. Third, state capacity: because of the size of their populations and economies relative to many foreign countries, states have an enormous stake in how those countries differentiate among them, and conversely, an ability to differentiate among those countries on issues such as the latter's human rights practices.

None of these three factors seems likely to wane in the near future. Their combined force is fundamentally altering the nation's political and constitutional landscape. In part, their effect is to nudge the nation back to federalism's early days, an era in which the states played a much larger role internationally. The succeeding chapters of this book explore the extent to which federal jurisprudence, chiefly that of the Supreme Court, is flexible enough to accommodate these forces and the extent to which it may need to adapt to them. Adaptation, of course, must be realistic. It is therefore prudent to begin with a close examination of the three forces that have motivated states and cities to increase their activities in foreign affairs.

I. The Globalization Driver

The term "globalization" is an imprecise, broad, and poorly understood phenomenon. In its most expansive sense, it is both a mélange and a paradox.

Globalization is a mélange because it consists of multiple phenomena. The term subsumes, among other developments, political events such as the end of the Cold War and the dissolution of the Soviet Union; technological innovations such as instantaneous worldwide communication and access to vast stores of previously inaccessible information, largely courtesy of the Internet; a related information explosion, bringing enhanced opportunities for people to learn more about what governments do, and to criticize them and organize against them; easy and efficient international travel, resulting in more porous national borders and the growth of transnational business; cosmopolitanism; swelling populations, generating mass migration, mostly from south to north—and often illegal; both cultural conflict and convergence; increased transborder pollution and other uncontrolled externalities, exacerbating global warming and threatening biodiversity; and ethereal economic competition, represented by rootless multinational corporations with offshore supply chains capable of producing better products at lower prices by competing in global markets for the friendliest regulatory environments and the cheapest labor.

Globalization is also paradoxical because it is an amalgam of conflicting elements. It often pushes people and developments in opposite directions simultaneously. Globalization improves standards of living by making available better, cheaper goods and services. But it also undermines quality of life by requiring, for example, greater mobility and retraining to chase new jobs. Globalization educates people about and reminds them of how much they have in common with those in other countries. But it also exacerbates insecurities, and in this regard, threatens to encourage various forms of tribalism, driving populations to seek shelter in rigid, intolerant religious, ethnic, and national identities. Globalization encourages greater consensus globally by providing more news sources that broadens minds. But it also narrows minds by enabling people to avoid unsupportive data that challenges their presuppositions.[1] Globalization drives many to care about human rights in other countries. But it also makes them defensive about their own nation's practices. Arthur Schlesinger captured the contradiction succinctly. "Integration and disintegration," he wrote, "are the opposites that feed on one another. The more the world integrates, the more people cling to their own . . . ."[2] And globalization's risks at times countermand its benefits. In retrospect,

> the immediate post-Cold War era now looms as a time of "global optimism," when many commentators were exuberantly optimistic about the constructive possibilities posed by the globalization of transport, commerce, finance, and communications. In the age of global optimism, we marveled at the potential of the growing global network of information, trade, and transportation to create genuinely global solutions to global problems. But then we learned that the same coin has a dark side: that terrorists can exploit that same interconnectedness to turn airplanes into missiles, to use the global financial system to move money across borders, to turn ordinary mail into a delivery system for biological weapons, and to plant viruses into email as a tool for cyberterrorism. Since September 11, we have almost literally left the light and entered the shadows of a new age of global pessimism, in which we have realized with alarm that all of the interdependent dimensions of the age of globalization could be equally turned against us.[3]

So what, exactly, is going on? How is globalization affecting interactions between the states and the federal government on foreign affairs issues? Pankaj

---

1. In a 2009 op-ed, Nichoas Kristof aptly observed that, today, "When we go online, each of us is our own editor, our own gatekeeper. We select the kind of news and opinions that we care most about." Nicholas Kristof, Op-Ed, *The Daily Me*, N.Y. TIMES, Mar. 18, 2009, at A31. "That's because there's pretty good evidence that we generally don't truly want good information—but rather information that confirms our prejudices. We may believe intellectually in the clash of opinions, but in practice we like to embed ourselves in the reassuring womb of an echo chamber." *Id.*

2. ARTHUR M. SCHLESINGER, JR., THE DISUNITING OF AMERICA: REFLECTIONS ON A MULTICULTURAL SOCIETY 12 (1998).

3. Harold Hongju Koh, *On American Exceptionalism*, 55 STAN. L. REV. 1479, 1496 (2003).

Ghemawat offers compelling evidence that "most types of economic activity that could be carried out within or across national borders are actually still concentrated domestically."[4] For Ghemawat, consequently, all this talk of the "flattening of the world"[5] and the "death of distance" adds up to a lot of "globaloney."[6] Ghemawat's data highlight the continued centrality of local producers, local consumers, and thus local markets. If local markets remain as or more important than ever, so too do local governments. Moreover, the conflicting incentives and trends generated by globalization—at once local and global—partially explain the paralysis that increasingly characterizes the federal government's efforts (or lack thereof) to resolve the problems caused by globalization. Absent national action, states increasingly have sought to tackle those problems themselves. At least eleven powerful developments animate the growing participation of states in foreign affairs:

1. *Increasingly, social and economic problems can be addressed effectively only through cross-border collaboration—necessitating cooperative arrangements between states and foreign nations.* Because of their geographic proximity, U.S. states have joined with Canadian provinces to form a number of organizations. The Alberta Bilateral Advisory Council and Task Forces includes its namesake Canadian province, plus Alaska, Idaho, and Montana. The Council of Great Lakes Governors consists of Quebec, Ontario, Illinois, Indiana, Michigan, Minnesota, New York, Ohio, Pennsylvania, and Wisconsin. The Northeast Regional Homeland Security Directors Group (Connecticut, Delaware, Maine, Massachusetts, New Hampshire, New York, Pennsylvania, Rhode Island, Vermont; Ontario, Quebec, New Brunswick, Nova Scotia) and the Western Canadian Premiers and Western Governors Association, which

---

4. *See* Pankaj Ghemawat, *Globalization Myths versus Reality*, HARV. BUS. REV. BLOG (Sept. 5, 2007), http://blogs.hbr.org/ghemawat/2007/09/globalization_myths_versus_rea_1.html; *see also* Pankaj Ghemawat, *Semiglobalization and International Business Strategy*, 34 J. INT'L BUS. STUD. 138 (2003). The enduring importance of local markets is fleshed out further in Ghemawat's book-length treatment of the issue. PANKAJ GHEMAWAT, REDEFINING GLOBAL STRATEGY: CROSSING BORDERS IN A WORLD WHERE DIFFERENCES STILL MATTER (2007); *see also* Alan Rugman & Alain Verbeke, *Liabilities of Regional Foreignness and the Use of Firm-Level versus Country-Level Data: A Response to Dunning et al.*, 38 J. INT'L BUS. STUD. (2007) (arguing that with the exception of a few outliers, such as Google, IBM, Nokia, and the like, most multinational enterprises (MNEs) still operate intra-regionally because of the high costs of doing business abroad and other cultural, administrative, geographic, and economic factors).

5. *See generally* THOMAS FRIEDMAN, THE WORLD IS FLAT 3.0: A BRIEF HISTORY OF THE TWENTY-FIRST CENTURY (2007).

6. Pankaj Ghemawat, *Globalization in the World We Live in Now: World 3.0*, HARV. BUS. REV. BLOG (May 31, 2011), http://blogs.hbr.org/2011/05/globalization-in-the-world-we/.

includes four provinces and twenty-one states who send representatives to one another's annual meetings, represent additional prominent partnerships.[7] To be sure, partnerships, agreements, and cooperation of this sort predate globalization.[8] Yet it can no longer be said with confidence, as Louis Henkin did as recently as 1996, that none of these forms of collaboration "involve[] local intrusion on matters of foreign policy."[9] And this raises questions about the efficacy, prudence, and constitutionality of these newly robust and expansive forms of state action in foreign affairs.

2. *More transnational problems generate more international standards, backed by complex empirical research and global political momentum that spans continents and crosses borders—incentivizing states and cities to participate.* The most prominent issues raised by globalization include immigration, human rights, global warming, and other environmental concerns, among others that may be sensibly ameliorated by the establishment of international standards. States and cities increasingly adopt global standards applicable to such issues, as well as global health,[10] disease control, and human services. This, in turn, naturally motivates local officials and their constituents to participate in the formation of "global best practices." The Federation of State Medical Boards, for example, which represents the seventy medical and osteopathic boards of the U.S. states and territories, serves as the Secretariat for the International Association of Medical Regulatory Authorities and assists in the development of global best practices for medical regulators. Its goal is to "anticipate trends in medical regulation, licensure and discipline and act to strengthen the role of state medical boards in a global health care environment."[11]

3. *Globalization creates more opportunities for trade, tourism, and investment, which can be pursued most effectively through direct personal presence in the form of official visits and permanent overseas offices.* According to the 2010 census, international visitors to the United States totaled 29.4 million people in 2008, up 15 percent from just two years earlier.[12] California, New York, and

7. *See* Earl Fry, *Federalism and the Evolving Cross-Border Role of Provincial, State and Municipal Governments*, 60 INT'L J. 479–80 (2005).

8. LOUIS HENKIN, FOREIGN AFFAIRS AND THE U.S. CONSTITUTION 155 (2d ed. 1996).

9. *Id.* at 154.

10. *See* Drew Altman & Douglas Morgan, *The Role of State and Local Government in Health*, 2 HEALTH AFF. 1 (1983).

11. Federation of State Medical Boards, *Strategic Plan* (2000), https://www.fsmb.org/Media/Default/PDF/FSMB/Advocacy/2002_grpol_License_Portability.pdf.

12. U.S. CENSUS BUREAU, THE NATIONAL DATA BOOK: STATES AND LOCAL AREAS (2010), https://www.census.gov/library/publications/2010/compendia/databooks.html.

Florida together attracted almost 14.5 million visitors. From 1997 to 2006, governors led 512 U.S. state trade missions abroad, an average of 55 per year.[13] Japan was the most frequent destination, visited 67 times.[14] China (45) and Taiwan (31) combined accounted for another 76 visits, while Mexico (39) and Germany (37) were also popular destinations.[15] Virginia was the most active of the states. Its representatives visited foreign nations 31 times in ten years.[16] Others with a large number of trips included Wisconsin (30), Nebraska (23), and Ohio (21).[17]

4. *Foreign investors enjoy more alternatives, encouraging states and cities to offer them comparatively superior incentives to beat the competition.* This rivalry leads to state and local governments offering bigger tax breaks and other favorable conditions to attract businesses. Tax incentives can play a decisive role in the decisions of foreign businesses once they narrow their choices to a handful of otherwise desirable locations with similar characteristics.[18] Whether these incentives, in the aggregate, actually benefit local economic development is debatable. Data support both sides.[19] It appears that lower taxes often do attract investment from international businesses.[20] Despite initial gains, however, states that fail to write effective "clawback" provisions into investor-friendly agreements ultimately may suffer losses. States use clawback provisions to recapture at least part of the benefits that they award companies after, for example, promising to create jobs in a specified location.[21] If a state fails to incorporate such provisions, it often ends up holding the bag. Heavily courted

---

13. Andrew Cassey, *State Trade Missions* 15 (Wash. State U., Working Paper Series WP-2010-13, 2010), http://faculty.ses.wsu.edu/WorkingPapers/Cassey/WP2010-13.pdf.

14. *Id.* at 16.

15. *Id.*

16. *Id.*

17. *Id.*

18. *See* Jacques Morisset, *Tax Incentives: Using Tax Incentives to Attract Foreign Direct Investment*, The World Bank Group [WBG]), Note No. 253 (Feb. 2003) 1; *see also* Gustavo Bobonis & Howard Schatz, *Agglomeration, Adjustment and State Policies in the Location of Foreign Direct Investment in the United States*, 89 REV. ECON & STAT. 30 (2007) (finding that unitary taxation and state foreign office policies do influence foreign direct investment decisions).

19. *See generally* Terry F. Buss, *The Effect of State Tax Incentives on Economic Growth and Firm Location Decisions: An Overview of the Literature*, 15 ECON. DEV. Q. 90 (2001).

20. *A Survey of Globalisation and Tax: To the Victor Go the Spoils*, THE ECONOMIST (Jan. 27, 2000), http://www.economist.com/node/277006.

21. Kathleen A. Norat & Eileen M. Lomoriello, *Clawbacks: A Help or Hindrance in Negotiating Incentive Benefits?*, J. MULTISTATE TAX'N & INCENTIVES 24, 26 (2003).

and widely wooed major international businesses—deep-pocketed multinational corporations—generally emerge as the real winners in global tax competition. But that hasn't stopped states from falling over each other to be the next landing spot for Mercedes-Benz, Nestlé, or Google.

5. *More companies believe that to survive they need to "internationalize" their business models, creating a perpetual search for underserved markets.* Despite, or perhaps because of, the damage to the U.S. economy from the 2008 financial crisis, U.S. markets continue to attract companies looking to expand. Particular regions of the United States have become centers for specialized sectors of global business, such as technology and pharmaceutical companies. State-funded universities provide much of the research and intellectual capital that enables these companies to thrive, and state-funded projects supply infrastructure that contributes substantially to business efficiency. Regions with a high concentration of particular industries tend over time to develop their own identity and culture. Silicon Valley attracts "new school" social media, web advertising, and software companies from around the world, such as Facebook and Google, while the region also attracts "old school" computing technology companies, including Hewlett-Packard and IBM.[22] New Jersey and Pennsylvania have become epicenters for huge multinational pharmaceutical conglomerates, including Bristol Meyers-Squibb, Novo-Nordisk, Novartis, and Merck, while the Route 128 corridor surrounding Boston and Cambridge serves as a center of gravity for defense research, electronics development, and high-tech industrial innovation.[23]

6. *More Americans travel abroad—generating a desire to establish ongoing political, cultural, and educational relationships with local entities and people in foreign countries.* The total number of U.S. international visitors totaled 60.3 million in 2010, which despite amounting to a 2 percent decrease from 2009, set records for visits to several international locations, including the Dominican Republic, South Africa, Aruba, and Israel.[24] The desire of

---

22. For an overview of the development of high-technology culture in Silicon Valley, see EVERETT M. ROGERS & JUDITH K. LARSEN, SILICON VALLEY FEVER: THE GROWTH OF HIGH-TECHNOLOGY CULTURE (1984). The story of Facebook's migration from Cambridge, Massachusetts, to Palo Alto, California, is recounted in BEN MEZRICH, THE ACCIDENTAL BILLIONAIRES: THE FOUNDING OF FACEBOOK: A TALE OF SEX, MONEY, GENIUS AND BETRAYAL (2010).

23. *See* SUSAN ROSEGRANT & DAVID R. LAMPE, ROUTE 128: LESSONS FROM BOSTON'S HIGH-TECH COMMUNITY (1993). For an interesting comparison of the Silicon Valley and Route 128 cultures, see Paul Mackun, *Silicon Valley and Route 128: Two Faces of the American Technopolis*, NETVALLEY.COM, http://www.netvalley.com/silicon_valley/Silicon_Valley_and_Route_128.html (last visited Mar. 10, 2012).

24. U.S DEP'T OF COMMERCE, INT'L TRADE ADMIN., U.S. CITIZEN AIR TRAFFIC TO OVERSEAS REGIONS, CANADA AND MEXICO 2011, http://tinet.ita.doc.gov/view/

Americans to connect and engage internationally manifests itself in cultural and educational exchanges and "sister-city" relationships.[25]

7. *More Americans pay attention to international news, in part because of its greater prominence today, and in part because it increasingly affects them directly, and they therefore develop opinions about foreign policy issues, which, in turn, leads them to place pressure on accessible public officials to reflect those opinions in policy statements and regulatory laws.* Globalization creates winners and losers. High-income, high-ability workers tend to benefit from globalization and therefore demand less from government.[26] Low-income, low-ability workers generally lose; in response, they often demand greater income redistribution by various means. Policy preferences tend to reflect these differential effects of globalization.[27] State constituents increasingly push their governors to take stands on trade, investment, and other foreign policy issues and to engage visibly with foreign leaders, demonstrating forceful advocacy for their states. This has already led to the establishment of new state offices and institutions, such as the Secretary of Foreign Affairs in California, the Office of International Affairs in Hawaii, and the Office of Federal and International Relations in Kentucky.[28] Voters occasionally have put elected foreign policy officials, such as Bill Richardson, in office as governor, hoping that these leaders can use their international experience and expertise for the state's benefit.[29]

8. *More American jobs are going abroad, incentivizing governments at all levels to require that goods and services be purchased in the United States.*

---

m-2011-O-001/index.html (last visited Feb. 25, 2012); U.S. DEP'T OF COMMERCE, INT'L TRADE ADMIN., U.S. TRAVEL ABROAD DECREASED TWO PERCENT IN 2010 (Nov. 10, 2011), http://tinet.ita.doc.gov/outreachpages/download_data_table/2010_Outbound_Analysis.pdf.

25. *See* Sister-Cities International, http://sister-cities.org/mission-and-history (last visited May 24, 2014).

26. Stephanie Walter & Linda Maduz, *How Globalization Shapes Individual Risk Perceptions and Policy Preferences: A Cross-National Analysis of Differences between Globalization Winners and Losers* 10 (Weatherhead Center for Int'l Affairs, Harvard University, Working Paper No. 2009-0015, 2009) ("Low-ability workers exposed to the international economy face lower wages and higher risk of unemployment, and can therefore be characterized as globalization losers. In contrast, high-ability workers receive higher wages when they are exposed to international competition and, are therefore identified as globalization winners."). *See also id.* at 2–3.

27. Walter & Maduz, *supra* note 26, at 1 ("Overall, . . . studies typically find that in developed countries, high-skilled individuals are more pro-trade and pro-immigration than low-skilled individuals, and that individuals employed in exporting or tradables industries tend to have different policy preferences than those working in the non-tradable sector.").

28. *See* Samuel Lucas McMillan, *Subnational Foreign Policy Actors: How and Why Governors Participate in U.S. Foreign Policy*, 4 FOREIGN POL'Y ANALYSIS 227, 244 (2008).

29. *See id.* at 244–45.

Estimated net U.S. job loss (gross job gains minus gross job losses) because of "offshoring" is approximately 3 percent.[30] The total number since 2001 is generally believed to be in the millions.[31] At the same time, more and more consumer goods and services consumed by Americans come from overseas, where their jobs have relocated. The nation's international trade deficit in goods and services increased from $500 billion in 2010 to $558 billion in 2011.[32] Some states have been hit particularly hard. In a single year, from 2008 to 2009, Montana's exports decreased by 17.9 percent; North Dakota's by 15.4 percent; and South Dakota's by 16.7 percent.[33] During that same period, the number of manufacturing companies engaged in export decreased nationwide by 4.1 percent. In an effort to keep American companies in business, state and local governments, which spend close to $2 trillion annually on goods and services, increasingly try to leverage their purchasing power to favor local businesses and create jobs.[34] Twenty-one states had "Buy American" laws as of 2009, according to the National Association of State Procurement Officials, and nearly every state has implemented preference statutes for buying from in-state producers.[35]

9. *More goods and services sold in the United States are produced abroad and marketed within the United States by geographically-ethereal multinational corporations, encouraging states to devise new, nontraditional schemes to curb tax avoidance.* Imports of goods and services into the United States have increased nationwide. The combined value of imported goods and services increased dramatically in the past half century, from $22.4 billion in 1960 to $2.85 trillion in 2014,[36] with the pace of change accelerating in recent years. The trade deficit in goods rose from $645.9 billion in 2010 to $741.5 billion in 2014.[37] In 2008, some 83 of the 100 largest publicly-traded U.S. corporations

---

30. *See* LINDA LEVINE, CONG. RESEARCH SERV., RL32292, OFFSHORING (AKA OFFSHORE OUTSOURCING) AND JOB INSECURITY AMONG U.S. WORKERS 1 (2011).

31. *See id.* at 6–7.

32. U.S. CENSUS BUREAU, FOREIGN TRADE, U.S. INTERNATIONAL TRADE DATA, http://www.census.gov/foreign-trade/data/index.html (last visited Feb. 27, 2012).

33. U.S. CENSUS BUREAU, PROFILE OF U.S. IMPORTING AND EXPORTING COMPANIES, 2008–2009 HIGHLIGHTS (2009), http://www.census.gov/foreign-trade/Press-Release/edb/2009/2009Highlights.pdf.

34. Devin Dwyer, *More States Using Purchasing Power to "Buy American," Create Jobs*, ABC NEWS, Mar. 8, 2011, http://abcnews.go.com/Politics/MadeInAmerica/state-governments-push-made-america-create-jobs-economic/story?id=13078351#.ToAAqFF2N3I.

35. *Id.*

36. U.S. CENSUS BUREAU, FOREIGN TRADE, U.S. INTERNATIONAL TRADE DATA, http://www.census.gov/foreign-trade/statistics/historical/gands.pdf (last visited July 21, 2015).

37. *Id.*

maintained partially or wholly owned subsidiaries in jurisdictions listed as tax havens or financial privacy jurisdictions.[38] Some states attempting to clamp down on these global tax evaders have closed potential loopholes through "unitary taxation" and other comprehensive schemes designed to tax multinational corporations on all of their earnings, regardless of the locus.[39]

10. *More foreigners want to live in the United States, leading to more illegal immigration, and straining public services.* The number of unauthorized immigrants in the United States rose from 8.46 million in 2000 to 10.79 million in 2010, an increase of 28 percent.[40] Of that total, approximately 2.57 million (24 percent) live in California; 1.77 million in Texas (16 percent), and 760,000 in Florida (7 percent). These three states thus accounted for 47 percent, nearly half, of all unauthorized immigrants. Approximately 11 percent of the unauthorized immigrant population (1.23 million) are under the age of eighteen. In some states this number is growing quickly, adding to the largest single expenditure in state and local budgets—education.[41] In California alone, by one estimate, unauthorized immigrant students enrolled in K-12 institutions cost the state government $3.2 billion in annual education expenses.[42] California

38. *See* U.S. GOV'T ACCOUNTABILITY OFFICE, GAO-09-157, LARGE U.S. CORPORATIONS AND FEDERAL CONTRACTORS WITH SUBSIDIARIES IN JURISDICTIONS LISTED AS TAX HAVENS OR FINANCIAL PRIVACY JURISDICTIONS (2008).

39. *See generally* Michael S. Schadewald, *State Taxation of U.S.-Controlled Foreign Corporations: How Big Is the Tax Bite?*, 36 INT'L TAX J. 73 (2010) (assessing the tax policies of California, Illinois, New York, Florida, and Texas).

40. *See* MICHAEL HOEFER, NANCY RYTINA & BRIAN BAKER, DEP'T OF HOMELAND SEC., ESTIMATES OF THE UNAUTHORIZED IMMIGRATION POPULATION LIVING IN THE UNITED STATES: JANUARY 2010, at 2 (Feb. 2011), http://www.dhs.gov/xlibrary/assets/statistics/publications/ois_ill_pe_2010.pdf. Although the population of illegal immigrants peaked in 2007 at 11.78 million and dropped to 10.75 million by 2009, it appears to be rising again. *Id.* The financial crisis of 2008 may explain some of this fluctuation.

41. *See* CONG. BUDGET OFFICE, THE IMPACT OF UNAUTHORIZED IMMIGRANTS ON THE BUDGETS OF STATE AND LOCAL GOVERNMENTS (Dec. 2007), http://www.cbo.gov/sites/default/files/cbofiles/ftpdocs/87xx/doc8711/12-6-immigration.pdf. Accurate statistics for the number of school-aged unauthorized immigrants in each state as well as the costs that they impose on state and local governments are difficult to come by, reflecting the need for additional data and study. For a review of the practical and methodological impediments, see generally U.S. GOV'T ACCOUNTABILITY OFFICE, GAO-04-733, REPORT TO THE CHAIRMAN, COMMITTEE OF THE JUDICIARY, HOUSE OF REPRESENTATIVES, ILLEGAL ALIEN SCHOOLCHILDREN: ISSUES IN ESTIMATING STATE-BY-STATE COSTS (June 2004), http://www.gao.gov/assets/250/243050.pdf.

42. Federation for American Immigration Reform, *The Costs of Illegal Immigration to Californians* (Nov. 2004), http://www.fairus.org/site/DocServer/ca_costs.pdf?docID=141. The FAIR study was based on an estimated total of 425,000 K-12-aged unauthorized immigrants and 597,000 U.S.-born children of unauthorized immigrants.

spends another $4.5 billion each year to educate the U.S.-born children (and therefore new citizens)[43] of illegal immigrants.[44]

11. *Transnational security threats, such as terrorism and drug trafficking, affect more and more Americans, leading to increased involvement by local law-enforcement and police personnel.* The National Governors Association (NGA) maintains a special committee on homeland security, the mandate of which includes homeland security policy, emergency management, cybersecurity, and combating substance abuse and drug trafficking.[45] The preamble to the NGA's Homeland Security Policy highlights state and local responsibilities:

> States continue to face unprecedented, permanent responsibilities and challenges to provide for the security of all Americans. Although the U.S. Constitution delegates to Congress the power and responsibility to provide for the common defense, homeland security requires coordination between all levels of government. Multifaceted threats can materialize at any time and cross any borders. As a result, strategic intergovernmental preparedness and interagency cooperation at all levels of government are essential to preventing loss of life and major economic damage.[46]

Governments at all levels must handle these and other consequences of globalization. How has the federal government responded?

Not well.

II. *Federal Incapacity*

To be fair, the extent of federal gridlock is often overstated. Powerful images prevail in the media of disconnected politicians in Washington grinding the gears of government to a halt. In fact, although opinions of course differ on its merits or demerits, significant federal legislation has been enacted in recent years,

---

43. U.S. CONST. amend. XIV, § 1.

44. Federation for American Immigration Reform, *The Costs of Illegal Immigration to Californians* (Nov. 2004), http://www.fairus.org/site/DocServer/ca_costs.pdf?docID=141.

45. *See* National Governors Association, Special Committee on Homeland Security, *Policy Positions*, http://www.nga.org/cms/home/federal-relations/nga-policy-positions/page-hsps-policies.html (last visited July 21, 2015).

46. *See* National Governors Association, *EC-05 Homeland Security Policy* (July 19, 2009).

including national healthcare, an economic stimulus package, financial regulatory reform, and other legislative initiatives. And federal inaction is sometimes deliberate; no policy is sometimes preferable to unwise or risky policy. Further, relative to individual states, the federal government inevitably confronts a broader array of interests that it must try to accommodate or balance. What may seem like an obvious and uncontroversial policy prescription in Providence or Sacramento may look a lot more complicated to the Office of the Special Trade Representative or the Department of Homeland Security, which must weigh competing interests.

But such qualifications aside, it is not unfair to say that the federal government has neglected a host of festering problems that have and continue to harm the states.

Illegal immigration is perhaps the most prominent example. Despite years of intermittent effort, Congress and the White House remain unable to reach consensus on an immigration reform package. "The federal government's failure to enforce our border has functionally turned every state into a border state," said Randy Terrill, a Republican representative from Oklahoma who has led the drive for laws against illegal immigration there. "This is federalism in action," he continued: "The states are stepping in and filling the void left by the federal government."[47]

Environmental protection is another major issue. The United Nations convened a climate summit in Copenhagen in December 2009 to develop a treaty or other arrangement to succeed the Kyoto Protocol. It failed. At the Bali climate summit two years earlier, the parties to the Kyoto Protocol agreed to put the final touches on a binding global treaty to cut greenhouse gas emissions. But the parties abandoned that objective even before Copenhagen convened. Participating nations then agreed that at Copenhagen they would resolve issues such as mid-term reduction commitments by developed countries, monitoring those commitments, and funding adaptation and mitigation in developing countries. They again made no progress.[48]

---

47. Julia Preston, *Political Battle on Illegal Immigration Shifts to States*, N.Y. TIMES (Dec. 31, 2010), http://www.nytimes.com/2011/01/01/us/01immig.html?_r=0; *see also* Shannon O'Neil, *Immigration Reform Is Happening: With the Federal Government Paralyzed by Partisan Bickering over Undocumented Immigrants, States and Cities Are Leading the Way*, FOREIGN POL'Y, July 11, 2014, http://foreignpolicy.com/2014/07/11/immigration-reform-is-happening/. *See generally* Juliet P. Stumpf, *States of Confusion: The Rise of State and Local Power over Immigration*, 86 N.C. L. REV. 1557 (2008).

48. Ronald Baily, *Copenhagen Climate Conference Collapses*, REASON.COM (Dec. 18, 2009), http://reason.com/archives/2009/12/18/copenhagen-climate-conference.

Still another area of federal deficiency, if not dereliction, is cybersecurity. Federal officials as prominent as the Secretary of Defense have warned of a "cyber-Pearl Harbor."[49] Yet Washington remains deadlocked on how to prevent it and related issues. Targets in the United States have suffered a number of significant cyberattacks in recent years, and protecting the nation's networks has supposedly been among the federal government's top priorities. But the federal government has not imposed even minimal security standards for private operators of critical information systems.[50]

Why the federal gridlock? Analysts routinely cite several obvious causes:

- Increasingly safe congressional districts reduce the need for representatives to appeal to a broad spectrum of voters and thus tend to encourage political extremism.
- Use of the filibuster has increased dramatically in the Senate, preventing that body from even considering legislation on major controversial issues.[51]
- Nonpartisan, professional committee staff members in both houses of Congress have become a relic of past eras, replaced by political appointees who answer to either the majority or minority and who have little inclination to understand, still less accommodate, opposing interests.
- Campaign finance limits have all but collapsed, particularly in the wake of *Citizens United* and *McCutcheon*,[52] while voter identification requirements

---

49. Elisabeth Bumiller & Thom Shanker, *Panetta Warns of Dire Threat of Cyberattack on U.S.*, N.Y. Times, Oct. 11, 2012, http://www.nytimes.com/2012/10/12/world/panetta-warns-of-dire-threat-of-cyberattack.html?pagewanted=all.

50. Jonathan Masters, *Securing U.S. Cyberspace*, Council on Foreign Rel., Feb. 22, 2012, http://www.cfr.org/united-states/securing-us-cyberspace/p27430 (last visited June 9, 2014); *see also* U.S. Dep't of Defense, Department of Defense Cyber Strategy 21 (Apr. 17, 2015), http://www.defense.gov/Portals/1/features/2015/0415_cyber-strategy/Final_2015_DoD_CYBER_STRATEGY_for_web.pdf (detailing five strategic objectives: "Build and maintain ready forces and capabilities to conduct cyberspace operations; Defend the DoD information network, secure DoD data, and mitigate risks to DoD missions; Be prepared to defend the U.S. homeland and U.S. vital interests from disruptive or destructive cyberattacks of significant consequence; Build and maintain viable cyber options and plan to use those options to control conflict escalation and to shape the conflict environment at all stages; Build and maintain robust international alliances and partnerships to deter shared threats and increase international security and stability.").

51. Norman J. Ornstein et al., *Vital Statistics on Congress*, Brookings Inst. (July 2013), http://www.brookings.edu/research/reports/2013/07/vital-statistics-congress-mann-ornstein (last visited June 21, 2015); *see also* Fred Dews, *Chart: A Recent History of Senate Cloture Votes Taken to End Filibusters*, Brookings Inst., Nov. 21, 2013, http://www.brookings.edu/blogs/brookings-now/posts/2013/11/chart-recent-history-of-senate-cloture-votes-to-end-filibusters (last visited July 21, 2015).

52. McCutcheon v. FEC, 134 S. Ct. 1434 (2014); Citizens United v. FEC, 558 U.S. 310 (2010).

and similar impediments to broad voting rights have diminished the voice of the comparatively disenfranchised,[53] leading to aggregation of de facto political power among the wealthiest Americans.

- Open meeting requirements mean government in the sunshine for everyone—including, in particular, lobbyists for special interests, who can more capably and effectively monitor and reward friendly legislators.
- Ideological media, concentrated in cable television and talk radio, and enhanced greatly by the online publications, blogs, Twitter, and other media enabled by the Internet, encourages dogmatism and ideologues.[54]
- Negative attack ads, often sponsored by supposedly unaffiliated political action committees (PACs), exercise an outsize influence on the political process, eroding public respect for electoral victors, discouraging newcomers, and engendering cynicism about the electoral process generally.

Many pundits ascribe such factors to the same forces responsible for Washington's creeping paralysis. In fact, they may well be more symptoms than causes, epiphenomena that distract from the deeper currents responsible for political dysfunction. Serious scholars have begun to examine those currents,[55] which, although largely beyond the scope of this book, relate in substantial part to the dislocations and insecurities associated with globalization and mistaken expectations concerning the benefits of economic integration.

At least since the classical work of David Ricardo in 1817,[56] economists have known that a nation profits by exporting goods in which it has a comparative advantage and importing goods from other nations in which those nations

53. Shelby County v. Holder, 133 S. Ct. 2612 (2013); Crawford v. Marion County Election Bd., 553 U.S. 181 (2008); *see also* John Schwatz, *Judge in Landmark Case Disavows Support for Voter ID*, N.Y. Times, Oct. 15, 2013, http://www.nytimes.com/2013/10/16/us/politics/judge-in-landmark-case-disavows-support-for-voter-id.html?_r=0 (last visited July 21, 2015), print version. For more information on voter ID laws across the United States, see Wendy Underhill, *Voter Identification Requirements*, National Conference of State Legislatures (last updated Apr. 30, 2014), http://www.ncsl.org/research/elections-and-campaigns/voter-id.aspx (last visited July 21, 2015).

54. Kristof, *supra* note 1.

55. *See, e.g.*, Congress Reconsidered (Lawrence C. Dodd & Bruce I. Oppenheimer eds., 9th ed. 2008); Thomas F. Mann & Norman J. Ornstein, The Broken Branch: How Congress Is Failing American and How to Get It Back (2006); Barbara Sinclair, Unorthodox Lawmaking: New Legislative Processes in the U.S. Congress (4th ed. 2011); Sean M. Theriault, Party Polarization in Congress (2008); The U.S. Senate: From Deliberation to Dysfunction (Burdett Loomis ed., 2011).

56. David Ricardo, On the Principles of Political Economy and Taxation (1817).

maintain a comparative advantage. Consequently, all nations, by engaging in free trade with one other and capitalizing on their disparate efficiencies and costs of production, can benefit and increase their overall wealth.[57] That seems like an unmitigated good.

It is not.[58]

The first problem is that overall wealth says nothing about its distribution. A nation may become wealthier through free international trade, but all or most of that additional wealth may flow to only a tiny fraction of the population. That is precisely the situation in the United States today, a consequence of consistent trends beginning roughly thirty-five years ago. From 1993 to 2010, the incomes of the top 1 percent of Americans grew 58 percent while those of the remaining 99 percent grew only 6.4 percent.[59] In 2010, the top 1 percent captured 93 percent of additional income generated by the economy that year.[60] And in terms of net wealth (in contrast to income alone), the disparity is even more dramatic. According to a 2009 study by the Economic Policy Institute, "The wealthiest 1% of U.S. households had net worth that was 225 times greater than the median or typical household's net worth in 2009. This is the highest ratio on record."[61] The disparity between the top .01 percent, 1 percent, next 19 percent, and remaining 80 percent is breathtaking:

> As of 2010, the top 1% of households (the upper class) owned 35.4% of all privately held wealth, and the next 19% (the managerial, professional, and small business stratum) had 53.5%, which means that just 20% of the people owned a remarkable 89%, leaving only 11% of the wealth for the bottom 80% (wage and salary workers). In terms of financial wealth (total

---

57. *Cf.* Jesus Felipe & Matias Vernengo, *Demystifying the Principles of Comparative Advantage: Implications for Developing Countries*, 32 INT'L J. POL. ECON. 32, 50–51 (2002–2003).

58. Consider, for example, debates over the success of NAFTA. *E.g.*, IAN FERGUSSON & M. VILLARREAL, CONG. RESEARCH SERV., R42965, NAFTA AT 20: OVERVIEW AND TRADE EFFECTS 10 (2014).

59. Eduardo Porter, *Inequality Undermines Democracy*, N.Y. TIMES, Mar. 21, 2012, at B1.

60. *Id.* at B4.

61. Sylvia A. Allegretto, *The State of Working America's Wealth, 2011: Through Volatility and Turmoil, the Gap Widens*, ECON. POL'Y INST., at 2 (Mar. 23, 2011), http://epi.3cdn.net/2a7ccb3e9e618f0bbc_3nm6idnax.pdf; *see also* R.A. *Capital in the Long Run*, THE ECONOMIST, Jan. 9, 2014, http://www.economist.com/blogs/freeexchange/2014/01/inequality; Estelle Sommeiller & Mark Price, *The Increasingly Unequal States of America*, ECON. POL'Y INST. (Feb. 19, 2014), http://www.epi.org/publication/unequal-states/ (last visited June 9, 2014).

> net worth minus the value of one's home), the top 1% of households had an even greater share: 42.1%.[62]

Data since 2010 indicate that this disparity is continuing to grow. One 2014 Federal Reserve study found that between 2010 and 2013, only "families at the very top of the income distribution saw widespread income gains."[63] The dramatic growth in income inequality has now made the United States the most economically unequal nation in the industrialized world.[64] Federal taxation policies have done little to even things out. The results are pernicious. Research consistently shows that extreme economic polarization creates corrosive social problems and instability.[65] Witness, for example, the chronic instability in South American countries where a few rich families have lived for generations in enclaves, enjoying private and exclusive forms of education, transportation, entertainment, and the like, while the rest of the population is relegated to a dilapidated infrastructure of potholed roads, sporadic electricity, and crumbling schools. The *New York Times* concisely summed up the threat:

> Once inequality becomes very acute, it breeds resentment and political instability, eroding the legitimacy of democratic institutions. It can produce political polarization and gridlock, splitting the political system between haves and have-nots, making it more difficult for governments to address imbalances and respond to brewing crises.

The danger, the *Times* concluded, is that "the United States could become a hereditary plutocracy under the trappings of liberal democracy."[66]

---

62. G. William Domhof, *Wealth, Income, and Power*, WHO RULES AMERICA? (July 30, 2015), http://www2.ucsc.edu/whorulesamerica/power/wealth.html (summarizing data drawn from the work of NYU economist Edward N. Wolff); *see* Edward N. Wolff et al., *Growth and Inequality in the United States*, *in* GROWTH WITH INEQUALITY: AN INTERNATIONAL COMPARISON OF INCOME DISTRIBUTION 53 (Jinjun Xue ed., World Scientific Press 2012); Edward N. Wolff, *The Asset Price Meltdown and the Wealth of the Middle Class* (Nat'l Bureau of Econ. Research, Working Paper No. 18559, 2012), http://appam.confex.com/data/extendedabstract/appam/2012/Paper_2134_extendedabstract_151_0.pdf.

63. Jesse Bricker et al., *Division of Research & Statistics, Changes in U.S. Family Finances from 2010 to 2013: Evidence from the Survey of Consumer Finances*, 100 FED. RESERVE BULL. (Sept. 5, 2014), http://www.federalreserve.gov/pubs/bulletin/2014/pdf/scf14.pdf.

64. Charles A. Kupchan, *The Democratic Malaise: Globalization and the Threat to the West*, 91 FOREIGN AFF. 62, 64 (Jan./Feb. 2012).

65. *See, e.g.*, Peter M. Lewis, *Nigeria: Assessing Risks to Stability*, CTR. FOR STRATEGIC & INT'L STUDIES (June 2011), http://csis.org/files/publication/110623_Lewis_Nigeria_Web.pdf.

66. Porter, *supra* note 59, at B4.

The second, and related, problem is that fairly distributing the increased wealth acquired by international trade presupposes social mobility: to chase the newly arriving dollars, people must have the opportunity to educate themselves, learn new skills, change jobs, and, often, move to new cities where newfound income may be disproportionately concentrated. A study by the Brookings Institution shows that social mobility in the United States, contrary to the nation's historic and still-widespread Horatio Alger mythology,[67] is extremely low and compares unfavorably to Canada, much of Western Europe, and other industrialized nations.[68] Although the trends of stagnating or decreasing social mobility predate the phenomena and changes collectively referred to as globalization, including the growth of international trade,[69] globalization only entrenches or exacerbates those trends.

Many of these changes are deeply unsettling. In part, their effects can be economically mitigated by "adjustment assistance," that is, financial assistance in the form of subsidies, educational programs, training, and so forth, provided to workers in industries that become uncompetitive because of import pressures. But money can only buy so much. Even when governments offer sufficient adjustment assistance, which they seldom do, it cannot compensate for socioeconomic and physical dislocations such as pulling children out of schools, selling a beloved old house, or moving away from family and friends.

Free trade's benefits, including cheaper consumer goods and at least nominally higher standards of living, can sometimes be so great as to dwarf its social costs—but not always. If the resulting distributional imbalance is sufficiently intense and the social dislocation sufficiently extreme, a nation (or state) might be better off, on balance, if it were to preserve or revert to earlier, economically *un*integrated arrangements. And even if a semblance of balance can be achieved, the aggregate societal costs can be enormous. Over the last decade, average household income in the United States has fallen by 10 percent. This decline is in part a

67. *See* John Cassidy, *Social Mobility Hasn't Fallen: What It Means and Doesn't Mean*, NEW YORKER, Jan. 23, 2014, http://www.newyorker.com/online/blogs/johncassidy/2014/01/social-mobility-hasnt-fallen-what-it-means-and-doesnt-mean.html (last visited July 21, 2015).

68. *See* Michael Greenstone et al., *Thirteen Economic Facts about Social Mobility and the Role of Education*, THE HAMILTON PROJECT (June 2012), http://www.brookings.edu/~/media/research/files/reports/2013/06/13%20facts%20higher%20education/thp_13econfacts_final.pdf; *see also* Jason DeParle, *Harder for Americans to Rise from Lower Rungs*, N.Y. TIMES, Jan. 4, 2012, at A1 (summarizing a host of studies reaching the same conclusion); *Nomencracy*, THE ECONOMIST, Feb. 9, 2013, at 75 (discussing the extent to which social mobility is limited across various nations, including Sweden, the United Kingdom, Spain, and China).

69. *See* Cassidy, *supra* note 67; *see also Mobility, Measured; Class in America*, THE ECONOMIST, Feb. 1, 2014, at 23.

result of technological innovation, which has improved productivity. But it also reflects the consequences of the entry into the labor force of billions of low-wage workers from less developed nations.[70] Millions of America's lost jobs have gone overseas.[71]

These socioeconomic dislocations and new and unfamiliar challenges breed insecurity and create psychological strains. People often respond by rejecting the "other" and seeking out the familiar, especially by adopting or reinforcing collective (group or tribal) identities and memberships. Religious, racial, national, and other collective identities become critical sources of pride.[72] The impulse to be surrounded by the familiar reflects itself in many ways, for example, where people choose to live. Americans increasingly make their homes near people with similar political views.[73] They also choose to live around people in their own income bracket. Peter Orszag has summarized recent research on America's growing political segregation:

> [I]n 1970, almost two-thirds of American families lived in middle-income neighborhoods. By 2007, only 44 percent did. The share of those living in a poor neighborhood, in the same period, more than doubled, from 8 percent to 17 percent. So did the share living in an affluent neighborhood—from 7 percent to 14 percent.[74]

Whether voting patterns reflect growing trends in income inequality represents an area for further research, but emerging evidence suggests that higher-income people are more likely to vote Republican, especially in Republican

70. *See* DANIEL ALPERT, ROBERT HOCKETT & NOURIEL ROUBINI, THE WAY FORWARD (2012).

71. *See* LEVINE, *supra* note 30, at 6–7.

72. *See* Shobha Pais, Indiana University School of Medicine, Presentation to the 4th Viennese Conference on Mediation (May 5, 2006) (transcript *available at* http://www.bildungsmanagement.ac.at/download/Konferenz%202006/Pais.pdf). On the larger issue of the psychological impact of globalization, see generally Jeffrey Jansen Arnett, *The Psychology of Globalization*, 57 AM. PSYCHOLOGIST 774–83 (2002) (concluding that globalization creates new challenges and obstacles to the formation of a viable identity for individuals).

73. *See* Peter R. Orszag, *Blame Supercommittee's Failure on the Income Gap*, BLOOMBERG (Nov. 22, 2011), http://www.bloombergview.com/articles/2011-11-23/blame-supercommittee-failure-on-the-income-gap-commentary-by-peter-orszag; *see generally* BILL BISHOP & ROBERT CUSHING, THE BIG SORT (2011).

74. *See* Sean Reardon & Kendra Bischoff, *Growth in the Residential Segregation of Families by Income 1970–2009*, US 2010 PROJECT (Nov. 2011), at 11, http://cepa.stanford.edu/sites/default/files/RussellSageIncomeSegregationreport.pdf; Orszag, *supra* note 73.

states.[75] Furthermore, as noted earlier, high-income, high-ability workers, those likely to benefit from globalization, tend to demand less economic redistribution, while low-income, low-ability workers, those likely to be hurt by globalization, tend to demand increased economic redistribution.[76] And voting patterns undoubtedly reflect race: 89 percent of Republican voters are white, while the percentage of Democratic voters is split more evenly, 65 percent white and 35 percent nonwhite.[77]

In democratic nations, a polarized population leads quickly to a polarized political system, and a polarized political environment, in turn, makes governing difficult. Orszag summarizes the feedback loop:

> Residential segregation by income has been increasing markedly, and since income is strongly related to voting patterns, this phenomenon may help explain the rise in residential segregation by political party. As we surround ourselves with people like us, we reinforce our own views, and the result is a more polarized population.[78]

Unsurprisingly, insecurity also leads to an increased perception of risk;[79] when loss seems imminent, it is far more difficult to summon the courage to place more chips on the table.

The inevitable upshot is governmental gridlock. As Norman Ornstein has noted,

> [f]or the first time ever, in the 111th Congress that convened during the first two years of the Obama presidency, . . . the most conservative

---

75. *See generally* Andrew Gelman, Lane Kenworthy & Yu-Sung Su, *Income Inequality and Partisan Voting in the United States*, 91 SOCIAL SCI. Q. 1203 (2010) (concluding that high-income Americans are more likely to vote Republican than low-income Americans); *see also* ANDREW GELMAN, RED STATE, BLUE STATE, RICH STATE, POOR STATE (2009).

76. Walter & Maduz, *supra* note 26, at 3.

77. A 2009 Gallup Poll showed a huge discrepancy in the racial makeup of the Republican, Democratic, and Independent parties. *See* Frank Newport, *Republican Base Heavily White, Conservative, Religious*, GALLUP (June 1, 2009), http://www.gallup.com/poll/118937/republican-base-heavily-white-conservative-religious.aspx (last visited July 21, 2015).

78. Orszag, *supra* note 73.

79. See Walter & Maduz, *supra* note 26, at 25. Because the "losers" of globalization, namely low-skilled individuals working in highly-exposed occupations, are the individuals feeling insecure, they are the ones experiencing an increased perception of risk. These individuals also, not surprisingly, demand greater income redistribution and social protection. *Id.* at 4.

> Democratic senator was to the left of the most liberal Republican. There is now no overlap ideologically at all between the parties. Only nine of the remaining small number of conservative House Democrats . . . were to the right of the most liberal House Republican.[80]

This ideological polarization drives legislative paralysis, which is reflected, for example, in increased use of the filibuster.[81] Former senator and now Secretary of State John Kerry provides a telling historical perspective and explains the debilitating effect that routine use of the filibuster has had on the Senate:

> [I]n the entire 19th century, including the struggle against slavery, fewer than two dozen filibusters were mounted. Between 1933 and the coming of World War II, it was attempted only twice. During the Eisenhower administration, twice. During John Kennedy's presidency, four times—and then eight during Lyndon Johnson's push for civil rights and voting rights bills. By the time Jimmy Carter and Ronald Reagan occupied the White House, there were about 20 filibusters a year.
>
> But in the 110th Congress of 2007-2008, there were a record 112 cloture votes. And in the 111th Congress, there were 136, one of which even delayed a vote to authorize funding for the Army, Navy, Air Force and Marine Corps during a time of war.[82]

The resulting perception of government among its constituents is unsurprising. In a recent CNN/Opinion Research survey, 86 percent of Americans said they believe the federal government is broken; only 14 percent felt that it worked.[83] Approval ratings for Congress, in particular, have reached an all-time low. In a February 2012 Gallup poll, only 10 percent of Americans approved of

---

80. Norman Ornstein, *Worst. Congress. Ever.*, FOREIGN POLICY (July 19, 2011), http://foreignpolicy.com/2011/07/19/worst-congress-ever/.

81. Charts from the Brookings Institute and Mother Jones show when filibusters and cloture votes have increased in recent years as either party has gained or lost majority rule in Congress. *See* Dews, *supra* note 51; Kevin Drum & Jaeah Lee, *3 Charts Explain Why Democrats Went Nuclear on the Filibuster*, MOTHER JONES (Nov. 22, 2013), http://www.motherjones.com/kevin-drum/2013/11/charts-explain-why-democrats-went-nuclear-filibuster.

82. Ezra Klein, *If You Read Only One John Kerry Speech Today . . .*, WASH. POST (Jan. 11, 2011), http://voices.washingtonpost.com/ezraklein/2011/01/if_you_read_only_one_john_kerr.html.

83. Darrel M. West, *Broken Politics*, BROOKINGS INST. No. 33 (March 2010), http://www.brookings.edu/~/media/research/files/papers/2010/3/broken%20politics%20west/03_broken_politics_west.pdf.

the job Congress is doing, down from 13 percent in January and 11 percent in December 2011.[84]

III. State Capacity

State governments have hardly been insulated from these global gale-force winds. Nor have political polarization and gridlock been confined to Washington.[85] With fifty different state governments fighting the global headwinds, some inevitably fare better than others, not just socioeconomically, but in resisting such political sclerosis. The precise qualities and institutions that contribute to a healthy political environment and effective democratic government may well vary from state to state in the Union—just as they may from nation to nation, and just as the Anglo-Saxon adversarial and Continental inquisitorial legal traditions, despite very distinct approaches, can equally well satisfy due process and the rule of law. Nonetheless, citizens and officials within any democratic nation tend to share certain virtues that almost invariably contribute to efficient, functional, and sound governance. Prominent among these are a willingness to compromise, understanding of the issues, commitment to fair process, empathy, revulsion toward demagoguery, commitment to the common welfare, and personal responsibility. Unfortunately, it is often precisely these civic virtues that globalization makes it more difficult to cultivate in polities that comprise the several states of the Union.

It would be facile to blame globalization for all of the problems faced by the states today. A serious and endemic ill that predates globalization and continues to plague government at all levels, not least states and cities, is corruption. The non-partisan Center for Public Integrity examined several aspects of good governance, including campaign finance reform, transparency, ethics

84. Frank Newport, *Congress' Job Approval at New Low of 10%*, GALLUP (Feb. 8, 2012) http://www.gallup.com/poll/152528/congress-job-approval-new-low.aspx (last visited Mar. 10, 2012).

85. *See* Peter R. Orszag, Op-Ed, *State Lawmakers Can't Find Common Ground Either*, BLOOMBERG (Dec. 20, 2011) [hereinafter Orszag, *State*], http://www.cfr.org/world/state-lawmakers-cant-find-common-ground-either/p26895; Peter R. Orszag, *Won't You Be My (Hyper-Partisan) Neighbor?*, BLOOMBERG (Jan. 8, 2011) [hereinafter Orszag, *(Hyper-Partisan) Neighbor?*], http://www.cfr.org/congresses-parliaments-national-legislatures/wont-you-my-hyper-partisan-neighbor/p25233. *See generally* Boris Shor & Nolen McCarty, *The Ideological Mapping of American Legislatures*, 105 AM. POL. SCI. REV. 530 (Aug. 2011) (examining the ideologies and degrees of polarization within the individual state legislatures). The legislatures of Arizona, California, and Colorado have seen the most dramatic increases in polarization. *See* Orszag, *State, supra*. California has (by far) the most polarized state legislature; Rhode Island and Louisiana the least. *See* Shor & McCarty, *supra*.

enforcement, and auditing, and found state performance to be abysmal along these dimensions:

> Not a single state—not one—earned an A grade from the months-long probe. Only five states earned a B grade: New Jersey, Connecticut, Washington, California, and Nebraska. Nineteen states got C's and 18 received D's. Eight states earned failing grades of 59 or below from the project, which is a collaboration of the Center for Public Integrity, Global Integrity, and Public Radio International.
>
> The F's went to Michigan, North Dakota, South Carolina, Maine, Virginia, Wyoming, South Dakota, and Georgia.[86]

States and cities also suffer from an overarching weakness in the global marketplace that the federal government does not: they can be played off against one another.[87] The United States is the fortunate recipient of more foreign direct investment than any other nation in the world. In 2009, foreign companies invested $130 billion in the United States. By way of comparison, $95 billion flowed into China and $60 billion into France, the next two successive competitors; and more than 6 million Americans worked for foreign-controlled businesses on U.S. soil.[88] Foreign investment benefits the national economy, but in a federalist system, it also means that potential state or city hosts to foreign investors will not sit idly by while these businesses decide where to invest.

To the contrary, local polities engage feverishly in "incentive wars" in an effort to win often intense competitions. Incentives take various forms. One of the most common is tax breaks. Although states and cities of course offer them to domestic as well as foreign businesses, a look at the numbers is sobering. A 2011 study examined the 265 Fortune 500 companies that fully disclosed their state and local income tax payments. The average statutory state corporate-tax rate is about 6.2 percent. Between 2008 and 2010, these 265 companies paid state income taxes equal to only 3.0 percent of their U.S. profits. Half of their profits, in other words, escaped state taxes entirely. Of the same 265 companies, 68 managed to pay no state income tax at all, even though they told their shareholders that they earned almost $117 billion in pretax U.S. profits in those same

---

86. Caitlin Ginley, *50 States and No Winners*, STATE INTEGRITY INVESTIGATION (Mar. 2012), http://www.stateintegrity.org/state_integrity_invesitgation_overview_story.

87. This is not to suggest, of course, that nations cannot be played off against one another by other nations.

88. Earl Fry, *The United States of America*, *in* FOREIGN RELATIONS IN FEDERAL STATES 306 (Hans Michelman ed., 2009).

years; during the 2008–2010 period, these 265 corporations avoided paying a total of $42.7 billion in state corporate income tax on profits reported to their shareholders.[89]

This study scrutinizes only domestic, not foreign, companies. But there can be no question that the states spend enormous amounts of their revenues to attract foreign businesses. By the end of 2010, the total amount of foreign direct investment in the United States stood at $2.3 trillion.[90] In the last ten years alone, the amount added up to $1.7 trillion.[91] State and local governments spend approximately $50 billion annually on promotions and incentives to attract domestic and foreign companies.[92] Yet these massive expenditures have often generated disappointingly low numbers of jobs. In 1993, for example, Alabama spent $253 million to bring in approximately 1500 jobs from Mercedes-Benz, amounting to a measly 0.039 percent increase in its employment rate.[93] Taxpayers often have no choice but to stand idly by as their political representatives sell the farm to feed the livestock. In 2006, the Supreme Court threw out a claim challenging the constitutionality of $300 million in tax inducements offered by Ohio to Daimler-Chrysler, holding that the taxpayers who filed the suit lacked standing.[94]

For many states, tax and similar incentives of this sort represent a Faustian bargain. Businesses want to locate in areas with good social services, superior schools, educated workers, low crime, high-quality, diverse transportation, and solid local infrastructure. But such social goods require tax revenues, and states sacrifice those tax revenues to attract the very businesses that would benefit from them. Furthermore, as Michael Ettlinger emphasized in testimony to the Task Force on Interstate Competition of the Pennsylvania General Assembly, "Business tax incentives provided to some firms put competing firms at a disadvantage. Hence, increases in output and employment by firms receiving incentives may be at least somewhat offset, and perhaps even outweighed, by the decreases in output and

---

89. *Corporate Tax Dodging in the Fifty States*, 2008–2010, ITEP.ORG (Dec. 2010), http://www.itep.org/pdf/CorporateTaxDodgers50StatesReport.pdf.

90. U.S. DEP'T OF COMMERCE, BUREAU OF ECON. ANALYSIS, FOREIGN DIRECT INVESTMENT IN THE UNITED STATES TABLES (Sept. 2011), http://www.bea.gov/scb/pdf/2011/09%20September/0911_fdius_tables.pdf.

91. DAVID PAYNE & FENWICK YU, FOREIGN DIRECT INVESTMENT IN THE UNITED STATES (June 2011), http://www.esa.doc.gov/sites/default/files/fdiesaissuebriefno2061411final_0.pdf.

92. Fry, *supra* note 88, at 306.

93. Timothy C. Ford, Jonathan C. Rork & Bruce T. Elmslie, *Foreign Direct Investment, Economic Growth, and the Human Capital Threshold: Evidence from US States*, 16 REV. OF INT'L ECON. 96, 104 (2008).

94. DaimlerChrysler Corp. v. Cuno, 547 U.S. 332 (2006).

employment of competing firms."[95] Financially healthy businesses that do not receive favorable tax treatment relative to their competitors may be driven out of business—counterintuitively culminating in a net increase rather than decrease in state unemployment. Some state officials have tried to opt out of these incentive wars, but they are sailing into the wind. Because no politician wants to be on the wrong side of job creation, typically, the best option seems to be to strike a balance between economic development and taxpayer interests.

The states do not face globalization's challenges empty-handed. In fact, many have greater resources than many countries. It is often noted that if California were a country, it would have the eighth-largest economy in the world.[96] It is less often appreciated that other states compare favorably with foreign countries in the size and health of both their populations and economies.[97] In population, New York State is roughly the size of Cameroon. Texas is about the size of Saudi Arabia. Florida is larger than Angola. Iowa is nearly as large as Armenia. Minnesota is about the size of Finland. Alabama is approximately the size of Norway. Louisiana is larger than Ireland. South Carolina is as big as Costa Rica. Arizona is about the size of Libya. The gross domestic products (GDPs) of the states likewise often rival or surpass those of foreign countries. California's GDP is nearly as large as Italy's. Oregon's is larger than Pakistan's. Washington's is larger than that of Greece. Nevada's is about the size of Peru's. Kansas's is larger than New Zealand's. Massachusetts's is nearly as large as Saudi Arabia's. Kentucky's is larger than the Philippines's. Georgia's is larger than Austria's. Maryland's is nearly as large as South Africa's. Pennsylvania's is larger than Indonesia's. New Jersey's is almost as large as Switzerland's. Michigan's is almost as large as Taiwan's. Illinois's is larger than Turkey's. Hawaii's is larger than Croatia's. By one count, all fifty states rank among the largest seventy-seven national GDPs in the world.[98]

The growing international clout of the states of the Union is part of a global trend toward dynamic regionalism that has seen important cities, in particular, assume increasing importance. Ivo Daalder has suggested that "[t]he most important characteristic of the 21st century is the rise of cities." "For the first time in

---

95. Michael Ettlinger, Tax Policy Director, Citizens for Tax Justice, Testimony Before the Task Force on Interstate Competition at the Pennsylvania General Assembly (Sept. 25, 1997), http://www.ctj.org/html/patest.htm (last visited July 21, 2015).

96. *The Size of States If They Were Countries*, THE ECONOMIST, Jan. 13, 2011, http://www.economist.com/node/17910000.

97. The population and GDP statistics in this section are from *Graphic Detail*, THE ECONOMIST, Jan. 13, 2011, http://www.economist.com/blogs/dailychart/2011/01/comparing_us_states_countries (last visited July 21, 2015).

98. Fry, *supra* note 88, at 308.

human history, more people now live in cities than in rural areas. By 2050, 6.5bn people, two-thirds of all humanity, will live and work in cities. In 1950 fewer than one billion did so." Global cities, Daalder suggests, are

> beginning to resemble the Hanseatic League of medieval cities, with global centres trading and working together to address common problems in ways that large nations do not. While not sovereign, global cities are increasingly independent—driving policies that stimulate wider change.
>
> They drive the world's economy. The 600 biggest cities account for more than 60 per cent of global gross domestic product. The top 20 are home to one-third of all large corporations, and almost half of their combined revenues. Tokyo leads the pack—in population size, economic punch and number of corporate headquarters—ahead of New York, London and Paris.[99]

Why does the size of a polity's population and GDP matter? For at least three reasons: first, they supply rough indicia of (potential) geoeconomic clout, that is, of a polity's ability to fend for itself in the global arena and advance its interests. High GDP economies can effectively locate high-growth, distant markets for their exports. They also attract unique imports and large-scale investment from other powerful players. Of course, other characteristics of political entities matter—and may matter more. China and India, for example, have long exercised international influence disproportionately small relative to the sizes of their populations, although China's global influence (and, to a lesser extent, India's) is doubtless on the rise.[100] In contrast, the influence of Japan and Switzerland internationally has been disproportionately low relative to the size of their economies, and Great Britain has long exercised a degree of influence disproportionately high relative to the size of its population and economy. But all else equal, the size of a polity's economy and population tends to correlate with and predict its comparative power internationally.

Second, the same two factors indicate in a general way the extent of a polity's stake in the international economic order. What happens internationally affects larger nations and individual states of the Union more than smaller ones simply because their "foreign affairs" affect more people and more economic interests.

---

99. Ivo Daalder, Opinion, *A New Global Order of Cities*, FIN. TIMES (May 26, 2015), http://www.ft.com/cms/s/2/a5230756-0395-11e5-a70f-00144feabdc0.html#axzz3gjgWUY4j.

100. *See* C. FRED BERGSTEN ET AL., CHINA'S RISE: CHALLENGES AND OPPORTUNITIES (2008).

Their greater international presence typically reflects that interest. Size supplies motive.

Third, greater and richer resources enable larger nations and states to engage more effectively in foreign affairs. Diplomacy is expensive, and yet even small countries maintain embassies and consulates, run by highly trained diplomats, worldwide. Larger states, like larger nations, exercise greater influence in foreign affairs. Size supplies capacity. State and local government employee pension funds now hold about $2.9 trillion in assets,[101] enough to exert substantial influence on the deliberations of a company seeking investors and considering doing business in a place such as South Africa or Burma.

Accordingly, the several states increasingly decline to stand idly by while global issues threaten their interests or offer new opportunities. They have both the motive and capacity to act. And they do.

IV. State Activities in the International Realm

As noted earlier, the record belies the shibboleth that the federal government alone conducts foreign policy. An overview of comparatively recent international activities by states and cities reveals that federal exclusivity is a fiction.[102]

A. Compacts and Agreements with Foreign Countries

In recent decades, state and local governments have entered into thousands of compacts and agreements with national and subnational governments around the world.[103] More than four hundred agreements exist between the states and Canadian provinces, with some 46 states parties.[104] For example, Alaska, Idaho, Oregon, Montana, and Washington joined several Canadian provinces to coordinate provincial and state policies throughout the region, enhance competitiveness

---

101. U.S. Census Bureau, Statistical Abstract of the United States: 2012, Assets of Private and Public Pension Funds by Type: 1990–2010 (2012), https://www.census.gov/library/publications/2011/compendia/statab/131ed/banking-finance-insurance.html.

102. Few of these initiatives have been subjected to judicial challenge. It should be noted, however, that among those that have been contested, a number have been struck down. By reviewing these activities, we do not address their constitutionality. The point is descriptive: contrary to common assumptions, states and cities engage in many and diverse activities in foreign affairs. Sometimes, these activities, or forms of expression, may be in tension or inconsistent with federal foreign policy. But often they will not be.

103. Earl H. Fry, The Expanding Role of State and Local Governments in U.S. Foreign Affairs 5 (1998).

104. *Id.* at 73.

of the region in international and domestic markets, and maintain the region's natural resources, among other goals.[105] On the opposite end of the United States, New England governors and Eastern Canadian premiers came together in 1997 to work together on projects pertaining to acid rain deposition and impacts and reduce mercury in the northeast.[106] Later plans have included efforts to address climate change generally and transportation and air quality.[107] For the past seventeen years, Maine has done well for itself developing international trade relations with a number of foreign nations, including South Korea, Chile, and Brazil, and now the United Kingdom and Iceland.[108] What makes Maine's initiative unique, perhaps, is the extent to which the state and federal agencies work together to encourage and "smooth the way" for such economic partnerships.[109]

Not all of these foreign agreements conform to federal policy, and some affirmatively contravene it. Residents of the United States seldom receive economic assistance from developing countries, for example, but some Massachusetts residents can now claim that distinction by virtue of a deal with Venezuela's state-owned oil company, Petróleos de Venezuela S.A. (PDVSA). Under its terms, PDVSA agreed to supply oil to low-income Massachusetts families.[110] At the time of the agreement's negotiation by U.S. representative Bill Delahunt, Hugo Chavez, a close ally of Cuba and boisterous critic of U.S. foreign policy, was president of Venezuela. Boulder, Colorado made a name for itself when it created a

---

105. *Background and History*, PNWER.ORG (July 21, 2015), http://www.pnwer.org/about-us.html.

106. *Action Plans, Policy Reports, and Other Publications*, NEW ENGLAND GOVERNORS' CONFERENCE, INC. (June 26, 2007), http://www.mercvt.org/PDF/Addendum%20File%20for%20CD%20ROM.pdf.

107. *Id.*

108. Douglas Brooks, *Are Maine's Overseas Trade Missions Worth the Time and Money?*, MAINEBIZ, May 5, 2014, http://www.mainebiz.biz/article/20140505/CURRENT-EDITION/305019999/are-maine's-overseas-trade-missions-worth-the-time-and-money.

109. *Id.*

110. During the winter of 2005–2006, CITGO provided oil for heating to the residents of Maine, Massachusetts, New York, and Rhode Island at approximately 40 percent below market rates. The Venezuelan government said that it would provide 12 million gallons of fuel to Massachusetts and approximately 8 million gallons to the Bronx, New York. Participating households would receive a discount of 60 to 80 cents per gallon, totaling $10 to $14 million in savings for the whole winter. OFFICE OF LEGIS. RESEARCH, 2006-R-0079, VENEZUELAN SUBSIDIZED HEATING OIL PROGRAM (2006), http://www.cga.ct.gov/2006/rpt/2006-R-0079.htm; *see also Venezuela Gives US Cheap Oil Deal*, BBC, Nov. 3, 2005, http://news.bbc.co.uk/2/hi/americas/4461946.stm (last visited July 21, 2015). For a discussion on the subsequent political questions raised by the agreement, see Kate Phillips, *Kennedy Connection to Chavez and Citgo*, Sept. 6, 2009, N.Y. TIMES BLOG, http://thecaucus.blogs.nytimes.com/2009/09/06/kennedy-connection-to-chavez-and-citgo/?_php=true&_type=blogs&_r=0.

sister-city relationship with Jalapa, Nicaragua, at the height of the Iran-Contra Affair and, in 2013, attempted to do so with Nablus, Palestine.[111]

B. Adoption of International Standards

The states have also adopted a variety of international standards, even when the United States has declined or neglected to take action. Many states and cities, for example, have adopted international standards, entered into agreements, or otherwise taken prophylactic action against global warming and other environmental threats despite the federal government's failure to ratify the Kyoto Protocol.[112] Subsequent rounds of international climate negotiations among nations have yielded few if any concrete results. Yet local laws and ordinances implementing or emulating the Protocol have been adopted by at least 185 cities. Martin Chavez, the former mayor of Albuquerque, New Mexico, in a telling comment to the *Washington Post* in 2006, expressed a common sentiment among many cities that have taken action: "Like most mayors, I'm disappointed the federal government has not taken more of a lead on this issue, but so be it. We're moving forward."[113] Similarly, nine northeastern states have enacted state laws establishing cap-and-trade programs modeled on the Kyoto Protocol.[114] These initiatives require electricity generators located within the states to reduce carbon dioxide emissions.[115] On November 18, 2008, former California governor Arnold Schwarzenegger met with the governors of Illinois, Florida, Kansas, and Wisconsin at the Governors' Global Climate Summit in Beverly Hills to explore mutual economic, environmental, and security interests in reducing greenhouse gas emissions.[116] Two years earlier, Schwarzenegger met with former British Prime Minister Tony Blair, and they agreed to work together on ways for California and Great Britain to

---

111. FRY, *supra* note 103, at 93; Amy Bounds, *Bounds City Council Denies Making Nablus a Sister City*, THE BOULDER DAILY CAMERA, June 11, 2013, http://www.huffingtonpost.com/2013/06/11/boulder-city-council-deni_n_3420515.html.

112. Kyoto Protocol to the United Nations Framework Convention on Climate Change, Dec. 10, 1997, U.N. Doc FCCC/CP/1997/7/Add.1, 37 I.L.M. 22.

113. Mayor Chavez was quoted in John Dinan, *Defying Washington, U.S. State Capitols Take on Policy Making*, 5(3) FORUM OF FEDERATIONS 27 (Oct./Nov. 2006).

114. *See* Regional Greenhouse Gas Initiative (RGGI), http://rggi.org/ (last visited Feb. 24, 2012).

115. THOMAS M. FRANCK, MICHAEL J. GLENNON, SEAN D. MURPHY & EDWARD T. SWAINE, FOREIGN RELATIONS AND NATIONAL SECURITY LAW: CASES, MATERIALS, AND SIMULATIONS 751 (4th ed. 2012).

116. Thomas Eatmon, *Paradiplomacy and Climate Change: American States as Actors in Global Climate Governance*, 1 J. NAT. RESOURCES POL'Y RES. 153 (Apr. 2009).

address global warming.[117] The California Global Warming Solutions Act of 2006 (known as AB 32) mandates these activities, requiring California to reduce its carbon emissions to 1990 levels by 2020. AB32 envisions the state exercising a "global leadership role" in the battle against climate change.[118]

To pursue environmental protection goals, the states have also looked to international standards regulating certain dangerous chemicals. Language from the Stockholm Convention on Persistent Organic Pollutants,[119] which President George W. Bush signed in 2001 but the United States has thus far failed to ratify, appears in the regulations of Maine and Washington.[120] California's ban on lindane, one of the pollutants targeted by the Stockholm Convention for elimination, subsequently led New York, Washington, Maine, and Michigan to adopt similar legislation.[121] Cities have likewise been active in this regard. Buffalo, Boston, San Francisco, Seattle, and Oakland have all taken steps to eliminate the use of persistent organic pollutants.[122]

Local action has by no means been limited to environmental issues. Human rights have been another common concern. The United States declined to ratify the Convention on the Elimination of All Forms of Discrimination Against Women (CEDAW).[123] But that did not deter San Francisco from adopting local ordinances to implement portions of it.[124] San Francisco's efforts, in turn, prompted other states and cities to call for regulations and implementation. Coalitions in Chicago, Los Angeles, and Atlanta have urged federal legislators to approve CEDAW.[125] Similarly, the federal government's recalcitrance in implementing the

---

117. *California and UK in Climate Pact,* BBC, Aug. 1, 2006, http://news.bbc.co.uk/2/hi/5233466.stm; *see also* Patrick Wintour, *Blair Signs Climate Pact with Schwarzenegger*, THE GUARDIAN, July 31, 2006, http://www.theguardian.com/environment/2006/aug/01/greenpolitics.usnews (describing the deal as an obvious way of sidestepping the Bush administration).

118. CAL. CODE REGS. The California Global Warming Solutions Act of 2006, §§ 38501(e), 38550 (2006), http://www.leginfo.ca.gov/pub/05-06/bill/asm/ab_0001-0050/ab_32_bill_20060927_chaptered.pdf.

119. Stockholm Convention on Persistent Organic Pollutants, May 22, 2001, 40 I.L.M. 532.

120. *See* Lesley Wexler, *Take the Long Way Home: Sub-federal Integration of Unratified and Non-self-executing Treaty Law*, 28 MICH. J. INT'L L. 1, 22 (2006).

121. *Id.* at 23.

122. *Id.*

123. Convention on the Elimination of All Forms of Discrimination Against Women, Dec. 18, 1978, 1249 U.N.T.S. 13.

124. S.F., CAL. ADMIN. CODE CH. 12K (2001); *see* FRANCK ET AL., *supra* note 115, at 750.

125. *See* Wexler, *supra* note 120, at 25–26. In fact, the initiative has sparked a campaign, "Cities for CEDAW," that focuses on major cities throughout the United States to promote the

Convention on the Elimination of All Forms of Racial Discrimination,[126] which the United States ratified but declared non-self-executing,[127] did not deter local officials in Iowa, California, and New York from enacting local implementing legislation.[128]

C. State Offices in Foreign Countries

The states operate almost as many permanent offices overseas as the federal government does embassies.[129] Florida maintains fifteen offices in fourteen foreign countries.[130] New York has established six, in Montreal, Toronto, Hong Kong, London, Paris, and Beit Shemesh (Israel). It also shares offices in Sydney, São Paolo, Santiago, and Highveld (South Africa) with the other states of the Council of

---

adoption of CEDAW. United Nations Association—UNA-SF Women's Committee, *Cities for CEDAW from Win-CAWA*, UNA-SF.ORG (Feb. 28, 2014), http://www.una-sf.org/cities-for-cedaw-posted-by-una-sf-womens-committee/.

126. International Convention on the Elimination of All Forms of Racial Discrimination, Mar. 7, 1966, 660 U.N.T.S. 195, 5 I.L.M. 352.

127. U.S. Senate Resolution of Advice and Consent to Ratification of the Convention on the Elimination of Racial Discrimination, 140 CONG. REC. S7634 (1994). As discussed further in Chapter 6, the Constitution makes treaties "the supreme law of the land; and the judges in every state shall be bound thereby, anything in the Constitution or laws of any State to the contrary notwithstanding." U.S. CONST. art. VI, cl. 2. But since Chief Justice Marshall's opinion in *Foster v. Neilson*, 27 U.S. (2 Pet.) 253 (1829), the Supreme Court has distinguished so-called self-executing from non-self-executing treaties. In the words of *Foster*:

> Our constitution declares a treaty to be the law of the land. It is, consequently, to be regarded in courts of justice as equivalent to an act of the legislature, whenever it operates of itself without the aid of any legislative provision. But when the terms of the stipulation import a contract, when either of the parties engages to perform a particular act, the treaty addresses itself to the political, not the judicial department; and the legislature must execute the contract before it can become a rule for the Court.

Id. at 314. The essence of the doctrine is that the latter, "non-self-executing treaties," do not "operate of [themselves]"; rather, they must be implemented by an act of Congress before the judiciary will take cognizance of them as rules of decision. The precise doctrine of non-self-executing treaties, however, has developed considerably since *Foster* and remains a subject of controversy. The most recent Supreme Court decision on this issue, which, not coincidentally, involved a quintessential issue of foreign affairs federalism, is *Medellín v. Texas*, 552 U.S. 491 (2008), discussed in Chapter 6. For analysis, see generally Carlos Manuel Vázquez, *The Four Doctrines of Self-Executing Treaties*, 89 AM. J. INT'L L. 695 (1995).

128. *See* Wexler, *supra* note 120, at 27–28.

129. FRY, *supra* note 103, at 4.

130. Enterprise Florida, *International Office Network*, http://www.eflorida.com/ContentSubpage.aspx?id=360 (last visited Feb. 24, 2012). These are the result of public-private partnerships.

Great Lakes Governors.[131] International activities in the trade sector are not limited to the largest states. Wisconsin, for example, has state representatives in Shanghai, Toronto, Mexico City, and São Paolo,[132] while West Virginia has trade offices in Nagoya (Japan) and Munich, mediating its interests in Asian and European markets, respectively.[133] In 2011, Governor Deval Patrick of Massachusetts traveled to Chile to start cooperative initiatives regarding clean energy, biotechnology, and education.[134] The existence of state trade missions is not new, but their exponential growth in the past few decades is remarkable. As of 2009, the states operated a total of 230 trade offices worldwide; although this is down from a peak of 243 offices in 2002, it far exceeds the mere 4 that existed in 1980.[135]

From 2000 to 2010, budget shortfalls compelled the states to close a number of foreign offices and programs. But through innovative public-private partnerships, states have found ways to maintain a foothold in foreign markets. A rising state deficit in California, for example, forced it to close twelve taxpayer-funded offices in 2003. But on February 18, 2012, Governor Jerry Brown announced that the state would be opening two new trade offices in Shanghai and Beijing, to be funded by "partners in the private sector."[136]

Beyond permanent offices, the mayors of major cities and state governors often lead trade delegations to foreign countries in an effort to attract foreign direct investment and promote their local exports. Indeed, almost every state has sponsored such missions to other countries,[137] and most governors have led at least one.[138]

---

131. *New York State Economic and International Development Official Website*, N.Y. STATE, EMPIRE STATE DEV., http://www.nylovesbiz.com/International.html (last visited Feb. 24, 2012). The Council of Great Lakes Governors includes Illinois, Indiana, Michigan, Minnesota, New York, Ohio, Wisconsin, and Pennsylvania, and the Canadian provinces of Ontario and Quebec. *See* COUNCIL OF GREAT LAKES GOVERNORS, http://www.cglg.org/governors/index.asp (last visited May 10, 2014).

132. WISCONSIN DEP'T OF COMMERCE, INTERNATIONAL STAFF & OFFICES, http://www.commerce.wi.gov/IE/IE-MeetOurStaff.html (last visited Feb. 24, 2012).

133. WEST VIRGINIA COMMERCE DEP'T, INTERNATIONAL OFFICES LISTINGS, http://www.wvcommerce.org/business/businessassistance/investinginwestvirginia/internationaloffices.aspx (last visited Feb. 24, 2012).

134. Deval Patrick, *Governor Patrick Signs Agreement with Chilean President Sebastian Pinera to Grow Innovation Economy Partnerships*, MASS.GOV (Dec. 1, 2011).

135. Fry, *supra* note 88, at 308.

136. Kevin Riggs, *Jerry Brown Re-Opens California Trade Offices*, NBCS SAN DIEGO, Feb. 7, 2012, http://www.nbcsandiego.com/blogs/prop-zero/Jerry-Brown-Re-Opens-California-Trade-Offices-China-139531163.html.

137. Richard B. Bilder, *Role of the States and Cities in Foreign Relations, in* HENKIN, *supra* note 8, at 116.

138. FRY, *supra* note 103, at 15.

Although the federal government generally tolerates (or pays little attention) to state trade and economic initiatives abroad, at times, state conduct in tension with U.S. foreign policy leads to conflict. The State Department objected, for example, after several states, including Texas, sent observers to meetings of the Organization of Petroleum Exporting Countries (OPEC), in an effort to influence decisions relating to supply and pricing.[139] And in the late 1970s, despite the United States' adverse, if not hostile, relations with Libya, Idaho sponsored trade missions to the nation.[140] In 1986, Maine, Massachusetts, and Vermont refused to send National Guard units to Honduras for training.[141] The refusal encouraged several midwestern states to follow suit, eventually culminating in a Supreme Court case that affirmed the federal government's authority to send National Guard units overseas without the consent of a state's governor.[142] Despite the long-time U.S. embargo on Cuba, in 1996, the mayor of Pasadena, California, traveled to Cuba, courtesy of the Cuban government. Although he later denied the remarks, he was quoted by Cuban news agencies as speaking out against the U.S. embargo.[143] Following the September 11 attacks, many local governments passed resolutions condemning the Patriot Act. The small town of Arcata, California was the first of dozens to denounce what they saw as an unprecedented expansion of power.[144] At times, the differences result in lawsuits. In 2005, then-governor Rod Blageovich signed the Illinois Sudan Act that prohibited certain types of investments in Sudan's government and companies doing business with Sudan.[145] The federal government had taken its own steps to encourage peace in Sudan, including Executive Order No. 13067, revisions of the Trade Sanctions Reform and Export Enhancement Act, and the Sudan Peace Act.[146] Illinois's Act, in similar ways to Massachusetts's law regarding Burma, seemed to go further in

---

139. *Id.* at 45, 95.

140. *Id.* at 92.

141. *Id.* at 93.

142. Perpich v. Dep't of Defense, 496 U.S. 334 (1990); Bernard E. Trainor, *Rehearing Sought on Curb on Militia*, N.Y. TIMES, Dec. 14, 1988, http://www.nytimes.com/1988/12/14/us/rehearing-sought-on-curb-on-militia.html; David Evans, *Supreme Court Confirms U.S. Control over Guard*, CHI. TRIB., June 12, 1990, http://articles.chicagotribune.com/1990-06-12/news/9002170920_1_montgomery-amendment-guard-members-minnesota-national-guard.

143. FRY, *supra* note 103, at 93.

144. Evelyn Nieves, *Local Officials Rise Up to Defy the Patriot Act*, WASH. POST, Apr. 21, 2003, http://www.washingtonpost.com/wp-dyn/content/article/2005/11/04/AR2005110401088.html.

145. Nat'l Foreign Trade Council, Inc. v. Giannoulias, 523 F. Supp. 2d 731, 733 (N.D. Ill. 2007).

146. *Id.* at 735–36.

directly affecting business relations with Sudan. The Act functioned in two ways. First, it amended the Deposit of State Moneys Act to prevent the Illinois Treasurer from depositing state funds into any financial institution not certified to have policies and practices in place to exclude "forbidden entities" as defined in the Act.[147] Second, it amended the Illinois Pension Code so that pension funds established under the Code could not be invested in any entity unless it fulfilled three specific conditions as to its relations with "forbidden entities."[148] The National Foreign Trade Council (NFTC) challenged the law, arguing that the Act was preempted by federal law, interfered with the federal government's ability to conduct foreign affairs, violated the Constitution's Foreign Commerce Clause, and was preempted by the National Bank Act.[149] In the end, the district court issued a permanent injunction on the basis that the "Act's lack of flexibility, extended geographic reach, and impact on foreign entities interefere[d] with the national government's conduct of foreign affairs," and was thus "preempted by federal law."[150] Additionally, the court held that the Act violated the Constitution's Foreign Commerce Clause found in Article I, section 8, as the "conduct the Illinois Sudan Act seeks to proscribe involves foreign commerce."[151]

D. State Representatives to Foreign Countries

The policy objectives of state and city quasi-diplomatic missions are not exclusively economic. The mayor of Irvine, California, accompanied by a California state senator, traveled to Vietnam in 1989 to lobby for the release of thirty individuals whose California families had emigrated from Vietnam.[152] Massachusetts representative Paul Heroux traveled to North Korea in 2013 on a diplomatic mission. He described

---

147. *Id.* at 733.

148. The three conditions were that "(1) the fund managing company has not loaned to, invested in, or otherwise transferred any of the retirement system or pension fund's assets to a forbidden entity any time after the effective day of this Act [January 27, 2006]; (2) at least 60% of the retirement system or pension fund's assets are not invested in forbidden entities at any time more than twelve months after the effective date of this Act [January 27, 2007]; [and] (3) at least 100% of the retirement system or pension fund's assets are not invested in forbidden entities at any time more than eighteen months after the effective date of this act [July 27, 2007]." *Id.* at 734.

149. *Id.* at 737.

150. *Id.* at 741. For a discussion of the concept of preemption, see Chapter 9.

151. 523 F. Supp. 2d at 747.

152. Sarah H. Cleveland, *Crosby and the 'One-Voice' Myth in U.S. Foreign Relations*, 46 Vill. L. Rev. 975, 994 (2001).

his goal in terms of learning more about North Korea's people, history, and culture.[153] After returning, he published a brief article explaining the key ways in which, he believed, discussions and interactions with North Korea could be improved.[154]

E. State Incentives to Attract Foreign Business

State governments issue more export grants and loan guarantees to foreign businesses than do agencies of the federal government.[155] Some 37 percent of American cities host the main office of one or more foreign corporations,[156] and foreign-owned businesses provide some 5.3 million jobs for American workers.[157] It is therefore little wonder that states and cities create incentives in an effort to attract foreign investment. These incentives include programs for training workers, site preparation, infrastructure improvement, and various forms of subsidies and tax breaks.[158] Nearly all states now offer tax incentives to new as well as existing foreign-owned businesses in an effort to discourage them from relocating; indeed, some 75 percent of medium- and large-size foreign-owned companies receive special tax breaks.[159] State right-to-work laws provide another major incentive.[160] It should be noted, however, that the overall economic consequences of this trend remain contentious, for states and cities naturally compete with one another, culminating in enormous aggregate costs. Bidding wars cost local governments billions of dollars in lost tax revenues.

F. Sister-City Relationships

More than 1,200 U.S. cities have established nearly 2,200 official sister-city relationships in 121 different countries or autonomous regions.[161] These relationships commonly involve cultural and educational agreements, facilitating the exchange

---

153. Zarchary Keck, *A US State Representative to Visit North Korea*, THE DIPLOMAT, July 31, 2013, http://thediplomat.com/2013/07/a-us-state-representative-to-visit-north-korea/.

154. Paul Heroux, *Inside North Korea: Lessons for Diplomacy*, THE HUFFINGTON POST, Jan. 16, 2014, http://www.huffingtonpost.com/paul-heroux/inside-north-korea_b_4499273.html.

155. FRY, *supra* note 103, at 4.

156. JAMES BROOKS, MANAGING YOUR CITY'S GLOBAL CONNECTIONS, NAT'L LEAGUE OF CITIES (2002), http://www.nlc.org/Documents/Build%20Skills%20Networks/Networks/Committees%20and%20Councils/Advisory%20Groups/International%20Council/managing-cities-global-connections-book-2005.pdf.

157. Micheline Maynard, *A Lifeline Not Made in the USA*, N.Y. TIMES, Oct. 17, 2009, at BU1.

158. FRY, *supra* note 103, at 81.

159. *Id.* at 81.

160. *Id.* at 82.

161. Brooks, *supra* note 108.

of students, teachers, artists, and performers.[162] Some of them also include cooperative economic projects.[163] About 36 percent of U.S. cities sponsor educational "study abroad" programs at local high schools or universities.[164] Indeed, some universities require students to study abroad in order to graduate.[165] At times, cities use these relationships to pursue human rights objectives, for example, placing pressure on the apartheid South African government to stop the forced removal of black communities in areas of South Africa.[166] And at times, cities use sister-city relationships in an effort to advance political objectives that do not entirely conform to federal foreign policy (or at least not that of the executive branch). During the Reagan administration, for example, several U.S. cities whose citizens and officials disagreed with federal policy toward Central America established sister-city relationships with municipalities in Nicaragua.[167] Recently, the sister-city relationship between Baltimore, Maryland, and Odessa, Ukraine, has been beneficial for those in need at the time of the crisis in Ukraine in 2014. A local Baltimore organization, The Associated, has made significant efforts to use that relationship to provide food, medicine, heating, and cooking fuel to those in Odessa.[168]

G. State Foreign Policy Statements

During the 1980s more than twenty-eight cities and communities declared themselves sanctuaries for refugees from Central America.[169] Some ordered their law enforcement officials not to cooperate with agents of the United States

162. FRY, *supra* note 103, at 90.

163. *Id.* at 86.

164. Brooks, *supra* note 108.

165. Devon Haynie, *10 Universities Where the Most Students Study Outside the U.S.*, U.S. NEWS, May 20, 2014, http://www.usnews.com/education/best-colleges/articles/2014/05/20/10-universities-where-the-most-students-study-outside-the-us.

166. Cleveland, *supra* note 152, at 994. Atlanta, Berkeley, Louisville, Milwaukee, St. Paul, and Wichita used their sister-city relationships to halt the forced removal of black townships in South Africa.

167. FRY, *supra* note 103, at 90.

168. Melissa Gerr & March Shapiro, *Eyes on Ukraine*, BALT. JEWISH TIMES, Mar. 20, 2014, http://jewishtimes.com/20591/eyes-on-ukraine/#.U4pqP5RdVbw.

169. Bilder, *supra* note 137, at 116. For examples, see FRANCK, ET AL., *supra* note 115, at 788–91; FRY, *supra* note 103, at 93; *see also New Mexico Is Declared Sanctuary for Refugees*, N.Y. TIMES, Mar. 30, 1986, http://www.nytimes.com/1986/03/30/us/new-mexico-is-declared-sanctuary-for-refugees.html; Daniel B. Wroblewksi, *One Year of Sanctuary in Cambridge, Mass.*, THE HARVARD CRIMSON, Apr. 11, 1986, http://www.thecrimson.com/article/1986/4/11/one-year-of-sanctuary-in-cambridge/.

Immigration and Naturalization Service seeking to track down undocumented immigrants from Central America.[170] In 1985, New York City mayor Edward Koch prohibited city employees from reporting non-criminal illegal immigrants.[171] In the 1980s, more than two hundred cities adopted resolutions supporting a treaty banning the testing of nuclear weapons.[172] During the Vietnam War, at least seven cities held referenda on the conflict, and three measures opposing the war received majority support.[173] More recently, more than one hundred cities adopted resolutions disapproving the 2003 U.S. invasion of Iraq.[174] As Ivo Daalder has pointed out, U.S. cities have hardly been alone in venturing into the international realm:

> Cities are also increasingly pursuing their own foreign policies. Shanghai has its own foreign affairs office, while São Paulo has established diplomatic relations with dozens of states. These nations, in turn, have larger diplomatic representations there than they have in the capital Brasília.
>
> Major capital cities, such as London, Tokyo and Paris, are integral to the foreign policies of their national governments. But global cities that are not national seats of government, such as Chicago or Shanghai, increasingly need to forge foreign policies of their own by co-ordinating the global engagement of [sic] corporations, top academic centres, cultural institutions and civic bodies in ways that benefit the city and its citizens as a whole.[175]

H. State Economic Sanctions and Trade Bans

States increasingly seek to use their economic clout to encourage political change in target countries. In the 1970s, some states enacted laws barring companies that did business with their governments from complying with the Arab League's boycott of Israel.[176] About 150 states, cities, and counties, as well as the Virgin Islands, adopted divestment or procurement laws and enacted sanctions on U.S. and foreign companies doing business in apartheid South Africa well

---

170. FRY, *supra* note 103, at 5.

171. *Id.* at 91.

172. *Id.* at 93.

173. *Id.* at 92.

174. FRANCK ET AL., *supra* note 115, at 751.

175. Daalder, *supra* note 99.

176. *See* FRY, *supra* note 103, at 94; Cleveland, *supra* note 152, at 996.

before Congress enacted comprehensive federal legislation to similar effect in 1986.[177] In 1996, Massachusetts enacted a statute that restricted the authority of its agencies to purchase goods or services from companies doing business with Burma (Myanmar). The Supreme Court struck the law down on preemption grounds several years later.[178] In 1997, New York City's comptroller banned certain Swiss banks from bidding on billions of dollars in bond offerings, dissatisfied with their explanation of the disposition of gold and other assets taken from Holocaust victims. The State Department harshly criticized the ban.[179] In 2003, California enacted the Holocaust Victim Insurance Relief Act of 1999,[180] requiring any insurer doing business in California to disclose information about all policies sold in Europe between 1920 and 1945 by the insurer itself or any affiliated business or person. The Court invalidated this law as well, although on a distinct and more contentious basis.[181] About half the states had imposed some form of sanctions on Iran at the time the Obama administration began to negotiate the deal under which Iran agreed to accept limits on its nuclear program in return for sanctions relief.[182]

I. "Buy American" Requirements

International trade laws and regimes have sought to limit or eliminate altogether requirements that goods and services be purchased locally. When Congress enacted the American Recovery and Reinvestment Act of 2009, it included provisions forbidding the use of stimulus funds for the construction, repair, or maintenance of a public building or public work unless all of the project's iron, steel, and manufactured goods used were made in the United States.[183] Policies of this sort raise concerns that other countries will retaliate with comparable protectionist policies,[184] for the World Trade Organization rules disallow favoring

---

177. Fry, *supra* note 103, at 5; *see also* Bilder, *supra* note 137, at 116. Comprehensive Anti-Apartheid Act, Pub. L. No. 99-440,100 Stat 1086 (1986).

178. Crosby v. Nat'l Foreign Trade Council, 530 U.S. 363 (2000). For a discussion of the case, see Chapter 9.

179. Fry, *supra* note 103, at 5.

180. Cal. Ins. Code Ann. §§ 13800–13807 (West Cum. Supp. 2003).

181. Am. Ins. Ass'n v. Garamendi, 539 U.S. 396 (2003). For a discussion of the case, see Chapter 4.

182. Patrick Clawson, *The Iran Primer: U.S. Sanctions*, U.S. Institute of Peace, http://iranprimer.usip.org/resource/us-sanctions (last visited Nov. 11, 2015).

183. Jonathon Watson, *"Buy American" Clause Raises Tensions*, 63 Int'l B. News 10, 11 (2009).

184. *Id.*

local suppliers,[185] and this provision applies to subfederal units.[186] States and cities nonetheless continue, increasingly, to promulgate such requirements.[187]

J. State Taxation of Foreign Businesses

States regularly seek to tax foreign enterprises, and several such recent efforts have come before the Supreme Court. California imposed a nondiscriminatory ad valorem property tax on foreign-owned cargo containers, which the Court struck down in 1979.[188] In 1983, however, the Court upheld California's income-based corporate franchise tax as applied to a multinational enterprise.[189] The decision did not address the constitutionality of California's taxing scheme as applied to domestic corporations with foreign parents or to foreign corporations with either foreign parents or foreign subsidiaries. Eleven years later, the Court sustained California's "unitary taxation" scheme,[190] under which California imposed taxes on foreign corporations based on their worldwide earnings rather than their California earnings alone. Some such corporations had threatened to withdraw their investments from California and refuse to invest in the future unless California terminated or at least modified the unitary taxation system.[191]

K. State Restrictions on Immigrants

States have, over the years, imposed a variety of restrictions on immigrants. These include, for example, a Maryland policy under which non-immigrant aliens, even though domiciled within the state, were rendered ineligible for in-state

185. World Trade Organization, Uruguay Round, Agreement on Government Procurement, art. III, IV, https://www.wto.org/english/docs_e/legal_e/gpr-94_e.pdf. For a debate over the legality of "Buy American" provisions, see The Editors, *That "Buy American" Provision*, N.Y. Times Blog, Feb. 11, 2009, http://roomfordebate.blogs.nytimes.com/2009/02/11/that-buy-american-provision/#.

186. *See* World Trade Organization, Uruguay Round, Agreement on Government Procurement, annex 2; John H. Jackson, The World Trading System: Law and Policy of International Economic Relations 228 (2d ed. 1997).

187. *See* Edward T. Swaine, *Negotiating Federalism: State Bargaining and the Dormant Treaty Power*, 49 Duke L.J. 1127, 1132 (2000).

188. *See* Japan Line, Ltd. v. County of Los Angeles, 441 U.S. 434, 449 (1979).

189. Container Corp. of Am. v. Franchise Tax Bd., 463 U.S. 159 (1983). For a discussion of the case, see Chapter 5.

190. Barclays Bank Plc v. Franchise Tax Bd., 512 U.S. 298 (1994). For a discussion of the case, see Chapter 5.

191. Fry, *supra* note 103, at 26–27.

preferential treatment relative to tuition and fees. The Supreme Court struck down Maryland's policy in 1982.[192] The same year, the Supreme Court also struck down a Texas statute that denied undocumented child immigrants the ability to enroll in public schools.[193] Since then, education for undocumented immigrants has continued to be a divisive issue. In 2001, Texas and California were the first of several states to enact legislation that permits undocumented students to receive in-state tuition rates.[194] Colorado, Arizona,[195] Georgia, and Indiana enacted bans against receiving in-state tuition, although Colorado repealed the ban in 2013.[196] Further restrictions on immigrants include an Arizona law from 2011 that provided for the suspension or revocation of the licenses of state employers who knowingly or intentionally employed unauthorized aliens, and also required those employers to use an Internet-based system to check the work authorization status of their employees.[197]

L. State Regulatory Prohibitions and Restrictions

States and cities have occasionally enacted laws with a direct regulatory effect on foreign affairs. In the 1970s, the Regents of the University of New Mexico denied admission to foreign students whose governments had held or permitted the holding of U.S. citizens as hostages. A federal district court invalidated the policy.[198]

Ordinances establishing nuclear free zones became common during the 1980s. Over 150 local jurisdictions adopted some type of nuclear free zone law. Most such ordinances were largely symbolic, but some prohibited contracts between the governmental entity in question and vendors that produced components used in nuclear weapons.[199] More than 120 cities and counties adopted

---

192. Toll v. Moreno, 458 U.S. 1 (1982).

193. Plyler v. Doe, 457 U.S. 202 (1982).

194. *Undocumented Student Tuition: State Action*, NAT'L CONFERENCE OF STATE LEGISLATURES (June 12, 2014) [hereinafter *Undocumented Student Tuition*], http://www.ncsl.org/research/education/undocumented-student-tuition-state-action.aspx. As of this writing, at least eighteen states have laws allowing undocumented students to receive in-state tuition rates.

195. Arizona v. United States, 132 S. Ct. 2492, 2498 (2012).

196. *Undocumented Student Tuition*, *supra* note 194.

197. Chamber of Commerce of the United States v. Whiting, 131 S. Ct. 1968 (2011).

198. Tayyari v. New Mexico State Univ., 495 F. Supp. 1365 (D.N.M. 1980).

199. Patrick J. Borchers & Paul F. Dauer, *Taming the New Breed of Nuclear Free Zone Ordinances: Statutory and Constitutional Infirmities in Local Procurement Ordinances Blacklisting the Producers of Nuclear Weapons Components*, 40 HASTINGS L.J. 87, 87–90 (1988).

resolutions banning nuclear weapons production within their boundaries.[200] The U.S. Department of Justice challenged one such ordinance, adopted by the city of Oakland,[201] and a federal district court invalidated it.[202] Oakland later adopted a modified version. Yet the courts have not been uniformly hostile to such efforts. The city of Cambridge, Massachusetts, adopted an ordinance prohibiting the testing, storage, transportation, or disposal within the city of chemical warfare agents. Unlike the Oakland ordinance, the Cambridge ordinance was upheld by the Massachusetts Supreme Judicial Court.[203]

In 1983, in response to the downing of a South Korean passenger airplane by a Soviet military jet on September 1, 1983, the governors of New York and New Jersey ordered the Port Authority of New York and New Jersey not to grant clearance for the landing of a Soviet airplane carrying Soviet foreign minister Andrei Gromyko to a meeting of the U.N. General Assembly. The United States took no action to prevent implementation of the order.[204]

One effort at local regulation seemed like the plot of a Woody Allen movie. In May 1982, a two-year dispute began among the city of Glen Cove, New York, the federal government, and the Soviet Union[205] when the mayor of Glen Cove revoked permits for recreational facilities for Soviet citizens living at their government's Glen Cove estate of Killenworth. Without permits, the Soviets were forbidden use of Glen Cove's beaches, tennis courts, and golf courses. The State Department wrote to the mayor that the "conduct of foreign affairs, a function within the exclusive competence of the federal government, requires that the federal government exercise full control over these matters. Discriminatory actions such as that taken by Glen Cove interfere with the conduct of foreign relations by the United States." The mayor, referring to reports that the Soviets had been conducting electronic surveillance of telephone conversations from the facilities, replied that "[our] government should not allow this to exist. The spying is against this country's best interest." Three days later, the *New York Times* editorialized as follows: "Here's how [the Mayor] should have put it: 'The State

---

200. FRY, *supra* note 103, at 93.

201. *See* FRANCK ET AL., *supra* note 115, at 830–32.

202. United States v. Oakland, No. C-89-3305 JPV 13-14 (N.D. Cal. Aug. 20, 1990), *aff'd*, United States v. City of Oakland, 958 F.2d 300 (9th Cir. 1992).

203. Arthur D. Little, Inc., v. Comm'r of Health & Hosps., 481 N.E.2d 441 (Mass. 1985).

204. See Note, *Acts by State Governments Affecting Foreign Relations—Decision of New York and New Jersey Governors to Deny Soviet Airplane Clearance to Land, Sept. 1983*, 25 HARV. INT'L L.J. 200 (1984).

205. For a detailed description of this episode, and relevant references and citations, see FRANCK ET AL., *supra* note 115, at 837–48.

Department's impertinent intrusion in decisions relating to our security is a mockery of accepted norms, a threat to all small territories. It is hegemony in the name of patriotism and will be repudiated by the common conscience of mankind."[206] The appropriate solution, the *Times* suggested, might be for the mayor and city council to "secede from the country they embarrass."[207]

Several days later, the State Department received a cable from the U.S. embassy in Moscow indicating that the embassy had encountered increasing evidence of Soviet foot-dragging on two projects of a recreational nature for use by the embassy staff and their family members in Moscow. The embassy speculated that this reflected retaliation for Glen Cove's action, which Soviet authorities had raised several times. *Pravda*, meanwhile, quoted an elderly woman in Glen Cove as complaining that "[t]hose Soviet diplomats interfere with my TV watching," and described a beach attendant as "even worse off. He can't have a minute's rest, watching the horizon for Soviet battleships."[208]

At this point, the mayor and State Department exchanged a spate of correspondence. The State Department explained that "[t]he current impasse is not in the interest of the United States." Banning Soviet diplomats from Glen Cove's beaches "threatens to lead to a cycle of retaliations and counter-retaliations which will only add more problems to our already troubled relations with the Soviets." And the Soviets did retaliate. On August 6, the Soviets barred American diplomats from using a beach on the Moskva River that is reserved for the city's diplomatic community.[209] The State Department therefore proposed a solution involving a yearly lump sum payment and limits on the number of Soviets using Glen Cove's beaches at any given time.

The mayor responded that the ban also applied to all Glen Cove golf courses and tennis courts, not only its beaches. The annual lump sum proposed by the State Department, he suggested, would not suffice because the demonstrations, marches, and prayer vigils conducted outside the Soviet facilities required costly protection by Glen Cove's police. The State Department, "naturally disappointed" with the mayor's reply, said it would not consider the police expenses, and asked the mayor to reconsider.

---

206. *Rebellions and Relief; Insurgent Glen Cove*, N.Y. TIMES, July 25, 1982, http://www.nytimes.com/1982/07/25/opinion/topics-rebellions-and-relief-insurgent-glen-cove.html.

207. *Id.*

208. John F. Burns, *Moscow Derides Glen Cove Curb on the Russians*, N.Y. TIMES, Aug. 11, 1982, http://www.nytimes.com/1982/08/11/nyregion/moscow-derides-glen-cove-curb-on-the-russians.html.

209. James Barron, *Glen Cove and Russians: What's Next?*, N.Y. TIMES, Aug. 29, 1982, http://www.nytimes.com/1982/08/29/nyregion/glen-cove-and-russians-what-s-next.html.

The mayor replied by pointing out that the FBI recently had "caught three Soviet spies 'redhanded,' (one in a neighboring community)," arguing that Killenworth should not enjoy tax-exempt status, and threatening to "pursue our legal remedies." He then wrote to the *Charge d'Affaires* of the Soviet Mission to the United Nations, announcing that because Killenworth was "not being used for the specific purpose for which it was intended," all passes and permits for recreational facilities for Soviet residents of Killenworth were being revoked. The mayor then wrote another letter to the State Department, suggesting that they risked becoming "involuntary pen pals" and expressing, again, concern about "the recent revelation of KGB activity in Long Island . . . ."

The controversy ended when, on April 24, 1984, the City Council voted five to two to lift the ban. This followed a settlement worked out by Glen Cove officials, Soviet officials, the State Department, and the Justice Department.

V. Conclusion

The German jurist Eugen Ehrlich argued over ninety years ago that much law emerges from the spontaneous ordering of social relations.[210] In the United States, the Constitution of course supplies the foundational blueprint, but not infrequently with vague or uncertain parameters. This is especially so in the realm of foreign relations.[211] The patterns of state practice that we have recounted reflect a spontaneous ordering vis-à-vis federal-state relations in the realm of foreign affairs. That ought not, on reflection, be surprising. Indeed, it could hardly have been otherwise, and there is every reason to believe that the Framers foresaw precisely the need for such adaptation in a document intended, as Chief Justice Marshall famously wrote, to "endure for ages to come, and consequently, to be adapted to the various *crises* of human affairs."[212]

---

210. Eugen Ehrlich, *The Sociology of Law*, 36 HARV. L. REV. 130, 133 (1922); *see also* FRIEDRICH A. HAYEK, LAW, LEGISLATION, AND LIBERTY, VOLUME 1: RULES AND ORDER (1973).

211. *See generally* HENKIN, *supra* note 8, at 87–121.

212. McCulloch v. Maryland, 17 U.S. (4 Wheat.) 316, 415 (1819).

3

Constitutional Methodology and the Role of the Courts

THE AGENDA OF the following chapters is twofold. The first objective is descriptive: we describe and clarify the current state of the law on foreign affairs federalism, the black-letter doctrine that governs the scope and limits of state authority relative to the federal government in the realm of foreign affairs. We emphasize those areas in which the relevant law is either unclear or subject to more than one reasonable interpretation, some of which will inevitably be in tension with one another. The second part of the agenda is normative: we appraise the relevant doctrine in view of its coherence with constitutional doctrine and actual practice, as well as, at times, its relationship to international law.

The latter part of the agenda poses something of a dilemma. This is not a treatise on constitutional theory. Given the focus and scope of this book, it would be both impracticable and imprudent for us to purport to defend in any depth a particular thesis concerning constitutional interpretation. Yet we would be remiss to neglect the subject altogether. To do so would expose any normative analysis to the justified critique that it offers no more than the personal values or political preferences of the authors.

So without belaboring the many vexing issues of constitutional theory, a brief word about our general approach to the main theoretical questions is in order, followed by a more specific word on our notion of the proper role of the courts in this realm.

I. Constitutional Methodology

Although we tend to reject the various incarnations of originalism for reasons explored in depth by its critics,[1] we decline to adopt a global or "field" theory of constitutional interpretation, that is, a uniform methodology that applies to any and all issues of constitutional interpretation, adjudication, and practice. When it comes to the general enterprise of constitutional interpretation, we agree with Laurence Tribe's call for "self-conscious humility in the face of a task about which none of us is entitled to feel too self-assured,"[2] and with his view that:

> [t]o prevent the interpretive task from degenerating into the imposition of one's personal preferences or values under the guise of constitutional exegesis, one must concede how difficult the task is; avoid all pretence that it can be reduced to a passive process of *discovering* rather than *constructing* an interpretation; and replace such pretense with a forthright account, incomplete and inconclusive though it might be, of why one deems his or her proposed construction of the text to be worthy of acceptance, in light of the Constitution as a whole and the history of its interpretation.[3]

Of course, we take and defend particular positions on the jurisprudence. We try to evaluate them critically and fairly relative to reasonable alternatives. And naturally, we hope that our normative appraisal of existing doctrine, even if it does not persuade, will contribute original or at least sensible perspectives and arguments that merit serious consideration from scholars, judges, and policymakers. Above all, however, we reject any dogmatic approach to constitutional interpretation, for we see the paramount objective of the particular set of normative appraisals in this book as a comparatively modest one: to motivate an unduly neglected conversation about an increasingly important area of the law that has long been enveloped in the cobwebs of outdated doctrine.

Second, whatever the theoretical merits of originalism as an interpretive theory, not even the most doctrinaire originalist would claim that the

---

1. *See, e.g.*, SOTIRIOS A. BARBER & JAMES E. FLEMING, CONSTITUTIONAL INTERPRETATION: THE BASIC QUESTIONS 79–116 (2007); FRANK CROSS, THE FAILED PROMISE OF ORIGINALISM (2013); Jack M. Balkin, *The New Originalism and the Uses of History*, 82 FORDHAM L. REV. 641 (2013); Mitchell N. Berman, *Originalism Is Bunk*, 84 N.Y.U. L. REV. 1 (2009). For a summary of common critiques that is particularly accessible to the lay reader, see DAVID STRAUSS, THE LIVING CONSTITUTION 7–31 (2010).

2. Laurence H. Tribe, Comment, *in* ANTONIN SCALIA, A MATTER OF INTERPRETATION: FEDERAL COURTS AND THE LAW 65, 72 (1997).

3. *Id.*

U.S. constitutional order can be sustained by a static approach to constitutional adjudication that neglects context.[4] When the text and history do not supply clear answers, the most widely subscribed variant of originalism today, embraced by Justice Antonin Scalia among others,[5] asks what the Constitution's text would have meant to a reasonable person of that era—and seeks to resolve contemporary controversies in constitutional adjudication in a manner consistent with the putatively best inference of original meaning. Yet those controversies often lie well beyond the scope of what the Framers, ratifiers, engaged civic constituents, or any other ideal candidate reader, did—or could—have had in mind. Because no one regards the original meaning of the text as irrelevant to constitutional interpretation and adjudication,[6] the real normative question is what weight the original meaning and arguable inferences from it merit relative to other factors to which the justices commonly look: history, precedent, structure, practice, political theory, and so forth.

Seldom if ever does the text alone answer any question that reaches the Supreme Court, especially in the modern era in which federal law gives the Court virtually complete discretion over its docket. Supreme Court decisions on constitutional law commonly intone the relevant textual provisions of the Constitution as a kind of ritual before turning to the considerations that do the real work in the opinions, viz., complex analyses that combine scrutiny of historical and judicial precedent, comparative functional capacities, considerations of policy, social interests, principles, values, and the broader potential consequences of different approaches to the issues (often teased out at oral argument by the skillful construction of hypotheticals)—assigning different weights to each depending on the nature of the issue and the context in which it arises.[7] And the results of constitutional adjudication contribute to a tapestry woven by history, practice,

---

4. *Cf.* Randy E. Barnett, *Scalia's Infidelity: A Critique of "Faint-Hearted" Originalism*, 75 U. CIN. L. REV. 7, 21 (2005).

5. Antonin Scalia, *Originalism: The Lesser Evil*, 57 U. CIN. L. REV. 849 (1989); *see also* John O. McGinnis & Michael B. Rappaport, *Original Methods Originalism: A New Theory of Interpretation and the Case against Construction*, 103 NW. U. L. REV. 751 (2009).

6. JOHN HART ELY, DEMOCRACY AND DISTRUST 1–2, 14–16 (1980). On the distinction drawn by some scholars between constitutional interpretation and adjudication, see Gary Lawson, *On Reading Recipes . . . and Constitutions*, 85 GEO. L.J. 1823, 1824 (1997). We use the former phrase for the sake of convention and clarity—for without minimizing the role of the judiciary, it is important to recognize that foreign relations law often evolves outside the context of courts and adjudication, for example, from precedents established by periodic struggles between the political branches, legislation, practice, tradition, and so forth. Despite our doctrinal focus on the Court's jurisprudence, adjudication of foreign affairs issues is rare, and often plays an interstitial role in the evolution of constitutional law in this area.

7. *See* STRAUSS, *supra* note 1, at 33–35.

precedent, shared (or conflicting) political assumptions about the meaning of constitutional democracy, and explicit and implicit values embodied in the text and the circumstances of its adoption.

An eclectic approach to constitutional adjudication that considers and accepts the validity of different perspectives and methodologies also conforms, not coincidentally, to the actual practice of the Court. No one method describes the uniform preference of the Court as a whole, or even that of a particular Supreme Court justice, protests to the contrary notwithstanding.[8] Nor is it clear why one *should*: adjudication can be *principled* without relying on a single principle or methodology. Different issues may well lend themselves more readily or appropriately to different methods. It is indeed "doubtful that any defensible set of ultimate 'rules' exists. Insights and perspectives, yes; rules, no."[9] For a document and body of jurisprudence intended to endure and govern a nation in perpetuity, Justice Holmes's famous words—not coincidentally, in a case central to issues explored in this book—remain apt:

> [W]hen we are dealing with words that also are a constituent act, like the Constitution of the United States, we must realize that they have called into life a being the development of which could not have been foreseen completely by the most gifted of its begetters. It was enough for them to realize or to hope that they had created an organism; it has taken a century and has cost their successors much sweat and blood to prove that they created a nation. The case before us must be considered in the light of our whole experience, and not merely in that of what was said a hundred years ago.[10]

A century earlier, Chief Justice Marshall emphasized to similar effect that "[t]o have prescribed the means by which government should, in all future time, execute its powers, would have been to change, entirely, the character of the instrument, and give it the properties of a legal code. It would have been an unwise attempt to provide, by immutable rules, for exigencies which, if foreseen at all, must have been seen dimly, and which can be best provided for as they occur."[11]

It is therefore fair to say that we incline toward what some would characterize as a functional or pragmatic approach to constitutional adjudication. Vexing

---

8. Tribe, *supra* note 2, at 66.

9. *Id.* at 73.

10. Missouri v. Holland, 252 U.S. 416, 433 (1920).

11. McCulloch v. Maryland, 17 U.S. (4 Wheat.) 316, 415 (1819).

constitutional questions require attending to empirical issues and the comparative consequences of different outcomes.[12] At times, tradeoffs, often between the incommensurable, will be unavoidable and inevitable. Constitutional interpretation should also, in our view, be sensitive to concrete political and social circumstances. The consequences of and rationales for alternative decisions should, if possible, promote the efficient functioning of the U.S. constitutional order—based, as it is, on a document adopted nearly two and half centuries ago by people with whom we have comparatively little in common. There is no non-normative way for a responsible judge to decide a difficult constitutional question. There are only different normative approaches, more or less defensible in context, from which to choose.

Finally, it bears emphasis that in the realm of foreign affairs, methods of interpretation other than textual exegesis seem not only especially appropriate, but likely indispensable. Louis Henkin began his seminal treatise *Foreign Affairs and the US Constitution* by observing that "where foreign relations are concerned the Constitution seems a strange, laconic document: although it explicitly lodges important foreign affairs powers in one branch or another of the federal government, and explicitly denies important foreign affairs powers to the states, many powers of government are not mentioned."[13] For that reason, among others, the constitutional law of U.S. foreign affairs—perhaps more than any other subfield of constitutional law—relies routinely on history, practice, structure, inference, precedent, the alleged incidents of sovereignty or independent statehood, and other methods that some might regard as unorthodox or inappropriate. The point is not that "judicial legislation" based on cherry-picking and motivated reasoning from among the foregoing sources and methodologies is any more appropriate in the realm of foreign affairs than elsewhere in constitutional law; it is rather that constitutional interpretation in this particular area compels scrutiny of questions well beyond the Constitution's text; and it depends more than many other areas of constitutional law on inferences, structure, traditions, and past practice—including, but far from limited to, judicial precedent.

II. The Role of the Courts

"Unelected." Critics of decisions that they consider wrongheaded routinely characterize the judicial authors of those decisions with this (contextually pejorative) term. From all points on the political spectrum, elected officials stress their

---

12. *See generally* Richard Posner, Reflections on Judging (2013).

13. Louis Henkin, Foreign Affairs and the US Constitution 13–14 (2d ed. 1996).

democratic bona fides when judges who cannot claim the same pedigree strike down their handiwork. And in a nation avowedly governed by "We the People,"[14] citizen-critics inveigh against the disliked decisions of unelected judges. Few arguments in a democracy seem so compelling as the argument that some judicial act conflicts with the will of the governed. Popular approval or disapproval, to many, is the ultimate trump.

There are good reasons to constrain judicial power. But the fact that most judges (and all federal judges) are appointed rather than elected is not among them.[15] Federal judges do not, after all, appoint themselves. An elected president appoints them. An elected Senate confirms them. And except for justices of the Supreme Court, the establishment of which the Constitution expressly requires,[16] judges sit on courts that can in theory be abolished by Congress.[17] The Constitution also renders federal appellate jurisdiction subject to "such exceptions, and . . . such regulations as the Congress shall make,"[18] which some argue empowers Congress to exclude almost any issue from federal judicial review.[19]

---

14. U.S. CONST. pmbl.

15. Some states elect some of their judges. For example, Alabama, Illinois, Louisiana, and others hold partisan elections for state high courts, intermediate appellate courts, and trial courts. Others states, including Arkansas, Mississippi, and Washington, hold nonpartisan elections for the same courts. *See* American Bar Association, Fact Sheet on Judicial Selection Methods in the States, http://www.americanbar.org/content/dam/aba/migrated/leadership/fact_sheet.authcheckdam.pdf, (last visited Nov. 11, 2015).

16. U.S. CONST. art. III, § 1. Technically, the Constitution mandates only a single judge, the Chief Justice of the Supreme Court. *See* JAMES E. PFANDER, PRINCIPLES OF FEDERAL JURISDICTION 1–2 (2006).

17. U.S. CONST. art. III, § 1. *See, e.g.*, Theodore Eisenberg, *Congressional Authority to Restrict Lower Federal Court Jurisdiction*, 83 YALE L.J. 498, 500 (1974); *see also* LARRY W. YACKLE, FEDERAL COURTS 66 (3d ed. 2009). Justice Story argued in an early decision that the Constitution requires Congress to establish at least some inferior federal courts, *Martin v. Hunter's Lessee*, 14 U.S. (1 Wheat.) 304 (1816), but most scholars now reject that view. *See* YACKLE, *supra*, at 66–67. And at any rate, in practice, it would be all but unimaginable for Congress to abolish lower federal courts, which have been established and continually in operation since 1789. *Id.*

18. U.S. CONST. art. III, § 2.

19. A debate has long raged over the extent to which Congress may limit the courts' appellate jurisdiction, thereby effectively insulating certain (potentially unconstitutional) statutes and issues altogether from federal judicial review. Virtually the only decision on point is *Ex parte McCardle*, 74 U.S. (7 Wall.) 506, 513 (1869), which some suggest affirms Congress's plenary power in this regard. But that is hardly clear. Because of the unusual circumstances and limited nature of the question decided in *McCardle*, it is doubtful that the Court truly suggested that Congress's so-called jurisdiction-stripping power under Article III, section 2, is limitless. *See* YACKLE, *supra* note 17, at 60–62; *see also* Steven G. Calabresi & Gary Lawson, *The Unitary Executive, Jurisdiction Stripping, and the* Hamdan *Opinions: A Textualist Response to Justice Scalia*, 107 COLUM. L. REV. 1002, 1008 (2007).

At any rate, since 1803, when Chief Justice Marshall delivered the seminal opinion for the Court in *Marbury v. Madison*,[20] the Court has reviewed and invalidated as incompatible with the Constitution some 176 acts of Congress and 1318 state and local measures.[21] It's a bit late in the game to claim that an unelected judiciary renders the practice of judicial review in the United States democratically illegitimate. Indeed, for all the ink spilled in debates over the so-called counter-majoritarian difficulty, judicial review is hardly the sole, or even the most troubling, offender against democracy within the republican political structure established by the Constitution.[22] Wyoming's 550,000 citizens receive the same two votes in the Senate as California's 37 million citizens, which means its two senators exercise about *thirty times* more political power than California's two senators. This and other features of the U.S. constitutional legal order seem as or more "counter-majoritarian" than judicial review. And properly understood and practiced, the institution of judicial review—which serves, among other functions, to check the tyranny of the majority[23] that afflicts any sophomoric equation of democracy with majoritarianism—is arguably among America's greatest constitutional innovations. It is no accident that it has been incorporated worldwide into the constitutions or foundational charters of dozens of other nations.

It is doubly prudent in a liberal democracy to limit the power of all public officials, judges included. But the reasons for restricting judicial review relate less to majoritarian legitimacy than to determinacy and the allocation of authority. Cases that call for judges to base their decisions on vague, nebulous, or ethereal standards, which admit of multiple, conflicting and perhaps equally plausible interpretations, virtually compel the judiciary to exceed the conventional limits of the judicial role—to "legislate from the bench," in colloquial terms.[24] This intuition is

20. 5. U.S. (1 Cranch) 137 (1803).

21. *See* Gov't Printing Office, Acts of Congress Held Unconstitutional in Whole or in Part by the Supreme Court of the United States (2013), http://www.gpo.gov/fdsys/pkg/GPO-CONAN-2013/pdf/GPO-CONAN-2013-11.pdf; Gov't Printing Office, State Constitutional and Statutory Provisions and Municipal Ordinances Held Unconstitutional or Held to Be Preempted by Federal Law (2013), http://www.gpo.gov/fdsys/pkg/GPO-CONAN-2013/pdf/GPO-CONAN-2013-12.pdf.

22. *See* Robert A. Dahl, How Democratic Is the American Constitution? (2d ed. 2003); Sanford Levinson, Our Undemocratic Constitution: Where the Constitution Goes Wrong (And How We the People Can Correct It) (2008).

23. John Stuart Mill, On Liberty and Other Writings 8 (Stefan Collini ed., 1989).

24. It is of course true that state and, less often, federal judges do, in a largely unobjectionable sense, "make law" within the United States, as in other, Anglo-American common-law legal systems—most prominently, through common law adjudication, but also, at times, in the course of statutory or regulatory interpretation and exposition. Yet precedent constrains the nature and extent of judicial lawmaking, and except for decisions involving constitutional

widely shared, not least by judges themselves. In the seminal case on the political question doctrine, *Baker v. Carr*,[25] the Supreme Court itself explained the difficulty with requiring judges to decide cases without a manageable standard of review, and disavowed its authority or willingness to do so.

The Court has of course decided countless cases that require it to apply nebulous standards, involving, for example, the Equal Protection and Due Process Clauses, the rights of criminal defendants, and the scope of Congress's power to regulate interstate commerce. The Constitution's text itself requires the application of broad and abstract principles to concrete facts and new circumstances. Yet a long line of precedent constrains the Court's decisions in most such constitutional cases.[26] Their limits are woven into the fabric of U.S. legal history. *Why* these cases were decided as they were has eventually become less relevant than the simple historical fact that they *were* decided as they were. Perhaps the clearest and most notorious example of this path-dependency is the extent to which the *Slaughter-House Cases*[27] eviscerated, for all practical purposes, the Privileges or Immunities Clause of the Fourteenth Amendment shortly after its adoption.[28] Despite consensus across the political spectrum that Justice Miller's opinion in the *Slaughter-House Cases* dramatically misconstrued this part of the Fourteenth Amendment, the decision's holding persists and has affected a vast range of substantive constitutional doctrine. The same may be said for the *Insular Cases*.[29] Theorists across the methodological and political spectrum regard them as almost as misguided, and in some ways also as racist, as *Dred Scott v. Sanford*.[30] But the Supreme Court nevertheless continues to rely upon them in critical and

---

interpretation, judicial common-law or statutory interpretation can be replaced or superseded by new legislation.

25. 369 U.S. 186 (1962).

26. STRAUSS, *supra* note 1, at 36; David A. Strauss, *Common Law Constitutional Interpretation*, 63 U. CHI. L. REV. 877, 883 (1996).

27. 83 U.S. (16 Wall.) 36 (1873).

28. U.S. CONST. art. XIV, § 1.

29. The *Insular Cases* refer collectively to a series of decisions rendered in the early 1900s that restricted the application of the Constitution in U.S. territories, mostly those acquired from Spain as colonies after the Spanish-American War of 1898. *See, e.g.*, Balzac v. Porto Rico, 258 U.S. 298 (1922); Dorr v. United States, 195 U.S. 138 (1904); Hawaii v. Mankichi, 190 U.S. 197 (1903); De Lima v. Bidwell, 182 U.S. 1 (1901); Dooley v. United States, 182 U.S. 222 (1901); Armstrong v. United States, 182 U.S. 243 (1901); Downes v. Bidwell, 182 U.S. 244 (1901); Fourteen Diamond Rings v. United States, 183 U.S. 176 (1901).

30. 60 U.S. (19 How.) 393 (1857), *superseded by constitutional amendment*, U.S. CONST. amend. XIV.

controversial situations.[31] Even in cases far more defensible than the *Insular Cases*, such as *Gibbons v. Ogden*,[32] *Yick Wo v. Hopkins*,[33] and *Griswold v. Connecticut*,[34] it is hard to imagine the United States as it exists today had those cases been decided differently. These opinions are now of primary interest to legal historians and scholars, not litigators seeking to ferret out a weak rationale for judicial reassessment.

Many of the cases that we proceed to discuss, however, do not fall into this category. They are comparatively more recent. Most could easily have been decided differently, likely with little effect on the nation's history. The decisions do, however, often involve the courts in applying or formulating indeterminate standards—indeed, sometimes *no* standards. Foreign affairs federalism cases also, not infrequently, arise where there is not only no congressional enactment to interpret or apply; there is also no obvious *constitutional* standard to apply. Both dormant foreign-affairs preemption (see Chapter 4) and dormant Foreign Commerce Clause preemption (see Chapter 5) were manufactured by the courts in recent years virtually out of whole cloth. Consistent and overwhelming state practices, including, but not limited to, those canvassed in Chapter 2, cannot always be reconciled with their perplexing holdings. The effect of these cases has been to muddy the waters badly, giving inadequate guidance to state officials and to individuals and businesses who need to know the rules—who need to know when the courts might step in and say no. The "dormancy" case law discussed in these chapters cries out for realistic simplification, which would likely have the laudable effect of returning judges to their institutional role of interpreting and applying constitutional standards, not creating them. However desirable a given case's substantive outcome, it remains a compelling criticism that, constitutionally, the issue is not one that a judge ought properly decide.

---

31. *See, e.g.*, Boumediene v. Bush, 553 U.S. 723, 726 (2008).

32. 22 U.S. (9 Wheat.) 1 (1824).

33. 118 U.S. 356 (1886).

34. 381 U.S. 479 (1965).

4

Dormant Foreign-Affairs Preemption

I. Introduction

The Constitution, both expressly[1] and by clear implication elsewhere,[2] prohibits certain state activities in the realm of foreign affairs. But the Constitution does not tell us what states *may* do in the realm of foreign affairs—either categorically or without congressional consent.[3] More precisely, it does not say what states may do unless and until the federal government takes action constitutionally sufficient to prohibit it—for example, by enacting a preemptive federal law. Nor does any language in the Constitution prohibit the states generally from engaging in activities that might affect foreign affairs. There is, in other words, no affirmative textual basis for the common and popular claim that the federal government's role in the realm of foreign affairs is *exclusive*;[4] there are only the express prohibitions and

1. U.S. CONST. art. I, § 10.

2. LOUIS HENKIN, FOREIGN AFFAIRS AND THE US CONSTITUTION 156 & n.33 (2d ed. 1996). The Court has held, for example, that Congress's express power to "establish a uniform rule of naturalization," U.S. CONST. art. I, § 8, cl. 4, implicitly excludes the states from exercising the power to "naturalize or denaturalize persons." *Id.* (citing Chirac v. Chirac, 15 U.S. (2 Wheat.) 259, 269 (1817)).

3. Clause 1 provides, without qualification, that "[n]o state shall enter into any treaty, alliance, or confederation; [or] grant letters of marque and reprisal," while clauses 2 and 3 say that, absent congressional consent, "[n]o state shall . . . lay any imposts or duties on imports or exports, except what may be absolutely necessary for executing it's inspection laws," "lay any duty of tonnage, keep troops, or ships of war in time of peace, enter into any agreement or compact . . . with a foreign power, or engage in war, unless actually invaded, or in such imminent danger as will not admit of delay." U.S. CONST. art. I, § 10. These provisions, as noted in Chapter 1, originate in the nation's experience under the Articles—in particular, widespread state malfeasance in foreign affairs, including neglect and repudiation of the nation's international obligations.

4. The Supreme Court itself has not been immune from such simplification, as noted in the Preface to this book.

limitations in Article I, section 10, and, arguably, others that should be inferred. Hence, when Henkin wrote that "[t]he language, the spirit, and the history of the Constitution *deny* the states authority to participate in foreign affairs,"[5] he seems to have overstated the case. True, the federal government has the constitutional power, *if* it exercises it, to deny the states authority to participate in most or all aspects of foreign affairs. But the Constitution's language, spirit, and history do not themselves do so. At any rate, in practice, as Henkin hastened to add, "despite careless, flat statements to the contrary, the foreign relations of the United States are not in fact wholly insulated from the states, are not conducted as though the United States were a unitary state."[6] And although we might reasonably identify "core" cases of foreign as opposed to domestic affairs, the distinction between foreign and domestic affairs today is, as noted earlier, seldom obvious.

It is in fact a mistake to think that the Constitution excludes the states from foreign affairs. Arguments for exclusion generally rely on dubious inferences from history, or from the Constitution's textual allocation of certain foreign-affairs powers to the federal government. Virtually no one would deny the force of many inferred constitutional limits on state action in foreign affairs. Most everyone agrees, for example, that the president's power under Article II, section 2, clause 2, "to appoint ambassadors and to receive foreign ambassadors 'results' in the power to recognize governments," and that, in turn, implies authority to conduct diplomatic relations.[7] Because of the weight of historical evidence of state interference in foreign affairs under the Articles of Confederation, and the grants and denials of foreign affairs powers in the Constitution's text, any other conclusion would be difficult to defend. At the same time, other common inferences do not follow as uncontroversially from the text or history—for example, those about the extent of state authority in the field of immigration regulation (see Chapter 9). For these reasons, it is necessary to analyze particular foreign-affairs powers carefully at a *practical* level, for as Chapter 2 shows, the truth is that states participate in foreign affairs all the time. And they always have.[8]

5. HENKIN, *supra* note 2, at 150 (emphasis added).

6. *Id.*

7. *Id.* at 15; *see* Zivotofsky *ex rel.* Zivotofsky v. Kerry, 135 S. Ct. 2076, 2085–87 (2015).

8. That does not, of course, mean all such participation is or has been constitutional. It does, however, cast further and considerable doubt on assertions that the Constitution excludes the states from foreign affairs, as the Court has sometimes misleadingly suggested in dicta. In *Hines v. Davidowitz*, 312 U.S. 52 (1941), for example, the Court said that "[t]he Federal Government, representing as it does the collective interests of the forty-eight states, is entrusted with full and *exclusive* responsibility for the conduct of affairs with foreign sovereignties." *Id.* at 62 (emphasis added).

Because the Constitution delegates certain powers to the federal government, with the states presumptively retaining the balance of authority under the Tenth Amendment,[9] it is difficult as a practical matter to see how the states could be excluded from foreign affairs. Theory alone would be misleading and unavailing.[10] Immigration regulation, for example, falls within the plenary power of the federal government *if* the federal government chooses to preempt all state law on the issue. The Constitution itself does not exclude state regulation in this area. Constitutional jurisprudence on immigration, like the jurisprudence in certain other areas, relies on inferences from America's status as an independent nation and alleged incidents of sovereignty under international law.[11] Whatever the merits of such jurisprudence, for purposes of considering foreign-affairs federalism under the Constitution, the word "sovereignty" tends to be unhelpful and, at times, misleading.[12] International law does not dictate to nations *how* their sovereign powers should be exercised or allocated.

9. Several influential cases infer national foreign-affairs powers from either conceptions of the necessary implications of sovereign national independence in international law or historical speculation. *See, e.g.*, Hines v. Davidowitz, 312 U.S. 52, 62 (1941); United States v. Curtiss-Wright Export Corp., 299 U.S. 304, 319 (1936); Chae Chan Ping v. United States (The Chinese Exclusion Case), 130 U.S. 581, 600 (1888). We do not here suggest any view on the merits of such decisions.

10. The Constitution technically empowers the federal government to exercise virtually plenary power in foreign affairs—virtually, because all governmental powers remain subject to limits imposed elsewhere in the Constitution, especially the Bill of Rights. *See* Reid v. Covert, 354 U.S. 1, 6 (1957). In theory, however, Article I, sections 8 and 10, Article II, Article VI, clause 2, and Article III combine to empower the federal government, *if* it were to invoke the full extent of that constitutional authority, to exercise plenary foreign-affairs power. *See* Jack L. Goldsmith, *Federal Courts, Foreign Affairs, and Federalism*, 83 VA. L. REV. 1617, 1619 (1997). But even were it deemed desirable as a matter of policy, in practice, in the U.S. federal system, the national government lacks the institutional, personal, and financial resources to exercise such broad power.

11. Arizona v. United States, 132 S. Ct. 2492, 2498 (2012) (federal immigration authority rests in part on the federal government's "inherent power as sovereign to control and conduct relations with foreign nations"). This idea originated in late nineteenth-century jurisprudence. *See* Wong Wing v. United States, 163 U.S. 228, 231 (1896); Fong Yue Ting v. United States, 149 U.S. 698, 705 (1893); *The Chinese Exclusion Case*, 130 U.S. at 603–04. The power of Congress "[t]o establish a uniform Rule of Naturalization," U.S. Const. art. I, § 8, cl. 4, in contrast, is express and also supplies federal authority over immigration. *Arizona*, 132 S. Ct. at 2498; Toll v. Moreno, 458 U.S. 1, 10 (1982). None of these decisions require or imply exclusive federal authority over immigration absent preemption by Congress. *See* De Canas v. Bica, 424 U.S. 351, 355 (1976), *superseded by statute as stated in*, Chamber of Commerce of the United States v. Whiting, 131 S. Ct. 1968, 1973–75 (2011).

12. The Rehnquist Court's development of a robust concept of "state sovereign immunity," as the gravamen of Eleventh Amendment analysis, *see, e.g.*, Alden v. Maine, 527 U.S. 706 (1999); Seminole Tribe of Fla. v. Florida, 517 U.S. 44 (1996), is an arguable example. *Alden* for example, relied on the view that this immunity constituted "a fundamental aspect of the sovereignty which the States enjoyed before the ratification of the Constitution." *Alden*, 527 U.S. at 713.

At first blush, the very idea of a (figurative) dormant foreign-affairs clause may therefore seem odd. The dormant Foreign Commerce Clause, despite our reservations about the Court's current approach to the doctrine (see Chapter 5), at least rests on an express textual basis, the Foreign Commerce Clause.[13] But the Constitution does not give Congress any express—*non*-dormant—power by virtue of a "Foreign Affairs Clause." So it should probably not be surprising that nearly two centuries passed before the Supreme Court, in its 1968 opinion in *Zschernig v. Miller*,[14] introduced the idea of dormant foreign-affairs preemption, according to which state laws might be preempted even in the absence of action by the political branches—indeed, even in the face of indications by the political branches opposing preemption.[15]

As we will see, quite apart from the lack of a textual basis for the doctrine, its support in jurisprudence before and after *Zschernig* is weak, and despite its apparent reaffirmation in *American Insurance Association v. Garamendi* (2003),[16] history and the Court's own cases cast considerable doubt on the constitutional validity of dormant foreign-affairs preemption. Further, whatever the doctrine's theoretical merit, it has, in practice, predictably proved impossible for the Court to articulate a workable standard with some intelligible limiting principle. Absent such a standard, we suggest that judicial intervention on this ground will, absent extraordinary circumstances, be arbitrary. Finally, in almost every imaginable case, dormant Foreign Commerce Clause standards, which the Court could, with equal logic, apply to state measures challenged on dormant foreign-affairs grounds, suffice to enable the appropriate kind and degree of judicial review.

When did the dormant foreign-affairs doctrine originate? The common understanding is it did not exist before the Supreme Court's 1968 decision in *Zschernig v. Miller*.[17] Suggestions of federal exclusivity in foreign affairs and arguable precedents for a dormant foreign-affairs doctrine may be found in

---

Justice Souter argued with considerable force, however, that the Court misunderstood what sovereignty meant at the time and how it applied to the several states—before and after the Constitution's ratification. *See id.* at 762–98 (Souter, J., dissenting).

13. U.S. CONST. art. I, § 8, cl. 3. See Chapter 5.

14. 389 U.S. 429 (1968). As the analysis below suggests, earlier intimations notwithstanding, only in *Zschernig* did the Court—apparently—first establish dormant foreign-affairs preemption as new constitutional doctrine. *See also* HENKIN, *supra* note 2, at 163–64.

15. *See Zschernig*, 389 U.S. at 434 ("The government does not . . . contend that the application of the Oregon escheat statute in the circumstance of this case unduly interferes with the United States' conduct of foreign relations.").

16. 539 U.S. 396 (2003).

17. 389 U.S. 429 (1968); *see* HENKIN, *supra* note 2, at 162.

several earlier decisions, in particular, *Holmes v. Jennison* (1840),[18] *United States v. Curtiss-Wright Export Corp.* (1936),[19] and *Hines v. Davidowitz* (1941).[20] The Court's 1947 opinion in *Clark v. Allen*,[21] however, which relied on earlier contrary precedents, seemed to put the idea of a dormant foreign-affairs doctrine to rest. Justice William O. Douglas, writing for a unanimous Court in *Clark*, characterized it as "extraordinary" and "far fetched."[22]

For that reason, among others, *Zschernig v. Miller*,[23] which, ironically, Justice Douglas also authored, struck many as perplexing. *Zschernig* invalidated an Oregon statute as an unconstitutional intrusion into a *dormant* federal foreign-affairs power, meaning, apparently, a federal prerogative inferred by the Court despite the absence of any constitutional text, treaty, federal statute—or even federal policy—that preempted Oregon's local law. In fact, in an amicus brief, the executive branch told the Court that it did not object to Oregon's statute and that the statute had not interfered with federal foreign relations.[24] Decades passed before the Court again relied upon *Zschernig* or otherwise implied the existence of a dormant foreign-affairs doctrine. Some scholars began to dismiss the case as sui generis, perhaps no more than a relic from the Cold War, an aberration, surely not a constitutional doctrine.[25] Yet thirty-five years later, the Court seems to have resurrected the dormant foreign-affairs preemption doctrine in *American Insurance Ass'n v. Garamendi* (2003).[26]

The pedigree of the dormant foreign-affairs doctrine is weak, the doctrine ill-defined, and its application capricious. We ultimately suggest that it be abandoned. Still, because the Court in *Garamendi* suggested that the doctrine persists

---

18. 39 U.S. 540 (1840).

19. 299 U.S. 304 (1936).

20. 312 U.S. 52 (1941).

21. 331 U.S. 503 (1947).

22. *Id.* at 517. In *Blythe v. Hinckley*, 180 U.S. 333 (1901), the Court had remarked to the same effect that "[t]he absence of such a claim is not so extraordinary as is the claim itself," *id.* at 340, referring to the plaintiff's claim that "the attempt of the state of California to legislate upon this subject was therefore an invasion of and an encroachment upon, the treaty-making power of the United States." *Id.* at 333.

23. 389 U.S. 429 (1968).

24. *Id.* at 434.

25. *See, e.g.*, Emily Chiang, *Think Locally, Act Globally? Dormant Federal Common Law Preemption of State and Local Activities Affecting Foreign Affairs*, 53 SYRACUSE L. REV. 923, 951 (2003); Joseph B. Crace, Jr., *Gara-Mending the Doctrine of Foreign Affairs Preemption*, 90 CORNELL L. REV. 203, 235 (2004).

26. 539 U.S. 396 (2003).

in some form, our assessment will also consider what can be said about the doctrine at this stage and what may be the best way to understand and address the concerns that seem to animate it.

II. Origins

A. *Holmes v. Jennison* (1840)

Some scholars trace the dormant foreign-affairs doctrine to *The Federalist*.[27] Madison wrote, in an oft cited passage, "If we are to be one nation in any respect, it clearly ought to be in respect to other nations."[28] Yet close attention to the language and context, here as elsewhere in *The Federalist*,[29] makes clear that none of the Framers who contributed to *The Federalist* suggested federal exclusivity in foreign affairs, still less a dormant foreign-affairs doctrine. Madison's statement, like similar essays in *The Federalist* by Alexander Hamilton and John Jay, emphasized the rationale for uniformity in foreign affairs and for plenary foreign-affairs authority in the federal government in certain spheres.[30] But there is scant if any support—whether in *The Federalist*, the ratification debates,[31] or other historical materials—for the idea that the Constitution vests a generic "foreign affairs power," whatever that might mean today, in the federal government.[32]

The first intimation of a dormant foreign-relations doctrine appears in Justice Roger B. Taney's plurality opinion in *Holmes v. Jennison*.[33] Holmes, a resident

---

27. *See, e.g.*, Brannon P. Denning & Jack H. McCall, Jr., *The Constitutionality of State and Local "Sanctions" against Foreign Countries: Affairs of State, States' Affairs, or a Sorry State of Affairs*, 26 HASTINGS CONST. L.Q. 307, 307 n.1, 310, 317 n.51 (1999).

28. THE FEDERALIST NO. 42, at 279 (James Madison) (Jacob E. Cook ed., 1961). John Jay and Alexander Hamilton expressed similar sentiments. *E.g.*, THE FEDERALIST NO. 3 (John Jay), at 14–15 (respecting international law "will be more perfectly and punctually done by one national government than it could be either by thirteen separate States, or by three or four distinct confederacies"); THE FEDERALIST NO. 80 (Alexander Hamilton), at 535 (Jacob E. Cook ed., 1961) ("[T]he peace of the WHOLE ought not to be left at the disposal of a PART.").

29. *See also, e.g.*, THE FEDERALIST NOS. 4, 5 (John Jay). (Jacob E. Cook ed., 1961).

30. THE FEDERALIST NO. 42, at 279–82 (James Madison) (Jacob E. Cook ed., 1961).

31. James Wilson, Pennsylvania Convention of 1787, *reprinted in* DEBATES ON THE ADOPTION OF THE FEDERAL CONSTITUTION 424–25 (Jonathan Elliot ed., 2d ed. 1836).

32. The constructivist argument that "the various provisions related to foreign affairs *can* be read to contain a structural or 'penumbral' restriction on state actions affecting foreign affairs, even in the absence of a congressional enactment," while defensible, is ultimately unpersuasive. Denning & McCall, Jr., *supra* note 27, at 337 (emphasis added).

33. 39 U.S. (14 Pet.) 540 (1840) (4-4 decision, *aff'd* New York *ex rel.* Bryant v. Zimmerman, 278 U.S. 63 (1928)).

of Canada, fled to Vermont after his indictment by a Québec grand jury. At the presumed request of Canadian authorities, Vermont governor Silas H. Jennison issued a warrant for Holmes's arrest and extradition to the custody of William Brown, Canada's agent, to stand trial in Canada under British law. Holmes sought habeas corpus, and the Supreme Court of Vermont issued the writ to consider his arguments. He argued in part that extradition by Vermont would be an unconstitutional state intrusion upon the federal government's exclusive power over extradition. The Supreme Court of Vermont found this argument unconvincing and ordered Holmes remanded, at which point he brought a writ of error to the Supreme Court.[34]

Taney framed the question as follows: "Can a state, since the adoption of the Constitution of the United States, deliver up an individual found within its territory, to a foreign government, to be tried there for offences alleged to have been committed against it?"[35] After disposing of preliminary jurisdictional objections,[36] he considered, first, whether Vermont had violated Article I, section 10, by entering into a prohibited international agreement with a foreign nation, and second, whether the Constitution in any event prohibited Holmes's extradition by one of the states.

Taney concluded that the extradition arrangement did not technically qualify as an Article II *treaty* under international law.[37] But the influential treatise of Emer de Vattel, an eighteenth-century Swiss jurist,[38] persuaded Taney that the extradition arrangement nonetheless fell within the scope of those international agreements prohibited to the states, absent congressional consent, under Article I, section 10: The "framers of the Constitution . . . use[d] the broadest and most comprehensive terms" to prohibit "all intercourse with foreign nations," for "they anxiously desired to cut off all connection or communication between a state and a foreign power."[39] Taney thus held, on behalf of the Court, that Vermont lacked

---

34. *Id.* at 561–62.

35. *Id.* at. 561.

36. *Id.* at 561–68.

37. *Id.* at 571.

38. Emer de Vattel, The Law of Nations (Knud Haakonssen ed., 2008) (1758). In the late eighteenth and nineteenth centuries, U.S. judges, lawyers, scholars, and diplomats commonly regarded *The Law of Nations* as an authoritative source on international law. *But see* Brian Richardson, *The Use of Vattel in the American Law of Nations*, 106 Am. J. Int'l L. 547 (2012) (arguing that Vattel's influence on early U.S. understandings of international law has been overstated).

39. *Holmes*, 39 U.S. at 572.

authority to extradite Holmes because the arrangement qualified as a prohibited international agreement—in substance if not form.[40]

But in dicta he went much further. In particular, he considered whether, absent a prohibited Article I, section 10 international agreement, "the exercise of such a power [by a state] is inconsistent with the power upon the same subject conferred on the United States."[41] Taney recognized that the Constitution's investment of the federal government with a particular power does not generally compel the conclusion that it prohibits the same power to the states; the Constitution often makes concurrent jurisdiction the norm. But Taney perceived a tacit *policy* on the part of the federal government, which, in his view, precluded Vermont's extradition of Holmes. His plurality opinion, which relied on this policy, anticipated the majority opinion of the Court, more than 150 years later, in *Garamendi*,[42] suggesting that his rationale for the doctrine may persist today despite the very distinct circumstances in which the two cases arose.

Taney began by pointing out that no extradition agreement existed between the United States and Great Britain. The former agreement had expired in 1793. Since then, the federal government had adopted an implicit policy against extradition of which the Court, Taney argued, should take judicial notice. He wrote:

> [T]he general government appears to have adopted the policy of refusing to surrender persons, who, having committed offenses in a foreign nation, have taken shelter in this [one]. It is believed that the general government has entered into no treaty stipulations upon this subject since the one above mentioned; and in every instance where there was no engagement by treaty to deliver, and a demand has been made, they have uniformly refused, and have denied the right of the executive to surrender, because there was not a treaty, and no law of Congress to authorize it. And acting upon this principle throughout, they have never demanded from a foreign government any one who fled from this country in order to escape from the punishment due to his crimes. This being the *policy* of the general government, is not the possession of the power by the states totally contradictory and repugnant to the authority conferred on the federal government?[43]

---

40. *Id.* at 573.

41. *Id.* at 574.

42. Am. Ins. Ass'n v. Garamendi, 539 U.S. 396 (2003).

43. *Holmes*, 39 U.S. at 574 (emphasis added).

Taney thus believed, accurately or not, that the federal government had deliberately adopted a policy *against* extradition, and in his view, Vermont's decision to extradite a murder suspect, even if it had not been carried out to implement the terms of an unconstitutional international agreement, as the Court had held, would interfere with the federal policy; indeed, Taney considered Vermont's conduct "totally contradictory and repugnant" to the federal policy.[44] That, in his view, sufficed for preemption.

Taney's dicta did not stop there, however. It is worth distinguishing two arguments he advanced, for he regarded the supposed policy of the federal government against extradition as evidence of—but not a necessary condition for—dormant foreign-affairs preemption. Even without a clear federal policy, Taney suggested, the Constitution implicitly gives the federal government alone the power to extradite, excluding state law or activity in this domain.[45] He therefore embraced the broader and more extreme of two rationales for dormant foreign-affairs preemption that can be discerned in *Holmes*.

First, one might argue narrowly, as Taney did, that *if* the federal government has adopted a uniform national policy on some aspect of foreign affairs (in *Holmes*, for example, a policy against extradition), even a tacit one without a clear textual basis, that suffices to prohibit state action in the same field. Contrary state and federal policies, this argument runs, may threaten national credibility in foreign relations, or risk repercussions for the nation as a whole—rationales that motivated the Framers to lodge potentially plenary power over foreign affairs in the federal government.[46]

Second, one might argue more broadly, as Taney also did, that even if the federal government has *not* expressed a clear policy in some domain of foreign affairs, the federal courts may and should, at times, assume the authority to decide that a particular unenumerated foreign-affairs power nonetheless falls within the *exclusive* power of the federal government.

---

44. As we will see, a similar inference seems to have been drawn, and prevailed by a single vote, in *Garamendi*: there too, despite the absence of any statute, treaty, or other federal law requiring the states to defer to federal *policy*, the Court inferred that the relevant federal policy should preempt state *law* on the issue.

45. *Holmes*, 39 U.S. at 575.

46. *See id.* at 575–77. Again, the analogy to *Garamendi*, decided 150 years later, is apt: despite the absence of federal law or treaty on point, Justice Souter found state law preempted because the federal government had adopted a particular policy on a foreign affairs issue (reparations for Holocaust-era insurance fraud), and California law interfered with that policy. *Garamendi*, 539 U.S. at 439 ("Despite the absence of express preemption, the Court holds that the HVIRA interferes with foreign policy objectives implicit in the executive agreements.").

While Taney advanced both arguments in dicta, he seems to have embraced more firmly the second, more extreme view. He compared extradition to a hypothetically unexecuted power on the part of the federal government to appoint ambassadors. He reasoned that just as "the general government [and only the federal government] must act" to appoint ambassadors, because "it is the only nation known to foreign powers," so too, and notwithstanding that the Constitution does not mention extradition, international law and the incidents of sovereignty should be understood to render extradition a dormant constitutional power that belongs exclusively to the national government.[47]

Only this latter view led to Taney's oft-quoted dictum: "It was one of the main objects of the Constitution to make us, so far as regarded our foreign relations, one people, and one nation; and to cut off *all* communications between foreign governments, and the several state authorities."[48] The Constitution as a whole, he wrote, "[e]very part of that instrument," including the powers to make treaties and appoint ambassadors, commits *all* foreign intercourse to the federal government.[49] In short, Taney understood the Constitution to vest foreign affairs powers exclusively in the federal government, sometimes excluding state action by implication even in the absence of an enumerated constitutional power or federal action.

Holmes has had little precedential force. That has not deterred subsequent writers from quoting Taney's plurality opinion selectively. Yet that opinion's adoption of a dormant foreign-affairs doctrine was, again, dicta—and four of the *Holmes* Court's justices expressly rejected that dicta, three in dissent and one in a concurrence. Further, even the broadest reading of Taney's opinion does not imply an omnibus doctrine that prohibits all state action in foreign affairs.[50] His view appears to have been that dormant foreign-affairs preemption is appropriate in circumstances in which "an authority is granted to the Union, to which a similar authority in the States would be *absolutely and totally contradictory and*

47. *Holmes*, 39 U.S. at 577. Taney clearly erred in this regard to the extent that he relied on international law. No principle of international law requires that the power to extradite be vested solely in the national government. The allocation of political authority within a nation is a matter solely within that nation's domestic competence. Then as now, under international law, the federal government may give the states authority to extradite if it so chooses. It would, of course, still be responsible for their conduct under international law. *See* Articles on the Responsibility of States for Intentionally Wrongful Acts, *in* Report of the International Law Commission to the General Assembly on Its Fifty-Third Session, 56 U.N. GAOR Supp. No. 10, at 1, 43, U.N. Doc. A/56/10 (2001).

48. *Holmes*, 39 U.S. at 575–76 (emphasis added).

49. *Id.*

50. *See* HENKIN, *supra* note 2, at 434.

repugnant," because only in that event is "the authority to the Federal government . . . *necessarily exclusive*, and the same power cannot be constitutionally exercised by the States."[51] Taney regarded *Holmes* as a paradigm of such circumstances. But he did not suggest that such "absolutely and totally contradictory and repugnant" federal-state conflicts were the constitutional norm.

Nine years later, in *Smith v. Turner*, Justice Wayne, writing for the Court's majority, characterized Taney's plurality opinion in *Holmes* narrowly: "All that is decided in the case of *Holmes v. Jennison* is, that the States of this Union have no constitutional power to give up fugitives from justice to the authorities of a nation from which they have fled. That it is not an international obligation to do so, and that all authority to make treaties for such a purpose is in the United States."[52]

The handful of relevant lower-court precedents over the next century also lent little credence to the idea of a dormant foreign-affairs doctrine. In 1847, in *United States v. New Bedford Bridge*,[53] a federal circuit court discussed *Holmes* and expressly rejected the idea that it proclaimed a dormant foreign-affairs doctrine. Circuit Judge Woodbury wrote, "I think it the safer and sounder opinion, that a mere naked power, unexercised and *dormant* in the general government, with no prohibition, express or implied, to the states, to act on the same matter, could not make the state legislation upon it nugatory or unconstitutional, much less render acts crimes, which are done under state laws of that description."[54] Woodbury also rejected the idea that congressional silence implies federal exclusivity: "The idea, that because congress can act on the matter, but have [*sic*] not, all state action, though favorable and assisting the object, is ipso facto void, seems to me entirely untenable."[55]

At the turn of the twentieth century, in *Blythe v. Hinckley*,[56] the plaintiff argued that the defendant, a citizen of the United Kingdom, could not inherit under California law because of the absence of a treaty between the United States and the United Kingdom on the subject, there being "no power in the state of California to legislate upon the subject" by reason of the prohibition in Article I,

---

51. *Holmes*, 39 U.S. at 574 (emphasis added).

52. Smith v. Turner, 48 U.S. (7 How.) 283, 427 (1847). The two other Supreme Court decisions to mention *Holmes* in the nineteenth century raised jurisdictional rather than substantive issues. Neither decision lends support to the doctrine subsequently announced and applied in *Zschernig v. Miller*, 389 U.S. 429 (1968), discussed later in this chapter. *See* Scott v. Jones, 46 U.S. (5 How.) 343, 381 (1847) (McLean, J., dissenting); Barry v. Mercein, 46 U.S. (5 How.) 103 (1847).

53. 27 F. Cas. 91 (Mass. 1847).

54. *Id.* at 99 (emphasis added).

55. *Id.* at 100.

56. 180 U.S. 333 (1901).

Reviewing the evidence in *Zschernig*, Douglas explained the problem as it "now appears":

> [I]n this reciprocity area under inheritance statutes, the probate courts of various States have launched inquiries into the type of governments that obtain in particular foreign nations—whether aliens under their law have enforceable rights, whether the so-called "rights" are merely dispensations turning upon the whim or caprice of government officials, whether the representation of consuls, ambassadors, and other representatives of foreign nations is credible or made in good faith, whether there is in the actual administration in the particular foreign system of law any element of confiscation.[114]

Clark had therefore been correct insofar as it went, but only because the Court had no reason, or so Justice Douglas said in *Zschernig*, to think that California courts—and, as it turned out, state courts elsewhere—had been deploying state probate laws to criticize foreign nations and laws.[115] The evidence since *Clark*, however, revealed that, in practice even if not by legislative design, state courts were using their probate laws to scrutinize and pass judgment on foreign nations.[116]

> exercise of state authority, by the same token, it could regulate aliens in other respects, by requiring registration, payment of fees, etc.,—all matters within the exclusive federal field . . . . Granted the patriotic impulse prompting the enactment of the State statute, nevertheless it invades the federal field. . . . The California statute is invalid and unconstitutional because the State of California attempted, by the probate statute in question, to enter the field of foreign relations, a domain reserved exclusively to the federal government, free from local interference.

Id. at 854. Perhaps the Court relied on the petitioner's representation without reading *Crowley*, but that seems unlikely. More probable is that the Cold War cast a new light on the challenged state probate laws and their application by state courts.

114. *Zschernig*, 389 U.S. at 433–34.

115. *Id.* at 440.

116. State decisions after *Clark*, the Court further explained, "radiate some of the attitudes of the 'cold war,' where the search is for the 'democracy quotient' of a foreign regime as opposed to the Marxist theory." *Id.* at 435. In Oregon's state courts in particular, "it seems that foreign policy attitudes, the freezing or thawing of the 'cold war,' and the like are the real desiderata. Yet they of course are matters for the Federal Government, not for local probate courts." *Id.* at 437–38 (footnotes omitted). The Court intimated that beneath the veneer of routine probate law, the Oregon legislature sought to criticize authoritarian governments, whether extreme left or right. "The same [difficulty] seems to be true if enforcement may require approval of a Fascist dictator." *Id.* The state's motives were thus improper, and the law, in the Court's view, had invidious effects: "It seems inescapable that the type of probate law that Oregon enforces affects international relations in a persistent and subtle way," by means of the "notorious" practices of

section 10 of the Constitution.[57] California's probate statute, the plaintiff further argued, amounted to "an invasion of and an encroachment upon, the [exclusive] treaty-making power of the United States."[58] The Supreme Court characterized this claim as just short of preposterous:

> Plaintiff urges that never before has the question been directly passed upon by this court. If he means that it has never heretofore been asserted that in the absence of any treaty whatever upon the subject, the State had no right to pass a law in regard to the inheritance of property within its borders by an alien, counsel may be correct. *The absence of such a claim is not so extraordinary as is the claim itself.*[59]

A treaty can, of course, if the federal government so provides, suspend the right of a state to legislate on certain probate issues affecting foreign affairs. But no such prohibition, the court found, may be inferred from congressional silence. "If the law of a state is contrary to a treaty, the treaty is superior under the Federal Constitution, but there is no intimation that when there is no treaty the right of the state does not exist in full force."[60] California thus retained complete freedom to legislate as to the inheritance of property, whether real or personal. Absent an act of Congress or a treaty, the Court held, the fact that California law would affect foreign nationals (as innumerable state laws do) could not mean that an amorphous "dormant" federal power preempted that law.[61] Half a century later, *Clark v. Allen*[62] affirmed the same in no uncertain terms.

B. *United States v. Curtiss-Wright Export Corp.* (1936)

In the interim, however, the Supreme Court decided one of the most misguided precedents in U.S. foreign relations law, *United States v. Curtiss-Wright Export Corp.*[63] Despite serious errors, amply documented by scholars,[64] *Curtiss-Wright*

57. *Id.* at 334.

58. *Id.* at 333–34.

59. *Id.* at 340 (emphasis added).

60. *Id.* at 341.

61. *Id.* at 340–41.

62. *See infra* Section C.

63. 299 U.S. 304 (1936).

64. *See, e.g.*, Michael D. Ramsay, *The Myth of Extraconstitutional Foreign Affairs Power*, 42 WILLIAM & MARY L. REV. 379 (1997).

remains a favorite, for obvious reasons, of the executive branch.[65] One would be hard-pressed to identify anyone who still defends the decision's sweeping dicta.[66] Nonetheless, the opinion has continued to exert a tremendous and pernicious influence on U.S. foreign relations law.[67] In part, its purported relevance to the dormant foreign-affairs doctrine reflects just that, for *Curtiss-Wright* did not raise any issue of state power relative to the federal government in foreign affairs. It did not involve Tenth Amendment rights. Claims about the powers of the federal government, especially those of the president, relative to the states in foreign affairs nonetheless permeate Sutherland's opinion in dicta.[68]

On its face, *Curtiss-Wright* raised only a question about the so-called non-delegation doctrine.[69] The Department of Justice indicted the defendants for conspiring to sell arms to Bolivia in violation of a criminal prohibition promulgated by President Franklin D. Roosevelt under the authority of Congress's May 24, 1934 Joint Resolution. Congress had empowered the president to prohibit the sale of arms to countries involved in the Chaco War, subject to certain findings and conditions, mainly that the prohibition would help to re-establish peace.[70] Roosevelt exercised this authority immediately and issued a proclamation criminalizing such arms sales. Following their indictment, the defendants argued that

65. The Supreme Court has continued to cite *Curtiss-Wright* in, among other recent decisions, Zivotofsky *ex rel.* Zivotofsky v. Kerry, 135 S. Ct. 2076, 2085-87 (2015); and Am. Ins. Ass'n v. Garamendi, 539 U.S. 396 (2003). The *Zivotofsky* Court underscored, however, that those portions of the opinion dealing with plenary presidential power are dicta. *See* Michael J. Glennon, *Recognizable Power: The Supreme Court Deals a Blow to Presidential Authority*, FOREIGN AFF. (snapshot), June 23, 2015, https://www.foreignaffairs.com/articles/united-states/2015-06-23/recognizable-power.

66. *See* H. Jefferson Powell, *The Story of Curtiss-Wright Export Corporation*, *in* PRESIDENTIAL POWER STORIES 195, 231 (Curtis A. Bradley & Christopher H. Schroeder eds., 2009).

67. *See generally* MICHAEL J. GLENNON, CONSTITUTIONAL DIPLOMACY 18–34 (1991).

68. *Id.*

69. The non-delegation doctrine theoretically prohibits Congress from delegating its legislative power. *See* Loving v. United States, 517 U.S. 748, 758–59 (1996); Mistretta v. United States, 488 U.S. 361, 371–72 (1989); Field v. Clark, 143 U.S. 649, 692 (1892). Yet the Supreme Court has long held that it applies only if the delegation does not supply an "intelligible principle to which the person or body authorized . . . is directed to conform." J.W. Hampton, Jr. & Co. v. United States, 276 U.S. 394, 409 (1928); *see also* Cargo of the Brig Aurora v. United States (The Brig Aurora), 11 U.S. (7 Cranch) 382 (1813). The Court has also recognized "that in our increasingly complex society, replete with ever changing and more technical problems, Congress simply cannot do its job absent an ability to delegate power under broad general directives," *Mistretta*, 488 U.S. at 372. The doctrine persists in theory as a separation-of-powers constraint on Congress, but in practice, the Court has not applied it to strike down legislation since the New Deal. *See* Carter v. Carter Coal Co. 298 U.S. 238 (1936); A. L. A. Schechter Poultry Corp. v. United States, 295 U.S. 495 (1935); Panama Refining Co. v. Ryan, 293 U.S. 388 (1935).

70. *See* United States v. Curtiss-Wright, 299 U.S. 304, 311–12 (1936).

the law constituted an unconstitutional delegation of the power to enact criminal legislation to the executive branch. The facts thus raised no question of states' rights.

Justice Sutherland, however, seized the opportunity to launch into an essay on the purported exclusivity of presidential power in "external relations." In perhaps the most frequently quoted passage, he wrote:

> It is important to bear in mind that we are here dealing not alone with an authority vested in the President by an exertion of legislative power, but with such an authority plus the very delicate, plenary and *exclusive* power of the President as the sole organ of the federal government in the field of international relations—a power which does not require as a basis for its exercise an act of Congress, but which, of course, like every other governmental power, must be exercised in subordination to the applicable provisions of the Constitution.[71]

Sutherland's assertion about exclusivity speaks to the comparative competence of the federal executive and legislative branches in foreign relations—not that of the states.[72] Nonetheless, *Curtiss-Wright* has been invoked in the context of foreign affairs federalism because the opinion relies upon a theory about the federal government's historical relationship to the states in the realm of external or foreign affairs. According to Sutherland,

> The broad statement that the federal government can exercise no powers except those specifically enumerated in the Constitution, and such implied powers as are necessary and proper to carry into effect the enumerated powers, is categorically true only in respect of our internal affairs. In that field, the primary purpose of the Constitution was to carve from the general mass of legislative powers *then possessed by the states* such portions as it was thought desirable to vest in the federal government, leaving those not included in the enumeration still in the states.[73]

But in Sutherland's view, "the states severally never possessed international powers" in the first place;[74] rather, those powers were transmitted directly from

---

71. *Id.* 319–20 (emphasis added).

72. See, in particular, *id.*

73. *Id.* at 316 (emphasis in original).

74. *Id.*

the Crown "to the colonies in their collective and corporate capacity" and thereafter to the federal government.[75] Sutherland therefore concluded that the states, individually, never possessed foreign-affairs powers: "the colonies were a unit in foreign affairs, acting through a common agency."[76]

"By *Curtiss-Wright*," as Henkin pointed out, "the federal government would have had all foreign relations powers, and the states none, even if the Constitution had said nothing on the subject."[77] That cannot be right.[78] If it were, *Curtiss-Wright* overturned decades of constitutional jurisprudence sustaining state laws with incidental effects, intentional or unintentional, on foreign affairs. These include, among others, a New York labor law that imposed citizenship requirements on the employees of government contractors,[79] a Washington statute that denied aliens the right to own land within the state's borders unless they declared their good-faith intention to become U.S. citizens,[80] a California law that similarly limited the right of certain aliens to acquire interests in real property,[81] and Cincinnati's refusal to grant an alien a license to conduct a billiard and pool room.[82] Indeed, under the exclusion principle of *Curtiss-Wright*, none of the state conduct in foreign affairs detailed in Chapter 2 would be constitutional.

C. *Clark v. Allen* (1947)

Just over a decade later, the Supreme Court retreated from any theory of sweeping federal exclusivity and confirmed its rejection of dormant foreign-affairs preemption. In *Clark v. Allen*,[83] the will of a deceased California resident left real and personal property to German heirs. Six U.S. citizens and heirs-at-law of California disputed the will based on California's probate code, which, they argued, prohibited the named heirs, East German nationals, from inheriting.[84] California's probate code contained a reciprocity condition: It allowed foreign nationals to

---

75. *Id.*

76. *Id.*; *see also id.* at 317.

77. HENKIN, *supra* note 2, at 151 (footnote omitted).

78. For elaboration, see, for example, GLENNON, *supra* note 67, at 18–27.

79. Heim v. McCall, 239 U.S. 175 (1915).

80. Terrace v. Thompson, 263 U.S. 197 (1923).

81. Webb v. O'Brien, 263 U.S. 313 (1923); *see also* Frick v. Webb, 263 U.S. 326 (1923).

82. Ohio *ex rel.* Clarke v. Deckebach, 274 U.S. 392 (1927).

83. 331 U.S. 503 (1947).

84. *Id.* at 506.

inherit property only if U.S. citizens could likewise inherit from nationals of the relevant foreign country; failing satisfaction of this reciprocity condition, the foreign national's inheritance would escheat to the state.[85] *Clark* raised two issues: first, whether a 1923 bilateral treaty with Germany preempted California's probate law despite a state of war (World War II) between the two nations at the time the testator died, and second, whether dormant foreign-affairs preemption prohibited California's reciprocity condition in any event.

The Court quickly disposed of the former issue, reiterating that war does not, in general, abrogate treaty relations except insofar as particular treaty provisions prove incompatible with the state of war.[86] Consequently, under the Supremacy Clause, the 1923 treaty preempted California's law prohibiting the East German nationals from inheriting real property. Yet for reasons of treaty interpretation that need not be recited here, the Court concluded that the treaty did not extend to personal property,[87] thus requiring analysis of whether a dormant foreign-affairs doctrine preempted the state law as to personal property, as well. Tellingly, the Court devoted a mere four paragraphs to this claim (by contrast to the ten pages or so in which it analyzed the treaty issue).

"The challenge to the statute," Justice Douglas explained, "is that it is an extension of state power into the field of foreign affairs, which is exclusively reserved by the Constitution to the Federal Government."[88] By conditioning inheritance on reciprocity, California "seeks to promote the right of American citizens to inherit abroad," which is "said to be a matter for settlement by the Federal Government on a nation-wide basis."[89] Citing *Blythe v. Hinckley*,[90] which involved a similar situation with Great Britain relative to California probate law, Douglas reiterated the Court's characterization of the very idea of dormant foreign-affairs preemption as "extraordinary," and remarked that the "objection to the present statute is equally far fetched."[91]

Douglas briefly explained why: state law traditionally governs inheritance rights. Treaties may, as in *Clark*, preempt conflicting state law under the Supremacy Clause. But absent federal law to the contrary, the simple fact that

85. *Id.* at 506 n.1.

86. *Id.* at 50.

87. *Id.* at 516.

88. *Id.*

89. *Id.* at 517.

90. 180 U.S. 333 (1901).

91. *Clark*, 331 U.S. at 517.

"what California has done will have some incidental or indirect effect in foreign countries," a routine and common consequence of diverse state laws nationwide, did not mean those laws "cross the forbidden line" or raise a constitutional conflict.[92] The Court appropriately dismissed the relevance of *Curtiss-Wright*, observing that California had not sought to negotiate with a foreign country.[93] Less than a decade after *Curtiss-Wright*, the Court thus rejected Justice Sutherland's broadside as the correct test of state authority in foreign affairs.

III. Invention of the Dormant Foreign-Affairs Doctrine

A. *Zschernig v. Miller* (1968) and Its Progeny

It therefore came as a considerable surprise when the Supreme Court held in *Zschernig v. Miller* (1968) that Oregon had crossed the "forbidden line."[94] Everything about the case suggested that the Court would sustain Oregon's challenged probate law. The state law at issue in *Zschernig* seemed virtually indistinguishable from the California law sustained in *Clark*. The facts were also similar: *Zschernig* involved, in part, the same provision (article IV) of the same 1923 bilateral treaty with Germany.[95] Justice Douglas, who authored *Zschernig*, had written *Clark*, rejecting dormant foreign-affairs preemption as "farfetched."[96] Further, the Johnson administration had filed an amicus brief in *Zschernig* asking the Court to revisit *Clark*'s interpretation of the 1923 treaty so as to construe article IV as applicable to both real and personal property;[97] had the Court accepted this invitation, it could have reached the same conclusion in *Zschernig* by uncontroversial (express) preemption principles, avoiding the need to create a new and questionable constitutional doctrine.[98] In the same amicus brief,

---

92. *Id.*

93. *Id.*

94. 389 U.S. 429, 458 (1968).

95. Treaty of Friendship, Commerce and Consular Rights, Dec. 8, 1923, United States-Germany, 44 Stat. 2132, T.S. No. 725.; *see Zschernig*, 389 U.S. at 431–32; *Clark*, 331 U.S. at 506. After the post-WWII division of Germany, the United States entered into a new, superseding treaty with West Germany. But the 1923 treaty continued to govern U.S. relations with East Germany.

96. *Clark*, 331 U.S. at 517.

97. *Zschernig*, 389 U.S. at 432; *see id.* at 449–57 (Harlan, J., concurring in the judgment).

98. *Id.* at 444–45 (Harlan, J., concurring in the judgment); *see also id.* at 432 (noting that the executive branch had asked the Court to reexamine *Clark*'s interpretation of the 1923 treaty's provision governing the inheritance of personalty).

the administration also denied that the Oregon law "unduly interferes with the United States' conduct of foreign relations."[99]

Why, then, did the Court decide to overturn Oregon's law based on a newfangled theory of dormant foreign-affairs preemption? This question bears close scrutiny. *Zschernig* might once have been dismissed as a Cold War aberration. In 2003, however, the Court's decision in *Garamendi* made clear that the doctrine for which it stands remains good law.[100]

At the outset, it is worth reviewing the opinions in *Zschernig* to determine what, exactly, the Court formally held. It seems at first glance that only three justices (Chief Justice Warren and Justices Goldberg and Fortas) joined Douglas's principal opinion, forming only a plurality and thus depriving *Zschernig* of precedential force. Yet Justice Stewart, with whom Justice Brennan joined, concurred, and he began by saying that he and Brennan, too, "join[ed] the opinion of the Court." Stewart wrote separately only because, in their view, the Court should "go *further*,"[101] embracing the federal-exclusivity position proclaimed in *Curtiss-Wright* and assorted dicta elsewhere.[102] Six justices therefore adopted the doctrine of dormant foreign-affairs preemption as formulated in Douglas's opinion, making *Zschernig* precedential.[103] But what *is* that precedent?

As *Clark*'s author two decades earlier, it may seem curious that Douglas would have decided *Zschernig* differently than *Clark* despite almost identical laws and facts. Douglas seems to have adopted in *Zschernig* the very doctrine he had characterized as "extraordinary" and "farfetched" in *Clark*. And yet Douglas insisted in *Zschernig* that it did not overrule *Clark*.[104] Why the seeming change of heart?

---

99. *Id.* at 429. Justice Harlan argued that the Court might therefore have neglected the cardinal constitutional-avoidance canon of statutory interpretation: to avoid decisions on constitutional grounds if a case may be decided on other grounds. *Id.* at 460 (Harlan, J., concurring in the judgment).

100. Am. Ins. Ass'n v. Garamendi, 539 U.S. 396 (2003).

101. *Zschernig*, 389 U.S. at 441–42 (Stewart, J., concurring) (emphasis added).

102. *See, e.g., id.* at 441–43. Dicta supporting the exclusivity position can be found in, among other cases, Hines v. Davidowitz, 312 U.S. 52, 63 (1941); United States v. Belmont, 301 U.S. 324, 331 (1937); Chae Chan Ping v. United States (The Chinese Exclusion Case), 130 U.S. 581, 600 (1888); and Holmes v. Jennison, 39 U.S. (14 Pet.) 540, 574 (1840).

103. Justice Harlan concurred in the judgment only on distinct grounds. He argued that the 1923 treaty should be reinterpreted to apply to personalty. Had the Court agreed, the treaty alone would have preempted the Oregon statute, disposing of the case on routine preemption grounds. But Harlan rejected the Court's dormant foreign-affairs rationale. *Zschernig*, 389 U.S. at 457–62 (Harlan, J., concurring in the judgment). Justice White, for his part, incorporated Harlan's critique of dormant foreign-affairs preemption by reference but, in a three-sentence dissent, noted his disagreement with Harlan's reinterpretation of the 1923 treaty. *Id.* at 462 (White, J., dissenting). Justice Marshall did not participate in the case, *id.* at 441, because he had argued it as Solicitor General before joining the Court. *See id.* at 429.

104. *Id.* at 433–36.

Douglas located the dispositive differences between *Clark* and *Zschernig* in both the specific terms of the state statutes and their application, in practice, by state courts.

Under both the California and Oregon laws challenged in *Clark* and *Zschernig*, respectively, estate proceeds claimed by foreigners would escheat to the state unless U.S. citizens were, first, entitled to inherit on the same terms as citizens of the relevant foreign nation, and second, allowed to receive the funds in the United States. The Oregon law differed in that it imposed a third condition: it required that foreign heirs be entitled to receive the proceeds due from an Oregon estate "without confiscation,"[105] by law or in practice, in the heir's nation. Because this is the sole substantive distinction between the California and Oregon probate statutes,[106] Justice Douglas must have reasoned either that the confiscation condition made all the difference or that the factual circumstances differed relevantly from those in *Clark*. A close reading of *Zschernig* suggests both.

Douglas concluded that the confiscation provision was itself problematic. Yet he also saw it as emblematic of a general constitutional defect in the statute. Douglas confirmed in *Zschernig*, thus conceding no error in *Clark*, that California's law, which conditioned inheritance on simple reciprocity, "did not *on its face* intrude on the federal domain," for it had "only some incidental or indirect effect in foreign countries."[107] Or so it seemed in 1947, when the Court decided *Clark*. Such a routine "matching of laws"[108] raised no constitutional issue.

But Justice Douglas concluded that the "without confiscation" condition of the Oregon statute encouraged, if not required, Oregon's judiciary to scrutinize not only the text of foreign laws, but their actual application abroad, and the bona fides of the officials charged with their administration. Douglas clarified the import of this distinction in an extended footnote:[109]

> In *Clark v. Allen*, . . . the District Court had held the California reciprocity statute unconstitutional because of legislative history indicating that the purpose of the statute was to prevent American assets from reaching hostile nations preparing for war on this country. . . . But when the case reached this Court, petitioner contended that the statute was invalid, not

105. *Id.* at 431.

106. *Zschernig*, 389 U.S. at 432. *Compare id.* at 432–33 nn.1–2, *with* Clark v. Allen, 331 U.S. 503, 506 n.1 (1947).

107. *Zschernig*, 389 U.S. at 433 (quoting *Clark*, 331 U.S. at 517) (emphasis added) (internal quotation marks omitted).

108. *Id.* at 433 n.5.

109. *Id.*

> because of the legislature's motive, but because on its face the statute constituted "an invasion of the exclusively Federal field of control over our foreign relations." In discussing how the statute was applied, petitioner noted that a California court had accepted as conclusive proof of reciprocity the statement of a foreign ambassador that reciprocal rights existed in his nation. . . . Thus we had no reason to suspect that the California statute in *Clark v. Allen* was to be applied as anything other than a general reciprocity provision requiring just matching of laws. Had we been reviewing the later California decision of [*In re Gogabashvele*]. . . , the additional problems we now find with the Oregon provision would have been presented.[110]

The *Clark* petitioner's argument, in other words, had (whether deliberately or not) misleadingly characterized the district court's decision. According to the petitioner, the district court accepted the East German official's testimony as conclusive proof of reciprocity. Such routine examination of foreign law, Douglas reiterated, is no more troubling, constitutionally, than any other situation in which a court takes judicial notice of foreign law, which is generally a question of fact in domestic litigation.[111] Echoing *Clark*, Douglas thus reaffirmed in *Zschernig*: "It has never been seriously suggested that state courts are precluded from performing that function [namely, to 'read, construe, and apply laws of foreign nations'], albeit there is a remote possibility that any holding may disturb a foreign nation—whether the matter involves commercial cases, tort cases, or some other type of controversy. At the time *Clark v. Allen* was decided, the case seemed to involve no more than a routine reading of foreign laws."[112] The *Clark* Court therefore had insufficient information to see the real constitutional difficulty.[113]

---

110. *Id.* (internal citations omitted).

111. *E.g.*, Adam v. Saenger, 303 U.S. 59, 63–64 (1938).

112. *Zschernig*, 389 U.S. at 433.

113. The district court's decision casts some doubt on this account. *See* Crowley v. Allen, 52 F. Supp. 850 (N.D. Cal. 1943). *Crowley* did not, as Douglas suggested in *Zschernig*, obscure the basis on which the district court had struck down the California statute. Nor did *Crowley* refer to a routine matching of laws or the court's general obligation to accept a foreign official's testimony about the relevant foreign law. Rather, the court wrote, in terms that anticipate the concerns in *Zschernig*:

> The emphasized portions of the above "purpose" clause disclose that the California State Legislature did not adopt the probate statute as an orthodox procedural rule to regulate succession to property in the ordinary course. To the contrary, the expressed design was to fix a policy of international relations, which, the Legislature thought, would aid the United States in anticipated hostilities with a foreign government. If this were a valid

Oregon had its own geopolitical agenda in foreign relations. It effectuated that agenda through the vehicle of state courts adjudicating what would otherwise have been garden-variety probate cases. The majority in *Zschernig* thus pointed to what it regarded as inappropriate legislative motives.[117] It also observed that because of the Oregon law, in practice, inappropriate institutions (state courts) were routinely opining on federal foreign-affairs policies in an inappropriate legal context (probate). Oregon's courts were routinely transgressing the "forbidden line" separating legitimate state activities from exclusively federal foreign-affairs concerns by means of a law that "ma[de] unavoidable judicial criticism of nations established on a more authoritarian basis than our own."[118]

That explains why much of Douglas's opinion is occupied with examples of what the *Zschernig* majority saw as constitutionally objectionable criticism of foreign laws by state courts in Oregon and elsewhere. His point was empirical: the evidence showed that state courts routinely arrogated to themselves the right to speculate about the "democracy quotient"[119] of foreign regimes, the credibility of foreign laws and official representations about them, or the true implementation of foreign law abroad. The Court focused, among several other examples, on *In re* Gogabashvele's Estate.[120] In *Gogabashvele*, a California court critiqued the Soviet law and government at length, glibly comparing the Soviet Union's Civil Code, as interpreted by a Soviet jurist, to Humpty Dumpty's attitude toward words in *Through the Looking Glass*.[121] Douglas explained that if the evidence in *Clark* had

---

withholding remittances to otherwise qualified recipients in communist countries or blocking remittances coming from those countries. *Id.* at 440. Nor did it matter to the Court that probate falls within an area of traditional state competence. "The several States, of course, have traditionally regulated the descent and distribution of estates," Douglas acknowledged. "But those regulations must give way if they impair the effective exercise of the Nation's foreign policy." *Id.*

117. *Id.* at 433 n.5. Ordinarily the Court does not inquire into the legislature's motives. It applies so-called "rational basis" review, sustaining the law if a rational basis for it exists unless its history and purpose show an invidious motive such as racism. *See, e.g.*, Williamson v. Lee Optical Co., 348 U.S. 483 (1955). If a statute is constitutionally valid, the legislature's motive is considered irrelevant. One of the chief reasons for avoiding judicial inquiry into legislative motivation is that, often, no single motivation exists; there may be several competing ones. Provided the motive is not unconstitutional, the question is simply whether the statute itself has a rational basis.

118. *Zschernig*, 389 U.S. at 440.

119. *Id.* at 435.

120. 195 Cal. App. 2d 503 (1961).

121. "When *I* use a word . . . , it means just what I choose it to mean—neither more nor less." *Zschernig*, 389 U.S. at 433 n.6 (quoting LEWIS CARROLL, ALICE IN WONDERLAND AND THROUGH THE LOOKING GLASS 197 (Weekly Reader Books 1983) (originally published 1872)) (internal quotation marks omitted). *See also id.* at 433–39 nn. 5–9 (describing several other, similar examples).

similarly disclosed state-court conduct of this sort, "a different result would have obtained"; the *Clark* Court had been misled because it focused on the law's text rather than its judicial application and state legislative motives.[122]

The *Zschernig* Court seems to have been intent upon ensuring that state courts not adjudicate foreign-affairs issues that, in its view, the Constitution vests in the federal political branches. It is worth pausing to note that this theme recurs throughout U.S. foreign-relations law. In promulgating the act of state doctrine (see Chapter 7), the Court expressed a similar worry (also, not coincidentally, in the context of the Cold War) that the courts might adjudicate contentious ideological issues, a practice that could obstruct or complicate delicate foreign-affairs policies of the federal political branches. Applying that doctrine, the Court has thus refused to decide and apply customary international law on expropriation and the standard of compensation, if any, owed to foreign nationals by expropriating nations "established on a more authoritarian basis than our own,"[123] to quote *Zschernig*. As in the act-of-state cases, in *Zschernig* the Court suggested that courts must avoid certain foreign-affairs issues for which they're institutionally ill-suited as compared to the federal political branches, and it suggested further that constitutionally, federalism, like separation-of-powers, principles require that the courts not intrude into a domain—the conduct of U.S. foreign affairs—that the Constitution entrusts to the federal political branches.[124]

Zschernig's majority therefore appears to have been animated by a concern about the institutional competence of state courts, their lack of authority and constitutional role in foreign affairs—amplified by the Supreme Court's concern at the time about the parochial perspectives of the several states vis-à-vis

122. *Id.* at 433.

123. *Id.* at 440. The *Sabbatino* Court had in mind, not just communist nations such as Cuba but, more generally, the G-77 coalition of developing states that at the time were seeking to modify customary international law on these issues. *See, e.g.*, Charter of Economic Rights and Duties of States, G.A. Res. 3281, U.N. GAOR, 29th Sess., Supp. No. 31, at 50, U.N. Doc. A/9631 (1974); Permanent Sovereignty Over Natural Resources, G.A. Res. 3171, U.N. GAOR, 28th Sess., U.N. Doc. A/RES/3171 (1974). As Justice White pointed out in his famous dissent in *Sabbatino*, the Court, by deciding *not* to adjudicate the issues in *Sabbatino*, effectively *did* just that—resolving them in favor of Cuba. *See* Banco Nacional De Cuba v. Sabbatino, 376 U.S. 398, 455–56 (1964) (White, J., dissenting). For further analysis, see Chapter 7.

124. In *Zschernig*, unlike *Sabbatino*, the Court decided the issue on a constitutional basis, precluding superseding legislation. In *Sabbatino*, it invoked constitutional "separation of powers principles," *Sabbatino*, 376 U.S. at 423–24, but did not hold the act of state doctrine constitutionally compelled. Yet it is telling that the Supreme Court has resisted efforts to erode the act of state doctrine, in particular, by the Hickenlooper Amendment, 22 U.S.C. § 2370 (1961), which the court has construed narrowly. *See* First Nat'l City Bank v. Banco Nacional de Cuba, 406 U.S. 759, 771 (1972). For further analysis, see Chapter 7.

Cold War politics.[125] The Constitution entrusts "*[t]hat* kind of state involvement in foreign affairs . . . *solely* to the Federal Government."[126] In sum, Douglas saw the key distinction between *Clark* and *Zschernig* as between, on the one hand, what the state law *said*—did it, for example, simply tell the state court to apply a reciprocity condition that could be satisfied by a routine review of evidence of foreign law ("matching of laws")?—and, on the other, how the state law *applied*—did it, whether by legislative design or in practice, lead the state courts to scrutinize foreign legal systems, critique their credibility and fairness, express ideological views, or otherwise convey animosity toward foreign countries?[127] In the latter case, the state law could redound to the disadvantage of the whole nation and unconstitutionally interfere with the federal government's conduct of foreign affairs.[128]

The distinction between facial and as-applied challenges to laws is familiar to constitutional jurisprudence.[129] But does it, as Douglas insisted, explain the different outcomes in *Zschernig* and *Clark*? Justice Harlan, for one, found the Court's effort to reconcile the two decisions on this basis unpersuasive: "To say that the additional conditions imposed by the Oregon statute [namely, that foreign heirs must receive the benefit, use, and control of the inherited property 'without confiscation']" explain the differing outcomes of *Clark* and *Zschernig* "would be to suggest that while a State may legitimately place inheritance by aliens on a reciprocity basis, it may not take measures to assure that reciprocity exists in practice and that the inheritance will actually be enjoyed by the person whom the testator intended to benefit."[130] Federal and state courts alike necessarily inquire into the content and actual administration of foreign laws all the time. To be sure, Harlan conceded, courts at times indulge in ill-considered remarks about foreign laws and governments.[131] It is certainly possible that a state court opinion of this sort could adversely affect or interfere with federal foreign-affairs policy. But as Harlan aptly observed, despite the examples recited by Douglas, scant evidence

---

125. *E.g.*, *Zschernig*, 389 U.S. at 435, 437.

126. *Id.* at 436 (emphasis added).

127. *See id.* at 433 (characterizing the Court's decision in *Clark*, in contrast to *Zschernig*, as "concerned with the words of a statute on its face, not the manner of its application").

128. *Cf.* THE FEDERALIST NO. 80, at 535 (Alexander Hamilton) (Jacob E. Cooke ed., 1961) ("[T]he peace of the WHOLE ought not to be left at the disposal of a PART.").

129. *E.g.*, Citizens United v. FEC, 558 U.S. 310, 331–32 (2010).

130. *Zschernig*, 389 U.S. at 458 (Harlan, J., concurring in the judgment).

131. Federal courts have hardly been innocent of injudicious conduct of this sort. *See, e.g.*, National Iranian Oil Co. v. Ashland Oil, 817 F.2d 326 (5th Cir. 1987).

suggested that this had been a general or widespread problem.[132] At any rate, the Oregon probate law could hardly be deemed unique in this regard:

> Essentially, the Court's basis for decision appears to be that alien inheritance laws afford state court judges an opportunity to criticize in dictum the policies of foreign governments, and that these dicta may adversely affect our foreign relations. In addition to finding no evidence of adverse effect in the record, I believe this rationale to be untenable because logically it would apply to many other types of litigation which come before the state courts. It is true that, in addition to the many state court judges who have applied alien inheritance statutes with proper judicial decorum, some judges have seized the opportunity to make derogatory remarks about foreign governments. However, judges have been known to utter dicta critical of foreign governmental policies even in purely domestic cases, so that the mere possibility of offensive utterances can hardly be the test.[133]

Justice Stewart, joined by Justice Brennan, concurred in the *Zschernig* majority opinion and judgment. Leaving aside treaty interpretation, Stewart's concurrence largely echoed Douglas's opinion for the Court. Stewart, too, condemned the Oregon legislature for giving its courts competence and reason to critique foreign nations through the vehicle of probate litigation. While conceding, as Justice Harlan stressed in dissent, that "state courts must routinely construe foreign law," Stewart replied that "here the courts of Oregon are thrust into these inquiries only because the Oregon Legislature has framed its inheritance laws to the prejudice of nations whose policies it disapproves and thus has trespassed upon an area where the Constitution contemplates that only the National Government shall operate."[134]

Yet Stewart went further. Taking a cue from *Curtiss-Wright*, he argued that "*any* realistic attempt to apply" the Oregon statute would "launch the State upon a prohibited voyage into a domain of *exclusively* federal competence."[135] Stewart

---

132. *Zschernig*, 389 U.S. at 460 (Harlan, J., concurring in the judgment). The Department of Justice agreed. *See id.* at 460, 460 n.27. With very few exceptions, as noted below, it is also difficult to identify post-*Zschernig* examples of the sort that concerned Douglas.

133. *Id.* at 461–62 (Harlan, J., concurring in the judgment).

134. *Id.* at 442 (Stewart, J., concurring).

135. *Id.* at 442 (Stewart, J., concurring) (emphasis added). Justice Douglas's opinion, in contrast, suggested that concurrent competence might in theory be unobjectionable. The evidence showed, however, that in practice state courts had been applying the Oregon probate law

thus suggested that *Clark* had been wrongly decided: probate laws of the sort at issue in *Clark* and *Zschernig* were objectionable as such, on their face; they compelled, not just risked, improper state court intrusion into an exclusively federal domain. This suggestion, however, raises a puzzling and important question about Stewart's concurrence: if its rationale is to avoid interference with foreign affairs that the Constitution commits *exclusively* to the political branches, why did Stewart dismiss the Solicitor General's express disavowal of the Court's premise: that "the Oregon escheat statute in the circumstances of this case unduly interferes with the United States' conduct of foreign relations."[136] After all, if the Constitution really does commit such issues exclusively to the president and Congress, by what right did the Court contradict the former's judgment? Stewart answered:

> Resolution of so fundamental a constitutional issue cannot vary from day to day with the shifting winds at the State Department. Today, we are told, Oregon's statute does not conflict with the national interest. Tomorrow it may. But, however that may be, the fact remains that the conduct of our foreign affairs is entrusted under the Constitution to the National Government, not to the probate courts of the several States.[137]

Before concluding analysis of *Zschernig*, it is instructive to return to Justice Harlan's concurrence in the judgment, for it has since exerted considerable influence.[138] Recall that Harlan concurred in the judgment only because he concluded that Article IV of the 1923 treaty with Germany applied to Oregon's statute, and he would therefore have overruled *Clark*'s holding in this regard, resolving the

---

unconstitutionally, consistent with the Oregon legislature's real motivation. Stewart focused on dicta in the *Chinese Exclusion Case* and *Hines v. Davidowitz* that imply complete exclusion of the states from foreign affairs. (Neither case, in fact, so held). *See Zschernig*, 389 U.S. at 442–43 (Stewart, J., concurring in the judgment) (quoting Chae Chan Ping v. United States (The Chinese Exclusion Case), 130 U.S. 581, 606 (1888); and Hines v. Davidowitz, 312 U.S. 52, 63 (1941)).

136. *Id.* at 442 (Stewart, J., concurring).

137. *Id.* at 443 (Stewart, J., concurring).

138. *See, e.g.*, Am. Ins. Ass'n v. Garamendi, 539 U.S. 396, 439 (2003); Constitutionality of South African Divestment Statutes Enacted by State and Local Governments, 10 Op. O.L.C. 49 (Apr. 9, 1986). As we will see, the constitutional-avoidance canon that Harlan invoked in the course of his concurrence is also vital to an understanding of the most prominent case on foreign affairs federalism in recent years, *Bond v. United States*, 529 U.S. 334, 338 (2000), in which the Court sought to avoid the major constitutional question raised by the interaction of treaties and federalism. *See* Missouri v. Holland, 252 U.S. 416 (1920). For analysis, see Chapter 6.

case based on ordinary preemption principles and enabling the Court to avoid any constitutional question.[139] He devoted much of his concurrence to explaining why he believed this to be the correct and preferable basis for resolving *Zschernig*. The Court had, as it has continued to, long adhered to the prudential principle that deciding constitutional issues should be avoided if a case may be resolved on other grounds.[140] Against the backdrop of the 1923 treaty, as he interpreted it, Harlan therefore admonished the majority for violating this cardinal principle of constitutional adjudication.[141]

The constitutional-avoidance doctrine strives to limit the cost of judicial error. Non-constitutional decisions may be legislatively "overruled" or superseded by Congress. It can generally revise laws that the Court interprets contrary to its intentions or policy objectives. In contrast, decisions on constitutional grounds can be changed only by a later decision of the Court or a constitutional amendment, an exceedingly difficult and rare process. That is no license, however, for the Court to evade a constitutional question by strained statutory or treaty construction. It seems fair to say that, in *Zschernig*, reasonable arguments supported Harlan's interpretation of the treaty. But reasonable arguments also supported the majority's interpretation, including stare decisis and the treaty analysis in *Clark*. Douglas probably cannot be faulted for deciding *Zschernig* on constitutional grounds; no non-constitutional basis existed in his view. Harlan understood this, and recognizing the significance of the Court's new constitutional doctrine, he therefore devoted five pages to a trenchant critique of dormant foreign-affairs preemption,[142] with which Justice White concurred.[143]

Harlan's critique merits a close look because it influenced the most recent articulation by the Court of the dormant foreign-affairs doctrine in *American Insurance Ass'n v. Garamendi*.[144] Harlan began by explaining that he found *Clark* and *Zschernig* indistinguishable.[145] True, he acknowledged, "[t]he years since the

---

139. *Zschernig*, 429 U.S. at 457–62 (Harlan, J., concurring in the judgment).

140. The canonical statement of this principle and its rationale is found in Justice Louis Brandeis's opinion in *Ashwander v. TVA*, 297 U.S. 288, 341 (1936).

141. *Zschernig*, 389 U.S. at 444–45 (Harlan, J., concurring in the judgment). In its amicus brief, the Department of Justice, too, urged the Court to reexamine *Clark*'s interpretation of provisions on inheritance of personal property in the 1923 treaty with Germany. *Id.* at 445.

142. *See Zschernig*, 429 U.S. at 443–57 (Harlan, J., concurring in the judgment).

143. Justice White dissented "[g]enerally for the reasons stated" by Justice Harlan, stating simply, "I do not consider the Oregon statute to be an impermissible interference with foreign affairs." *Id.* at 462; *see also Garamendi*, 539 U.S. at 418 & n.10.

144. *See Garamendi*, 539 U.S. at 418–20.

145. *Zschernig*, 389 U.S. at 458.

Clark decision have revealed some instances in which state court judges have delivered intemperate or ill-advised remarks about foreign governments in the course of applying such statutes, but nothing has occurred which could not readily have been foreseen at the time *Clark* v. *Allen* was decided."[146] He agreed with *Clark*'s rule, to which the majority purported to adhere, that incidental or indirect effects in foreign nations caused by state laws do not "cross the forbidden line."[147] In *Zschernig*, he noted, Oregon had legislated in an area of traditional state competence.[148] Given *Clark* and its antecedents, he argued, "in the absence of a conflicting federal policy or violation of the express mandates of the Constitution the States may legislate in areas of their traditional competence even though their statutes may have an incidental effect on foreign relations. Application of this rule to the case before us compels the conclusion that the Oregon statute is constitutional."[149]

Oregon's law neither did nor could impinge on any federal foreign-affairs power. "[T]here is no specific interest of the Federal Government which might be interfered with by this statute"; "the Court does not mention, nor does the record reveal, any instance in which such an occurrence has been the occasion for a diplomatic protest, or, indeed, has had any foreign relations consequence whatsoever."[150] Yet Harlan's concurrence may not have categorically rejected dormant foreign-affairs preemption. He arguably left open the possibility that it could be warranted in extreme circumstances involving, for example, a state law that intruded upon areas well beyond the traditional legal powers of the states, or that produced much more than an "incidental and indirect effect" on foreign affairs, or that seriously interfered with a clear federal policy. But Harlan did not speculate on a test or standard to decide the propriety of dormant foreign-affairs preemption. Nor did he discuss whether preemption under the Supremacy Clause might be appropriate in circumstances in which a clear and consistent federal *policy* exists (of the sort emphasized by Justice Taney in *Holmes*) but not

---

146. *Id.*

147. *Id.* (Harlan, J., concurring in the judgment) (quoting Clark v. Allen, 331 U.S. 503, 517 (1947)).

148. "Prior decisions," he wrote, "have established [that] . . . Oregon has so legislated in the course of regulating the descent and distribution of estates of Oregon decedents, a matter traditionally within the power of a State." *Id.* at 459. (Harlan, J., concurring in the judgment).

149. *Id.*

150. *Id.* (Harlan, J., concurring in the judgment). In fact, Oregon's reciprocity requirement was "a measure wisely designed to avoid any offense to foreign governments and thus any conflict with general federal interests: a foreign government can hardly object to the denial of rights which it does not itself accord to the citizens of other countries." *Id.* at 459.

a statute, treaty, or other binding federal *law* in the realm of foreign affairs. The latter, by the plain language of the Supremacy Clause, would take precedence over state law. The former, however, raised an issue that would not be picked up until *Garamendi*, some thirty-five years later.

Before we turn to that case, however, a brief review of the intervening years will be helpful. During the decades between *Zschernig* and *Garamendi*, local officials and courts sought to understand and apply *Zschernig*'s new constitutional doctrine. At a minimum, the *Zschernig* majority held that *some* dormant foreign-affairs doctrine of *some* kind constrains state and other local laws and activities, including adjudication, *if* they actually or potentially have more than an indirect or incidental effect on foreign relations. Yet for the reasons elaborated earlier, those limits were exceedingly unclear. Few knew what to make of the case.[151]

The majority opinion did not offer much guidance. Local courts and officials were left to distinguish (1) the incidental (*Clark*) from the non-incidental (*Zschernig*); (2) the indirect (*Clark*) from the direct (*Zschernig*); (3) routine review of foreign law (*Clark*) from review that implies or expresses judgment on foreign laws or nations and interferes with the federal government's conduct of foreign affairs (*Zschernig*); (4) proper from improper legislative motives; and (5) traditional from nontraditional exercises of state power; and other distinctions apparently relevant to the dormant foreign affairs doctrine.

The majority, after all, not only did *not* purport to overrule *Clark*; it suggested, to the puzzlement of many, that it was fully consistent with *Zschernig*.[152] Only a handful of cases, state and federal, grappled with how to reconcile *Clark* and *Zschernig*, as well as, and perhaps most significant, a Department of Justice memorandum[153] analyzing the many local divestment statutes that had imposed sanctions on apartheid-era South Africa despite federal silence—arguably, in fact, an implicitly contrary policy toward South Africa before the federal government enacted the Comprehensive Anti-Apartheid Act in 1986.[154] No consensus on *Zschernig*'s meaning emerged. But a sample of the cases during this era

---

151. Before *Garamendi*, some commentators criticized or marginalized *Zschernig* as an anomaly of the Cold War. *See, e.g.*, Chiang, *supra* note 25, at 951.

152. Goldstein v. Cox, 299 F. Supp. 1389, 1392 (S.D.N.Y. 1968) ("In *Zschernig*, the Supreme Court expressly declined to overrule *Clark v. Allen*."). *Zschernig* repeatedly insisted on this point. *See Zschernig*, 389 U.S. at 429, 432-34. It is nonetheless questionable, as Harlan (and subsequently scholars) pointed out, whether the two cases can be reconciled.

153. Constitutionality of South African Divestment Statutes Enacted by State and Local Governments, 10 Op. O.L.C. 49 (Apr. 9, 1986).

154. Comprehensive Anti-Apartheid Act of 1986, Pub. L. No. 99-440 606, 100 Stat. 1086 (1986), repealed by South African Democratic Transition Support Act of 1993, Pub. L. No. 103-149, 4(a)(2), 107 Stat. 1505, 1505 (2000) (codified as amended at 22 U.S.C. § 5001(4)(c)(1)).

is illuminating. It suggests that most courts understood the "forbidden line" referred to in *Zschernig* to lie between the incidental and indirect effects of local law, on the one hand, and direct, manifest, and (at least potentially) substantial interference with federal foreign-relations prerogatives that might be caused by applying local law, on the other.

The first case to construe *Zschernig* followed closely on its heels. In 1968, in *In re Leikind's Estate*,[155] the New York Court of Appeals dismissed a challenge predicated on *Zschernig* to a New York statute comparable to the Oregon statute in *Zschernig*. The Court of Appeals held that *Zschernig* prohibited only those local statutes that, in practice or application, required "minute inquiries" into "the actual administration of foreign law."[156] The Supreme Court, in its view, had condemned only those local statutes that threatened "palpable interference with foreign relations," especially "animadversions" to foreign laws or nations.[157] *Zschernig* therefore did not, according to *Leikind's Estate*, reject *Clark*'s affirmation that local courts could otherwise, as they did and inevitably would, engage in the routine review and application of foreign law in diverse legal contexts.[158] Later in 1968, a three-judge federal district court reached much the same conclusion.[159] As in *Leikind*, the court stressed the distinction between a local statute on its face and as applied:

> Two justices concurring in a separate opinion stated that, while joining the opinion of the Court, they would go further and hold the Oregon statute unconstitutional on its face. Obviously, it was manifest to these two justices, as it is to us, that the opinion of the Court did *not* go this far, but held only that the Oregon statute was unconstitutional because of the manner of its application.[160]

This interpretation of *Zschernig* meant the dismissal of most dormant foreign-affairs challenges. In 1990, for example, the Third Circuit, which interpreted *Zschernig* in the same way, sustained Pennsylvania's "Buy American"

155. 239 N.E.2d 550 (N.Y. 1968).

156. *Id.* at 552 (quoting *Zschernig*, 389 U.S. at 434–35) (internal quotation marks omitted).

157. *Id.* at 553; *see also* Shames v. Nebraska, 323 F. Supp. 1321 (D. Neb. 1971); *Goldstein*, 299 F. Supp. at 1389.

158. *Leikind's Estate*, 239 N.E.2d at 552; *see also Zschernig*, 389 U.S. at 433.

159. *Goldstein*, 299 F. Supp. at 1389.

160. *Id.* at 1393.

statute, which required "suppliers contracting with a public agency in connection with a public works project to provide products whose steel is American made."[161] Judge Pollak, writing for the circuit court, concluded that *Zschernig*, the only case in which the Supreme Court had found a state statute unconstitutional based on dormant foreign-affairs preemption, had involved an unusual situation in which the Oregon law led local probate courts to express foreign policy judgments about other nations, which "held great potential for disruption or embarrassment."[162] Pennsylvania's "Buy American" statute, in contrast, did not require or encourage state courts to critique or judicially appraise foreign regimes and their laws. The law did not distinguish between foreign source countries based on their governments, selectively applying, say, only to those with fascist or communist regimes.[163]

A final example of an unavailing effort to invoke *Zschernig* in the years preceding *Garamendi* arose in an action brought by Nigeria and supporters. They sued the New York City Council to enjoin it from enacting Local Law No. 93, which named the northeast corner of Second Avenue and East 44th Street in Manhattan "Kudirat Abiola Corner." The Council had proposed Law No. 93 to honor the assassinated wife of Mashood K.O. Abiola, a candidate in Nigeria's 1993 presidential election who had later been jailed as a dissident and remained in prison at the time of the lawsuit. Nigeria informed the State Department that New York City's law would "politically embarrass" it because the building across the street from this corner housed the Nigerian Consulate and U.N. Mission.[164]

Relying on *Zschernig*, the plaintiffs thus argued that if New York City enacted Law No. 93, the affected street corner's offensive new moniker would constitute a "targeted political statement," an expression of hostile local views that intruded upon the federal government's amiable diplomatic relations with Nigeria. Unfortunately for the plaintiffs, the State Department disavowed this claim and "elected not to participate" in the case.[165] Consistent with the other post-*Zschernig* cases, the trial court concluded that the defect of the Oregon law had been that, as applied, it risked direct, substantial, and demonstrable interference with federal foreign-affairs policy because state probate courts had inappropriately been

161. Trojan Tech. v. Pennsylvania, 916 F.2d 903, 903 (3d Cir. 1990).

162. *Id.* at 913 (quoting *Zschernig*, 389 U.S. at 435) (internal quotation marks omitted).

163. *Id.*

164. Opusunju v. Giuliani, 669 N.Y.S.2d 156, 157 (N.Y. Sup. Ct. 1997).

165. *Id.* at 159.

tasked with sitting in judgment on foreign laws and nations.[166] Law No. 93, the court somewhat comically observed, did not pose a similar risk:

> Petitioners warn that Local Law No. 93 could cause the Nigerian government to retaliate by adversely renaming the street next to the United States Embassy in Nigeria, which, they contend, unconstitutionally creates the "dangers" of international repercussions noted in *Zschernig*. But what dangerous adverse name-calling could occur? Might Nigeria offend New York City by naming the street outside the United States Embassy "Boston Red Sox Boulevard" or "Los Angeles Symphony Orchestra Drive"?[167]

"Local Law 93," it concluded, "has not been demonstrated to have a direct impact upon foreign relations but instead falls within the category of a diplomatic bagatelle."[168]

Beyond the legal academy, perhaps the most in-depth legal analysis of *Zschernig* during the years between *Zschernig* and *Garamendi* appeared in a memorandum by the Department of Justice Office of Legal Counsel (OLC) responding to the proliferation of local divestment statutes sanctioning South Africa's apartheid regime.[169] Unlike most of the challenged statutes in post-*Zschernig* cases, the OLC memo focused on state and local divestment laws that could reasonably have been expected to fall within the scope of the dormant foreign-affairs doctrine implied by the *Zschernig* Court.

The local laws at issue "requir[ed] the divestment of pension funds from companies that do business in South Africa or prohibit[ed] governmental bodies from entering into contracts with such companies."[170] Although they did not conflict with any express federal treaty or law, they intentionally, directly, and significantly affected a foreign nation. And they risked complicating U.S. foreign relations with South Africa, a delicate diplomatic issue at the time. Indeed, in comparison to the Oregon statute held bad in *Zschernig*, which, as Justice Harlan pointed out, had only a speculative effect on foreign affairs, the local divestment laws almost surely had a real, and probably not trivial, effect on foreign relations. They implicitly passed judgment on a foreign regime; and they were overtly motivated by and intentionally designed to influence South Africa's apartheid regime.

166. *Id.* at 157.

167. *Id.* at 159–160 (internal citation omitted).

168. *Id.* (citation and internal quotation marks omitted).

169. Constitutionality of South African Divestment Statutes Enacted by State and Local Governments, 10 Op. O.L.C. 49 (Apr. 9, 1986).

170. *Id.* at 49.

States and other localities hoped that mass divestment would disrupt the stability, security, and economic welfare of the apartheid regime and thereby contribute to ending apartheid. But however laudatory from an ethical standpoint, these laws seemingly violated the letter and spirit of *Zschernig*. Like the Oregon law in *Zschernig*, they discriminated against a foreign nation, not just in effect, but by design; unlike the Oregon law, they also demonstrably, not just speculatively, influenced a sensitive federal foreign-relations policy.

The OLC considered whether the divestment laws "constitute[d] an impermissible intrusion into a field, foreign affairs, that is uniquely the concern of the federal government[.]"[171] It read *Zschernig* narrowly to mean "that the Court will scrutinize state statutes to determine whether such statutes have a direct impact on foreign relations" and also concluded that "[r]ead together, *Zschernig* and *Clark* suggest that even in scrutinizing state statutes that have an impact on foreign affairs, the Court will balance the degree to which the statute intrudes on foreign affairs against the degree to which the exercise of the state power falls within traditional state powers."[172] The divestment statutes would survive constitutional challenge, in the OLC's view, because they did not require judicial inquiry into the credibility of foreign officials or the operation of South African law. The OLC further argued that *Zschernig* had been limited to state regulatory power, not proprietary power,[173] and that states might have legitimately decided not to invest in companies doing business in South Africa because of the "large risk of revolution and, thus, of expropriation in that country."[174]

Although the latter decision might well be legitimate under *Zschernig*, the OLC's suggestion that financial issues in fact animated the divestment ordinances seemed an obvious fiction. Everyone understood the intent of the local divestment laws: to contribute to the demise of apartheid and, if necessary, the South African regime. And the majority in *Zschernig* had said that it regarded legislative motive and statutory purpose, as well as the local law's potentially deleterious effect on foreign relations, as relevant to dormant foreign-affairs preemption.

The OLC's analysis is dubious for other reasons. Nowhere in *Zschernig* did the majority suggest that dormant foreign-affairs preemption calls for courts to balance local conduct in a realm of traditional state competence[175] against the

---

171. *Id.* at 50.

172. *Id.* at 61–62.

173. *Id.* at 50, 63–64.

174. *Id.* at 62.

175. Only Justice Harlan's concurrence mentioned areas of traditional state competence. Although this concept assumed significance in *Am. Ins. Ass'n v. Garamendi*, 539 U.S. 396, 418 (2003), at the time the OLC wrote, neither *Zschernig* nor any lower court precedent suggested

degree of intrusion into federal foreign-affairs policy. *Clark* likewise says nothing of this sort. Nor did the *Zschernig* Court limit its holding to "*judicial* criticism."[176] The rationale for the Court's decision did not depend on the particular local institution whose conduct potentially interfered with federal foreign-policy prerogatives. *Zschernig* also did not rely in any obvious way on a distinction between state laws enacted in the state's regulatory as opposed to proprietary capacity: the rationale for the majority decision rested on the potential effect of state laws and activities; it is unclear why the regulatory-proprietary distinction would make any difference in this regard. Finally, the OLC's characterization of the local statutes and ordinances directed at South Africa's apartheid government as *less* rather than more of an intrusion into foreign affairs than the Oregon law was implausible.[177] The divestment laws and other local sanctions had a measurable effect on South Africa's apartheid regime and did, in fact, contribute to its ultimate demise.

Despite the OLC's questionable interpretation of *Zschernig*, it was a reasonable effort to make sense of a puzzling precedent in light of the Court's other relevant precedents. The OLC opinion was also emblematic of the fairly common assumption among courts and commentators that *Zschernig* had been an anomaly, a case the Court would be unlikely to rely on often, if at all, in the future. Perhaps it set forth new constitutional doctrine. But that doctrine would seldom apply, and only in unusual circumstances.[178] The only court to rule on the constitutionality of the local South Africa divestment statutes concluded that *Zschernig* should be read narrowly and applied only rarely in cases of substantial, manifest state interference with federal foreign affairs.[179] Many scholars and lawyers thus came to regard *Zschernig* as a relic of the Cold War and a very narrow, fact-intensive decision; some doubted that it remained good law.[180]

---

such a federal-state "balancing" theory of the case. In any event, although pension investment may be within the state's traditional competence, de facto economic sanctions against foreign nations are surely not.

176. *See* Constitutionality of South African Divestment Statutes Enacted by State and Local Governments, 10 Op. O.L.C. 49, 62 (Apr. 9, 1986) (emphasis added). *Compare* Zschernig v. Miller, 389 U.S. 429, 440–41 (1968).

177. Constitutionality of South African Divestment Statutes Enacted by State and Local Governments, 10 Op. O.L.C. at 66 (Apr. 9, 1986).

178. *Cf.* Constitutionality of South African Divestment Statutes Enacted by State and Local Governments, 10 Op. O.L.C. 49 (Apr. 9, 1986).

179. *See* Bd. of Trustees. v. Mayor of Baltimore, 562 A.2d 720, 744–47 (Md. Ct. Spec. App. 1989).

180. *See, e.g.*, Peter J. Spiro, *Foreign Relations Federalism*, 70 U. COLO. L. REV. 1223, 1274 (1999).

Then in 2003, thirty-five years after *Zschernig*, the Court unexpectedly resurrected the dormant foreign-affairs doctrine.

B. *American Insurance Ass'n v. Garamendi* (2003)

In *American Insurance Ass'n v. Garamendi*,[181] the plaintiff, an association of insurance companies, challenged a California statute, the Holocaust Victim Insurance Relief Act (HVIRA), mandating that insurers currently doing business in California disclose the details of all insurance policies sold by the insurer or "related"[182] companies in Europe between 1920 and 1945.[183] Justice Souter wrote for the Court's 5-4 majority, joined by Chief Justice Rehnquist and Justices O'Connor, Kennedy, and Breyer, while Justice Ginsburg, joined by Justices Scalia, Stevens, and Thomas, dissented. The decision not only confirmed *Zschernig*'s status as good law, but arguably went even further by expanding the dormant foreign-affairs doctrine introduced in *Zschernig*.

Garamendi arose out of efforts to provide reparations to the surviving victims and relatives of decedents who had suffered theft of their assets at the hands of Nazi Germany and its collaborators. Nazi Germany and officials of occupied France and Austria had engaged in the mass theft of Jewish assets in the years preceding and during World War II, including life insurance policies, a form of financial security held by many Jews in Europe in those decades. Life insurance companies either refused to honor or seized the value and proceeds of policies issued to Jews before and during the war.[184] Further, after the war, "even a policy that had escaped confiscation was likely to be dishonored, whether because insurers denied its existence or claimed it had lapsed from unpaid premiums" during the years of the Holocaust.[185] The Allies sought by diplomacy to secure reparations for the victims shortly after the war, but the effort waned as the concerns grew about crippling the German economy, and "[d]espite a payout of more than 100 billion deutsch marks as of 2000," many claimants remained uncompensated.[186] Following the treaty reunifying Germany in 1990, which German courts read to lift a moratorium on Holocaust litigation brought by foreign nationals,

181. 539 U.S. 396 (2003).

182. *Id.* at 401.

183. *Id.* at 409–10.

184. *Id.* at 402.

185. *Id.* at 403.

186. *Id.* at 405.

class action lawsuits against the relevant insurers proliferated, both within the United States and Germany, leading to political pressure to resolve the claims through negotiation.

This culminated in an executive agreement between Germany and the United States involving Germany, the insurers, various representatives of the remaining victims, and the International Commission on Holocaust Era Insurance Claims (ICHEIC). The agreement established a claims-settlement procedure that the parties supposed would be more efficient. It also created a 10 billion deutsch mark fund contributed to by Germany and certain German companies, from which payment would be made to the survivors and relatives of the decedents.

The United States, in turn, offered Germany some security from U.S. lawsuits. First, the federal government agreed that in the event of a lawsuit on a Holocaust-era insurance claim, it would "submit a statement that it would be in the foreign policy interests of the United States for the Foundation to be the exclusive forum and remedy for the resolution of all asserted claims against German companies arising from their involvement in the National Socialist era and World War 2."[187] Second, the government agreed to "use its 'best efforts, in a manner it considers appropriate,' to get state and local governments to respect the foundation as the exclusive mechanism."[188] Yet the government expressly declined to guarantee dismissal of U.S. lawsuits, "that being an issue for the courts."[189] Not only did nothing in the executive agreement preempt state law under ordinary preemption principles,[190] but also, by declining to guarantee dismissal of relevant state and local lawsuits, the federal government put Germany on notice that it might *not* be able to ensure the exclusivity of the Foundation's settlement procedures. Indeed, Justice Ginsburg noted in dissent that "ambiguity on this point appears to have been the

187. *Id.* at 406 (quoting Agreement Concerning the Foundation "Remembrance, Responsibility and the Future", U.S.-Ger., July 17, 2000, 39 I.L.M. 1298, 1303) (internal quotation marks omitted). To similar effect, the government said it would notify the courts "that U.S. policy interests favor dismissal on any valid legal ground." *Id.* (quoting Agreement Concerning the Foundation "Remembrance, Responsibility and the Future," *supra*, at 1304) (internal quotation marks omitted).

188. *Id.* at 406 (quoting Agreement Concerning the Foundation "Remembrance, Responsibility and the Future," *supra* note 187, at 1300).

189. *Id.* Both the insurers challenging HVIRA and "the United States as *amicus curiae* ... acknowledge[d] that the agreements include[d] no preemption clause," and that "their claim of preemption" could only "rest on asserted interference with the foreign policy those agreements embody." *Id.* at 417.

190. *See, e.g.*, Crosby v. Nat'l Foreign Trade Council, 530 U.S. 363, 372 n.6 (2000). The Court has held, as it reiterated in *Garamendi*, 539 U.S. at 415, that sole executive agreements, those made by the president alone without congressional participation in any form, preempt state law at least in the context of mass claims settlement. *See, e.g.*, Dames & Moore v. Regan, 453 U.S. 654 (1981); United States v. Pink, 315 U.S. 203 (1942); United States v. Belmont, 301 U.S. 324 (1937).

studied aim of the American negotiating team."[191] The federal government later concluded substantially identical agreements with Austria and France.[192]

In the meantime, California enacted HVIRA. The new law did not authorize litigation based on Holocaust-era insurance fraud. It instead established disclosure requirements for all insurers doing business in California, added a provision to California law making it an unfair business practice to refuse to pay valid Holocaust survivor claims, and instructed the California insurance department to take an active role in investigating insurers for evidence of their responsibility for reparations.[193] The executive branch, as it had promised, tried to persuade California to repeal HVIRA, but to no avail. The plaintiffs in *Garamendi* then filed suit, supported by the United States as amicus curiae.

Because of the conceded absence of a preemption clause or any language to the same effect, the insurers and the federal government relied on *Zschernig* to argue that "HVIRA interferes with foreign policy of the Executive Branch *as expressed principally in* the executive agreements."[194] Perhaps with the exception of *Zschernig*,[195] it was a novel argument to contend that a mere *policy* reflected in executive agreements—rather than those agreements themselves or another federal law—preempted a valid state law.[196]

---

191. *Garamendi*, 539 U.S. at 440 (Ginsburg, J., dissenting) (emphasis added).

192. *Id.* at 408.

193. *Id.* at 409–10.

194. *Id.* at 413 (emphasis added).

195. Perhaps: in *Zschernig*, unlike in *Garamendi*, the federal government did not say that its foreign policy interests would be served by, or still less required, preemption of Oregon law. To the contrary, it filed an amicus brief expressly disavowing that the law interfered with its conduct of foreign relations. Zschernig v. Miller, 389 U.S. 429, 443 (1968). To be sure, if the Court may, as it held in *Zschernig*, infer dormant foreign-affairs preemption of state law even *in the face of* federal opposition to preemption, then it seems to stand to reason that the Court may, a fortiori, preempt state law when the federal government affirmatively requests it or indicates that the state law indeed interferes with its foreign policy. Recall, however, that Justice Stewart suggested in his *Zschernig* concurrence that dormant foreign-affairs preemption is an issue for the *Court*, not the political branches. Joined by Justice Brennan, he wrote, "We deal here with the basic allocation of power between the States and the Nation. Resolution of so fundamental a constitutional issue cannot vary from day to day with the shifting winds at the State Department. Today, we are told, Oregon's statute does not conflict with the national interest. Tomorrow it may." *Id.* at 443 (Stewart, J., concurring); *see also Garamendi*, 539 U.S. at 417. Of course, if it *does* turn out that, tomorrow, the Oregon statute interferes with the national interest, Congress has ample constitutional authority to affirmatively preempt it. Yet because the Court held, as a matter of constitutional law, that Oregon's statute conflicts with the national interest, the political branches no longer have the authority to deal with such a shift in the national interest; it has been judicially determined for all time.

196. Justice Souter began his analysis with the assertion that "[t]here is . . . no question that at some point an exercise of state power that touches on foreign relations must yield to the National Government's policy, given the concern for uniformity in this country's dealings with foreign nations, that animated the Constitution's allocation of the foreign relations power to

The Court thus naturally turned to *Zschernig*. Yet it reframed that decision by considering and giving precedential weight, not only to Justice Douglas's majority opinion, but also to Justice Stewart's concurrence and Justice Harlan's concurrence in the judgment. The *Garamendi* Court first observed that "[t]he *Zschernig* majority relied on statements in a number of previous cases open to the reading that state action with more than an incidental effect on foreign affairs is preempted, even absent any affirmative federal activity in the subject area of the state law, and hence without any showing of conflict."[197] But the Court then shifted to Justice Harlan's concurrence in the judgment, which it construed to endorse a narrower dormant foreign-affairs doctrine—one that would apply to preempt state law "in a case of conflicting federal policy" evinced by the state law's interference with a "specific interest" of the federal government. The Court also wrote that Justice White "basically agreed" with Harlan "in this regard."[198]

This characterization of Harlan's concurrence in the judgment (and hence also White's brief dissent) is questionable. Justice Harlan did not indicate, as the *Garamendi* majority characterized his view, that "[h]e would have found [dormant] preemption in a case of conflicting federal policy."[199] What he said is that "[p]rior decisions have established that in the absence of a conflicting federal policy or violation of the express mandates of the Constitution the States may legislate in areas of their traditional competence even though their statutes may have an incidental effect on foreign relations."[200] It is not, in fact, clear that Harlan

---

the National Government in the first place." *Garamendi*, 539 U.S. at 413 (citations and internal quotation marks omitted). The general principle of federal supremacy in foreign affairs is uncontroversial. But absent a preemptive federal law or treaty under the Supremacy Clause, Souter's assertion is indeed questionable. Apart from *Zschernig*, the Court had never held that the courts should preempt valid state laws based on (what judges perceive to be) the foreign-affairs policy of the federal political branches. No precedent or other authority in the string-citation following Justice Souter's assertion supports it, and the four justices in dissent indeed questioned, if not rejected, it.

197. *Id.* at 418. The citations in *Zschernig*, which the *Garamendi* Court reiterated to support this reading, included dicta from *Hines v. Davidowitz*, 312 U.S. 52, 63 (1941); Stewart's concurrence in *Zschernig* itself, in which he described foreign relations as "a domain of *exclusively* federal competence," *Zschernig*, 389 U.S. at 432 (Stewart, J., concurring) (emphasis added); and *United States v. Belmont*, 301 U.S. 324, 331 (1937), which quoted *United States v. Curtiss-Wright Export Corp.*, 299 U.S. 304, 316 (1936), to the effect that the federal government has "*complete* power over international affairs," which is not "subject to *any* curtailment or interference" by the states (emphasis added). None of these cases held that federal foreign-affairs powers wholly exclude state laws or other activities in the realm of foreign affairs.

198. *Garamendi*, 539 U.S. at 418–19.

199. *Id.* at 419.

200. *Zschernig*, 389 U.S. at 458–59 (Harlan, J., concurring in the judgment) (emphasis added). Harlan's intended meaning here is ambiguous, in part because he phrased this statement in the

accepted the validity of any doctrine of dormant foreign-affairs preemption. There is ample reason to doubt the *Garamendi* majority's assertion that if there had there been evidence of a true conflict between federal policy and Oregon law in *Zschernig*, Justice Harlan, too, would have voted to strike the state law down based on some theory of dormant foreign-affairs preemption, and it is, at best, unclear that the *Garamendi* majority correctly characterized his concurrence in *Zschernig* to mean that he accepted dormant foreign-affairs preemption based on a "conflict" rather than "field" theory.[201] In fact, at the outset of Part IV of his concurrence, Justice Harlan apparently rejected the very idea of dormant foreign-affairs preemption, remarking, "Upon my view of this case, it would be unnecessary to reach the issue [of dormant foreign-affairs preemption]. However, since this is the basis upon which the Court has chosen to rest its decision, I feel that I should indicate briefly *why I believe the decision to be wrong on that score, too*."[202]

The *Garamendi* Court declined to endorse either the view of the majority in *Zschernig* or Justice Harlan's supposedly narrower conception of dormant preemption. Justice Souter remarked that "[i]t is a fair question whether" the president may preempt state law on a dormant foreign-affairs "field" or "conflict" basis. He also stressed what he regarded as Harlan's focus on whether the challenged state law falls within an area of traditional state power.[203] But the majority

---

negative, and in part because none of the precedents he cited involved only a conflicting federal *policy*. *See id.* at 459 n.25. At any rate, it would be a stretch to conclude from these words alone that Harlan accepted a narrower doctrine of dormant foreign-affairs preemption—especially because he concurred in the judgment only, on wholly distinct grounds. The balance of his concurrence casts further doubt on this conclusion.

201. *See Garamendi*, 539 U.S. at 419 & n.11. Established constitutional doctrine recognizes express and implied (conflict, obstacle, or field) preemption of state law. *See, e.g.*, Crosby v. Nat'l Foreign Trade Council, 530 U.S. 363, 372–73 (2000). Because the Supremacy Clause makes the Constitution, federal laws, and treaties "the supreme Law of the Land," U.S. CONST. art. VI, cl. 2, the Court has long held that Congress (or, for treaties, the president and Senate) can preempt state law expressly and implicitly in several ways—based on a direct conflict between the federal and state laws, based on a state law that stands as an obstacle to the implementation or goals of federal law, or based on federal law indicating a congressional intention to occupy a particular field. Before *Zschernig*, however, the Court had never suggested that a mere foreign-affairs *policy* may implicitly preempt state *law*. The Supremacy Clause, after all, does not make federal policy the supreme law of the land. The *Garamendi* majority apparently read Harlan's concurrence to embrace dormant foreign-affairs preemption in the context of conflict but not field preemption. Only Justices Stewart and Brennan arguably suggested dormant foreign-affairs *field* preemption, that is, that the new doctrine announced in *Zschernig* should categorically preempt state law in the field of foreign affairs. It is at best unclear that Justice Harlan accepted a narrower doctrine of dormant foreign-affairs preemption, limited to conflicts—or indeed, any variation of *Zschernig*'s new doctrine.

202. *Zschernig*, 389 U.S. at 457 (Harlan, J., concurring in the judgment) (emphasis added).

203. *Garamendi*, 539 U.S. at 419–20.

concluded that it did not need to explore these issues because HVIRA should be preempted under even the narrower view of dormant foreign-affairs preemption. The facts, Justice Souter wrote, "demonstrated a sufficiently clear conflict" to invalidate the California law under a field or a conflict approach to dormant preemption.[204]

Like the OLC, the Court also understood Justice Harlan's opinion in *Zschernig* to suggest a test that required the judiciary to balance state and federal interests.[205] For this proposition, however, it did not cite anything in Harlan's opinion; rather, it invoked a dormant Commerce Clause case with no foreign relations dimension, *Southern Pacific Co. v. Arizona ex rel. Sullivan*,[206] which is famous for its balancing test. If the effect on foreign relations were balanced against California's interests, the Court concluded, the federal interests would prevail.[207]

---

204. *Id.* at 420.

205. Again, this does not seem accurate. Justice Harlan did not suggest in *Zschernig*, as the *Garamendi* majority characterized his concurrence in the judgment, that "on his view it is legislation within areas of . . . traditional competence that gives a State any claim to prevail." *Id.* (quoting *Zschernig*, 389 U.S. at 458–58) (Harlan, J., concurring in the judgment) (internal citation and quotation marks omitted). Nor did he propose a balancing test. To be sure, as the *Garamendi* Court suggested, perhaps "it would be reasonable to consider the strength of the state interest, judged by standards of traditional practice, when deciding how serious a conflict must be shown before declaring the state law preempted." *Id.* But Justice Harlan's opinion in *Zschernig* did not say so. The *Garamendi* Court nonetheless speculated about the propriety of balancing and the relative virtues of the *Zschernig* majority's and Justice Harlan's (supposed) alternative approaches to dormant foreign-affairs preemption. *Id.* at 420 n.11.

206. 325 U.S. 761 (1945). The Court read *Southern Pacific* to suggest that "reconciliation of the conflicting claims of state and national power is to be attained only by some appraisal and accommodation of the competing demands of the state and national interests involved." *Garamendi*, 539 U.S. at 420. It then referred to Henkin's suggested test, namely, to "balance the state's interest in a regulation against the impact on U.S. foreign relations." *Id.* (quoting HENKIN, *supra* note 2, at 164).

207. The Court concluded that the California law "undercuts the President's diplomatic discretion and the choice he has made exercising it. . . . Quite simply, if the [California] law is enforceable the President has less to offer and less economic and diplomatic leverage as a consequence. The law thus compromise[s] the very capacity of the President to speak for the Nation with one voice in dealing with other governments to resolve claims against European companies arising out of World War II." *Garamendi*, 539 U.S. at 423–24 (2003) (citations and internal quotation marks omitted). "If any doubt about the clarity of the conflict remained, however, it would have to be resolved in the National Government's favor, given the weakness of the State's interest, against the backdrop of traditional state legislative subject matter, in regulating disclosure of European Holocaust-era insurance policies in the manner of HVIRA." *Id.* at 425. And although HVIRA and the Foundation process shared a goal, the Court, citing *Crosby*, noted that "[t]he fact of a common end hardly neutralizes conflicting means," *id.* (citations and internal quotation marks omitted), for "California seeks to use an iron fist where the President has consistently chosen kid gloves," *id.* at 427; and "the evidence here is more than sufficient to demonstrate that the state Act stands in the way of [the President's] diplomatic

Justice Ginsburg, joined by Justices Stevens, Scalia, and Thomas, forcefully dissented. At the outset, she observed that "no executive agreement or other formal expression of foreign policy disapproves state disclosure laws like HVIRA."[208] While she agreed that a sole executive agreement concluded in the context of the long-standing tradition of executive foreign-claims settlement would likely suffice to preempt a state law such as HVIRA,[209] she emphasized that preemption from a sole executive agreement must be express, not implied.[210] In *Barclays Bank PLC v. Franchise Tax Board of California*,[211] for example, a seminal Foreign Commerce Clause case decided nine years earlier, the Court held that "'[e]xecutive branch actions—press releases, letters, and *amicus* briefs' that 'express federal policy but lack the force of law'—cannot render a state law unconstitutional under the Foreign Commerce Clause."[212] And yet, "[a]s the Court acknowledges, no executive agreement before us expressly preempts the HVIRA. . . . Indeed, no agreement so much as mentions the HVIRA's sole concern: public disclosure."[213] Mere

objectives." *Id.* (quoting *Crosby*, 530 U.S. at 386) (citations and internal quotation marks omitted). The Court's heavy reliance on *Crosby* is arguably misplaced. *Crosby*, a unanimous decision, applied established (non-dormant) preemption principles and found that the challenged state law stood as an obstacle to the federal law concerning the same foreign-affairs issue. The Supremacy Clause's text supplies a sound doctrinal basis for non-dormant preemption in foreign, as in domestic, affairs. But there is no freestanding "foreign affairs power" that supplies a clear constitutional basis for dormant foreign-affairs preemption. Article VI, clause 2, makes the Constitution, federal laws, and treaties the supreme law of the land; it says nothing about federal policy. The analogy between *Crosby* and *Garamendi* is dubious, as Justice Ginsburg indeed pointed out in dissent. *Garamendi*, 539 U.S. at 440 n.4 (Ginsburg, J., dissenting). For analysis of *Crosby*, see Chapter 9.

208. *Garamendi*, 539 U.S. at 430.

209. *Id.* at 436–38; *see* Dames & Moore v. Regan, 453 U.S. 654, 688 (1981). Justice Ginsburg pointed out, however, that "[t]he executive agreements to which we have accorded preemptive effect . . . warrant closer inspection than the Court today endeavors." *Garamendi*, 539 U.S. at 436 (Ginsburg, J., dissenting). Both *United States v. Belmont*, 301 U.S. 324 (1937), and *United States v. Pink*, 315 U.S. 203 (1942), for example, sustained preemption by sole executive agreement in part because of the president's well-established power to settle claims incidental to the recognition of foreign governments, *see* Zivotofsky *ex rel.* Zivotofsky v. Kerry, 135 S. Ct. 2076 (2015), or to "the resolution of a major foreign policy dispute between our country and another." *Garamendi*, 539 U.S. at 438 (Ginsburg, J., dissenting) (citations and internal quotation marks omitted). Ginsburg further pointed out that "the Court in *Dames & Moore* was emphatic about the narrowness of its decision," disavowing any general holding that "the President possesses plenary power to settle claims, even as against foreign governmental entities." *Garamendi*, 539 U.S. at 438 (Ginsburg, J., dissenting) (quoting *Dames & Moore*, 453 U.S. at 688) (internal quotation marks omitted).

210. *Garamendi*, 539 U.S. at 440 (Ginsburg, J., dissenting).

211. 512 U.S. 298 (1994).

212. *Garamendi*, 539 U.S. at 442 (Ginsburg, J., dissenting) (quoting *Barclays Bank*, 512 U.S. at 329–30).

213. *Id.* at 438.

expressions of federal policy should not, Ginsburg concluded, preempt California law.[214] Never before had the Court "premised foreign affairs preemption on statements of that order."[215] Nor should it, in the dissent's view, for the precedent would effectively empower "sub-Cabinet members of the Executive Branch" to displace state law, even though, as the majority conceded, "no authoritative text accords such officials the power to invalidate state law simply by conveying the Executive's views on matters of federal policy."[216]

The dissent also critiqued the majority's reliance on *Zschernig*, observing that since that decision, the Court had not relied on it and that she "would not resurrect that decision here."[217] Like virtually all of the lower courts that examined *Zschernig* before *Garamendi*, Justice Ginsburg construed *Zschernig* narrowly, highlighting the degree to which the Court had underscored the effects of Oregon's law and, in particular, the idea that it is problematic for states to "sit in judgment" on foreign nations. The California law, in contrast, "takes no position on any contemporary foreign government and requires no assessment of any existing foreign regime."[218] California's law had no direct impact on the nation's foreign relations and did not threaten to impair the effective exercise of the nation's foreign policy.[219]

Finally, Ginsburg pointed out that, as in *Zschernig*, the *Garamendi* Court had arrogated to itself a power that properly belongs to the political branches. If, as the facts suggested, Congress and the president were unable or unwilling to preempt state law by express federal law or provisions in the sole executive agreements,[220] on the basis of what constitutional principle did the Court

---

214. *See id.* at 440.

215. *Id.* at 442. "The United States," Ginsburg clarified, "has agreed to file precatory statements advising courts that dismissing Holocaust-era claims accords with American foreign policy, but the German Foundation agreement confirms that such statements have no legally binding effect. . . . Indeed, ambiguity on ['whether even *litigation* . . . must be abated'] appears to have been the studied aim of the American negotiating team." *Id.* at 440–41.

216. *Id.* at 442. She allowed that "[e]xecutive officials of any rank may of course be expected 'faithfully [to] represen[t] the President's policy,' . . . . [But] [t]he displacement of state law by preemption properly requires a considerably more formal and binding federal instrument." *Id.*

217. *Id.* at 439.

218. *Id.* (citation omitted).

219. *Id.*

220. Indeed, the sole executive agreements between the United States and Austria, France, and Germany, respectively, said only that the United States would in effect "do its best" to ensure the exclusivity of the federal Holocaust-era insurance reparations policy, implicitly acknowledging that no legally binding obligation existed in this regard. Despite the federal government's lukewarm assurances that it would make an effort to ensure exclusivity, it understood

see fit to substitute its own judgment on foreign affairs policy for that of the executive branch? For *Garamendi* effectively replaced the president's agreement to file *precatory* statements with binding federal law prohibiting all state legislation on the broad subject of Holocaust-era insurance reparations. The majority, Justice Ginsburg argued, had thus, in effect, rewritten the executive agreements. This was improper, for "judges should not be the expositors of the Nation's foreign policy, which is the role they play by acting when the President himself has not taken a clear stand. As I see it, courts step out of their proper role when they rely on no legislative or even executive text, but only on inference and implication, to preempt state laws on foreign affairs grounds."[221]

IV. Assessment

Should the Constitution be read to disable a state from acting if its conduct, in the judgment of the courts, interferes with the federal government's conduct of foreign relations? The answer turns on several questions raised most directly in *Zschernig* and *Garamendi*, both of which continue to generate disagreement among judges and scholars. On balance, we conclude that in principle as well as practice, the concept of dormant foreign-affairs preemption should be abandoned in all but the most exigent and unforeseeable circumstances. Furthermore, as we will suggest in Chapter 5, dormant Foreign Commerce Clause jurisprudence offers a more coherent, determinate, and constitutionally defensible basis for resolving almost any case in which dormant foreign-affairs preemption might be thought relevant. A look at the principal issues addressed by these two cases reveals why their approach should be abandoned.

---

and, by promising only to "do its best," clearly conveyed to Austria, France, and Germany that the several states might enact their own laws on the subject. By saying it would *try* to ensure exclusivity, it put Austria, France, and Germany on notice that it might not succeed, and that it would not be able or willing to invest the political capital or other resources required to ensure federal exclusivity. The federal government could, after all, have preempted state law on the issue by the direct and simple expedient of a statute or international agreement. (Whether a sole executive agreement should suffice in this regard is debatable.) It did not, likely because it did not want to alienate certain constituents or instigate controversy with the states. For the federal courts to take on the right or, a fortiori, the alleged legal obligation to, in effect, *judicially* supply the missing political will and resources to preempt state law enables the political branches to evade and displace responsibility for its decision onto an institutional actor that is not accountable to the electorate.

221. *Id.* at 442–43.

A. Federal Exclusivity

Should an exclusivity standard apply? Two justices in *Zschernig* (Stewart and Brennan) would have held that federal authority over foreign affairs is exclusive, while four (Warren, Douglas, Black, and Fortas) believed that a state's actions could permissibly have some indirect or incidental effect on the nation's foreign affairs but, as Justice Souter put it, "at some point an exercise of state power that touches on foreign relations must yield to the National Government's policy, given the concern for uniformity in this country's dealings with foreign nations, that animated the Constitution's allocation of the foreign relations power to the National Government in the first place."[222] According to the *Garamendi* Court, Justices Harlan and White, too, accepted a narrower version of this proposition, embracing "conflict" but not "field" preemption.

In *Garamendi*, the majority declined to choose between an exclusivity standard and a narrower standard that would require preemption only if state legislation would likely produce more than an indirect or incidental effect in conflict with express federal foreign policy. The *Garamendi* majority thus confirmed *Zschernig*'s conclusion that a federal foreign-affairs policy—as inferred by the judiciary—should in some circumstances preempt state law. But it left open the question whether an actual conflict between the state law and federal policy is necessary for preemption. Only two justices (Stewart, joined by Brennan) explicitly reached this issue in *Zschernig*. In their view, no conflict is required. Although there is reason to doubt the *Garamendi* Court's interpretation of Justice Harlan's concurrence in the *Zschernig* judgment,[223] the majority opinion of Justice Souter read Justice Harlan to agree that dormant foreign-affairs preemption would be appropriate, even within a realm of traditional state competence, if state action is more than indirect and incidental, and also conflicts with a clear policy of the federal government.

To place all this in perspective, three possible standards are available: (1) a rule of per se federal exclusivity; (2) some kind of balancing test that considers the effects of state activity on federal foreign-affairs policy, perhaps providing greater leeway for such state conduct in legal realms of traditional state competence; and (3) the hands-off, pre-*Zschernig* approach—judicial deference to the states absent affirmative preemption, with a possible exception for exigent circumstances. Each approach has potential advantages and disadvantages; the most sensible approach, however, is the third—judicial deference to the states in the absence

---

222. *Id.* at 413 (citations omitted).

223. *See supra* text accompanying and notes 199-202, 205.

of affirmative federal preemption under accepted doctrine or genuine exigency. Yet such exigencies, as we explain in the next chapter, can be resolved more easily, predictably, and defensibly under standards available from dormant Foreign Commerce Clause jurisprudence.[224]

1. Per Se Federal Exclusivity

A standard of per se federal exclusivity supplies a clear rule rather than a standard, reducing if not eliminating (in theory) judicial discretion. It therefore has the potential advantage of avoiding the need for judges to sort out comparative federal and state interests, as well as the degree or kind of effects produced by challenged state conduct. If virtually any state intrusion into foreign policy is per se invalid, the judiciary need not engage in highly speculative assessments of whether state activities have only an indirect and incidental, rather than direct and substantial, effect; whether the state activities fall within a realm of traditional competence; whether and to what extent those activities conflict with federal foreign policy; what, precisely, that foreign policy *is*; and so forth. Nor would courts need to engage in the equally speculative and imprecise tasks of balancing incommensurable state and federal interests. Doing so inevitably thrusts the courts into matters consigned by the Constitution to the political branches.

But the disadvantages far outweigh the virtues, if they are virtues, of a categorical rule of exclusivity. The issue is not merely judicial capacity. If the dormant foreign-affairs doctrine is constitutional in nature, as the Court has held, the doctrine must have a constitutional basis—not necessarily a clear textual basis but at least some structural, functional, or other principled rationale embodied in the document. There is, of course, no general "Foreign Affairs Clause" that assigns foreign affairs exclusively to the federal government. Nor, as we have pointed out, does the Constitution implicitly establish federal exclusivity in foreign affairs. The Constitution gives the federal government potentially plenary, but not exclusive, power, through its delegation of particular foreign affairs powers to the national government.[225] Article I, section 10 makes little sense if the Constitution excludes the states categorically from acting in the realm of foreign affairs.

Further, virtually all state laws and activities have an effect of some kind on foreign relations. This was true in 1789, and it is true today, so true, as we have suggested, that it is difficult even to demarcate the boundary between foreign

---

224. That jurisprudence can and, we will argue, should be applied by the courts in virtually any case involving a state law that arguably interferes unduly with the federal government's conduct of foreign affairs.

225. *See* Goldsmith, *supra* note 10, at 1619, and accompanying text.

and domestic affairs. The exclusivity rule therefore would not, in practice, liberate the courts from the task of making numerous speculative judgments about the comparative weight of state and federal interests, as well as inferences about federal foreign-policy objectives. Every exclusivity case would require the courts to determine at the outset that some state's action has had *too great* an international effect. It would load the dice by establishing a default presumption, or shifting the burden of proof, in close cases.

To do so by purporting to differentiate between incidental and non-incidental effects, or between direct and indirect effects, would also open the door to unprincipled adjudication of the sort discredited in earlier decades—in particular, when the Supreme Court saw itself as able and constitutionally obliged to distinguish between federal action with direct as opposed to indirect effects on intrastate commerce. A draconian insistence that the states stay out of the international realm altogether would also mean barring the states from doing virtually anything described in Chapter 2—it would mean, in other words, disrupting patterns of settled behavior that have been established over two hundred years. And for what purpose? Scant evidence exists that any of those activities have hurt either the nation or the state that undertook them. To the contrary, most of these activities have proved constructive or, at worst, innocuous.

Finally, the federal government can always preempt problematic state conduct in foreign affairs through established doctrine. Express, conflict, field, and obstacle preemption give the federal government ample means to calibrate whether and how to preempt state law. But if the political branches, for whatever reason, do not clearly preempt state law in foreign affairs, what license have the courts to substitute their judgment that preemption is nonetheless required?

In both *Zschernig* and *Garamendi*, the Court purported to be protecting from state intrusion the authority and capacity of the political branches to conduct national foreign policy. But it inexplicably substituted its own judgment about what that policy entailed and required for the judgment of the executive branch. In *Garamendi*, as Justice Ginsburg pointed out in dissent, it appears to have been the "studied aim of the American negotiating team" to leave certain issues of potential state interference, including the potential for litigation, ambiguous. She cited evidence to this effect, namely, "the 'double negative' that satisfied German negotiators and preserved the flexibility sought by Justice Department litigators."[226] The executive agreement with Germany (and later those with France and Austria) committed the United States only "to file precatory statements advising courts that dismissing Holocaust-era claims accords with American foreign policy, but the German Foundation agreement confirms that such statements have

226. *Garamendi*, 539 U.S. at 440–41 (Ginsburg, J., dissenting) (citations omitted).

no legally binding effect."[227] The majority thus effectively substituted the Court's opinion about what the executive agreements should have said for the actual agreements, which, it should be borne in mind, had been carefully negotiated by the executive branch with three foreign nations in the context of a diplomatically complex and sensitive issue.

Yet as Justice Ginsburg asked in *Garamendi*, why should judicial opinions serve, in effect, to "fill the . . . silences" left by the absence of an ordinary basis for preemption with "statements by individual members of the Executive Branch" or otherwise?[228] If the "studied aim" of the executive negotiating teams that concluded the Foundation Agreements in *Garamendi* was indeed to leave the status of future Holocaust-era insurance litigation ambiguous,[229] the Court not only failed to protect federal prerogatives in foreign policy, it actually subverted them by inferring and establishing a categorical rule precluding state litigation. In *Zschernig*, the executive branch stated clearly that Oregon's probate law did not interfere with its foreign policy. But the Court appropriated to itself the prerogative to decide that Oregon's law interfered with federal foreign policy. In sum, the idea of an exclusive rule dictating dormant foreign-affairs preemption lacks a principled basis in the Constitution and, indeed, while purporting to respect the federal political branches, actually shifts power away from them—and to the courts.

2. *Balancing Tests*

A second option would be for the Court to adopt a balancing test of the sort ascribed to Justice Harlan in *Garamendi*. On this view, courts should weigh the strength of the state interest in an area of traditional state competence or the degree of state interference with foreign affairs against the federal government's prerogative to conduct the nation's foreign policy—perhaps taking into account

227. *Id.* at 440.

228. *Id.* at 440–41.

229. The executive branch might have decided for any number of reasons not to include a provision promising that it would protect foreign nations from litigation (or, in the case of HVIRA, mere transparency obligations). Perhaps it concluded that it would be imprudent or inadvisable to give up this bargaining chip. Perhaps it knew that Congress could not be counted upon to enact the federal laws required to affirmatively preempt all state law on the subject of the executive agreements. Perhaps it recognized that it had been precisely such "litigation in American courts [that] provided a spur to [federal] action," contributing to the willingness of foreign governments in Germany, Austria, and France to negotiate the executive agreements in the first place. *Id.* at 432. It does not matter: whatever the reason, it is doubtful that the judiciary has the constitutional prerogative—still less the obligation—to substitute its opinion about what federal foreign policy requires for what federal laws and treaties, as negotiated by the political branches, actually say.

"the strength of the federal foreign policy" as well.[230] The advantage of a balancing test of this sort is that, in theory, it could avoid overturning settled state behavior in areas of traditional state competence that has had no pernicious consequences for federal foreign affairs, while preserving the ability of the judiciary to preempt state law or conduct if it unreasonably interferes with federal foreign policy. It would also save the courts from pretending to identify an objective threshold needed to enforce a per se rule of federal exclusivity, for there is and can be no such standard. As the case law illustrates, efforts by the courts to understand and apply *Zschernig* in the three-and-a-half decades before *Garamendi* yielded no intelligible standard. *Garamendi*, unsurprisingly, has not ameliorated the confusion. Nor did it offer any prospective standard for the courts to apply in future cases.

Here again, the theoretical advantages of the approach do not withstand practical scrutiny. In reality, a balancing test would be all but impossible to define or administer. The courts would first need to determine some threshold of state involvement in foreign affairs that triggers judicial scrutiny under the putative dormant foreign-affairs doctrine. What sorts of effects on foreign affairs qualify as both direct and more than incidental? Then they would be required to assess how much state involvement is too much—to determine when affectation becomes, to quote the *Garamendi* Court, "interference." Interference is a tricky notion; among other things, it requires deciding whether *no* federal policy *is* the federal policy—determining when the federal government is truly silent and whether that federal silence is intentional. Often, these questions are not susceptible to judicial fact-finding, especially because, notwithstanding the "one-voice principle," the federal government does not always speak with one voice;[231] indeed, the Constitution's allocation of foreign affairs powers almost ensures that it won't.[232]

This is as it should be. The Constitution is "an invitation to struggle for the privilege of directing American foreign policy."[233] It deliberately compromises efficiency to safeguard the people against tyranny.[234] Except in limited situations

---

230. *See id.* at 420 & n.11 (Souter, J., majority opinion).

231. *See, e.g.*, Zivotofsky v. Clinton, 132 S. Ct. 1421, 1433 (2015).

232. *See* Sarah H. Cleveland, *Crosby and the "One-Voice" Myth in U.S. Foreign Relations*, 46 VILL. L. REV. 975 (2001); David H. Moore, *Beyond One Voice*, 98 MINN. L. REV. 953 (2015).

233. EDWARD S. CORWIN, THE PRESIDENT: OFFICE AND POWERS 1787–1984, at 201 (Randall Bland et al. eds., 5th rev. ed. 1984).

234. "The doctrine of the separation of powers," Justice Brandeis wrote, "was adopted by the convention of 1787 not to promote efficiency but to preclude the exercise of arbitrary power. The purpose was not to avoid friction, but, by means of the inevitable friction incident to the distribution of the governmental powers among three departments, to save the people from autocracy." Myers v. United States, 272 U.S. 52, 85 (1926) (Brandeis, J., dissenting).

(such as mass claims settlements incident to diplomatic recognition or resolution of a foreign affairs crisis),[235] the president cannot unilaterally preempt state law.[236] He or she must cooperate with Congress to achieve certain foreign policy goals.

Further, case-by-case balancing would produce little meaningful guidance for the states. Ad hoc judicial judgments based on particular factual situations would seldom be susceptible to generalization. It would be difficult for state officials to predict what would fall on one side of the line or the other, potentially wreaking havoc on federal-state relations and depriving businesses and individuals of the ability to predict what law will govern future international dealings.

B. Judicial Abstention

That leaves the third approach: allow the states to act absent federal preemption or manifest and egregious abuse. Recall, again, that for present purposes federal (political-branch) inaction is assumed. By one reading, *Garamendi* is not a "dormancy" case at all because it involved a supposed *conflict* between state and federal policy, and for that reason falls more correctly in Chapter 9, on preemption. Yet preemption, being rooted in the Supremacy Clause, elsewhere requires conflicts between state and federal *law*, not expressions of policy. If the real issue is in fact state power to engage in conduct affecting foreign affairs when Congress and the president have not acted, it's hard to see how the Constitution has anything to say about the matter—let alone that it somehow contains an implicit ban on state action. In fact, the usual assumption is to the contrary: the states may act except in those legal domains that the Constitution has delegated to the federal government.

The advantages of judicial abstention under these circumstances mirror the disadvantages of federal exclusivity and case-by-case balancing. Judicial abstention would mean leaving political decisions about the relationship between local and foreign affairs to the political branches, where the Constitution assigns them. It would liberate the courts from exercising arbitrary, standardless review—or review so stringent that it overturns settled historical practice.

Finally, state conduct in foreign affairs may be constructive and valuable within the U.S. constitutional system. *Garamendi* illustrates a situation in which a state adopted a more effective means of achieving a foreign policy goal that it

---

235. *See, e.g.*, Dames & Moore v. Regan, 453 U.S. 654 (1981); United States v. Pink, 315 U.S. 203 (1942); United States v. Belmont, 301 U.S. 324 (1937).

236. Hence President Bush's unilateral attempt to "hav[e] State courts give effect to the decision in accordance with general principles of comity" did not constitutionally suffice to displace or modify state criminal law so as to provide "review and reconsideration" of the criminal sentences at issue in *Medellín*. Medellín v. Texas, 552 U.S. 491, 503 (2008).

shared with the federal government,[237] obtaining compensation for victims of Holocaust-era insurance fraud.[238]

Of course, as in *Garamendi*, the federal government has the constitutional power to preempt state law affirmatively under the Supremacy Clause; if it exercises that power, then, even if state measures taken to advance the shared foreign-policy goal prove far more effective than federal measures, state law must give way.[239] But if the federal government is silent, there is no constitutional justification or reason to preclude states from experimenting with solutions to problems that their electoral constituencies want addressed.

In *Garamendi*, Justice Souter wrote, "Our thoughts on the efficacy of the one approach [HVIRA] versus the other [the Foundation] are beside the point, since our business is not to judge the wisdom of the National Government's policy; dissatisfaction should be addressed to the President, or perhaps, Congress."[240] But that is just the point. True, the federal government had not enacted a law affirmatively preempting California's disclosure requirements. But it had not promised that it would. Again, there was reason to believe that the federal negotiating team's "studied aim" had been to leave the potential for further litigation ambiguous.[241] And "[i]f it is uncertain whether insurance *litigation* may continue given the executive agreements on which the Court relies, it should be abundantly clear that those agreements leave *disclosure* laws like HVIRA untouched."[242]

---

237. *See Garamendi*, 539 U.S. at 432–33 (Ginsburg, J., dissenting). It is also worth emphasizing that class-action "litigation in American courts," including state courts, had "provided a spur to" the federal government's negotiations with Germany that culminated in the Foundation process in the first place, and it "propelled a number of European companies to agree on a framework for resolving unpaid claims outside the courts." State court litigation, in other words, deserves some of the credit for bringing to the federal government's attention a serious foreign-policy concern of its constituents, that is, the extent of unaddressed Holocaust-era insurance fraud. *Id.* at 431–32. The ability of states and local government to hear and respond to the concerns of their constituents, compared to the remoteness and delay that may characterize the federal government, is one of the virtues of federalism, in foreign as in domestic affairs. See Chapter 2.

238. *Id.* at 424. As Justice Ginsburg observed, the federal process—voluntary claims settlement carried out under the auspices of the International Commission on Holocaust Era Insurance Claims (ICHEIC)—had been "[a]t least until very recently, . . . slow and insecure." *Id.* at 432 (Ginsburg, J., dissenting). "[A] 2001 press account describ[ed] ICHEIC as having 'repeatedly been at the point of collapse since its inception in 1998.'" *Id.* In the three years following its establishment, it had resolved only 797 of 77,000 claims. *Id.* at 433. And perhaps most to the point, "although ICHEIC has directed its members to publish lists of unpaid Holocaust-era policies, that non-binding directive had not yielded significant compliance at the time this case reached the Court." *Id.* HVIRA, in contrast, which created binding disclosure obligations, had been more successful.

239. *Id.* at 424–25.

240. *Id.* at 427.

241. *Id.* at 441 (Ginsburg, J., dissenting).

242. *Id.* at 440.

Absent true federal preemption, the courts have no business prohibiting state conduct that neither the Constitution nor federal laws or treaties prohibit. State laws may well advance national foreign policy interests, especially in circumstances of federal paralysis, neglect, or ineffective means. Fears about state interference with federal foreign-affairs supremacy generally ring hollow. The federal government can always preempt a problematic or parochial state law that interferes with its conduct of foreign affairs. But as Justice Souter (ironically but correctly) said, the political branches, not the courts, should do that work. Instead, the Court transformed a limited executive-branch promise "to file *precatory* statements"[243] with the courts into a federal legal *obligation* that preempted state law—not just those authorizing state litigation but California's state disclosure requirements, which were nowhere mentioned in the executive agreements.[244]

An extraordinary, unforeseeable case could someday arise that requires a need for judicial intervention justified by a much more limited dormant foreign-affairs doctrine. But, historically, that case has yet to arise—not coincidentally. For it's hard to imagine an egregious abuse of state power in the realm of foreign affairs that the federal government would not step in to preempt. Given federal gridlock, the "case from hell" can't completely be ruled out. If and when it arises, however, the courts can fashion an appropriately narrow precedent that tells the states, Congress, and the president where the outer boundary is to be drawn; and even in this unlikely scenario, for reasons explained in Chapter 5, the dormant Foreign Commerce Clause will almost surely suffice to handle an egregious abuse of state power in the realm of foreign affairs. Judicial deference to the states—in the form of a strong presumption of the validity of state law and conduct —is the most compelling approach, and the one most consistent with the structure and values of the Constitution.

C. Alternative Limiting Principles

Not so quick, one might reply: there are a variety of possible limiting principles that might yet save the doctrine. What about looking at the state's motive? Or the subject matter of the regulation? Or, similarly, whether the matter is one of traditional state competence? Or whether the state is negotiating with a foreign

---

243. *Id.* at 438 (emphasis added).

244. The Court thus modified an informal, limited assurance reflecting one sort of diplomatic commitment (to seek to persuade the states and U.S. courts to defer to the federal ICHEIC approach) into a very different sort of diplomatic commitment (to preempt state laws reflecting alternatives that arguably interfered with the ICHEIC process). It is hard to see how the Court's obligation "to say what the law is," *Marbury v. Madison*, 5 U.S. (1 Cranch) 137, 177 (1803), extends to modifying the law—in *Garamendi*, by transforming a limited promise to file precatory statements into a de facto federal law capable of preemption under the Supremacy Clause.

government? Or sitting in judgment on one? Or whether the executive objects to what the state is doing? Respectable arguments have been made for all these approaches. None, however, is convincing.

1. State Motive

Four justices in *Zschernig* (Warren, Douglas, Black, and Fortas) believed that the state "desiderata" relating to the condemnation of a given foreign government, or at least of a type of government—authoritarianism—are matters for the federal government. Justices Harlan, White, Stewart and Brennan, on the other hand, focused only on the effects of the Oregon law and did not delve into the state's motives in enacting the law. Similarly, neither the majority nor the dissent in *Garamendi* examined California's motives; they looked only at the law's effects.

These justices were right. Looking to the state's intent is misguided. Virtually everything states do has one effect or another on international relations, and of course those effects are all, at some level, intended to the extent that those effects are reasonably foreseeable consequences of state law or conduct. If intent were the real issue, therefore, and if states cannot constitutionally affect foreign affairs, then state intent is always necessarily invidious. The courts should in any event be leery of claims of legislative intent, for the reasons that Justice Scalia and others have emphasized.[245] It has been eighty years since Max Radin debunked the myth of "the intent of the legislature,"[246] but U.S. constitutional jurisprudence has not, alas, caught up. Here is one opportunity to do so. Neither a state nor Congress nor the president is a unitary actor. Different subsets of each often express different views at different procedural stages at different points in time. A focus on whose voice, among these, should prevail is a question that invites cherry-picked answers.[247]

2. State Negotiation with a Foreign Government

If a state negotiates with a foreign government, the Court warned in *Clark*, it has entered a constitutionally "forbidden domain."[248] Edward Swaine has argued, similarly, that the Constitution should be seen as implying a dormant treaty power, which would preclude states from bargaining with foreign governments

---

245. *See, e.g.*, Antonin Scalia, *Common-Law Courts in a Civil-Law System: The Role of United States Federal Courts in Interpreting the Constitution and Laws*, *in* A MATTER OF INTERPRETATION: FEDERAL COURTS AND THE LAW 3 (Amy Gutmann ed., 1997).

246. Max Radin, *Statutory Interpretation*, 43 HARV. L. REV. 863 (1930).

247. This is also a reason for courts to hesitate before inferring congressional intent to preempt state action. See Chapter 9.

248. *See* Clark v. Allen, 331 U.S. 503, 517 (1947).

on matters of national concern.[249] State measures contingent on the policies of foreign nations would thus be prohibited.[250] A standard that simply prohibits state negotiation with foreign governments would surely be more realistic than rote insistence upon federal exclusivity. It would rely upon a clear grant of constitutional authority, the treaty power, and it would largely save the courts from the impracticable job of evaluating the effects of a state's action on the nation's foreign relations. Still, there are reasons to hesitate.

First, the Constitution gives the states authority to negotiate compacts and agreements with foreign governments provided Congress consents and, in practice, that has generally also meant in the event of congressional silence. The constitutional text does not require that Congress consent before the negotiation begins, and the Court has held that it need not.[251] One factor that affects whether congressional approval ultimately is necessary is whether the agreement increases the political power of the state, encroaching upon national supremacy.[252] But that can't be assessed until the conclusion of negotiations. As some topics negotiated by states with foreign countries might also fall within the power of the federal government to negotiate with those countries as treaties, overlap exists. The Constitution cannot be construed to give the federal government the exclusive power to negotiate with foreign governments; it explicitly recognizes concurrent state authority to do so in the Compact Clause.[253]

Second, an enormous amount of state activity is directly or indirectly contingent upon the policies of foreign nations—and would therefore, presumably, be prohibited under a dormant treaty-power doctrine. Chapter 2 has described, for example, the incentive wars waged by states to land businesses that are also considering locating in foreign countries. Those businesses, however, are often not the real negotiators; they are proxies for the foreign governments, which play off state governments against each other for the lowest-bid tax breaks. Whether the state strikes a deal with that business depends greatly on action taken or not taken by the foreign government in question. Many of the other state activities detailed in Chapter 2 could involve direct negotiating with a foreign government, but it's

249. Edward T. Swaine, *Negotiating Federalism: State Bargaining and the Dormant Treaty Power*, 49 DUKE L. J. 1127, 1134 n.23 (2000).

250. *Id.* at 1140.

251. In *Virginia v. Tennessee*, 148 U.S. 503, 521 (1893), the Court held that "[t]he Constitution does not state when the consent of Congress shall be given, whether it shall precede or may follow the compact made, or whether it shall be express or may be implied." *See also* RESTATEMENT (THIRD) OF THE FOREIGN RELATIONS LAW OF THE UNITED STATES § 302 cmt. f. (1987).

252. *Virginia*, 148 U.S. at 503.

253. U.S. CONST. art. I, § 10. For a discussion of the Compact Clause, see Chapter 8.

hard to know for sure because many of those activities—for example, trade delegations, sister-city relationships, oil purchases, and the like—could well entail behind-the-scenes, off-the-record meetings that, as a practical matter, would be hard to police or, once completed, to penalize. There is no question, in any event, that many of the projects states have undertaken over the years could have altered foreign governments' actions and, thus, state action as well,[254] which undercuts one of the benefits the approach is advertised to provide, namely, bringing constitutional theory more in line with modern practice.

3. *Sitting in Judgment on a Foreign Government*

In *Zschernig*, the Court expressed concern that the Oregon probate law, in practice, required or led state courts to criticize foreign governments "established on a more authoritarian basis than our own."[255] This particular worry did not arise in *Garamendi* because the government in question, Nazi Germany, no longer existed, and no contemporary foreign government came to its defense.[256]

Yet to the extent that this concern continues to animate the dormant foreign-affairs doctrine, the Court's apprehension seems misplaced. As Justice Harlan noted in *Zschernig*, state courts regularly "sit in judgment" on foreign governments in the course of routine litigation of all kinds without provoking retaliation that interferes with federal foreign policy.[257] Various states and cities, as described in Chapter 2, have also decried human rights abuses in countries such as South Africa and elsewhere.[258] These actions have seldom had a demonstrable negative impact on the achievement of national foreign policy goals and may, to the contrary, actually have enhanced the nation's reputation abroad. In the rare

254. Swaine lists a number: in the 1960s, some states targeted Eastern Bloc countries through trade boycotts and reciprocal inheritance laws; in the 1970s, they shunned firms supporting the Arab boycott of Israel; in the 1980s, they used their economic clout to attack South African apartheid; in the 1990s, they campaigned against European banks holding Holocaust-related assets and against repressive regimes in Burma (Myanmar) and elsewhere, and they increasingly adopted "Buy American" laws, notwithstanding international procurement reform. Swaine, *supra* note 249, at 1130–31 (citations omitted).

255. Zschernig v. Miller, 389 U.S. 429, 440 (1968).

256. Am. Ins. Ass'n v. Garamendi, 539 U.S. 396, 420–21 (2003).

257. *Zschernig*, 389 U.S. at 460–61 (Harlan, J., concurring in the judgement).

258. Unless preempted by federal law, these statutes have, almost without exception, been upheld against challenges based on post-*Zschernig* dormant foreign-affairs doctrine. *See, e.g.*, Bd. of Trustees v. Mayor of Baltimore, 562 A.2d 720 (Md. Ct. Spec. App. 1989); *see also* Trojan Tech. v. Pennsylvania, 916 F.2d 903, 903 (3d Cir. 1990); Shames v. Nebraska, 323 F. Supp. 1321 (D. Neb. 1971); *In re* Estate of Leikind, 239 N.E.2d 550 (N.Y. 1968). *But see* Springfield Rare Coin Galleries, Inc. v. Johnson, 503 N.E.2d 300, 305 (Ill. 1986) (invalidating an Illinois statute that imposed discriminatory taxes on South African Krugerrands).

cases in which a state law does interfere with federal policy or risk provoking foreign retaliation, the federal government can, as it has, preempt that law under established preemption doctrine. In *Crosby v. National Foreign Trade Council*,[259] for example, the Massachusetts Burma Law created diplomatic tension between the United States and its allies, Japan and the European Union (leading, among other things, to threats of an international trade dispute), and interfered with the policy established by the president and Congress. The Court unanimously struck down the law based on obstacle preemption.[260] Such rare cases of troubling state interference with federal foreign policy will inevitably come to the attention of the federal government, which has ample constitutional means to remedy such problems. It would be surprising if this were not the case, given the history of state malfeasance under the Articles of Confederation described in Chapter 1. When such issues do come to federal attention, it may in fact be advisable to let the states act, given that foreign governments sometimes have shared the sentiments of particular states, which often have been at greater liberty to express these sentiments.

4. *Challenges to Federal National Security Policy*

State initiatives critical of *foreign* government policies should be distinguished from state initiatives critical, or potentially obstructive, of *federal* government policies. Typical of the latter have been an Oakland, California, ordinance declaring Oakland a "nuclear free zone," and a Cambridge, Massachusetts, regulation prohibiting the testing, storage, transportation, and disposal within Cambridge of chemical warfare agents. Operative provisions of the Oakland ordinance prohibited any person within the City from engaging in "any work that has as its purpose the development, testing, production, maintenance or storage of nuclear weapons, the components of nuclear weapons, or any secret or classified research or evaluation of nuclear weapons."[261] The ordinance also restricted the transportation of nuclear weapons and materials within Oakland.

A federal district court struck down the Oakland ordinance, citing *Tarble's Case*,[262] and holding it violative of "the War Powers Clauses of the Constitution,"[263] for "the exercise of war powers is the exclusive province of the federal government

259. 530 U.S. 363 (2000).

260. *Id.* at 381.

261. For a copy of the ordinance, see Thomas M. Franck & Michael J. Glennon, Foreign Relations and National Security Law: Cases, Materials, and Simulations 830 (2d ed. 1987).

262. 80 U.S. (13 Wall.) 397, 409 (1871).

263. United States v. City of Oakland, No. C-89-3305 JPV (N.D. Cal. 1990).

under the Constitution."[264] The Massachusetts Supreme Judicial Court, in contrast, upheld the Cambridge regulation.[265] It "recognize[ed] that Congress has plenary authority in exercising war and defense powers" but found that the regulation would have, at most, a speculative and indirect impact on national defense.[266] Absent any congressional action that clearly conflicted with the regulation or intent to occupy the field, the court sustained the regulation.[267]

The approach of the Massachusetts Supreme Judicial Court seems more sensible. If achieving a federal policy objective is so vital to the protection of national security that state and local opposition cannot be brooked, it hardly seems too much to expect citizens to understand the overriding importance of that policy when they go to the polls, or failing that, to expect Congress to enact preemptive legislation that explicitly precludes state or local obstruction. To look to the courts to invent some test for invalidating state or city measures absent congressional action requires the courts to exercise powers that, again, properly belong to political branches, and call for judicial standards that cannot be articulated and applied clearly. One risk must be weighed against another; in this realm, based on the historical record, the risk of judicial overreaching seems greater than the risk of state or local overreaching.[268]

5. *Traditional State Competence*

Why not assess whether the state action in question falls within a subject matter within which the states exercise "traditional competence"—or conversely, whether the federal government has customarily exercised responsibility in the area? *Zschernig* is not entirely clear on this point. But it appears that two justices in *Zschernig* (Harlan and White) believed that traditional state competences were relevant, while seven (Warren, Douglas, Black, Fortas, Brennan, Stewart and White) did not. In *Garamendi*, the majority went further. It read Justice Harlan's concurrence in the *Zschernig* judgment to assert that not only does it matter; it's crucial. Harlan, the majority opined, would have held that "it is legislation within

---

264. FRANCK & GLENNON, *supra* note 261, at 837; *see also* Fossella v. Dinkins, 110 A.D.2d 227, 229–31 (N.Y. App. Div. 2d Dep't 1985).

265. Arthur D. Little, Inc., v. Comm'r of Health, 481 N.E.2d 441, 556 (Mass. 1985).

266. *Id.* at 551.

267. *Id.* at 550.

268. For the argument that Congress has not enacted legislation precluding the establishment of nuclear free zones of the sort generally at issue in the Oakland case, see Luis Li, *State Sovereignty and Nuclear Free Zones*, 79 CAL. L. REV. 1169 (1991). *But see* Lori A. Martin, Comment, *The Legality of Nuclear Free Zones*, 55 U. CHI. L. REV. 965, 1009 (1988) ("[M]any of the recent Nuclear Free Zone ordinances are invalid as unconstitutional intrusions on the federal power to provide for national defense and to conduct foreign affairs.").

'areas of . . . traditional competence' that gives a State any claim to prevail."[269] The *Garamendi* majority viewed the characterization of a subject as within federal or state authority as equally if not more important to dormant foreign-affairs preemption: resolving Holocaust-era insurance claims fell "well within the Executive's responsibility for foreign affairs," and mass foreign-claims settlement had been a "longstanding practice" of the executive branch.[270]

A focus on traditional state competence thus, necessarily, pays implicit homage to Justice Holmes's axiom that the life of the law is not logic but experience.[271] Looking to custom, which Justice Frankfurter described as a gloss on the constitutional text,[272] is common in separation-of-powers cases,[273] and it has the advantage of invoking historical precedents to resolve disputes—diminishing the risk of disrupting settled expectations by avoiding reliance upon a judicial construct. It has the disadvantage, however, of dissemblance—because custom *is* a judicial construct. Custom does not exist "out there": it is an artifact of human imagination. The historical events and practices that comprise a putative custom are selected without reference to any objective guideline. The resulting "tradition" is therefore susceptible to arbitrary particularization or generalization, with the outcome of the analysis dictated by the original premises of event selection.

Consider two concrete examples. In *Zschernig*, was the matter in which the states had traditionally legislated "conditions for inheritance," in which case the state wins, or "sitting in judgment on the political structure of a foreign government," in which case the federal government wins? In *Garamendi*, was the tradition "[v]indicating victims injured by acts and omissions of enemy corporations in wartime,"[274] as the majority narrowly defined the tradition, or "mandate[ing] only information disclosure,"[275] as the dissent, in effect, more broadly characterized it?[276] Neither formulation is objectively correct or incorrect in either case.

---

269. Am. Ins. Ass'n v. Garamendi, 539 U.S. 396, 420 (2003).

270. *Id.*

271. Oliver Wendell Holmes, Jr., The Common Law 5 (Mark DeWolfe Howe ed., Harvard Univ. Press 1963) (1881).

272. Youngstown Sheet & Tube v. Sawyer, 343 U.S. 579, 610–11 (1952) (Frankfurter, J., concurring).

273. *See* Glennon, *supra* note 67, at 18–27.

274. *Garamendi*, 539 U.S. at 421.

275. *Id.* at 435.

276. In *Movsesian v. Victoria Versicherung AG*, 629 F.3d 901, 907–08 (9th Cir. 2010), the court of appeals upheld against a preemption challenge a California statute that extended the statute of limitations for claims arising out of life insurance policies issued to victims of the

If the outcome of the case turns upon which formulation judges select (or construct), the result will often be arbitrary and unpredictable.

Indeed, that is a chief reason the Supreme Court, formally at least, abandoned the very idea of traditional state functions. *Garcia v. San Antonio Metro Transit Auth.* (1985)[277] "reject[ed], as unsound in principle and unworkable in practice, . . . judicial appraisal of whether a particular governmental function is 'integral' or 'traditional.'"[278] The Court has never been able to articulate a clear standard for identifying traditional state functions. An approach to dormant foreign-affairs preemption that gives the same concept an indispensable role in judicial appraisal thus seems, in the first place, to be inconsistent with *Garcia*. Yet the Court has since decided a number of cases, *Garamendi* among them,[279] that call into question whether *Garcia* remains good law.[280] Be that as it may, it would be troubling for such an arbitrary and indeterminate concept to play a decisive role in the context of dormant foreign-affairs preemption. Reliance upon tradition is an illusory method of keeping the courts out of foreign policy. A better approach is to forgo deciding cases based upon the irretrievably nebulous and manipulable dormant foreign-affairs doctrine.

V. Conclusion

The futile search for a sound limiting principle need not, of course, be confronted if the judiciary were simply to abandon dormant foreign-affairs preemption. If a state interferes with federal foreign policy or intrudes upon federal foreign-affairs powers, the political branches can preempt the state's law or conduct. Sometimes the executive branch can do so alone by entering into a sole executive agreement;[281] other times, preemption will require congressional participation,

---

Armenian genocide, finding that the regulation of insurance fell within the area of traditional state responsibility.

277. 469 U.S. 528 (1985). *Garcia* overruled *Nat'l League of Cities v. Usery*, 426 U.S. 833 (1976), which had held that the Tenth Amendment protects traditional or integral state functions from regulation. *See id.*, 426 U.S. at 854–55.

278. *Garcia*, 469 U.S. at 546–47; *see also id.* at 530.

279. *See Garamendi*, 539 U.S. at 420; *see also*, e.g., Bond v. United States, 134 S. Ct. 2077 (2014). For analysis of *Bond*, see Chapter 6.

280. *See* John C. Yoo, *The Judicial Safeguards of Federalism*, 70 S. CAL. L. REV. 1311, 1334–57 (1997). Since 1997, the Court has continued to invoke traditional state functions, lending additional support to Yoo's contention that *Garcia* has been de facto overruled. *See id.* at 1311.

281. *See, e.g.*, Dames & Moore v. Regan, 453 U.S. 654 (1981); United States v. Pink, 315 U.S. 203 (1942); United States v. Belmont, 301 U.S. 324 (1937).

whether by statute, congressional-executive agreement, or treaty.[282] It's hard to see how a state's activities could be so objectionable as to warrant judicial invalidation if the political branches lack the will or capacity to preempt those activities. But if state recalcitrance persists and federal action is for legitimate reasons infeasible, the president can always bring a legal action against the state, arguing for application of some sort of *Zschernig* principle and leaving no need for judicial guesswork. The issue of relative power would then be placed squarely before the courts. Absent exigent, unforeseeable circumstances, however, the courts should afford state action in the face of federal silence a strong presumption of constitutionality. And as we will see in the following chapter, existing dormant Foreign Commerce Clause jurisprudence already provides the judiciary with all the authority it needs to handle exigencies that might arise were the dormant foreign-affairs doctrine abandoned—as it should be.

282. *See, e.g.*, Crosby v. Nat'l Foreign Trade Council, 530 U.S. 363, 372–73 (2000).

5

Dormant Foreign Commerce Preemption

LIKE MOST EVERY author in the twenty-first century, we typed this book on computers. Is a twenty-first century computer an article of foreign or domestic commerce? Massachusetts has authority to protect its residents from potentially noxious chemicals in computers[1] by virtue of what the Supreme Court refers to as the state's "police power"—to provide for the polity's general health, safety, welfare, and the like.[2] The federal government, however, may limit the state's authority in the exercise of its constitutional powers under the Constitution's Foreign or Interstate Commerce Clause[3] power—which is it? And what if the federal government has said nothing, deliberately or otherwise (does *that* matter?)? Does a "dormant" Commerce Clause still limit Massachusetts's authority under the state police power?

The Court has struggled with these issues almost from the time of the Constitution's adoption, in part because of the sheer breadth and diversity of commerce and in part because the Court has recognized, repeatedly and almost from the outset of the nation's history, that Congress cannot conceivably "keep track of and override all of the laws that discriminate against or unduly burden

---

1. Toxic chemicals used to manufacture a notebook computer include beryllium, lead, chromium, and mercury compounds. *See* Dylan Tweney, *What's Inside Your Laptop? Toxic Electronics?*, PC MAG. (Mar. 14, 2007), http://www.pcmag.com/article2/0,2817,2102893,00.asp (last visited June 10, 2014).

2. Gibbons v. Ogden, 22 U.S. (9 Wheat.) 1, 19 (1824).

3. U.S. CONST. art. I, § 8, cl. 3 (vesting Congress with the power "[t]o regulate commerce with foreign nations, and among the several states, and with the Indian tribes").

interstate commerce that may be enacted by any of the fifty states and thousands of local governments."[4]

Consider one expert's account of how a modern notebook computer reaches its final purchaser. Behind each of a notebook computer's components, and behind each of the sequential processes of the manufacture, sale, and delivery of the final product to its final purchaser, lies a complex, distinct—and distinctively *transnational*—story. In fact, it would "be impossible to trace, [at least within the confines of] a magazine article, the origin of every single component in your notebook, because it contains hundreds of parts, including microchips, the hard drive, the battery pack, the LCD, circuit boards, resistors, capacitors, wires, and even the pieces of metal and plastic that make up the casing. But we can take a look at the web of production leading up to one component—the CPU—and use that to shed some light on just how global the PC industry has become."[5] Consider just the computer's nucleus, its microprocessor, a tiny silicon flake with millions of microscopic, precision-engineered circuits responsible for making the computer compute.

A microprocessor begins as a pile of quartz chips, perhaps in Brazil. A company there—it might be a Brazilian corporate national but, more likely, a subsidiary owned or controlled by a foreign multinational enterprise—processes and partially purifies the chips into silicon metal ingots. Then it ships them to a refining company, perhaps in Germany, for further purification and distillation into a liquid called trichlorosilane. The refining company then sends this substance to another nation, perhaps Japan, to be converted to polysilicon. From Japan, it typically goes to an Intel wafer fabrication factory, probably in the United States. The principal domestic contribution takes place at this stage, for "[i]n the entire PC production chain, this is the one step in which the United States still has a stake in production." The Intel factory thereafter ships the wafers to the Philippines or Malaysia for further testing and assembly into chips. Those chips go on to a factory, frequently in Shanghai, China, where workers insert them into a printed circuit board. All of the preceding steps culminate in the creation of the core of the computer's motherboard.

Yet the motherboard has "hundreds of other components, including transistors, resistors, diodes, LEDs, capacitors, and more, all of which are plugged or soldered into place." And the motherboard, in turn, must be connected with still other components, including the "hard drive, optical drive, battery pack,

---

4. Michael C. Dorf, *Is the Dormant Commerce Clause a "Judicial Fraud"?*, VERDICT (May 20, 2015), https://verdict.justia.com/2015/05/20/is-the-dormant-commerce-clause-a-judicial-fraud.

5. Tweney, *supra* note 1.

LCD, keyboard and track pad," as well as the notebook's external casing, which is branded in the final stages with a "logo identifying a notebook's ostensible 'manufacturer.'" Once fully assembled, the notebook computer is sent to a wholesale distribution center, which, in turn, sells it to a retailer and, finally, to the consumer. "The end result of this long production chain is that a supposedly American product from a company such as HP, Dell, or Apple is actually built overseas, almost entirely from overseas components."

This condensed account of a computer's production and sale is instructive because a computer is emblematic of virtually every product in our globalized world: cars, locomotives, refrigerators, clocks, pens, aircraft engines, and so on—all of which go through a serpentine international odyssey similar to a computer's before reaching their final destinations and purchasers. It is hardly obvious how to answer the question whether they should be characterized as foreign or domestic commerce under the Constitution. In an earlier era, tea arrived in Boston harbor on clipper ships from China, or cloth manufactured from cotton grown and woven in South Carolina was transported to other states for sale. The distinction between foreign and domestic commerce made sense. It seldom does today.

Yet the Supreme Court has suggested that distinct constitutional rules apply to state authority to regulate, respectively, foreign and domestic (interstate) commerce in the absence of congressional action. For almost two centuries after the Constitution's ratification, the Court prudently made no such distinction. It applied the same doctrinal standards to evaluate all state commercial regulation under the Constitution. But in *Japan Line, Ltd. v. County of Los Angeles* (1979),[6] the Court decided—mistakenly, in our judgment—that foreign commerce should be subject to a more rigorous constitutional test than interstate commerce. We suggest below that, barring exceptional circumstances, the Court should return to its traditional approach, with minor modifications. It is simpler, clearer, and fully adequate in the vastly more transnational twenty-first century.

To understand why the Court succumbed to the temptation, comparatively recently, to complicate dormant Commerce Clause doctrine by distinguishing between its application to foreign and interstate commercial regulation, it is instructive to consider the traditional approach and its jurisprudential evolution in the nearly two centuries before *Japan Line*. We begin with the Court's interpretation of Congress's dormant interstate-commerce power because, despite *Japan Line*, it continues to comprise the bedrock of the analysis in dormant Foreign Commerce Clause cases: the doctrinal standards that govern the former apply equally to the latter; the sole difference is that, after *Japan Line*, foreign commerce must comply with two supplemental criteria of constitutional scrutiny.

---

6. 441 U.S. 434 (1979).

Textually, the Constitution, with characteristic brevity, simply vests Congress with power "[t]o regulate Commerce with foreign Nations, and among the several States." It thus empowers the federal government to govern the most pervasive and amorphous of goods, services, and other commercial activities, viz., all those that move from place to place, cross state or international borders, or "substantially affect" commerce.[7] By implication, it limits state power to do the same. The story of the evolution of the Commerce Clause is woven through the fabric of U.S. history and federalism.[8] In practice, it is the federal power that most often functions as the flip side of the Tenth Amendment:[9] The Tenth Amendment reserves to the states,[10] among other powers, what the federal government may not regulate under the Commerce Clause; conversely, what the Tenth Amendment reserves to the states is, by definition, not within the ambit of the Commerce Clause. Where the Constitution draws the line is a perennial frontier of federalism: as a rule, it is where federal power ends and state power begins.

---

7. United States v. Lopez, 514 U.S. 549, 558 (1995).

8. Justice Robert Jackson aptly summarized that history:

> When victory had relieved the Colonies from the pressure for solidarity that war had exerted, a drift toward anarchy and commercial warfare between states began. "[E]ach State would legislate according to its estimate of its own interests, the importance of its own products, and the local advantages or disadvantages of its position in a political or commercial view." This came to threaten at once the peace and safety of the Union. The sole purpose for which Virginia initiated the movement which ultimately produced the Constitution was "to take into consideration the trade of the United States; to examine the relative situations and trade of the said States; to consider how far a uniform system in their commercial regulations may be necessary to the common interest and their permanent harmony" and for that purpose the General Assembly of Virginia in January of 1786 named commissioners and proposed their meeting with those from other states. The desire of the Forefathers to federalize regulation of foreign and interstate commerce stands in sharp contrast to their jealous preservation of the state's power over its internal affairs. No other federal power was so universally assumed to be necessary, no other state power was so readily relinquished. [Madison] indicated [that] "want of a general power over Commerce led to an exercise of this power separately, by the States, wch [sic] not only proved abortive, but engendered rivaled, conflicting and angry regulations." The necessity of centralized regulation of commerce among the states was so obvious and so fully recognized that the few words of the Commerce Clause were little illuminated by debate.

H.P. Hood & Sons v. DuMond, 336 U.S. 525, 533–34 (1949).

9. *Cf.* LAURENCE H. TRIBE, AMERICAN CONSTITUTIONAL LAW 1173 (3d ed. 2000) ("Most problems pertaining to federal preemption have arisen in close connection with the Commerce Clause, involving federal legislation enacted pursuant to that clause, and involving state or local action vulnerable to dormant Commerce Clause attack as well as to what are, strictly speaking, preemption arguments.").

10. Or "the People." U.S. CONST. amend. X.

I. Evolution of the Dormant Interstate Commerce Clause

Hundreds of cases have been decided based on challenges to state and local laws that allegedly encroached upon federal authority under the dormant Commerce Clause. [11] Each case shared the presumption that Congress had been silent relative to the challenged law. All agree that Congress may say no (that is, prohibit state regulation within the scope of the Commerce Clause), and all agree that Congress may say yes (that is, permit state commercial regulation that the Clause would otherwise prohibit). The hard questions arise when Congress says nothing, and the courts must infer, or decline to infer, preemption. The Supreme Court has resolved these questions piecemeal over the course of U.S. history and modified the resulting doctrine several times. But among the seminal decisions in this area, none is more significant, influential, and enduring than the first, *Gibbons v. Ogden* (1824).[12]

A. From *Gibbons* to *Blackbird Creek*

In *Gibbons*, New York State had granted two of its citizens, Livingston and Fulton, an exclusive right (a de facto monopoly) over steamboat navigation in New York State waters for a thirty-year period.[13] Livingston and Fulton assigned their steamboat navigation rights in the waters between New York City and New Jersey to Ogden, and the latter subsequently brought suit to enjoin defendant Gibbons from operating steamships under the auspices of a federal license granted by Congress. Because the state-granted monopoly conflicted with a license granted by the federal government, Congress had not been silent as to the subject of litigation.[14] Yet Gibbons's challenge to the New York-granted license assumed that it

11. The dormant commerce power has generated an avalanche of criticism from certain members of the Court, most recently, Justices Scalia and Thomas. *See, e.g.*, Comptroller of Treasury of Md. v. Wynne, 135 S. Ct. 1787, 1807 (2015) (Scalia, J., dissenting, joined by Thomas, J.); S. Pac. Co. v. Arizona, 325 U.S. 761, 790 (1945) (Black, J., dissenting). Whether it should be retained generally is beyond the scope of this book. It suffices to note that as a practical matter, there is zero chance that the dormant Commerce Clause doctrine will disappear anytime soon. We therefore assume its continuing vitality as constitutional doctrine.

12. 22 U.S. (9 Wheat) 1 (1824).

13. *Id.* at 6.

14. *Gibbons* therefore did not directly raise questions under the dormant Foreign Commerce Clause. That did not stop Chief Justice Marshall from observing, however, that "[t]he States are unknown to foreign nations. . . . Whatever regulations foreign commerce should be subjected to in the ports of the Union, the general government would be held responsible for them . . . ." *Id.* at 228–29. Furthermore, in the course of his dicta in this regard, Marshall "first coined the

did not matter: whether Congress expressly prohibited New York's commercial regulation or said nothing about it, he argued, the Commerce Clause precluded New York from regulating navigation that qualified as interstate commerce within the meaning of the Constitution.

As Chief Justice Marshall summarized Gibbons's argument, "to regulate" implies full power over the subject to be regulated. It therefore necessarily excludes state regulation of the same subject. On this view, Congress's Commerce Clause power, even when it has not been exercised, "produces a uniform whole, which is as much disturbed and deranged"[15] if the states regulate in areas that Congress has left untouched as it would be if they acted in conflict with express congressional regulation. Marshall neither accepted nor rejected this argument, leaving its resolution for another day, although he made clear that he found it plausible.[16] He decided the case on the more straightforward and less disputatious ground of express preemption, holding simply that because Congress had acted within the scope of its constitutional power under the Commerce Clause, New York's inconsistent grant of a monopoly could not stand.

Five years later, however, in *Willson v. Black Bird Creek Marsh Co.* (1829),[17] Marshall answered the question he had declined to decide in *Gibbons*. In *Willson*, Delaware had enacted a statute authorizing Black Bird Creek Marsh Company to build a dam in order to drain a marshy creek. The Supreme Court sustained Delaware's action even though it obstructed a navigable tributary of the Delaware River, an interstate waterway within the meaning of the Commerce Clause. The Court observed that because of "[t]he value of the property on [Delaware's] banks [would] be enhanced" by the dam and "the health of the inhabitants probably

term 'dormant' to describe the power of the clause, even in the absence of conflicting federal statutes, to preempt state regulation affecting interstate commerce." Richard H. Seamon, *The Market Participant Test in Dormant Commerce Clause Analysis—Protecting Protectionism?*, 1985 DUKE L.J. 697, 699–700 (1985).

15. Transcript of Oral Argument, Gibbons v. Ogden, 22 U.S. (9 Wheat.) 1 (1824).

16. "There is great force in this argument," he wrote, "and the court is not satisfied that it has been refuted." *Gibbons*, 22 U.S. at 209. Five years earlier, Marshall had expressed a less categorical but analogous view in the bankruptcy context—intimating that a similar decision might well be forthcoming were a comparable case to arise in the context of the Commerce Clause. *See* Sturges v. Crowninshield, 17 U.S. (4 Wheat.) 122, 193 (1819) ("Whenever the terms in which a power is granted to congress, or the nature of the power, require that it should be exercised exclusively by congress, the subject is as completely taken from the state legislature as if they had been expressly forbidden to act on it."). *Sturges* thus suggested that the exclusivity of an enumerated congressional power turns on its nature or how the Constitution frames it.

17. 27 U.S. (2 Pet.) 245 (1829).

improved,"[18] Delaware's goals fell squarely within the state's general police power. And although the dam, strictly speaking, regulated interstate commerce in a certain respect, Chief Justice Marshall concluded that such a formal conflict alone should not be understood to offend the Constitution:

> Measures calculated to produce these objects, provided they do not come into collision with the powers of the general government, are undoubtedly within those which are reserved to the states. But the measure authorised by this act stops a navigable creek, and must be supposed to abridge the rights of those who have been accustomed to use it. But this abridgement, *unless it comes in conflict with the constitution or a law of the United States*, is an affair between the government of Delaware and its citizens, of which this Court can take no cognizance.[19]

Congress, in other words, clearly had power to regulate the interstate waterway at issue. But it had not. Against the background of congressional silence, could a state regulate as Delaware had? Yes, the Court answered:[20] state action that has an effect on interstate and foreign commerce is not categorically unconstitutional under the Commerce Clause absent inconsistent congressional action.

But was this true of *all* such state regulation? Were there no circumstances in which state activity that affected interstate or foreign commerce was forbidden? Do circumstances exist that differ relevantly from those in *Willson*, such that the Constitution prohibits state regulation of commerce despite congressional silence? Put simply, how far could states go in this regard? The Supreme Court's 1851 decision in *Cooley v. Board of Wardens of the Port of Philadelphia*[21] provided an answer—for a time.

---

18. *Willson*, 27 U.S. at 251.

19. *Id.* (emphasis added).

20. The Court reasoned:

> [T]he repugnancy of the law of Delaware to the Constitution is placed entirely on its repugnance to the power to regulate commerce with foreign nations and among the several states; a power which has not been so exercised as to affect the question. We do not think that the act empowering the [company] to place a dam across the creek, can, under all the circumstances of the case, be considered as repugnant to the power to regulate commerce in its dormant state, or as being in conflict with any law passed on the subject.

Id. at 252.

21. 53 U.S. (12 How.) 299 (1851).

B. The Rise and Fall of the *Cooley* Doctrines

In *Cooley*, the Board of Wardens of the Port of Philadelphia sued two vessels for debts allegedly owed under an 1803 state law requiring vessels entering or leaving the port of Philadelphia to hire a local pilot for assistance in navigating the harbor.[22] The Court upheld the law against constitutional challenges based on its inconsistency with, among other provisions, the Commerce Clause. Speaking for the Court, Justice Curtis reiterated that interstate or cross-border navigation does, of course, constitute commerce under the Constitution, and further agreed that, in several ways, Pennsylvania's law regulated commerce.[23] But the question, the Court said, is "whether the grant of the commercial power to Congress, did per se deprive the states of all power to regulate pilots,"[24] especially against the backdrop of a 1789 federal law that seemingly countenanced state regulation in this very area.[25]

As Chief Justice Marshall had intimated in earlier decisions,[26] the answer turned upon "the nature of the power," in particular whether its conferral by the Constitution upon Congress "requires that a similar authority should not exist in the states."[27] The Court thus distinguished power over commercial subject matters "absolutely and totally repugnant to the existence of a similar power in the states" from those "compatible with the existence of a similar power in the states."[28] Only the former, it concluded, exclude concurrent federal and state power.[29]

---

22. Presumably *Cooley* therefore involved foreign, not just interstate, commerce. The Court said in this regard that "the regulation of pilots and pilotage has an intimate connection with, and an important relation to, the general subject of commerce with foreign nations and among the several states," and that the Constitution vested the commerce power in the national government in part to avoid state "discriminations favorable or adverse to commerce with particular foreign nations." *Id.* at 316–17. Chief Justice Marshall expressed a similar view in *Brown v. Maryland*, 25 U.S. (12 Wheat.) 419, 447 (1827).

23. *Cooley*, 53 U.S. at 315–16.

24. *Id.* at 318.

25. The 1789 federal law said that "all pilots in the . . . ports of the United States shall continue to be regulated in conformity with the existing laws of the states, respectively, wherein such pilots may be, or with such laws as the states may respectively hereafter enact for such purpose, until further legislative provision shall be made by Congress." *Id.* at 317 (citation and internal quotation marks omitted).

26. *See* Sturges v. Crowninshield, 17 U.S. (4 Wheat.) 122, 193 (1819).

27. *Cooley*, 53 U.S. at 318.

28. *Id.*

29. Marshall reasoned that

> the power to regulate commerce, embraces a vast field, containing not only many, but exceedingly various subjects, quite unlike in their nature; some imperatively demanding a single uniform rule, operating equally on the commerce of the United States in

The Court apparently regarded Pennsylvania's purposes and the state legislature's motives for enacting the local statute at issue as immaterial. *Cooley* instead held that the subject matter of the regulation, its "nature," controls: if the subject matter demands uniform national regulation, the Commerce Clause precludes state action in the area; in contrast, if the subject matter "imperatively demand[s] that diversity, which alone can meet . . . local necessities" in character, the states may act unless and until Congress says otherwise or preempts the state law under established preemption doctrine. This so-called "first *Cooley* doctrine" thus held that the subject matter of the commercial regulation, its local or national character, and the consequent need or lack thereof for uniform regulation, determines whether the Constitution compels federal exclusivity in the face of congressional silence.

Although the law in *Cooley* did not concern a subject that the Court deemed exclusively federal, the case also came to be understood to establish a second doctrine. This so-called "second *Cooley* doctrine" answered a distinct question, albeit in dicta: What if, in contrast to the facts in *Cooley*, the nature of the subject matter *did*—in the Court's view, at any rate—require uniform, national regulation and therefore, presumably, federal exclusivity? May Congress nonetheless decide to allow the states to regulate such subject matters by affirmative action? No, the *Cooley* Court concluded: Congress may not authorize what the Constitution, in its view, forbids.[30] To Justice Curtis, the syllogism supporting this conclusion, an

> every port; and some, like the subject now in question, imperatively demanding that diversity, which alone can meet the local necessities of navigation. Either absolutely to affirm, or deny that the nature of this power requires exclusive legislation by Congress, is to lose sight of the nature of the subjects of this power, and to assert concerning all of them, what is really applicable but to a part. Whatever subjects of this power are in their nature national, or admit only of one uniform system, or plan of regulation, may justly be said to be of such a nature as to require exclusive legislation by Congress. That this cannot be affirmed of laws for the regulation of pilots and pilotage is plain. The act of 1789 contains a clear and authoritative declaration by the first Congress, that the nature of this subject is such, that until Congress should find it necessary to exert its power, it should be left to the legislation of the states; that it is local and not national; that it is likely to be the best provided for, not by one system, or plan of regulations, but by as many as the legislative discretion of the several states should deem applicable to the local peculiarities of the ports within their limits.

Id. at 2684–85.

30. Two current members of the Court, Justices Thomas and Scalia, continue to insist, in effect if not by name, on the second *Cooley* doctrine. *See, e.g.*, Camps Newfound/Owatonna v. Town of Harrison, 520 U.S. 564, 1608–30 (1997); Tyler Pipe Indus., Inc. v. Wash. State Dep't of Revenue, 483 U.S. 232, 254–65 (1987) (Scalia, J., concurring in part and dissenting in part). Indeed, Justice Scalia recently went so far as to describe the dormant Commerce Clause generally as "a judicial fraud"; in this context, he suggested that the best evidence for its speciousness is "the utterly illogical holding that congressional consent enables States to enact laws that would otherwise constitute impermissible burdens upon interstate commerce. . . . How could congressional consent lift a constitutional prohibition?" Comptroller of Treasury of Md. v. Wynne, 135 S. Ct. 1787, 1808 (2015) (Scalia, J., dissenting) (citations omitted).

echo of *Marbury v. Madison*,[31] seemed self-evident to the Court: if, as the Court held, the Constitution "divested [the states] of the power to legislate on [certain] subject[s] by the grant of the commercial power to Congress, it is plain" that Congress may "not confer upon them power thus to legislate."[32] Congress may not "re-grant" or "re-convey" to the states what the Constitution expressly forbids them.[33]

The *Cooley* Court's careful analysis and resulting doctrines, at first blush, may well seem sensible. The first doctrine provided an apparently reasonable standard for determining the constitutionality of state commercial regulations absent congressional action; the second established a comparatively modest, but nontrivial, limit on Congress's Commerce Clause power. Yet for reasons that quickly become apparent upon further reflection, neither *Cooley* doctrine proved enduring.[34]

It was doubtful from the start that the Court would adhere to the second *Cooley* doctrine, for it dubiously insisted on the Court's prerogative to substitute its judgment for that of Congress on the question of the "true" nature of the commercial subject matter to be regulated (and therefore the constitutionality of state regulation of that subject matter). Whether a particular subject matter should be deemed permissibly local or exclusively national is seldom obvious. Nor is it a question of fact susceptible to judicial determination. It is hardly clear why judgments of this sort should be regarded as questions of law for judicial determination rather than fact-intensive questions of policy that call for the exercise of sound congressional judgment.[35]

---

31. Marbury v. Madison, 5 U.S. (1 Cranch) 137 (1803).

32. *Cooley*, 53 U.S. at 318.

33. *Id.*

34. The Court has never explicitly overruled or disavowed *Cooley*'s doctrines, but both have been superseded or abrogated. *See* Okla. Tax Comm'n v. Jefferson Lines, Inc., 514 U.S. 175, 181–83 (1995); United Haulers Ass'n, Inc. v. Oneida-Herkimer Solid Waste Mgmt. Auth., 550 U.S. 330, 349–50 (2007) (Scalia, J., dissenting); Tarrant Reg'l Water Dist. v. Herrmann, 656 F.3d 1222, 1233 (10th Cir. 2011); Conservation Force, Inc. v. Manning, 301 F.3d 985, 991 (9th Cir. 2002). *Cooley* nonetheless continues to be cited in dormant Commerce Clause cases. *See* LOUIS HENKIN, FOREIGN AFFAIRS AND THE US CONSTITUTION 159 (2d ed. 1996).

35. Indeed, the *Cooley* Court might have inadvertently recognized just that: in the key passage quoted above, it emphasized that "[t]he act of 1789 contains a clear and authoritative declaration by the first Congress, that the nature of this subject is such, that until Congress should find it necessary to exert its power, it should be left to the legislation of the states . . . ." Had the *Cooley* Court actually adhered to the "second *Cooley* doctrine," why should Congress's judgment in 1789 be deemed "authoritative"? Presumably it should instead have been treated as, at most, persuasive (not conclusive) evidence to assist the Court's judicial determination of the "true" (permissibly local or exclusively national) nature of the subject at issue. *Cooley*, 53 U.S. at 319. *But see* TRIBE, *supra* note 9, at 1047 n.7 (noting ambiguity in the role of the 1789 statute).

Liquor clarified the Court's thinking. In *Leisy v. Hardin* (1890),[36] the Court, citing and applying *Cooley*,[37] held that a state could not forbid the sale of liquor brought into its territory in its original package from another state. A need for uniform regulation obtained so long as Congress had not enacted any legislation to regulate a subject. Congress responded that same year by enacting the Wilson Act, which permitted state regulation of such liquor imports. The next year, in *Wilkerson v. Rahrer* (1891),[38] the Court upheld the constitutionality of the Wilson Act, thus burying the second *Cooley* doctrine.

At any rate, the Court's subsequent jurisprudence, for example, in *Prudential Insurance Co. v. Benjamin* (1946),[39] makes clear that, contrary to the second *Cooley* doctrine, Congress can indeed authorize or validate state commercial regulations on subjects that might otherwise impose unconstitutional burdens under the dormant Commerce Clause; and Congress, not the Court, authoritatively decides this question—the only limit being that its decision to grant or withhold authorization must, of course, be about commerce.

For similar reasons, the first *Cooley* doctrine did not withstand scrutiny. A moment's reflection, and later cases,[40] revealed the fragility of the putative distinction between commercial subjects that "imperatively demand" national regulation and those that may be regulated locally. And the *Cooley* doctrines proved insufficiently nuanced to resolve many of the concrete questions that arose in practice. "[J]ust 35 years after *Cooley*, it had already become clear that the classification of regulatory subject matter as 'national' or 'local,' like the earlier dichotomy between 'police' and 'commerce' regulations, was more conclusory than explanatory."[41]

---

36. 135 U.S. 100 (1890).

37. *Id.* at 109.

38. 140 U.S. 545 (1891).

39. 328 U.S. 408, 434 (1946); *see also* Camps Newfound/Owatonna v. Town of Harrison, 520 U.S. 564, 572 n.8 (1997) (collecting cases); New York v. United States, 505 U.S. 144, 171 (1992).

40. *See, e.g.*, Okla. Tax Comm'n v. Jefferson Lines, 514 U.S. 175 (1995); Tarrant Reg'l Water Dist. v. Herrmann, 656 F.3d 1222 (10th Cir. 2011).

41. Further, "[w]hether a given subject matter should be judged appropriate for state regulation often depended upon how the state proposed to regulate it in the particular case. *What the states did*, and not *what subject they did it to*, came to be seen as the crucial question . . . ." TRIBE, *supra* note 9, at 1049. Nevertheless, *Cooley* remains an important milestone in dormant Commerce Clause jurisprudence because its "basic theme" endures to this day: "the validity of state action affecting interstate commerce must be judged in light of the desirability, in terms of the Constitution's structure and goals, of permitting diverse responses to local needs and the undesirability, again evaluated by a constitutional metric, of permitting local interference with such uniformity as the unimpeded flow of interstate commerce may require." *Id.* at 1048. This principle, however, differs markedly from *Cooley*'s presumption that commercial subjects fall,

Consider, for example, the hypothetical possibility that not enough qualified local pilots had been available to guide ships through Philadelphia's harbor, causing a three-week delay to enlist the help of a licensed pilot. Or suppose Pennsylvania had enacted a law privileging its own shipping. Uniformity and diversity clearly were not the only relevant considerations. A state could regulate a commercial subject matter susceptible to, or that admitted of a need for, diverse local regulations—but in a manner that either unduly burdened interstate commerce or discriminated against other states (or foreign nations). Precisely these threats culminated in what remain, today, the chief cases that define the core of the dormant Commerce Clause doctrine.

C. The Modern Standard: *Philadelphia v. New Jersey* and *Pike v. Bruce Church*

In *Pike*,[42] the plaintiff, Bruce Church, Inc., which grew, harvested, and processed fresh produce, including cantaloupe, a highly perishable fruit, for sale throughout the United States, challenged the constitutionality of an Arizona law that required all cantaloupe grown in Arizona to be packaged in the state. The Bruce Church corporation had no packaging facility in Parker, Arizona, where it had recently spent some $3 million dollars cultivating 6,400 acres of formerly arid land for the purpose of growing high quality cantaloupe. It had therefore been transporting the uncrated Arizona cantaloupes to its nearby California packaging facility. Compliance with Arizona's statute would have required Bruce Church to build a new packing plant in Parker, Arizona, at a cost of some $200,000. The Court did not question that Arizona's law, which the state had enacted in 1929 in response to fears that "some growers were shipping inferior or deceptively packaged produce"; Arizona sought "simply to protect and enhance the reputation of growers within the State," which were legitimate state interests under longstanding precedents.[43] Yet it emphasized that the state law nonetheless unduly impeded the business of out-of-state companies such as Bruce Church. As the Court pointed out, Bruce Church would, under the Arizona law, actually end up paying a nontrivial part of the cost of enhancing the reputation of Arizona's cantaloupe producers: "If the Commerce Clause forbids a State to require work to be done within its jurisdiction to promote local employment," as the Court had held in an earlier decision,[44] "then surely it cannot permit a State to require a person to

---

by nature, into either the local or national category; or that the Court's judgment in this regard conclusively determines the reach of the dormant Commerce Clause.

42. 397 U.S. 137 (1970).

43. *Id.* at 143, 145.

44. *Id.*

go into a local packing business solely for the sake of enhancing the reputation of other producers within its borders."[45]

The Court's decision in *Pike*, as it was at pains to make clear, applied a more "general rule that emerges" from its prior precedents, which "can be phrased as follows":

> Where the statute regulates even-handedly to effectuate a legitimate local public interest, and its effects on interstate commerce are only incidental, it will be upheld unless the burden imposed on such commerce is clearly excessive in relation to the putative local benefits. If a legitimate local purpose is found, then the question becomes one of degree. And the extent of the burden that will be tolerated will of course depend on the nature of the local interest involved, and on whether it could be promoted as well with a lesser impact on interstate activities.[46]

Pike's "general rule" remains "the starting point for dormant Commerce Clause cases."[47]

In *Philadelphia v. New Jersey*,[48] widely taken to be the classic "discrimination" case in Commerce Clause jurisprudence, the Court considered, not an undue burden on interstate commerce caused by a facially nondiscriminatory law promoting legitimate state interests, but rather a state law that, in effect if not by design, discriminated against out-of-state commerce. Philadelphia challenged New Jersey's law prohibiting "the importation of most solid or liquid waste which originated or was collected outside the territorial limits of the State,"[49] arguing, in relevant part, that the New Jersey legislature's parochial interest in economic protectionism had motivated the law. But the Court held that nothing turned on the state legislature's motivation: "[T]he evils of protectionism can reside in legislative means as well as legislative ends.... [W]hatever New Jersey's ultimate purpose, it may not be accomplished by discriminating against articles of commerce coming from outside the State unless there is some reason, apart from their origin, to treat them differently. Both on its face and in its plain effect, [the law] violates this principle of nondiscrimination."[50] In an opinion by Justice Potter Stewart,

45. *Id.*

46. *Id.* at 142 (internal citations omitted).

47. HENKIN, *supra* note 34, at 160 nn.12–14.

48. 437 U.S. 617 (1978).

49. *Id.* at 618 (internal quotation marks omitted).

50. *Id.* at 626–27.

the Court struck down the statute because, it found, articles coming from outside New Jersey were treated differently for no constitutionally legitimate reason.[51]

Combining *Pike* and *Philadelphia*, the Court today examines, first, whether a state law discriminates against commerce, looking to *Philadelphia* for guidance; and second, absent a finding of discrimination, whether, under *Pike*, the law imposes a burden on interstate commerce that is clearly excessive in relation to the putative local benefits. To decide these issues, it often looks to several later decisions, which helped to clarify what makes a burden constitutionally undue or excessive. In *Healy v. Beer Institute* (1989),[52] for example, the Court said that "a state law that has the practical effect of regulating commerce occurring wholly outside that State's borders, is invalid under the Commerce Clause."[53] And in *Complete Auto Transit, Inc. v. Brady* (1977), it held that when a state tax is at issue, that tax will not invalidated as an impermissible burden provided it "is applied to an activity with a substantial nexus with the taxing State, is fairly apportioned, does not discriminate against interstate commerce, and is fairly related to the services provided by the State."[54]

D. The Market Participant Exception to the Dormant Commerce Clause

Dormant Commerce Clause doctrine is subject to a significant exception. Beginning in 1976, a series of Supreme Court cases established that when a state acts as a market "participant" rather than a market "regulator," the dormant Commerce Clause does not similarly constrain its activities.[55] The first, *Hughes*

---

51. In an effort to preserve a scarce natural resource—landfill sites—New Jersey had "impose[d] on out-of-state commercial interests the full burden of conserving the State's remaining landfill space." *Id.* at 628. It had "overtly moved to slow or freeze the flow of commerce for protectionist reasons. . . . What is crucial is the attempt by one State to isolate itself from a problem common to many like erecting a barrier against the movement of interstate trade." *Id.* When the state does not treat interstate commerce even-handedly, the state regulation is almost always per se invalid. Justice Rehnquist, writing in dissent, saw the New Jersey statute as similar to quarantine laws that had not been considered forbidden protectionist measures, even though they were directed against out-of-state commerce. "I simply see no way to distinguish solid waste . . . from germ-infected rags, diseased meat, and other noxious items . . . ." *Id.* at 632 (Rehnquist, J., dissenting).

52. 491 U.S. 324 (1989). In *Healy*, the Court invalidated a Connecticut law requiring beer companies to affirm that they were not selling beer at a lower price in Connecticut than in four neighboring states.

53. *Id.* at 332.

54. Complete Auto Transit, Inc. v. Brady, 430 U.S. 274, 279 (1977). In *Brady*, Justice Blackmun, writing for a unanimous Court, sustained a Mississippi tax against a dormant Commerce Clause challenge.

55. These cases were summarized by Justice Byron White for a plurality of the Court in South-Central Timber Development, Inc. v. Wunnicke, 467 U.S. 82, 100–01 (1984).

v. Alexandria Scrap Corp. (1976),[56] involved a Maryland program intended to cut down on the number of junked automobiles in the state by paying for junked cars. But Maryland insisted on stricter documentation from out-of-state than in-state scrap processors. Alexandria Scrap Corporation challenged the program on the ground that it impeded interstate commerce. The Court rejected this contention, holding that "[n]othing in the purposes animating the Commerce Clause prohibits a State, in the absence of congressional action, from participating in the market and [insofar as it acts as such a participant] exercising the right to favor its own citizens over others."[57] In 1980, for substantially the same reason, the Court upheld a South Dakota policy of restricting the sale of cement from a state-owned plant to state residents.[58] And in *White v. Mass. Council of Construction Employers, Inc.* (1983), the Court upheld an order of the mayor of Boston requiring that construction projects funded in whole or in part by the city be performed by a workforce of at least 50 percent city residents.[59]

In two more recent cases, however, the Court limited the market participant exception. In *South-Central Timber Development, Inc. v. Wunnicke* (1984), it invalidated an Alaska program under which the state sold state-owned timber on condition that the purchaser process the timber in Alaska before shipping it out of the state. The Court found that although Alaska participated in the timber market, it could not claim the same status in the context of the "downstream" processing market.[60] "Participation," in other words, has its limits and does not extend to every stage in a sequential commercial activity:

> The limit of the market-participant doctrine must be that it allows a State to impose burdens on commerce within the market in which it is a participant, but allows it to go no further. The State may not impose conditions, whether by statute, regulation, or contract that have a substantial regulatory effect outside of that particular market.[61]

---

56. 426 U.S. 794 (1976).

57. *Id.* at 809.

58. "The basic distinction . . . between States as market participants and States as market regulators," the Court said, "makes good sense and sound law." It noted that there was a "'long recognized right of trader or manufacturer, engaged in an entirely private business, freely to exercise his own independent discretion as to parties with whom he will deal.'" Reeves, Inc. v. Stake, 447 U.S. 429, 438–39 (1980) (quoting United States v. Colgate & Co., 250 U.S. 300, 307 (1919)).

59. White v. Mass. Council of Constr. Emps., Inc., 460 U.S. 204, 215 (1983).

60. *Wunnicke*, 467 U.S. at 95.

61. *Id.* at 97.

The market-participant exception therefore did not immunize Alaska's downstream regulation of a market in which the state did not participate merely because the state acted as a market participant at an earlier stage in the same industry.[62]

Most recently, in *Camps Newfound/Owatonna v. Town of Harrison* (1997),[63] the Court considered "whether an otherwise generally applicable state property tax violates the [dormant] Commerce Clause . . . because its exemption for property owned by charitable institutions excludes organizations operated principally for the benefit of nonresidents."[64] The Town of Harrison had enacted a local law under which it refused the exemption at issue to a Maine nonprofit corporation operating a religious camp because it served principally (about 95 percent) nonresidents.

Once again, the Court stressed the limits of the market-participant exception, rejecting Maine's contention that the tax exemption constituted a state "proprietary activity," and stating in no uncertain terms that such an "exemption is not the sort of direct state involvement in the market that falls within the market-participation doctrine."[65] Justice Stevens reasoned that "nothing short of a dramatic expansion of the market-participant exception would support its application to this case. . . . Maine's tax exemption—which sweeps to cover broad swathes of the nonprofit sector—must be viewed as action taken in the State's sovereign capacity rather than a proprietary decision to make an entry into all of the markets in which the exempted charities function. . . . The Town's version of the market-participant exception would swallow the rule against discriminatory tax schemes."[66]

II. Origins and Development of the Dormant Foreign Commerce Clause

For years, the Court did not distinguish between foreign and interstate commerce in its elaboration of the dormant Commerce Clause. In *Brown v. Maryland* (1827),[67] Chief Justice Marshall applied dormant *interstate* Commerce Clause analysis to foreign commerce in striking down a state law that required a

62. *Id.* at 98.

63. 520 U.S. 564 (1997).

64. *Id.* at 657.

65. *Id.* at 593.

66. *Id.* at 593–94 (citations and internal quotation marks omitted).

67. 25 U.S. (12 Wheat.) 419 (1827).

state-issued license to sell a package imported from a foreign country.[68] By 1847, Chief Justice Taney's words in the *License Cases* had come to represent the conventional wisdom. "The power to regulate commerce among the several states," he wrote, "is granted to Congress in the same clause, and by the same words, as the power to regulate commerce with foreign nations, and is co-extensive with it."[69]

A. *Japan Line, Ltd. v. County of Los Angeles* (1979)

In 1979, that changed. No longer would Congress's foreign and interstate powers, and consequently limits on the states, be coextensive in the context of dormant Commerce Clause analysis. *Japan Line, Ltd. v. County of Los Angeles* (1979)[70] involved a nondiscriminatory ad valorem property tax levied on foreign-owned cargo containers. The president filed an amicus curiae brief opposing the tax.[71] Los Angeles argued, however, that its tax met the criteria imposed by the test that the Court applied to determine the constitutionality of a state tax under the Interstate Commerce Clause,[72] and it maintained that dormant Commerce Clause analysis is the same whether it involves interstate or foreign commerce.[73]

The Court found two reasons to reject this contention, however, and fashioned two commensurate doctrinal requirements that would thereafter be applied to dormant foreign-commerce cases—beyond those enumerated in the canonical test contained in *Lopez*. It held that Congress's power to "regulate Commerce with foreign Nations" required a more extensive constitutional

---

68. "What would be the language of a foreign government," Chief Justice Marshall asked rhetorically, "which should be informed that its merchants, after importing according to law, were forbidden to sell the merchandise imported? What answer would the United States give to the complaints and just reproaches to which such an extraordinary circumstance would expose them? No apology could be received, or even offered. Such a state of things would break up commerce." *Id.* at 447.

69. 46 U.S. (5 How.) 504, 548 (1847). This is not strictly accurate, for the Constitution does not confer the foreign and interstate commerce powers "by the same words." It distinguishes *interstate* commerce, which Congress may regulate "*among* the several states," from foreign commerce, which Congress may regulate "*with* foreign nations." U.S. CONST. art. I, § 8, cl. 3 (emphasis added). On the arguable import of this distinction, see Anthony J. Colangelo, *The Foreign Commerce Clause*, 96 VA. L. REV. 949, 954 (2010). *But see* HENKIN, *supra* note 34, at 356 n.9.

70. 441 U.S. 434 (1979).

71. *Id.* at 435. In later decisions, the Court has made clear that amicus briefs filed by the executive branch cannot affect the constitutionality of a particular state tax under the Commerce Clause. *See, e.g.*, Barclays Bank PLC v. Franchise Tax Bd., 512 U.S. 298, 299–300 (1994).

72. Complete Auto Transit, Inc. v. Brady, 430 U.S. 274 (1977).

73. *See* HENKIN, *supra* note 34, at 356 n.9 (collecting cases).

inquiry to supplement the usual *Lopez* standards:[74] "When a State seeks to tax the instrumentalities of foreign commerce, two additional considerations . . . come into play. The first is the enhanced risk of multiple taxation. It is a commonplace of constitutional jurisprudence that multiple taxation may well be offensive to the Commerce Clause."[75]

"Second," the Court said, "a state tax on the instrumentalities of foreign commerce may impair federal uniformity in an area where federal uniformity is essential. Foreign commerce is preeminently a matter of national concern. 'In international relations and with respect to foreign intercourse and trade the people of the United States act through a single government with unified and adequate national power.' "[76] The Court proceeded to spell out that it understood the imperative of federal uniformity to require that the nation "speak with one voice," lest foreign nations retaliate against other states or the United States as a whole.[77] Under this new, supplemental test, it found California's ad valorem tax, as applied to the Japanese plaintiff corporation's cargo containers, unconstitutional—both because the tax risked multiple taxation and because it offended the one-voice principle. Notably, the Court rejected California's contention that any multiple taxation caused by the tax could be cured with congressional action or international agreement, remarking that where Congress has not acted, the Court and not the state legislature is the final arbiter of competing state and national interests.

---

74. *Japan Line*, 441 U.S. at 446.

75. *Id.*

76. *Id.* at 448 (quoting Bd. of Trustees v. United States, 289 U.S. 48, 59 (1933)).

77. It reasoned as follows:

> [I]n discussing the Import–Export Clause, this Court . . . spoke of the Framers' overriding concern that "the Federal Government must speak with one voice when regulating commercial relations with foreign governments." The need for federal uniformity is no less paramount in ascertaining the negative implications of Congress' power to "regulate Commerce with foreign Nations" under the Commerce Clause.
>
> A state tax on instrumentalities of foreign commerce may frustrate the achievement of federal uniformity in several ways. If the State imposes an apportioned tax, international disputes over reconciling apportionment formulae may arise. If a novel state tax creates an asymmetry in the international tax structure, foreign nations disadvantaged by the levy may retaliate against American-owned instrumentalities present in their jurisdictions. Such retaliation of necessity would be directed at American transportation equipment in general, not just that of the taxing State, so that the Nation as a whole would suffer. If other States followed the taxing State's example, various instrumentalities of commerce could be subjected to varying degrees of multiple taxation, a result that would plainly prevent this Nation from "speaking with one voice" in regulating foreign commerce. . . . If a state tax contravenes either of these precepts, it is unconstitutional under the Commerce Clause.

Id. at 450–51.

Japan Line did not, however, make clear how far the Court would go in applying the new one-voice doctrine[78] to strike down state laws under the dormant Foreign Commerce Clause. It had occasion to clarify matters in cases in 1983, 1986, and 1994. Each time, its answer seemed the same: not far at all. The state statutes in each of these cases were upheld against claims that they ran afoul of the two supplemental *Japan Line* criteria.

In 1983, in *Container Corp. of America. v. Franchise Tax Board*,[79] the Court upheld California's income-based corporate franchise tax, as applied to a multinational enterprise, against a comprehensive challenge under the Foreign Commerce Clause. The case involved a corporate taxpayer domiciled and headquartered in the United States; in addition to its stateside components, the taxpayer had a number of overseas subsidiaries incorporated in the countries in which they operated. The Court quickly dispelled concerns that the one-voice doctrine called for drastic new limits on the breadth of state power under the dormant Foreign Commerce Clause. It observed that it had little competence to determine whether or when foreign nations might be offended by a particular state act. At any rate, the United States had the right, as a sovereign nation, to let the states do what they will, although it would, of course, remain liable for any foreign-affairs consequences or violations of international obligations.[80] The

78. The one-voice concept preexisted *Japan Line*, *see, e.g.,* Brown v. Maryland, 25 U.S. (12 Wheat.) 419 (1827), but the Court had never before suggested that it required a limit on state commercial regulations absent congressional action.

79. 463 U.S. 159 (1983).

80. The Court reasoned in this regard:

> We come finally to the second inquiry suggested by *Japan Line*—whether California's decision to adopt formula apportionment in the international context was impermissible because it may impair federal uniformity . . . and prevents the Federal Government from speaking with one voice in international trade. [W]e must keep in mind that if a state tax merely has foreign resonances, but does not implicate foreign affairs, we cannot infer, [absent] some explicit directive from Congress, . . . that treatment of foreign income at the federal level mandates identical treatment by the States. Thus, a state tax at variance with federal policy will violate the one voice standard if it either implicates foreign policy issues which must be left to the Federal Government or violates a clear federal directive. The second of these considerations is, of course, essentially a species of pre-emption analysis.
>
> The most obvious foreign policy implication of a state tax is the threat it might pose of offending our foreign trading partners and leading them to retaliate against the Nation as a whole. [H]owever . . . [t]his Court has little competence in determining precisely when foreign nations will be offended by particular acts, and even less competence in deciding how to balance a particular risk of retaliation against the sovereign right of the United States as a whole to let the States tax as they please. The best that we can do, in the absence of explicit action by Congress, is to attempt to develop objective standards that reflect very general observations about the imperatives of international trade and international relations.

Container Corp. of Am. v. Franchise Tax Bd., 463 U.S. 159, 193–94 (1983) (citations omitted) (internal quotations omitted).

Court also observed that in *Container Corp.*, the executive had not opposed the tax, as it had in *Japan Line*,[81] while making clear that the views of the president could not be conclusive of a constitutional question under the Commerce Clause.

In 1986, the Court continued to retreat from the one-voice doctrine in the dormant foreign-commerce context. In *Wardair Canada, Inc. v. Florida Dept. of Revenue* (1986),[82] it assessed the constitutionality of a Florida tax on all aviation fuel purchased in Florida, without regard to the amount the carrier consumed within the state or the amount of its in-state business. The United States, again expressing its views as amicus curiae, contended that Florida's tax threatened the federal government's capacity to speak with one voice for the nation in its international relations. The Court found, however, that nothing in federal statutory or treaty law barred the challenged state tax. To the contrary, the law as it stood "acquiesce[d] in taxation of the sale of that fuel by political subdivisions of countries."[83] It therefore let Florida's tax stand.

B. *Barclays Bank PLC v. Franchise Tax Board* (1994)

In 1994, the Court seemed to bury the one-voice doctrine further in the context of the dormant Foreign Commerce Clause. The 1983 *Container Corp.* decision had not ruled on the constitutionality of California's worldwide taxing scheme as applied to domestic corporations with foreign parents, or to foreign corporations with either foreign parents or foreign subsidiaries. In *Barclays Bank PLC v. Franchise Tax Board* (1994),[84] it revisited the validity of California's taxing system and answered these questions. In *Barclays Bank*, the Court began by reiterating, as it had said in *Japan Line*, that "in the unique context of foreign

81.

> A state tax may, of course, have foreign policy implications other than the threat of retaliation. We note, however, that in this case, unlike *Japan Line*, the Executive Branch has decided not to file an amicus curiae brief in opposition to the state tax. The lack of such a submission is by no means dispositive. Nevertheless, when combined with all the other considerations we have discussed, it does suggest that the foreign policy of the United States—whose nuances, we must emphasize again, are much more the province of the Executive Branch and Congress than of this Court—is not seriously threatened by California's decision to apply the unitary business concept and formula apportionment in calculating appellant's taxable income.

Id. at 195–96 (citations omitted).

82. 477 U.S. 1 (1986).

83. *Id.* at 10.

84. 512 U.S. 298 (1994).

commerce, a State's power is further constrained because of the special need for federal authority."[85] And it repeated that a tax affecting foreign commerce raises the additional concerns of an enhanced risk of multiple taxation and a need for the federal government to speak with one voice when regulating commercial relations with foreign governments. But the Court said that it had "left the ball in Congress' court" in *Container Corp.* Congress could have enacted legislation preempting California's method of taxation. It had not.[86] California's method, in its view, should therefore be deemed constitutional absent congressional indication to the contrary. Oddly, the Court did not seem to see any tension between this reasoning and its rejection, in *Japan Line*, of California's similar contention that, if Congress found its ad valorem tax problematic, it had plenary power under the Commerce Clause to preempt it.

C. *National Foreign Trade Council v. Natsios* (1994)

National Foreign Trade Council v. Natsios,[87] a case decided by the U.S. Court of Appeals for the First Circuit, is, despite its formal limitation to the geographical limits of the First Circuit, the most significant dormant Foreign Commerce Clause case decided since the Supreme Court last addressed the issue in 1994—for three reasons. First, whereas the U.S. Supreme Court had not relied upon the doctrine to invalidate a state law since its 1979 decision in *Japan Line* (leading to speculation that aggressive enforcement of the clause had fallen into disfavor), the Court of Appeals applied the doctrine, as an alternative to its dormant foreign-affairs doctrine analysis (see Chapter 4) to invalidate a prominent state statute, and it reasoned in terms quite different from those found in the Supreme Court's more recent pronouncements on the doctrine. Second, the Supreme Court, reviewing *Natsios*, declined to reach the First Circuit's treatment of the dormant Foreign Commerce Clause.[88] Third, the Court of Appeals inferred from the doctrine a breathtaking new prohibition against *non*-protectionist state regulation of extraterritorial conduct—whatever the effect of that conduct within the state's

85. *Id.* at 311 (internal quotation marks and citations to *Japan Line* omitted).

86. "[H]ad Congress, the branch responsible for the regulation of foreign commerce . . . considered nationally uniform use of separate accounting 'essential,' it could have enacted legislation prohibiting the States from taxing corporate income based on the worldwide combined reporting method. In the 11 years that have elapsed since our decision in *Container Corp.*, Congress has failed to enact such legislation." *Id.* at 324.

87. 181 F.3d 38 (1st Cir. 1999), *aff'd on other grounds*, Crosby v. NFTC, 530 U.S. 363 (2000).

88. *Crosby*, 530 U.S. at 374 n.8. Or the Court's questionable treatment of the dormant foreign-affairs doctrine. The Supreme Court instead upheld the First Circuit's invalidation of the statute based on ordinary preemption principles.

territory or on its residents, and whatever its validity under international law. The ramifications of this new prohibition would be far-reaching were it ever endorsed by the Supreme Court.

Natsios overturned the Massachusetts Burma law.[89] Enacted by the state in 1996, the law sharply limited the ability of Massachusetts and its agents to purchase goods from or engage the services of individuals or companies doing business (broadly defined) in Myanmar (Burma). The state enacted it in an effort to condemn and impede the autocratic rule and human rights violations of the State Law and Order Council (SLORC), which had nullified Burma's elections and imposed martial law in 1989. The First Circuit found that the Massachusetts law facially discriminated against foreign commerce,[90] interfered with the federal government's ability to speak with one voice,[91] and violated the Foreign Commerce Clause merely because Massachusetts, in its view, sought to "regulate conduct beyond its borders and beyond the borders of this country." (We discuss extraterritoriality in Chapter 7 in connection with the relationship among federal common law, customary international law, and state law.) Although the breadth of its decision potentially raised serious issues, the Supreme Court's decision in *Crosby*, affirming unanimously on straightforward preemption grounds, may suggest that the Court found much of the First Circuit's analysis—its dormant Foreign Commerce Clause reasoning included—dubious.

D. The Market Participant Exception to the Dormant Foreign Commerce Clause

The Supreme Court has not yet decided whether the market-participant exception applies to the dormant foreign-commerce doctrine. In *Reeves*,[92] however, the Court hinted in a footnote that if the exception *does* apply, it would likely be a narrower one: "We have no occasion to explore the limits imposed on state

---

89. "An Act Regarding State Contracts with Companies Doing Business with or in Burma (Myanmar)," MASS. GEN. LAWS CH. 130, §§7:22G–7:22M, 40 F. ½ (West 1997).

90. "When the Constitution speaks of foreign commerce," the court wrote, "it is not referring only to attempts to regulate the conduct of foreign companies; it is also referring to attempts to restrict the actions of American companies overseas." Citing *Cooley*, the court said that "[l]ong-standing Supreme Court precedent indicates that the Framers were concerned with 'discriminations favorable or adverse to commerce with particular foreign nations [under] state laws.'" *Natsios*, 181 F.3d at 68 (internal citation omitted).

91. Nothing in *Barclays Bank*, the court said, dismantled the one-voice test or suggested that "we should reduce the amount of scrutiny that a state law that directly regulates foreign commerce should receive." *Id.* at 69.

92. Reeves, Inc. v. Stake, 447 U.S. 429 (1980).

proprietary actions by the 'foreign commerce' Clause. . . . We note, however, that Commerce Clause scrutiny may well be more rigorous when a restraint on foreign commerce is alleged."[93] That the exception does apply, however, has been a common view among lower state and federal courts, discussed below.[94] A number of these opinions concern the constitutionality of "Buy American" laws, which require generally that materials purchased under government contracts be produced in the United States. The Supreme Court has not ruled on the constitutionality of these laws, and some of them predate *Japan Line* and therefore assumed that the dormant interstate-commerce and foreign-commerce doctrine analyses were identical. But there is good reason to believe that they would be sustained.[95]

In the 1977 case of *K.S B. Technical Sales Corp. v. North Jersey District Water Supply Commission*,[96] for example, the New Jersey Supreme Court observed that "the cases scrutinizing state regulations affecting commerce, in the absence of interference with the foreign affairs power, seem to have made no distinction between interstate and foreign commerce."[97] Whether it would have come to the same conclusion after *Japan Line* is unclear; the court did note that "some differences between interstate and foreign commerce exist," but it saw "no need in this factual context to differentiate between the two."[98] The *K.S.B.* court upheld New Jersey's Buy American laws, citing *Alexandria Scrap* and reasoning that a state's legislation with respect to its purchase of goods and materials for its own end use, absent federal action, is not subject to the usual Commerce Clause restrictions.[99]

---

93. *Id.* at 437 n.9.

94. *See, e.g.*, Tri-M Group, LLC v. Sharp, 638 F.3d 406 (3d Cir. 2011).

95. *See* TRIBE, *supra* note 9.

96. 381 A.2d 774, 784–89 (N.J. 1977).

97. *Id.*

98. *Id.* at 788.

99. *Id.* at 787. The court further rejected the argument that the laws were invalid under *Zschernig*, noting that New Jersey had not, in enacting the restrictions, made any negative judgment concerning foreign countries' domestic policies:

> It is quite clear that the New Jersey Legislature, by means of the statutory provisions under review, has not authorized its local units of government to engage in the sensitive business of evaluating the politics of countries whose citizens seek to market their products in this State. The Buy American provisions apply without any discrimination based on the ideology of the seller's country. Nor is there any evidence to suggest that the political climate in a potential foreign bidder's nation has ever motivated the inclusion of the Buy American condition in an invitation for bids or that its inclusion is predicated on an assessment of the internal policies of any foreign country.

A similar Pennsylvania statute was also found to be immune from a dormant Foreign Commerce Clause challenge under the market-participant exception. The law required certain suppliers that provided a public agency with products containing steel to use American-made steel. In 1990, in *Trojan Techs. v. Pennsylvania*,[100] the U.S. Court of Appeals for the Third Circuit read *White* as on point.[101] *National Foreign Trade Council, Inc. v. Giannoulias* (2007)[102] involved a challenge to the Illinois Sudan Act, which restricted the deposit of state funds in financial institutions whose customers had certain types of connections with Sudan. It also restricted the investment of public pension funds in certain Sudan-connected entities.

The Third Circuit found the law preempted by federal law but also said that it ran afoul of the dormant foreign-affairs power. Turning to the dormant foreign-commerce doctrine, it concluded that it need not decide whether the market-participant exception applied because the doctrine does not, at any rate, apply to local subdivisions.[103] In *Natsios*, the First Circuit indicated that the market-participant exception might not apply at all in dormant Foreign Commerce Clause analysis,[104] or if it did, would require a much more rigorous degree of scrutiny.[105]

---

100. 916 F.2d 903 (3d Cir. 1990).

101. "If employees of a private contractor can be thought to be in relationship with the city," the appeals court reasoned, "we think it equally clear that suppliers of a local public entity can be thought to be 'supplying for the state.'" It continued: "As the ultimately controlling public purchaser, the Commonwealth enjoys the same right to specify to its suppliers the source of steel to be used in any supplies provided as is enjoyed by similarly situated private purchasers." *Trojan Techs.*, 916 F.2d at 911. The court was "not persuaded that the fact that the products being excluded are of foreign origin countenances a different result." *Id.* at 912. It noted the Supreme Court's suggestion that statutes affecting foreign commerce are subject to a more searching review, *Reeves*, 447 U.S. at 437 n.9, but found that the "the Pennsylvania statute survives even the most searching review." *Trojan Techs.*, 916 F.2d at 912.

102. 523 F. Supp. 2d 731 (N.D. Ill. 2007).

103. "Illinois is not acting exclusively as a market participant through its enforcement of the . . . Act. The Act's amendment to the Pension Code affects not just state-controlled pension funds but also the pension funds of municipal entities [and] the market participant doctrine does not apply to the state when the market participants are local political subdivisions." *Id.* at 748.

104. *Natsios*, 181 F.3d at 65.

105. The court said that "[t]he Supreme Court has repeatedly suggested that state regulations that touch on foreign commerce receive a greater degree of scrutiny than do regulations that affect only domestic commerce." *Id.* at 66. In any event, the court concluded, Massachusetts was not a market participant: Massachusetts "had crossed over the line from market participant to market regulator." *Id.* at 63. The state was engaged, in effect, in downstream regulation: "the Massachusetts law, by creating a selective purchasing list, creates a mechanism to monitor the ongoing activities of private actors. This monitoring is not limited to individual

III. Assessment

The dormant foreign-commerce doctrine begins with and includes the same two-part analysis as the dormant interstate-commerce doctrine.[106] First, a state statute that discriminates, whether on its face or in effect, against interstate commerce is virtually per se invalid.[107] Second, nondiscriminatory state regulations with no more than incidental effects on commerce are valid unless the burden imposed on commerce is clearly excessive in relation to the local benefits.[108] In addition, if the issue is a state tax on interstate commerce, then, absent congressional approval, that tax will not survive dormant Commerce Clause scrutiny if the taxpayer challenging it demonstrates that the tax either (1) applies to an activity lacking a substantial nexus to the taxing state, (2) is not fairly apportioned, (3) discriminates against interstate commerce, or (4) is not fairly related to the services provided by the state.[109] These criteria also apply to state restrictions on foreign commerce but call for a more extensive constitutional inquiry "because matters of concern to the entire nation are implicated."[110]

In *Japan Line*, however, the Court decided that a state tax on foreign commerce implicates two additional considerations: first, the enhanced risk of multiple taxation, and second, the risk that a state tax on foreign commerce may impair federal uniformity in an area that demands federal uniformity.[111] As the Court said in 1976, "the Federal Government must speak with one voice when regulating commercial relations with foreign governments."[112] There is, finally,

---

purchasing decisions. Further, Massachusetts is attempting to regulate unrelated activities of its contractors once a contract is signed but before its performance is completed." *Id.* at 64. The court rejected Massachusetts's argument that "it acts as private actors do because some companies have ceased doing business with Burma due to human rights concerns." *Id.* at 65. The court acknowledged that "Massachusetts has created a market," but, it said, Massachusetts "cannot regulate the market that it has created so as to regulate conduct elsewhere not related to that market.... Massachusetts's action here is akin to prohibiting purchases from companies that do business in states that have policies with which Massachusetts disagrees. This would plainly be unconstitutional under the domestic Commerce Clause. Massachusetts surely cannot do the same in the international context, as state actions that affect international commerce receive even greater scrutiny than do actions that affect interstate commerce." *Id.* at 65.

106. Japan Line, Ltd. v. County of Los Angeles, 441 U.S. 434 (1979).

107. Oregon Waste Sys., Inc. v. Dep't of Envtl. Quality, 511 U.S. 93, 93–94 (1994).

108. Pike v. Bruce Church, Inc., 397 U.S. 137, 142 (1970).

109. Barclays Bank Plc v. Franchise Tax Bd., 512 U.S. 298 (1994).

110. Kraft General Foods v. Iowa Dep't of Revenue & Fin., 505 U.S. 71, 79 (1992).

111. Japan Line, Ltd. v. County of Los Angeles, 441 U.S. 434 (1979).

112. Michelin Tire Corp. v. Wages, 423 U.S. 276, 285 (1976).

authority to the effect that the dormant Commerce Clause limits state authority to project their laws extraterritorially. (See Chapter 7.) Yet the gravamen of the Court's rationale for *Japan Line*—a decision that stands all but alone in its departure from traditional dormant Commerce Clause analysis, as well as in its bifurcation of foreign and interstate commerce for these purposes—lies in the two rationales stressed by Justice Blackmun: the risk of multiple taxation and the need for national uniformity.

Neither withstands scrutiny. Barring exceptional circumstances, the Court's traditional approach, with certain minor modifications, not only suffices but would restore doctrinal clarity and simplicity.

The first reason for distinguishing foreign from interstate commerce concerned the risk of multiple taxation. Foreign commerce, the Court supposed, unlike domestic commerce, may be taxed by both a state and a foreign government. A more searching judicial inquiry, it believed, is therefore appropriate to vitiate any worry about clogging the channels of foreign commerce. Concern about the burden of multiple taxation is in general well founded. But the conclusion that traditional dormant Commerce Clause analysis can't handle the concern is not.

Recall that the Court's settled approach is to strike down state regulations if "the burden imposed on . . . commerce is clearly excessive in relation to the putative local benefits."[113] A state regulatory scheme that imposes multiple taxes on the same articles or instrumentalities clearly could constitute an excessive burden, whether it involves foreign or domestic commerce. Judicial application of this approach might therefore differ in degree; a court's evaluation of the nature and scope of the burden on commerce in diverse contexts involving foreign commerce and state regulations should, of course, be sensitive to the facts. Yet there is no need for a supplemental judicial standard. *Pike*'s balancing standard suffices. Indeed, assuming the Court has applied *Pike*'s standard correctly in the first place, the application of *Japan Line*'s first supplemental criterion may well be substantively duplicative in practice. Before some courts, plaintiffs might get, in effect, two bites at the "constitutional apple."

The second reason *Japan Line* gave to hold state regulations on foreign commerce to a tighter standard under dormant foreign-commerce doctrine is the need for national uniformity—the imperative for the nation to "speak with one voice" in international trade and relations. The one-voice concern not only threads through the Court's dormant Foreign Commerce Clause opinions:[114] it

113. *Pike*, 397 U.S. at 142.

114. *See* Container Corp. of Am. v. Franchise Tax Bd., 463 U.S. 159, 195 (1983); Wardair Canada v. Florida Dep't of Revenue, 477 U.S. 1, 4 (1986).

has since been invoked in a host of other foreign relations contexts. It animates, for example, the Court's analysis of presumptions governing statutory shipping regulations,[115] state-imposed economic sanctions in the Massachusetts Burma law at issue in *Crosby*,[116] the insurance-disclosure requirements struck down in *Garamendi*,[117] and most recently, the exclusivity of the president's power to recognize foreign governments even in the face of inconsistent congressional action.[118] With respect to the latter, note that the one-voice doctrine has now migrated from the context of foreign relations federalism, in which it originated, to that of federal separation of powers. Especially in the latter context, it is not at all obvious that the one-voice principle is appropriate, and the doctrine's growing traction is unfortunate even in its original federalism context. A closer look reveals why.

First, in the separation-of-powers context, its premise is simply wrong. The Constitution does not presuppose national uniformity in foreign policy; to the contrary, it recognizes the inevitability of fractiousness, as reflected in Edward Corwin's famous observation that the Constitution is an invitation to struggle for the privilege of directing American foreign policy.[119] Struggle implies cacophony, discord, and parlous, disagreeing voices, not one nation singing together in harmony from the same hymnal. Sarah Cleveland has detailed many of the recent clashes between Congress and the president over foreign policy issues.[120]

Second, in the federalism context, as emphasized throughout this book, although the federal government possesses *theoretically* plenary power, the simple fact is that it has neither the desire nor the capacity to exercise plenary foreign-affairs power, exclusive of state and local activities and initiatives. The state activities described in Chapter 2 typically benefit rather than harm the national interest, and if particular local activities turn out to be problematic for the nation, Congress always retains the power to preempt them. The realm of government foreign-affairs activities is also vast. Even if it had sufficient resources, the federal government almost surely would be unable to monopolize foreign affairs—and again, has no reason to.

---

115. *See* Ray v. Atlantic Richfield Co., 435 U.S. 151, 166 (1978) (stating that "the Nation was to speak with one voice with respect to tanker-design standards").

116. *See* Crosby v. Nat'l Foreign Trade Council, 530 U.S. 363, 381 (2000).

117. *See* Am. Ins. Ass'n v. Garamendi, 539 U.S. 396, 399 (2003). For analysis of *Garamendi* and the dormant foreign-affairs doctrine, see Chapter 4.

118. Zivotofsky *ex rel.* Zivotofsky v. Kerry, 135 S. Ct. 2076 (2015).

119. *See* Edward Corwin, The President 1787–1984, at 201 (Randall Bland et al. eds., 5th ed. 1984).

120. Sarah H. Cleveland, *Crosby and 'One-Voice' Myth in U.S. Foreign Relations*, 46 Vill. L. Rev. 975 (2001).

The Supreme Court itself has declined to abide by the supposed one-voice edict absent congressional action. In *Barclays Bank*, the Court upheld California's controversial worldwide-reporting method of taxation even in the face of a series of executive-branch actions, statements, and amicus filings criticizing that method.[121] *Barclays Bank* conforms to numerous earlier foreign-relations cases in which the Court did not hesitate to speak with a voice different from that of the executive branch—from *Youngstown Sheet & Tube Co. v. Sawyer*,[122] where the Court invalidated President Truman's seizure of the steel mills during the Korean War, to *Medellín v. Texas*,[123] where it overturned President George Bush's order directing that the courts of the State of Texas review certain convictions. *Medellín* almost surely threatened the interest of the nation and its citizens, and risked retaliation by foreign nations (e.g., failure to comply with consular obligations toward U.S. citizens) far more than the ad valorem tax at issue in *Japan Line*.

Third, although the presumptively supreme "one voice" invoked is typically that of the executive,[124] Congress, not the executive, is constitutionally empowered to regulate foreign commerce. Congress, not the executive, is constitutionally empowered to grant exemptions for state regulation of foreign commerce through silence or express statutory approval.[125] Once again, the Court has acknowledged this. In *Barclays Bank*, Justice Ginsburg dismissed the various indicia of the federal government's "one voice" proffered by the plaintiff taxpayers, including "a series of Executive Branch statements, and *amicus* filings, made both before and after [the Court's] decision in *Container Corp*," rejecting the argument that these documents collectively constituted "a 'clear federal directive'" prohibiting California's worldwide combined reporting method.[126] But the reason for Justice Ginsburg's decision had far less to do with the nature of the documents than with their source: "The *Executive* statements . . . cannot perform the service for which [plaintiff] Colgate would enlist them. The Constitution expressly

121. Barclays Bank Plc v. Franchise Tax Bd., 512 U.S. 298, 327–28 (1994).

122. 343 U.S. 579, 587 (1952).

123. 552 U.S. 491 (2008).

124. In *Japan Line* and *Zschernig*, in the form of an amicus brief, *see* Brief for the United States as Amicus Curiae Supporting Appellant, Japan Line, Ltd. v. County of Los Angeles, 441 U.S.343 (1979) (No. 77-1378); Brief for the United States as Amicus Curiae Supporting Appellant, Zschernig v. Miller, 389 U.S. 429 (1968) (No. 21); in *Garamendi*, in the form of policy statements by executive branch officials; and in Zivotofsky *ex rel.* Zivotofsky v. Kerry, 135 S. Ct. 2076 (2015), as a matter of one of the few presidential powers deemed exclusive of Congress.

125. *See Barclays Bank*, 512 U.S. at 329.

126. *Id.* at 328.

grants Congress, not the President, the power to 'regulate Commerce with foreign Nations.'"[127]

Were a state to undertake some initiative to regulate foreign commerce that is utterly beyond the pale, causing real, not just judicially speculative, injury either to other states or the nation as a whole, its recklessness would surely come to the attention of Congress—and Congress would have ample opportunity to correct it.[128] If Congress declines to take action in such a situation, its judgment, prudent or not, nonetheless remains its constitutional prerogative. The Constitution vests Congress, not the Court, with the power to make these mistakes. Nothing in the Constitution prohibits Congress, or, derivatively, the states, from making what the Supreme Court might consider risky or embarrassing foreign policy.

Fourth is a related point: the judicial capacity to make the necessary findings of fact is limited. Judges, after all, find facts for purposes of resolving disputes—not determining national foreign policy, or speculating on the potential risk of foreign retaliation. Once again, the Court's own self-admonition is on point. In *Container Corp.*, it conceded:

> This Court has little competence in determining precisely when foreign nations will be offended by particular acts, and even less competence in deciding how to balance a particular risk of retaliation against the sovereign right of the United States as a whole to let the States tax as they please. The best that we can do, in the absence of explicit action by Congress, is to attempt to develop objective standards that reflect very general observations about the imperatives of international trade and international relations.[129]

The Constitution confides these quintessentially political calculations and policy judgments in Congress. The courts are not the appropriate forum for resolving them.[130]

---

127. *Id.* at 328–29; *see also id.* at 329 ("That the Executive Branch proposed legislation to outlaw a state taxation practice, but encountered an unreceptive Congress, is not evidence that the practice interfered with the Nation's ability to speak with one voice, but is rather evidence that the preeminent speaker decided to yield the floor to others.").

128. "[I]f a state regulation escaped congressional attention, then it is unlikely to meet the necessary threshold to implicate foreign affairs, and it likely only has foreign resonances." Leanne M. Wilson, *The Fate of the Dormant Foreign Commerce Clause after* Garamendi *and* Crosby, 107 Colum. L. Rev. 746, 788 (2007).

129. Container Corp. of Am. v. Franchise Tax Bd., 463 U.S. 159, 193–94 (1983) (citations omitted).

130. The argument that California's worldwide combined reporting requirement was unconstitutional, the Court said, "because it is likely to provoke retaliatory action by foreign

Fourth, and relatedly, the risk of foreign retaliation against the nation as a whole might seem real or high from the comparatively abstract vantage point of the courts, but in reality, it may well be overblown. The judiciary necessarily (and appropriately) considers this risk from the concrete vantage point of particular plaintiffs and defendants in the course of resolving their disputes. It typically lacks the institutional competence to assess the broader foreign policy implications of a particular state initiative. To be sure, as noted in Chapter 1, the states created serious international problems for the United States in the post-Revolutionary War era and, to a lesser extent, during the nation's infancy in the early eighteenth century. Yet one searches in vain for evidence of *any* case of foreign retaliation against the United States for *any* of the modern state activities detailed in Chapter 2.[131]

Fear of foreign retaliation seems largely a vestige of federalist-era anxieties, reflected in Washington's farewell address,[132] warning against entry into entangling alliances. The concern was that the fragile new nation and its constituents could ill-afford to offend powerful foreign adversaries, which, at that time, could have imperiled the fledgling nation's survival. That concern is far less pertinent today. The geopolitical landscape differs dramatically. The point is not that constitutional law itself changes simply because the world, and the United States' relative power and position within it, have changed; it is that the gravity of foreign threats, among other facts, has changed, yielding different legal conclusions despite applying the same constitutional standards. The judiciary is, if anything, less suited to assess the risks and ramifications of state commercial regulations today than in 1789. The political, economic, social, and other factors required to make an informed judgment of this sort are not, as a rule, available to the courts. Nor is it obvious that courts should appropriately take them into account in the context of litigation. Judicial speculation about the probability or nature of a foreign nation's response to a particular state law is a dubious way to regulate foreign commerce absent congressional guidance. At any rate, it is doubtful that the Constitution licenses it.

Fifth, judicial review of state laws under the dormant Foreign Commerce Clause should in one respect be less, not more, restrictive, than review under

---

governments is directed to the wrong forum. The judiciary is not vested with power to decide 'how to balance a particular risk of retaliation against the sovereign right of the United States as a whole to let the States tax as they please.'" *Barclays Bank*, 512 U.S. at 327–28 (citation omitted).

131. *See* John M. Kline, State Government Influence in U.S. International Economic Policy 97 (1983).

132. George Washington, Farewell Address (1796), avalon.law.yale.edu/18th_century/washing.asp.

the dormant Interstate Commerce Clause. One key inquiry under the dormant Foreign Commerce Clause is discriminatory effects: if a state law discriminates against interstate commerce, it is virtually per se invalid. The concern underpinning this prohibition, however, is for *other states and residents of other states*—not for foreign countries or residents of foreign countries. The concern is that, by attempting to get a leg up on other states through discrimination against interstate commerce, national unity will be undermined. Nothing in the Constitution prohibits a state from attempting to gain an advantage over foreign nations or businesses. Discrimination of the sort prohibited by the Fifth and Fourteenth Amendments, outlawing racial, ethnic, and religious discrimination, for example, has no necessary application to purely economic discrimination against foreign entities. Such discrimination against foreign commerce may be and, to differing extents, is prohibited by treaties,[133] but not by the Constitution. Alleviating potential discrimination can be an important bargaining chip in the federal government's international negotiations. The discrimination prong of the Court's traditional dormant Commerce Clause analysis should therefore apply with much less force to foreign nations.

Synthesizing and Simplifying Dormancy Standards

We've considered, in this and the preceding chapter, two constitutional hurdles to state action: the dormant foreign-affairs doctrine and the dormant Foreign Commerce Clause. Both presuppose that, at times, the Constitution tasks the courts with a role in managing the foreign affairs of the United States by rendering interim judgments based on judicial presumptions about which state and local foreign-affairs activities the federal political branches would tolerate. Such activities, as Chapter 2 illustrates, have proliferated in recent years, arguably rendering one of the main rationales for the dormant Foreign Commerce Clause—that Congress would assess and preempt certain state and local laws if it had the capacity and resources to monitor them—compelling. At the same time, as we have seen, it's a virtual certainty that genuinely problematic state foreign-affairs activities would come to Congress's attention. And as Chapter 8 explains, Congress has ample doctrinal authority to preempt state and local laws, expressly or implicitly. Almost by definition, therefore, these dormancy doctrines deal with

133. *See, e.g.*, General Agreement on Tariffs and Trade, *opened for signature* Oct. 30, 1947, 61 Stat. pts. 5 & 6, T.I.A.S. No. 1700, 55 U.N.T.S. 187, *reprinted in* IV GATT, Basic Instruments and Selected Documents 1–78 (1969); North American Free Trade Agreement, Dec. 17, 1992, § 1710, 107 Stat. 2057, 32 I.L.M. 612.

less visible state foreign-affairs activities, those that do *not* seriously interfere with vital national foreign-policy interests.

Which, if either, doctrine should therefore be retained today? Only, we suggest, the dormant Foreign Commerce Clause—and only as modified, first, by eliminating *Japan Line*'s two supplemental criteria for the reasons described; and second, by substantially lowering, for state and local foreign-affairs activities, the discrimination threshold set forth in *Philadelphia* from a rule of (virtually) per se invalidity to one of (virtually) presumptive validity. Absent exigent circumstances, however, the dormant foreign-affairs doctrine is ill-advised. It is also needless, for it is difficult even to imagine circumstances in which it would not be duplicative of the dormant Foreign Commerce Clause.

Superficially, the two doctrines seem similar and (affirmatively applied) seem to yield identical outcomes, viz., preemption of state or local foreign-affairs activities. But their constitutional bases and functional rationales differ markedly, and the contrast between the two is stark. Begin with the dormant Foreign Commerce Clause. It rests on a firm constitutional footing: textually, Article I gives Congress clear authority to regulate foreign commerce. Historically, the dormant Commerce Clause doctrine has been a consistent part of the Court's jurisprudence for the nearly two centuries since Chief Justice Marshall's 1824 decision in *Gibbons v. Ogden*.[134] Doctrinally, albeit principally in the interstate context, it has evolved over that time, supplying ample precedent and judicial guidance today. Indeed, it is a testament to the resilience of the doctrine that Justice Scalia, a major critic of the dormant Commerce Clause, has said that he will nonetheless adhere to it "(1) against a state law that facially discriminates against interstate commerce, and (2) against a state law that is indistinguishable from a type of law previously held unconstitutional by this Court."[135] The stare decisis values that motivate this position—commitment to a legal system characterized by stability, predictability, reliance interests, and so on—equally counsel maintaining the dormant Foreign Commerce Clause, although not, it should be noted, the new criteria introduced in *Japan Line* (and not applied since). Finally, the combination of globalization, the muddying of the putative distinction between foreign and domestic commerce, the increase in local and state foreign-affairs activities, and congressional gridlock—suggest that the traditional rationale for the dormant Foreign Commerce Clause persists.

Along each of these constitutional baselines, the dormant foreign-affairs doctrine fares poorly. First, it lacks a textual basis; there is, as noted in Chapter 4, no

134. 22 U.S. (9 Wheat.) 1 (1824).

135. Itel Containers Int'l Corp. v. Huddleston, 507 U.S. 60, 79 (1993) (Scalia, J., concurring in part and concurring in the judgment).

non-dormant "Foreign Affairs Clause"; there are only particular foreign-affairs powers, allocated by the Constitution among the branches of the federal government. Historically, the Court had, until *Zschernig*, repeatedly dismissed the doctrine as "extraordinary" and "far-fetched."[136] To date, the dormant foreign-affairs doctrine has been applied by the Supreme Court in just two cases, *Zschernig* and *Garamendi*, and as Chapter 4 suggested, they have bred only confusion in lower state and federal courts. Neither case provided state and local officials with helpful guidance or enhanced stare decisis values such as stability, predictability, and reliance interests—quite the contrary.

While the full spectrum of problems the dormant foreign-affairs doctrine faces is outlined in Chapter 4, two bear special emphasis here. First, state and local foreign-affairs initiatives struck down on the basis of the dormant foreign-affairs doctrine cannot be restored; *Zschernig* and *Garamendi* alike suggested that the judiciary has the final word on whether a state or local initiative, such as Oregon's probate law or California's insurance-disclosure requirements, conflicts with national foreign policy. As Justice Stewart wrote in *Zschernig*:

> Resolution of so fundamental a constitutional issue cannot vary from day to day with the shifting winds at the State Department. Today, we are told, Oregon's statute does not conflict with the national interest. Tomorrow it may. But, however that may be, the fact remains that the conduct of our foreign affairs is entrusted under the Constitution to the National Government, not to the probate courts of the several States.[137]

In effect, Stewart's view means that under the dormant foreign-affairs doctrine, the federal judiciary, not the federal political branches, has the final word. Consequently, if, tomorrow, Oregon's probate law turned out to comport with or even advance national foreign-relations interests, it could not be re-enacted. Congress could not authorize the states to enact similar probate laws—as it could (after the second *Cooley* doctrine's demise) were the case decided under the dormant Foreign Commerce Clause.

Second, the dormant foreign-affairs doctrine, unlike the dormant Foreign Commerce Clause, pits state or local *law* against national foreign *policy* (as characterized by the courts, who, under the doctrine, have the final word in this regard). In *Zschernig*, the Court thus struck down Oregon's probate law based on its assertion that the state law interfered with federal foreign policy—the executive's

136. Clark v. Allen, 331 U.S. 503 (1947).

137. Zschernig v. Miller, 389 U.S. 429, 443 (1968) (Stewart, J. concurring).

contrary view notwithstanding. In *Garamendi*, similarly, the Court struck down California's law on Holocaust-era insurance disclosure based on its assertion that the state law interfered with a tacit policy to prohibit state laws on the issue—the executive agreements with Germany, France, and Austria, and presidential statements to the contrary, notwithstanding.

This *seems* like classic preemption. But technically it is not. Congress plays no role in the dormant foreign-affairs doctrine; if it did, the issue would involve a clash of state and federal laws that would be resolved by the Supremacy Clause. But no federal law is at issue under the dormant foreign-affairs doctrine—only a judicial inference about national foreign policy. The judiciary's intuitions concerning federal foreign policy trump state law. That is hard to square with the Supremacy Clause, for the clause applies to *laws*; it accords no status to judicially inferred foreign policies. Further, once a state law has been struck down based on the dormant foreign-affairs doctrine, Congress cannot, so it seems, reauthorize it. That may be because the supposed foreign-affairs policy at issue was not Congress's in the first place; it was the president's—or more accurately, it was the foreign policy that the judiciary supposed to be that of the president. Applying the dormant foreign-affairs doctrine, the Court thus purports to accomplish what the president either could not do or chose not to do. To be sure, the president represents the nation abroad and communicates on its behalf. But his foreign *policy* does not enact supreme federal *law* under the Supremacy Clause. The Court has never explained why an executive foreign policy constitutionally can preempt state law. Worse, in the doctrine's most recent iteration, it is not even (really) the president's policy that does the work under the dormant foreign-affairs doctrine. It is rather the Court's own opinion about the content of national foreign policy and how it should best be advanced.

Finally, because of the scope of the contemporary Commerce Clause, the dormant foreign-affairs doctrine, even were it constitutionally sound, is simply needless. Almost any imaginable state or local foreign-affairs activity that might be challenged on the basis of the dormant foreign-affairs doctrine could equally, and with greater doctrinal clarity, be challenged as a violation of the dormant Foreign Commerce Clause. In theory, the dormant foreign-affairs doctrine and the dormant Foreign Commerce Clause differ in that the latter applies only in situations involving commerce. In reality, virtually every dormant foreign-affairs doctrine situation involves commerce and is susceptible to evaluation under the same judicial standards that have been established in the context of the dormant Foreign Commerce Clause. A law held unconstitutional under the former would likewise be invalid under the latter. (Consider, for example, the analysis of the First Circuit in *Natsios v. National Foreign Trade Council*, which, predictably, found the law invalid under both the dormant foreign-affairs doctrine and the dormant Foreign Commerce Clause—for substantially the same reasons.) Hence, without judicially inventing a dormant foreign-affairs doctrine out of whole cloth, the Court could decide would-be dormant foreign-affairs doctrine challenges under the standards established by the Court in its dormant Commerce Clause cases, in particular, *Pike* and *Philadelphia*, as modified by one key distinction explained below. Last, even if the two novel criteria identified by the Court in *Japan Line* (the alleged need for federal uniformity, or "one voice," and the risk of foreign retaliation) reflected real concerns, the dormant foreign-affairs doctrine and dormant Foreign Commerce Clause would share them, with the result that the dormant foreign-affairs doctrine offers no practical advantage over the dormant Foreign Commerce Clause.

The dormant Foreign Commerce Clause, in contrast, in addition to its firm constitutional footing, provides clear, administrable standards for judicial evaluation of state foreign-affairs laws and regulations. As noted earlier, the core of dormant Commerce Clause analysis, whether foreign or interstate, is a two-part standard derived from *Pike* and *Philadelphia*: first consider whether the challenged law has discriminatory effects on commerce, and second, ask whether the burden on commerce imposed by the law is "clearly excessive" relative to that law's local benefits.[138] Few state or local laws in the realm of foreign affairs will be invalidated under this test. Genuinely problematic state laws can always be invalidated by Congress. But absent congressional action, rarely will the burden on foreign commerce be clearly excessive in relation to a local law that pursues a constitutionally legitimate aim within the scope of the state's police powers. And this is as it should be. Consider the documented benefits of the numerous state foreign-affairs initiatives described in Chapter 2. It is not obvious how any of them impose a burden, still less a *clearly excessive* burden, on foreign commerce.

As noted, however, the discrimination prong of the traditional dormant Commerce Clause test must be adjusted in the case of foreign commercial activities carried out by states and municipalities. The dormant Foreign Commerce Clause's prohibition on discrimination, animating its rule of per se invalidity, reflects the Constitution's effort to establish national unity and a uniform, fair economy within the nation. That requires equal treatment of other states and their residents. But the Constitution does not prohibit the states from seeking economic advantages over foreign nations or private business entities. International trade, investment, and other foreign commerce is regulated by international agreements, with which the states must, of course, abide. Local, no less than federal, officials, as well as private economic actors, operate within a framework of international treaty commitments in the realms of trade (e.g., the World Trade Organization, free trade agreements) and investment (e.g., the North American

---

138. Pike v. Bruce Church, Inc., 397 U.S. 137, 142 (1970).

Free Trade Agreement, bilateral investment treaties, and so forth). But recall that the justification for a dormant Foreign Commerce Clause, like the justification for the dormant Interstate Commerce Clause, is that Congress cannot perpetually and comprehensively monitor the countless local commercial transactions that take place throughout the nation. For that reason, the Court has said the judiciary may invalidate certain local activities that Congress presumably *would* preempt if it knew about them and had the resources (and in some cases, perhaps the institutional or political will) to handle. Yet it is hardly self-evident that, if only Congress had the capacity to monitor state laws that discriminate against foreign nations (assuming they remain within the limits of any treaty or national legal obligations, of course), it would presumably preempt them. Only in very extreme cases would or should the courts make that assumption.

One such extreme case might have been *Crosby*. In *Crosby*, before Congress had enacted its own law sanctioning Myanmar (Burma), it would not have been unreasonable for a federal court to assume that the Massachusetts Burma Law would be preempted by Congress because of its interference with national policy toward Myanmar's authoritarian regime. Among other evidence, Japan and the European Union had threatened legal action and initiated a dispute-resolution process with the WTO, and a host of foreign businesses had objected. The evidence disclosed that the Massachusetts Burma Law discriminated strongly against a number of foreign nations and private business entities abroad *and* that, as a consequence, the nation as a whole (not just the state) might well suffer retaliation or other negative repercussions. Under such circumstances, application of the dormant Foreign Commerce Clause would be appropriate as an *interim* measure. Note, however, the contrast with the dormant foreign-affairs doctrine: if Congress subsequently decided that the Massachusetts law in fact did not interfere with national foreign policy, it could affirmatively authorize the state to re-enact the Massachusetts Burma Law.

Hence, although the *Philadelphia* discrimination prong of the Court's traditional dormant Commerce Clause analysis would ordinarily apply with far less force to foreign nations and private business entities—in contrast to the per se invalidity standard that applies in the interstate context—the dormant Foreign Commerce Clause doctrine would still leave the courts equipped with the tools and enough discretionary leeway to handle the occasional case of unusually burdensome discrimination against foreign commerce. The dormant Foreign Commerce Clause standards also would enable the courts to preempt manifestly problematic local laws in the event of a gridlocked federal government.

In sum, the dormant Foreign Commerce Clause, stripped of the *Japan Line* criteria and modified to require a very high threshold for discrimination (contrary to *Philadelphia*), would provide a synthesis of the Court's dormancy doctrines that suffices to handle legitimate concerns about local initiatives in foreign affairs that risk damage to the nation while at the same time denying the courts the latitude to determine national foreign policy or invalidate state law based on speculation or their own political preferences. Although it is difficult to imagine, an extraordinary situation might arise, the "case from hell," involving a state foreign-affairs initiative that both (1) could not be characterized legally as commerce under the Constitution, and (2) could not be preempted by Congress because of gridlock, government shutdown, or some similar malfunction. If and when that happens, the federal judiciary might rely on dormant foreign-affairs doctrine precedents for an interim solution. But except for this highly improbable potential exception, the Constitution's analytic framework can be simplified, without sacrificing anything important, by relying upon slightly modified dormant Foreign Commerce Clause jurisprudence. Every case in this or the preceding chapter in which dormant foreign-affairs or dormant Foreign Commerce Clause doctrine was applied could be more fairly, predictably, and coherently resolved by this suggested standard.

6

The Treaty Power

The treaties of the United States, under the [Articles of Confederation] are liable to infractions of thirteen [states]. The faith, the reputation, the peace of the whole union, are thus continually at the mercy of the prejudices, the passions, and the interests of every member of which it is composed. Is it possible that foreign nations can either respect or confide in such a government?

—ALEXANDER HAMILTON[1]

I. Introduction

Missouri v. Holland[2] was to the federal treaty power what *McCulloch v. Maryland*[3] is to its legislative power. In *McCulloch*, Chief Justice Marshall wrote that "we must never forget that it is a *Constitution* we are expounding."[4] In *Holland*, Justice Holmes interpreted the treaty power in the spirit of Marshall's dictum by adopting a functional, adaptivist approach to its relationship to the Tenth Amendment. Referring to the degree to which the federal government may make treaties that trench upon what might ordinarily be traditional state functions, he wrote, "We must consider what this country has become in deciding what that Amendment has reserved."[5] *Holland* was therefore far more than what generations of law

1. THE FEDERALIST NO. 22, at 144 (Alexander Hamilton) (Jacob E. Cooke ed., 1961).

2. 252 U.S. 416 (1920).

3. 17 U.S. (4 Wheat.) 316 (1819).

4. *Id.* at 407.

5. *Holland*, 252 U.S. at 434.

students might recall as the curious case about migratory birds written by the Supreme Court's most eminent justice since Marshall; it was a case, like *McCulloch*, that would have vindicated their professors in claiming that we live today, not only in Marshall's America, but in Holmes's, too. The Constitution's remarkable durability and resilience over 230 years should be ascribed in no small part to the prescient spirit of pragmatism that infuses cases such as *McCulloch* and *Holland*.

Yet *Holland*, alas, should now be discussed in the past tense. On June 2, 2014, in *Bond v. United States*,[6] the Supreme Court abandoned *Holland*. It did not say so. Nor did the justices themselves believe *Bond* did so. Chief Justice Roberts, for the majority, and Justices Scalia, Alito, and Thomas, who concurred in the judgment only, arguing *Holland should* be overruled, all nonetheless wrote as though *Bond* did not disturb *Holland*. Commentators, too, did not see *Holland*'s demise.[7] A consensus rapidly emerged that the Court had decided *Bond* on a narrow statutory basis, successfully—even if, to the concurring justices, objectionably—eliding the constitutional issue in *Holland*. But the consensus was premature, and it is mistaken. The Court *tried*, of course, to avoid the constitutional issues raised by *Holland*. But it failed. In fact, holding all else constant, had *Bond* honored *Holland*, the Court would have reached the opposite result; had *Holland* applied *Bond*'s analysis—a federalism background principle and commensurate canon of avoidance that will henceforth govern laws implementing treaties—*Holland*, too, would have reached the opposite result.[8]

We lament *Holland*'s passing. We argue in this chapter that it represented the most sensible reconciliation of the tension between the Treaty Clause and the Tenth Amendment. We further suggest that *Bond* is inconsistent with the Court's treaty jurisprudence in *Medellín v. Texas*,[9] for the Court there suggested that the federal government can do what *Bond* has now held that it constitutionally cannot do. Yet the problem *Bond* creates is not limited to one inconsistency; it runs deeper. By abandoning *Holland*, the Court has handicapped the nation in

---

6. 134 S. Ct. 2077 (2014).

7. *E.g.*, Curtis A. Bradley, *Federalism, Treaty Implementation, and Political Process*: Bond v. United States, 108 AM. J. INT'L L. 486, 486, 495 (2014); Jean Galbraith, *Congress's Treaty-Implementing Power in Historical Practice*, 56 WM. & MARY L. REV. 59, 73 (2014); Heather K. Gerken, *Slipping the Bonds of Federalism*, 128 HARV. L. REV. 85, 89 (2014); Nicholas Quinn Rosenkranz, Bond v. United States: *Concurring in the Judgment*, 2014 CATO SUP. CT. REV. 285, 306 (2014). For examples of earlier media commentary to the same effect, *see infra* note 95.

8. We assume, in other words, that no alternative rationale or tacit consideration existed in either case; holding the facts, law, and judicial analyses constant, both decisions would have reached the opposite result at the times *Holland* and *Bond*, respectively, were decided.

9. 552 U.S. 491 (2008).

a globalizing world and risked impeding the ability and reliability of the United States as a treaty partner. Without *Holland*, it will be well-nigh impossible for the nation to honor certain treaties—treaties that the nation has routinely concluded since its founding and, today more than ever, it can be expected, increasingly will. Mindful of the origins of the Treaty Clause in the experience with state practice under the Articles of Confederation, it is not only unfortunate but hazardous for the Court to have unwittingly recreated one of the paramount problems the Framers sought to remedy in Philadelphia.

Granted, the Court surely will not soon explicitly regard *Bond* as having overruled *Holland*. But for the reasons we will develop, adherence to *Bond*'s analysis would effectively undermine *Holland*—notwithstanding the majority's effort in *Bond* to avoid constitutional questions. Indeed, ironically, it is the Court's insistence on a background principle and constitutional-avoidance canon based on *pre-Holland* federalism that renders *Bond* inconsistent with *Holland*. At most, *Holland* survives in name only. Unless the Court repudiates *Bond*'s analysis, it will have abandoned *Holland*'s core doctrine. We conclude, however, by noting that the Court could choose to reorient and expand its remarks in *Bond* so as to reinvigorate the *Holland* doctrine—without conceding error in the case (and thus saving institutional face). Such a reorientation would likely have the additional virtue of clarifying *Holland*'s holding in conformity with the actual principles that animated Holmes's opinion.

We develop the argument in five parts. In the first section, "The Treaty Clause versus the Tenth Amendment?," we clarify the conundrum created by the treaty power's interaction with the Tenth Amendment. In the second section, "Deciphering Holmes's Cryptic Opinion in *Holland*," we argue that a close reading of *Holland* reveals that its true rationale is far more subtle and forceful than the textual-delegation rationale often ascribed to Justice Holmes. We also consider how two oft-neglected decisions on which Holmes relied, *Andrews v. Andrews*[10] and *Carey v. South Dakota*,[11] offer critical insight into what *Holland* held—and why.

In the third section, "How *Bond* Hobbled *Holland*," we scrutinize *Bond* and argue that, contrary to the consensus that it left *Holland* untouched, *Bond* gutted *Holland* by rejecting at least two indispensable predicates of Holmes's analysis: first, that a treaty and its implementing legislation must be considered together, and second, that a treaty's validity under the Tenth Amendment immunizes that treaty's implementing legislation against a generic federalism challenge. In contrast, *Bond* held that a treaty and its implementing legislation may

10. 188 U.S. 14 (1903), *abrogated by* Sherrer v. Sherrer, 334 U.S. 343 (1948).

11. 250 U.S. 118 (1919).

be assessed separately under the Tenth Amendment—without considering the implementing statute in view of the treaty it implements—and further, that in doing so, the "statute—unlike the [treaty]—*must* be read consistent with principles of federalism inherent in our constitutional structure."[12] Further, the Court erred by treating those "principles of federalism" as excluding, rather than incorporating, *Holland*'s interpretation of the Tenth Amendment and the Article II treaty power.

A careful analysis of what Justice Holmes actually held in *Holland* makes clear that *Bond* and *Holland* cannot be reconciled. We do not find it plausible to dismiss the Court's troubling premise ("the statute—unlike the [treaty]—*must* be read consistent with principles of federalism inherent in our constitutional structure") as a mere case of careless or ill-considered language. The quoted premise does not exist in isolation. It both motivated and enabled the majority's approach to statutory interpretation and, in particular, Chief Justice Roberts's reliance on the canon of constitutional avoidance based on background federalism concerns. Had the majority honored *Holland*, no such concerns would have arisen.

The Court could have plausibly decided *Bond* on the basis of non-constitutional principles of statutory interpretation—resolving what it saw as an ambiguity in the implementing legislation without resort to a federalism-based canon of constitutional avoidance. But tellingly, it did not. To the contrary, the proposition that a treaty's legislation, unlike the treaty, "must be read consistent with principles of federalism inherent in our constitutional structure"[13] constituted *an indispensable predicate* of the majority's statutory analysis—the chief factor that resolved the putative ambiguity of the implementing legislation. The same predicate is also emblematic of the *Bond* Court's central mistake. Assuming, as every justice correctly did, the constitutionality of the treaty,[14] "there can be no dispute about the validity of the statute"[15] based only on general "principles of federalism inherent in our constitutional structure."[16]

In the fourth section, "Critiques of *Holland*: Theory and Practice," we argue that perennial critiques of *Holland* and the risks it allegedly entails ring hollow. No theoretical consideration or practical development since *Holland* has suggested any reason to disturb its doctrine. Indeed, critics have been unable to point

12. Bond v. United States, 134 S. Ct. 2077, 2088 (2014) (emphasis added).

13. *Id.* at 2088.

14. *See id.* at 2098 (Scalia, J., concurring in the judgment) (noting the Court's consensus that the treaty is valid).

15. Missouri v. Holland, 252 U.S. 416, 432 (1920).

16. *Bond*, 134 S. Ct. at 2088.

to a single incident of abuse or concrete, nonhypothetical example of any risk that the decision supposedly poses, including the parade of horribles *Holland* allegedly set to march. Nor does *Holland* threaten to abrogate individual rights or other constitutional limits. It does not, as the Court wrote in 1957, "confer power on the Congress, or on any other branch of Government, which is free from the restraints of the Constitution,"[17] in particular, individual rights set forth in the Bill of Rights and other provisions of the Constitution.

In the fifth section, "*Holland* and the Modern Law of Treaties after *Bond:* The Treaty Power and Federalism in Contemporary Perspective," we consider *Bond*'s likely future consequences, especially its potentially deleterious implications for modern U.S. treaty practice. We suggest that the Court's decision in *Medellín v. Texas*[18] implicitly required *Holland*'s doctrine. *Bond*'s abandonment of *Holland* therefore renders a core holding in *Medellín*, which is likely the most significant decision on the domestic U.S. law of treaties in decades, incoherent. More generally, *Bond* needlessly complicates the conduct of U.S. foreign affairs. It diminishes the nation's diplomatic capacity, handicapping it in its relations with foreign nations and threatening its ability to cooperate with them to tackle some of the most serious global issues in the twenty-first century.

We conclude that the nation's response to its experience under the Articles of Confederation, which motivated the Framers to lodge the treaty power in the federal government and to make treaties supreme federal law, remains equally vital today. *Bond*'s short-term effects may seem modest. But we expect that the nation will come to regret abandoning *Holland*. For that reason, we suggest how the Court might resolve the problems *Bond* created. Without calling into question the result in *Bond*, the Court could recast its copious references to federalism to bring its jurisprudence back into conformity with *Holland*—because the very "principles of federalism inherent in our constitutional structure,"[19] on which the Court placed such emphasis, *include* Holmes's reconciliation of the treaty power and federalism.

II. The Treaty Clause Versus the Tenth Amendment?

The treaty power and the Tenth Amendment, read together, present a conundrum. The Tenth Amendment provides simply, "The powers not delegated to the United States by the Constitution, nor prohibited by it to the States, are reserved

17. Reid v. Covert, 354 U.S. 1, 16–17 (1957); *see also* Boos v. Barry, 485 U.S. 312 (1988).

18. 552 U.S. 491 (2008).

19. *Bond*, 134 S. Ct. at 2081.

to the States respectively, or to the people."[20] Article II gives the president "power, by and with the advice and consent of the Senate, to make treaties, provided two thirds of the Senators present concur."[21] The conundrum lies in the consequences of applying, or not applying, Tenth Amendment limits to the treaty power in the event that the federal government were to ratify an Article II treaty[22] regulating a subject generally reserved to the states—that is, an area of law that falls within the traditional power of the states to legislate on matters not delegated by the Constitution to the federal government.[23]

If the Tenth Amendment limits the treaty power, a treaty obliging the United States to legislate on a subject reserved to the states would by definition be unconstitutional. The federal government would be powerless to enter into the potentially broad class of treaties obliging the United States to enact domestic federal laws regulating areas of traditional state competence. In practice, foreign nations would also lack an alternative way to conclude such treaties with the United States. They would be compelled to negotiate with each state individually in an effort to conclude fifty identical international agreements, which, under the Constitution, would be "compacts."[24]

The Compact Clause requires that agreements between states and foreign nations receive congressional approval.[25] That a foreign nation might negotiate fifty substantially identical compacts with the states, each contingent on congressional approval, is implausible, not to mention inefficient. And even if a series of state compacts could be concluded, the United States, as a nation, would not be legally bound by them under federal law; it would not be a party. The nation would be all but powerless to enforce an international obligation in the event of a state's breach.

---

20. U.S. CONST. amend. X

21. *Id.* art. II, § 2, cl. 2.

22. *Holland* relied on the proposition that Article II treaties differ from other types of U.S. international agreements. References to treaties, unless otherwise indicated, are therefore only to international agreements made in conformity with Article II.

23. International law refers to countries as nation-states or simply states. Because we discuss both nation-states and U.S. states, for clarity and convenience, we refer to nation-states as "countries" or "nations" and to the states of the Union as "states."

24. U.S. CONST. art. I, § 10. International law is indifferent to the denomination of an international agreement (compact, treaty, convention, etc.). Vienna Convention on the Law of Treaties art. 2(1)(a), May 23, 1969, 1155 U.N.T.S. 331. Under the Constitution, however, even though neither the Court nor anyone else has managed to explain what differentiates treaties from compacts, terminology matters. *See* LOUIS HENKIN, FOREIGN AFFAIRS AND THE US CONSTITUTION 152 & nn.12–13 (2d ed. 1996) (citing, inter alia, Felix Frankfurter & James M. Landis, *The Compact Clause of the Constitution—A Study in Interstate Adjustments*, 34 YALE L.J. 685, 695 n.37 (1925)).

25. U.S. CONST. art. I, § 10, cl. 3.

Because any federal law intended to implement international legal obligations under these compacts would be unconstitutional, it would also be left to the states to agree how to implement those obligations uniformly under their respective laws and constitutions. This scenario, including the level of cooperation it would require, is—to say the least—improbable.[26] Yet as a rule, international law recognizes and governs relations between nations, not their political subdivisions. So the United States, not the states, might incur international legal responsibility for any breach.[27] That prospect, of course, ranked among the foremost defects of the Articles of Confederation. It is difficult to imagine that the Framers understood the Tenth Amendment and the treaty power, in conjunction, to create one of the very problems they sought to resolve at Philadelphia. At any rate, today, with more and more problems requiring global cooperation and with the proliferation of multilateral treaties, the detrimental consequences of this reading of the Constitution could be serious and far-reaching. The United States could find itself increasingly isolated in foreign affairs and handicapped in its relations with other nations.

Yet the alternative resolution to the conundrum is also problematic. If the Tenth Amendment does not limit the treaty power, the rights reserved to the states would be theoretically defeasible at the whim of the federal government. With the right treaty partner, it would seem that the federal government could enter into a treaty on a subject ordinarily reserved to the states and then enact legislation to implement its treaty obligations under the Necessary and Proper Clause.[28] The treaty and its implementing legislation, in turn, would preempt inconsistent state law under the Supremacy Clause. The principal obstacle to a federal government intent upon usurping state authority over a local issue would be finding another nation able and willing to enter into a treaty including the necessary obligations. Echoing other critics, Justice Scalia thus suggested in *Bond* that "the holding that a statute prohibiting the carrying of firearms near schools went beyond Congress's enumerated powers, . . . could be reversed by negotiating a treaty with Latvia providing that neither sovereign would permit the carrying of guns near schools."[29] If the treaty power enables the federal government to co-opt

---

26. *Cf.* New York v. United States, 505 U.S. 144 (1992) (concluding that Congress may not constitutionally commandeer the states to enter into compacts by which they would cooperate to dispose of radioactive waste produced within their respective jurisdictions).

27. Articles on the Responsibility of States for Internationally Wrongful Acts art. 4, *in* Report of the International Law Commission on the Work of Its Fifty-Third Session, UN GAOR, 56th Sess., Supp. No. 10, at 43, UN Doc. A/56/10 (2001).

28. U.S. CONST. art. I, § 8, cl. 18. Indeed, depending on its details, the implementing legislation could preempt state regulation of an entire field of law ordinarily reserved to the states.

29. Bond v. United States, 134 S. Ct. 2077, 2100 (2014) (Scalia, J., concurring in the judgment). Since *Missouri v. Holland*, 252 U.S. 416 (1920), commentators have expressed concerns about

powers reserved to the states in this way, the Tenth Amendment would become no more than a "parchment barrier," in Madison's felicitous phrase.[30] State authority over traditional state functions could atrophy as globalization, and the consequent need for international cooperation on issues once deemed quintessentially local, relentlessly broadens and advances.

For most of the nineteenth century and into the twentieth, the United States remained a largely agrarian, inward-looking country and a comparatively minor player on the international stage. The 1823 Monroe Doctrine,[31] although principally intended to convey to the major European powers that the United States would not tolerate their intrusion in the Western hemisphere, also reflected a policy against being drawn into the maelstrom of European diplomatic maneuvering, colonial politics, and wars—a prudent stance for a fledgling nation that persisted, with some exceptions, into the twentieth century.[32] Also, for much of the nineteenth century, custom remained the principal source of international law. Treaties, particularly multilateral treaties, were less common.[33] And because treaties seldom implicated local issues, the conundrum raised by the potential tension between the treaty power and the Tenth Amendment remained largely academic.

Nations began to conclude more treaties after the 1814 Congress of Vienna, however, and by the turn of the century, the number of treaties had proliferated. Even then, bilateral treaties remained the norm, and multilateral treaties focused

---

this risk. We're aware of no evidence that it has ever materialized. Comparable hypotheticals, however, have become a staple of courses in foreign relations law. *Holland* is often deemed a "liberal" decision because of such hypotheticals. Yet the issue does not, in fact, track any partisan divide. Consider, by way of contrast to Justice Scalia's example, what might be characterized as a "conservative" example: the Supreme Court, hypothetically, overrules *Roe v. Wade*, 410 U.S. 113 (1973), holding that abortion's regulation falls within the realm of rights reserved to the states. Thereafter, some states prohibit abortion while others legalize and regulate it. The president and Senate, dissatisfied with the unwieldy patchwork of state laws and believing abortion should be nationally prohibited, ratify the American Convention on Human Rights, Nov. 22, 1969, 1144 U.N.T.S. 123. Article 4 of the Convention says that everyone has the right to life, which "shall be protected by law, in general, from the moment of conception." *Id.* art. 4. Congress might then enact implementing legislation to uniformly prohibit abortion in all or virtually all circumstances, preempting state laws that authorize it. Countless similar hypotheticals, culminating in conventionally liberal or conservative outcomes, may be constructed. *Holland*'s political valence is de minimis.

30. THE FEDERALIST NO. 48, at 333 (James Madison) (Jacob E. Cooke ed., 1961).

31. 41 ANNALS OF CONG. 22–23 (1823) (statement of Pres. James Monroe).

32. JOHN LEWIS GADDIS, THE COLD WAR: A NEW HISTORY 206 (2005).

33. *See* Curtis A. Bradley, *The Treaty Power and American Federalism*, 97 MICH. L. REV. 390, 396 (1998).

almost exclusively on bread-and-butter international issues. Nations rarely perceived the need for international regulation of local issues. Research discloses few jurists at the time who considered whether treaties could regulate matters that traditionally fall within the province of state law.[34] Nor had the Supreme Court considered the issue directly.[35] But it would have been at least reasonable to suppose that the federal government could not sidestep the Tenth Amendment with a minuet patterned by the Treaty Clause.

III. Deciphering Holmes's Cryptic Opinion in Holland

That changed in 1920. The issue confronted the Court squarely in *Missouri v. Holland*.[36] In 1913, Congress had enacted one of the nation's first environmental laws, regulating the taking of game and migratory birds.[37] Yet less than two decades earlier, in *Geer v. Connecticut*, the Court had said that "the right to preserve game flows from the undoubted existence in the State of a police power,"[38] notwithstanding incidental effects on interstate commerce. Relying in part on *Geer*, two federal district courts held that the 1913 statute usurped powers reserved to the states.[39]

---

34. *But see* HENKIN, *supra* note 24, at 189–90, 456 n.57. Some scholars sought to establish "that the executive and legislative branches of the government in the period 1830-60 believed that treaties could not deal with matters not otherwise in the federal domain." *Id.* at 456 n.57 (citing, inter alia, Ralston Hayden, *The States' Rights Doctrine and the Treaty-Making Power*, 22 AM. HIST. REV. 556 (1917)). According to Henkin, however, these scholars "represented a minority view." *Id.* at 462 n.57.

35. In *Bond v. United States*, 134 S. Ct. 2077, 2098 & n.4 (2014), Justice Scalia noted that *Neely v. Henkel*, 180 U.S. 109, 121 (1901), and *Prigg v. Pennsylvania*, 41 U.S. (16 Pet.) 539, 619 (1842), respectively, "embraced" and "arguably favor[ed]" the rationale in *Holland*—albeit, in his view, "without reasoning." In contrast, in *Mayor of New Orleans v. United* States, 35 U.S. (10 Pet.) 662 (1836), the Court said that treaties may not expand the scope of the powers delegated by the Constitution to the federal government. Henkin suggests that "the basic principles of . . . *Holland* were laid down in the early years of the Republic." HENKIN, *supra* note 24, at 463 n.65 (citing Ware v. Hylton, 3 U.S. (3 Dall.) 199 (1796)).

36. 252 U.S. 416 (1920).

37. Act of Mar. 4, 1913, c. 145, 37 Stat. 828, 847 (codified as amended at 16 U.S.C. 673 (2012)).

38. 161 U.S. 519, 534 (1896).

39. United States v. McCullagh, 221 F. 288 (D. Kan. 1915); United States v. Shauver, 214 F. 154 (E.D. Ark. 1914). These decisions have been thought to show that, before *Holland*, no one thought treaties could empower the federal government to act in realms otherwise reserved to the states. Not so. Before *Holland*, at least three district courts had sustained the Migratory Bird Treaty Act notwithstanding that substantially the same law might be constitutionally beyond federal power absent the treaty. *See* United States v. Thompson, 258 F. 257 (E.D. Ark. 1919); United States v. Rockefeller, 260 F. 346, 348 (D. Mont. 1919); United States v. Samples,

Undeterred, the United States entered into a treaty with the United Kingdom, which, at the time, controlled Canadian territory. Migratory birds of value to both nations routinely traversed the border. The treaty thus required each nation to enact laws protecting migratory birds within its territories. Congress then enacted legislation substantially identical to the 1913 statute that two federal district courts had struck down[40]—but this time in the exercise of its Necessary and Proper Clause power to implement the treaty. Missouri brought suit claiming a Tenth Amendment violation. The Court therefore faced the core issue directly: May Congress legislate under the Necessary and Proper Clause to implement an Article II treaty if the implementing legislation might otherwise exceed Congress's enumerated powers,[41] intruding upon an area of law ordinarily reserved to the states by the Tenth Amendment?

Justice Holmes answered in the affirmative with characteristic eloquence and brevity. Whether he truly intended to offer arguments in the alternative, *Holland* has been read to supply at least two rationales for the Court's decision: one textual, the other functionalist or adaptivist. Much literature focuses on or presupposes the former (textual) rationale. Yet as we will see, it is implausible. We nonetheless explain and critique it briefly at the outset—in part because of its prominence in the literature, but more significantly, to situate it within the context of *Holland*'s actual, and far more compelling, rationale.

A. The Textual Rationale

The textual rationale seizes upon Holmes's self-evident observation that Article II of the Constitution delegates the whole treaty power to the federal government.[42] At first blush, Holmes thus seems to have supposed simply that any treaty, and any law made to implement a treaty, is by definition not reserved to the states. But that argument rests on a semantic error. The Treaty Clause, which says that the president has "Power, by and with the Advice and Consent of the Senate, to make Treaties," is not a delegated power comparable to Congress's Article I,

258 F. 479 (W.D. Miss. 1919); *see also Bond*, 134 S. Ct. at 2098 (Scalia, J., concurring in the judgment) (citing two earlier Supreme Court opinions favorable to *Holland*).

40. *Holland*, 252 U.S. at 431.

41. Many have framed the issue posed by *Holland* solely in terms of Congress's Article I, Section 8, delegated powers. That is misleading, for it is not the question Holmes answered. The Constitution does not limit the federal government's delegated powers to those of Congress. Nor is there a "plausible reason to suppose that the treaty power can extend only to subjects within Congress's enumerated powers." Gary Lawson & Guy Seidman, *The Jeffersonian Treaty Clause*, 2006 U. ILL. L. REV. 1, 11 (2006).

42. *See Holland*, 252 U.S. at 432.

section 8 delegated (enumerated) powers; rather, it is a *mode of exercising* power. It enables the federal government to make treaties to regulate international issues, including but not limited to, trade, extradition, military alliances, borders, fishing and navigation rights, and diplomatic relations. Unlike Congress's Article I, section 8 powers, the text of Article II, section 2 neither specifies nor limits the subjects about which treaties may be concluded.

Congress's legislative power, insofar as that refers to its power to make laws, is likewise properly understood as a *mode of exercising* the powers "herein granted,"[43] by Article I, section 8, over enumerated subjects: regulating commerce, coining money, establishing post offices, making rules to govern the army, and so forth.[44] The Constitution does not say that Congress has the "power to make laws"; rather, it vests "[a]ll legislative Powers herein granted" in "a Congress of the United States."[45] Hence, the word "Power[]" in Article I, section 1 is not semantically equivalent to "Power" in Article II, section 2, Clause 2. When we speak of Congress's delegated powers, we typically mean the Article I, section 8 "list" of enumerated powers, not Congress's authority to make laws about the items on that list. In short, the word "delegated" can be ambiguous and therefore misunderstood in this context. Were we to conceptualize the treaty and legislative modes as freestanding powers that the Constitution delegates to the federal government, then the Tenth Amendment, which reserves to the states those powers not delegated to the federal government, would limit the operation of *neither*. That construction would effectively read the Tenth Amendment out of the Constitution. It would have nothing on which to operate.

To avoid this absurd result, neither the legislative nor the treaty mode should be understood as a delegated power within the meaning of the Tenth Amendment. The textual rationale alone would not only sweep too broadly; it is simply implausible. The other, and far better, rationale, as Holmes surely recognized, would likely be characterized in modern constitutional theory as functionalist or adaptivist. Our analysis of *Holland* will focus on this dimension of its rationale—for despite, or perhaps because of, the perennial debate about

43. U.S. Const. art. I, § 1.

44. The Constitution does not, of course, delegate the power to make treaties to the states; it expressly prohibits them from exercising this mode of power. *Id.* art. I, § 10, cl. 1. But delegating the treaty mode to the federal government—without enumerating (as Article I, section 8, does for Congress) or otherwise indicating the scope of the *substantive* legal issues delegated—does not tell us which, if any, such substantive issues the Tenth Amendment might nonetheless reserve to the states.

45. *Id.* art. I, § 1.

Holmes's "cryptic" opinion,[46] it has not, we suggest, been correctly or fully understood in the literature.

B. The Force of Functionalism and Adaptivism in *Holland*

Holmes made short work of the facts in *Holland*, recounting them briefly only to remark that "it is enough that the bill is a reasonable and proper means to assert the alleged quasi sovereign rights of a State," for "the question raised is the general one whether the treaty and statute are void as an interference with the rights reserved to the States."[47] But after so posing the question, Holmes appropriately reframed it. The issue, he said, cannot be resolved simply by reference to the Tenth Amendment. That amendment reserves to the states only what the Constitution does not delegate to the federal government—and yet Article II delegates the treaty power to the federal government. Holmes did not, however, rest his argument upon this observation alone, which, as noted, would be misguided.

1. How Holmes Framed the Constitutional Question—And Why

It is nonetheless worth pausing here to emphasize how and why Holmes reframed the constitutional question as he did. Missouri had argued that the federal statute interfered with its Tenth Amendment right to regulate migratory birds within its territory—not to make treaties.[48] That is, of course, exactly as one would have expected. After all, the Court had previously characterized this right as an aspect of "the undoubted existence in the State of a police power."[49] And just one year before *Holland*, in *Carey v. South Dakota*, the Court had applied the canon of constitutional avoidance to avoid deciding the constitutionality under the Tenth Amendment of the *pre*-treaty 1913 Migratory Bird Act relative to a state law that regulated the shipping of migratory birds. Justice Brandeis, speaking for the Court, construed the 1913 Act narrowly, sidestepping the federalism issue and reiterating essentially what the Court had said in *Geer*: "a state has exclusive power to control wild game within its borders, and the South Dakota law was valid when enacted, although it incidentally affected interstate commerce."[50] The Missouri law at issue in *Holland* also did not affect interstate commerce more than incidentally, for the Court construed the Commerce Clause more narrowly at the time. Missouri

46. *E.g.*, Rosenkranz, *supra* note 7, at 295.

47. *Holland*, 252 U.S. at 431–32.

48. *See id.* at 431.

49. Geer v. Connecticut, 161 U.S. 519, 534 (1896).

50. Carey v. South Dakota, 250 U.S. 118, 120 (1919).

therefore had every reason to conclude that the Tenth Amendment reserved to it the right to regulate migratory birds, free from federal interference.

But Justice Holmes correctly reoriented the analysis to focus on the true—and constitutionally distinct—question. Rather than ask whether the Tenth Amendment reserves to the states *power over the subject* of the legislation (migratory birds), the question raised in *Geer* and *Carey*, he observed that the Amendment does not, of course, reserve to the states the *power to make treaties.* To the contrary, the Constitution expressly delegates that power to the federal government and denies it to the states.[51] That was and is uncontroversial. It is not the gravamen of Holmes's rationale, as noted in the preceding section. Yet it enabled him to clarify an indispensable point: that the "question before us is narrowed to an inquiry into the ground upon which the present supposed *exception* is placed."[52]

Holmes clarified, in other words, that the appropriate way to frame the constitutional question in *Holland*, in contrast to *Carey* and *Geer*, is not to ask whether the treaty power compels an exception to the Tenth Amendment but the converse: whether the Tenth Amendment compels an exception to the federal government's otherwise plenary power to make treaties. Recall in this regard that the federal government's power to make treaties, unlike Congress's power to make laws, is not textually limited to enumerated subjects. That is why, as Holmes thereafter emphasized, "[w]hether the two cases [striking down on Tenth Amendment grounds the earlier federal law regulating migratory birds] were decided rightly or not, they cannot be accepted *as a test of the treaty power*."[53] As he remarked in a critical but often misunderstood sentence, "If the treaty is valid there can be no dispute [under the Tenth Amendment] about the validity of the statute under Article 1, Section 8, as a necessary and proper means to execute the powers of the Government."[54] *Holland* therefore focused on the Tenth Amendment validity of the *treaty*—and only derivatively on its implementing legislation.

---

51. U.S. CONST. art. II, § 2; art. I, § 10.

52. *Holland*, 252 U.S. at 432 (emphasis added).

53. *Id.* at 433 (emphasis added).

54. *Id.* at 432. This sentence has caused needless confusion and has often been criticized, most recently by Justice Scalia's characterization of it as "unreasoned and citation-less." Bond v. United States, 134 S. Ct. 2077, 2098 (Scalia, J., concurring in the judgment); *cf.* Bradley, *supra* note 33, at 424 (speculating about this sentence's interpretation). In context, it is clear that Holmes meant only to refer to the Tenth Amendment validity of the legislation, that is, valid in the sense of necessary and proper despite otherwise potentially-applicable federalism limits. Legislation to implement a treaty may, of course, be invalid for many reasons that have nothing to do with the Tenth Amendment. It might, for example, bear an insufficiently rational

Holland, Holmes continued, raised an issue quite distinct from those in *Geer*, *Carey*, and the two federal district court decisions that had struck down the earlier 1913 Migratory Bird Act—namely, whether the Tenth Amendment compels an exception to the otherwise (textually) plenary federal power to make treaties. The Court held that it does not. Holmes's rationale for this conclusion is worth quoting here at length:

> It is said that a treaty cannot be valid if it infringes the Constitution, that there are limits, therefore, to the treaty-making power, and that one such limit is that what an act of Congress could not do unaided, in derogation of the powers reserved to the States, a treaty cannot do....
>
> [But that] cannot be accepted as a test of the treaty power [under the Tenth Amendment]. We do not mean to imply that there are no qualifications to the treaty-making power; but they must be ascertained in a different way. It is obvious that there may be matters of the sharpest exigency for the national well being that an act of Congress could not deal with but that a treaty followed by such an act could, and it is not lightly to be assumed that, in matters requiring national action, "a power which must belong to and somewhere reside in every civilized government" is not to be found. *Andrews v. Andrews* .... What was said in that case with regard to the powers of the States applies with equal force to the powers of the nation in cases where the States individually are incompetent to act .... [W]hen we are dealing with words that also are a constituent act, like the Constitution of the United States, we must realize that they have called into life a being the development of which could not have been foreseen completely by the most gifted of its begetters. It was enough for them to realize or to hope that they had created an organism; it has taken a century and has cost their successors much sweat and blood to prove that they created a nation. The case before us must be considered in the light of our whole experience and not merely in that of what was said a hundred years ago. The treaty in question does not contravene any prohibitory words to be found in the Constitution. The only question is whether it is forbidden by some invisible radiation from the general terms of the Tenth Amendment. We must consider what this country has become in deciding what that Amendment has reserved.[55]

---

relationship to the treaty under the Necessary and Proper Clause, or abrogate express individual rights. *See* Boos v. Barry, 485 U.S. 312 (1988); Reid v. Covert, 354 U.S. 1 (1957). Holmes did not—because nothing in *Holland* required him to—speculate about such other arguable "qualifications to the treaty-making power." *Holland*, 252 U.S. at 432.

55. *Holland*, 252 U.S. at 432–34 (internal citations omitted).

2. Holland's *Functionalist Rationale*

This quotation has become famous, not only for its significance to the central holding in *Holland*, but also because it captures a particular, albeit controversial, view of political theory, judicial interpretation, and the relevance of history to constitutional adjudication. Were it adopted generally, it would exert an especially forceful influence on the broader field of foreign affairs law, which frequently invokes history, practice, tradition, and similar non-textual considerations. It is also essential to understanding what *Holland* necessarily held—and why *Bond* and *Holland* cannot be reconciled. So at the risk of belaboring *Holland*'s analysis, it is instructive to consider this passage in greater depth.

Holmes began with the proposition that the treaty power is not just an alternative method by which the federal government may exercise in the international sphere the same congressional powers enumerated in Article I, section 8; rather, Article II, section 2, the treaty power, is a separate and independent *source* of federal lawmaking power. It both complements and augments Congress's enumerated powers. The Treaty Clause gives the federal government—in particular, the "treaty-makers,"[56] viz., the president plus two-thirds of the Senate[57]—the power to make national law by international means: "It is obvious," Holmes wrote, "that there may be matters of the sharpest exigency that an act of Congress could not deal with but that a treaty followed by such an act could."[58]

For *Holland*'s critics, of course, it was, and is, not at all obvious. But Holmes did not believe that the Framers, with the experience under the Articles fresh in their minds, created a Constitution that would disable the United States as a nation from exercising the same powers as other nations, including the power to make internationally lawful treaties. International law, of course, does not place federalism constraints on treaties, and it is definitional of a nation that it has full capacity to enter into relations with other nations.[59] The Constitution *itself*, for Holmes, established a fully empowered and functional nation. That is why, as he concluded, this authority must be found somewhere in the nation's government.[60] Yet in the federalist structure of the United States, it does not reside in the states. Nor could it. The national experience under the Articles established as much. And

---

56. *See generally* HENKIN, *supra* note 24, at 175–214.

57. U.S. CONST. art. II, § 2, cl. 2.

58. *Holland*, 252 U.S. at 433.

59. *See, e.g.*, Montevideo Convention on the Rights and Duties of States art. 1, Dec. 26, 1933, 165 L.N.T.S. 19.

60. This conclusion might at first seem redolent of Justice Sutherland's notoriously problematic theory in *United States v. Curtiss-Wright Export Co.*, 299 U.S. 304 (1936)—viz., that sovereignty provides the federal government, and in particular, in Sutherland's view, the President,

the nation's history and experience since 1789, especially the Civil War (in which Holmes fought and to which he alluded in *Holland*) put any residual doubts on this issue to rest.

Not coincidentally, Holmes's reference to "matters of the sharpest exigency for the national well being" echoes Marshall's proclamation in *McCulloch v. Maryland*. For the Treaty Clause, like the Necessary and Proper Clause, is part of

> a constitution, intended to endure for ages to come, and consequently, to be adapted to the various *crises* of human affairs. To have prescribed the means by which government should, in all future time, execute its powers, would have been to change, entirely, the character of the instrument, and give it the properties of a legal code. It would have been an unwise attempt to provide, by immutable rules, for exigencies which, if foreseen at all, must have been seen dimly, and which can be best provided for as they occur.[61]

Marshall's words aptly capture Holmes's answer to the question of the appropriate test, as he put it, of the treaty power. Given the "character of the [Constitution]," the treaty power's scope and limits were not frozen for all time by "immutable rules," which the Constitution set out in 1789. It is not accidental that the Article II power to make treaties, unlike Congress's Article I power to make laws, does not enumerate an exclusive list of allowable subjects for treaties. The treaty power must be sufficiently flexible to adapt to the exigencies of governing a nation "for ages to come." It must be robust enough to handle crises "which, if foreseen at all, must have been seen dimly, and which can be best provided for as they occur."

3. The Andrews *Analogy*

Holmes's reference to *Andrews v. Andrews*[62] is far more significant in this regard than scholars have recognized. It clarifies the nature and force of *Holland*'s rationale. A routine estate dispute in Massachusetts, *Andrews* may at first seem to be no more than a convenient source for a poignant quotation. It reached the Supreme

---

with an extra Constitutional source of power—although *Curtiss-Wright* postdates *Holland*. Yet Holmes clearly meant to interpret the Constitution *itself*. Nothing in *Holland* suggests any dubious thesis about extraconstitutional foreign-affairs powers. *See* Michael D. Ramsey, *The Myth of Extraconstitutional Foreign Affairs Power*, 42 WM. & M. L. REV. 379 (2000).

61. McCulloch v. Maryland, 17 U.S. (4 Wheat.) 316, 415 (1819); *see also* THE FEDERALIST NO. 23, at 147 (Alexander Hamilton) (Jacob E. Cooke ed., 1961).

62. 188 U.S. 14, 33 (1903), *abrogated by* Sherrer v. Sherrer, 334 U.S. 343 (1948). *Sherrer*'s abrogation of *Andrews* does not affect how the latter informs the rationale in *Holland*: what matters is Justice White's rationale, his constitutional methodology, not the validity of his conclusion.

Court only because the plaintiff invoked the Full Faith and Credit Clause,[63] injecting a federal question into an otherwise quintessential state-law dispute in which the decedent's ex-wife and second wife each sought appointment as administratrix of his estate. The local issues in *Andrews* scarcely seem relevant to the international issues in *Holland*.

Yet *Andrews* clarifies *Holland*'s functional rationale. Although Holmes did not offer details about the case, his remark on it is informative: "What was said in [*Andrews*] with regard to the powers of the States applies with equal force to the powers of the nation in cases where the States individually are incompetent to act."[64] The gravamen of Justice White's opinion for the Court in *Andrews* was that the Constitution established a functional *nation*. It should therefore be construed, in the event of ambiguity or uncertainty, to effectively lodge every legal power indispensable to a well-ordered nation in *a* government, state or federal, of that nation. Understanding *Andrews*'s relevance to *Holland* requires a brief review of the former's facts.

Charles Andrews sought to divorce his first wife, Kate. But the law of his domicile, Massachusetts, disallowed it. He therefore moved to South Dakota for the short period of time needed to establish residence, secured a divorce decree in South Dakota state court, and then returned to Massachusetts. A year later, he married his second wife, Annie. When he died five years later, Annie and Kate each claimed the right to administer his estate. The trial court, while observing that Kate had unscrupulously "connived at and acquiesced in the South Dakota divorce decree," found that she nonetheless retained the "right to administer his estate as his lawful widow,"[65] for Massachusetts law prohibited Charles's conduct, and directed its courts not to recognize the South Dakota divorce decree.[66] Because that decree could not be enforced in Massachusetts, Kate remained the decedent's lawful spouse and administratrix of his estate. Annie countered that the Full Faith and Credit Clause preempted Massachusetts state law and compelled its courts to enforce the decree, making her, not Kate, the administratrix.

Andrews's relevance can now be fully appreciated. In the United States of 1903, legally codified cultural norms conceived of marriage as a vital social institution. *Andrews*, citing earlier decisions, went so far as to describe marriage as "an essential attribute of government ... upon which the *existence* of civilized

63. U.S. CONST. art. IV, § 1.

64. Missouri v. Holland, 252 U.S. 416, 433 (1920).

65. *Andrews*, 188 U.S. at 27.

66. *Id.* at 29.

society depends."[67] The Constitution does not, obviously, delegate power over marriage to the federal government; it is a power reserved to the states. But just as in *Holland* applying the treaty power despite what might ordinarily be Tenth Amendment reserved rights over the legal regulation of migratory birds generated a conundrum, so too, in *Andrews*, did applying the Full Faith and Credit Clause to the reserved authority of the states over marriage. The Constitution apparently required Massachusetts to give full faith and credit to, and hence enforce, the very divorce decree that its own law prohibited. One law or the other, state or federal, had to yield.

A formal reading of the Constitution would have required that federal law prevail: a decree rendered in one state must be given full faith and credit in the courts of every other.[68] The Constitution therefore seemed to require Massachusetts to enforce the South Dakota divorce decree in its courts even though its own state law prohibited just that. But the *Andrews* Court reasoned that so applying the Full Faith and Credit Clause to marriage in this way would effectively deprive the domiciliary state of its reserved right under the Tenth Amendment to regulate marriage: a citizen of one state could evade its marriage laws, as did Charles, by the expedient of residing briefly in another state with lax marriage laws, obtaining a divorce decree there, returning to his domicile, and then enforcing the out-of-state decree in its courts—notwithstanding any domiciliary state law to the contrary, which the Constitution would preempt.

Justice White declined to construe the Constitution to require this dysfunctional result. Because, he noted, the Full Faith and Credit Clause could divest the states of their reserved right to regulate marriage, and yet the Constitution does not delegate that power to the federal government, it would result that, in practice, *neither* the states *nor* the federal government would be able to effectively regulate marriage—a social institution "upon which the existence of civilized society depends," and further, one which "ha[d] always been subject to the control of the [state] legislature."[69] To interpret the Constitution in *Andrews* to nullify Massachusetts state law would therefore be to prioritize form over substance. It would "presuppos[e] that the determination of what powers are reserved and what delegated by the Constitution is to be ascertained by a blind adherence to mere form, in disregard of the substance of things. But the settled rule is directly to the contrary."[70] The Court concluded that it would be untenable to interpret the Constitution to "destroy"—that is, to deprive government in the aggregate

67. *Id.* at 30–31 (emphasis added).

68. U.S. CONST. art IV, § 1.

69. *Andrews*, 188 U.S. at 30.

70. *Id.* at 33.

(state *and* federal) of—the effective legal power to regulate marriage, a social institution indispensable to government.[71]

The same principle, Holmes held in *Holland*, applies, *mutatis mutandis*, to the treaty power. It would be untenable to construe the Constitution to deprive the federal government of the power to make and implement treaties indispensable to the nation the Constitution established "for ages to come."[72] Treaties, like the social institution of marriage in the *Andrews* era, are "an essential attribute of government."[73] To insist that the treaty power cannot be exercised if the subject would otherwise be reserved to the states would be to render an important class of treaties beyond the authority of *any* government of the United States—state or federal. For it would be implausible to suppose that treaties could be coordinated and enforced uniformly by the states. The treaty power is among the "powers of the nation . . . where the States individually are incompetent to act."[74]

Holland, in brief, applied the constitutional logic of *Andrews*—viz., to oversimplify somewhat, that the Court should construe tensions in the text to enable the Constitution to function effectively given national interests and needs—to the converse situation in terms of whether federal or state law should prevail: in *Andrews*, that logic prioritized state law; in *Holland*, federal. But the principle in each case is the same: a contrary holding would interpret the Constitution to deprive government (in the aggregate, state and federal) of power to regulate "a subject . . . upon which the existence of civilized society depends,"[75] a power indispensable to the nation's "well being,"[76] perhaps even to its "existence."[77] Neither Justice White nor Justice Holmes thought a sound interpretation of the Constitution, which *establishes* the United States as a nation, compels a conclusion that *disempowers and diminishes* that nation.

C. An Anachronism?

The preservation of migratory birds may not strike the modern reader as a "national interest of very nearly the first magnitude."[78] Nor would many citizens

71. *Id.* ("This would be but to declare that, in a necessary aspect, government had been destroyed by the adoption of the Constitution."); *cf.* Missouri v. Holland, 252 U.S. 416, 435 (1920).

72. McCulloch v. Maryland, 17 U.S. (4 Wheat.) 316, 415 (1819).

73. *Andrews*, 188 U.S. at 31.

74. *Holland*, 252 U.S. at 433.

75. *Andrews*, 188 U.S. at 31.

76. *Holland*, 252 U.S. at 433.

77. *Andrews*, 188 U.S. at 31; *cf. Holland*, 252 U.S. at 435.

78. *Holland*, 252 U.S. at 435.

today describe the social institution of marriage as indispensable to the "existence" of civilized society.[79] But it would be mistaken to dismiss the logic of these cases as anachronistic. At the time of *Holland*, migratory birds were, the Court emphasized, a crucial "food supply" and "protectors of our forests and our crops."[80] The federal government's need to prevent their extinction by entering into a treaty—after lower courts had struck down its earlier effort to accomplish the same objective through the use of Congress's Article I powers alone—is itself evidence of just how important this national interest was at the time. And whatever the truth of Justice Holmes's characterization of the need to protect migratory birds, or of Justice White's description of marriage, the principle advanced in both cases is no less forceful: the Constitution need not and should not be read to disable government (again, in the aggregate, federal *and* state) from legislating effectively on matters of national significance.

Holmes stressed in *Holland* that a vital national interest could "be protected *only* by national action in concert with that of another power."[81] Without the doctrine established in *Holland*, such vital national interests, then as now, would be beyond the power of the United States to safeguard and promote. That is the gravamen of Holmes's argument: *a Constitution intended to function effectively for the ages and to adapt to the exigencies of a constantly evolving nation should not be read to deny government the power to protect indispensable interests of the nation it constitutes.*[82]

As we will see in Section VI, despite its relatively modest influence in the past century, contemporary international law and dramatic changes in the global order mean that *Holland*'s reconciliation of the treaty power with federalism remains even more vital to the national interest today. Only that reconciliation enables the Constitution to endure in this regard and to "adapt[] to the various *crises* of human affairs" we face in the twenty-first century.[83] Given the consensus that *Bond* did not overrule or substantially modify *Holland*'s core doctrine, however,

---

79. One the other hand, *Obergefell v. Hodges*, 135 S. Ct. 2584 (2015), suggests that citizens continue to perceive marriage as a critical social institution.

80. *Holland*, 252 U.S. at 435.

81. *Id.* (emphasis added).

82. Holmes did not argue that "need implies power," a dangerously illiberal argument. He accepted that the Constitution limits as well as empowers government, and he suggested in particular that limits on the treaty power exist. He denied, however, that those limits were properly to be ascertained simply by checking the list of Congress's enumerated powers. Again, there is no "plausible reason to suppose that the treaty power can extend only to subjects within Congress's enumerated powers." Lawson & Seidman, *supra* note 41, at 11.

83. McCulloch v. Maryland, 17 U.S. (4 Wheat.) 316, 415 (1819).

why is there cause for concern? Because, as we explain in the next section, the consensus is wrong: *Bond* eviscerated *Holland.*

IV. How Bond *Hobbled* Holland

In 2014, the Supreme Court granted certiorari to review *United States v. Bond*,[84] which squarely posed the issue in *Holland* for the first time in nearly a century. The film noir facts of the case generated no few chuckles. In 1997, the United States ratified the Convention on Chemical Weapons ("CWC" or Convention).[85] It requires the parties to prohibit certain activities set forth in the Convention, including by "enacting penal legislation."[86] The prohibited activities include the development, possession, or use of chemical weapons, which the CWC defines as "[t]oxic chemicals and their precursors," which, in turn, it defines broadly as "[a]ny chemical which through its chemical action on life processes can cause death, temporary incapacitation or permanent harm to humans or animals. This includes all such chemicals, regardless of their origin or of their method of production, and regardless of whether they are produced in facilities, in munitions or elsewhere."[87] Congress implemented the CWC in 1998.[88] The CWC Implementation Act ("Act"), modeled closely on the Convention's language, made it a federal crime to develop, possess, or use chemical weapons.[89]

In 2006, Carol Anne Bond, a microbiologist, discovered that her friend Myrlinda Haynes was pregnant by Bond's husband. Seeking revenge, Bond stole toxic chemicals from her employer and ordered others on the Internet. On at least twenty-four occasions between November 2006 and June 2007, she spread these chemicals on Haynes's car door, mailbox, and doorknob. Bond did not intend to kill Haynes; rather, she "hoped that Haynes would touch the chemicals and develop an uncomfortable rash."[90] Because the chemicals were readily noticeable, however, Haynes avoided them except on one occasion, when she suffered a minor burn to her thumb. Haynes repeatedly reported Bond's conduct to the

---

84. 681 F.3d 149, 149–70 (3d Cir. 2012).

85. Convention on the Prohibition of the Development, Production, Stockpiling, and Use of Chemical Weapons and on Their Destruction, *opened for signature* Jan. 13, 1993, 1974 U.N.T.S. 317.

86. *Id.* art. VII.

87. *Id.* art. II.

88. Bond v. United States, 134 S. Ct. 2077, 2083 (2014).

89. *Id.* at 2085.

90. *Id.*

police. Eventually, they referred her reports to the postal service, which set up surveillance and filmed Bond stealing an envelope from Haynes's mailbox and stuffing chemicals into her car muffler.

Federal prosecutors indicted Bond for mail theft and—perhaps because this charge alone failed to capture the seriousness of Bond's attempted assaults—for a violation of 18 U.S.C. section 229, the main criminal provision of the Act. Bond moved to dismiss this charge on two grounds. First, while conceding that her conduct could not technically be characterized as a statutorily exempt "peaceful purpose[],"[91] she argued that this exemption implied that the Act should not be read to reach non-"warlike" conduct. Second, she argued that, if it did, the Act "exceeded Congress's enumerated powers and invaded powers reserved to the States by the Tenth Amendment."[92] The Third Circuit rejected her arguments, relying, in the latter case, on *Holland* to sustain section 229 as "necessary and proper to carry the [CWC] into effect."[93]

A. The Court's Attempt to Sidestep *Holland*

Because the federal government disavowed reliance on the Commerce Clause as the basis for section 229,[94] leaving implementation of the CWC through the Necessary and Proper Clause as the statute's only potential constitutional basis, *Bond* offered the Court an opportunity, were it so inclined, to overrule *Holland*. But the majority did not seem so inclined. It instead chose to decide the case on statutory grounds, thereby avoiding—or so it thought—the need to revisit the constitutional issue it had decided in *Holland*. And since the Court's decision, a consensus has indeed emerged that, for better or worse, the *Bond* Court successfully elided *Holland* and managed to leave its core holding undisturbed.[95]

According to this view, the Supreme Court effectively dodged the issue in *Holland* by applying the canon of constitutional avoidance and resolving *Bond* on statutory grounds alone. That is, in fact, not only the consensus among

91. *Id.* at 2086.

92. *Id.*

93. United States v. Bond, 681 F.3d 149, 162 (3d Cir. 2012).

94. *See id.* at 168–69.

95. To the best of our knowledge, all commentary on *Bond* to date takes this position. *See supra* note 7. For earlier media commentary, see, amoung many other examples, Adam Liptak, *Chemical Weapons Treaty Does Not Apply to Petty Crime, Justices Rule*, N.Y. TIMES, June 2, 2014, at A13; and Ronald J. Bettauer, *Supreme Court Limits Holding in Bond, Not Reaching Constitutional Treaty Implementation Authority*, AM. SOC'Y INT'L L. INSIGHTS, June 25, 2014.

commentators; it is how all of the justices evidently understood the majority opinion, written by Chief Justice Roberts and joined by Justices Kennedy, Ginsburg, Breyer, Sotomayor, and Kagan. Justices Scalia, Thomas, and Alito, who concurred in the judgment despite vehement disagreement with the majority opinion, nonetheless understood it as the majority did.[96]

The Supreme Court, so this reading of the case continues, essentially embraced the statutory interpretation of the Act that the Third Circuit had rejected.[97] Avoiding consideration of the Tenth Amendment's interaction with the Treaty Clause, the Court read the Act narrowly such that it did not need to revisit *Holland*: Roberts found it implausible to construe the Act as criminalizing Bond's rather pedestrian efforts at revenge for marital infidelity. Congress enacted the Act, he concluded, to implement the CWC's ban on chemical *weapons*—not, as he colorfully wrote, to define chemical weapons so broadly as to "sweep in everything from the detergent under the kitchen sink to the stain remover in the laundry room," or to "make[] it a federal offense to poison goldfish."[98]

A cursory reading of the majority opinion indeed seems to bear out this view of the majority and therefore to minimize *Bond*'s import. Roberts summarized the potential stakes in the *Holland* debate only to dismiss it as needless to resolve *Bond*.[99] He began with the canon of constitutional avoidance: that, as a rule, "the Court will not decide a constitutional question if there is some other ground upon which to dispose of the case."[100] Consequently, he considered whether a non-constitutional ground to resolve *Bond* existed and concluded that Bond's statutory interpretation argument—the Act, properly interpreted, did not reach her misconduct—supplied a sound one.

Despite the Act's broad language, Roberts found "no reason to think the sovereign nations that ratified the Convention were interested in anything

96. *See Bond*, 134 S. Ct. at 2094–97 (Scalia, J., concurring in the judgment). Justices Thomas and Alito adopted by reference Justice Scalia's analysis in this regard. *See id.* at 2102 (Thomas, J., concurring in the judgment); *id.* at 2111 (Alito, J., concurring in the judgment).

97. The Third Circuit, like the concurring Supreme Court Justices, concluded that the constitutional question could not be avoided because "while one may well question whether Congress envisioned the Act being applied in a case like this, the language itself does cover Bond's criminal conduct. . . . [T]he statute speaks with sufficient certainty that we feel compelled to consider the hard question presented in this appeal." *Bond*, 681 F.3d at 155.

98. *Bond*, 134 S. Ct. at 2091; The majority concluded that "[t]here is no reason to suppose that Congress—in implementing the Convention on Chemical Weapons—thought" that "the global need to prevent chemical warfare [requires] the Federal Government to reach into the kitchen cupboard, or to treat a local assault with a chemical irritant as the deployment of a chemical weapon." *Id.* at 2093.

99. *Id.* at 2087.

100. *Id.*

like Bond's common law assault," and "nothing prevents Congress from implementing the Convention in the same manner it legislates with respect to innumerable other matters—observing the Constitution's division of responsibility between sovereigns and leaving the prosecution of purely local crimes to the States."[101] The gravamen of Roberts's argument is therefore clear: the Act excludes Bond's conduct because the correct statutory construction of section 229, the one consistent with its text and Congress's presumed intent, renders it inapplicable to "purely local crimes."[102]

B. Why the Court's Attempt to Sidestep *Holland* Failed

1. The Neglect of Holland*'s Own Federalism Principles*

Despite the Court's efforts, a close analysis of *Bond* reveals that it failed to sidestep the constitutional issues in *Holland* for at least three related reasons, summarized here and further elaborated below:

First, recall that after citing the canon of constitutional avoidance, the Court proceeded from the premise that it "[f]ortunately [had] no need to interpret the scope of the Convention .... Bond was prosecuted under [§ 229], and the statute—unlike the Convention—must be read consistent with principles of federalism inherent in our constitutional structure."[103] So framed by the Court, this premise is mistaken. To be sure, it is conceivable that this quotation reflects no more than ill-considered language. But the balance of the majority opinion suggests otherwise, and it is difficult to reconcile this statement with *Holland.* If the majority meant that treaty-implementing legislation must be read "consistent with" the *same* "principles of federalism inherent in our constitutional structure" as those that apply to legislation that does not implement a treaty, that proposition is manifestly inconsistent with *Holland.*[104] Whatever else *Holland* held, there can be no question that it distinguished between federalism constraints on laws that do and do not implement treaties.

Second: The same quotation reflects the Court's struggle to avoid revisiting *Holland.* If we assume, as did every member of the Court, that the majority succeeded, then *Holland* remains good law and binding precedent. That, in turn,

---

101. *Id.*

102. *Id.* at 2090.

103. *See id.* at 2088.

104. Had *Holland* truly been treated as good law by the majority, the Act at issue in *Bond* would not have presented an ordinary case of statutory interpretation—to be resolved in conformity with the same federalism principles that apply to a statute that does not implement a treaty. *Bond* mistakenly applied the same methodology as the federal district courts that had appraised the 1916 Migratory Bird Treaty Act *before* the Court's decision in *Holland.*

means that "principles of federalism inherent in our constitutional structure," as authoritatively interpreted by the Court itself, don't *conflict* with *Holland*'s doctrine; they *incorporate* it. *Holland*'s resolution of the tension between the treaty power and the Tenth Amendment, in other words, is among the "principles of federalism inherent in our constitutional structure." It is also among the federalism principles that the Court invoked and therefore should have applied when it enlisted the constitutional avoidance canon in support of its resolution of section 229's perceived ambiguity. Yet the *Bond* Court did not—as *stare decisis* and respect for precedent generally require—adhere to *Holland*'s conclusion about federalism principles in the context of a treaty-implementing statute.

Third: *Holland* held that a treaty and its implementing legislation must be appraised together under the Tenth Amendment; if the treaty is valid in this regard, so too is its implementing legislation. *Bond* proceeded from the contrary premise that the "statute—unlike the [treaty]—must be read consistent with principles of federalism inherent in our constitutional structure."[105] The majority further reasoned that "nothing prevents Congress from implementing the Convention in the same manner it legislates with respect to innumerable other matters—observing the Constitution's division of responsibility between sovereigns and leaving the prosecution of purely local crimes to the States."[106] The majority's assertion would ordinarily be unobjectionable. Nations frame multilateral treaties in terms that enable them to implement international legal obligations so as not to violate internal laws. *Bond*'s conflict with *Holland* in this regard arises because the majority's premise—viz., that legislation to implement treaties must comply with the *same* federalism principles as apply to legislation that does not—directly contravenes *Holland*. Were that so, a treaty and its implementing legislation could be assessed independently under the Tenth Amendment, notwithstanding *Holland*'s insistence to the contrary, viz., that a treaty's validity vis-à-vis federalism renders its implementing legislation valid under the Tenth Amendment—as necessary and proper to implement the treaty.[107]

2. Holland*'s Uniform Standard: Treaties and Implementing Legislation*

Each prong of the majority's analysis depended ineluctably on the last of these flawed reasons—never acknowledged as such, still less justified—namely, that the implementing legislation (the Act) and the treaty it implements (the CWC) may

105. *Bond*, 134 S. Ct. at 2088.

106. *Id.* at 2087.

107. *See* Missouri v. Holland, 252 U.S. 416, 432 (1920).

be appraised independently under the Tenth Amendment. Introducing the balance of the majority's analysis, Roberts thus wrote that "the statute—unlike the Convention—must be read consistent with principles of federalism inherent in our constitutional structure."[108] Under *Holland*, that's wrong. The validity of the CWC and the Act must be assessed together; logically, the two are inextricably linked. *Holland* held, among other things, that under the Tenth Amendment, if the treaty is constitutionally valid so too is its implementing legislation; if the treaty is not, neither is its implementing legislation. Roberts could interpret the Act not to reach purely local crimes only by neglecting, indeed subverting, this essential premise of *Holland: The constitutional validity of an Article II treaty determines the validity under the Tenth Amendment of its implementing legislation.*

Holmes could not have made this more explicit: "If the *treaty* is valid, there can be no dispute about the [Tenth Amendment] validity of the statute under Article I, § 8, as a necessary and proper means to execute the powers of the Government."[109] That is why, recall, Holmes recast the constitutional question in *Holland* to focus on the *treaty*'s validity rather than that of the implementing legislation: "The language of the Constitution as to the supremacy of *treaties* being general, the question before us is narrowed to an inquiry into the ground upon which the present supposed *exception* [to the treaty power] is placed."[110] Recall, too, that by "exception," Holmes meant exception to the treaty power based on the Tenth Amendment, not exception to the Necessary and Proper Clause.[111] In

108. *Bond*, 134 S. Ct. at 2088.

109. *Holland*, 252 U.S. at 432 (emphasis added).

110. *Id.* (emphasis added).

111. As part of the resurgence of federalism in the 1980s and 1990s, the Supreme Court established federalism limits on the Necessary and Proper Clause itself. It is therefore arguable that, even before *Bond*, these limits abrogated *Holland*'s holding that the treaty power enables Congress to regulate some subjects beyond those enumerated in Article I, section 8 (or delegated elsewhere to the federal government). Principles of federalism now apply also, and directly, to limit the ambit of the Necessary and Proper Clause, U.S. CONST. art. I, § 8, cl. 18. *See, e.g.*, Printz v. United States, 521 U.S. 898, 924 (1997) (finding that a federal law that "violates the principle of state sovereignty" can never be necessary and proper to execute Congress's powers); New York v. United States, 505 U.S. 144, 160-62 (1992) (holding that although the federal government had the power to regulate the radioactive waste at issue, the Tenth Amendment limited the *means* by which it could do so because federalism limits the Necessary and Proper Clause itself); *accord* Nat'l Fed'n of Indep. Bus. v. Sebelius, 132 S. Ct. 2566, 2592 (2012); Alden v. Maine, 527 U.S. 706, 728-29 (1999). Because federalism now directly constrains the Necessary and Proper Clause vis-à-vis Article I, it is technically an open question (especially bearing in mind that this body of case law postdates *Holland* by decades) whether the same constraints apply to legislation necessary and proper to implement an otherwise valid treaty. In other words, do federalism limits on the Necessary and Proper Clause in the context of Congress's Article I enumerated powers *alone* apply equally to Congress's powers to implement

other words, the Tenth Amendment validity of the implementing legislation is derivative of and determined by the Tenth Amendment validity of the treaty.[112] That is why Holmes could conclude without hesitation that the holdings of the two federal district courts striking down similar laws—laws that did *not*, however, implement a treaty—were irrelevant to the real issue in *Holland*. In contrast, *Carey v. South Dakota*,[113] which found the 1913 Migratory Bird Act unconstitutional, did not raise the "test of the treaty power"[114] at issue in *Holland*. Holmes accordingly prioritized analysis of the *treaty*. He assessed the validity of the treaty, not its implementing legislation, in light of the Tenth Amendment.

Holland therefore began with the text of the 1916 treaty between the United States and the United Kingdom concerning the preservation of migratory birds. It "provided . . . that the two powers would take or propose to their lawmaking bodies the necessary measures for carrying the treaty out."[115] Those measures, the implementing legislation challenged by Missouri, were passed "to give effect to the convention."[116] For the *Holland* Court, however, the validity of that convention, not its implementing legislation, determined the Tenth Amendment's relevance *vel non*.

After reframing the question, appropriately, as an "inquiry into the ground upon which the present supposed exception [to the treaty power based on the Tenth Amendment] is placed,"[117] Holmes thus considered the state's principal argument: that "a *treaty* cannot be valid if it infringes the Constitution," in particular federalism limits, and that "what an act of Congress could not do unaided,

---

a treaty concluded by the President and Senate under Article II? In our view, the arguments advanced in this chapter in support of *Holland*'s analysis of putative Tenth Amendment limits on Congress's *substantive* enumerated powers to effectuate a treaty apply with equal force to the limits now imposed by the Court on the *means* at Congress's disposal under the Necessary and Proper Clause. The logic of *Holland* does not depend in any obvious way on such a means-ends distinction. But it is conceivable that the prohibition on commandeering state political institutions, for example, might apply to a statute that would otherwise be necessary and proper to implement a treaty.

112. Again, implementing legislation might, of course, be unconstitutional for other reasons, such as a violation of the Bill of Rights. *E.g.*, Reid v. Covert, 354 U.S. 1, 16 (1957). *Holland* involved only its constitutionality under the Tenth Amendment. Holmes did not consider issues like prosecutorial discretion (surely a question in *Bond*) or the Necessary and Proper Clause's rational basis requirement.

113. 250 U.S. 118 (1919).

114. *Holland*, 252 U.S. at 432.

115. *Id.* at 431.

116. *Id.*

117. *Id.* at 432.

in derogation of the powers reserved to the States, a *treaty* cannot do."[118] This is the core argument—an argument that turns on the *treaty's* validity—that *Holland* considered and rejected: "The treaty in question," Holmes reasoned, not the implementing legislation, "does not contravene any prohibitory words to be found in the Constitution."[119] He also recognized that "but for the treaty," not the implementing legislation, "the State would be free to regulate this subject itself."[120] Consequently, he concluded, "the *treaty* and statute must be upheld."[121]

3. *The Unavoidable Conflict Between* Holland *and* Bond

Now reconsider *Bond*. The justices took the constitutional validity of the treaty for granted.[122] They did not question that the CWC involves "a national interest of very nearly the first magnitude," deals with an issue as to which "the States individually are incompetent to act," or requires "action in concert" with other nations.[123] In short, they did not regard the CWC's constitutionality as the relevant issue. Here again, the *Bond* Court's abandonment of *Holland* emerges clearly in Roberts's proclamation that the Court had "no need to interpret the scope of the Convention" because "Bond was prosecuted under [section 229], and the statute—unlike the Convention—must be read consistent with principles of federalism inherent in our constitutional structure."[124]

These words, and the balance of the analysis that relied upon them, mark a dramatic departure from *Holland*. The *Holland* defendants, too, were prosecuted under a law that Congress had enacted to implement a treaty. Unlike the *Bond* Court, however, the *Holland* Court did not state or imply that this law "must be read consistent with principles of federalism inherent in our constitutional structure."[125] Justice Holmes held to the contrary that for Tenth Amendment purposes, a valid treaty renders generic "principles of federalism inherent in our constitutional structure" nugatory as putative limits on congressional power to implement

---

118. *Id.* (emphasis added).

119. *Id.* at 433 (emphasis added).

120. *Id.* at 434 ("No doubt the great body of private relations usually fall within the control of the State, but a treaty may override its power.").

121. *Id.* at 435 (emphasis added).

122. Bond v. United States, 134 S. Ct. 2077, 2087 (2014); *accord id.* at 2098 (Scalia, J., concurring in the judgment); *id.* at 2111 (Alito, J., concurring in the judgment).

123. *See id.* at 2083–84.

124. *Id.* at 2088.

125. *Id.*

that treaty. Assuming, as both Chief Justice Roberts and Justice Holmes did, an otherwise constitutional treaty, *Holland* thus held *immaterial* the very same canon of statutory construction that *Bond* held *mandatory*. Stated otherwise, in the context of treaty-implementing legislation, Holmes characterized *Bond's* "principles of federalism inherent in our constitutional structure" as an irrelevant "invisible radiation from the general terms of the Tenth Amendment."[126]

Consider also the sharp (and irreconcilable) distinction between how Justice Holmes and Chief Justice Roberts framed the issue in, respectively, *Holland* and *Bond*—notwithstanding that each case arose in substantially the same posture and raised substantially the same constitutional question. Holmes focused first and foremost on the *treaty*: the precise "question before us," he wrote, "[can now be] narrowed to an inquiry into the ground upon which the present supposed exception [to the treaty power] is placed."[127] For Chief Justice Roberts, in contrast, the implementing legislation, not the treaty, raised the central question. He focused foremost, indeed exclusively, on the implementing legislation: "The question presented . . . is whether the *Implementation Act* . . . reaches a purely local crime."[128] In fact, in the *Bond* Court's view, this focus obviated the need to consider the treaty.

4. Bond's *Misguided "Background Principle"*

Only by rejecting *Holland's* insistence on the mutual dependence of the treaty and its implementing legislation for Tenth Amendment purposes could the *Bond* Court shift its focus to the statute alone, which it then analyzed as though it were a routine exercise in statutory interpretation. And only by effectively abandoning *Holland* could the *Bond* Court conclude that the Tenth Amendment constrained the reach of the Act. In contrast to *Holland, Bond* treated the federalism-based canon of constitutional avoidance as mandatory.

The orthodox reading of *Bond* interprets the majority opinion to introduce a clear statement rule in the context of laws implementing treaties: Congress must be explicit if it intends implementing legislation to abrogate the usual limitations imposed by federalism. Illustrative of this reading is Professor Bradley's conclusion that "[*Bond*] extends a federalism-based clear statement requirement, which was originally developed by the Supreme Court in the context of purely domestic legislation, into the realm of treaty-implementing legislation."[129]

---

126. Missouri v. Holland, 252 U.S. 416, 434 (1920).

127. *Id.* at 432.

128. *Bond*, 134 S. Ct. at 2083 (emphasis added); *see also id.* at 2088.

129. Bradley, *supra* note 7, at 493.

To be sure, much language in the *Bond* opinion seemingly lends itself to this view. The Court characterized the clear statement rule as a "background principle[] of construction"[130] and "conclude[d] that, in this curious case, we can insist on a clear indication that Congress meant to reach purely local crimes before interpreting the statute's expansive language in a way that intrudes on the police power of the States."[131] In part because of such statements, it is understandable that *Bond* has been read to impose a modest clear-statement rule on treaty-implementing legislation rather than to abandon (or even reach) the constitutional issue in *Holland*.

The Supreme Court could have, plausibly if controversially,[132] held that the Act did not reach Bond's conduct by means of a variety of canons of statutory interpretation—*without* invoking the canon of constitutional avoidance based on federalism; after all, as Karl Llewelyn famously pointed out, there's no shortage of these canons available to support particular results.[133] But the Court saw the federalism background principle and canon as all but determinative, the principal factor that resolved section 229's perceived ambiguity.

We have repeatedly quoted the Court's analytic predicate "the statute—unlike the Convention—must be read consistent with principles of federalism in our constitutional structure"[134] because it so clearly underscores *Bond*'s abandonment of *Holland*. It also directly illustrates the Court's misguided assumptions, first, that a mandatory federalism limit applies to laws implementing valid treaties; and second, that the statute and treaty may be assessed separately under the Tenth Amendment. *Holland* rejected both of these assumptions. Still, lest it seem that this is a case of cherry-picking one misguided quotation, note that the proposition is not an anomaly. The majority's analysis relied on it. Roberts stressed, time and again, that interpreting section 229 to reach Bond's local crimes would raise serious constitutional questions based on the structural principle that the federal government exercises only delegated powers, and that crimes such as Bond's would ordinarily fall within the state's "police power." In sum, the Court's pervasive reliance on a federalism "background principle" and canon of constitutional

130. *Bond*, 134 S. Ct. at 2088.

131. *Id.* at 2090.

132. Justice Scalia, like the Third Circuit, argued that textualism sufficed to show that the Act reached Bond's conduct and left no room for ambiguity. *Id.* at 2094.

133. Karl N. Llewelyn, *Remarks on the Theory of Appellate Decision and the Rules or Canons about How Statutes Are to Be Construed*, 3 VAND. L. REV. 395 (1950).

134. *Bond*, 134 S. Ct. at 2088.

avoidance to resolve section 229's ambiguity was not just one factor among many; it was, in the majority's view, the dispositive one.[135]

From the perspective of the orthodox reading, one might raise the following objection: Leave aside the Tenth Amendment. The majority did not try to avoid deciding whether the Act violates that amendment; it only sought to resolve section 229's perceived ambiguity without deciding whether *Holland* remains good law.[136] The easiest way to accomplish this was to apply a routine canon of avoidance that counsels construing the Act such that *Holland*'s continuing validity would not affect the Act's analysis regardless. That is why the Court insisted on "a clear indication that Congress meant to reach purely local crimes, before interpreting the statute's expansive language in a way that intrudes on the police power of the States."[137] For if the Court had *not* required this clear indication, then it *would* have needed to decide whether the statute's expansive language intruded on police powers vouchsafed to the states by the Tenth Amendment. That is all, one might argue, the Court did; it avoided the constitutional issue in *Holland* by assuming that for treaty-implementing legislation, as for other federal statutes, Congress legislates mindful of the background principle that federalism limits the reach of federal criminal law.

Yet if that characterization of the Court's approach is accurate, the majority misunderstood the implications of its analysis. After *Holland*, generic federalism principles are no longer a sound reason to believe that a treaty-implementing statute violates the Tenth Amendment. The *Bond* Court's application of the constitutional avoidance canon on this basis, however, assumes the contrary. *Holland* held, in relevant part, that an "invisible radiation from the Tenth Amendment,"[138] or in Chief Justice Roberts's substantively equivalent words, general "principles of federalism inherent in our constitutional structure,"[139] do not carve out an

135. *See id.* at 2086. It is unnecessary to catalog every instance where the Court relied on the avoidance canon predicated on pre-*Holland* federalism to construe section 229. A few examples suffice to show the extent to which it pervades the Court's statutory analysis. *See, e.g., id.* at 2086 ("A criminal act committed wholly within a State cannot be made an offence against the United States, unless it have some relation to the execution of a power of Congress, or to some matter within the jurisdiction of the United States.") (internal quotation marks omitted); *id.* at 2088 (stating that a contrary interpretation would "dramatically intrude upon traditional state criminal jurisdiction") (internal quotation marks omitted); *id.* at 2088–89 (mentioning federalism as a "background principle" of construction); *id.* at 2090 ("[I]t is appropriate to refer to basic principles of federalism embodied in the Constitution to resolve ambiguity in a federal statute.").

136. We thank Mike Dorf for pointing to the need for this clarification.

137. *Bond*, 134 S. Ct. at 2090.

138. *Holland*, 252 U.S. at 434.

139. *Bond*, 134 U.S. at 2088.

exception to the otherwise plenary federal treaty power. That does not mean, as Holmes said, that there are *no* limits on the treaty power.[140] It does, however, mean that in the context of a statute implementing a treaty, there are no limits based on general principles of federalism.[141] *Holland*, like any other precedent of the Supreme Court interpreting the Constitution, is (or was) itself *part of* the constitutional principles (here, of federalism) that, according to the Court, Congress must be presumed to respect when it legislates.[142] The Court's constitutional decisions have the same legal status as the document's text—Congress may not supersede them.[143] The Court's federalism background principle and associated canon of constitutional avoidance are themselves inconsistent with the Court's own authoritative interpretation of the Tenth Amendment in *Holland*,[144] unless and until the Court expressly overrules the case.

The point merits further elaboration. The Court began its analysis of federalism in Part III.A of the *Bond* opinion by criticizing the government's interpretation of section 229, according to which the statute reaches local crimes such as Bond's. It said that "this interpretation would dramatically intrude upon traditional state criminal jurisdiction, and we avoid reading statutes to have such reach in the absence of a clear indication that they do."[145] Then, at the close of this section, after exploring a series of cases (none involving treaties) that invoked

140. *Holland,* 252 U.S. at 433.

141. *See* HENKIN, *supra* note 24, at 193. Citing several scholars, Henkin speculates that "[t]he Constitution probably protects some few states' rights, activities, and properties against federal invasion, even by treaty." Though the Court has held that the Guarantee Clause, U.S. CONST., art. IV, § 4, is non-justiciable, given these specific "prohibitory words," *Holland*, 252 U.S. at 433, it would, for example, be doubtful that the treaty-makers could enter into a treaty requiring a state to adopt an authoritarian government. *See id. Holland* rejected the notion that abstract or general principles of federalism, without more, constrain the federal government's power to make treaties under Article II or to implement them by means of Congress's Article I, section 8 power to make laws necessary and proper to carry those treaties into effect.

142. *See generally* DAVID STRAUSS, THE LIVING CONSTITUTION (2012); David Strauss, *Common Law Constitutional Interpretation*, 63 U. CHI. L. REV. 877 (1996).

143. *See* Dickerson v. United States, 530 U.S. 428, 437 (2000) (citing City of Boerne v. Flores, 521 U.S. 507, 517-21 (1997)).

144. Roberts invoked the avoidance canon in an effort to decide *Bond* without being compelled to revisit the constitutional issue in *Holland*. But the only reason there *was* a constitutional issue to avoid was that the Court had tacitly rejected *Holland*. In the treaty context, the principles of federalism inherent in our constitutional structure, which emanate from the Tenth Amendment, *as the Court has construed it*, include *Holland,* thus obviating the same federalism concerns that, in *Bond*, animated its invocation of the avoidance canon in the first place.

145. Bond v. United States, 134 S. Ct. 2077, 2088 (2014) (internal quotation marks omitted).

federalism as a background principle of statutory interpretation, the Court concluded:

> These precedents make clear that it is appropriate to refer to basic principles of federalism embodied in the Constitution to resolve ambiguity in a federal statute. In this case, the ambiguity derives from the improbably broad reach of the key statutory definition given the term—"chemical weapon"—being defined; the deeply serious consequences of adopting such a boundless reading; and the lack of any apparent need to do so in light of the context from which the statute arose—a treaty about chemical warfare and terrorism. We conclude that, in this curious case, we can insist on a clear indication that Congress meant to reach purely local crimes, before interpreting the statute's expansive language in a way that intrudes on the police power of the States.[146]

The problem with this conclusion is twofold. First, because section 229 implements a treaty, there *is* no dramatic intrusion upon traditional state criminal jurisdiction—unless the Court has tacitly abandoned *Holland*. Second, assuming, as the *Bond* Court implicitly did by trying to avoid the constitutional issue in *Holland*, that the latter case remains good law, the presumption that Congress legislates against a federalism background principle cannot do the interpretative work that the majority supposed. In the treaty context, after *Holland*, there is no reason to presume that Congress sought to preserve the usual federal-state balance that obtains outside the treaty context. Rather, the "principles of federalism inherent in our constitutional structure" include *Holland*'s doctrine that those principles do *not* compel federalism constraints on statutes implementing treaties.[147] Provided the Act were enacted to implement a constitutionally valid treaty (as all of the justices in *Bond* regarded the CWC), generic "principles of

---

146. *Id.* at 2090.

147. *Id.* The Court might, of course, have logically concluded that because the CWC does not require implementation by federal criminal law, Congress exercised its discretion to respect general, non-doctrinal federalism concerns in implementing the CWC. After all, the federal government routinely does consider federalism when it negotiates treaties, and Congress may and likely does consider it as well in deciding how to implement treaties. In *Holland*, in contrast, the 1916 treaty arguably required Congress to intrude upon traditional federalism limits, and the evidence could not have been clearer that Congress also intended to transgress those limits. *Bond*'s assumption that Congress sought to respect the usual federal-state balance despite the CWC might be right; the legislative history behind the Act apparently did not clarify Congress's intent in this regard. But after *Holland* the Court cannot assume that legislation implementing a treaty should be construed, if possible, to adhere to the *same* federal-state balance as in a purely domestic context.

federalism inherent in our constitutional structure" would have been immaterial to, not the mandatory lodestar of, statutory construction. And it would have been equally immaterial that the Act, *absent the* treaty, might have intruded upon background principles of federalism against which Congress may be assumed ordinarily to legislate.

5. Carey v. South Dakota*: The Constitutional Avoidance Canon in Context*

The prudential rationale for the canon of constitutional avoidance bears emphasis. It adjures judges to avoid interpreting an ambiguous statute in a manner that might raise a constitutional doubt—but only *if* another construction is equally plausible. We need not defend any position here on the merits of the *Bond* majority opinion's approach to the Act's statutory interpretation in contrast to that of Justice Scalia's concurrence.[148] But it is instructive to call attention to Scalia's exasperation that, in his view, the majority misapplied the canon of constitutional avoidance *in order to find* the implementing legislation ambiguous based on federalism rather than, as it should have done, applied that canon only *if and after* finding the statute ambiguous—and only *because* of that ambiguity.[149]

It is ironic in this regard, but not coincidental, that in the absence of a treaty, Justice Brandeis in *Carey*, like Chief Justice Roberts in *Bond*, also applied the canon of constitutional avoidance to a federal statute (for Brandeis, the 1913 Migratory Bird Act). For Brandeis's opinion in *Carey* reveals how Roberts misunderstood the real issue in *Bond*. In short, Roberts treated *Bond* as the functional equivalent of *Carey* rather than *Holland*. But *Carey* arose under a federal law that did *not* implement a treaty. That law, the 1913 Migratory Bird Act, like the CWC Act in *Bond*, arguably raised Tenth Amendment issues, especially given the Court's precedents affirming state authority over the regulation of migratory birds.[150] But because of the treaty in *Holland*, unlike in *Carey* (decided only the previous year), Justice Holmes found no place for the canon of constitutional avoidance that Brandeis had applied in *Carey*. Brandeis agreed—for in *Holland*, unlike in *Carey*, the question had been the constitutional validity of the treaty and only derivatively that of the implementing legislation.

In *Carey*, by contrast, the question had been the constitutionality of the 1913 law, which substantively resembled the 1916 Migratory Bird Treaty Act, but did

---

148. *Bond*, 134 S. Ct. at 2094 (Scalia, J., concurring in the judgment).

149. *Id.* at 2095–97 (Scalia, J., concurring in the judgment).

150. *See* Carey v. South Dakota, 250 U.S. 118, 120, 122 (1919).

not implement a treaty. Yet in *Bond*, Chief Justice Roberts followed the *non*-treaty analysis in *Carey* rather than the treaty analysis in *Holland*. It is telling that Brandeis, *Carey*'s author, joined *Holland* without reservation.[151] His distinct approaches to *Carey* and *Holland*, which he regarded as constitutionally consistent, show that Brandeis agreed with Holmes that a treaty fundamentally reorients the Tenth Amendment analysis.[152]

In sum, had Chief Justice Roberts honored *Holland*, the real question in *Bond* would have been the federal government's authority to enter into the CWC itself *notwithstanding potential limits imposed by the Tenth Amendment*.[153] Justice Holmes did not (because he had no need to) speculate on the comparable issue in *Holland*. He simply said that the Court did not mean to imply that the treaty power has no limits.[154] Under *Holland*, then, either a treaty is beyond the federal government's Article II power—that is, an international agreement that the president plus two-thirds of the Senate may never constitutionally conclude—or it is not. If it is beyond the treaty power, then of course no statute to implement it could be constitutional. If it is not, then "principles of federalism inherent in our constitutional structure" would not apply to its implementing legislation, just as they would not apply to the same treaty were it self-executing. Either Tenth Amendment limits apply to both, or they apply to neither. And in the event of an arguable ambiguity in the implementing legislation, mandatory application of the canon of constitutional avoidance based on federalism principles would be erroneous—or at least, contrary to what the *Bond* Court suggested, inconsistent with *Holland*.

Bond's application of that canon, which it deemed mandatory, not precatory, cannot be reconciled with *Holland*. There is only a reason to apply the canon—only a constitutional issue to avoid—if one assumes, as the Court did, that the

151. The Tenth Amendment, that is, motivated Justice Brandeis to apply the constitutional avoidance canon in *Carey*. Chief Justice Roberts reasoned that the same goes for *Bond*. But *Carey* did not consider the constitutional test of the treaty power. Nor did *Carey* require the Supreme Court to consider whether that test should include a federalism exemption to the treaty power, as did *Missouri v. Holland*, 252 U.S. 416, 434 (1920).

152. *Id.* at 432–33. Just as the 1916 migratory bird treaty in *Holland* rendered general Tenth Amendment limits irrelevant to its implementing statute, so too, in *Bond*—were it truly the case that it did not overrule *Holland*—should the CWC have rendered Tenth Amendment limits irrelevant to *its* implementing legislation.

153. In theory, Congress might enact an absurdly broad or otherwise manifestly inappropriate statute, ostensibly to implement a treaty—and that statute would be invalid. But it would not be invalid because of the Tenth Amendment; it would be invalid because it would not be a genuinely necessary and proper means to implement the treaty. Not surprisingly, given the political safeguards of federalism, the Supreme Court has never had occasion to consider this issue.

154. *See Holland*, 252 U.S. at 433.

statute might otherwise conflict with general principles of federalism. But if the Court did not disturb *Holland*, there *is* no worry that generic federalism principles call into question the Tenth Amendment validity of a statute that implements a concededly constitutional treaty—rendering the canon of constitutional avoidance superfluous. Instead, the *Bond* Court relied on that canon, albeit among other principles of statutory interpretation, to interpret a purportedly ambiguous statute one way rather than another.

Because the Court did not see the presence of the CWC as relevant to the Tenth Amendment appraisal of the Act, it decided *Bond* by asking if the Act would be valid absent the treaty.[155] And absent the treaty, the *Bond* Court held that it was not only "appropriate to apply the background assumption that Congress normally preserves the constitutional balance between the National Government and the States," but also required by "the very structure of the constitution."[156] Had the Court, holding all else constant, employed that same background assumption in *Holland*, Missouri would have prevailed: the law implementing the 1916 treaty would have been constitutionally required to conform to the same "principles of federalism inherent in our constitutional structure"[157] that would have applied in the absence of the treaty, and the Supreme Court had held in *Geer* and *Carey*, both of which arose in a non-treaty context, that the regulation of migratory birds falls within the state's police power despite incidental effects on commerce. Applying *Bond*'s methodology in *Holland*, the Court would therefore have been obliged to strike down the Migratory Bird Treaty Act as a violation of the Tenth Amendment—for as Holmes affirmed, "but for the treaty . . . the State would be free to regulate this subject itself."[158] Consensus to the contrary notwithstanding, *Bond* abandoned *Holland*.

V. Critiques of Holland: *Theory and Practice*

Whether *Holland*'s substantive demise is cause for celebration is, of course, a different question. Fears of *Holland*'s supposed implications have never entirely receded. If we are right that *Bond* either effectively overruled *Holland* or, at a minimum, eviscerated its foundations, a word on the likely effects of this development is in order. In this and the following parts, we consider, respectively, the force of the chief critiques of *Holland* and the probable consequences, in a vastly changed international legal order, of the Court having now hobbled *Bond*. We

155. Bond v. United States, 134 S. Ct. 2077, 2087 (2014).

156. *Id.* at 2091.

157. *Id.* at 2088.

158. *Holland*, 252 U.S. at 434.

point out how abandoning *Holland* will impede the United States' ability to carry out certain international obligations. We begin in the first section with a brief review of the nation's experience with *Holland* in the century before *Bond*, for it supplies the appropriate empirical light in which to assess the chief objections to and critiques of *Holland*. In the latter two sections, we then turn to the political and legal constraints, which, we suggest, dramatically mitigate, if not obviate, the threats *Holland* allegedly poses to our constitutional order.

A. Before *Bond*: States' Rights, Individual Rights, and the Lessons of History, Experience, and Jurisprudence

Holmes's opinion has never lacked critics.[159] It generated controversy from the outset. Scholars almost immediately speculated about potential threats *Holland* might pose to both state and individual rights.[160] Nine years after *Holland*, former Secretary of State and later Chief Justice Hughes launched a broadside against *Holland* in a speech to the American Society of International Law, arguing that the treaty power extends only to "properly" international issues.[161]

After World War II, *Holland* also provoked a political backlash. The postwar rise of international institutions and multilateral human rights treaties raised fears among some politicians that treaties would intrude upon national sovereignty. Foremost in the mind of many were worries that such treaties might empower the federal government to enact civil rights legislation that would preempt state segregation and other racially discriminatory laws. In 1953, these fears culminated in Ohio Senator Bricker's proposal of the infamous Bricker Amendment, which sought to overrule *Holland* by amending the Constitution to add that "[a] treaty shall become effective as internal law in the United States only through legislation

---

159. Some commentators therefore bemoaned the *Bond* Court's perceived refusal to revisit the constitutional issue. *See, e.g.*, John C. Yoo & Julian Ku, *The Supreme Court Misses Its Chance to Limit the Treaty Power*, FORBES, June 12, 2014, http://www.forbes.com/sites/realspin/2014/06/12/the-supreme-court-misses-its-chance-to-limit-the-treaty-power/.

160. *E.g.*, Thomas Reid Powell, *Constitutional Law in 1919–20*, 19 MICH. L. REV. 1, 12–13 (1920).

161. *See* Power Auth. of New York v. Fed. Power Comm'n, 247 F.2d 538, 543 (D.C. Cir. 1957) (quoting Proc. Am. Soc'y Int'l L. 194, 196 (1929)), *vacated as moot*, 355 U.S. 64 (1957); *see also* HENKIN, *supra* note 24, at 197 and 471–72 n.87; Louis Henkin, *The Treaty Makers and the Law Makers: The Niagara Reservation*, 56 COLUM. L. REV. 1151 (1956); *accord* RESTATEMENT (SECOND) OF FOREIGN RELATIONS LAW § 117 (1965); *see also Bond*, 134 S. Ct. at 2110 (Thomas, J., concurring in the judgment). Hughes's objections reflected those made by Thomas Jefferson early in the nation's history. *See* David M. Golove, *Treaty-Making and the Nation: The Historical Foundations of the Nationalist Conception of the Treaty Power*, 98 MICH. L. REV. 1075, 1187–88 (2000); Lawson & Seidman, *supra* note 41, at 15–16.

that would be valid in the absence of a treaty."[162] The most prominent variation of the Amendment narrowly failed after President Eisenhower opposed it.[163] But many continued to fear that *Holland* could be used to avoid *all* constitutional limits—not only, as Holmes had more judiciously put it, "some invisible radiation from the general terms of the Tenth Amendment."[164] The Supreme Court found a welcome opportunity to put that fear to rest—or at least attempt to do so—in 1957.

In *Reid v. Covert,*[165] the plaintiffs argued that Article 2(11) of the Uniform Code of Military Justice—which, in conformity with executive status-of-forces agreements, authorized the trial of civilian dependents of military servicemembers abroad by court-martial—deprived them of due process under the Constitution.[166] Echoing *Holland*, the government countered that Article 2(11) could be "sustained as legislation that is necessary and proper to carry out the United States' obligations under the international agreements made with" the host states.[167] Justice Black, writing for a plurality, replied that "no agreement with a foreign nation can confer power on the Congress, or on any other branch of Government, which is free from the restraints of the Constitution .... The prohibitions of the Constitution ... cannot be nullified by the Executive *or by the Executive and the Senate combined*,"[168] thus implying that the same result would be forthcoming under an Article II treaty as opposed to the executive agreements at issue in *Reid*.[169] The *Reid* plurality also carefully distinguished *Holland*, in which, Black stressed, "the treaty involved was not inconsistent with any specific provision of the Constitution. The Court was concerned with the Tenth Amendment which reserves to the States or the people all power not delegated to the National Government."[170]

---

162. S. REP. NO. 412, at 1, amend. 2 (1953).

163. Jide Nzelibe, *Partisan Conflicts over Presidential Authority*, 53 WM & MARY L. REV. 389, 428 (2011); *see generally* DUANE TANANBAUM, THE BRICKER AMENDMENT CONTROVERSY: A TEST OF EISENHOWER'S POLITICAL LEADERSHIP (1988).

164. Missouri v. Holland, 252 U.S. 416, 434 (1920).

165. 354 U.S. 1 (1957).

166. *Id.* at 3–4, 15–16; *see* U.S. CONST. art. III, § 2, *id.* amends. V & VI.

167. *Reid*, 354 U.S. at 16.

168. *Id.* at 16–17 (emphasis added). Because *Reid* involved only sole executive agreements, its reference to Article II treaties ("the Executive and Senate combined") is dicta (in a plurality opinion); it therefore did not and could not overrule *Holland.*

169. *Id.* at 5–6. Justice Harlan concurred on the narrow ground that the defendants were tried for capital offenses. *Id.* at 65. But a majority of the Court found that distinction irrelevant three years later. Kinsella v. United States *ex rel.* Singleton, 361 U.S. 234 (1960). *Accord* RESTATEMENT (THIRD) OF THE FOREIGN RELATIONS LAW OF THE UNITED STATES § 721 (1987); *see also* Boos v. Barry, 485 U.S. 312, 323–24 (1988).

170. *Reid*, 354 U.S. at 18.

Reid has long been understood, correctly, to allay fears that *Holland* implies that treaties can supersede clear constitutional constraints. In 1987, the American Law Institute did not hesitate to codify in the new *Restatement* that "[n]o provision of an agreement may contravene any of the prohibitions or limitations of the Constitution applicable to the exercise of authority by the United States."[171] The following year, the Supreme Court, citing *Reid*, struck down on First Amendment grounds a provision of the D.C. Code prohibiting the display of any sign, or the congregation of three or more persons, within 500 feet of a foreign embassy, if the display or congregation tended to bring that foreign government into public "odium" or "disrepute."[172] The Court so held even though, first, Congress enacted it pursuant to its power to "define and punish . . . Offenses against the Law of Nations,"[173] and second, the Vienna Convention on Diplomatic Relations, to which the United States is a party and which "represents the current state of international law," requires states "to take all appropriate steps to protect the premises of the mission against any intrusion or damage and to prevent any disturbance of the peace of the mission or impairment of its dignity."[174]

By the late twentieth century, it therefore seemed clear that *Holland* did not affect constitutional provisions apart from arguable Tenth Amendment limits. But the vitality of the Tenth Amendment as a check on the treaty power remained unclear. The Supreme Court continued to cite *Holland* in cases in which the Tenth Amendment might otherwise have presented a fatal barrier.[175] In fact, as of 2006, the Court's justices had cited *Holland* in thirty-four opinions, none of which overturned it.[176] Lower courts, too, have applied and cited *Holland* as good law.[177]

---

171. Restatement (Third) of the Foreign Relations Law of the United States § 302(2) & cmt. (b) (1987).

172. *Boos*, 485 U.S. at 315 (quoting D.C. Code § 22-1115 (1987)). *But see* Lawson & Seidman, *supra* note 41, at 6, 16–18 (arguing that the First Amendment does not apply to the treaty power).

173. U.S. Const. art. I, § 8, cl. 10. *See Boos*, 485 U.S. at 316.

174. Vienna Convention on Diplomatic Relations art. 22, Apr. 18, 1961, 23 U.S.T. 3227, 500 U.N.T.S. 95.

175. *E.g.*, United States v. Lara, 541 U.S. 193 (2004); Minnesota v. Mille Lacs Band of Chippewa Indians, 526 U.S. 172 (1999).

176. *See* Duncan B. Hollis, *Executive Federalism: Forging New Federalist Constraints on the Treaty Power*, 79 S. Cal. L. Rev. 1327, 1353 (2006).

177. *E.g.*, United States v. Lue, 134 F.3d 79, 82–85 (2d Cir. 1998); United States v. Belfast, 611 F.3d 783, 805–06 (11th Cir. 2010); Cunard S.S. Co. v. Lucci, 222 A.2d 522, 527 (N.J. Sup. Ct. 1966); *see also* Martin v. State, 24 Ill. Ct. Cl. 6, 10 (1960).

Yet for most intents and purposes, *Holland* scarcely mattered for decades. Roughly between the Bricker Amendment's defeat in 1953 and the resurgence of states' rights jurisprudence in the 1980s, the Court's broad reading of the Commerce Clause enabled Congress to regulate virtually any activity, however attenuated its connection to federal interests. Canonical cases such as *Wickard v. Filburn*,[178] *Katzenbach v. McClung*,[179] and other post-New Deal and Civil Rights era cases expanded the scope of the Commerce Clause to all but eliminate constraints on Congress's power to regulate issues that once might have been deemed clearly reserved to the states. To be sure, as late as 1976, in *National League of Cities v. Usery*,[180] the Supreme Court, 5-4, said that the Tenth Amendment protects certain traditional or integral state functions from federal regulation (although it did not identify them). But a decade later, in *Garcia v. San Antonio Metropolitan Transit Authority*, a similarly divided Court overturned *National League*, concluding that the distinction between traditional and nontraditional state functions could not be sustained "for purposes of state immunity under the Commerce Clause."[181] It "reject[ed], as unsound in principle and unworkable in practice, a rule of state immunity from federal regulation that turns on a judicial appraisal of whether a particular governmental function is 'integral' or 'traditional.'"[182]

The Court thus embraced the idea that limits on federal power reside solely in the political safeguards of federalism,[183] that is, structural features of the Constitution that "protect the States from overreaching by Congress," for example, by giving the states prominent "role[s] in the selection both of the Executive and the Legislative Branches of the Federal Government."[184] For as long as this view prevailed, *Holland*'s merits seemed mostly academic. Jurisprudential developments since 1920 would have rendered it unnecessary for the federal government to conclude a treaty to protect migratory birds that routinely cross international and state borders. The Commerce Clause would have sufficed. No longer, in other words, did it seem "obvious" that there were "matters of the sharpest exigency

---

178. 317 U.S. 111 (1942).

179. 379 U.S. 294 (1964).

180. 426 U.S. 833, 854–55 (1976).

181. 469 U.S. 528, 530 (1985).

182. *Id.* at 546–47.

183. *See* Herbert Wechsler, *The Political Safeguards of Federalism: The Role of the States in the Composition and Selection of the National Government*, 54 COLUM. L. REV. 543 (1954). The Supreme Court has expressly adopted this view in several cases. *E.g., Wickard*, 317 U.S. at 120.

184. *Garcia*, 469 U.S. at 551.

for the national well being that an act of Congress could not deal with but that a treaty followed by such an act could."[185]

But the jurisprudential tide shifted under Chief Justice Rehnquist's leadership as the Court breathed new life into federalism. Among other developments reinvigorating federalism, the Rehnquist Court invalidated federal laws commandeering state legislatures and executive officials,[186] expanded the scope of the Eleventh Amendment to confer upon the states immunity from suit in most cases,[187] and for the first time since the New Deal, struck down federal laws as beyond the reach of the Commerce Clause.[188] Furthermore, although the Court has not overruled *Garcia* explicitly, it has decided several cases that seem to be in considerable tension with *Garcia*'s rejection of the idea of traditional state functions.[189] *Holland*'s potential implications therefore began to resurface insofar as it might enable the federal government to accomplish by treaty what is now foreclosed by the Tenth Amendment. This prospect has long been among the chief critiques of *Holland*,[190] and it has re-emerged because of developments in both national and international law.

B. The Political and Legal Limits of *Holland*

1. Political Constraints: A Short, Not-So-Horrible Parade

Before considering *Bond*'s future consequences more closely, it will be prudent to put into some perspective a recurrent red herring that persists despite a century of experience with *Holland*: the parade of horribles that *Holland* supposedly set to march. Critics of *Holland* have long constructed a variety of implausible hypothetical scenarios. Justice Scalia's concurrence in *Bond* is a recent exemplar:

> [T]he possibilities of what the Federal Government may accomplish, with the right treaty in hand, are endless and hardly farfetched.... For example,

185. Missouri v. Holland, 252 U.S. 416, 433 (1920).

186. Printz v. United States, 521 U.S. 898 (1997); New York v. United States, 505 U.S. 144 (1992).

187. Alden v. Maine, 527 U.S. 706 (1999); Seminole Tribe of Florida v. Florida, 517 U.S. 44 (1996).

188. United States v. Morrison, 529 U.S. 598 (2000); United States v. Lopez, 514 U.S. 549 (1995).

189. *See, e.g.*, Am. Ins. Ass'n v. Garamendi, 539 U.S. 396 (2003). *See generally* John C. Yoo, *The Judicial Safeguards of Federalism*, 70 S. Cal. L. Rev. 1311 (1997).

190. *E.g.*, Bond v. United States, 134 S. Ct. 2077, 2100 (2014) (Scalia, J., concurring in the judgment).

> the holding that a statute prohibiting the carrying of firearms near schools went beyond Congress's enumerated powers, *United States v. Lopez*, 514 U.S. 549, 512 (1995), could be reversed by negotiating a treaty with Latvia providing that neither sovereign would permit the carrying of guns near schools.[191]

Similarly, Justice Scalia suggested, the United States could bar "state inheritance taxes on real property" to implement a treaty. Among other jurists over the years, he concluded based on such speculation that "*Holland* places Congress only one treaty away from acquiring a general police power."[192]

Hypotheticals of this sort have been bandied about since the Court decided *Holland*. Any competent law professor could construct countless others. Senator Bricker and his colleagues took them seriously, and Justice Scalia's concurrence shows that this worry persists. Yet it is both fair and accurate to describe such hypotheticals as farfetched. *Holland* has been good law for almost a century. No one can point to a single real example of abuse. In the ninety-four years since *Holland*—through World War II, global economic integration, massive immigration flows, the modern conflict with transnational terrorism, and all the familiar dislocations that beset the modern world—the federal government has never, *never*, sought to evade a Supreme Court decision or otherwise circumvent the Constitution by concluding a contrived treaty with a foreign nation. It is not difficult to see why.

First, whatever the general force of the political safeguards of federalism, they prove manifestly effective in the treaty realm.[193] The Constitution deliberately makes it difficult to conclude treaties. Under Article II, the president may ratify a treaty only with the concurrence of two-thirds of the Senate.[194] Securing that concurrence is no simple matter—and it shows.[195] Consider a few examples: the United States has refused to ratify, among other treaties, the Convention on the Rights of Persons with Disabilities,[196] which essentially codified U.S. law

---

191. *Id.*

192. *Id.* at 2101.

193. Wechsler, *supra* note 183; Martin S. Flaherty, *Are We to Be a Nation? Federal Power vs. "States' Rights" in Foreign Affairs*, 70 U. COLO. L. REV. 1277, 1308–09 (1999).

194. U.S. CONST. art. II, § 2.

195. *See, e.g.*, GLEN S. KRUTZ & JEFFREY S. PEAKE, TREATY POLITICS AND THE RISE OF THE EXECUTIVE AGREEMENTS 32–35 (2009).

196. Convention on the Rights of Persons with Disabilities, Dec. 13, 2006, 2515 U.N.T.S. 3. President Bush signed the Convention, but despite former senator Dole's memorable appearance in a wheelchair to encourage Senate approval, the treaty did not even make it out

internationally;[197] the Convention on the Rights of the Child, which only the United States has not ratified;[198] and the Convention on the Law of the Sea, despite a widespread belief that it would further the national interest.[199]

Second, constituents hold senators accountable. Except perhaps in (historically unprecedented) exigent circumstances, senators would be highly unlikely to agree to an ersatz treaty crafted by the executive branch simply to override state authority or "overrule" a disfavored Supreme Court decision. As Professor Epps observed, commenting on Justice Scalia's hypothetical treaty with Latvia, "67 senators or so (depending on the number voting), after a public debate, would have to agree that Latvian-U.S. relations should govern guns in American high schools," and because the Constitution guarantees all states two senators regardless of their populations, "[e]ven in a harmonious Senate, senators representing roughly 7.5 percent of the population could block a gun treaty."[200]

Third, it is unclear why the federal government would have an interest in arrogating to itself power over traditional state functions such as probate. It is no accident that it has never sought to conclude a treaty for the purpose of taking over a traditional state police power. To the contrary, it has become commonplace for the federal government to insert federalism clauses in international agreements in order to protect the states from intrusion upon their traditional powers.[201]

---

of committee. Michael Kranish, *The Story of Washington Gridlock Seen Through the Eyes of Bob Dole*, Bos. Globe, Mar. 24, 2013, http://www.boston.com/news/politics/2013/03/23/the-story-washington-gridlock-seen-through-the-eyes-bob-dole/zyQo5CKoGMKjPBDcNJGAVP/story.html.

197. *Convention on the Rights of Persons with Disabilities Before the S. Comm. on Foreign Relations*, 113th Cong. (2013) (statement of C. Boyden Gray), http://www.foreign.senate.gov/imo/media/doc/Gray_Testimony.pdf.

198. Convention on the Rights of the Child, Nov. 20, 1989, 1577 U.N.T.S. 3. Federalism is one reason the United States has not ratified the Convention. Some fear that the Convention will interfere with family matters traditionally reserved to the states. *Why Won't America Ratify the UN Convention on Children's Rights?*, Economist (Oct. 6, 2013), http://www.economist.com/blogs/economist-explains/2013/10/economist-explains-2.

199. *See, e.g.*, Thomas Wright, *Outlaw of the Sea*, Foreign Aff. (Aug. 7, 2012), https://www.foreignaffairs.com/articles/oceans/2012-08-07/outlaw-sea.

200. Garrett Epps, Bond v. U.S. *Doesn't Mean Latvian Cops Are Coming for Your Guns*, The Atlantic, June 5, 2014, http://www.theatlantic.com/politics/archive/2014/06/bond-v-us-doesnt-mean-that-latvian-cops-are-coming-for-your-guns/372263/.

201. *See* Hollis, *supra* note 176, at 1373–75. The federalism clause in the International Labor Organization's Constitution encouraged federal states, such as the United States, Australia, and Canada, to seek similar clauses in other international agreements. The United States inserted federal-state clauses in the 1967 Protocol to the Convention Relating to the Status of Refugees and the Cybercrime Convention. *Id.* at 1375–76. *See also* David M. Golove, *Treaty-Making and the Nation: The Historical Foundations of the Nationalist Conception of the Treaty Power*, 98 Mich. L. Rev. 1075, 1273 (2000).

Senators often insist upon these provisions as a condition of their consent, often because the states carry out their functions ably, and senators see no need to fix what does not need fixing.

Finally, of course, treaties require two parties: the United Kingdom and the United States had a mutual interest in cooperating to preserve migratory birds that traversed international, not just state, borders. Absent a similar mutual interest, it would require a good measure of (passing strange) collusion for Latvia, or any foreign nation, to enter into a contrived treaty with the United States to enable the federal government to keep guns out of school zones—or, in general, to expand federal power at the expense of the states.[202] And it is a virtual certainty that any such contrivance would become evident long before the treaty received the consideration, still less approval, of the Senate.

In sum, "*Holland* places Congress only one treaty away from acquiring a general police power"[203] only in an imaginary world—not the one in which we live.

2. *Legal Constraints: The Scope of* Holland

The lessons of practice, experience, and history notwithstanding, some critics object to *Holland*'s supposed theoretical scope: Did the Framers really vest the federal government with the potential power to vitiate the Tenth Amendment altogether, subject to finding the right treaty partner? How could that be consistent with the foundational principle that the Constitution establishes a federal government with delegated powers only, all residual authority remaining with the states? Tellingly, Holmes did not offer a general theory of the scope and limits of the treaty power. *Holland* did not require it. Extensive dicta on such a critical constitutional issue would have been, literally and figuratively, injudicious. We cannot and should not, therefore, try to draw any firm conclusions about Holmes's view of issues beyond those he addressed. Indeed, far from offering needless, imprudent speculation in *Holland*, the dicta in Holmes's brief opinion served only to reinforce the limited scope of his decision. Properly understood, Holmes's analysis does not conflict with the principle that the Constitution established a federal government of delegated, limited powers.

---

202. "The United States and Latvia have not in fact negotiated such a treaty. Why not? Could it be that countries do not enter into treaties that regulate internal matters because they have no reason to do so?" *Bond v. United States*, ERIC POSNER, June 2, 2014, http://ericposner.com/bond-v-united-states. Posner is likely correct that the "unstated target of the [concurrence] is the international human rights treaty." *Id.* The ghost of Senator Bricker lives on. Louis Henkin, *U.S. Ratification of Human Rights Conventions: The Ghost of Senator Bricker*, 89 AM. J. INT'L L. 341 (1995).

203. Bond v. United States, 134 S. Ct. 2077, 2101 (2014) (Scalia, J., concurring in the judgment).

Holmes predicated his analysis in *Holland* on an Article II treaty.[204] The decision's logic is properly limited to that context. Holmes presupposed that Article II establishes a federal lawmaking power in the president and Senate that is conceptually and in its scope distinct from that of Congress under Article I. That is why, Holmes argued, an act of Congress to implement an Article II treaty may sometimes accomplish what an act of Congress under Article I, section 8, alone, may not. Beyond doubts in some scholarly quarters about the constitutionality of other types of U.S. international agreements,[205] it is therefore clear that neither congressional-executive nor sole executive agreements suffice under *Holland*. Henkin aptly summarized Holmes's logic in this regard:

> What he said, simply, was that the Constitution delegated powers to various branches of the federal government, not only to Congress; the Treaty Power was delegated to the federal treaty-makers, a delegation additional to and independent of the delegations to Congress. Since the Treaty Power was delegated to the federal government, whatever is within its scope is not reserved to the states: the Tenth Amendment is not material. Many matters, then, may appear to be "reserved to the States" as regards domestic legislation if Congress does not have power to regulate them; but they are not reserved to the states so as to exclude their regulation by international agreement.[206]

In other words, certain matters fall within the domain of the treaty power, and hence the federal government, even though they do not fall within the domain of congressional power.

Henkin's insight posits two additional legal limits on *Holland*'s doctrinal scope. First, *Holland* "did not say that there were no limitations on the Treaty Power in favor of the states, only that there were none in any 'invisible radiation' from the Tenth Amendment."[207] The phrase "invisible radiation" is a rhetorical flourish, but Holmes's essential point is clear. The general terms of the Tenth Amendment

---

204. Because *Holland*'s doctrine is limited to Article II treaties, the federalism issue it raises will almost always arise in the context of what Hughes, Jefferson, and others have described as "genuine" or "proper" international treaties. Lawson & Seidman, *supra* note 41, at 13; *cf. Bond*, 134 S. Ct. at 2110 (Thomas, J., concurring in the judgment). The principal exception is the international human rights treaty, which does not conform to the contractual model dominant in earlier centuries. *Cf.* Henkin, *Ghost of Senator Bricker*, *supra* note 202.

205. *See, e.g.*, Laurence H. Tribe, *Taking Text and Structure Seriously: Reflections on Free-Form Method in Constitutional Interpretation*, 108 HARV. L. REV. 1221 (1995).

206. HENKIN, *supra* note 24, at 191.

207. *Id.* at 193.

(reserving to the states or the people what the Constitution does not delegate to the federal government) do not establish a nebulous penumbra of state authority that limits the treaty power. Scholars have argued, however, that *specific* federalism constraints exist: for example, that the federal government may not, by treaty, cede state territory to a foreign nation without that state's consent; deny to any state a republican form of government; or abolish state militias.[208] We take no position on these issues here, except to say that we see no basis for the limitation suggested by Justice Thomas in *Bond*, and by Hughes and others before him, namely, the supposed distinction between "proper" international and domestic issues.[209]

Second, *Holland*'s doctrine is limited to the structural *allocation* of power between the federal and state governments. "Many matters," Henkin wrote, "may appear to be 'reserved to the States' as regards domestic legislation if Congress does not have power to regulate them; but they are not reserved to the states so as to exclude their regulation by international agreement."[210] Justice Holmes interpreted the Treaty Clause relative to the Tenth Amendment, not any other provision of the Constitution. In particular, he neither said nor implied anything about the Bill of Rights. As the Court has since held, no treaty may infringe individual rights, such as the right to grand jury indictment, jury trial, and freedom of expression. Note, therefore, that after *District of Columbia v. Heller*,[211] not only would a hypothetical gun treaty with Latvia, as a political matter, stand no chance of being concluded, it would also, as a legal matter, be presumptively unconstitutional under *Reid* insofar as it infringed upon the right to possess a handgun for lawful purposes as affirmed in *Heller*.

It may be objected, as it has been, that there is no principled basis upon which to limit *Holland* to the Tenth Amendment alone, insulating the rights of individuals, but not states, from the doctrine's ambit. Not so. *Holland* speaks to a structural issue raised by the Tenth Amendment about the allocation of federal and state authority. It does not increase the aggregate power of government within the United States (state and federal) at the expense of the governed. In other words, *Holland* holds that treaties may adjust *which* government has authority to exercise a particular power.[212] But nowhere does Holmes suggest that treaties confer on

---

208. *See* HENKIN, *supra* note 24, at 193 and nn.72–75. Nor, almost surely, could a treaty deprive a state of its voice in the Senate. *See* U.S. CONST. art. V.

209. 134 S. Ct. at 2110 (Thomas, J., concurring in the judgment).

210. HENKIN, *supra* note 24, at 191.

211. 554 U.S. 570 (2008).

212. From an originalist perspective, this limitation on *Holland*'s doctrine makes sense. The Tenth Amendment deals with an issue of structure and the allocation of authority. The reasonable person of 1789 surely understood that one of the virtues of the new Constitution would be its amelioration of the problems created by state refusal under the Articles of Confederation

government, state or federal, any power that the Constitution otherwise denies to government in the aggregate.

Consider *Holland* itself: it established that to the extent necessary to carry out treaty obligations to the United Kingdom, federal rather than state government had the power to regulate migratory birds. Absent the 1916 treaty, the same power existed; it is just that the power would have remained with the states rather than the federal government. No one argued (it would have been absurd) that the Constitution protects the people from governmental regulation of migratory birds—as it protects the people from, for example, deprivation of liberty without due process of law. Nor did Justice Holmes suggest that the 1916 treaty gave government, state and federal, any power it would otherwise lack under the Constitution. In *Bond*, similarly, Bond challenged the *federal* government's right to make it a crime to prosecute her for a "purely local" assault with a chemical weapon.[213] She did not dispute that Pennsylvania, the relevant *state* government, had the power to make precisely the same conduct a crime and to prosecute her under its laws. The Court agreed: "It is . . . clear that the laws of the Commonwealth of Pennsylvania (and every other State) are sufficient to prosecute Bond. Pennsylvania has several statutes that would likely cover her assault. . . . And state authorities regularly enforce these laws in poisoning cases."[214] All this is to reaffirm from another perspective the abiding truth of Justice Black's reassurance in *Reid v. Covert*.[215]

Finally, *Holland* may not have proclaimed as broad a doctrine as some of its critics suppose. To see why, reconsider two passages from the opinion. First, early in the analysis, Holmes wrote:

> We do not mean to imply that there are no qualifications to the treaty-making power; but they must be ascertained in a different way. It is obvious that there may be matters of the sharpest exigency for the national

to abide by national treaty obligations. Because international law, today as in 1789, regards nations, not their political subdivisions, as the repository of state responsibility, see Articles on Responsibility of States for Internationally Wrongful Acts, in Report of the International Law Commission on the Work of its Fifty-third Session art. 4, UN GAOR 56th Sess., Supp. No. 10, at 43, U.N. Doc. A/56/10 (2001), violation of, for example, the Jay Treaty, would have placed the nation as a whole at risk, potentially the risk of war, in 1789. *See* THE FEDERALIST NO. 28, at 102 (Alexander Hamilton) (J. Cooke ed., 1961). Enabling treaties to ameliorate this risk by empowering the federal government, under a treaty, to exert greater authority relative to the states than usual would be a logical response to this risk.

213. Bond v. United States, 134 S.Ct. 2077, 2087-88 (2014).

214. *Id.* at 2092.

215. 354 U.S. 1, 3, 16 (1957).

> well being that an act of Congress could not deal with but that a treaty followed by such an act could, and it is not lightly to be assumed that, in matters requiring national action, "a power which must belong to and somewhere reside in every civilized government" is not to be found. *Andrews v. Andrews*, 188 U.S. 14 (1903). What was said in that case with regard to the powers of the States applies with equal force to the powers of the nation in cases where the States individually are incompetent to act.[216]

Later, he concluded:

> Here a national interest of very nearly the first magnitude is involved. It can be protected only by national action in concert with that of another power. . . . It is not sufficient to rely upon the States. The reliance is vain, and were it otherwise, the question is whether the United States is forbidden to act.[217]

These passages may suggest a narrower legal doctrine, which, quite apart from the political safeguards of federalism, does not necessarily place traditional state powers at the mere whim of the federal government. Holmes began with the "general question" of the test of the treaty power's scope in the face of a claimed Tenth Amendment "exemption." He rejected the argument that the Tenth Amendment, *as such*, creates an omnibus exemption. Article II, he observed, delegates the treaty power to the federal government, and hence, "whatever is *within its scope* is not reserved to the states: the Tenth Amendment is not material."[218] That observation need not, and presumably does not, mean that just anything is "within its scope"; if anything, it implies the contrary. Holmes said only that the limits of the treaty power "must be ascertained in a different way."[219] With reference to the rationale of *Andrews* and *Holland*, that way may depend on the ability of the United States to vindicate national interests in circumstances where, first, effective regulation necessitates "national action in concert with that of another power"; and second, either the states would be "incompetent to act" or reliance upon them would be "vain"—a more circumscribed conception of *Holland*'s doctrinal reach.

Holmes, again, took a pragmatic view of constitutional adjudication. He saw "nothing in the *Constitution* that compels the Government" to stay its hand

---

216. Missouri v. Holland, 252 U.S. 416, 433 (1920).

217. *Id.* at 435.

218. HENKIN, *supra* note 24, at 191 (emphasis added).

219. *Holland*, 252 U.S. at 433.

despite the manifest inability of the states to handle a pressing national issue.[220] The Constitution establishes a functional and durable government for the whole nation. It should not be interpreted to deprive government in the aggregate, state and federal, of the ability to act effectively to address a critical need. In *Andrews*, Justice White confronted a situation in which the interaction of the Full Faith and Credit Clause and a Massachusetts state law might yield the conclusion that neither federal nor state government could effectively regulate a vital legal issue—the institution of marriage, as it was understood at the time. Holmes therefore quoted *Andrews* for the proposition that "it is not lightly to be assumed that, in matters requiring national action, 'a power which must belong to and somewhere reside in every civilized government' is not to be found . . . . What was said in that case with regard to the powers of the States applies with equal force to the powers of the nation in cases where the States individually are incompetent to act."[221]

Both *Andrews* and *Holland* resolved perceived conflicts between state and federal power *internal* to the Constitution. We need not, in other words, read the passages in these cases about "civilized government" and the like to refer to extraconstitutional conceptions of law inherent in sovereignty or nationhood.[222]

---

220. *Id.* at 435 (emphasis added).

221. *Id.* at 433.

222. It would be mistaken to read *Holland* to endorse any doctrine comparable to Justice Sutherland's notoriously flawed theory in *United States v. Curtiss-Wright Export Co.*, 299 U.S. 304 (1936), especially insofar as it suggests plenary presidential power in foreign affairs. We have both critiqued *Curtiss-Wright* elsewhere. Robert D. Sloane, *The Puzzling Persistence of* Curtiss-Wright-*Based Theories of Executive Power*, 37 WM. MITCHELL L. REV. 5072 (2011); Michael J. Glennon, *Two Views of Presidential Foreign Affairs Power:* Little v. Barreme *or* Curtiss-Wright? 13 YALE J. INT'L L. 5 (1988). And the Supreme Court recently rejected the broad reading of *Curtiss-Wright* long advocated by the executive branch. Zivotofsky v. Kerry, 135 S. Ct. 2076 (2015). The most plausible, which is not to say persuasive, argument in favor of presidentialism today is a functional claim about the national security needs of the nation since World War II. Functionalism takes two different forms, however, only one of which we attribute to Holmes. The first is a claim that, in the event of ambiguity, the Constitution should be construed in a manner that allows it to work—to create a competent government that integrates, rather than contravenes, the structural values that animate the instrument as a whole. Among those values, institutional pluralism is preeminent. That functionalist claim, however, is quite distinct from the kind of functionalist argument that Sutherland advanced for extraconstitutional presidential power beyond what Article II spells out. As Justice Brandeis reminded us, "The doctrine of the separation of powers was adopted by the convention of 1787 not to promote efficiency but to preclude the exercise of arbitrary power. The purpose was not to avoid friction, but, by means of the inevitable friction incident to the distribution of the governmental powers among three departments, to save the people from autocracy." Myers v. United States, 272 U.S. 52, 293 (1926). There is nothing functional in this regard about sweeping presidential power; to the contrary, it is *dysfunctional* in that, from a U.S. constitutional perspective, it institutionalizes the executive role by deinstitutionalizing the roles of the legislature and courts. Valorization of the president's potential capacities and resources in foreign affairs may be factually true (e.g., he has greater

Nor should we. It is well-known that Holmes disdained such metaphysical or transcendental conceptions of natural law.[223]

Because the Constitution establishes a government intended to endure and function for ages to come, it would be dysfunctional for the Constitution—hence "not lightly to be assumed"—to disable the federalist system it establishes from enabling *government*, state or federal as the case may be, from meeting real though unforeseen, and perhaps unforeseeable, challenges. *Holland*, read in light of *Andrews*, construed the treaty power to extend to situations where the nation seeks to vindicate an interest of "very nearly the first magnitude"; reliance upon the states would be in vain, and action in concert with another country would empower government to address the issue effectively. There is no reason to construe the Constitution to disallow *Holland*'s reading of the treaty power based on an "invisible radiation from the general terms of the Tenth Amendment."

Holland's doctrine therefore does not, as a matter of law, risk the kind of expansion of federal power at the expense of the states that worries its critics. *Andrews* and *Holland* alike imply legal, as well as political, limits on the latter's doctrine. Justice Black's opinion in *Reid* suggests the same, for its consistency with *Holland* rests on Black's statement that *Holland* had not been concerned with "any specific provision of the Constitution," only the scope of the Tenth Amendment.[224]

VI. Holland *and the Modern Law of Treaties*

A. After *Bond*: The Treaty Power and Federalism in Contemporary Perspective

Scholars have, as noted, criticized *Holland* on historical, structural, textual, and other grounds.[225] Many of these critiques can be, and have been, answered on their own terms,[226] persuasively or not, and it would be superfluous to rehearse them. Yet the scholarly debate over *Holland* has taken place largely within the

---

access to information, the ability to respond more quickly and decisively than Congress, and so forth). But the Framers deliberately rejected this vision of functionalism and efficiency, and the Constitution should not be interpreted to the contrary.

223. Oliver Wendell Holmes, Jr., *Natural Law*, 32 HARV. L. REV. 40 (1918); *cf.* S. Pac. Co. v. Jensen, 244 U.S. 205, 222 (1917).

224. Reid v. Covert, 354 U.S. 1, 18 (1957).

225. *See, e.g.*, Michael D. Ramsey, Missouri v. Holland *and Historical Textualism*, 72 MO. L. REV. 969 (2008); Lawson & Seidman, *supra* note 41; Rosenkranz, *supra* note 7.

226. *E.g.*, Carlos Manuel Vazquez, Missouri v. Holland'*s Second Holding*, 73 MO. L. REV. 939 (2008); Edward T. Swaine, *Putting* Missouri v. Holland *on the Map*, 73 MO. L. REV 1007 (2008).

confines of constitutional methodologies that Justice Holmes would have rejected. Consequently, they tend to miss the force of *Holland*'s abiding functionalist, adaptivist rationale.

Holmes was a pragmatist.[227] His methodology of constitutional adjudication reflected it,[228] as, of course, did *Holland*. The decision relied, as Holmes candidly wrote, on a vision of the Constitution as an organic document that has adapted, as it should, to evolving national conditions in the light of history, practice, and experience. Constitutional adjudication should preserve and contribute to the strong foundation established by the Constitution for the United States as "a *nation*."[229] Holmes did not believe the Tenth Amendment froze in time a static set of rights reserved to thirteen agrarian states in a precarious seaboard republic of 3.5 million people.[230]

Echoing Chief Justice Marshall, he wrote of the Constitution as a foundational but organic document, constitutive of a nation, and "intended to endure for ages to come, and consequently, to be adapted to the various *crises* of human affairs."[231] The Constitution therefore does not establish a set of "immutable rules," which could disable the nation's government from responding to future "exigencies which, if foreseen at all, must have been seen dimly, and which can be best provided for as they occur."[232] To the contrary, like Justice White in *Andrews*, Justice Holmes sought to interpret the Constitution to *work*—to function as durable, foundational law for the system of government it establishes, including, but not limited to, the federal structure of the United States. *Holland* interpreted the Article II treaty power to enable a functional, but interstitial, adjustment of the allocation of authority between the states and the federal government, which the Constitution, respectively, presupposed and established.

One may, of course, reject Holmes's jurisprudential approach. By describing it, we do not blithely dismiss critiques of *Holland* that sound in other approaches to constitutional adjudication. We do, however, consider it appropriate to assess *Holland* on its own terms. Assuming, as Holmes did, that the Constitution is a document "intended to endure for ages to come"[233]—that it must adapt to

---

227. *See* LOUIS MENAND, THE METAPHYSICAL CLUB 432–33 (2002).

228. *See* RICHARD POSNER, *Introduction*, *in* THE ESSENTIAL HOLMES, at xi (Richard Posner ed., 1992).

229. Missouri v. Holland, 252 U.S. 416, 433 (1920) (emphasis added).

230. *Id.* at 434.

231. McCulloch v. Maryland, 17 U.S. (4 Wheat.) 316, 415 (1819).

232. *Id.*

233. *Id.*

"exigencies which, if foreseen at all, must have been seen dimly, and which can be best provided for as they occur"[234]—what might be the consequences for the nation of abandoning *Holland*? If *Bond* effectively eviscerated *Holland*, as we have argued, what effects might we expect in the future?

Despite *Holland*'s periodic citation by the courts,[235] its real-world effects to date, as noted earlier, have been modest. In part, the reason for this is historical and traces to the post-New Deal expansion of congressional power. But the reason is also diplomatic, reflecting the federal government's reluctance to conclude treaties that intrude on traditional state functions. When it has concluded such treaties, it has often included federalism clauses or textual reservations intended to reassure the states or protect traditional state authority.[236] If the federal government's practices in this regard continue, the issue in *Holland* may not recur in the near future or with any frequency.

B. What the Future Holds

Yet *Holland*'s limited influence in the past may be an unreliable barometer of its impact in the future. Today, more than ever before, the nation's needs often require state deference to federal foreign-affairs interests. If this historical trajectory continues, *Bond*'s effects may begin to look both serious and unwelcome.[237] The federal government had substantial reasons for submitting a brief that implored the Court not to overrule *Holland*.[238] Whether *Holland* remains good law might, for example, "alter U.S. positions in international negotiations."[239] The federal government, as noted, has long sought, often successfully, to accommodate state concerns and interests in the course of treaty negotiations, and the political safeguards of federalism all but guarantee that the government's practices in this regard will persist. Furthermore, if, as we suggested earlier, the most common concerns have been overstated, and if, as we also noted earlier, the effect

234. *Id.*

235. *See* Duncan B. Hollis, *Executive Federalism: Forging New Federalist Constraints on the Treaty Power*, 79 S. CAL. L. REV. 1327, 1353–54 (2006).

236. *See id.* at 1361–62, 1372–75.

237. *Cf.* John C. Yoo, *Globalization and the Constitution: Treaties, Non-Self-Execution, and the Original Understanding*, 99 COLUM. L. REV. 1955, 1956–58 (1999) (observing that modern treaties permeate virtually every aspect of international law, with growing effects on domestic law, including in the realms of environmental, trade, and human rights).

238. Brief for Respondent at 47-55, Bond v. United States, 134 S. Ct. 2077 (2014) (No. 12-158).

239. *See* INTERNATIONAL LAW: NORMS, ACTORS, PROCESS 256 (Jeffrey Dunoff et al. eds., 3d ed. 2010).

of *Holland* has thus far been marginal, why might the *Holland* doctrine nonetheless prove to be of more than academic interest? The answer revolves around postwar changes in international law, in particular, the modern law of treaties, which constitute the predominant source of international law today in contrast to custom's predominance in the past.[240]

C. The Postwar Evolution of Treaty Law

It is a truism that international law now governs far more than relations between nations. What some scholars call transnational law includes issues of trade, foreign investment, war, international crime, national security, international organizations, jurisdiction, global commons, human rights, and international administrative law. It also subsumes the full spectrum of international dispute-resolution: the International Court of Justice; WTO panels; the International Tribunal for the Law of the Sea; private international arbitral tribunals for commercial, investment, and other disputes; ad hoc, hybrid, and permanent international criminal courts; and diverse committees and quasi-judicial bodies established by treaty. The United States participates in all these areas of international law. As the world's largest economic and military power, it has an especially strong interest in its ability to shape and sustain them.

Today, however, the principal source of international law is no longer custom but treaties, often multilateral treaties. Some treaties, such as the U.N. Convention on the Law of the Sea,[241] comprehensively regulate fields that were once governed by custom. The law of treaties has also evolved substantially since 1789, as reflected in the Vienna Convention on the Law of Treaties.[242] Many contemporary treaties differ from the contractual paradigm of the nineteenth century.[243] Some multilateral treaties, chiefly international human rights treaties, also govern how a nation treats its own citizens or other traditionally domestic matters.

---

240. Yoo, *supra* note 237, at 1956–57. *See also* Duncan B. Hollis, *Why State Consent Still Matters—Non-state Actors, Treaties, and the Changing Sources of International Law*, 23 BERKELEY J. INT'L L. 137 (2005).

241. United Nations Convention on the Law of the Sea, Dec. 10, 1982, 21 I.L.M. 1261.

242. Vienna Convention on the Law of Treaties, May 23, 1969, 1155 U.N.T.S. 331, 8 I.L.M. 679 (1969).

243. United States v. Old Settlers, 148 U.S. 427, 467 (1893); Whitney v. Robertson, 124 U.S. 190, 194 (1888); The Amiable Isabella, 19 U.S. 1, 21 (1821). The ICJ's *Reservations to the Genocide Convention* advisory opinion notably led international lawyers to replace the traditional principle of unanimity, requiring each party to agree precisely on the treaty's terms, with a less contractual, more flexible model, authorizing reservations subject to a modest limitation based on the object and purpose of the treaty. Reservations to Convention on the Prevention and Punishment of Crime of Genocide, Advisory Opinion, 1951 I.C.J. 15, 24 (May 28).

The idea that only properly international issues may be the subject of treaties—as Charles Evans Hughes, Thomas Jefferson, and others once suggested—is anachronistic. It assumes an unrealistic (and often arbitrary) bright-line distinction between domestic and international issues.[244] Most treaties still do not intrude upon "purely local" issues within the realm of traditional state functions. But some do—and as in 1789, reliance on the states to carry out, or uniformly interpret, national treaty obligations may sometimes be in vain. Modern multilateral treaties that deal with matters such as trade, investment, the environment, and international organizations, among other issues, may entail obligations that involve, which need not mean intrude upon, traditional state functions.

With more and more issues requiring international cooperation—for example, global warming—the need to avoid bright-line subject-matter limitations on treaties is more pressing than ever. Absent *Holland*'s sensible doctrine, the limitations imposed by the Tenth Amendment would risk undermining confidence in the United States as a treaty partner, as the United States emphasized in its brief in *Bond*.[245] The United States can sometimes accommodate or allay the concerns of potential treaty partners by crafting federalism clauses or including reservations—but not always. Reservations may be at odds with the object and purpose of the treaty. This might be true, for example, of a treaty requiring intrastate environmental regulations. Yet even before *Bond*, the Court suggested that federal regulation of an intrastate body of water might well be in violation of the Tenth Amendment.[246] Other reservations might be excluded by the terms of the treaty, as they are, for example, by the Convention on the Law of the Sea.[247]

---

244. *But see Bond*, 134 S. Ct. at 2110–11 (Thomas, J., concurring in the judgment) (suggesting that "hypothetical difficulties in line-drawing are no reason to ignore a constitutional limit on federal power").

245. Brief for Respondent at 47-55, Bond v. United States, 134 S. Ct. 2077 (2014) (No. 12-158). One example of a post-*Lopez* situation in which *Holland* influenced treaty negotiations is U.S. opposition to the draft Framework Convention on Tobacco Control. INTERNATIONAL LAW: NORMS, ACTORS, PROCESS, *supra* note 239, at 256. The treaty "would have prohibited the distribution of free tobacco samples to children, because the federal government allegedly lacked authority to regulate the samples under the Commerce Clause," culminating in the treaty's revision to the softer language "prohibit or promote the prohibition." Yet if the United States were to ratify the treaty (it has signed but not ratified), and if *Holland* no longer remains good law, it is still unclear whether it would be constitutional for the federal government to require the states to take action under the treaty as opposed, for example, to merely exhorting them to act. *See id.; cf.* Peter Spiro, *Resurrecting* Missouri v. Holland, 73 MO. L. REV. 1029, 1040 (2008); Vasquez, *supra* note 226, at 965.

246. Solid Waste Agency of Northern Cook County v. U.S. Army Corp of Engineers, 531 U.S. 159 (2001).

247. United Nations Convention on the Law of the Sea art. 309, Dec. 10, 1982, 183 U.N.T.S. 397.

These changes reinforce the need to preserve *Holland's* doctrine. It alone enables the Treaty Clause to deal flexibly with powers and rights that might otherwise be deemed integral state functions and hence immune from even vital national regulation. On balance, then, we suggest that it would have been at least valuable, and may well turn out to be critical, to preserve *Holland.* The United States must remain able to adapt to an era in which most international law is based on treaties and in which participation in the international legal system will at times require flexibility in the allocation of federal and state power. Flexibility is imperative in the practice of diplomacy no less than in the Court's own case law concerning diplomacy. Indeed, one consequence of abandoning *Holland* is evident in its effect on one of the most significant Supreme Court decisions on U.S. treaty law in decades, *Medellín v. Texas.*[248] *Bond* has rendered it all but incoherent.

D. *Medellín's* New Incoherence

Beginning with the International Court of Justice's (ICJ) decision in *Breard*[249] and, as a consequence, the Court's brief opinion in *Breard v. Greene,*[250] the ICJ decided a trio of cases under the Optional Protocol to the Vienna Convention on Consular Relations ("Optional Protocol").[251] In each, states had convicted and sentenced foreign nationals to death following their convictions in trials in which the defendants were denied the right to consular assistance under Article 38 of the Vienna Convention on Consular Relations (VCCR).[252] The United States is a party to the VCCR, and Article 38 is self-executing in that it imposes obligations on the United States, including all relevant federal and state officials who act on the nation's behalf, without the need for implementing legislation.[253] Article 38 is, under the Supremacy Clause, the "Law of the Land."[254] In *Avena*, the last

248. 552 U.S. 491 (2008).

249. Case Concerning the Vienna Convention on Consular Relations (Para. v. U.S.), 37 I.L.M. 810 (1998).

250. 523 U.S. 371 (1998).

251. The other two are LaGrand, (F.R.G. v. U. S.), 1999 I.C.J. 9 (Order of Mar. 3), and Avena and Other Mexican Nationals (Mex. v. U.S.), Judgment, 2004 I.C.J. 12 (Mar. 31). These cases led to numerous decisions in both state and federal U.S. courts, including, in addition to *Breard,* Federal Republic of Germany v. United States (LaGrand), 526 U.S. 111 (1999), Sanchez-Llamas v. Oregon, 548 U.S. 331 (2006), and Medellín v. Texas, 552 U.S. 491 (2008).

252. Vienna Convention on Consular Relations art. 38, Apr. 24, 1963, 23 U.S.T. 3227, 500 U.N.T.S. 95.

253. *Medellín*, 552 U.S. at 505.

254. U.S. CONST. art. VI

of the ICJ cases, the ICJ held that the United States was under an obligation to allow some fifty Mexican nationals on death row in various states, all of whom had been denied their Article 38 right to consular assistance under the VCCR, to have their convictions and sentences reviewed and reconsidered.[255] The ICJ also held that the requirement of review and reconsideration should be carried out by the judiciary.[256]

After *Avena*, President George W. Bush withdrew from the Optional Protocol,[257] which had supplied the ICJ with the jurisdiction to decide the VCCR disputes.[258] But under the U.N. Charter, "Each Member of the United Nations undertakes to comply with the decision of the International Court of Justice in any case to which it is a party."[259] As a matter of international law, the United States therefore remained under a treaty obligation to comply with the ICJ's final judgment in *Avena*,[260] which the Court rendered before U.S. withdrawal from the Optional Protocol. President Bush accordingly issued a statement indicating that he had determined that in order to give effect to the ICJ's decision, state courts that had sentenced the Mexican nationals named in *Avena* should give effect to the ICJ requirement of review and reconsideration by applying general principles of comity.[261] Many states refused, even though every state official (governors, state court judges, attorney generals, line prosecutors, and so forth) is part of, and acts on behalf of, the United States as a nation—the legal entity to which the ICJ properly directed its judgment under international law.[262]

---

255. *Avena*, 2004 I.C.J. ¶¶ 57, 105.

256. *Id.* ¶ 122.

257. Steve Charnovitz, *Correcting America's Continuing Failure to Comply with the* Avena *Judgment*, 106 AM. J. INT'L L. 572, 573 (2012).

258. Optional Protocol to the Vienna Convention on Consular Relations Concerning the Compulsory Settlement of Disputes art. 1, *opened for signature* Apr. 24, 1963, 21 U.S.T. 77, 596 U.N.T.S. 261.

259. U.N. CHARTER art. 94(1).

260. Medellín v. Texas, 552 U.S. 491, 504 (2008).

261. Charnovitz, *supra* note 257, at 573.

262. Before *LaGrand*, the ICJ had never held clearly that provisional measures were binding. State (and federal) officials therefore arguably had the discretion to decline to abide by them. But in *LaGrand*, the ICJ held that provisional measures are binding, LaGrand (F.R.G. v. U. S.), 1999 I.C.J. 9, ¶ 29 (Order of Mar. 3), and so in *Avena*, both the Court's provisional measures and the final judgment it rendered bound the United States, including everyone who acts for the United States under U.S. law. *Cf.* Louis Henkin, *Provisional Measures, U.S. Treaty Obligations, and the States*, 92 AM. J. INT'L L. 679 (1998).

Most states either did not recognize the international obligation as legally binding or simply refused to abide by it,[263] conduct that cannot fail to call to mind the problems experienced by the nation under the Articles of Confederation. But apart from President Bush's unilateral directive, the federal government, too, failed to take action to respect the international obligation imposed by *Avena* (in combination with the VCCR, the Optional Protocol, and the U.N. Charter): Congress did not try to enact legislation authorizing compliance, the U.S. Attorney General did not bring suit to compel enforcement of the international obligation against recalcitrant state officials, and both federal and state judicial officers, by and large, gave the ICJ's judgment, at best, the "respectful consideration" that the Supreme Court had suggested in its brief per curiam opinion from 1998 denying Breard's application for a stay of execution based on a prior provisional order of the ICJ.[264]

When these issues reached the Supreme Court, it, too, declined to see itself as under a direct obligation to give judicial effect to the ICJ's judgment, in part because it found the U.N. Charter (the treaty that imposed the obligation on the United States to undertake to comply with *Avena*) non-self-executing.[265] It further held that President Bush's directive to the state courts to effectuate the decision by reviewing the convictions and sentences in conformity with general principles of comity exceeded his power: "The President has an array of political and diplomatic means available to enforce international obligations, but unilaterally converting a non-self-executing treaty into a self-executing one is not among them. The responsibility for transforming an international obligation arising from a non-self-executing treaty into domestic law falls to Congress."[266] Nor, the Court held, did the president have power, in effect, to rewrite state judicial standards—that is, rules of decision—to be applied to pending (or any) criminal cases.[267]

Medellín is problematic in many respects; what is relevant here, however, is not its arguable doctrinal deficiencies but its conclusion that responsibility for effectuating U.S. international obligations under *Avena* "falls to Congress."[268]

---

263. *See* Robert D. Sloane, *Measures Necessary to Ensure: The ICJ's Provisional Measures Order in* Avena and Other Mexican Nationals, 17 LEIDEN J. INT'L L. 673, 688 (2004); Letter from Advocates for Human Rights et al., on the Implementation of the *Avena* Decision, to Attorney Gen. Eric Holder and Secretary of State, Hillary Clinton, http://www.constitutionproject.org/pdf/375.pdf.

264. Breard v. Greene, 523 U.S. 371, 375 (1998).

265. Medellín v. Texas, 552 U.S. 491, 517-18 (2008).

266. *Id.* at 525-26.

267. *Id.* at 530.

268. *Id.* at 526.

In particular, the Court held that the United States may give "domestic effect to an international treaty obligation under the Constitution" in two potential ways—but in either case, compliance "requires joint action by the Executive and Legislative Branches: The Senate can ratify a self-executing treaty made by the Executive, or, if the ratified treaty is not self-executing, Congress can enact implementing legislation approved by the President."[269]

This resolution seems plausible under *Holland*: Congress could exercise its Necessary and Proper Clause powers to enact federal law to carry into effect U.S. treaty obligations under the U.N. Charter (emanating from the final *Avena* judgment), and the implementing legislation would bind the states even if, absent treaty obligations, Congress would lack the power to require state courts to review and reconsider the relevant capital convictions and sentences of Mexican nationals. After *Bond*, however, this route to discharging the *Avena* judgment's obligations would be unconstitutional. After *Bond*, had the federal government sought to effectuate the international obligation imposed by Article 94 of the U.N. Charter, which the Supreme Court found to be non-self-executing,[270] by passing implementing legislation, that law would have violated the Tenth Amendment. As the *Bond* Court said, a treaty's implementing legislation, that is, "the statute—unlike the Convention—must be read consistent with principles of federalism inherent in our constitutional structure."[271] It is difficult to imagine a state function more integral or traditional than the general police power to define and punish "purely local" crimes.[272] The criminal law at issue in *Bond*, as the Court there insisted, would ordinarily be of "the sort . . . regulated by the States."[273]

The Mexican nationals within the ambit of *Avena* had likewise been convicted and sentenced under "purely local" state criminal laws. As horrendous as their capital crimes were, none of them fell within the scope of the federal government's powers under Article I, section 8—or any other delegated federal power. Absent the interpretation given to the Treaty Clause's interaction with the Tenth Amendment in *Holland*, the federal government lacks power to interfere with purely local criminal laws and their administration. Congress has no power to compel state courts to review and reconsider state criminal convictions and sentences under a retroactive standard. The *only* way in which Congress could have carried out acknowledged U.S. international obligations emanating from the

269. *Id.* at 527 (internal quotation marks and alterations omitted).

270. *See id.* at 508–10.

271. Bond v. United States, 134 S. Ct. 2077, 2088 (2014).

272. *Id.* at 2090.

273. *Id.* at 2111 (Alito, J., concurring in the judgment); *see also id.* at 2088 (opinion of Roberts, C.J.) (enumerating similar federalism presumptions).

treaties at issue, as the *Medellín* Court held that it alone could do,[274] would have been by resorting to the Necessary and Proper Clause.[275] In particular, it would have needed to enact legislation necessary and proper to implement the international obligation incurred by the United States based on the combination of four treaties: the VCCR, Optional Protocol, *Avena* decision, and U.N. Charter.

Had *Holland* survived *Bond*, then the means by which the *Medellín* Court suggested that the United States can discharge non-self-executing treaty obligations would at least be intelligible. Congress would have the authority to enact legislation to require the states to carry out U.S. international obligations—notwithstanding that, absent the treaties at issue, authority over "purely local" criminal laws would remain within the reserved powers of the states under the Tenth Amendment. But if *Holland* is no longer good law, then the Supreme Court has held in *Medellín* that the United States, as a nation, is incapable of complying with its international legal obligations under *Avena—or any similar obligation in the future*. The president cannot bring the nation into compliance by unilateral declaration.[276] The federal courts cannot require compliance because of the doctrine of non-self-executing treaties, as interpreted in *Medellín*.[277] And now, after *Bond*, Congress too, despite what the Court said in *Medellín*, cannot enforce the nation's international obligations under *either* Article I, section 8, *or* Article I in combination with the Article II treaty power. *Holland's* doctrine—that "there may be matters of the sharpest exigency for the national well being that an act of Congress could not deal with but that a treaty followed by such an act could"[278]—was the sole route to compliance with the ICJ's judgment. *Bond* has blocked that route.

E. U.S. Treaty Practice After *Bond*

Avena aptly illustrates the predicament the United States faces today because of the complexity and nature of modern treaty law.[279] Today, as in 1789 and before, the states cannot always be relied upon to carry out the international obligations of the United States. The resistance of the states to treaty obligations they found distasteful—a significant motivation for the Philadelphia Convention

---

274. *Medellín*, 552 U.S. at 520.

275. *Id.* at 536.

276. *Id.* at 529–30.

277. *Id.* at 504.

278. Missouri v. Holland, 252 U.S. 416, 433 (1920).

279. *Avena*, recall, involved an international obligation that arose from (1) the U.N. Charter, triggered by (2) *Avena*, which had been litigated under (3) the Optional Protocol based on violations of (4) the VCCR, and then decided under (5) the Statute of the ICJ—also a treaty.

culminating in the Constitution—did not cease in 1789. And although the United States is obviously not at risk of war with Mexico, the states in *Avena* placed the nation in an awkward, diplomatically harmful situation. To paraphrase Hamilton's remark in *The Federalist*, after *Bond* and contrary to the clear intent of the Framers, "the peace of the WHOLE" may now indeed "be left at the disposal of a PART."[280]

In *Bond*, the Court reasoned that Pennsylvania criminal law would suffice to carry out the nation's CWC international obligation to punish violations under the treaty. Perhaps. But that is merely adventitious. Another state might not have enacted a law that suffices to carry out CWC prosecution obligations—or those contained in other treaties that require conduct in legal domains traditionally deemed "purely local." Why should the ability of the United States to comply with a legitimate treaty obligation depend on the fortuity of whether a state happens to have passed a law sufficient for that purpose?

Avena also reinforces the contemporary need to understand the Tenth Amendment within the context of a functional Constitution—one that respects federalism and preserves its value in our constitutional order but does not set it up as a constraint on the nation's ability to act internationally or adhere to international obligations. Justice Holmes's words in *Holland* still ring true today: "We must consider what this country has become in deciding what that Amendment has reserved."[281] By abandoning *Holland*, as the wreckage of *Medellín* suggests, the Supreme Court took a potentially dangerous step backward toward recreating one of the foremost problems that beset the new nation under the Articles of Confederation. The Framers sought to resolve that problem by making treaties the supreme law of the land and vesting the treaty power exclusively in the federal government, thus giving it the power to enforce international obligations against recalcitrant states. *Bond* makes that, not only more difficult, but at times unconstitutional.

VII. Conclusion

"[I]t is not lightly to be assumed," Holmes wrote, "that, in matters requiring national action, 'a power which must belong to and somewhere reside in every civilized government' is not to be found."[282] To have found a Tenth Amendment impediment to a treaty regulating migratory waterfowl would have denied the federal government the authority to make that agreement. It would have required would-be treaty partners to negotiate with the forty-eight states of the Union instead—forty-eight different negotiations, state by state. That cannot be the system established by the Framers under the Constitution.

---

280. THE FEDERALIST NO. 80, at 535 (Alexander Hamilton) (Jacob E. Cook ed., 1961).

281. *Holland*, 252 U.S. at 432–34.

282. *Id.* at 433 (quoting Andrews v. Andrews, 188 U.S. 14, 33 (1903)) (citation omitted).

True, the federal government retains domestic discretion to refuse to implement a treaty. But the option of dishonoring U.S. obligations internationally ought not be cavalierly embraced. Vindicating the high purposes of the Constitution, so eloquently set forth in its Preamble, depends upon preserving the nation's credibility. It does not do to waive off this enduring imperative, as the *Bond* Court did, with a thin, formal reference to Congress's discretion to disregard U.S. international obligations—all the while purporting to apply a mere (but, after *Bond*, mandatory) canon of construction to laws implementing treaties.[283] Preserving national credibility requires honoring rather than betraying treaty commitments. This, in the final analysis, is *Holland*'s raison d'être, to which *Bond* is oblivious.

Treaty law in the United States, like so much else in U.S. foreign relations law, has always been shaped by history, tradition, principle, and practice—by experience, as Holmes wrote elsewhere, rather than logic alone.[284] Nothing in the experience of the United States revealed a need to abandon *Holland*. And if experience establishes the need, at times, to make treaties that arguably intrude on traditional conceptions of the boundaries of federalism in domestic circumstances, it is difficult to see why the constitutional law of treaties is not properly read to accommodate the needs of the nation that the Constitution established for ages to come. *Bond* debilitated *Holland*. The Court—and, we fear, the nation—will come to regret it.

Yet *Holland* can likely be salvaged without retreating explicitly from *Bond*. Precisely because the Court did not expressly overrule *Holland*, it need not reverse itself again in a future decision in order to revive *Holland*. As we have suggested, the Court could have, as indeed it should have, treated background principles and statutory canons of federalism as incorporating the Court's own interpretation of those principles in *Holland*. The Court could simply make clear that, consistent with what it held in *Holland*, the federalism principles that Congress should be presumed to bear in mind when it legislates *include* Justice Holmes's analysis of the interaction between the Article II treaty power and the Tenth Amendment.

Like other structural principles of the Constitution, such as the separation of powers, federalism cannot be reduced to bright-line rules or formulae. The Court should, as it has in the past, consider the values that the principles of federalism serve in the U.S. constitutional system. In the spirit of *McCulloch*, those principles must be adapted to the exigencies, needs, and global context of the nation the Constitution established "to endure for ages to come."[285] The spirit of *McCulloch* is also the spirit of *Holland*.

---

283. Bond v. United States, 134 S.Ct. 2077, 2089, slip op. at 13 (2014).

284. Oliver Wendell Holmes, Jr., The Common Law 1 (1881).

285. 17 U.S. at 415.

7

Federal Common Law and State Power

I. Introduction: Federal Common Law's Status and Legitimacy

Common law refers to "judge-made law",[1] the body of legal rules, principles, and procedural rules that judges make in the course of deciding disputes. Colonial legal systems adopted much of British common law,[2] and since 1789, state and federal courts alike have continued to adapt, develop, and expand upon the Anglo-American common law that existed at the time of the Constitution's ratification. The legal status of federal common law, however, and the authority of federal judges to make it,[3] has long been a controversial aspect of federalism. In part, the reason for this traces to the Supremacy Clause, which reads:

> This Constitution, and the laws of the United States which shall be made in pursuance thereof; and all treaties made, or which shall be made, under the authority of the United States, shall be the supreme law of the land;

1. Banco Nacional de Cuba v. Sabbatino, 376 U.S. 398, 426 (1964).

2. *See* Rogers v. Tennessee, 532 U.S. 451, 475–76, 476 n.3 (Scalia, J., dissenting); *see also* Stewart Jay, *Origins of Federal Common Law: Part II*, 133 U. PA. L. REV. 1231, 1234–40 (1985).

3. In the late-eighteenth and nineteenth centuries, many adhered to the natural-law view that common law courts found, rather than made, common law—looking to what Justice Holmes memorably described as "a brooding omnipresence in the sky," S. Pac. Co. v. Jensen, 244 U.S. 205, 222 (1917) (Holmes, J., dissenting), or as a "transcendental body of law outside of any particular State," Black & White Taxicab & Transfer Co. v. Brown & Yellow Taxicab & Transfer Co., 276 U.S. 518, 533 (1928) (Holmes, J., dissenting).

> and the judges in every state shall be bound thereby, anything in the Constitution or laws of any state to the contrary notwithstanding.[4]

Do the "laws of the United States" include those made by judges in the exercise of their putative authority to make federal common law? Do such laws bind state court judges "anything in the Constitution or laws of any state to the contrary notwithstanding"?

In *United States v. Hudson & Goodwin*, the Supreme Court held that the federal courts lack common-law criminal jurisdiction.[5] Yet thirty years later, in *Swift v. Tyson*,[6] the Court found no constitutional impediment to common-law jurisdiction in federal civil cases. *Swift* involved "principles established in the *general* commercial law."[7] Speaking for the Court, Justice Story held that under the 1789 Judiciary Act,[8] federal courts should decide "questions of a more general nature, not at all dependent upon local statutes" just as state courts would were they "called upon to perform the like functions as ourselves, that is, to ascertain, upon general reasoning and legal analogies, what is the true exposition of the contract or instrument, or what is the just rule furnished by the principles of commercial law to govern the case."[9]

For nearly a century thereafter, between the bookends of *Swift* and *Erie Railroad Co. v. Tompkins*,[10] federal courts exercising diversity jurisdiction, that is, cases or controversies between citizens of different states or between U.S. and foreign citizens,[11] continued to make federal common law without regard for or

---

4. U.S. CONST. art. VI, cl. 2.

5. United States v. Hudson & Goodwin, 11 U.S. (7 Cranch) 32 (1812). The Court's somewhat opaque opinion suggested a federalism rationale, viz., that "[t]he powers of the general Government are made up of concessions from the several states," none of which included common-law criminal jurisdiction. *Id.* at 33. Yet it did not clarify whether such jurisdiction would be unconstitutional, remarking only that "whether the general Government . . . possesses the power of conferring on its Courts a jurisdiction in cases similar to the present; it is enough that such jurisdiction has not been conferred by any legislative act[.]" *Id.* Regardless, *Hudson & Goodwin*'s holding persists. *See, e.g.*, Dowling v. United States, 473 U.S. 207, 213 (1985). Justice Story joined *Hudson & Goodwin* without comment even though, as noted in the text, he later authored *Swift v. Tyson*, 41 U.S. (16 Pet.) 1 (1842), which reached the contrary conclusion with respect to civil common-law jurisdiction.

6. 41 U.S. (16 Pet.) 1 (1842).

7. *Id.* at 18 (emphasis added).

8. 1789 Judiciary Act, 1 Stat. 73.

9. *Swift*, 41 U.S. at 18–19.

10. Erie Railroad Co. v. Tompkins, 304 U.S. 64 (1938).

11. U.S. CONST. art. III, § 2, cl. 1; 28 U.S.C. § 1332 (2012).

deference to the common law of the states in which they sat. The issues they confronted in these cases typically dealt with the same traditional state-law fields on which the common law has long focused, for example, torts, contracts, property, wills, corporations, and family relations. Yet federal courts exercising common-law jurisdiction would not infrequently make or apply legal norms different from those of the states: hence the outcome of a case could depend on the fortuity of whether the parties were completely diverse.[12]

As one would expect, the states were not overjoyed to have their common law ignored by federal courts. Especially after the demise of legal formalism in the late 1800s, the states, with growing support from the legal academy and practitioners, argued that the Constitution required federal judges to apply state common-law rules in diversity cases. In 1938, this position finally prevailed. In *Erie*, Justice Brandeis famously held that "[e]xcept in matters governed by the Federal Constitution or by acts of Congress, the law to be applied in any case is the law of the state. . . . *There is no federal general common law*."[13] The era of *Swift v. Tyson* was at an end.

Well, almost at an end. *Erie* did away with federal *general* common law, not all federal common law; "few and restricted" enclaves of federal *specialized* common law persist.[14] Indeed, on the same day the Court decided *Erie*, it held, in a unanimous opinion also authored by Justice Brandeis, that a dispute between Colorado and New Mexico over interstate waters "is a question of 'federal common law' upon which neither the statutes nor the decisions of either State can be conclusive."[15]

Since *Erie*, the Court has continued to make and apply federal common law in the context of various special enclaves that constitute exceptions to

12. The Court has long interpreted 28 U.S.C. section 1332 to require complete diversity of citizenship, although the Constitution does not require it. State Farm Fire & Casualty Co. v. Tashire, 386 U.S. 523, 530–31 (1967); Strawbridge v. Curtiss, 7 U.S. (3 Cranch) 267 (1806).

13. *Erie R.R.*, 304 U.S. at 78 (emphasis added). "Congress," the Court explained, "has no power to declare substantive rules of common law applicable in a state. . . . [N]o clause in the Constitution purports to confer such a power upon the federal courts." *Id.* Quoting Holmes, a long-standing critic of *Swift*, Brandeis stressed that there is no "transcendental law outside of any particular State," and therefore that "law in the sense in which courts speak of it today does not exist without some definite authority behind it. The common law so far as it is enforced in a State, . . . is not the common law generally but the law of that State existing by the authority of that State without regard to what it may have been in England or anywhere else." *Id.* at 78–79 (citations and internal quotation marks omitted).

14. Texas Indus. v. Radcliff Materials, 451 U.S. 630, 640–41 (1981); Wheeldin v. Wheeler, 373 U.S. 647, 651 (1963).

15. Hinderlinder v. La Plata River & Cherry Creek Ditch Co., 304 U.S. 92, 110 (1938).

Erie's general rule. These include interstate disputes,[16] admiralty,[17] labor relations,[18] federal Indian law,[19] and federal negotiable instruments.[20] Occasionally, Congress also expressly authorizes the federal courts to make common law. A prominent example is Rule 501 of the Federal Rules of Evidence, which instructs the federal courts to make common law governing evidentiary privileges in federal-question cases in "the light of reason and experience."[21] Two principles, according to the Court, unify most federal common-law issues: "those in which a federal rule of decision is necessary to protect uniquely federal interests, and those in which Congress has given the courts the power to develop substantive law . . . ."[22]

Few would regard federal common law, literally, as legislation. Yet in substance even if not form, federal common law functions as federal legislation by another name: like legislation, it creates public rights and obligations, and if a state law that might otherwise govern exists, federal common law, like federal statutory law, supersedes it to the extent of any conflict. The one real difference is that federal common law is interstitial: federal courts "legislate" when they make specialized federal common law—but they do so at the sufferance of Congress, often by filling statutory gaps. Justice Jackson wrote in this regard that federal common law reflects "the recognized futility of attempting all-complete statutory codes."[23] But for that reason, the legislative handiwork of the federal courts stands only so long as Congress permits it.

---

16. The Constitution established this long-standing category as part of the Supreme Court's original jurisdiction in Aricle III, section 2, clause 1, as suggested by the quotations Justice Brandeis inserted around the phrase "federal common law." *Hinderlinder*, 304 U.S. at 110. Such cases preceded *Erie*, see, for example, Kentucky v. Indiana, 281 U.S. 163 (1930), and *Erie* did not affect this area of federal common-law jurisdiction. *See, e.g.*, New Jersey v. New York, 523 U.S. 767 (1998).

17. *See, e.g.*, Norfolk S. Ry. Co. v. Kirby, 543 U.S. 14, 23 (2004); Moragne v. States Marine Lines, Inc., 398 U.S. 375 (1970). This enclave of federal common law, too, by dint of Article III, section 2, clause. 1, preceded *Erie*. *See, e.g.*, S. Pac. Co. v. Jensen, 244 U.S. 205 (1917).

18. Textile Workers Union v. Lincoln Mills, 353 U.S. 448, 456–57 (1957).

19. Oneida County v. Oneida Indian Nation, 470 U.S. 226, 235 (1985); *see also* Nat'l Farmers Ins. Co. v. Crow Tribe, 471 U.S. 845 (1985).

20. Clearfield Trust v. United States, 318 U.S. 363, 366–67 (1943).

21. FED. R. EVID. 501.

22. Texas Indus. v. Radcliff Materials, 451 U.S. 630, 640 (1981) (internal citations and quotation marks omitted). Filling statutory "gaps" must be distinguished from interpreting federal statutes, which is, of course, a large part of the business of the federal courts.

23. D'Onench, Duhme & Co. v. Fed. Deposit Ins. Corp., 315 U.S. 447, 470 (1942).

In *City of Milwaukee v. Illinois*,[24] former Chief Justice Rehnquist—seldom regarded as a proponent of what some would characterize as judicial activism—defended federal common law in part because it is always "subject to the paramount authority of the Congress."[25] He stressed in this regard that "[t]he enactment of a federal rule in an area of national concern, and the decision whether to displace state law in doing so, is generally made not by the federal judiciary, purposefully insulated from democratic pressures, but by the people through their elected representatives in Congress."[26] But he observed that Congress knows full well when the federal courts have made common law, and, assuming Congress has not objected, has implicitly delegated authority to the federal judiciary to do so.[27] Because the federal courts act in Congress's stead when they make federal common law, such law binds the states to the same extent as federal legislation. Indeed, this has long been clear. "All constitutional acts of power, whether in the executive or in the judicial department," John Jay wrote in *The Federalist*, "have as much legal validity and obligation as if they proceeded from the legislature."[28]

A. The Act of State Doctrine

The quintessential post-*Erie* federal common-law decision, *Banco Nacional de Cuba v. Sabbatino*,[29] arose, not coincidentally, in the context of foreign affairs. In *Sabbatino*, Cuba had purported to seize from a U.S.-controlled corporation the proceeds from a sale of sugar that had been brokered by an intermediary, one of many such seizures carried out under the authority of a law authorizing the expropriation of all "property or enterprises in which American nationals had an interest."[30] *Banco Nacional*, the Cuban instrumentality to which the expropriated proceeds had ultimately been assigned, sued Sabbatino, a temporary receiver of the proceeds appointed by a New York state court. (*Banco Nacional* later removed the case to federal court.)

24. City of Milwaukee v. Illinois, 451 U.S. 304 (1981).

25. *Id.* at 313–14 (internal quotation marks omitted).

26. *Id.* at 312–13.

27. *See* Michael J. Glennon, *1997 Survey of Books Relating to the Law: Constitutional Law: Process versus Policy in Foreign Relations*, 95 MICH. L. REV. 1542, 1552–53 (1997) (reviewing LOUIS HENKIN, FOREIGN AFFAIRS AND THE UNITED STATES CONSTITUTION (2d ed. 1996)).

28. THE FEDERALIST NO. 64, at 394 (John Jay) (Clinton Rossiter ed., 1961).

29. 376 U.S. 398 (1964).

30. *Id.* at 401. Cuba passed the law in retaliation for President Eisenhower's reduction of Cuba's sugar quota, which, given the Cuban economy's reliance on sugar exports, Cuba had characterized as "an act of aggression for political purposes on the part of the United States." *Id.* (internal quotation marks omitted).

The Supreme Court therefore had to decide which party had the right to the proceeds, a question of substantive *state* common law to be resolved in conformity with the laws of the State of New York—or so it seemed. As in *Erie*, the plaintiff sought recovery based on state law,[31] and consistent with *Erie*, state, not federal, law presumably applied in *Sabbatino*, a federal diversity action. Yet *Banco Nacional* had argued, and the Supreme Court agreed, that the act-of-state doctrine applied, obviating the substantive tort claim, for under that doctrine, as the Court wrote in 1897, "the courts of one country will not sit in judgment on"—viz., adjudicate and determine the validity of—"the acts of the government of another, done within its own territory."[32] The Court acknowledged that neither international law nor comity, the doctrine's original rationale,[33] nor the Constitution's text, required it to apply the act-of-state doctrine.[34] Yet the Court reasoned that, nonetheless, the doctrine "does have 'constitutional' underpinnings. It arises out of the basic relationships between branches of government in a system of separation of powers."[35] To be sure, the act-of-state doctrine was not new; it had been kicking around for a while since the late eighteenth century. But after *Erie* sounded the death knell for federal general common law, the doctrine could only be sustained as "necessary to protect uniquely federal interests."[36] In other words, the *Sabbatino* Court announced that the act-of-state doctrine fell within one of the few surviving enclaves of special federal common law. After all, Congress had said nothing about it.

Nothing, that is, until the Court decided *Sabbatino*. A Supreme Court decision siding, in effect, with Fidel Castro just two years after the Cuban Missle Crisis could not be expected to excite broad public enthusiasm. Nor did it. Shortly after *Sabbatino*, Congress enacted the so-called Second Hickenlooper Amendment,[37]

---

31. Banco Nacional sought recovery based on the intentional tort of conversion, unlike, in *Erie*, a tort of negligence. *Id.* at 407. Both, however, were common-law, not statutory, claims.

32. *Id.* at 416 (internal quotation marks omitted) (quoting Underhill v. Hernandez, 168 U.S. 250, 252 (1897)). This is (still) the traditional linguistic expression of the doctrine. But it's misleading. As Justice White emphasized in dissent, the act-of-state doctrine is not an abstention doctrine. In practice, it means the judiciary will choose and apply the law of the foreign country. *Id.* at 441 (White, J., dissenting). The Court's most recent act-of-state doctrine case makes this unmistakably clear. *See* W.S. Kirkpatrick & Co. v. Envtl. Tectonics Corp., 493 U.S. 400 (1990).

33. *See* Oetjen v. Cent. Leather Co., 246 U.S. 297, 303–04 (1918); *see also Sabbatino*, 376 U.S. at 445–50 (White, J., dissenting).

34. *Sabbatino*, 375 U.S. at 421–23.

35. *Id.* at 423.

36. Texas Indus. v. Radcliff Materials, 451 U.S. 630, 640 (1981) (internal citations and quotation marks omitted).

37. 22 U.S.C. § 2370(e)(2) (2012).

limiting the doctrine's application to cases not involving a violation of international law and thus effectively overturning the result in *Sabbatino*. The Second Circuit upheld the amendment, deciding against Cuba.[38] Yet the courts have since construed the Hickenlooper Amendment narrowly and preserved the core holding of *Sabbatino*.[39]

B. Customary International Law

Sabbatino's most significant contribution to foreign affairs federalism undoubtedly lies in its forceful establishment of what had theretofore been a controversial exception to *Erie*'s general prohibition on federal common law: the *Sabbatino* Court, expressly and implicitly, asserted judicial authority to make a federal common law of foreign relations, binding on the states:

> We are constrained to make it clear that an issue concerned with a basic choice regarding the competence and function of the Judiciary and the National Executive in ordering our relationships with other members of the international community must be treated exclusively as an aspect of federal law. It seems fair to assume that the Court did not have rules like the act of state doctrine in mind when it decided *Erie R. Co. v. Tompkins*.[40]

Yet *Sabbatino*'s implications, as we will see, extend further. According to most commentators, *Sabbatino* further supported, if not established, federal judicial authority to interpret and incorporate, in some circumstances, customary international law as post-*Erie* federal common law, likewise binding on the states.[41]

Early in Justice Harlan's analysis of the act-of-state doctrine, he concluded that "international law does not require application of the doctrine," based on a

---

38. Banco Nacional de Cuba v. Farr, 383 F.2d 166 (2d Cir. 1967), *cert. denied*, 390 U.S. 956 (1968).

39. *See* Banco Nacional de Cuba v. First Nat'l City Bank, 431 F.2d 394 (2d Cir. 1970), *rev'd on other grounds*, 406 U.S. 759 (1972).

40. *Sabbatino*, 375 U.S. at 425; *see also Texas Indus.*, 451 U.S. at 640–41 (describing "relations with foreign nations" as an area in which it is "necessary to protect uniquely federal interests" and therefore as an enclave of post-*Erie* federal common law).

41. *See, e.g.*, Harold Hongju Koh, *Is International Law Really State Law?*, 111 Harv. L. Rev. 1824 (1997); Louis Henkin, *International Law as Law in the United States*, 82 Mich. L. Rev. 1555, 1559–61 (1984). The *Restatement* takes the same position. Restatement (Third) of the Foreign Relations Law of the United States § 131 (1987). *But see* Curtis Bradley & Jack Goldsmith, *Customary International Law as Federal Common Law: A Critique of the Modern Position*, 110 Harv. L. Rev. 186, 849–61 (1997).

careful review of "the practice of nations" and other traditional authorities for discerning customary international law.[42] Because, as he had concluded, the Court's references to (non-binding) international comity in earlier precedents such as *Underhill v. Hernandez*[43] did not require application of the act-of-state doctrine, Harlan considered whether customary international law required the Court to apply the doctrine in the circumstances presented. He concluded that although "international law does not prescribe use of the doctrine, neither does it forbid application of the rule even if it is claimed that the act of state in question violated international law."[44] At this stage of the analysis, one might have concluded that the states were free to decide whether to apply the doctrine as a matter of state common law or, potentially, legislation. But notice the implication: Why, after all, would it matter whether the Supreme Court found that customary international law required the act-of-state doctrine *unless* one were to assume that customary international law, as interpreted by the federal judiciary, is supreme law under the Constitution, that is, post-*Erie* federal common law that would trump New York State common law in a state claim for conversion?

Did *Sabbatino* therefore hold that federal interpretations of customary international law constrain state court judges—or, for that matter, legislators and governors? If a state statute authorizes the death penalty, could it be struck down by a federal court based on that court's interpretation of a rule of customary international law prohibiting capital punishment?[45] Could a state's law-enforcement authorities arrest and prosecute a visiting head of state who bears criminal responsibility for presiding over, say, systematic war crimes, ethnic cleansing, and

---

42. *Sabbatino*, 376 U.S. at 421–23; *see also id.* at 421 n.21 (canvassing the status of the act-of-state doctrine in foreign and international tribunals, among other sources relevant to customary international law analysis).

43. 168 U.S. 250 (1897).

44. *Sabbatino*, 376 U.S. at 422.

45. For a time, this question may not have been hypothetical. The Convention on the Rights of the Child, G.A. Res. 44/25, U.N. GAOR, 44th Sess., Supp. No. 49, U.N. Doc. A/Res/44/25 (1989), which only the United States has not ratified, prohibits executing juvenile offenders for crimes perpetrated as juveniles under the age of eighteen, *id.* at art. 37(a), and according to many commentators, this prohibition has become customary international law. *See, e.g.*, Roper v. Simmons, 543 U.S. 551, 576–77 (2005) (collecting evidence of an international consensus against the juvenile death penalty). Yet until the Supreme Court's 2005 decision in *Roper*, which held unconstitutional the execution of juvenile offenders for crimes they had committed before the age of eighteen, twenty states retained statutes authorizing the execution of juvenile offenders—and a handful of these had been carried out. *See id.* at 564–65. If customary international law is federal common law, these state statutes and executions of juvenile offenders may have been unconstitutional violations of the Supremacy Clause.

torture—notwithstanding that customary international law apparently mandates head-of-state immunity even in such circumstances?[46] Could a state legislature enact a statute criminalizing the growing of cocoa in the territory of another country despite customary international law's prohibition against the exercise of unreasonable or exorbitant jurisdiction?

Before considering such questions, a clarifying note: these issues arise in two legal systems, the domestic legal system of the United States and the international legal system. Thus far in this book, we've discussed domestic legal constraints, for example, the dormant foreign-affairs doctrine and the dormant Foreign Commerce Clause of the Constitution. In principle, a state law might be constitutional but run afoul of international law, or vice versa, that is, it might be consistent with international law but run afoul of the Constitution. It is axiomatic that the domestic validity of a law does not affect its international validity.[47] Here, the question we're considering is whether a violation of international law affects the domestic legal system such that it should be addressed by either or both federal and state courts, and, if the former, whether the federal judiciary's interpretation of customary international law has a constitutional status that requires state courts to defer to its interpretation.

Conventionally, international lawyers speak of three sources of international law: treaties, customary international law, and general principles of law, as well as "judicial decisions and the teachings of the most highly qualified publicists of the various nations, as *subsidiary means* for the determination of rules of law."[48] Yet in the context of domestic legal systems, the issue of how international legal norms should be given effect (or not) generally arises only in the case of treaty or customary international obligations—all the more so in the context of U.S. federalism. Chapter 6 considered the domestic legal effect of treaties under the Supremacy Clause and the controversial constitutional interpretation that empowers the federal government to comply with those that might otherwise intrude upon

46. *See* Arrest Warrant of 11 April 2000 (D.R.C. v. Belg.), 2002 I.C.J. 3 (Feb. 14) (finding head-of-state immunity applicable under customary international law despite credible allegations of similar international crimes); Tachiona v. Mugabe, 169 F. Supp. 2d 259 (S.D.N.Y. 2001) (dismissing action for human rights violations based on head-of-state immunity).

47. Int'l Law Comm'n, Articles on the Responsibility of States for Internationally Wrongful Acts, in Rep. on the Work of Its Fifty-Third Session, U.N. Doc. A/56/10 (2001), annexed to G.A. Res. 56/83 (Dec. 12, 2001) ("The characterization of an act of a State as internationally wrongful is governed by international law. Such characterization is not affected by the characterization of the same act as lawful by internal law.").

48. Statute of the International Court of Justice art. 38(1)(d), June 26, 1945, 59 Stat. 1055 (emphasis added); *see also* The Paquete Habana, 175 U.S. 677, 700 (1900).

traditional state functions under the Tenth Amendment. Here we consider domestic constraints imposed on the states by customary international law.

The paramount question, then, is whether, and if so how, U.S. domestic law incorporates customary international law. The specific question is properly tackled here because it arises most often when the federal government is silent. (A statute within the constitutional powers of the federal government, say, one criminalizing piracy under the Define and Punish Clause,[49] implements customary international law and binds the states directly under the Supremacy Clause.[50]) As we will see in Chapter 9 (Federal Disapproval), a federal green light to the states, federal *approval*, authorizes states to act in the realm of international law, whether for a state legislative initiative or as a rule of decision for the state courts; in contrast, a federal red light—federal *disapproval*—renders the rule moot as a matter of domestic law under basic principles of statutory preemption. Before turning to the question of international law's domestic incorporation, it will be useful to consider briefly what is generally meant by customary international law. Where do the supposed rules of international custom come from, and why might they appropriately be thought operative in domestic law at all?

II. *What is Customary International Law?*

Conventionally, it is said that customary international law results from a general and consistent practice of nations followed by them from a sense of legal obligation.[51] Although near-unanimity and the passage of substantial time is typical of customary international norms, neither is required:

> The practice necessary to create customary law may be of comparatively short duration.... A practice can be general even if it is not universally followed; there is no precise formula to indicate how widespread a practice must be, but it should reflect wide acceptance among the states particularly involved in the relevant activity. Failure of a significant number of important states to adopt a practice can prevent a principle from becoming general customary law.[52]

---

49. U.S. CONST. art I, § 8, cl. 10.

50. *Id.* art. VI, cl. 2.

51. RESTATEMENT (THIRD) OF THE FOREIGN RELATIONS LAW OF THE UNITED STATES, *supra* note 41, § 102(4).

52. *Id.* § 102 cmt. b. The establishment of international custom on the continental shelf after the 1945 Truman Proclamation, for example, required only about fifteen years, and it involved sufficient, but far from unanimous, state practice. *Cf.* North Sea Continental Shelf Cases

Practice itself, however, does not suffice; a putative norm must also be accompanied by what's known as *opinio juris*: states must engage in the practice out of a sense that it has become legally obligatory—*because* they believe it is legally obligatory. A practice states generally, or even uniformly, follow but feel legally free to disregard isn't customary international law.[53] Further, because the international legal system is (theoretically at least) based on consent, states may sometimes opt out of a particular customary norm *provided* they make their rejection of that norm known publicly, clearly, and repeatedly during the process of its formation: "[A] state that indicates its dissent from a practice while the law is still in the process of development is not bound by that rule even after it matures."[54] This is known as the persistent objector rule. Yet there's an exception to the exception. States may not opt out of so-called jus cogens, or peremptory, norms of international law—for example, the prohibition on genocide. In the treaty context, a peremptory norm is a "norm of general international law . . . accepted and recognized by the international community of States as a whole as a norm from which no derogation is permitted and which can be modified only by a subsequent norm of general international law having the same character."[55] Peremptory norms of customary international law likewise permit no derogation; they prevail over and invalidate treaties and customary international norms alike to the extent of any conflict.

That, in a nutshell, is what's commonly meant by customary international law. Suffice it to say that all of this has extensively been questioned and criticized, including by the authors.[56] Our aim here is only to offer a brief overview of the

---

(FRG/Den.; FRG/Neth.), 1969 I.C.J. REP. 3, 43 (Feb. 20) ("[A]n indispensable requirement would be that within the period in question, short though it might be, State practice, including that of States whose interests are specially affected, should have been both extensive and virtually uniform in the sense of the provision invoked; and should moreover have occurred in such a way as to show a general recognition that a rule of law or legal obligation is involved.").

53. RESTATEMENT (THIRD) OF THE FOREIGN RELATIONS LAW OF THE UNITED STATES, *supra* note 41, § 102 cmt. c.

54. *See id.* § 102 cmt. d; *see also* Ted Stein, *The Approach of the Different Drummer: The Principle of the Persistent Objector in International Law*, 26 HARV. INT'L. L.J. 457 (1985).

55. Vienna Convention on the Law of Treaties, May 23, 1969, art. 2, 1155 U.N.T.S. 331; RESTATEMENT (THIRD) OF THE FOREIGN RELATIONS LAW OF THE UNITED STATES, *supra* note 41, § 102, cmt. k.

56. The literature is vast. *See, e.g.*, ANTHONY D'AMATO, THE CONCEPT OF CUSTOM IN INTERNATIONAL LAW (1971); Jack Goldsmith & Eric Posner, *A Theory of Customary International Law*, 66 U. CHI. L. REV. 1113 (1999). For commentary by one of the authors, see generally MICHAEL J. GLENNON, THE FOG OF LAW: PRAGMATISM, SECURITY, AND INTERNATIONAL LAW (2010); MICHAEL J. GLENNON, LIMITS OF LAW, PREROGATIVES OF POWER: INTERVENTION AFTER KOSOVO (2001).

orthodox perspective on customary international law, and this summary comes as close as anything to what most international lawyers regard as the basic principles of customary international law.

Where Does Customary International Law Fit into U.S. Federal and State Law?

One's first reaction in thinking about the role of customary international law in U.S. law might be: So what? Why should we care about customary international law in the context of the constitutional law of foreign affairs? After all, the Constitution says virtually nothing about it. The Supremacy Clause makes the Constitution, statutes, and treaties the supreme law of the land; it does not mention customary international law. In fact, customary international law, which was referred to as the law of nations in 1787 and for much of the nineteenth and early twentieth centuries, makes just one appearance in the Constitution. Article I, section 8, vests Congress with the power "to define and punish offenses against the law of nations."[57] One might logically infer that unless Congress has enacted federal law to define or criminally proscribe conduct as a violation of the law of nations, customary international law does not, of its own force, limit or contribute to domestic law, whether state or federal.

But that would be mistaken. Since the earliest days of the Republic, federal and state courts have applied customary international law as common law. The Constitution does not spell out this authority expressly only because, at the time, it was regarded as self-evident.[58] When the Framers met in Philadelphia to draft the Constitution, they worked against the backdrop of a common law system that had borrowed heavily from that of the English.[59] Eighteenth-century English and American judges typically conceived of their work as including the application of natural law and principles of the law of nations that fell within it. Long before the American Revolution, English judges had treated the law of nations as part of the common law of England.

After the American Revolution but before the Constitution took effect, English common law was regarded as part of the law of the several states, which then conducted themselves as independent nations. Recall that in the Declaration of Independence, the "thirteen united States of America" had proclaimed

57. U.S. CONST. art. I, § 8, cl. 10.

58. Louis Henkin, *supra* note 41, at 1566 ("Much is made . . . of the fact that, unlike treaties, customary law is not mentioned expressly in the Supremacy Clause. . . . The Supremacy Clause was addressed to the states, and was designed to assure federal supremacy. . . . The law of nations of the time was not seen as something imposed on the states by the new U.S. government; it had been binding on and accepted by the states before the U.S. government was even established.").

59. *See* MICHAEL J. GLENNON, CONSTITUTIONAL DIPLOMACY 252–54 (1990).

themselves "Free and Independent States" with "full Power to levy War, conclude Peace, contract Alliances, establish Commerce, and do all other Acts and Things which independent States may of right do."[60] In a 1784 Pennsylvania case involving an attack on a French diplomat, the state court wrote at the outset of the opinion that as a "case of first impression in the United States," the case "must be determined on the principles of the law of nations, which form part of the municipal [i.e., domestic or internal] law of Pennsylvania," and that "the law of nations, in its full extent, is part of the law of this state . . . ."[61] Application of the law of nations as binding common law was hardly novel for the the states under the Articles of Confederation.

Meeting in Philadelphia in 1787, the Framers believed that the application of the law of nations in the newly established federal courts would be necessary to avoid international harmony. The Constitutional Convention unanimously resolved "[t]hat the jurisdiction of the national Judiciary shall extend to cases arising under laws passed by the general Legislature, and to such other questions as involve the National peace and harmony."[62] John Jay, writing in *The Federalist*, later praised "[t]he wisdom of the Convention for committing questions concerning treaties and articles of treaties, as well as the laws of nations" to the federal courts.[63] The authority of the federal courts, like that of the state courts, to apply international law did not need to be enshrined in the Constitution's text; it remained a uniformly acknowledged part of the common law inherited from England and incorporated into the law of the United States upon independence. "In that country, from which the common law has been brought," James Wilson wrote, "the law of nations has always been most respectively and attentively adopted and regarded by the municipal tribunals, in all matters concerning which it is proper to have recourse to that rule of decision."[64] Alexander Hamilton declared the United States "a party to" the law of nations because it had not dissented from the law of nations upon independence;[65] that the law of nations is part of the law of the United States is, in a word, "indubitable."[66]

60. The Declaration of Independence (U.S. 1776).

61. Respublica v. De Longchamps, 1 U.S. (1 Dall.) 111, 114, 117 (1874).

62. 2 Records of the Federal Convention of 1787, at 39 (Max Farrand ed., 1911).

63. The Federalist No. 3, at 14–15 (John Jay) (Jacob E. Cooke ed., 1961).

64. James Wilson, Collected Works of James Wilson 374 (Kermit L. Hall & Mark David Hall eds., 1804).

65. Alexander Hamilton, The Works of Alexander Hamilton 436 (Henry Cabot Lodge ed., Fed. ed. 1971).

66. *Id.*

From the outset, the Supreme Court has affirmed this view. John Jay, the first chief justice of the United States, characterized the law of nations as "those laws by which nations are bound to regulate their conduct towards each other" and declared that, upon independence, "all those duties, as well as rights, which spring from the relation of nation to nation, have devolved upon us."[67] "The United States had, by taking a place among the nations of the earth, become amenable to the laws of nations," the Court said in 1793.[68] "[T]he Court is bound by the law of nations which is a part of the law of the land," Chief Justice Marshall wrote in 1815.[69]

Federal and state courts alike have long applied customary international law in appropriate cases—without specifying the precise rationale for doing so; it was simply accepted as part of the general common law, the "brooding omnipresence in the sky,"[70] as Justice Holmes would later disparage the idea of (general) common law. A federal district court, sitting in Pennsylvania in 1855, for example, considered whether a citizen of one state, which permitted slavery, could travel freely with his slaves through the territory of another, which prohibited slavery.[71] The court looked to the law of nations, suggesting that the same international restraints that existed before the establishment of the United States continued to bind the states afterward.[72] Nineteenth-century California courts looked to the law of nations in assessing the breadth of the obligation to protect private property rights.[73] In 1891, the Supreme Court confronted a claim that Massachusetts

---

67. *Reprinted in* Henfield's Case, 11 F. Cas. 1099 (C.C.D. Pa. No. 6360) (1793).

68. *See* Chisholm v. Georgia, 2 U.S. (2 Dall.) 419, 474 (1793); *see also* Ware v. Hylton, 3 U.S. (3 Dall.) 199, 201 (1796) (Wilson, J.) ("When the United States declared their independence, they were bound to receive the law of nations, in its modern state of purity and refinement.").

69. The Nereide, 13 U.S. (9 Cranch) 388, 423 (1815).

70. S. Pac. Co. v. Jensen, 244 U.S. 205, 222 (1917) (Holmes, J., dissenting).

71. United States *ex rel* Wheeler v. Williamson, 28 F.Cas. 686 (No. 16,726) (E.D. Pa. 1855).

72. The court continued:

> [B]efore the compact of union was formed between the states, each of them was an absolutely sovereign and independent community; and that, except so far as their relations to each other and to foreign nations have been qualified by the federal constitution, each of them remain so. As such, it is bound by that great moral code, which, because of its universal obligation, is called the "law of nations." What it could not do if freed from federative restrictions, it cannot do now: every restraint upon its policy, which duty to other states would in that case involve, binds it still, just as if the Union had been dissolved or had never been formed.

Id. at 692.

73. *See, e.g.*, Thompson v. Doaksum, 68 Cal. 593, 10 P. 199 (1886); Teschemacher v. Thompson, 18 Cal. 11 (1861).

had exceeded its jurisdiction, and it held that a state may define its boundaries—but only "[w]ithin what are generally recognized as the territorial limits of States by the law of nations."[74] By 1900, the Court could state what was, by then, a truism: "International law is part of our law, and must be ascertained and administered by the courts of justice of appropriate jurisdiction, as often as questions of right depending upon it are duly presented for their determination."[75] And despite some academic dissent from this position,[76] at present it remains difficult to contest the long-standing consensus that, after *Erie*, customary international law is an enclave of special federal common law,[77] as well as part of state common law.

In 1951, for example, the Oregon Supreme Court, reviewing the claims of heirs to a Dutch decedent to decide whether Germany's occupation of Holland during World War II had tolled the statute of limitations, looked to international law for an answer. *Erie* had by then put an end to general federal common law but not, as noted, to federal common law as such: enclaves survive, and customary international law is among them, as *Sabbatino* underscored in expressing its concern (echoing Philip Jessup's prescient article) that "rules of international law should not be left to divergent and perhaps parochial state interpretations."[78] Hence, the Oregon Supreme Court emphasized that

> international law is a part of the law of every state, which is enforced by its courts without any constitutional or statutory act of incorporation by reference, and while a court may be without jurisdiction to enforce

---

74. Manchester v. Massachusetts, 139 U.S. 240, 264 (1891).

75. The Paquete Habana, 175 U.S. 677, 700 (1900).

76. *See, e.g.*, Anthony J. Bellia Jr. & Bradford R. Clark, *The Federal Common Law of Nations*, 109 COLUM. L. REV. 1 (2009).

77. RESTATEMENT (THIRD) OF THE FOREIGN RELATIONS LAW OF THE UNITED STATES, *supra* note 41, § 131. Whatever the merits of the Supreme Court's recent case law on the Alien Tort Claims Act, 28 U.S.C. § 1350 (ATCA) (2012) (vesting federal district courts with "original jurisdiction of any civil action by an alien for a tort only, committed in violation of the law of nations or a treaty of the United States"), customary international law remains "part of our law," *The Paquete Habana*, 175 U.S. at 700, for both state and federal courts, subject to congressional override. Despite assertions to the contrary, neither *Sosa v. Alvarez-Machain*, 542 U.S. 692 (2004), nor *Kiobel v. Royal Dutch Petroleum Co.*, 133 S. Ct. 1659 (2013), changed this—or could have. The holdings of both cases were limited to interpretation of a particular federal statute, that is, the ATCA; all else is, at most, dicta.

78. Banco Nacional de Cuba v. Sabbatino, 376 U.S. 398, 425 (1964); *see* Philip C. Jessup, *The Doctrine of* Erie Railroad v. Tompkins *Applied to International Law*, 33 AM. J. INT'L L. 740 (1939).

> international law in a given case by reason of some controlling statute, nevertheless, relevant provisions of the law of nations are legally paramount whenever international rights and duties are involved before a court having jurisdiction to enforce them.[79]

That is as true today as in 1955. After *Erie*, however, it is also true that state decisions at odds with customary international law—as construed and incorporated by federal courts as federal common law—should be treated as preempted and, in appropriate cases, overruled.

It is difficult to find specific examples of these principles in modern case law. Courts have construed customary international law so as to assess whether particular state actions would violate it, and also used international custom to interpret statutes so as to avoid creating a conflict with it.[80] But in no modern case has a state law actually been struck down as violative of customary international law.[81] Why should that be so?

First, as a procedural matter, even though state courts called upon to resolve issues of customary international law to which federal courts have not spoken have a constitutional obligation to determine and apply it, federal questions (the content of specialized federal common law in addition, usually, to statutory issues) authorize litigants to remove cases from state to federal court,[82] which they almost invariably do. This is true even though state determinations of customary international law always remain subject to preemption by federal—statutory or common—law.

Second, the validity of a state law under customary international law rarely arises. Most of the time, what's unlawful under customary international law is also unlawful under federal or state law, and courts don't decide cases under customary international law if they can readily be resolved under federal or state law—whether constitutional, statutory, or common. Consider, for example, *Garcia-Mir v. Meese*.[83] Undocumented and excludable Cuban aliens, detained in an Alabama

---

79. Peters v. McKay, 238 P.2d 225, 231 (Or. 1951).

80. *See* Murray v. The Schooner Charming Betsy, 6 U.S. (2 Cranch) 64 (1804) (finding that congressional statutes should never be construed to violate international law if any other construction is possible).

81. Thomas M. Franck, Michael J. Glennon, Sean D. Murphy & Edward T. Swaine, Foreign Relations and National Security Law: Cases, Materials, and Simulations 803 (4th ed. 2012).

82. 28 U.S.C. § 1441 (2012).

83. Garcia-Mir v. Meese, 788 F.2d 1450, 1446 (11th Cir. 1986).

penitentiary, sought legal admittance to the United States. They argued that their continued detention violated the prohibition in customary international law against prolonged, arbitrary detention, as well as the Constitution's Due Process Clause. Although the district court reached the former claim and found that they were indeed being held in violation of international law, on appeal, the Eleventh Circuit resolved the case on constitutional grounds—without reference to customary international law.[84]

Third, state lawyers and judges, with few exceptions, lack expertise in international law. Given the sparse case law, few lawyers feel confident bringing a claim based on customary international law,[85] and few state judges feel confident resolving a case on such grounds. Fears of reversal and potential malpractice accusations animate more than a little conduct in American courtrooms.

Third, state officials rarely violate customary international law—at least not in any way that would not already be a violation under federal or state law. Hypothesizing a situation in which state officials might violate international custom (but not federal or state law) would require conjuring up unrealistic, indeed absurd, facts. The motivating restraint is not international law; it is simply that the contemplated action would be ridiculous. So profoundly have fundamental international customary rules worked their way into the ethos of the contemporary legislative process that their impact is no longer even consciously noticed. One of the scenarios hypothesized above—a state law making it illegal to grow cacao in a foreign country—borders on the absurd. As the Oregon Supreme Court put it, "States are not commonly disposed to defy by local statute recognized obligations imposed by international law. . . . Normally, it is taken for granted that international law prevails throughout the domain of a State and will be respected in the course of all the activities of its several agencies."[86]

Finally, not many emerging or potential norms of customary international law have "ripened," as the Court aptly put it in *The Paquete Habana*,[87] into sufficiently

---

84. *Id.*

85. Once again, there's also a technical barrier to be noted, which surely contributes to the sparse case law. Although customary international is part of our law, it seldom if ever *directly* supplies a domestic right of action enabling litigants to bring customary international claims in court; rather, to bring a claim based on customary international law in federal court, a litigant must be able to invoke a statute such as the ATCA, 28 U.S.C. § 1350 (2012), which authorizes the right of that litigant to make a claim based on customary international law. For state courts, rights of action may be implicit in general common law, as has long been the case for ordinary tort, contract, and similar claims. It is unclear, however, that state common law of its own force supplies a right of action for litigants to bring a claim based on customary international law.

86. Peters v. McKay, 238 P.2d 225, 231 (Or. 1951).

87. The Paquete Habana, 175 U.S. 677, 686 (1900).

clear rules to qualify for incorporation into U.S. law, a matter to which we now turn.

III. Which Rules of Customary International Law Apply?

Rules of customary international law fall on a spectrum, and because of the limited nature of the judicial role, not all of them will be appropriately applied by the courts. As Justice Harlan observed in *Sabbatino*:

> It should be apparent that the greater the degree of codification or consensus concerning a particular area of international law, the more appropriate it is for the judiciary to render decisions regarding it, since the courts can then focus on the application of an agreed principle to circumstances of fact rather than on the sensitive task of establishing a principle not inconsistent with the national interest or with internation[a]l justice.[88]

Judicial hesitance to resolve issues that depend on decisions about uncodified, debatable, or still emerging norms of customary international law has been an enduring theme of the Court's post-*Erie* jurisprudence on customary international law. Forty years after *Sabbatino*, for example, Justice Souter wrote to similar effect that the Court "ha[s] no congressional mandate to seek out and define new and debatable violations of the law of nations, and modern indications of congressional understanding of the judicial role in the field have not affirmatively encouraged greater judicial creativity."[89]

Judicial reluctance to resolve issues of customary international law reflects its nature. On one end of the spectrum, where little consensus surrounds a putative rule or where its scope is unsettled, the norm cannot be regarded as having crystalized to the extent necessary to permit judicial application.[90] Norms of this sort call to mind the Court's criteria for identifying a political question, viz., the "lack

88. Banco Nacional de Cuba v. Sabbatino, 376 U.S. 398, 428 (1964).

89. Sosa v. Alvarez-Machain, 542 U.S. 692, 728 (2004).

90. The Court declined to apply customary international law in *Sabbatino* in part because it found that "[t]here are few if any issues in international law today on which opinion seems to be so divided as the limitations on a state's power to expropriate the property of aliens." *Sabbatino*, 376 U.S. at 429. But the Court recognized that "[t]here are, of course, areas of international law in which consensus as to standards is greater and which do not represent a battleground for conflicting ideologies. This decision," concluded Justice Harlan, therefore "in no way intimates that the courts of this country are broadly foreclosed from considering questions of international law." *Id.* at 430 n.34.

of judicially discoverable and manageable standards," resulting in "the impossibility of deciding without an initial policy determination of a kind clearly for non-judicial discretion."[91] Cases exhibiting these features are thought to present political questions of a sort not fit for judicial resolution.[92] On the other end of the spectrum lie established rules of customary international law that, given both the regularity and uniformity of state practice and the solidity of *opinio juris*, can be regarded as fit for judicial resolution.

That class of norms that has crystalized into clearly defined, widely accepted customary rules of international law is far smaller than some suppose. It does not, for example, include a guaranteed right to education, as one federal district court correctly concluded.[93] Nor does customary international law, at present, prohibit capital punishment. In 2010, according to Amnesty International, twenty-three countries carried out 527 executions (excluding China, where thousands are believed to have been secretly executed),[94] which bars any putative prohibition from qualifying as a sufficiently general or consistent practice. The norm might be, in the words of the *Restatement*, "in the process of development."[95] But as the Supreme Court has made clear, the judiciary should not be in the business of "seek[ing] out and defin[ing] new and debatable violations of the law of nations."[96]

Further, even were state practice sufficient to justify a prohibition on capital punishment under customary international law, it is doubtful whether nations that have prohibited it have done so because they believe that international law prohibits it. The United States, whose status in the world today gives it a large influence on the development of customary international law in many areas, has also clearly "indicate[d] its dissent" from any such prohibition by continuing to conduct executions (forty-six in 2010)[97] and by having explicitly objected (by

---

91. Baker v. Carr, 369 U.S. 186, 217 (1962).

92. Not surprisingly, the Supreme Court has described the act-of-state doctrine as a species of the political question doctrine. First Nat'l City Bank v. Banco Nacional de Cuba, 406 U.S. 759, 787–88 (1972).

93. "[T]he court concludes that the right to education, while it represents an important international goal, has not acquired the status of customary international law." *In re* Alien Children Educ. Litig., 501 F. Supp. 544, 596 (S.D. Tex. 1980).

94. Amnesty Int'l, Death Sentences and Executions in 2010, (2011), https://www.amnesty.org/en/documents/act50/001/2011/en/.

95. Restatement (Third) of the Foreign Relations Law of the United States, *supra* note 41, § 102.

96. Sosa v. Alvarez-Machain, 542 U.S. 692, 728 (2004).

97. Amnesty Int'l, Death Sentences and Executions in 2010, *supra* note 94.

treaty reservation) to death penalty prohibitions in pertinent treaties that it has ratified, including the International Covenant on Civil and Political Rights[98] and the U.N. Convention against Torture.[99] The United States has expressed the same dissent in international fora. At least three federal appeals courts have declined to find that customary international law prohibits the death penalty.[100]

It is possible, of course, that state practice and *opinio juris* could continue to evolve and solidify such that customary international law might one day prohibit it. Yet even were that to eventuate, the United States would likely be exempt from the customary prohibition based on its status as a persistent objector.[101]

On the other end of the spectrum lie well-established customary international rules, for example, those governing the right of nations to exercise extraterritorial jurisdiction and, to some extent, also offering guidance on resolving international jurisdictional conflicts. These principles of customary international law permit a nation to prescribe law based on five internationally accepted bases or principles of international jurisdiction. Without one of these bases, jurisdiction is said to be "exorbitant" or unreasonable, meaning that the statute or regulation prescribing the rule, although valid as a matter of domestic law, is almost surely not valid as a

98. International Covenant on Civil and Political Rights, 999 U.N.T.S. 171 (Mar. 23, 1976). The U.S. reservation provides that "the United States reserves the right, subject to its Constitutional constraints, to impose capital punishment on any person (other than a pregnant woman) duly convicted under existing or future laws permitting the imposition of capital punishment, including such punishment for crimes committed by persons below eighteen years of age." 138 CONG. REC. H8068 (1992).

99. Convention Against Torture and Other Cruel, Inhuman or Degrading Treatment, Dec. 10, 1984, 1465 U.N.T.S. 85 (June 26, 1987). The U.S. reservation provides that "the United States understands that international law does not prohibit the death penalty, and does not consider this Convention to restrict or prohibit the United States from applying the death penalty consistent with the Fifth, Eighth and/or Fourteenth Amendments to the Constitution of the United States, including any constitutional period of confinement prior to the imposition of the death penalty." 136 CONG. REC. S17486-01 (daily ed., Oct. 27, 1990).

100. In *Hain v. Gibson*, the United States Court of Appeals for the Eleventh Circuit found that:

> It is far from certain that abolition of the death penalty for juveniles is a customary norm of international law that has "risen to the level that the international community as a whole recognizes it as . . . a norm from which no derogation is permitted." Instead, it appears the countries that have abolished the death penalty in these instances have done so for "moral" or "political" reasons (as opposed to any "sense of legal obligation").

287 F.3d 1224, 1243–44 (10th Cir. 2002); *see also* Beazley v. Johnson, 242 F.3d 248, 268 (5th Cir. 2001); Buell v. Mitchell, 274 F.3d 337, 373 (6th Cir. 2001) ("The prohibition of the death penalty is not so extensive and virtually uniform among the nations of the world that it is a customary international norm. . . . There is no indication that the countries that have abolished the death penalty have done so out of a sense of legal obligation, rather than for moral, political, or other reasons.").

101. On persistent objection, *see* Stein, *supra* note 54.

matter of customary international law. The American Law Institute's *Restatement* sets out those five bases:

First, the territoriality principle authorizes nations to prescribe law regulating conduct that, in whole or in substantial part, either takes place within its territory ("subjective territorial principle") or causes substantial effects within its territory ("objective territorial principle"). The former, the right of nations to govern conduct within their territorial borders, is, historically and today, the most well-established, uncontroversial basis for prescriptive jurisdiction.[102] The latter, too, has long been acknowledged, not least in what remains the seminal case by the International Court on prescriptive jurisdiction,[103] although at times, the reach of the principle is uncertain: some courts have held, for example, that actual effects in the prescribing nation need not be established if the defendant's conduct shows an intent to commit the proscribed act, combined with some objective indicia corroborating that intent—for example, a conspiracy between two people in Moldova to smuggle illegal firearms into the United States.

Second, and almost equally well-established, is the (active) nationality principle, which authorizes nations to regulate the conduct of their nationals abroad. The nationality principle applies to legal or juridical as well as to natural persons. A business entity incorporated and organized under the laws of a particular nation, even if it operates entirely abroad, would therefore fall well within the prescriptive jurisdiction of that nation.[104]

Third, under the passive personality principle (aka the passive nationality principle), a nation may regulate certain conduct abroad that harms one or more of its citizens. Although the reach of the passive personality principle remains controversial, the principle itself is accepted as a legitimate basis for jurisdiction. It would authorize, for example, jurisdiction to prosecute a foreign citizen for aircraft piracy based on the nationality of the victims.[105]

---

102. As Chief Justice Marshall wrote in 1812, "The jurisdiction of the nation within its own territory is necessarily exclusive and absolute. It is susceptible of no limitation not imposed by itself." The Schooner Exchange v. McFaddon, 11 U.S. (7 Cranch) 116, 136 (1812); *see also* American Banana Co. v. United Fruit Co., 213 U.S. 347, 356 (1909) (Holmes, J.) ("The general and almost universal rule is that the character of an act as lawful or unlawful must be determined wholly by the law of the country where the act is done.").

103. *See* The S.S. "Lotus" (Fr./Turk.), 1927 P.C.I.J. 4 (ser. A) No. 10 (Sep. 7).

104. The Supreme Court famously affirmed this principle domestically in *Blackmer v. United States*, 284 U.S. 421, 436–37 (1932), which involved the refusal of the defendant, a U.S. citizen residing in France, to comply with subpoenas requiring his appearance as a witness in a criminal trial in the United States.

105. *E.g.*, United States v. Rezaq, 134 F.3d 1121, 1133 (D.C. Cir. 1997); *see generally* RESTATEMENT (THIRD) OF THE FOREIGN RELATIONS LAW OF THE UNITED STATES, *supra* note 41, § 402 cmt. g.

Fourth, the protective principle authorizes a nation to regulate conduct outside its territory by foreign nationals that is directed against the security or a limited number of other core interests of the nation. Protective principle jurisdiction extends to activities such as espionage, counterfeiting, falsification of official documents, and perjury.[106]

Finally, nations may prescribe law regulating conduct abroad that has been recognized by the community of nations as being of universal concern. This conduct includes international piracy, the slave trade, attacks on or hijacking of aircraft, genocide, war crimes, and perhaps certain acts of terrorism.[107] Although the reach of this principle, too, is controversial, and its scope continues to develop, it has been accepted and applied by nations worldwide such that few today would deny its status as customary international law.[108]

Even when one or more of these five bases for jurisdiction is present, absent a governing treaty, customary international law requires that any prescriptive regulation be reasonable in light of, among other things, the countervailing interests of other nations.[109]

State and federal courts have long treated the jurisdictional limits imposed by customary international law as part of U.S. domestic law. *Strassheim v. Daily*,[110] for example, involved a defendant indicted in Michigan. While in Illinois, he had perpetrated bribery and theft by false pretenses in the course of trying to sell Michigan used machinery that he tried to pass off as new. Justice Holmes, writing for a unanimous Supreme Court, referred to customary international law to determine the constitutionality of Michigan's exercise of extraterritorial jurisdiction in the interstate context. If the jury found the evidence sufficient, he concluded, "the usage of the civilized world would warrant Michigan in punishing him," for "[a]cts done outside a jurisdiction, but intended to produce and producing detrimental effects within it, justify a State in punishing the cause of the harm as if he had been present at the effect, if the State should succeed in getting him within its power."[111] The Court thus incorporated the objective

106. *E.g.*, United States v. Pizzarusso, 388 F.2d 8 (2d Cir. 1968).

107. *See generally* RESTATEMENT (THIRD) OF THE FOREIGN RELATIONS LAW OF THE UNITED STATES, *supra* note 41, § 402 *et seq.*

108. *E.g.*, Demjanjuk v. Petrovsky, 776 F.2d 571, 582 (6th Cir. 1985). *But see* United States v. Yousef, 327 F.3d 56, 107–08 (2d Cir. 2003) (concluding that universal jurisdiction does not reach terrorism generally because of the persisting controversy over its definition, although it does supply the basis for prosecuting certain specific terrorist acts).

109. *See* RESTATEMENT (THIRD) OF THE FOREIGN RELATIONS LAW OF THE UNITED STATES, *supra* note 41, at § 403.

110. 221 U.S. 280 (1911).

111. *Id.* at 285.

territorial principle or "effects test," and its opinion can also be read to adopt a principle among the several states analogous to the protective principle: It was, after all, the integrity of Michigan's governmental activities that was threatened by the defendant's effort at deceiving Michigan officials in the conduct of their official duties.[112]

Thirty years later, in *Skiriotes v. Florida*,[113] the defendant, a Florida state citizen and, of course, also citizen of the United States, was convicted under Florida law for taking sponges off the Florida coast in the Gulf of Mexico. He challenged the statute's conferral of extraterritorial jurisdiction, arguing that its reach extended beyond Florida's maritime territorial boundaries. The Supreme Court held this objection "beside the point,"[114] even if Florida's law indeed applied beyond *its* territorial limits, for

> aside from the question of the extent of control which the United States may exert in the interest of self-protection over waters near its borders, although beyond its territorial limits, the United States is not debarred by any rule of international law from governing the conduct of its own citizens upon the high seas or even in foreign countries when the rights of other nations or their nationals are not infringed. With respect to such an exercise of authority there is no question of international law . . . .[115]

Rather, the Court explained, the validity of the law depends on domestic law.[116] Constitutionally, Congress could have validly enacted the law.[117] And because there existed no "legislation of Congress with which the state statute conflicts,"[118] the law fell within Florida's police power:

> If the United States may control the conduct of its citizens upon the high seas, we see no reason why the State of Florida may not likewise govern the conduct of its citizens upon the high seas with respect to matters in which the State has a legitimate interest and where there is no conflict with acts of Congress. Save for the powers committed by the Constitution to the

112. *See also* United States v. Bowman, 260 U.S. 94 (1922).

113. 313 U.S. 69 (1941).

114. *Id.* at 73.

115. *Id.* (footnotes omitted) (emphasis added).

116. *Id.*

117. *Id.* at 74.

118. *Id.*

> Union, the State of Florida has retained the status of a sovereign. Florida was admitted to the Union "on equal footing with the original States, in all respects whatsoever."[119]

The Court sustained the state law because, had it been enacted by Congress, the United States would not have thereby violated customary international law's jurisdictional limits. Florida's statute could be based on the nationality principle, among other international bases.[120] Citing *The Paquete Habana*, the Court affirmed that "[i]nternational law is a part of our law and as such is the law of all States of the Union, but it is a part of our law for the application of its own principles, and these are concerned with international rights and duties and not with domestic rights and duties."[121]

Federal and state courts routinely continue to consider the jurisdictional limits imposed by customary international law. "[T]he principles governing this case," Justice O'Connor wrote in 1983, "are common to both international law and federal common law."[122] In a landmark antitrust case ten years later, Justice Scalia wrote, in a dissent joined by three others, that "the practice of using international law to limit the extraterritorial reach of statutes is firmly established in our jurisprudence."[123] No justice in the majority disagreed with that statement; the majority's differences with the dissent lay in the substance of the analysis. The Court as a whole embraced the principle of applying customary international law limits on jurisdiction in its most recent decision on the extraterritorial reach of the Sherman Act.[124]

State courts have followed suit. In *State v. Miller*,[125] for example, an Arizona appellate court dismissed for lack of jurisdiction the indictment of an out-of-state defendant who had met two people in Colorado who had, in turn, stolen diamonds in Arizona; the defendant later helped them sell the diamonds without knowledge that the goods had been stolen. The court looked to international law to determine whether the exercise of jurisdiction over the defendant would be

119. *Id.* at 77 (footnote omitted); *see also id.* at 74.

120. *Id.* at 73.

121. *Id.* at 72–73 (citing The Paquete Habana, 175 U.S. 677, 700 (1900)).

122. First Nat'l City Bank v. Banco Para el Comercio Exterior do Cuba (Bancec), 462 U.S. 611, 623 (1983).

123. Hartford Fire Ins. Co. v. California, 509 U.S. 764, 818 (1993) (Scalia, J., dissenting).

124. F. Hoffman LaRoche v. Empagran, 542 U.S. 155, 164–65 (2004).

125. 755 P.2d 434 (Az. Ct. App. 1988).

unlawfully exorbitant:[126] "We look to international law to determine whether the state may assert jurisdiction based upon a statute that attempts to punish extraterritorial conduct.... The Supreme Court has also recognized that international law applies to the states of the United States in their relations with one another except as modified by the federal constitution."[127] The Court concluded that "Arizona must conform to international law in its exercise of extraterritorial jurisdiction.[128] *Miller*, among many other state cases,[129] thus supports the *Restatement* view that because "international and other foreign relations law are the law of the United States, under the Supremacy Clause of the Constitution an exercise of jurisdiction by a State that contravenes the limitations [of the *Restatement*] is invalid."[130] As the reporter notes:

> [E]xercise of jurisdiction to prescribe by States is governed by the same principles whether the exercise of jurisdiction has international or inter-State implications. States of the United States generally exercise jurisdiction on the basis of territoriality, including effects within the State. A State may not apply its laws to a person outside its territory merely on the basis that he is a national of the United States, but it may apply at least some laws to a person outside its territory on the basis that he is a citizen, resident, or domiciliary of the State.[131]

Federal—or State—Common Law?

It might be speculated that state common law includes rules of customary international law for many of the same historical reasons that federal common law

---

126. *Id.* at 435.

127. *Id.* at 436.

128. *Id.* at 439. The court reasoned that the defendant "is not an Arizona resident, all of his conduct occurred outside Arizona, and the conduct had, at most, only an insubstantial and indirect effect in Arizona. The . . . harm to the Arizona victim . . . had already occurred before [the defendant] had any connection with the stolen property." *Id.* at 438.

129. *See, e.g.*, Condon v. Inter-Religious Found. for Cmty. Org., Inc., 850 N.Y.S.2d 841, 847 (2008) ("Foreign policy is an area of law that is exclusively reserved for the federal government. Thus, neither the state nor any other local government can make laws or regulations regarding foreign policy . . . ."); *In re* Adoption of a Child by L.C., 425 A.2d 66 (N.J. 1980) (holding that federal law regarding locale of birthplace preempts state law).

130. Restatement (Third) of the Foreign Relations Law of the United States, *supra* note 41, § 402, cmt. k.

131. *Id.* § 403, reporters' note 5 (citations omitted).

includes such rules. Both, after all, originated in English common law. Both also emerged from the general common law that developed in both federal and state courts during the pre-*Erie* era. Yet customary international law seldom appears as common law in state court decisions—for two further reasons beyond those already mentioned.

First, issues of international law raise federal questions and will typically be decided by federal courts. The incorporation rationale would be undercut if every state were deemed capable of interpreting customary international law for itself, potentially leading to fifty-one versions of a particular rule of customary international law. The resulting chaos and opportunity for forum shopping and parochialism would be overwhelming. Hamilton feared that the entire nation might be blamed for "an unjust sentence against a foreigner" handed down by a state court.[132] When it comes to judicial interpretation of international law, federal, not state, courts should (and do) have the last word.

Second, common law, although it remains a greater part of the law on the state than the federal law,[133] is increasingly interstitial for both, filling gaps, if any, in statutory law. But all federal law is supreme. "International law [is] law of the United States," as the *Restatement* says, "supreme over the law of the several States."[134] Still,

> [q]uestions under international law or international agreements of the United States often arise in State courts. As law of the United States, international law is also the law of every State, is a basis for the exercise of judicial authority by State courts, and is cognizable in cases in State courts, in the same way as other United States law.[135]

IV. Assessment

Customary international law is part of federal common law. Federal common law is binding on the states. Congress *can*, as a practical matter, disregard customary international law, just as it *can* disregard treaty obligations—whether by a superseding statute, inconsistent conduct, or otherwise. Yet seldom is disregard for international law, customary or conventional (treaty-based), in the national

132. THE FEDERALIST NO. 80, at 477 (Alexander Hamilton) (Clinton Rossiter ed., 1961).

133. *See* GUIDO CALABRESI, A COMMON LAW FOR THE AGE OF STATUTES 1 (1982) (noting the "orgy" of statute-making that has displaced much of traditional state common law).

134. RESTATEMENT (THIRD) OF THE FOREIGN RELATIONS LAW OF THE UNITED STATES, *supra* note 41, § 111.

135. *Id.* § 111, cmt. d.

interest. It is not coincidental that overt breaches of international law by the federal government are few and far between. In general, the federal government incorporates international law in its rules—in some cases, construing or adapting it but rarely disregarding it.

Post-*Erie* federal common law is mostly interstitial. It typically fills statutory gaps. It most often supplies "a federal rule of decision" where "necessary to protect uniquely federal interests" or where "Congress has given the courts the power to develop substantive law."[136] Customary international law, and compliance with it, clearly qualify as "uniquely federal interests," and the federal courts do, as they should, incorporate customary international law as federal common law in appropriate cases. At times, Congress has been silent on issues of customary international law (for example, on general jurisdictional limits); at other times, Congress has given the courts a green light to incorporate it by making federal common law,[137] albeit perhaps subject to statutory limitations. But rules of decision made by the federal courts as specialized federal common law can, of course, always be superseded by federal statute or inconsistent law.[138] If Congress enacts a statute at odds or in tension with customary international law, the states can and should disregard the customary international law rule at issue, whether it had previously been incorporated via federal common law or not—just as federal courts, under those circumstances, would also be constitutionally obliged to follow the statute. But in the face of congressional silence, the states should respect clearly defined and widely accepted rules of customary international law, exercising judgment as to novel issues but deferring, where possible, to the incorporation of customary international rules by federal common law.

That is our view and still, we believe, that of the majority. Nonetheless, we acknowledge that considerable controversy exists about the nature and legitimacy of post-*Erie* federal common law, especially in the context of customary international law.[139] Some commentators have characterized all dormant foreign-affairs doctrine cases as federal common law. They reason, apparently, that Congress could legislatively "reverse" these cases because the federal courts that decided them were engaged in making federal common law in the absence of clear

---

136. Texas Indus. v. Radcliff Materials, 451 U.S. 630, 640 (1981) (internal citations and quotation marks omitted).

137. The ATCA is an especially clear example. *See* Sosa v. Alvarez-Machain, 542 U.S. 692, 739 (2004).

138. 28 U.S.C. § 1738 (2012).

139. *See, e.g., Sosa*, 542 U.S. at 739 (Scalia, J., concurring in the judgment); Tel-Oren v. Libyan Arab Republic, 726 F.2d 774, 799 (Bork, J., concurring in the judgment); *see generally* Bradley & Goldsmith, *supra* note 41.

congressional direction—as, for example, the Supreme Court did in *Sabbatino*, a classic post-*Erie* federal common law decision.

But that seems doubtful. Not all the dormant foreign affairs cases *were* clearly reversible. "In *Zschernig*," Henkin correctly wrote, "the Supreme Court was not making federal law about alien inheritance; the states were held excluded not by federal judge-made law but by the Constitution itself."[140] The majority clearly rejected the president's suggestion that the Oregon law need not be struck down and did not interfere with its foreign affairs priorities, and Justice Stewart's concurrence explicitly rejected the authority of the political branches.[141] There is every reason to believe that it would likewise have made no difference in *Zschernig* if Congress had passed a statute stating that it had no objection to such state laws. The *Zschernig* Court held that the Constitution—not any particular law, federal interest, or other consideration—precluded Oregon's probate statute. Congress could not have in effect delegated to the states a slice of the federal foreign-affairs power (as conceived by the Court), for the Constitution allocated that power to Congress and the president. The Court was interpreting the Constitution, just as it was in *Brown v. Board of Education*[142] and *Roe v. Wade*.[143] That, at least, seems to be what the Court was saying in *Zschernig*.

The same may also have been true in *Garamendi*, although that decision's reversibility is uncertain given the ambiguities in the Court's opinion concerning federal exclusivity. In neither *Zschernig* nor *Garamendi*, in any event, was the Court creating its *own* common-law rule—as it did in *Sabbatino* in the course of promulgating the modern act-of-state doctrine. Rather, in both *Zschernig* and *Garamendi*, the Court merely *invalidated* rules that would otherwise have applied (concerning, respectively, state inheritance rights and insurance disclosure requirements). Similarly, in dormant Commerce Clause cases, interstate as well as foreign, the Court has not created a new rule, as does Congress when it legislates, but merely set aside rules at odds with the Constitution. That these cases turn upon contingencies does not make them federal common law cases—any more than *Youngstown Sheet & Tube Co. v. Sawyer*,[144] *Dames & Moore v. Regan*,[145]

---

140. Louis Henkin, Foreign Affairs and the Constitution, *supra* note 27, at 456 n.46.

141. Zschernig v. Miller, 389 U.S. 429, 441 (1968) (Stewart, J., concurring).

142. 347 U.S. 483 (1954).

143. 410 U.S. 113 (1973).

144. 343 U.S. 579, 587 (1952).

145. 453 U.S. 654, 678 (1981).

Medellin v. Texas,[146] or various other separation-of-powers cases—the outcome of which also turned on the presence or absence of congressional action.

Perhaps clarity would be advanced by thinking of contingent constitutional law simply as "soft" constitutional law, soft in the sense that it is subject to congressional countermand or revision, as opposed to "hard" constitutional law that is not. Hard constitutional law, at issue in cases such as *Brown* and *Roe*, poses issues of ultimate validity; an act found wanting cannot be saved with stronger legislative support. Soft constitutional law cases, on the other hand, involve preemption, broadly speaking—cases in which the Court evaluates the act of one governmental entity, the validity of which depends upon the action or inaction of some other governmental entity. In the context of dormant foreign-affairs federalism, as in the context of interstate commerce analysis, the act being evaluated is the act of a state government; the other governmental entity is Congress. In the separation-of-powers context, the act being evaluated is the act of the president; the other governmental entity is again Congress. Preemption and contingency play no role in hard constitutional law, which is not a function of action taken or not taken by any other branch or department of government: a hard constitutional rule derives from interpretation of the Constitution, and nothing else. But soft constitutional law is all about contingency—the subject to which we now turn.

---

146. 552 U.S. 491 (2008).

8

Federal Approval

THE COMPACT CLAUSE

DESPITE THE FRAMING generation's experience with state malfeasance toward national treaty obligations under the Articles, the Constitution did not categorically preclude the states from entering into all international agreements. It instead distinguished international agreements that states may never enter into from those they may enter into with congressional approval. Article I, section 10, clause 1, thus categorically prohibits the states from entering into "any Treaty, Alliance, or Confederation," while clause 3 authorizes the states conditionally, subject to congressional approval, to "enter into any Agreement or Compact with another State, or with a foreign Power."[1]

The latter provision, generally known as the Compact Clause, leaves some obvious and theoretically perplexing questions unanswered. Yet as this chapter suggests, many of those questions need not be answered—at least not by the courts. Over more than two centuries of experience under the Constitution, Congress and the states have for all practical purposes worked out a modus operandi. In practice, issues raised by the Compact Clause have turned out to be few, to require minimal judicial—or, for that matter, congressional—intervention, and seldom if ever to raise concrete problems. Insofar as they do on occasion, the issues tend to arise in the context of interstate compacts rather than those

1. Among other things ordinarily prohibited to the states. The analysis in this chapter pertains only to that part of Art. I, section 10, clause 3, that authorizes states to enter into certain international agreements with congressional consent. We do not address the language from the same clause giving states conditional permission—likewise subject to the consent of Congress—to "lay any duty of tonnage, keep troops, or ships of war in time of peace, . . . or engage in war, unless actually invaded, or in such imminent danger as will not admit of delay." U.S. CONST. art. I, § 10, cl. 3.

between the states and foreign powers ("foreign state agreements," or FSAs).[2] As a matter of conceptual or historical interest, for example, it is natural to ask (among many other questions, such as those enumerated below): what distinguishes a categorically prohibited "Treaty" from a conditionally prohibited "Compact"? Yet so far as our national experience suggests, little turns on the answer to this and most of the other theoretically puzzling questions about the Compact Clause.

I. *From the Clear to the Unclear*

At the outset, it's nonetheless helpful to note what's legally uncontroversial. At least six principles governing the Compact Clause have been widely accepted: First, Congress can consent to a compact either before or after it has been made. Second, Congress can consent explicitly or implicitly. Third, a state compact that receives Congress's consent thereby acquires the status of federal law[3]—and consequently, presumably preempts state law to the contrary, although the case law on this issue is scarce to nonexistent. Fourth, by enacting a statute, Congress can preempt certain compacts in advance, obviating any need to consider consent later; in effect, the statute constitutes anticipatory refusal. Fifth, Congress can consent to a particular compact, but it can also, if it wishes, consent to a whole category of compacts on the same issue, such that states may later proceed without further legal hesitation. Sixth, Congress can withdraw its consent, explicitly or, under the last-in-time doctrine,[4] implicitly—although if the compact is with a "foreign Power," it presumably remains binding upon the United States, as a nation, under international law, which could render the nation in violation of international obligations.[5]

---

2. For the sake of brevity, we refer to agreements between a state and a foreign nation as foreign-state agreements, FSAs for short. Duncan B. Hollis, *Unpacking the Compact Clause*, 88 TEX. L. REV. 741, 742 (2009) [hereinafter Hollis I]. References to "compacts" below should similarly be understood as a shorthand for "any Agreement or Compact" under Article I, section 10, clause 3. As we will see, the nomenclature (i.e., agreement versus compact) almost surely does not matter.

3. Cuyler v. Adams, 449 U.S. 433, 440 (1981) (footnote omitted); *see also* Virginia v. West Virginia, 246 U.S. 565, 601 (1918) (affirming congressional authority to require state compliance with, at least interstate, compacts that have received congressional consent).

4. The last-in-time doctrine simply means that in the event of conflict between legal obligations under treaties and statutes, the instrument ratified or enacted, respectively, later in time prevails. *See* Whitney v. Robertson, 124 U.S. 190 (1888).

5. *See* Int'l Law Comm'n, Articles on the Responsibility of States for Internationally Wrongful Acts, in Rep. on the Work of Its Fifty-Third Session, U.N. Doc. A/56/10 (2001), annexed to G.A. Res. 56/83, art. 4 (Dec. 12, 2001) [hereinafter ASR].

The answers to (at least) ten other questions, however, remain unclear: First, how does a "Treaty, Alliance, or Confederation," which states may never conclude (and Congress lacks the power to authorize)[6] differ from an "Agreement or Compact," which states may conclude with congressional authorization? Second, what, if anything, differentiates an "Agreement" from a "Compact"? Third, how should a compact be distinguished from a simple contract that falls short of a compact? Is there a particular threshold and, if so, along what dimension or dimensions of the agreement? Fourth, whatever the answer to the preceding question, does it apply in the same way to an *interstate* compact, on the one hand, as to an FSA, on the other? Fifth, how does the requirement of congressional consent apply to a compact involving an intermediary, that is, one in which a state and foreign power, rather than deal with each other directly, transact through a third party? Sixth, may Congress place conditions on its consent to a compact? Seventh, when Congress consents, must it do so by means of the formal procedures set forth in the Presentment Clause,[7] including presidential signature (or congressional override of a presidential veto)—or does consent by a simple majority of each House suffice? Eighth, can Congress consent to a compact in which a state delegates certain of its powers to a foreign nation? Ninth, does the requirement of congressional consent apply to a compact between a state and an international or regional organization comprised of foreign nations—or between a state and the federal government? Tenth, if the Compact Clause requires the states to obtain congressional consent to compacts that falls within their exclusive, sovereign powers, does it potentially give rise to conflict with the Tenth Amendment?

II. Contemporary Practice

Despite, or perhaps because of, these lingering questions, Congress and the states have in practice arrived at a relatively stable modus vivendi and modus

---

6. Hence, even if Congress wanted to authorize a state-province "Alliance," which would, in its judgment, benefit the nation, the Constitution prohibits it from authorizing a state to conclude that agreement with a "foreign Power" (or consenting to the same). *See* U.S. CONST. art. I, § 10, cl. 1. Note, however, that, here too, this may well be an essentially academic issue. In the unlikely event, for instance, that Congress wanted one state, but not others, to enter into an alliance with a foreign nation, it could enter into an international agreement with a foreign nation that expressly makes clear that only, say, the State of Maine undertakes obligations on behalf of the nation and bears any and all international financial or other liability for breach of (formally national) obligations emanating from the alliance. Nothing in international law forbids this. International law simply establishes a default presumption that national authorities bear liability for all conduct attributable to the nation, however the subfederal entity, agent, or other actor may be characterized under that nation's internal law. *See* ASR, *supra* note 5, art. 4.

7. U.S. CONST. art. I, § 7.

operandi—with minimal guidance from the courts. Henkin's description of concrete practice remains apt two decades later:

> Whether by so narrowing the constitutional requirement of Congressional consent, or because consent was assumed, state and local authorities have in fact entered into agreements and arrangements with foreign counterparts without seeking consent of Congress, principally on matters of common local interest, such as the coordination of roads, police cooperation, and border control.[8]

According to one recent study, forty-one states "have concluded at least 340 FSAs since 1955,"[9] and "[v]irtually all of them have the same, limited function—coordinating activities by Border States in sharing information, resources or costs within a transboundary region."[10] Yet Congress has expressly approved a "mere handful" of them, which fall into "only four narrowly defined categories: (a) bridges; (b) fire fighting; (c) highways; and (d) emergency management."[11] Only once has Congress withheld its consent, in the case of "the 1968 Great Lakes Basin Compact (and even then only at the behest of a U.S. State Department concerned about conflicts with U.S. treaty obligations)"; and Congress has never withheld its consent on the ground that the FSA in question constitutes a "prohibited treaty" under Article I, section 10, clause 1.[12]

---

8. LOUIS HENKIN, FOREIGN AFFAIRS AND THE US CONSTITUTION 155 (2d ed. 1996).

9. Hollis I, *supra* note 2, at 744, 751. The evidence indicates that the number of FSAs "has increased dramatically in recent years." *Id.* at 750. But it's unclear that this evidence reflects an increase in the frequency with which states have been concluding FSAs or "simply . . . the rise of the Internet, making information on FSAs easier to acquire." *Id.* Congress approved the first recorded FSA in 1870, "New York and Canada's International Bridge Compact to construct a Niagara River bridge," *id.* at 1076, but other congressionally approved FSAs could, of course, have preceded it without available documentation.

10. Duncan B. Hollis, *The Elusive Foreign Compact*, 73 MO. L. REV. 1071, 1076 (2008) [hereinafter Hollis II].

11. *Id.* at 1075–76.

12. *Id.* at 1078. The fact remains today that "[n]o helpful, authoritative distinction has emerged [between a categorically prohibited "Treaty" and a conditionally prohibited "Compact"]. No agreement between a state and a foreign power has been successfully challenged on the ground that it is a treaty which the state was forbidden to make." HENKIN, *supra* note 8, at 153. Justice Story, in his *Commentaries*, grappled with the issue early in our constitutional history. But neither he nor Taney (nor anyone else) has arrived at an accepted distinction between the two. *See id.* at 153, 153 n.13. In fact, in this regard the only accepted "test," so to speak, is to defer to Congress's characterization. *Id.* (quoting Felix Frankfurter & James M. Landis, *The Compact Clause of the Constitution—A Study in Interstate Adjustments*, 34 YALE L.J. 685, 695 (1925)).

Nor has the Supreme Court ever objected on this ground. Cases on the Compact Clause, and especially FSAs, have been exceedingly rare.[13] Only once, in *Holmes v. Jennison*,[14] did the Supreme Court arguably invalidate an FSA on the grounds that Congress had not consented. Recall that despite Justice Taney's extensive dicta presaging the dormant foreign-affairs doctrine (see Chapter 4), *Holmes* held only, in a splintered judgment, that Vermont could not extradite a U.S. citizen to Canada absent a federal extradition treaty between the two nations (or the federal government's ad hoc agreement to surrender a fugitive). Taney concluded for a plurality that the extradition arrangement between Vermont and Canada substantively, even though not formally, qualified as a prohibited international agreement under Article I, section 10.[15] But the Court as a whole could not agree on whether the arrangement constituted a constitutional "agreement" within the ambit of section 10, clause 1 or 3.[16]

Because of the scarcity of cases on FSAs, the only real judicial guidance on what qualifies as a prohibited FSA is to be found in the (likewise minimal) case law on interstate compacts. In *Virginia v. Tennessee*,[17] the Court found implicit congressional consent to an interstate compact, stating in dicta that those compacts that do not involve an "increase of political power in the states, which may encroach upon or interfere with the just supremacy of the United States," may be concluded by the states without congressional consent.[18] The Court has since firmly established this standard for *interstate* compacts,[19] and it is has never invalidated such a compact based on a failure to obtain congressional consent—or for any other reason.

Yet in the context of foreign affairs, it is important to bear in mind that the Court "has never found the *Virginia v. Tennessee* standard or its progeny to apply to FSAs."[20] It is far from clear that the constitutional criteria for interstate

13. HENKIN, *supra* note 8, at 153 n.20.

14. 39 U.S. 540 (1840).

15. Taney wrote on behalf of a plurality that "[Vermont's] warrant of itself imports an agreement with the Canadian authorities.... [T]he act of delivery necessarily implies a mutual agreement." *Id.* at 573.

16. *See* HENKIN, *supra* note 8, at 153.

17. 148 U.S. 504 (1893).

18. *Id.* at 519.

19. *See* New Hampshire v. Maine, 426 U.S. 363, 369 (1976); *see also* Northeast Bancorp, Inc. v. Bd. of Governors of Fed. Res. Sys., 472 U.S. 159, 175–76 (1985); U.S. Steel Corp. v. Multistate Tax Comm'n, 434 U.S. 452, 473 (1978).

20. Hollis I, *supra* note 2, at 766.

compacts and FSAs, respectively, *should* be the same. The rationales for prohibiting FSAs overlap with, but also differ from, those for prohibiting interstate compacts. FSAs, for example, implicated the issue of state malfeasance with treaties and foreign affairs under the Articles. One might argue that this framing-era concern counsels a distinct, and stricter, standard.[21]

Further, in 1980, the Justice Department's Office of Legal Counsel surveyed the case law and opined that interstate compacts interfere with federal power "if (1) they involve a subject matter which the Congress is competent to regulate . . . , and (2) they purport to impose some legal obligation or disability"; the Office inferred from these cases that "[t]he test is whether the state action is truly independent or whether it is made instead in return for reciprocal action by other states."[22] Yet Congress is competent to regulate virtually *all* of the international activities undertaken by states (including those described in Chapter 2). *All* activities that qualify legally as international agreements impose some legal obligation or disability. *No* such agreement has ever been identified solely by reference to reciprocity. The Supreme Court's interstate compact cases therefore may not be sufficiently on point to justify the conclusion that the criteria for interstate compacts can be mechanically transposed to FSAs. The skeptics, one might well conclude, are therefore right:[23] the foreign prong of the clause means something different and should be evaluated under a distinct set of constitutional criteria. Yet this seemingly sound legal conclusion does not comport with established practice.

The reality is that, skeptical reservations notwithstanding, "the U.S. Department of State, at least one state court, the *Restatement (Third) of [] Foreign Relations Law*, and most scholars have all assumed that the Court's interstate compact doctrine does apply" to FSAs.[24] And in every instance in which the

---

21. *See, in particular*, Hollis I, *supra* note 2, at 760–61; Hollis II, *supra* note 10, at 1087–88.

22. *Applicability of the Compact Clause to Use of Multiple State Entities Under the Water Res. Planning Act*, 4B Op. O.L.C. 828 (1980).

23. *See* Edward T. Swaine, *Negotiating Federalism: State Bargaining and the Dormant Treaty Power*, 49 DUKE L. J. 1127, 1224 (2000); Hollis I, *supra* note 2, at 768, 783.

24. Hollis I, *supra* note 2, at 766–67 (footnotes and citations to the enumerated authorities omitted); *see also* McHenry County v. Brady, 163 N.W. 540 (N.D. 1917) (concluding, in a decision by the state court of last resort, that FSAs and interstate compacts alike should be held to the *Virginia v. Tennessee* standard). Henkin suggested that applying the interstate standard to FSAs makes good sense, "for one might extend and adapt the Court's distinction to such agreements as well," requiring congressional approval only "if the agreement tends to give the state elements of international sovereignty, interferes with the full and free exercise of federal authority, or deals locally with a matter on which there is or might be national policy." HENKIN, *supra* note 8, at 155.

states have sought consent to an FSA, Congress has provided it; none of them "involved local intrusion on matters of national policy."[25] In effect, the textual "default rule," so to speak, that appears on the face of Article I, section 10, clause 3, has changed by 180 degrees—from one that treats FSAs as presumptively invalid absent congressional approval to one that regards them as presumptively valid absent congressional disapproval. Indeed, today, "whether an agreement or compact requires Congressional consent will often be determined by *the state*."[26] How and why did this reversal come about?

III. The Problem Fades

The Compact Clause has gone slack for several reasons. First, the original problem that its drafters sought to avert has largely vanished. Second, congressional acquiescence or silence has for all practical purposes displaced the requirement of affirmative congressional consent, whether extended to the state before or after conclusion of the FSA. Third, another constitutional doctrine exists to handle those vestiges of the problem that remain and arise from time to time.

The Compact Clause's drafters sought to avert diplomatic anarchy. The text of the clause corroborates that "the framers contemplated adjustments" with foreign nations so as to avoid "political entanglements embarrassing to the national government."[27] Under the Articles of Confederation, the states made agreements haphazardly between and among themselves, with the Indian tribes, and with foreign nations, undermining concrete national interests.[28] Again, to paraphrase Hamilton, the parts threatened to imperil the well-being of the whole.[29] Because the Framers' experiences under the Articles were fresh in their minds, the rationales for the Compact Clause, Madison wrote in *The Federalist*, "are either so

---

25. Henkin, *supra* note 8, at 153.

26. *Id.* at 155 (emphasis added and footnote omitted). In the interstate context, the historical situation at the time of the Constitution's ratification also included "controversies between eleven states respecting their boundaries, which arose under their respective charters, and had continued from the first settlement of the Colonies." *Id.* (citing Rhode Island v. Massachusetts, 37 U.S. (12 Pet.) 657 (1838)).

27. Frankfurter & Landis, *supra* note 12, at 694.

28. As James Madison observed, despite a similar provision in the Articles of Confederation (Article VI), in the years leading up to the Constitution's ratification, Virginia, Maryland, Pennsylvania, and New Jersey all had entered into compacts "without previous application or apology." James Madison, *Preface to the Debates in the Convention of 1787*, *in* 3 Farrand's Records of the Constitutional Convention 548 (1911).

29. The Federalist No. 80, at 535 (Alexander Hamilton) (Jacob E. Cooke ed., 1961).

obvious, or have been so fully developed, that they may be passed over without remark."[30] Chief Justice Taney, summarizing what he understood to be those rationales fifty years later, opined that the Framers "manifestly believed that any intercourse between a state and a foreign nation was dangerous to the Union; that it would open a door of which foreign powers would avail themselves to obtain influence in separate states."[31]

For substantially this reason, Felix Frankfurter and James M. Landis suggested that the Framers concluded that Congress would be the "appropriate organ for determining what arrangements between States [and foreign Powers] might fall within the prohibited class of 'Treaty, Alliance, of Confederation', and what arrangements come within the permissive class of 'Agreement or Compact'"; and because the latter might "affect the interests of States other than those parties to the agreement," it followed for Frankfurter and Landis that "Congress must exercise national supervision through its power to grant or withhold consent, or to grant it under appropriate conditions."[32] The denomination of an FSA—as a categorically prohibited treaty or conditionally prohibited compact—has lost whatever meaning it may once have had. The Supreme Court has surmised that "treaties" and "compacts" were intended as terms of art but that their meaning has long been lost.[33] Nomenclature aside, the substantive issue is consent, and in that regard, it makes sense for the issue to be left to congressional judgment.

Yet even a cursory review of Chapter 2 reveals dozens of contemporary arrangements between states and foreign governments that might fairly be assumed (depending, of course, on the stipulated standard) to be substantive FSAs requiring congressional consent. Congress has neither affirmatively approved nor disapproved any of them. The courts, too, have been silent. How can this be explained?

The simple answer is that neither Congress nor the courts—nor, one might infer from the almost complete absence of litigation,[34] anyone else, whether a private entity or public official—see local FSA initiatives as harmful to any significant

30. THE FEDERALIST NO. 44, at 302 (James Madison) (Jacob E. Cooke ed., 1961). Madison wrote to similar effect that "[t]he prohibition against treaties, alliances and confederations, makes a part of the existing articles of Union; and for reasons which need no explanation, is copied into the new Constitution." *Id.* at 299.

31. Holmes v. Jennison, 39 U.S. (14 Pet.) 540, 541 (1840). As Chapter 4 explains, Taney almost surely overstated this point: the Framers neither said nor intended to preclude all intercourse whatsoever between the states and foreign nations.

32. Frankfurter & Landis, *supra* note 12, at 694–95.

33. *See* U.S. Steel Corp. v. Multistate Tax Comm'n, 434 U.S. 452, 460–63 (1978).

34. One reason for judicial silence on FSAs is that the courts can only speak in the context of resolving disputes. Those involving FSAs have historically been few and far between.

national interest;[35] indeed, often, quite the contrary: sister-city relationships, for example, which the Eisenhower administration initiated,[36] potentially advance national interests in amicable diplomatic relations, trade, cultural exchange, and peaceful dispute resolution. State trade missions to foreign countries advance the national interests in promoting American exports, encouraging foreign direct investment in the United States, and stimulating domestic employment. State offices in foreign countries encourage tourism to the United States.

Often, members of Congress don't even know about FSA initiatives. Institutionally, Congress has established no formal mechanism to monitor them. The Case-Zablocki Act[37] requires that sole executive agreements be reported to Congress. But no similar law requires that state and local governments report FSAs. Although many members of Congress formerly worked in state government, giving them a general familiarity with the nature of the FSAs and contacts between the states and foreign countries, few members have specific, day-to-day knowledge of what states and cities do internationally. And even when contentious local measures, such as nuclear free zones or sanctuary cities, come to Congress's attention, senators and representatives rarely have any incentive to interfere. Members of Congress avoid needlessly casting controversial votes. After all, little is to be gained politically by opposing a measure that local authorities pursued, in part at least, precisely because they expected it to garner popular support.

Some commentators have decried "the potential of corrupting foreign influences within the U.S. political process,"[38] suggesting that "the original problem of 'dangerous' or 'subversive' collaboration with foreign powers in the internal ordering and operation of the United States remains."[39] But evidence of this problem is scant,[40] and examples are hard to come by. One claimed example is a 2001

35. Congress would likely prevail if it challenged a compact for want of congressional consent, yet "ordinarily the state's judgment would not be reviewed unless some aggrieved private interest challenged the agreement in court." Henkin, *supra* note 8, at 155–56 (footnote omitted).

36. *See* Judith Resnik, *Law's Migration: American Exceptionalism, Silent Dialogues, and Federalism's Multiple Ports of Entry*, 115 Yale L.J. 1564, 1649 (2006).

37. 1 U.S.C. § 112b (2012).

38. Hollis I, *supra* note 2, at 805.

39. *Id.* at 787 (footnote omitted).

40. To be sure, foreign governments, such as China, do engage in (overt and tacit) lobbying efforts to influence elections or pending bills, and this is arguably a problem generally for the integrity of U.S. democracy. But it is seldom, especially if overt and in compliance with relevant federal regulations, illegal. At any rate, no evidence, so far as research discloses, suggests that states and foreign governments enter into compacts to manipulate local political processes.

memorandum of understanding between Missouri and the Canadian province of Manitoba, whereby the two agreed "to work cooperatively to the fullest extent possible consistent with law and existing treaties in their efforts to oppose water transfers between the Missouri River and Hudson Bay watersheds."[41] Yet the State Department Legal Adviser declined to find that the memorandum constituted an FSA.[42]

Another arguable example is a "secret" agreement concluded by then-Kansas governor Kathleen Sebelius in 2003 in an effort to encourage the Kansas congressional delegation to repeal trade and travel restrictions to Cuba in return for a Cuban commitment to buy $10 million worth of Kansas's agricultural produce.[43] In fact, however one chooses to characterize this arrangement politically, it did not constitute an FSA.[44] Kansas officials described it as non-binding.[45] And it was not, in any meaningful sense, a "secret": both Kansas's lieutenant governor and Cuba publicly announced the arrangement.[46]

In fact, the more likely victim of state "diplomacy" today is not the nation but the state. As Chapter 2 described, states and cities have virtually fallen all over themselves to offer the best incentives to foreign corporations to locate within them. Worker training programs, site preparation, tax breaks, and other subsidies—all have been placed on the table by states seeking foreign investment. The cost in tax revenues has been enormous. Yet states, locked in a kind of prisoners' dilemma, find themselves unable to escape the bidding war for fear of being cut out of the action entirely. The Compact Clause is not directly applicable because the agreements in most cases are not with "foreign powers" but rather with private businesses. There is also some dispute about whether the ultimate cost to states and cities is made up by net economic gains. Still, the situation cries out for federal review and, if the costs do outweigh the gains, federal action may be warranted—reviving, perhaps, the role of the Compact Clause.

---

41. Hollis II, *supra* note 10, at 1071–72 (internal quotation marks omitted).

42. Memorandum from William H. Taft, IV, Legal Adviser, U.S. Dep't of State, to Byron Dorgan, U.S. Senator (Nov. 20, 2001), *reprinted in* Thomas M. Franck, Michael J. Glennon, Sean D. Murphy & Edward T. Swaine, Foreign Relations and National Security Law: Cases, Materials, and Simulations 805, 809 (4th ed. 2012).

43. *See* Hollis I, *supra* note 2, at 741–42.

44. As discussed below, intent to be bound is the sine qua non of an international agreement.

45. Hollis I, *supra* note 2, at 741 n.3, 744.

46. *Id.* at 741.

IV. States' Rights and the Compact Clause

One plausible means to distinguish between FSAs that do and do not require Congress's consent might be sought in the idea of traditional state functions under the Tenth Amendment. A comparatively recent Compact Clause case, decided in 1978, might provide some guidance in this regard. In 1894, in a case involving fishing rights that hinged on a border dispute, the Court found congressional consent required for a compact that "might affect subjects placed under the control of Congress, such as commerce and the navigation of public waters, which is included under the power to regulate commerce."[47] In 1978, the Court clarified this consideration in the course of sustaining the "Multistate Tax Compact," to which Congress had not consented. The Court reasoned that the compact at issue conferred upon the states no powers that they could not already have exercised in its absence.[48] The opinion therefore may suggest that the reference point for assessing FSAs is preexisting state power: What power would the state have had to act alone, without the FSA?

This test also governs whether a sole executive agreement requires congressional consent (or concurrence of the Senate). The rationale is straightforward: what the president can do, he can agree with others to do. What falls within the president's authority to do without congressional approval also falls within his plenary agreement-making power. The executive agreement at issue in *Pink* and *Belmont* was lawful, for example, because it flowed from the exercise of the president's power to recognize a foreign government, as President Roosevelt did in recognizing the Soviet government.[49] No congressional approval was required. As the *Restatement* indicates, the president may "make an international agreement dealing with any matter that falls within his independent powers under the Constitution."[50] The president may, similarly, make an agreement to pardon an individual or negotiate a treaty without Senate or congressional approval.[51]

Constitutional custom, case law, and structure suggest that parallel principles govern FSAs. What the states can do, they can agree with foreign powers

47. Wharton v. Wise, 153 U.S. 155, 171 (1894).

48. U.S. Steel Corp. v. Multistate Tax Comm'n, 434 U.S. 452, 473 (1978).

49. *See* United States v. Pink, 315 U.S. 203, 229–30 (1942); United States v. Belmont, 301 U.S. 324, 330 (1937).

50. Restatement (Third) of the Foreign Relations Law of the United States § 303, cmt. e (1987).

51. *See* Michael J. Glennon, Constitutional Diplomacy 457 (1990).

to do. They can do things that lie within their reserved power under the Tenth Amendment, including, for example, permitting possession of firearms in a school zone,[52] or regulating purely intrastate violence.[53] They can therefore agree to do such things without congressional consent, given that such questions have been held by the Court to fall, again, within the ambit of the state police power safeguarded by the Tenth Amendment.

States can also do things that lie within at least some of the powers of Congress, such as the regulation of at least some foreign commerce.[54] But it is critical to bear in mind that these things are always subject to congressional preemption; the powers remain Congress's to exercise or reclaim under Article I, section 10, and a superseding statute would likewise suffice (under domestic law) to invalidate a problematic FSA under the last-in-time rule. Preemption is Congress's ultimate enforcement mechanism in this regard, the iron fist ever-present within the velvet glove of the Compact Clause. On the other hand, a state cannot, by making a foreign compact, confer upon itself a power that the Constitution denies it if the state were to act alone. The State of New Jersey, for example, could not, without congressional consent, make a compact with a Canadian province to discriminate against garbage headed for New Jersey landfills from Philadelphia, nor could the City of Los Angeles agree with a Mexican state to impose an ad valorem property tax levied on foreign-owned cargo containers; neither such act could be carried out on its own.[55] Congress presumably could approve such measures.[56] But even with congressional approval, some matters lie beyond the states' powers. A state may not, for example, join the European Union. It may not promise mutual assistance to a nation if either were attacked. A state could—as a legally non-binding political commitment—conform its own policies to policies required by a treaty, such as the Kyoto Protocol. But the state could not become a formal party to that treaty. These examples capture what the Constitution presumably meant to preclude altogether by barring, even with congressional consent, "Treaties, Alliances, or Confederations."[57]

---

52. United States v. Lopez, 514 U.S. 549 (1995).

53. United States v. Morrison, 529 U.S. 598 (2000).

54. See Chapter 5.

55. Philadelphia v. New Jersey, 437 U.S. 617 (1978); Japan Line, Ltd. v. County of Los Angeles, 441 U.S. 434 (1979).

56. *See* Prudential Ins. v. Benjamin, 328 U.S 408 (1946) (finding that Congress can authorize state action that the Commerce Clause would otherwise prohibit).

57. U.S. CONST. art. I, § 10, cl. 1.

V. Assessment

A focus on traditional state functions may well hold out the promise of a more coherent legal standard for assessing Compact Clause issues in the domain of foreign affairs. Yet with very few exceptions, today the problem of states endangering the national interest by making foreign compacts or agreements is far more theoretical than real. Congress seldom has any reason to object to state compacts—whether interstate compacts or FSAs. Often, it is simply unaware of them; again, no law requires that they be reported to Congress. And few of them cause any problem for the nation, as decades, if not centuries, of almost complete congressional silence suggest. Any nationally problematic state compact, interstate or FSA, would surely come to the attention of the federal government, which has ample means to nullify it by virtue of firmly established preemption doctrine. That is ultimately how Congress can, on a case-by-case basis, continue to exercise the power of consent that the Compact Clause gave it, if that becomes necessary (see Chapter 9).[58] In a sense, the Compact Clause as applied to FSAs has fallen into desuetude.[59]

---

58. *See* Frankfurter & Landis, *supra* note 12, at 694.

59. It would be implausible today to maintain that the states must obtain congressional consent every time they intend to enter into an FSA. That position is belied by two centuries of practice in which Congress has on only one occasion refused its consent, given it in a handful of instances, but in the vast majority of cases, simply said nothing. Literally thousands of such agreements, which, on their face, require congressional consent under the Compact Clause, have been concluded without it. HENKIN, *supra* note 8, at 156 n.26 (as of 1996); see Chapter 2 for other and more recent examples. *Cf.* Richard Bilder, *The Role of States and Cities in Foreign Relations*, *in* FOREIGN AFFAIRS AND THE U.S. CONSTITUTION 115, 116–17 (1990).

9

Federal Disapproval

PREEMPTION

IF ROOM FOR reasonable disagreement exists about the breadth of state foreign-affairs powers in the absence of an applicable federal law, as Chapters 4 and 5 suggested, no such disagreement exists in the presence of one. All agree that valid federal law governs. Unlike circumstances of federal silence or dormancy, in which any constitutional command is at best implicit, when the federal government has acted, an explicit constitutional command dominates: that command, of course, is the Supremacy Clause.

Contrary to popular impression, the Supremacy Clause does not itself establish a sources hierarchy among those it enumerates: legislation, treaties, and the Constitution. It reads: "This Constitution, and the laws of the United States which shall be made in pursuance thereof; and all treaties made, or which shall be made, under the authority of the United States, shall be the supreme law of the land . . . ."[1] Because the text itself does not privilege one source over another, it was left to the Supreme Court to establish a rank order of priority, beginning, above all else, with its decision in *Marbury v. Madison*;[2] and few if any constitutional lawyers today would question that the Constitution occupies the top rung on the ladder, with federal statutes and treaties on a lower rung.

The Supremacy Clause is clear, however, on the hierarchy among federal and state law: it makes the Constitution, treaties, and federal laws supreme over state law of any sort;[3] valid federal measures trump state constitutional provisions, statutes, common law rules, ordinances, and any other form of state or local law.

---

1. U.S. CONST. art. VI, cl. 2.

2. 5 U.S. (1 Cranch) 137 (1803).

3. Article VI, clause 2, mandates that "the judges in every state shall be bound thereby [i.e., by the Constitution, federal laws, and treaties], anything in the Constitution or laws of any State

All this assumes, of course, the constitutional *validity* of the federal measure; obviously, an unconstitutional federal measure trumps nothing.[4] Disputes involving claims of federal disapproval of state conduct thus often raise threshold questions about the constitutionality of the federal measure at issue. Challenges of this sort typically rely on the Commerce Clause or the Tenth Amendment, which, as noted earlier, often function as opposite sides of the same coin. Removing the federal predicate in such cases (by finding it constitutionally invalid) would render the Supremacy Clause inapplicable.

For purposes of this chapter, we therefore largely assume the constitutional validity of the federal measure disapproving a state foreign-affairs initiative. The question is the relationship between a *valid* federal statute or international agreement, on the one hand, and challenged state law or conduct, on the other. A single word—albeit one that describes a complex area of constitutional jurisprudence—captures this relationship: preemption. Before we address the issue of preemption relative to federal statutes and some international agreements, however, it will be helpful to pause to offer a brief summary of long-standing preemption doctrine.

Preemption may be express or implied. A federal measure might expressly state that it ousts state authority in some field of law. But in the realm of foreign affairs, such express preemption is rare. Implied preemption is far more common. It can take two basic forms: *conflict* and *field* preemption. Conflict preemption means that the relevant federal and state measures actually conflict with each other. Field preemption may, but need not, involve a conflict—but in either event, its rationale differs:

> Congress'[s] intent to supercede state law altogether may be found from a scheme of federal regulation so pervasive as to make reasonable the inference that Congress left no room to supplement it, because the Act of Congress may touch a field in which the federal interest is so dominant that the federal system will be assumed to preclude enforcement of state laws on the same subject, or because the object sought to be obtained by

---

to the contrary notwithstanding." U.S. CONST. art. VI, cl. 2. It should be noted that the Court's interpretation of the Tenth Amendment and federalism limits, especially the comparatively recent limits imposed on federal measures by dint of the Court's construction of the Necessary and Proper Clause, U.S. CONST. art. I, § 8, cl. 18, constrain or preclude altogether certain federal laws, arguably including those that implement treaties, discussed in Chapter 6. *See, e.g.*, Nat'l Fed'n of Indep. Bus. v. Sebelius, 132 S. Ct. 2566, 2591 (2012); Printz v. United States, 521 U.S. 898, 926 (1997); Alden v. Maine, 527 U.S. 706, 732 (1999); New York v. United States, 505 U.S. 144, 158 (1992).

4. We address the controversial issue of the validity under the Tenth Amendment of federal measures designed to carry treaties into effect in Chapter 6. The federal measures at issue here are typically statutes and, at times, international agreements other than those made as treaties in conformity with Article II.

> the federal law and the character of obligations imposed by it may reveal the same purpose.[5]

Field preemption may thus involve either a federal *scheme* so pervasive as to "occupy the field," implicitly precluding any state law within that realm;[6] or it may involve an "Act of Congress . . . in which the federal *interest* is so dominant that the federal system will be assumed to preclude enforcement of state laws on the same subject."[7]

There is considerable overlap among the forms of implied preemption. And although the doctrinal nomenclature can be convenient, as the Court has said, preemption does not fall into "rigidly distinct [categories]. Indeed, field preemption in a sense may be understood as a species of conflict preemption: A state law that falls within a preempted field conflicts with "Congress'[s] intent (either express or plainly implied) to exclude state regulation."[8] Similarly, conflict preemption might mean that it is literally impossible for a regulated entity to comply at one and the same time with state and federal law. Or it might mean that even though compliance with both laws simultaneously is theoretically feasible, in practice the state law nonetheless "stands as an obstacle to the accomplishment and execution of the full purposes and objectives of Congress"[9] in enacting the preemptive federal law.

In considering the possibility of preemption, judges often examine legislative intent, and they sometimes apply presumptions and canons of interpretation to aid in deciding cases where neither the statutory text nor Congress's purpose is clear—sometimes, but not always, for the relevant presumptions can conflict.[10]

---

5. Pac. Gas & Elec. Co. v. State Energy Res. Conservation & Dev. Comm'n, 461 U.S. 190, 203–04 (1983) (citations and internal quotation marks omitted).

6. *See, e.g.*, Pennsylvania v. Nelson, 350 U.S. 497, 503–04 (1956) (holding that Congress occupied the field of sedition); *see also* Rice v. Santa Fe Elevator Corp., 331 U.S. 218, 230 (1974) ("The scheme of federal regulation may be so pervasive as to make reasonable the inference that Congress left no room for the States to supplement it."); English v. Gen. Elec. Co., 496 U.S. 72, 79 (1990).

7. *Rice*, 331 U.S. at 230 (emphasis added).

8. *English*, 496 U.S. at 79 n.5.

9. *See, e.g.*, Gade v. Nat'l Solid Wastes Mgmt. Ass'n, 505 U.S. 88, 98 (1992); *English*, 496 U.S. at 79. The Court's opinion in *Crosby v. Nat'l Foreign Trade Council*, 530 U.S. 363 (2000), analyzed below, involved the obstacle variation on conflict preemption. It would not have been impossible for the regulated entities to comply with both federal and state (Massachusetts) law. But the latter stood as an obstacle to accomplishing the former's goals. *See Crosby*, 530 U.S. at 373.

10. *See generally* Curtis A. Bradley & Jack L. Goldsmith, Foreign Relations Law: Cases and Materials 326–27 (2d ed., 2006).

In the domestic context, the courts traditionally presume that Congress did not intend to preempt state law.[11] In the foreign-affairs context, in contrast, the Supreme Court at times has assumed the contrary view, that is, that Congress intended to preempt.[12] Whatever the basis for its decision, of course, when the Court or a lower federal court preempts state law based on non-constitutional, "soft law" preemption grounds,[13] it can always be superseded by Congress—for the linchpin of the analysis is a federal instrument—a statute, treaty, or other international agreement—that can always be removed.

A sample of the Court's many preemption cases illustrates how these principles emerged.

I. Preemption of State Law by Federal Statute

In *The Federalist*, James Madison painted a bleak picture of the straits in which, he argued, the United States would find itself absent the Supremacy Clause. Among other problems, because "the Constitutions of the States differ much from each other, it might happen that a treaty or national law of great and equal importance to the States, would interfere with some and not with other [State] Constitutions, and would consequently be valid in some of the States at the same time that it would have no effect in others."[14] And even if federal statutes and treaties were uniformly found valid under different state constitutions, their interpretation

11. *See, e.g.*, Medtronic, Inc. v. Lohr, 518 U.S. 470, 485 (1996); *see also Rice*, 331 U.S. at 230 (internal quotation marks omitted) ("The Court's prior cases indicate that when a State's exercise of its police power is challenged under the Supremacy Clause, we start with the assumption that the historic police powers of the States were not to be superseded by the Federal Act unless that was the clear and manifest purpose of Congress."). This presumption does not apply, however, where "the State regulates in an area where there has been a history of significant federal presence." United States v. Locke, 529 U.S. 89, 107–08 (2000).

12. *Cf. Locke*, 529 U.S. at 108; Hines v. Davidowitz, 312 U.S. 52, 62–63 (1941).

13. According to the Congressional Research Service, between 1789 and 2002 some 224 state and city laws were held to have been preempted by federal law. CONG. RESEARCH SERV., *State Constitutional and Statutory Provisions and Municipal Ordinances Held Unconstitutional or Held to Be Preempted by Federal Law (1789–2002)*, *in* THE CONSTITUTION OF THE UNITED STATES OF AMERICA: ANALYSIS AND INTERPRETATION 2161 (Johhny H. Killian et al. eds., 2004), *available at* http://www.gpo.gov/fdsys/pkg/GPO-CONAN-2002/pdf/GPO-CONAN-2002.pdf. During that same period, 935 state laws, 122 city ordinances, and 158 acts of Congress were held constitutionally invalid. *Id.*; CONG. RESEARCH SERV., *Acts of Congress Held Unconstitutional in Whole or in Part by the Supreme Court of the United States*, *in* THE CONSTITUTION OF THE UNITED STATES OF AMERICA: ANALYSIS AND INTERPRETATION 2117 (Johhny H. Killian et al. eds., 2004), *available at* http://www.gpo.gov/fdsys/pkg/GPO-CONAN-2002/pdf/GPO-CONAN-2002.pdf.

14. THE FEDERALIST NO. 44, at 306 (James Madison) (Jacob E. Cooke ed., 1961).

would inevitably vary from one state to the next. Absent the Supremacy Clause, Madison continued,

> [t]he world would have seen for the first time, a system of government founded on an inversion of the fundamental principles of all government; it would have seen the authority of the whole society every where subordinate to the authority of the parts; it would have seen a monster in which the head was under the direction of the members.[15]

Justice Holmes doubtless had similar concerns in mind when he commented, with reference to the institution of judicial review, "I do not think the United States would come to an end if we lost our power to declare an Act of Congress void. I do think the Union would be imperiled if we could not make that declaration as to the laws of the several States."[16]

State laws have regularly been struck down by the Court as preempted by federal statutes. An early example is *Tarble's Case*, an 1871 dispute involving a directive from the Wisconsin Supreme Court to the U.S. Army to release from military custody a soldier who had deserted after, it was claimed, enlisting unlawfully before he had reached the qualifying age of eighteen.[17] The Supreme Court reversed, pointing out that "among the powers assigned to the National government is the power 'to raise and support armies,' and the power 'to provide for the government and regulation of the land and naval forces.' "[18] State interference with these congressional prerogatives could not withstand constitutional scrutiny:

> The execution of these powers falls within the line of [the federal government's] duties; and its control over the subject is plenary and exclusive.... No interference with the execution of this power of the National government in the formation, organization, and government of its armies by any State officials could be permitted without greatly impairing the efficiency, if it did not utterly destroy, this branch of the public service .... It is manifest that the powers of the National government could not be exercised with energy and efficiency at all times, if its acts could be interfered with and controlled for any period by officers or tribunals of another sovereignty [i.e., that of the State].[19]

---

15. *Id.*

16. Oliver Wendell Holmes, Collected Legal Papers 295–96 (1921).

17. 80 U.S. (13 Wall.) 397 (1871).

18. *Id.* at 408.

19. *Id.* at 408–09.

American Ins. Ass'n v. Garamendi,[20] discussed in Chapter 4, presents an interesting contrast with *Tarble's Case*. The issue in each is federal disapproval. But the distinction between them lies in both the source of that disapproval (in *Garamendi*, an alleged policy of the executive branch; in *Tarble*'s *Case*, the Constitution's delegation of certain powers to Congress) and the nature of the alleged interference (in *Garamendi*, indirect; in *Tarble's Case*, direct). Recall that the *Garamendi* majority found that California's law conflicted with the federal government's policy, as inferred by the Court. *Tarble's Case*, in contrast, involved, in a sense, the reverse argument: the Court relied more on inferences from the Constitution's text and structure than on the federal government's conduct. Both cases indicate the critical point that the line between federal silence and federal disapproval is often blurry or controversial. The categories of federal approval, disapproval, and silence shade into one another. They comprise more of a spectrum than three neat pigeonholes.

A. *Crosby v. National Foreign Trade Council* (2000)

One recent example of a Supreme Court decision that falls squarely on the preemption side of that spectrum is *Crosby v. National Foreign Trade Council*,[21] colloquially known as the Massachusetts Burma Case. The federal district and circuit courts explored alternative grounds for decision, namely, dormant foreign-affairs preemption under *Zschernig* and the Foreign Commerce Clause.[22] But when *Crosby* reached the Supreme Court, the Court unanimously resolved it on the basis of implied preemption (in particular, obstacle preemption). The Court thus identified the Supremacy Clause, and only that clause, as the correct constitutional source of the law's infirmity: it struck down the Massachusetts law "owing to its threat of frustrating federal statutory objectives."[23]

Crosby originated in the mid-1990s as a response to the tragic political and human rights situation in Myanmar (Burma). In June 1996, Massachusetts enacted a statute barring state entities from procuring goods or services from any natural or legal persons "doing business," broadly defined, with the government

---

20. 539 U.S. 396, 425 (2003).

21. 530 U.S. 363 (2000).

22. *See, e.g.*, Nat'l Foreign Trade Council v. Baker, 26 F. Supp. 2d 287, 290–93 (1998). The district court found no sufficient basis for conflict preemption. *Id.* at 293. It also considered and rejected deciding the case based on the dormant Foreign Commerce Clause. *Id.* The First Circuit likewise considered all three grounds. Nat'l Foreign Trade Council v. Natsios, 181 F.3d 38 (1st Cir. 1999).

23. *Crosby*, 530 U.S. at 366.

of Myanmar.[24] The state compiled a "restricted purchase list" identifying such entities. In September 1996, three months later, Congress enacted its own statute imposing sanctions on Myanmar's authoritarian government, the State Law and Order Council (SLORC). Some of these sanctions were mandatory; others were conditional or subject to executive discretion.[25] The National Foreign Trade Council (NFTC), representing thirty-four of its members that were on Massachusetts's restricted purchase list, challenged the law.[26]

The facts culminating in *Crosby* also included events that cannot fail to call to mind, and to corroborate, the paramount concern of the Framers about state foreign-affairs activities, based on their experience under the Articles of Confederation: that, in Hamilton's words, "The peace of the WHOLE ought not to be left at the disposal of a PART."[27] Massachusetts's decision to enact a law based on the interests of its constituents led to international consequences that affected, not only or even primarily Massachusetts, but the United States as a whole, as a nation. Foreign nations and associations—Japan, the European Union (EU), and the Association of South East Asian Nations (ASEAN)—supported the NFTC by filing amicus briefs and otherwise, protested by note verbale to the federal government, and in the case of Japan and the EU, even "lodg[ed] formal complaints against the United States in the World Trade Organization (WTO), claiming that the state Act violates certain provisions of the Agreement on Government Procurement, and the consequence has been to embroil the National Government for some time now in international dispute proceedings under the auspices of the WTO."[28]

---

24. *Id.* at 367. The state law made exceptions for essential procurement unavailable elsewhere, medical supplies, and circumstances in which no other bids submitted were less than 10 percent higher than those of an otherwise statutorily barred enterprise. *Id.* at 367–68.

25. *See id.* at 368.

26. *Id.* at 370.

27. The Federalist No. 80, at 535 (Alexander Hamilton) (Jacob E. Cooke ed., 1961).

28. *Crosby*, 530 U.S. at 382–83 (internal citation omitted). It is worth noting here that the one-voice notion ritually intoned in many foreign-affairs cases once again proved a fiction. The federal government did not take a unified position in the *Crosby* litigation. Rather, "[w]ithin the U.S. Executive Branch, the Departments of State, Justice, Treasury, and Commerce, and the U.S. Trade Representative engaged in a vigorous inter-agency debate on whether the United States should file an amicus brief and, if so, what position it should take.... In the end, the [executive branch] filed a brief in the Supreme Court that supported the NFTC." In Congress, in contrast, seventy-eight members "filed an amicus brief urging reversal, arguing that Congress did not intend to preempt the Massachusetts law," while another twenty members filed a separate amicus "brief urging affirmance and calling on the court to declare all state and local sanctions law unconstitutional." Jeffrey L. Dunoff et al., International Law: Norms, Actors, Process 229 (3d ed. 2010). *Crosby* thus reflected, albeit modestly, the Constitution's "invitation to struggle for the privilege of directing American foreign policy." Edward S. Corwin, The President: Office and Powers, 1787–1957, at 201 (1940). *Cf.* Zivotofsky *ex rel.* Zivotofsky v. Kerry, 135 S. Ct. 2076 (2015).

The Court unanimously found the law preempted because, it concluded, Massachusetts's law stood as an "obstacle to the accomplishment and execution of the full purposes and objectives of Congress."[29] Applying this standard, the Court concluded that the Massachusetts Burma law implicitly stood as an obstacle in three respects to the accomplishment of Congress's full objectives.

First, "Congress clearly intended to provide the President with flexible and effective authority over economic sanctions against Burma," investing in him "as much discretion to exercise economic leverage against Burma, with an eye toward national security, as our law will admit."[30] Massachusetts, by mandating certain "immediate and perpetual" sanctions, "pull[ed] levers of influence that the federal Act [did] not reach,"[31] thereby "reduc[ing] the value of the [bargaining] chips created by the federal statute."[32]

Second, "Congress manifestly intended to limit economic pressure against the Burmese Government to a specific range," for example, by "confin[ing] [the federal law's] reach to United States persons";[33] Massachusetts, in contrast, penalized individuals and conduct that Congress had excluded from the sanctions—likely in an effort to avoid the very international friction that the Massachusetts Burma Law evidently caused.

Third and finally, Justice Souter pointed out that the federal law encouraged international cooperation, calling upon the president "to speak for the United States among the world's nations in developing a comprehensive, multilateral strategy to bring democracy to and improve human rights practices and the quality of life in Burma."[34] The Massachusetts Burma Law, Souter explained,

---

29. *Crosby*, 530 U.S. at 377 (internal quotation marks omitted). Souter explained that even though, in terms of conflict preemption, the regulated business entities could have complied with both the federal and state laws, the Massachusetts Burma Law nonetheless stood as an obstacle to the federal government's objectives and to the means by which it had decided to pursue them. Not all supposed state obstacles suffice for preemption; rather, "[w]hat is a sufficient obstacle is a matter of judgment, to be informed by examining the federal statute as a whole and identifying its purpose and intended effects. . . . For when the question is whether a Federal act overrides a state law, the entire scheme of the statute must of course be considered and that which must be implied is of no less force than that which is expressed." *Id.* at 373 (citations and internal quotation marks omitted). Further, "the fact of a common end hardly neutralizes conflicting means." *Id.* at 379 (citations omitted).

30. *Crosby*, 530 U.S. at 374–76.

31. *Id.* at 376.

32. *Id.* at 377 ("Quite simply, if the Massachusetts law is enforceable the President has less to offer and less economic and diplomatic leverage as a consequence.").

33. *Id.*

34. *Id.* at 380 (internal quotation marks omitted).

"undermines the President's capacity. . . for effective diplomacy"[35] in this regard, as the responses of foreign nations and associations to the Massachusetts law indeed suggested.[36]

Crosby is the quintessential example of direct foreign-affairs preemption. Yet beneath the seemingly straightforward reasoning of the Court several themes are worth noting. In the first place, Congress enacted the federal Burma law a few months after the Massachusetts law's enactment. Surely, it knew about the latter. Why, then, did Congress not simply preempt the Massachusetts Burma Law expressly? After all, had it done so, substantial financial and temporal resources that were devoted to litigation in the federal courts and potential clashes with our allies could have been avoided. Of course, we can only speculate. Perhaps Justice Souter is correct that "failure to provide for preemption expressly may reflect nothing more than the settled character of implied preemption that courts will dependably apply."[37] But it may also reflect Congress's interest in avoiding alienating state constituencies, and in general, human rights proponents and lobbying organizations nationwide. By declining to expressly preempt state law, Congress appears to pay more deference to state sovereignty while in fact merely displacing institutional responsibility for the very same decision (full preemption) from itself to the federal courts. The propriety of this form of "passing the buck" to the federal judiciary is questionable: it undercuts electoral accountability and runs counter to the Constitution's institutional allocation of governmental responsibility.

Also, on the other side of the ledger, note the *affirmative* role that Massachusetts played here. Again, we cannot know for sure, but with Burma, as with South Africa in the 1980s, local actors at the state and municipal levels took the initiative to advance values (e.g., political reform in Burma, international human rights protection) that might otherwise have been marginalized. Why *did* a law about human rights practices in Burma emerge first in a state rather than the federal government? Perhaps because state officials tend to be far less remote from, and far more accessible to, their constituents.

---

35. *Id.* at 381.

36. Because the Court decided *Crosby* wholly based on obstacle preemption, it did not, as did the First Circuit, see Nat'l Foreign Trade Council v. Natsios, 181 F.3d 38, 60 (1st Cir. 1999), discuss the market-participant exception to the dormant Foreign Commerce Clause; had it done so, it's at least arguable that some analog to the market-participant exception might have applied. The law, after all, regulated how the state spent its *own* money rather than regulating private entities, albeit the latter were, of course, indirectly affected.

37. *Crosby*, 530 U.S. at 387-88.

Concerns that might have been a low priority in Congress were taken up by the Massachusetts state legislature and rapidly culminated in an effective law (so effective, indeed, as to prompt international complaints). Several months later, Congress acted to address those concerns. Did state action prompt the federal action, or is it coincidental? We cannot know. But even if not in this case, it is certainly reasonable to think that state action has the laudable potential to prompt federal action on neglected foreign-affairs issues. Had the states not acted, or had they not acted as promptly, the federal government might not have prioritized using its leverage to promote human rights and political reform in Burma—even if, ultimately, a uniform national rather than state policy on these issues is more appropriate and effective because it might, for example, better promote international cooperation and avoid alienating allies economically.

Recall, similarly, that state and local divestment statutes preceded the 1986 Federal Comprehensive Anti-Apartheid Act by years. As in *Crosby*, these local activities may well have prompted national action—or brought it about years before it otherwise would have been at the forefront of the U.S. foreign policy agenda. In short, we tend to think of the states as more parochial in their perspective on foreign affairs. Yet their comparative liberation from the full array of diplomatic considerations that the federal government must consider and their distance from the Washington political environment sometimes enables the states to be *less* parochial about the national interest—to highlight and make headway on otherwise marginalized international issues.

B. Immigration

Immigration regulation is another example of the operation of the doctrine of preemption. Immigration policy is an essential government function. Few other issues provoke greater political controversy or as starkly pose one of the core tensions within foreign affairs federalism. About two-thirds of American citizens currently favor a path to citizenship for undocumented immigrants[38] (as, perhaps surprisingly, do majorities in every state in the Union).[39] Yet there can be little question that a large minority of citizens see immigration as the cause of countless problems: high crime rates; strains on state and local resources devoted to education, healthcare, disability, and welfare, and other public services; the loss of blue-collar jobs to immigrants who are willing to work for less or with few or

38. Jeffrey M. Jones, *In U.S., 65% Favor Path to Citizenship for Illegal Immigrants*, Gallup, Aug. 12, 2015, http://www.gallup.com/poll/184577/favor-path-citizenship-illegal-immigrants.aspx.

39. John Sides, *A Majority in Every State Favors a Path to Citizenship for Illegal Immigrants*, Wash. Post, Feb. 25, 2015, http://www.washingtonpost.com/blogs/monkey-cage/wp/2015/02/25/a-majority-in-every-state-favors-a-path-to-citizenship-for-illegal-immigrants/.

no benefits; and so forth. Whatever the truth of these perceptions,[40] for present purposes, the question is not *factual* accuracy; it is which government—federal or state (or local)—has the *legal* right to regulate immigration, especially in the presence of federal statutes that do not expressly preempt state law.

Immigration is in many ways a microcosm of foreign-affairs federalism. The federal government enjoys potentially plenary power, which it theoretically could exercise to assert full national control over immigration. But it has not, expressly or implicitly, "occupied the field" to preempt state regulation of immigration.[41] Nor, as a practical matter, could it probably do so. The simple fact is that the federal government lacks sufficient resources—financial, temporal, law-enforcement personnel, and so forth—to handle immigration entirely on its own. Consequently, whether because of congressional gridlock, substantive disagreements, a belief that some of the issues should be left to the states, or otherwise, the federal government has left major aspects of immigration regulation to the states. And at a time when national progress on immigration reform seems locked in a state of perpetual inertia, state and local officials have stepped into the breach, enacting a host of immigration initiatives. Contrary to popular belief, many of the most constructive and novel legal initiatives on immigration in recent years have begun at the state level. After describing the existing law, we note the substantial strides made by local authorities to cure a problem that the federal government, for now, seems unable or unwilling to address—as well as the role states and cities play in providing sanctuary to certain immigrant populations.

The Constitution says almost nothing about immigration. Article I authorizes Congress "[t]o establish a uniform rule of naturalization."[42] That's all. Like many other foreign affairs powers, the federal immigration power has consequently

---

40. The evidence varies, but several of these assertions, especially the alleged link between undocumented immigrants and crime, appear to be incorrect. *See, e.g.*, Shannon O'Neill, *Immigration Reform Is Happening*, July 11, 2014, Foreign Pol'y, http://www.cfr.org/immigration/immigration-reform-happening/p33235; *see also Lost in the Immigration Frenzy*, N.Y. Times, July 13, 2015 (noting that "immigrants—whether legal or unauthorized, and no matter their country of origin or education level—are less likely to be criminals than native-born Americans, that periods of high immigration correspond with lower crime rates, and that this has been true in this country as long as this issue has been studied").

41. Some have even argued that, despite the absence of field preemption, there exists a "dormant immigration clause," such that "Congress 'occupies the field' whether or not it exercises that power"; and further, that because "states have no power over immigration . . . [,] the exercise of any power they might possess interferes with federal power. . . . Thus, even when congressional power lies 'dormant,' states may not regulate in [an] exclusive area." Karl Manheim, *State Immigration Laws and Federal Supremacy*, 22 Hastings Const. L.Q. 939, 958-59 (1995).

42. U.S. Const. art. I, § 8, cl. 4. Article I, section 9, provides further: "The migration or importation of such persons as any of the states now existing shall think proper to admit, shall not be prohibited by the Congress prior to the year one thousand eight hundred and eight, but

developed over time on the basis of multiple sources beyond the text of the Constitution. One commentator, echoing many others, wrote recently that "[f]ederal immigration law is a renowned oddity where the normal rules of constitutional law simply do not apply."[43]

One of the principal reasons for the confusion is that in the late 1800s, the Court located the "true" foundation for federal authority over immigration not in Article I, but in an extraconstitutional source—the status of the United States as an independent nation. Given the centrality of territory in international law, the Court inferred that border control and authority over immigration resides in the government and emanates from the United States' mere existence as an independent nation.[44] "It is an accepted maxim of international law," Justice Gray wrote in 1892, "that every sovereign nation has the power, as inherent in sovereignty, and essential to self-preservation, to forbid the entrance of foreigners within its dominions, or to admit them only in such cases and upon such conditions as it may see fit to prescribe."[45]

Although this position continues to serve, in combination with the Naturalization Clause, as the chief rationale for federal supremacy,[46] it is worth pausing to note that international law neither presupposes nor requires that nations will vest control over immigration policy in national rather than subnational authorities. Sound policy may counsel giving the national government primary or exclusive power, but international law does not require it. Yet like some of the constitutional cases described at this book's outset—namely, those that few today think were rightly decided but that nonetheless survive as established law[47]—plenary national power over immigration is now an indelible axiom of U.S. constitutional law.

---

a tax or duty may be imposed on such importation, not exceeding ten dollars for each person." Yet this provision is not an authorization but an anachronistic compromise inserted by the Framers to temporarily protect the slave trade. The Court has never relied on it to elaborate constitutional authority over immigration.

43. David S. Rubenstein, *Immigration Structuralism: A Return to Form*, 8 DUKE J. CONST. L. & PUB. POL'Y 81, 97 (2013) (internal quotation marks omitted); *see also* Peter H. Schuck, *The Transformation of Immigration Law*, 84 COLUM. L. REV. 1, 1 (1984) ("Immigration has long been a maverick, a wild card, in our public law. Probably no other area of American law has been so radically insulated and divergent from those fundamental norms of constitutional right, administrative procedure, and judicial role that animate the rest of our legal system.").

44. *See* Chae Chan Ping v. United States, 130 U.S. 581, 603–04 (1889); Fong Yue Ting v. United States, 149 U.S. 698 (1893).

45. Nishimura v. United States, 142 U.S. 651, 659 (1892).

46. *See* Arizona v. United States, 132 S. Ct. 2492, 2498–99 (2012); Toll v. Moreno, 458 U.S. 1, 10 (1982).

47. *E.g.*, The Insular Cases, including Dorr v. United States, 195 U.S. 138 (1904); The Slaughter-House Cases, 83 U.S. (16 Wall.) 36 (1873).

Nonetheless, the Court's immigration jurisprudence often suggests a more dominant national role than contemporary practice might suggest. In the context of immigration, the Court has said, for example:

> The Federal Government, representing as it does the collective interests of the forty-eight states, is entrusted with full and exclusive responsibility for the conduct of affairs with foreign sovereignties. "For local interests the several states of the Union exist, but for national purposes, embracing our relations with foreign nations, we are but one people, one nation, one power."[48]

Statements to this effect permeate the Court's immigration decisions. Yet as a historical matter, states and localities, not the federal government, regulated immigration almost exclusively in the century following the Constitution's adoption.[49] As we will see, they continue to do so.

Because current constitutional law leaves no room for doubt that the federal government retains the right to supplant or preclude state measures concerning immigration, the general doctrines of preemption reviewed earlier in this chapter apply to state and local measures in the immigration field. In the Court's most recent major decision, prompted by Arizona's immigration laws, Justice Kennedy applied the plenary power doctrine of immigration and preemption principles to strike down several provisions of Arizona's immigration law, while remanding one provision for consideration of potential constitutional concerns.[50] The Court's preemption methodology was familiar.[51] Yet Arizona's laws, which some saw as parochial if not draconian,[52] helped to perpetuate an unfortunate myth about state and local immigration policy: that state and local immigration laws regularly

---

48. Hines v. Davidowitz, 312 U.S. 52, 63 (1941) (quoting *Chae Chan Ping*, 130 U.S. at 630).

49. GERALD L. NEUMAN, STRANGERS TO THE CONSTITUTION: IMMIGRANTS, BORDERS, AND FUNDAMENTAL LAW 19–20 (1996).

50. *Arizona*, 132 S. Ct. at 2492.

51. We express no opinion, however, on its application of preemption doctrine to the provisions of the Arizona law at issue or on the law's wisdom as a policy matter. The issue here, as elsewhere for us, is the locus of decision-making authority—who decides.

52. In Arizona, because of federal inaction, the state government began to enact laws that tightened enforcement and restricted benefits to undocumented immigrations, initiating a policy that has been dubbed "attrition through enforcement." *See* Kris Kobach, *Attrition through Enforcement: A Rational Approach to Illegal Immigration*, 15 TULSA J. COMP. & INT'L L. 155 (2007). One commentator characterized the goal of this policy as follows: Immigrants will "self-deport as the risks of detention or involuntary removal go up, and the probability of being able to obtain unauthorized employment goes down." Rubenstein, *supra* note 43, at 156. Indeed, Arizona's challenged law, S.B. 1070, specifically declared "that the intent of this act is to make attrition through enforcement the public policy." S. B. 1070, 50th Leg., 2d Reg. Sess. (Ariz. 2012).

reflect nativist attitudes, leading to harsh and unconstitutional crackdowns by local law-enforcement on immigrant populations.

This stereotype, regrettably, obscures other, very different measures that states and localities nationwide have often adopted. Because of the federal government's inertia or inefficiency in enacting comprehensive immigration reform, state legislatures have increasingly been picking up the slack. As Shannon O'Neill pointed out last year:

> With all the mudslinging and acrimony in Washington over unaccompanied minors and unauthorized immigrants, you might have missed it. Immigration reform has already happened—in fact, hundreds of times. With the federal government incapacitated, states, cities, and municipalities have stepped into the fray. In 2013 alone, 45 of the 50 state legislatures passed over 400 laws and resolutions on everything from law enforcement and employment to education and public benefits. Among this flurry were a few in the Arizona SB 1070 style—bills making life more miserable for undocumented immigrants. These laws ranged from blocking access to health care and schools to criminalizing common activities such as driving cars or buying homes. But the majority are actually designed to find ways to integrate undocumented immigrants—funding English language and citizenship classes and providing access to medical care and other social services.[53]

Among other local laws governing undocumented immigrants, O'Neill notes that some states and localities have authorized tuition for "all residents"; enabled immigrants to apply for drivers licenses; passed so-called "trust laws" to discourage local police from transferring undocumented migrants to federal immigration authorities unless they have been charged or convicted of a serious crime; created municipal identification cards that enable immigrants to open bank accounts, sign leases, borrow library books, and the like; and in one state (California), even authorized them to practice law.[54] Similar local initiatives have been enacted by municipalities, including New York, Los Angeles, San Francisco, and New Haven. Indeed, so far as the evidence suggests, local and municipal governments are often at least as well-suited to deal with the quotidian issues raised by immigrant populations as the federal government.[55] As early as 1994, well before the immigration

---

53. O'Neill, *supra* note 40.

54. *Id.*

55. *See generally* STRANGE NEIGHBORS, THE ROLE OF STATES IN IMMIGRATION POLICY (Carissa Byrne Hessick & Gabriel J. Chin eds., 2014); Juliet P. Stumpf, *States of Confusion: The Rise of State and Local Power over Immigration*, 86 N.C. L. REV. 1557 (2008).

crisis reached its current proportions, Peter Spiro wrote that "[a]s a practical matter, immigration is now largely a state-level concern."[56]

In the context of foreign-affairs federalism, therefore, we might profitably shift our perspective on federal preemption—from an increasingly "competitive" model, in which either the federal or the state government exercises authority—to a more cooperative model that seeks to locate areas in which federal and state governments can, as they already do in many areas, work together on issues of mutual concern. Challenges arising from immigration have long been addressed by the states, and a binary, light-switch analytical framework cannot capture the subtleties of federal-state cooperation that has emerged in practice.

Nonetheless, clear conflicts between federal and state authorities do emerge. One prominent conflict has involved so-called "sanctuary cities." San Francisco enacted one of the first such ordinances in 1989.[57] In general, these laws authorize local law-enforcement and other municipal officials to limit their participation in the enforcement of federal immigration policy by, for example, declining to report detained immigrants.

One might expect that such conflicts would be resolved by a straightforward application of the Supremacy Clause. State and municipal officials, not only federal officials, are bound by the U.S. Constitution, after all. Yet an early Supreme Court decision and subsequent jurisprudence suggest that the federal government is constitutionally unable to prevent the adoption of sanctuary ordinances or to compel states and cities to enforce federal immigration law.[58] In *Prigg v. Pennsylvania*,[59] the Supreme Court considered a number of sanctuary laws passed by states such as Pennsylvania and Massachusetts that were aimed at protecting fugitive slaves against the operation of federal laws that authorized their recapture. These state laws provided a variety of defenses, including due process, habeas corpus, and jury trial to those assisting fugitive slaves. Pennsylvania's law further prohibited removing a person from Pennsylvania for the purpose of enslaving that person. The *Prigg* Court held Pennsylvania's law

---

56. Peter J. Spiro, *The States and Immigration in an Era of Demi-sovereignties*, 35 VA. J. INT'L L. 121, 123 (1994).

57. City & County of San Francisco, Sanctuary Ordinance, SFGOV.ORG, http://sfgsa.org/index.aspx?page=1067 (last visited Aug. 28, 2015).

58. *See* Allan Colbern, *The House Is Picking a Fight with "Sanctuary City" Ordinances. How is This Like the Fugitive Slave Laws?*, WASH. POST., Aug. 13, 2015, https://www.washingtonpost.com/blogs/monkey-cage/wp/2015/08/13/the-house-is-picking-a-fight-with-sanctuary-city-ordinances-how-is-this-like-the-fugitive-slave-laws/.

59. 41 U.S. (16 Pet.) 539 (1842).

invalid as inconsistent with the federal fugitive slave act, the validity of which was affirmed.[60] The author of the Court's opinion, however, Justice Joseph Story, opined that state legislation could validly prohibit state officials from participating in recapture efforts.[61] A number of northern states proceeded to enact "a range of non-enforcement laws banning state and local officials from participating in recap[ture], and denying the federal government the right to use state and local courts to hear cases."[62]

The analogy to undocumented immigrants is straightforward; indeed, the Third Circuit Court of Appeals recently held that the federal government cannot require states and cities to enforce compliance with Immigrations and Customs Enforcement (ICE) directives, to obey ICE "detainers," or to expend financial and personnel resources on ICE priorities.[63] The court emphasized that the contrary result would be a clear violation of the anti-commandeering principles set forth in cases such as *New York v. United States*[64] and *Printz v. United States*:[65] "As in *New York* and *Printz*, immigration officials may not compel state and local agencies to expend funds and resources to effectuate a federal regulatory scheme."[66]

Immigration policy demonstrates how several states can serve, once again, as useful laboratories in discovering what works and what doesn't in tackling vexing national problems. No one suggests that their experiments will always be laudatory. If the states run afoul of constitutional limits of the sort embodied in the Fourth Amendment, the courts can and must step in. But barring such illegality, in the realm of immigration as in so many other areas, it must always be remembered that Congress has the last word. If the states' experiments turn out to be ill-advised, they at least will have provided valuable, real-world empirical data that can guide Congress in the enactment of a wiser solution—if and when it chooses to exercise the authority that the Constitution has given it.

---

60. The Court further found Pennsylvania's law to be inconsistent with Article IV, section 2 of the Constitution (a portion of which was repealed by the adoption of the Thirteenth Amendment, which outlawed slavery).

61. *Prigg*, 41 U.S. at 542.

62. Colbern, *supra* note 58.

63. *See* Galarza v. Lehigh County, 745 F.3d 634 (3d Cir. 2014); *see also* Miranda-Olivares v. Clackamas County, No. 3:12-CV-02317-ST, 2014 WL 1414305 (D. Or. Apr. 11, 2014).

64. 505 U.S. 144 (1992).

65. 521 U.S. 898 (1997).

66. *Galarza*, 745 F.3d at 644.

II. Preemption of State Law by Treaty

As we have seen,[67] concerns about the states dishonoring obligations undertaken by the national government under the Articles of Confederation comprised one of the principal incentives to draft a new Constitution. Hamilton stated the case forcefully:

> The treaties of the United States under the [Articles of Confederation] are liable to the infractions of thirteen different legislatures, and as many different courts of final jurisdiction, acting under the authority of those legislatures. The faith, the reputation, the peace of the whole Union are thus continually at the mercy of the prejudices, the passions, and the interests of every member of which it is composed. Is it possible that foreign nations can either respect or confide in such a government? Is it possible that the people of America will longer consent to trust their honor, their happiness, their safety, on so precarious a foundation?[68]

The Framers sought to stabilize the "precarious foundation" of the Articles with the new Constitution's Supremacy Clause,[69] ensuring that state constitutions, statutes, and judicial decisions would give way to treaties made by the federal government.

Indeed, this has been clear from the start. Although *Marbury v. Madison*[70] may forever be celebrated as the first case in which the Supreme Court exercised judicial review—asserted the authority of the federal courts to invalidate laws or acts inconsistent with the Constitution—it is not, in fact, the first instance in which the Court exercised this power. In *Ware v. Hylton*,[71] the Court invalidated a Virginia statute that blocked the recovery of debts covered by the Treaty of Paris of 1783, which guaranteed "no lawful impediment to the recovery . . . of all bona fide debts" owed to British creditors.[72] Justice Chase said what now seems self-evident: "A treaty cannot be the supreme law of the land, that is, of all the United States, if any act of a state legislature can stand in its way."[73] The Treaty of Paris

---

67. See Chapter 1.

68. THE FEDERALIST NO. 22, at 144 (Alexander Hamilton) (Jacob E. Cooke ed., 1961).

69. U.S. CONST. art. IV, cl. 2.

70. 5 U.S. (1 Cranch) 137 (1803).

71. 3 U.S. (3 Dall.) 199 (1796).

72. *Id.* at 213.

73. *Id.* at 236.

thus preempted the conflicting Virginia statute to the extent of any inconsistency under the Supremacy Clause.

To the same effect is *Asakura v. City of Seattle*.[74] *Asakura* involved a Seattle law that prohibited aliens from operating pawnbroking businesses. A Japanese national who owned such a business brought suit, arguing that the treaty of friendship, commerce, and navigation then in effect between the United States and Japan guaranteed that the citizens of each country could engage in commerce in the other on the same terms as its own citizens. The Supreme Court agreed: "The treaty is binding within the State of Washington. . . . It stands on the same footing of supremacy as do the provisions of the Constitution and the laws of the United States."[75]

As these two cases reveal, treaties may be used either offensively or defensively in litigation—to vindicate rights, as the *Ware* plaintiffs sought to do, or to safeguard from sanction activities vouchsafed by the treaty, as Asakura sought to do. Treaties thus represent a powerful tool for the assertion of federal supremacy, particularly because the Supreme Court has construed the general federalism principles of the Tenth Amendment not to limit the federal treaty power.[76]

This "carve-out" for treaties has, and continues to, prove controversial. State authorities naturally chafe under the possibility that to circumvent Tenth Amendment rights the federal government may choose the treaty route rather than legislation. For that reason, the federal government has often opted for the politically safer course of limiting the application of treaty provisions that might be seen as trenching upon traditional state prerogatives. It has done this by shaping treaty provisions or formulating reservations that effectively eliminate or at least mitigate potential federalism worries. The OAS Charter, the Instrument for Amendment of the Constitution of the International Labor Organization, the Protocol to the Convention Relating to the Status of Refugees, the International Covenant on Civil and Political Rights, and the Council of Europe Cybercrime Convention all provide examples.[77]

The Cybercrime Convention, discussed further in Chapter 10, illustrates the problem that arises when conduct that treaty parties seek to criminalize arguably falls at least in part within the exclusive authority of the states. Absent a reservation to the Convention, it would have obliged the United States to criminalize

74. 265 U.S. 332 (1924).

75. *Id.* at 341.

76. *See* Missouri v. Holland, 252 U.S. 416 (1920); Bond v. United States, 134 S. Ct. 2077, 2101 (2014), discussed in Chapter 6.

77. For discussion, see generally Thomas M. Franck, Michael J. Glennon, Sean D. Murphy & Edward T. Swaine, Foreign Relations and National Security Law: Cases, Materials, and Simulations 773–77 (4th ed. 2012).

conduct that Congress may lack the constitutional authority to criminalize. To meet this difficulty, the United States negotiated the inclusion of a provision in the Treaty that effectively pares down the scope of the U.S. obligation, as set out in Article 41:

> 1. A federal State may reserve the right to assume obligations under Chapter II of this Convention consistent with its fundamental principles governing the relationship between its central government and constituent States provided that it is still able to co-operate under Chapter III.
>
> 2. When making a reservation under paragraph 1, a federal State may not apply the terms of such reservation to exclude or substantially diminish its obligations to provide for measures set forth in Chapter II. Overall, it shall provide for a broad and effective law enforcement capability with respect to those measures.
>
> 3. With regard to the provisions of this Convention, the application of which comes under the jurisdiction of constituent States or other similar territorial entities, that are not obliged by the constitutional system of the federation to take legislative measures, the federal government shall inform the competent authorities of such States of the said provisions with its favourable opinion encouraging them to take appropriate action to give them effect.[78]

This provision is unusual: other negotiating parties can be expected in general to object to a condition of this sort, that is, one from which they cannot benefit because they are not federal states—and indeed, several nations initially did so object in the case of the Cybercrime Convention. In response, federal states might well decide to take a pass on the treaty in question. Yet this raises the curious possibility, discussed in Chapter 6, that the constitutions of at least some federal nations actually preclude them from ratifying treaties open to non-federal nations.

III. Preemption of State Law by Executive Agreement

Treaties are not the only instruments by which the United States undertakes legal obligations internationally. Presidents enter into two sorts of international agreements without the advice and consent of the Senate. The first is a congressional-executive agreement. These are made with the approval of a majority of both Houses of Congress, either before or after the agreement is concluded. In the

---

78. Council of Europe Convention on Cybercrime arts. 2–10, Nov. 23, 2001, http://www.coe.int/en/web/conventions/full-list/-/conventions/treaty/185.

modern era, the federal government uses congressional-executive agreements for major multinational treaties that might once have been concluded under Article II. The North American Free Trade Agreement is a prominent example, which reignited a debate about the so-called "interchangeability thesis"—that under the Constitution, the federal government can use a congressional-executive agreement to accomplish anything that it could accomplish with an Article II treaty.[79]

In *Made in the USA Foundation v. United States*,[80] the Eleventh Circuit concluded that whether NAFTA must be concluded as an Article II treaty, or whether it may be concluded as a congressional-executive agreement, is a political question.[81] Citing *Goldwater v. Carter*,[82] which involved a challenge to President Carter's unilateral termination of the U.S.-Taiwan mutual defense treaty, the Eleventh Circuit wrote that "just as the Treaty Clause fails to outline the Senate's role in the abrogation of treaties, we find that the Treaty Clause also fails to outline the circumstances, if any, under which its procedures must be adhered to when approving international commercial agreements."[83]

The Eleventh Circuit so held because it treated NAFTA as an instrument within the ambit of Congress's Foreign Commerce Clause power—and therefore as lawfully made by Congress with simple majorities of each House, even though it had been concluded as an international agreement with Canada and Mexico outside the parameters of Article II. Yet the court also denied that it meant "to suggest that the terms of the Treaty Clause effectively allow the political branches to exercise unfettered discretion in determining whether to subject a particular international agreement to the rigors of that Clause's procedural requirements; to state as much would be tantamount to rendering the terms of Art. II, § 2, cl. 2 a dead letter."[84] The problem, of course, before and after *Made in the USA Foundation*, is that, on the one hand, congressional-executive agreements have become a routine part of the U.S. law of international agreements; but on the other, unless one accepts the interchangeability thesis, there must be some treaties

79. *See* Oona A. Hathaway, *Treaties' End: The Past, Present, and Future of International Lawmaking in the United States*, 117 YALE L.J. 1236, 1244 (2008). *Compare* Bruce Ackerman & David Golove, *Is NAFTA Constitutional?*, 108 HARV. L. REV. 799, 867 (1995) *with* Laurence H. Tribe, *Taking Text and Structure Seriously: Reflections on Free-Form Method in Constitutional Interpretation*, 108 HARV. L. REV. 1221, 1276 (1995).

80. 242 F.3d 1300 (11th Cir. 2001).

81. *Id.* at 1302.

82. 444 U.S. 996 (1979).

83. *Made in the USA Found.*, 242 F.3d at 1315.

84. *Id.* at 1319.

that constitutionally must be "subject . . . to the rigors" of Article II. The Eleventh Circuit contributed no guidance in this regard. For those, including the authors, who reject the interchangeability thesis but accept the constitutional validity of at least some congressional-executive agreements, all that can be said—without a digression into the morass of literature on these issues—is that valid congressional-executive agreements, those that qualify as federal law, preempt state law to the same extent as federal statutes and treaties. But which congressional-executive agreements are valid is a question that is not addressed here.

The second form of U.S. international agreement (other than an Article II treaty) is the so-called "sole executive agreement." As the label suggests, such an agreement is made by the president alone, without Senate or congressional approval of any sort. Sole executive agreements break down into two subcategories: those that fall within the president's plenary constitutional power and those that fall within concurrent presidential and congressional power. Plenary presidential authority embraces authority exercised by the president pursuant to exclusive grants of power, such as those constitutional provisions empowering the president to serve as commander-in-chief, to grant pardons, and to receive ambassadors and ministers. Concurrent power, on the other hand, is also exercised by Congress, and, sometimes, by the president when Congress has not acted first and "occupied the field."[85] Foreign commerce is an example; Congress is granted power to regulate it, but presidents, too, have acted in the area when Congress has left certain matters untouched. Treaty termination is another example. Congress, or the Senate, may have the power to specify a procedure governing when and how a given treaty might be terminated. But absent such a directive, the president may be authorized to proceed on his own, as did Presidents Carter and Bush in terminating, respectively, the mutual security treaty with Taiwan and the ABM Treaty.[86] This issue, like the interchangeability thesis, remains controversial, but for Supremacy Clause purposes, it need not be resolved except to say, again, that insofar as it *is* valid federal law, a sole executive agreement preempts state law according to the accepted principles of preemption canvassed earlier. Fortunately, in the domain of sole executive agreements, the Supreme Court has supplied greater guidance on this particular issue.

85. For an explanation of plenary and concurrent power, see MICHAEL J. GLENNON, CONSTITUTIONAL DIPLOMACY 15–16 (1990).

86. See the several opinions in Goldwater v. Carter, 444 U.S. 996 (1979).

A. Judicial Precedents

The Court has had little difficulty in finding the first sort of sole executive agreement—one entered into under the president's plenary constitutional power—preemptive of state law. The Court's two landmark opinions establishing the validity of executive agreements both dealt with an exercise of plenary presidential power. In *United States v. Belmont*,[87] the Court upheld the validity of the "Litvinov Assignment," a sole executive agreement made by President Roosevelt with the Soviet Union upon the recognition of its government by the United States in 1933. In it, the Soviet government assigned certain outstanding claims to the U.S. government. Among them were claims made to accounts in New York banks. The claimants maintained, in effect, that the Soviet government had stolen their assets by nationalization decrees. After the agreement took effect, the federal government went to New York's courts and sought to recover the accounts on behalf of the Soviets, whom the courts had earlier rebuffed. But the state courts remained recalcitrant, holding that New York's public policy barred recovery by the federal government as well; the federal government, the state courts found, stood in this litigation on the same legal footing as the Soviet Union. The Supreme Court reversed. "[S]tate lines disappear," it said, "[i]n respect of all international negotiations and compacts and in respect of our foreign relations generally."[88] The Litvinov Assignment and recognition of the Soviet Union "were all parts of one transaction, resulting in an international compact between the two governments."[89]

Five years later, the Court had occasion to revisit the issue in *United States v. Pink*.[90] The Court backed off *Belmont*'s broad "package deal" approach and retreated to narrower grounds in upholding the Litvinov Assignment. But it still found that the agreement fell within the scope of the president's plenary power to recognize foreign nations as incident to the Constitution's express assignment to him of the power to receive ambassadors. The "power to remove such obstacles to full recognition . . . certainly is a modest implied power of the President. . . ."[91] Incidental to the exercise of the exclusive power of recognition, President Roosevelt, the Court found, had authority to settle claims that stood in the way of recognizing the Soviet Union.

---

87. 301 U.S. 324 (1937).

88. *Id.* at 331.

89. *Id.* at 330.

90. 315 U.S. 203 (1942).

91. *Id.* at 229.

A third case, *Dames & Moore v. Regan*,[92] took a different approach in reaffirming presidential power to settle international claims. The Court there considered the validity of the Algiers Accords, a de facto executive agreement with Iran in which President Carter settled outstanding claims against Iran arising out of the hostage crisis.[93] The agreement had the effect of extinguishing claims pending in both state and federal courts, under both state and federal law. It also had the effect of nullifying all attachments obtained in those courts and prohibiting future litigation based on those claims. In upholding the agreement, the Court relied not upon plenary constitutional power but rather upon a combination of custom—a historical practice of executive settlement of such agreements that had been "long-continued"—and congressional acquiescence—Congress, aware of the practice, failed to disapprove.[94]

None of these precedents, therefore, dealt with the preemptive effect of a sole executive agreement concluded in the zone of concurrent congressional-executive power. All fell, rather, within the realm in which the president acts under a grant of exclusive constitutional power or consistent with the explicit or implied approval of Congress. The Court thus did not confront the harder question: What would be the preemptive effect of a sole executive agreement falling within the sphere of concurrent power—and concluded with nary a peep from Congress, one way or the other?

Two federal courts of appeals have addressed the validity of executive agreements falling within the realm of concurrent power, but have not confronted the question whether those agreements preempted state laws. In *United States v. Guy W. Capps, Inc.*,[95] the Fourth Circuit invalidated a sole executive agreement concerning the export of potatoes from Canada into the United States. The agreement thus could have fallen within the concurrent power of Congress and the president, because the Constitution grants to Congress power to regulate commerce with foreign nations.[96] Parts of the opinion suggested that the agreement must be held invalid because Congress had disapproved it; other parts of the opinion, however, implied that the court considered the agreement invalid because the president lacked the power to conclude it in the face of congressional silence. In *Consumers Union of U.S., Inc. v. Kissinger*,[97] the D.C. Circuit upheld the validity of agreements

---

92. 453 U.S. 654, 678 (1981).

93. Because neither country would communicate with the other, the Algiers Accords, though effectively a sole executive agreement, consisted of joint declarations made by the governments of the United States and Iran, respectively, to Algeria.

94. *Dames & Moore*, 453 U.S. at 682, 686.

95. 204 F.2d 655 (4th Cir. 1953).

96. U.S. CONST. art. I, § 8, cl. 3.

97. 506 F.2d 136 (D.C. Cir. 1974).

entered into with foreign countries imposing voluntary restraints on steel imports into the United States, another activity clearly subject to congressional regulation under the Foreign Commerce Clause. The court found that the executive's actions did not constitute a "regulation of foreign commerce foreclosed to it generally by . . . the Constitution."[98] Little guidance exists in either opinion about whether conflicting state law would have been preempted; apparently, none existed.

B. Analytic Options

Three distinct analytic possibilities exist: first, such an agreement might be invalid altogether; second, it might be valid and preempt state law; or third, it might be valid yet lack any preemptive effect.

It's exceedingly unlikely today that the Court would hold such an agreement simply invalid. Whatever practice might have prevailed in the early days of the Republic, too many sole executive agreements have by this date been concluded,[99] concerning matters on which Congress also has the power to act, to suggest (as did the *Guy W. Capps* court) that those agreements were all ultra vires. A finding of invalidity would also raise controversial questions about whether the constitutionally invalid agreement was nonetheless binding within the international realm. The courts are not wont to complicate presidential diplomacy without weighty reasons.

On the other hand, difficulties also attend the argument for validity. There is, after all, nothing in the Supremacy Clause to suggest that the president can act alone—exercising a power that the Constitution assigns to Congress rather than to him—to preempt state law.[100] And there is, ex hypothesi, no suggestion that the state law in question runs afoul of any constitutional restraint; its validity was unquestioned before the president, acting on his own, claimed to preempt it. To permit the president alone to invalidate any unwanted state law merely by identifying a friendly foreign government willing to join in nullifying that law would upend traditional understandings of both federalism and separation of powers.[101]

---

98. *Id.* at 138.

99. For a compilation of recent studies, see CURTIS A. BRADLEY, INTERNATIONAL LAW IN THE U.S. LEGAL SYSTEM 74–75 (2013).

100. *Cf.* Medellín v. Texas, 552 U.S. 491, 533 (2008) (finding ineffective as constitutionally invalid a presidential directive to the states to carry out an international obligation to review and reconsider certain state criminal convictions in conformity with general principles of comity).

101. This scenario is at any rate only slightly less inconceivable than the idea that the federal government might enter into an Article II treaty with Latvia to "overrule" the holding in *United States v. Lopez*, 514 U.S. 549 (1995). *See* Bond v. United States, 134 S. Ct. 2077, 2100 (2014) (Scalia, J., concurring in the judgment). We discuss this issue in depth in Chapter 6.

A greater possibility is that a judge might balk at giving preemptive effect to a sole executive agreement concluded within the realm of concurrent congressional-executive power while still considering the agreement valid in other respects. Such an approach would constitute a judicial invitation to Congress, in effect, to express its intent on the issue of preemption, and would also constitute a guarantee to the states—and individuals and businesses operating in reliance upon state laws—that otherwise valid state laws will not be set aside on the initiative of the president alone. Henkin, noting the major limitation on state foreign-affairs actions posed by the Supremacy Clause, took care to opine that "[e]xecutive agreements *on the president's own authority* . . . enjoy such supremacy."[102] Others have picked up the distinction.[103] Yet this third situation seems to fall within the facts that arose in *Garamendi*. Recall that *Garamendi* involved executive policy statements rather than a directly preemptive executive agreement—yet the *Garamendi* Court did not hesitate to conclude that "valid executive agreements are fit to preempt state law, just as treaties are,"[104] and it proceeded to strike down the California law in question. It is conceivable, therefore, that the Court could reiterate that blanket statement in upholding the preemptive effect of any sole executive agreement, whether within the president's exclusive powers or the concurrent powers of a silent Congress.[105]

IV. Assessment

Treaties, congressional-executive agreements, and sole executive agreements, like federal statutes, all have the potential to preempt state law under the Supremacy

---

102. Louis Henkin, Foreign Affairs and the Constitution 242 (1972) (emphasis added).

103. For a convincing argument that "courts should permit a sole executive agreement to override preexisting legal rights only when the President has independent authority to do so," see Bradford R. Clark, *Domesticating Sole Executive Agreements*, 93 Va. L. Rev. 1573, 1577 (2007). *See also* Michael D. Ramsey, The Constitution's Text in Foreign Affairs 298 (2007) ("The core issue . . . is not whether states may resist the federal government, but *which branch* of the federal government can decide that the states must give way."). John Yoo has argued that "the normal statutory mode must be used to approve international agreements that regulate matters within Congress's Article I powers," and that treaties "must be used if the nation seeks to make agreements outside of Congress's competence or bind itself in areas where both President and Congress exercise competing, overlapping powers." John C. Yoo, *Laws as Treaties?: The Constitutionality of Congressional-Executive Agreements*, 99 Mich. L. Rev. 757, 764 (2001).

104. Am. Ins. Ass'n v. Garamendi, 539 U.S. 396, 416 (2003) (citing United States v. Pink, 315 U.S. 203, 223, 230–31 (1942); and United States v. Belmont, 301 U.S. 324, 331 (1937)).

105. One Court of Appeals has followed *Garamendi* in finding state law claims (also concerning Holocaust-era insurance policies) to have been preempted even though it could point to no executive agreement at odds with the claims. *See In re* Assicurazioni General, 592 F.3d 113 (2d Cir. 2010).

Clause. The issue in each case is not so much the Supremacy Clause, which clearly makes federal law supreme over state law and establishes a solid basis for the Court's preemption jurisprudence, as it is the *validity* of the federal law or other measure. In the constitutional law of foreign affairs, more than in domestic federal law, the Supreme Court has simply failed to speak unequivocally to many of the key questions on which the validity of the putatively preemptive federal measure turns.

Is a treaty on a subject that might otherwise be within the domain of the state police power under the Tenth Amendment a valid federal law for purposes of the Supremacy Clause?[106] May the president unilaterally terminate a treaty, and if so, under what circumstances (for surely a *validly* terminated treaty no longer preempts state law)?[107] Do only self-executing treaties qualify as valid federal law under the Supremacy Clause,[108] and if so, must non-self-executing treaties, although technically "the supreme Law of the Land,"[109] nonetheless first be "executed" by Congress before they can preempt inconsistent state law?[110] May the federal government enter into *all* international agreements as congressional-executive agreements rather than by the process set forth in Article II, or only those agreements that Congress could otherwise have concluded by virtue of its power to regulate foreign commerce?[111] Justice Frankfurter famously argued, and in cases such as *Dames & Moore*,[112] *Zivotofsky v. Kerry*,[113] and *NLRB v. Canning*,[114] the Supreme Court has seemingly concurred, that "a systematic, unbroken, executive practice, long pursued to the knowledge of the Congress and never before questioned, engaged in by presidents who have also sworn to uphold the Constitution, making as it were such exercise of power part of the structure of our Government, may be treated as a gloss on the 'executive Power' vested in the President by § 1 of Art. II."[115] But how should a court faced with a sole executive

---

106. *See* Missouri v. Holland, 252 U.S. 416 (1920). For analysis, see Chapter 6.

107. Goldwater v. Carter, 444 U.S. 996, 998 (1979).

108. Asakura v. City of Seattle, 265 U.S. 332 (1924).

109. U.S. CONST. art. VI, cl. 2.

110. Medellín v. Texas, 552 U.S. 491, 523 (2008).

111. Made in the USA Found. v. United States, 242 F.3d 1300, 1302 (11th Cir. 2001).

112. 453 U.S. 654 (1981).

113. 135 S. Ct. 2076 (2015).

114. 133 S. Ct. 2861 (2013).

115. Youngstown Sheet & Tube Co. v. Sawyer (*The Steel Seizure Case*), 343 U.S. 579, 610 (1952) (Frankfurter, J., concurring).

agreement determine whether it falls within the plenary "executive Power" of the president, so construed, such that the agreement qualifies as constitutionally valid federal law under the Supremacy Clause?

In short, the central problem that afflicts the issue of preemption in the constitutional law of foreign affairs in the event of federal disapproval is the dearth of legal controversies over the *validity* of the instruments of federal lawmaking in the international realm—Article II treaties, congressional-executive agreements, and sole executive agreements (and, one might add, federal common law, though that form of federal law arises less frequently in the context of the Supremacy Clause). This gap in the law of foreign-affairs federalism persists because questions of the sort posed above seldom reach the Supreme Court (or any court), and if and when they do, the Court routinely invokes the political question and other justiciability doctrines to dodge them. Until the Court provides more concrete guidance concerning the validity of the traditional federal foreign affairs instruments, the scope of state authority will on many questions involving federal preemption remain uncertain.

10

A Case Study

STATES AS CYBER-DEFENDERS

THE PARADE OF horribles potentially triggered by a cyberattack is by now familiar: no air traffic controllers or airport check ins; no electronically regulated rail traffic; no computer-dependent, overnight deliveries of packages or mail; no paychecks for millions of workers whose employers depend upon payroll software; no financial records of funds on deposit and no ATMs; no reliable medical records in hospitals and health centers; no electrical power, and hence no light, heat, operating oil refineries, or heating fuel or gasoline; no traffic signals; no telephone or Internet service; no or ineffective police protection—this is only a partial list of what could be disabled by an attack on America's computer networks.

Addressing this threat is generally thought to be a task for the federal government. But the dangers posed by cyberattacks frequently implicate traditional state police powers. And the states have significant interests at stake: among others, states maintain the most comprehensive collection of personal information about their residents, and their governments routinely rely upon the Internet to serve those residents: health data, driving records, educational and criminal records, professional licenses, and tax information—all are held by state governments.[1]

What role, then, might states play in promoting cybersecurity? Just how great is the threat from cyberattacks? What, indeed, is a "cyberattack"? How effective are federal and international safeguards? Isn't cybersecurity the proper domain of federal and international, rather than state, law?

1. *See* Fernando Pinguelo & Bradford Muller, *Virtual Crimes and Real Damages: A Primer on Cybercrimes in the United States and Efforts to Combat Cybercriminals*, 16 (1) VA. J.L. & TECH. 116, 120 (2011).

Let's begin with the gravity of the threat. So far as we know, hackers have caused serious damage to critical infrastructure in three cases, none of which occurred in the United States. In 2007, the Israeli Air Force disrupted Syrian air defenses during the destruction of a Syrian nuclear reactor. In 2010, the so-called Stuxnet attacks on Iranian nuclear reactors came to light.[2] And in 2014, hackers caused "massive damage" to a German steel mill.[3] It is also likely, however, that further damage has gone unreported; a recently declassified 2008 National Security Presidential directive indicates that "hackers and insiders have penetrated or shut down utilities in countries on at least three continents."[4]

These operations were appropriately called "cyberattacks." Because they involved destruction or disruption of a sort associated with war, they should be regulated by the international law of armed conflict. "Cyberespionage," in contrast, involves no destruction or disruption but is aimed at the surreptitious extraction of data. The term "cybercrime" has been used broadly to describe a wide variety of activities ranging from illegal interference and illegal access to the misuse of devices and content-related offenses.[5] Each of these terms refers as much to the perpetrators as to the act itself. Espionage conducted by other nations has been regarded as a matter for the federal government. Theft, property destruction, and related offenses perpetrated by individuals or criminal organizations have been thought to be within the purview of both the state and federal governments.

These distinctions provide some analytic clarity. Yet cyberattacks, cybercrimes, and cyberespionage do not fit well into existing legal categories. For one thing, they're not easily distinguishable from one another until well after their initiation, if then. All of them exploit vulnerabilities in computer networks, using similar techniques. Malware that has been unwittingly downloaded and sits silently on a computer may be intended simply to monitor keystrokes—or it may await the command of a distant operator who may be instructed to erase data, freeze an operating system, or participate in a botnet attack (explained below). Experts often cannot be sure what's afoot without conducting time-consuming

2. *See* James Lewis, *Cyber Attacks, Real or Imagined, and Cyber War*, CTR. FOR STRATEGIC & INT'L STUDIES, July 11, 2011, http://csis.org/publication/cyber-attacks-real-or-imagined-and-cyber-war.

3. *See* Kim Zetter, *A Cyberattack Has Caused Confirmed Physical Damage for the Second Time Ever*, WIRED, Jan. 8, 2015, http://www.wired.com/2015/01/german-steel-mill-hack-destruction.

4. *See* National Security Presidential Directive/NSPD-54 (Jan. 8, 2008), http://epic.org/privacy/cybersecurity/EPIC-FOIA-NSPD54.pdf.

5. *See* Council of Europe Convention on Cybercrime arts. 2–10, Nov. 23, 2001, http://www.coe.int/en/web/conventions/full-list/-/conventions/treaty/185.

and painstaking forensic analysis. Given the instantaneity of strike and counter-strike in cyberspace, this can be impractical. Further, the anonymity of cyberspace and the current state of information technology make it extremely difficult to identify transgressors and to attribute attacks with sufficient confidence, if at all. The attribution problem severely complicates the application of any legal regime to individual acts. Finally, as with terrorist attacks, vexing issues of legal categorization arise. Flying an airplane into a building is an offense under the criminal laws of states, the federal government, and if the attack originates from abroad, potentially international law as well. So too with a cyber-operation that derails a train or zeros-out a bank account.

For all these reasons, the term "cyber-intrusions," while simplistic, is a useful catch-all.

I. The Growing Threat from Cyber-Intrusions

All that said, and semantics aside, there's of course serious cause for concern. The frequency and severity of cyber-intrusions is proliferating. In 2009, computer hackers penetrated elements of the U.S. electrical grid into which they embedded malware that could have allowed malefactors to take control of at least parts of the system.[6] The security firm RSA disclosed in 2011 that information integral to the security of numerous government and corporate computer networks and email systems had been extracted from its servers.[7] During the 2013 holiday season, hackers compromised the credit and debit card information of at least 40 million Target customers, and in 2014, the personal data associated with 145 million eBay accounts was stolen.[8] In November of the same year, hackers penetrated Sony's network and released emails, salary lists, and other sensitive

6. *See* Duncan Hollis, *An e-SOS for Cyberspace*, 52(2) HARV. INT'L L.J. 373, 382 n.49 (2011).

7. *See* Open Letter from Art Coviello, Executive Chairman, RSA, to RSA Customers, http://www.sec.gov/Archives/edgar/data/790070/000119312511070159/dex991.htm (last visited Nov. 20, 2015); *see also* Rhonda Schwartz & Meg Chuchmach, *Department of Defense, Major Private Contractor Potentially Vulnerable in Cyber Attack*, ABC NEWS THE BLOTTER, Mar. 18, 2011, http://abcnews.go.com/Blotter/dod-private-contractors-potentially-vulnerable-rsa-cyber-attack/story?id=13162204 (discussing the potential fallout of an attack on RSA, which provides computer security to the U.S. government as well as to private clients, including Lockheed Martin).

8. *See* Elizabeth A. Harris & Nicole Perlroth, *Target Missed Signs of a Data Breach*, N.Y. TIMES, Mar. 13, 2014, http://www.nytimes.com/2014/03/14/business/target-missed-signs-of-a-data-breach.html?_r=0; *see also* Lauren Hertzler, *Scams Expected to Hit Customers Hard After eBay Data Breach*, PHILA. BUS. J., May 25, 2014, http://www.bizjournals.com/philadelphia/news/2014/05/25/scams-expected-to-hit-customers-hard-after-ebay.html?page=all.

data before launching a "wiper" attack that deleted data and disabled computers.[9] (President Obama and the FBI blamed North Korea, though private security researchers have since expressed doubts.[10]) The costs of these intrusions are high: The Ponemon Institute estimates that in 2014, cybercrime cost the average U.S. company $12.7 million, up 9 percent from 2013.[11] Intrusions against even U.S. government networks continue, as Chinese hackers breached the National Oceanographic and Atmospheric Administration in late 2014.[12] In April 2015, according to reports in the *New York Times* and elsewhere, Russian hackers penetrated deeply into the unclassified systems of the State Department and White House and swept up some of President Obama's email correspondence.[13]

These intrusions all occurred within the United States (or at least against U.S. targets). Foreign targets have been hit even harder. A 2007 botnet attack on the Estonian government's servers wrought havoc throughout the country. "All major commercial banks, telcos, media outlets, and name servers—the phone books of the Internet—felt the impact, and this affected the majority of the Estonian population," the defense minister said. "This was the first time that a botnet threatened the national security of an entire nation."[14] Georgia was the victim of a similar botnet attack in 2008.[15] A debilitating attack occurred in 2011

9. Ellen Nakashima, *Why the Sony Hack Drew an Unprecedented U.S. Response Against North Korea*, WASH. POST, Jan. 15, 2015, http://www.washingtonpost.com/world/national-security/why-the-sony-hack-drew-an-unprecedented-us-response-against-north-korea/2015/01/14/679185d4-9a63-11e4-96cc-e858eba91ced_story.html.

10. Nicole Perlroth, *New Study May Add to Skepticism among Security Experts That North Korea Was Behind Sony Hack*, N.Y. TIMES, Dec. 24, 2014, http://bits.blogs.nytimes.com/2014/12/24/new-study-adds-to-skepticism-among-security-experts-that-north-korea-was-behind-sony-hack/.

11. *See* THE PONEMON INSTITUTE, *2014 Global Report on the Cost of Cyber Crime*, Oct. 30, 2014, http://www.ponemon.org/library/2014-global-report-on-the-cost-of-cyber-crime.

12. *See* Mary Pat Flaherty, Jason Samenow & Lisa Rein, *Chinese Hack U.S. Weather Systems, Satellite Network*, WASH. POST, Nov. 12, 2014, https://www.washingtonpost.com/local/chinese-hack-us-weather-systems-satellite-network/2014/11/12/bef1206a-68e9-11e4-b053-65cea7903f2e_story.html.

13. Michael S. Schmidt & David E. Sanger, *Russian Hackers Read Obama's Unclassified Emails, Officials Say*, N.Y. TIMES, April 25, 2015, http://www.nytimes.com/2015/04/26/us/russian-hackers-read-obamas-unclassified-emails-officials-say.html?_r=0.

14. *See* Joshua Davis, *Hackers Take Down the Most Wired Country in Europe*, WIRED, Aug. 21, 2007, http://archive.wired.com/politics/security/magazine/15-09/ff_estonia?currentPage=all.

15. *See generally* Eneken Tikk et al., *Cyber Attacks Against Georgia: Legal Lessons Identified* (Coop. Cyber Def. Ctr. of Excellence, Draft Nov. 2008), *available at* http://www.ismlab.usf.edu/isec/files/Georgia-Cyber-Attack-NATO-Aug-2008.pdf (analyzing the cyberattacks against Georgia from 2008 and attempting to distill legal rules).

against a South Korean bank.[16] An American cybersecurity company reported later that year that it had identified a single perpetrator of cyberespionage who had continued to operate for as long as five years against a wide range of governments, American corporations, and U.N. groups; the pattern of targets suggested a government perpetrator, possibly the People's Republic of China.[17] Similarly, the cybersecurity firm Cylance reported that Iran has subverted the networks of major corporations such as Saudi Aramco and Korean Air.[18] Numerous other serious incidents have occurred,[19] but publicly available information is incomplete. Victims of cyber-intrusions tend to be tightlipped for fear of spreading panic, exposing vulnerabilities, or incurring financial liability.

The media attention focused on attacks on such big-name targets might lead one to believe that smaller organizations tend to be safer. Not so. As one McAfee executive recently put it, "[T]he only organizations that are exempt from [cyber-intrusions] are those that don't have anything valuable or interesting worth stealing."[20] Smaller businesses and low-level governmental entities have fewer protections in place and thus represent "low-hanging fruit."[21] Cyber-intrusions against such websites have provided a treasure trove of sensitive information. In August 2011, Anonymous revealed that it had accessed more than seventy (mostly rural) law-enforcement websites in the United States in retaliation for the arrest of its supporters.[22] The information Anonymous stole included the names and reports of police tipsters, profiles of gang members, data about security training, and credit card numbers.[23] Some county sheriffs were unaware that their websites had been hacked until they were contacted by journalists.[24] In August 2014, the

16. *See* Chico Harlan & Ellen Nakashima, *Suspected North Korean Cyberattack on a Bank Raises Fears for South Korea, Allies*, WASH. POST, Aug. 29, 2011, http://www.washingtonpost.com/world/national-security/suspected-north-korean-cyber-attack-on-a-bank-raises-fears-for-s-korea-allies/2011/08/07/gIQAvWwIoJ_story.html.

17. *See* DMITRI ALPEROVITCH, REVEALED: OPERATION SHADY RAT 6 (Aug. 2011), http://www.mcafee.com/us/resources/white-papers/wp-operation-shady-rat.pdf.

18. *See* Jim Finkle, *Iran Hackers Targeted Airlines, Energy Firms: Report*, REUTERS, Dec. 2, 2015, http://www.reuters.com/article/2014/12/02/us-cybersecurity-iran-idUSKCN0JG18I20141202.

19. *See Significant Cyber Incidents since 2006*, CTR. FOR STRATEGIC & INT'L STUDIES, http://csis.org/program/significant-cyber-events (last visited Nov. 20, 2015).

20. *See* ALPEROVITCH, *supra* note 17, at 14.

21. *Expert: Rural US Websites Easy Target for Hackers*, FOXNEWS.COM, Aug. 7, 2011, http://www.foxnews.com/us/2011/08/07/expert-rural-us-websites-easy-target-for-hackers/.

22. *See id.*

23. *See id.*

24. *See id.*

group attacked the city website of Ferguson, Missouri, and threatened to post online the personal information of city officials.[25]

Anonymous publicly took credit for these intrusions. Normally, however, identifying the source of an intrusion is extremely difficult. Sophisticated cyber-intrusions of the sort launched by governments are especially difficult to trace. Intrusions that don't originate from a given country can be made to appear as though they do, simply by planting a "false flag" in the virus's code. Even if the keyboard from which the intrusion originated can be identified, linking a perpetrator to that keyboard can be impossible—as can linking that perpetrator, if identified, to a government or other organization. Although many such intrusions might have been routed through the United States, what is significant for purposes of considering the cybersecurity powers of the states is that many apparently originate abroad,[26] particularly from China.[27] For that reason, one might look first to international law for at least part of the solution.

II. The Weakness of International Law

Alas, international law does little to thwart cyber-intrusions. For several reasons, that is not likely to change. First, it's not clear that traditional rules limiting the use of force are relevant to even the most severe form of cyber-intrusions—cyberattacks that are intended to cause destruction and harm. The United States and its allies have long argued that the current rules limit only "armed" attack—violence involving "kinetic" weaponry, not cutoffs of foreign aid, trade boycotts, travel bans, or other acts that might cause damage or have effects comparable to an armed attack. That interpretation is now widely accepted. Few will be persuaded if the United States and its newly vulnerable allies now reverse course and contend that it's really an attack's effects that count, not the means.

---

25. *See* Alex Rogers, *What Anonymous Is Doing in Ferguson*, TIME, Aug. 21, 2014, http://time.com/3148925/ferguson-michael-brown-anonymous/.

26. *See generally* Matthis G.T. von Polen, Giovane C.M. Maura & Aiko Pras, *Finding and Analyzing Evil Cities on the Internet*, *in* MANAGING THE DYNAMICS OF NETWORKS AND SERVICES 38 (Isabelle Crisment et al. eds. 2011) (ebook), *available at* http://doc.utwente.nl/76708/1/paper.pdf (using Internet protocol geolocation to identify the cities most responsible for cyber-security incidents).

27. *See generally Communist Chinese Cyber-Attacks, Cyber-Espionage and the Theft of American Technology: Hearing Before the Subcomm. on Oversight & Investigations of the H. Comm. on Foreign Affairs*, 112th Cong. 14 (2011) (statement of Richard D. Fisher, Jr., Senior Fellow, International Assessment and Strategy Center), http://frwebgate.access.gpo.gov/cgi-bin/getdoc.cgi?dbname=112_house_hearings&docid=f:65800.pdf (examining the issue of Chinese cyber-intrusions on the United States).

Second, it's doubtful that new international legal rules on cyberattacks are possible. Compliance with an international agreement probably could not be verified, as verification requires the ability to identify transgressors.[28] Some analysts hope that customary norms will emerge from ad hoc state practice, as they did long ago concerning diplomatic immunity and freedom of the seas. That's not likely. Nations' cyber-behavior is veiled in secrecy, which makes it impossible to find any dots to connect.

Third, even if nations could somehow agree upon international rules, it's doubtful those rules would be effective. Recall Stuxnet. The author of the Stuxnet virus that hamstrung the computer systems running Iran's nuclear centrifuges has never been positively identified, although signs point to the United States and Israel.[29] Some argue that this sort of cyberattack on a country's critical infrastructure should be off limits. Yet it's hard to see how such a ban could have any teeth. When no one knows whether rules are being honored, violators face no penalty and lack any incentive to comply.[30] The only treaty that addresses cyber-intrusions, the Convention on Cybercrime, discussed below, provides a framework for law enforcement. But its provisions have proven notoriously ineffective as nations have struggled to find the common ground necessary to keep pace with evolving threats.[31] Moreover, the Convention does nothing to address what many commentators see as the brunt of the problem: cyber-intrusions conducted by nations themselves.

Fourth, it's debatable whether effective international legal limits are desirable. Despite the controversy surrounding Stuxnet, its benefits were significant. It risked none of the casualties that air strikes could have entailed. It may well have been more effective. It was probably cheaper. Retaliation was less likely because the attack was anonymized. Indeed, the use of a cyber-weapon might have averted full-scale war. Some propose holding nations accountable for cyber-intrusions that come from within their territory. But the attribution problem would still loom large—and "strict liability" could easily boomerang; again, many cyber-intrusions originate within the United States.

---

28. *See generally* Michael J. Glennon, *The Road Ahead: Gaps, Leaks, and Drips,* 89 Int'l L. Stud. 362 (2013).

29. See David E. Sanger, *Obama Order Sped Up Wave of Cyberattacks Against Iran,* N.Y. Times, June 1, 2012, http://www.nytimes.com/2012/06/01/world/middleeast/obama-ordered-wave-of-cyberattacks-against-iran.html?_r=2&hp.

30. *See* Michael J. Glennon, *The Dark Future of Cyber-Security Regulation,* 6 J. Nat'l Sec. L. & Pol'y 563 (2013).

31. *See* Mikko Hypponen, *Fighting Viruses, Defending the Net,* TED, July 11, 2011, http://www.ted.com/talks/mikko_hypponen_fighting_viruses_defending_the_net/transcript?language=en.

International limits on cyber-intrusions are therefore likely to remain elusive. The central obstacle to legal restraints is the Internet's opaqueness, which allows attackers to disguise their identities and mask the source of the attack. Given the original design of the Internet, it's unlikely that nations will succeed in piercing that opaqueness through technological innovation. Absent an ability to attribute responsibility for cyber-intrusions, the best defense will therefore continue to lie not in international law but in national efforts to defend against them and mitigate their effects.

This is where the states can play a pivotal role. They can take steps to prevent cyber-intrusions, monitor malicious traffic, mandate cybersecurity measures, and mitigate the effects of cyber-intrusions when defensive safeguards fail. Indeed, many states have already quietly tightened the slack left by the federal government and the international community. Whatever else they may be called, most cyber-intrusions are, after all, crimes—which the states are especially well-situated to address.

III. The Crazy Quilt of Federal Statutory Law

Nothing is more integral to the traditional police power of the states than crime prevention.[32] Indeed, as the very term "police power" implies, ensuring the safety of their residents lies at the core of the states' responsibilities.[33] Statutes that prohibit and punish fraud, theft, conversion, criminal trespass, forgery, malicious destruction of property, and related offenses all have long been on the states' books. Cyber-intrusions cause, and are intended to cause, effects that fall within many of those traditional state statutes.

Yet it has somehow come to be assumed that cybersecurity is a federal responsibility. In 2015, President Obama urged Congress to enact legislation that would

32. *See, e.g.*, United States v. Morrison, 529 U.S. 598, 599 (2000) ("[W]e can think of no better example of the police power, which the Founders of the Constitution denied the National Government and reposed in the States, than the suppression of violent crime and vindication of its victims."); Rochin v. California, 342 U.S. 165, 168 (1952) ("Broadly speaking, crimes in the United States are what the laws of the individual States make them, subject to the limitations of Art. I, § 10, cl. 1, in the original Constitution, prohibiting bills of attainder and ex post facto laws, and of the Thirteenth and Fourteenth Amendments."); *see also* Bond v. United States, 134 S. Ct. 2077, 2083 (2014) ("Because our constitutional structure leaves local criminal activity primarily to the States, we have generally declined to read federal law as intruding on that responsibility, unless Congress has clearly indicated that the law should have such reach.").

33. *See* Leisy v. Hardin, 135 U.S. 100, 127 (1890) ("Among the powers thus reserved to the several states is what is commonly called the police power—that inherent and necessary power, essential to the very existence of civil society, and the safeguard of the inhabitants of the state against disorder, disease, poverty, and crime.").

relax privacy laws, allowing private firms to report breaches to the federal government.[34] After years of debate, Congress considered several versions of such a bill. None envisioned a role of any significance for state governments.[35] Most significant, however, no legislation was enacted that preempted the states' data security laws.

The reasons are understandable. An interconnected and borderless Internet means that most activity in cyberspace takes place without regard to state or international boundaries. The task of complying with multifarious state cybersecurity laws, each of which could impose varying levels of legal obligation, might easily become burdensome, complex, and costly. Then, too, dealing with threats from abroad has long been seen to be the province of the federal government. It is true that the consequences of a cyberattack that originates overseas can mirror the consequences of a military attack that employs traditional kinetic weaponry; a cyberattack can thus look more like war than crime. That's significant on many levels, not the least of which is that the Constitution prohibits the states from making war without congressional approval.[36] Add to this the fact that federal authority has now come to reach so pervasively into the daily lives of all Americans, and it is easy to understand why few notice or even question whether what's being done by the federal government should more properly be done by the states.

And so the federal government has acted—up to a point. Much of applicable federal law actually predates the advent of cyber-intrusions and simply happens, almost coincidently, to have some relevance to them. Fraud by wire, radio, or television, for example, has long been a federal offense.[37] Courts have adapted these prohibitions and recognized a variety of means of communications, including facsimile, telex, modem, and Internet transmissions, as constituting "wire, radio, or television communication[s]."[38] The Wiretap Act imposes criminal penalties on any person (including law enforcement personnel) who makes an

34. *See* Ellen Nakashima & Katie Zezima, *Obama to Propose Legislation to Protect Firms That Share Cyberthreat Data*, Wash. Post, Jan. 12, 2015, http://www.washingtonpost.com/politics/obama-proposes-legislation-to-protect-consumer-data-student-privacy/2015/01/12/539c4a06-9a8f-11e4-bcfb-059ec7a93ddc_story.html.

35. *See* Ellen Nakashima, *Congress Moving on Long-Sought Legislation to Thwart Cyberattacks*, Wash. Post, Mar. 24, 2015, http://www.washingtonpost.com/world/national-security/congress-moving-on-long-sought-legislation-to-thwart-cyberattacks/2015/03/24/32d20e98-d23c-11e4-ab77-9646eea6a4c7_story.html.

36. U.S. Const. art. I, § 10, cl. 3 ("No State shall . . . engage in War, unless actually invaded, or in such imminent Danger as will not admit of delay.").

37. *See* 18 U.S.C. § 1343 *et seq.* (2012).

38. *See* Office of Legal Educ., Exec. Office for U.S. Att'ys, U.S. Dep't of Justice, Comput. Crime & Intellectual Prop. Section Criminal Div., Prosecuting

illegal interception or who discloses illegally intercepted material.[39] A statute prohibiting unlawful access to stored communications protects the confidentiality, integrity, and availability of communications stored by the providers of electronic communication services.[40] Other statutes prohibit activities that might, but are not necessarily, carried out online, such as identity theft.[41]

Other federal statutes do specifically address Internet crimes. One, for example, prohibits "phishing," that is, the use of fraudulent emails to obtain bank account numbers, passwords, and other sensitive or confidential information.[42] The CAN-SPAM Act of 2003 provides a means of prosecuting individuals who send vast volumes of unsolicited commercial email.[43] Easily the most important federal statute, however, is the Computer Fraud and Abuse Act,[44] which addresses a number of offenses that relate specifically to computers. The Act makes it a felony to access classified information in a computer.[45] It makes it a misdemeanor to access financial records or credit history stored in a financial institution.[46] It penalizes the theft of property as part of a scheme to defraud with the use of the computer.[47] It prohibits altering, destroying, or damaging data that belongs to another.[48] All in all, at least forty additional federal statutes provide grounds for prosecuting cybercrime. Again, however, nowhere in the federal statutes is there an indication that Congress intended these prohibitions to preempt state law.[49]

Three aspects of the federal statutory scheme are noteworthy. First, the federal government has not done enough to *prevent* cyber-intrusions. It has engaged

---

COMPUTER CRIMES 110 (2d ed. 2010), *available at* http://www.justice.gov/sites/default/files/criminal-ccips/legacy/2015/01/14/ccmanual.pdf.

39. *See id.* at 59.

40. *See id.* at 89.

41. *See id.* at 96.

42. *See* 18 U.S.C. § 1029 *et seq.* (2012).

43. *See* 18 U.S.C. § 1037 *et seq.* (2012).

44. *See* 18 U.S.C. § 1030 *et seq.* (2012).

45. *See* 18 U.S.C. § 1030(a)(1), (c)(1)(A), (c)(1)(B) (2012).

46. *See* 18 U.S.C. § 1030(a)(2)(A), (c)(2)(A), (c)(2)(B), (c)(2)(C) (2012).

47. *See* 18 U.S.C. § 1030(a)(4) (2012).

48. *See* 18 U.S.C. § 1030(a)(5)(A) (2012).

49. *See, e.g.*, 18 U.S.C. § 1030(f) (2012) ("This section does not prohibit any lawfully authorized investigative, protective, or intelligence activity of a law enforcement agency of the United States, a State, or a political subdivision of a State, or of an intelligence agency of the United States.").

almost exclusively in efforts to punish conduct that has already occurred. This is partially the result of offensive asymmetries in cyberspace: Attackers need be successful only once, whereas defenses must be foolproof. But it is also a consequence of policy choices of convenience. It is much easier to be reactive than proactive. Preventive technology does exist, but it hasn't been implemented effectively. The federal government's Einstein 3 program was deployed in 2013. It is designed to provide real-time protection against cyberattacks on federal computer networks.[50] The program reportedly has the ability to "automatically detect and respond appropriately to cyber threats before harm is done, providing an intrusion prevention system supporting dynamic defense."[51] Concerns over potential violations of individual privacy, however, have prevented the deployment of the Einstein programs on the public Internet.[52] Instead of confronting this problem with creative solutions, perhaps along the lines of the minimization procedures already written into the Foreign Intelligence Surveillance Act,[53] the federal government has left the private sector to fend for itself.

When the federal government has been interested in providing security to the private sector, its programs have been poorly constructed. Its strongest actions have been executive orders: one in 2013, which encouraged information sharing among public and private entities making up "critical infrastructure,"[54] and another in 2015 stressing the importance of data sharing between firms and the

---

50. *See* William Jackson, *Einstein 3 Goes Live with Automated Malware Blocking*, GCN, July 24, 2013, http://gcn.com/articles/2013/07/24/einstein-3-automated-malware-blocking.aspx?s=security_080813&admgarea=TC_SecCybersSec&m=1.

51. *See The Comprehensive National Cybersecurity Initiative*, Exec. Office of the President 2-3 (Mar. 2010), *available at* http://www.whitehouse.gov/sites/default/files/cybersecurity.pdf [hereinafter CNCI].

52. For a review of the privacy issues at stake, see generally Dept. of Homeland Sec., *Privacy Impact Statement for EINSTEIN 3—Accelerated* (Apr. 19, 2013), *available at* http://www.dhs.gov/sites/default/files/publications/privacy/PIAs/PIA%20NPPD%20E3A%2020130419%20FINAL%20signed.pdf (disclosing that an exercise of the Einstein systems will analyze traffic that may contain personally identifiable information and assessing the impact the exercise may have on privacy rights of individuals); Legal Issues Relating to the Testing, Use, and Deployment of an Intrusion-Detection System (Einstein 2.0) to Protect Unclassified Computer Networks in the Executive Branch, 33 Op. O.L.C. (__) (Jan. 9, 2009) (Vol. 33 forthcoming), *available at* http://www.justice.gov/sites/default/files/olc/opinions/2009/01/31/e2-issues.pdf (analyzing the legality of the Einstein 2.0 program, including the burden it places upon "legitimate privacy rights").

53. *See* 50 U.S.C. § 1801 *et seq.* (2012).

54. Improving Critical Infrastructure Cybersecurity, Exec. Order No. 13,636, 78 Fed. Reg. 11739 (Feb. 12, 2013), http://www.gpo.gov/fdsys/pkg/FR-2013-02-19/pdf/2013-03915.pdf (building upon the 2011 Defense Industrial Base Cyber Pilot project, a voluntary network through which firms may share information on threats).

government.[55] The executive orders did not, however, resolve issues related to liability and proprietary information, which have made private firms reluctant to share information.[56] The necessary legislation was finally considered in 2015.[57] Congress's hesitation was understandable. As with the Einstein programs, the specter of government surveillance of the Internet raises legitimate civil liberties concerns. Federal officials are wary of potential criticism that they have violated the Fourth Amendment prohibition against unlawful searches and seizures. The results of such half measures are familiar: states, cities, private businesses and individuals are left to fight their own battles.[58]

The second key aspect of the current federal statutory scheme is that the federal government makes no meaningful effort at mitigation—at least not with respect to non-federal entities. States and local authorities along with businesses and private individuals must fend for themselves when it comes to alleviating the effects of cyberattacks and intrusions. Nothing in the current federal statutory framework, for example, brings the resources of the federal government to bear when a financial institution such as MasterCard or PayPal is subject to a botnet attack, as they were when they stopped processing transactions to WikiLeaks. The federal government's work thus far has focused mainly on safeguarding "critical infrastructure," to the exclusion of other private sector activity, and it has fallen short even in that regard. Efforts to build a stronger cyber "ecosystem" through the automation and convergence of best cybersecurity practices exist in theory but not practice.[59] Far from taking place in real time, federal response mechanisms

---

55. Promoting Private Sector Cybersecurity Information Sharing, Exec. Order No. 13,691, 80 Fed. Reg. 9349 (Feb. 13, 2015), http://www.gpo.gov/fdsys/pkg/FR-2015-02-20/pdf/2015-03714.pdf.

56. *See* ERIC A. FISCHER ET AL., CONG. RESEARCH SERV., 7-5700, THE 2013 CYBERSECURITY EXECUTIVE ORDER: OVERVIEW AND CONSIDERATIONS FOR CONGRESS (2013), http://www.fas.org/sgp/crs/misc/R42984.pdf.

57. Jennifer Steinhauer, *Senate Rejects Measure to Strengthen Cybersecurity*, N.Y. TIMES, June 11, 2015, http://www.nytimes.com/2015/06/12/us/politics/senate-rejects-measure-to-strengthen-cybersecurity.html?_r=0.

58. *See* RICHARD A. CLARKE & ROBERT KNAKE, CYBER WAR: THE NEXT THREAT TO NATIONAL SECURITY AND WHAT TO DO ABOUT IT 115, 118, 166–67 (2011); *see generally* INTELLIGENCE & NAT'L SEC. ALL., *Addressing Cyber Security through Public-Private Partnership: An Analysis of Existing Models* (Nov. 2009), *available at* http://www.insaonline.org/CMDownload.aspx?ContentKey=e1f31be3-e110-41b2-aa0c-966020051f5c&ContentItemKey=161e015c-670f-449a-8753-689cbc3de85e (surveying existing public-private partnerships to address cybersecurity and suggesting that future efforts should proceed on three fronts: private sector self-regulation, executive branch leadership, and congressional action).

59. For an overview and discussion of the "cyber ecosystem" idea, see generally DEP'T OF HOMELAND SEC., NAT'L PROT. & PROGRAMS DIRECTORATE, *Enabling Distributed Security in Cyberspace* (Mar. 23, 2011), *available at* http://www.dhs.gov/xlibrary/assets/

continue to be triggered by voluntary notification from victims; the haphazard nature of federal legislation means that many entities fall through the cracks. The Federal Information Security Management Act, for instance, requires all federal entities to report incidents of data breach,[60] but for the private sector, different laws apply to different businesses. Healthcare providers,[61] credit bureaus[62] and financial institutions[63] are subject to separate regulatory frameworks—while other industries are left unregulated altogether.[64] A 2013 Government Accountability Office report on federal cybersecurity strategy noted that "no overarching cybersecurity strategy has been developed," and lamented the effects of this failure on government entities, businesses, and individuals.[65]

This presages the third element in the federal framework, which is the lack of a comprehensive data protection regime. By adopting a "sectoral approach," federal initiatives impose varying levels of obligation across different industries and omit any mandated cybersecurity requirements for many private-sector entities.[66] Some legislators believe that market incentives will emerge to fill the security gap.[67] However, economists have suggested that the private sector is unlikely to protect

---

nppd-cyber-ecosystem-white-paper-03-23-2011.pdf (exploring the idea of a "healthy, resilient, cyber ecosystem" in which cyber participants, including cyber devices, are able to "work together in near-real time to anticipate and prevent cyber attacks, limit the spread of attacks across participating devices, minimize the consequences of attacks, and recover to a trusted state").

60. *See* 44 U.S.C.A § 3554(b)(7), § 3556 (Westlaw through Pub. L. No. 114-61 (excluding P.L. 114-52, 114-54, 114-59, and 114-60)).

61. *See* 42 U.S.C. § 1320(d) *et seq.* (2012).

62. *See* 15 U.S.C. § 1681–1681(x) (2012).

63. *See* Gramm-Leach-Bliley Act of 1999, 15 U.S.C. § 6801–6809 (2012); *see also* FTC Standards for Insuring the Security, Confidentiality, Integrity and Protection of Customer Records and Information, 16 C.F.R. Part 314 (2015) (also known as the "FTC Safeguard Rule," which implemented the Gramm-Leach-Bliley security standards for entities under the jurisdiction of the Federal Trade Commission).

64. *See generally* Gina Stevens, Cong. Research Serv., RL34120, Federal Information Security and Data Breach Notification Laws (2010), https://fas.org/sgp/crs/secrecy/RL34120.pdf (providing an overview of the relevant federal law).

65. *See* U.S. Gov't Accountability Office, GAO-13-187, Cybersecurity: National Strategy, Roles, and Responsibilities Need to Be Better Defined and More Effectively Implemented (2013), http://www.gao.gov/assets/660/652170.pdf at 28.

66. *See* Natasha Singer, *Data Protection Laws, an Ocean Apart*, N.Y. Times, Feb. 2, 2013, http://www.nytimes.com/2013/02/03/technology/consumer-data-protection-laws-an-ocean-apart.html?_r=0 (noting that the lack of a comprehensive scheme in the United States is in contrast to the European Union, whose countries began to implement data protection laws in 1995).

67. During an opening statement before the House Judiciary Committee in 2011, Representative Bob Goodlatte, Chairman of the Subcommittee on Intellectual Property,

itself from cyber-intrusions: market incentives favor those who spend less on security, not more.[68] Firms that do not prioritize security may not bear the costs of the resulting cyber-intrusions—a network externality that results in market failure.[69] Washington has failed to mandate the collective action necessary to resolve the problem, and consequently, the number of intrusions has continued to rise.[70] The offensive asymmetry in cyberspace therefore persists. Ideas for more aggressive protective action abound, but as its sense of insecurity mounts, Washington continues to suppose that any solution must come either from itself or through passive collaboration with private corporations, not the several states. The upshot has been lots of talk about the problem, but few, if any, concrete solutions.

IV. The States Step into the Void

As a result of this juridical void, the states have been increasingly active in taking on cyberthreats. Indeed, recent multistate surveys reveal a surprising volume of computer-related legislation. Every state has enacted laws directed at protecting state governments and businesses specifically from cyber-intrusions.[71] Much of the legislation is remarkably detailed and comprehensive.[72] The beginnings of such legislation can be traced to the California data privacy and breach notification law of 2003.[73] The California law requires state agencies and those

---

Competition, and the Internet, Committee on the Judiciary, claimed that "the private sector is best equipped to match the increasingly sophisticated threats to our cyber-security with sophisticated counter-efforts." *Cybersecurity: Innovative Solutions to Challenging Problems: Hearing Before the Subcomm. on Intellectual Property, Competition and the Internet of the H. Comm. on the Judiciary,* 112th Cong. 2 (2011).

68. *See* Ross Anderson & Tyler Moore, *The Economics of Information Security*, 314 SCI. 611 (Oct. 27, 2006) ("Consumers generally reward vendors for adding features, for being first to market . . . These motivations clash with the task of writing more secure software, which requires time-consuming testing and a focus on simplicity.").

69. *See generally* Johannes M. Bauer & Michel J.G. van Eeten, *Cybersecurity: Stakeholder Incentives, Externalities, and Policy Options,* 33 TELECOMM. POL'Y 706 (Nov.–Dec. 2009).

70. During his testimony before the House Judiciary Committee in May 2011, James Baker, Associate Deputy Attorney General, U.S. Department of Justice, noted that "[c]yber crime is on the rise and criminal syndicates are operating with increasing sophistication to steal from innocent Americans. . . . Despite the good work that has been going on in this area, the problem is far from resolved." *See supra* note 67, at 6.

71. *See* Pinguelo & Muller, *supra* note 1, at 151–88.

72. *See, e.g., id.* at 148–50 (discussing cybersecurity legislation in Virginia in detail).

73. *See* CAL. CIV. CODE § 1798.82 *et seq.* (West 2015). In 2002, California became the first state to legislate on the issue of data protection; however, the law was focused mainly on post-security breach notifications and response mechanisms, and not on the technical aspects of

conducting business in California, including foreign corporations, to notify a resident of California when his or her personal information has been acquired by an unauthorized person.[74] As of January 12, 2015, forty-seven other states had enacted similar data privacy and breach notification laws.[75]

On the issue of data security and protection (i.e., a "duty to protect" personal information), California has also led the way. In 2004 the state enacted a law requiring companies to "implement and maintain reasonable security procedures and practices" to protect personal information about California residents from unauthorized access, destruction, use, modification, or disclosure.[76] At least eight other states have now adopted similar legislation.[77] The statutes, like the earlier, more basic data privacy and data breach notification laws, also apply to entities headquartered outside the state in question—including in foreign countries.

One of the most far-reaching such statutes is the Massachusetts Data Security Act, enacted in 2009. This is one of a number of laws enacted by Massachusetts to curb cyber-intrusions.[78] Because its matrix is likely to be emulated by other states, the law is worth a close look, particularly with regard to its most controversial aspect—extraterritorial application of mandated security programs.

The actual law itself is brief. It merely directs the relevant state agency to adopt regulations to safeguard the personal information of residents of Massachusetts from unauthorized access.[79] The law then requires that those regulations apply

---

computer security. *See* California Database Security Breach Notification Act of 2003 (S.B. 1386). The law, which entered into effect in July 2003, became national almost immediately, as almost every company conducting business on the Internet collects the personal information of California residents.

74. *See* CAL. CIV. CODE § 1798.82 *et seq.* (West 2015).

75. *See Security Breach Notification Laws*, NAT'L CONFERENCE OF STATE LEGISLATURES, http://www.ncsl.org/research/telecommunications-and-information-technology/security-breach-notification-laws.aspx (last updated Oct. 22, 2015).

76. *See* CAL. CIV. CODE § 1798.81.5(b) (West 2015). The California law does not define the term "reasonable security."

77. *See, e.g.*, ARK. CODE ANN. § 4-110-104(b) (2015); CONN. GEN. STAT. ANN. § 42-471 (West 2015); MD. CODE ANN. COM. LAW § 14-3503 (West 2015); NEV. REV. STAT. § 603A.210 (2013); OREGON REV. STAT. § 646A.622 (2013); UTAH CODE ANN. §§ 13-44-201 to 202 (LexisNexis 2015); MASS. GEN. LAWS ch. 93H (2015); IND. CODE 24-4.9-3-3.5 (2014).

78. The Massachusetts data protection regime consists of MASS. GEN. LAWS ch. 93H *et seq.* (2015) and the implementing administrative regulation, 201 MASS. CODE REGS. 17.00 *et seq.* (LexisNexis 2015). On the issue of cyber crime, *see* MASS. GEN. LAWS ch. 266 §§ 30, 33A, 60A, 120F, 127 (2015).

79. *See* MASS. GEN. LAWS ch. 93H § 2(a) (2015), which states:

> The department of consumer affairs and business regulation shall adopt regulations relative to any person that owns or licenses personal information about a resident of the

to "any person that owns or licenses personal information about a resident of the Commonwealth." The regulations that have now been promulgated mandate the adoption of a "comprehensive information security program" by "every person that owns or licenses personal information about a resident of the Commonwealth."[80] The regulations then prescribe in guidelines what elements the security program should contain.[81] "Personal information" is defined in the regulations to include the resident's (1) social security number, (2) driver's license or other state-issued identification number, and (3) financial account or credit/debit card numbers.[82] The text of the statute and the regulations thus make clear that the protections apply to every Massachusetts resident regardless of where that resident is located. This includes those traveling abroad who are even momentarily in contact with a covered person. (Although it extends to those who "own[] or license[], receive[], store[], maintain[], process[], or otherwise [have] access to personal information",[83] the law does not apply to natural persons who are not engaged in commerce, or to businesses that merely "swipe" but don't retain credit card information, so long as the data is handled in accordance with industry standards.[84])

The plain language of the Massachusetts law therefore clearly gives it extraterritorial application—not only to persons in other states of the Union but to

---

commonwealth. Such regulations shall be designed to safeguard the personal information of residents of the commonwealth and shall be consistent with the safeguards for protection of personal information set forth in the federal regulations by which the person is regulated. The objectives of the regulations shall be to: insure the security and confidentiality of customer information in a manner fully consistent with industry standards; protect against anticipated threats or hazards to the security or integrity of such information; and protect against unauthorized access to or use of such information that may result in substantial harm or inconvenience to any consumer. The regulations shall take into account the person's size, scope and type of business, the amount of resources available to such person, the amount of stored data, and the need for security and confidentiality of both consumer and employee information.

80. *See* 201 MASS. CODE REGS. 17.03–04 (LexisNexis 2015).

81. *See* 201 MASS. CODE REGS. 17.03 (LexisNexis 2015); *see also* Commonwealth of Massachusetts, Office of Consumer Affairs and Business Regulation, 201 CMR [MASS. CODE REGS.] 17.00 Compliance Checklist, *available at* http://www.mass.gov/ocabr/docs/idtheft/compliance-checklist.pdf (providing a checklist for small business to help them comply with 201 CMR [MASS. CODE REGS.] 17.00); Commonwealth of Massachusetts, Office of Consumer Affairs and Business Regulation, Frequently Asked Questions regarding 201 CMR [MASS. CODE REGS.] 17.00, *available at* http://www.mass.gov/ocabr/docs/idtheft/201cmr17faqs.pdf (providing answers to common questions concerning 201 CMR [MASS. CODE REGS.] 17.00) [hereinafter MA OCABR FAQs].

82. *See* MASS. GEN. LAWS ch. 93H § 1(a) (2015).

83. *See* 201 MASS. CODE REGS. 17.02 (LexisNexis 2015).

84. *See* MA OCABR FAQs, *supra* note 81.

other countries.[85] Businesses expressed concern about this during the administrative hearings prior to the adoption of the regulations.[86] But the law's broad reach survived. Its requirements thus apply, for example, to a restaurant or hotel in Paris that maintains credit card information concerning a Massachusetts resident, as the regulations apply to any persons who "own or license" personal information about Massachusetts residents in connection with the provision of goods or services or in connection with employment. The requirements apply to Air France, the airline on which the resident may have traveled and whose ticket was purchased with a credit card (if that number is stored). And they apply to a small used-book store in Paris that maintains the resident's credit card number for making mail-order or Internet purchases. They would apply, indeed, to that bookstore even if the Massachusetts resident purchased a book through the Internet, without ever leaving his home in Massachusetts.

So far, Massachusetts has taken action only against domestic parties within the state. But it has won sizeable settlements, and related cases throughout the country have started to provide precedent for punishing parties who fail to protect

---

85. In *Taylor v. E. Connection Operating, Inc.*, 988 N.E.2d 408 (Mass. 2013), the Massachusetts Supreme Judicial Court summarized the Commonwealth's willingness to give extraterritorial effect to its statutes:

> [W]here no explicit limitation is placed on a statute's geographic reach, there is no presumption against its extraterritorial application in appropriate circumstances. *See* Hodas v. Morin, 814 N.E.2d 320[, 323 (Mass. 2004)] ("That the gestational carrier, her husband, and the plaintiffs all reside outside of Massachusetts does not bar the Probate and Family Court's subject matter jurisdiction under G.L. c. 215, § 6, because the equity statute poses no residency requirement"); O'Connell v. Chasdi, 511 N.E.2d 349[, 351 n.3] ([Mass.] 1987) (applying Civil Rights Act, G.L. c. 12, § 11I, to conduct occurring in South America where "the statute does not contain a provision limiting its application"). *See also* Gonyou v. Tri-Wire Eng'g Solutions, Inc., 717 F. Supp. 2d 152, 155 (D. Mass. 2010) ("Massachusetts has applied its statutory law to conduct outside its borders if sufficient contacts with the Commonwealth exist.").

86. *See, e.g.*, Testimony of Jon B. Hurst, President of the Retailers Association of Massachusetts, Before the Commonwealth of Massachusetts Office of Consumer Affairs and Business Regulation Re: 201 CMR [MASS. CODE REGS.] 17.00 (Jan. 16, 2009) (noting the difficulty of complying with separate state data protection regulations, and advocating for guidance on how to comply with 201 CMR [MASS. CODE REGS.] 17.00 and similar federal standards); Testimony of Tami Salmon, Investment Company Institute, Before the Commonwealth of Massachusetts Office of Consumer Affairs and Business Regulation Re: 201 CMR [MASS. CODE REGS.] 17.00 (Jan. 16, 2009) at 3 (reiterating concerns over extraterritorial impact of 201 CMR [MASS. CODE REGS.] 17.00). For a full write-up of the public hearing before the Office of Consumer Affairs and Business Regulation on January 16, 2009, see http://www.mass.gov/ocabr/docs/idtheft/201cmr17comments.pdf. The Office of Consumer Affairs and Business Regulation also maintains a website that provides useful information concerning the implementation of the regulations at http://www.mass.gov/ocabr/data-privacy-and-security/ (last visited Mar. 26, 2015).

their data.[87] In 2014, fewer data breaches occurred in Massachusetts than in any year since 2010, perhaps indicating that the law has had some effect—encouraging further emulation.[88]

With so extensive a reach, the obvious question is whether Massachusetts legally can do such a thing.

V. The Lawfulness of State Data Protection Initiatives

A number of different legal regimes address this question: international law, federal constitutional law, federal statutory law, and Massachusetts's own constitution. The answer is not simple. But the elements of the analysis go to the essence of what federalism means today in the United States.

A. International Legal Concerns

Let's begin with international law, if only because the Supreme Court said in 1900 that "international law is part of our law."[89] What precisely the Court meant by that phrase has been a topic of recurring controversy. One thing that is clear is that treaties, under the Supremacy Clause,[90] are the supreme law of the land—provided they are "self-executing," meaning that they operate as domestic law without implementing legislation.[91] Otherwise, implementing legislation is needed. Thus far only one treaty is in force to which the United States is a party that relates specifically to cyber-intrusions—the Convention on Cybercrime, noted earlier. The Cybercrime Convention requires parties, among other things, to establish laws against cybercrime, to ensure that their law enforcement officials have the necessary procedural authorities to investigate and prosecute cybercrime offenses effectively, and to cooperate with other parties in the fight against computer-related crime. It was

87. *See* Press Release, Office of Mass. Att'y Gen., South Shore Hospital to Pay $750,000 to Settle Data Breach Allegations (May 24, 2012), http://www.mass.gov/ago/news-and-updates/press-releases/2012/2012-05-24-south-shore-hospital-data-breach-settlement.html; *see also* Thomas Zeno & Lindsay Holmes, *Data Security Laws and Penalties*, TECHREPUBLIC, Dec. 4, 2013, http://www.techrepublic.com/blog/data-center/data-security-laws-and-penalties-pay-it-now-or-pay-out-later/ (referencing a $3.5 million settlement by a Florida company in a similar case).

88. Craig Douglas, *Here Are the Biggest Data Breaches Reported in Massachusetts in 2014*, BOS. BUS. J., Feb. 5, 2011, http://www.bizjournals.com/boston/blog/bbj_research_alert/2015/02/the-largest-data-breaches-reported-in-2014.html.

89. The Paquete Habana, 175 U.S. 677, 700 (1900) ("International law is part of our law, and must be ascertained and administered by the courts of justice of appropriate jurisdiction as often as questions of right depending upon it are duly presented for their determination.").

90. *See* U.S. CONST. art. VI, cl. 2.

91. *See* Medellín v. Texas, 552 U.S. 491, 505 (2008).

negotiated in 2001 under the auspices of the Council of Europe. President Bush signed the treaty and the Senate approved it on August 3, 2006. In his letter of transmittal, the president advised the Senate that the treaty would require no implementing legislation provided the Senate adopted the conditions that he recommended.[92] The secretary of state wrote in his letter of transmittal to the president that "federal substantive criminal law provides for broad overall coverage of the illegal conduct addressed by the Convention."[93] Significantly, for purposes of assessing the legitimate breadth of state authority, nothing in the Convention provides for, let alone requires, the preemption of legislation by sub-national units.

International legal limits on state power to engage in cybersecurity must therefore derive, not from the Convention or another treaty, but rather from customary international law. It is customary international law that imposes limits on assertions of extraterritorial jurisdiction by both nations and subnational governmental entities within them. It does so though the concept of jurisdiction. Five different bases of jurisdiction exist under which rules may be prescribed. Two of them relevant are to the Massachusetts Data Security Act: the territorial principle and the passive personality principle (also known as the passive nationality principle). Under the "subjective" dimension of the territorial principle, a nation may regulate all persons, events, conduct, and transactions within their territory, unless it has agreed to limit its jurisdiction in this regard by treaty or otherwise.[94] A nation's authority "within its own territory," Chief Justice Marshall wrote, "is necessarily exclusive and absolute. It is susceptible of no limitation not imposed by itself."[95] But a nation's territorial jurisdiction also includes an "objective" dimension, which authorizes the nation to regulate conduct beyond its territory if that conduct causes substantial effects within its territory, subject to the requirement that the assertion of jurisdiction be "reasonable" in view of the interests of other affected nations.[96] Under the passive personality principle, a nation can prescribe rules governing conduct abroad that harms its nationals. The scope of this jurisdictional basis remains uncertain and controversial, but it is significant that nations have relied upon it recently to criminalize certain acts of terrorism directed against their citizens located abroad.

92. *See* Message from the President of the United States Transmitting the Council of Europe Convention on Cybercrime, S. Treaty Doc. No. 108–11 (Nov. 17, 2003), *available at* https://www.congress.gov/108/cdoc/tdoc11/CDOC-108tdoc11.pdf.

93. *Id.* at XXII.

94. Restatement (Third) of the Foreign Relations Law of the United States § 402 (1987).

95. Schooner Exchange v. McFaddon, 11 U.S. (7 Cranch) 116, 136 (1812).

96. Restatement (Third) of the Foreign Relations Law of the United States § 403 (1987); *see, e.g.*, Hartford Fire Ins. Co. v. California, 509 U.S. 764, 815 (1993) (Scalia, J., dissenting) (citing the *Restatement*).

Citing both principles, nations in recent years have asserted broad authority to exercise extraterritorial jurisdiction—though not without nontrivial objections characterizing such jurisdictional assertions as "exorbitant."[97] Increasingly, these rules have involved Internet activities.[98] In one well-known case, a French court held in 2000 that French laws prohibiting Nazi propaganda applied to the operations of Yahoo!, which allowed Nazi paraphernalia and similar goods prohibited by those French laws to be obtained through its website.[99] Despite persisting uncertainty about the scope of effects jurisdiction, it seems doubtful that the effects of Yahoo!'s operations in France were sufficiently substantial for French jurisdiction to be reasonable under the objective territorial principle:[100] Yahoo!'s servers were not located in France, none of its personnel were present

---

97. *See, e.g.*, Simon v. Republic of Hungary, 37 F. Supp. 3d 381, 435 (D.D.C. 2014) (quoting Daimler AG v. Bauman, 134 S. Ct. 746, 761–62 (2014)).

98. The general problem with the objective territorial principle, or "effects jurisdiction," is that almost all conduct has effects abroad of a greater or lesser degree. Determining how substantial is substantial enough is no easy matter. What may be trivial to one nation may be substantial to another. The Internet exacerbates this issue tremendously because Internet "conduct" affects almost every nation in the world—provided it has an Internet connection. Clashes between competing assertions of jurisdiction over activities in cyberspace can therefore be expected to proliferate in the future.

99. *See* La Ligue Contra Le Racisme et Antisémitisme—Licra v. La Société Yahoo! Inc., Tribunal de Grande Instance [TGI] [ordinary court of original jurisdiction] Paris, Ordonnance de Référé [interim court order] (Nov. 20, 2000), *available at* https://www.legalis.net/spip.php?page=jurisprudence-decision&id_article=217. The U.S. judiciary's response to the French decision (when Yahoo! sought an injunction against its enforcement in the United States) raised more questions than it answered. *See* Yahoo!, Inc. v. Law Ligue Contre Le Racisme et l'Antisemitisme, 169 F. Supp. 2d 1181 (N.D. Cal. 2001), *rev'd* 433 F.3d 1199 (9th Cir. 2006) (en banc) (per curiam): the Ninth Circuit's decision reversed but by a per curiam opinion that failed to establish a clear basis for the resolution of comparable controversies in the future; at least three different theories for the reversal were set forth in separate opinions. For an excellent review of the issues under consideration in the *Yahoo!* controversy, see JACK GOLDSMITH & TIMOTHY WU, WHO CONTROLS THE INTERNET? ILLUSIONS OF A BORDERLESS WORLD 1-12 (2006). The *Yahoo!* saga is representative of many of the jurisdictional problems raised by the Internet. Concurrent jurisdiction by the United States and France over Yahoo!'s conduct meant that activities prohibited within France were simultaneously protected within the United States by the First Amendment. It was unclear, or so Yahoo! argued, *Yahoo!, Inc.* 169 F. Supp. at 1193, whether the technology existed to effectively prevent objectionable expression within cyberspace in France without also, inevitably, preventing it within U.S. cyberspace in violation of the Constitution. Cyberspace, after all, knows no territorial borders. A similar dispute arose when an Australian citizen sued Dow Jones for defamation based on an article uploaded in the United States that produced the allegedly defamatory effects within Australia, violating Australian defamation law, even though the same speech was protected under the U.S. First Amendment jurisprudence. *See Dow Jones and Co. v Gutnick*, (2002) HCA 56 (Austl.).

100. Yet it would also be difficult to say with confidence that France's law violated customary international law. Despite almost a century of uncertainty about the reach of the objective territorial, "effects" principle of jurisdiction, following the seminal but largely unhelpful decision in the S.S. Lotus (Fr. v. Turk.), 1927 P.C.I.J. (ser. A) No. 10 (Sept. 7), the scope of this jurisdictional

in France, and the conduct in question did not occur in France. And although customary international law has failed to clarify the limits of the passive personality principle, a case could certainly be made under an expansive construction of that principle that some French residents suffered a measure of harm because of Yahoo!'s conduct that sufficed to render French jurisdiction over Yahoo!'s sale of Nazi paraphernalia internationally lawful. But extraterritorial jurisdiction of the sort at issue in the *Yahoo!* case, which, depending on the facts, could be relevantly similar to the jurisdictional reach of the Massachusetts statute, might violate customary international law's limits on extraterritorial jurisdiction. At any rate, nations might object on this basis.

But, one might ask, so what? Why would it matter whether the Massachusetts statute violated customary international law? It's unlikely, after all, that any international tribunal or other entity with enforcement powers would, or could, effectively penalize Massachusetts for exercising arguably exorbitant jurisdiction in mandating measures aimed to enhance the data security of its residents. What difference should it make to lawmakers in other states who are considering emulating Massachusetts' approach?

B. Retaliation

First, other nations might enact retaliatory legislation—similar data security laws protecting the data of their own residents from sloppy Massachusetts businesses, or from businesses in other states of the Union with looser laws. Those states might not be thrilled to bear the brunt of foreign retaliation triggered by Massachusetts. Such "principled retaliation" is not at all uncommon in international law, which relies substantially on reciprocity dynamics. Yet foreign countries, too, can be made to feel the pain. France's anti-Holocaust laws might have been strengthened in the short-term by its rigorous enforcement actions, but in the long-term, the precedent may come back to haunt France, as other nations rely upon the tenuous jurisdictional foundation for the laws at issue in the *Yahoo!* case to justify their own extraterritorial cyber-protection laws.

C. Massachusetts Legal Concerns

Second, violation of customary international law by a state might be thought to create domestic legal problems for the state. Recall the Supreme Court's famous

---

principle remains both unclear and controversial under customary international law. *Id.* at 92; *see also* Case Concerning the Arrest Warrant of 11 Apr. 2000 (D.R.C. v. Belg.) Request for the Indication of Provisional Measures, 2000 I.C.J. 182, 233 (Dec. 8); *see generally* RESTATEMENT (THIRD) OF THE FOREIGN RELATIONS LAW OF THE UNITED STATES § 102 (1987).

observation that "international law is part of our law."[101] One theory that is widely, though not unanimously,[102] embraced by international legal scholars is that customary international law is part of federal common law. It is therefore binding domestically in the absence of federal legislation to the contrary.[103] Assuming so, the states, too, should presumably be obliged to respect principles of customary international law (unless Congress affirmatively authorizes them to violate those principles).

The federal government has the authority to place the nation in violation of customary international law.[104] But unless and until it does so, customary international law, as embodied in federal legislation or construed by the federal courts as a matter of federal common law, applies to the states.[105] It limits (as well as empowers) state legislatures, and in appropriate circumstances, serves as a source of decisional law for the state courts. There is apparently no case law squarely addressing the question of the obligation of the states to comply with customary international law. But there is good reason to suppose that customary international law binds the states under the Supremacy Clause, just as treaties do. Historically,

---

101. The Paquete Habana, 175 U.S. 677, 700 (1900).

102. See, in particular, Curtis Bradley & Jack Goldsmith, *Customary International Law as Part of Federal Common Law: A Critique of the Modern Position*, 110 HARV. L. REV. 815 (1997) (concluding that in the absence of authorization by the federal political branches, customary international law should not have the status of federal law). *But see* Harold Hongju Koh, *Is International Law Really State Law?*, 111 HARV. L. REV. 1824 (1998).

103. *See, e.g.*, RESTATEMENT (THIRD) OF THE FOREIGN RELATIONS LAW OF THE UNITED STATES §§ 111 cmt. d, 115 cmt. e (1987); Koh, *supra* note 102, at 1826; Louis Henkin, *International Law as Law in the United States*, 82 MICH. L. REV. 1555, 1560–62 (1984); *see also* Bradley & Goldsmith, *supra* note 102, at 817 n.151 (listing articles addressing the "federalization of [customary international law]").

104. As a matter of international law, "every nation-state [country] has the power—*I do not say the right*—to violate international law and obligation and to suffer the consequences." Louis Henkin, Foreign Affairs and the US Constitution 235 (2d ed. 1996) (footnotes omitted). The Constitution also, probably, does not prohibit the president from violating customary international law. *See, e.g.*, Barrera-Echavarria v. Rison, 44 F.3d 1441, 1451 (9th Cir. 1995), *superseded by statute on other grounds as stated in* Xi v. I.N.S., 298 F.3d 832, 837 (9th Cir. 2002) ("Barrera-Echavarria no longer exists . . . Instead we are bound by the Supreme Court's interpretation of the now-applicable statute, 8 U.S.C. § 1231(a)(6), which was added to the INA by the Illegal Immigration Reform and Immigrant Responsibility Act of 1996."); *see also* Garcia-Mir v. Meese, 788 F.2d 1446, 1454–55 (11th Cir. 1986). The case law on this point is controversial and scarce, and the president's authority may depend on the nature of the customary law at issue. Presumably the president could push the boundaries of jurisdictional limits but not, for example, authorize a violation of the customary international law prohibiting crimes against humanity.

105. The general *Charming Betsy* canon of construction also presumably applies, mutatis mutandis, to the states: "[a]n act of Congress ought never to be construed to violate the law of nations if any other construction remains." Murray v. Schooner Charming Betsy, 6 U.S. (2 Cranch) 64, 118 (1804).

following independence from Britain and prior to the advent of the Constitution, some courts of the "states"—technically, they were not then states of the Union but rather, in effect, independent nations under the Articles of Confederation—applied principles of customary international law as part of their own common law.[106] And there is no reason to think that, today, state common law no longer incorporates customary international law, albeit now as part of *federal* common law, insofar as it is bears on a judicial proceeding or proposed legislation.

Assuming, then, consistent with the predominant view, that after *Erie Railroad Co. v. Tompkins*,[107] customary international law has the status of federal common law, the states must heed any relevant customary international law limits, whether contained in a federal statute, elaborated in a federal common-law decision, or as independently determined. Any such limits would be potentially reviewable (and correctable) by a federal court on this view because international custom would raise a federal question.[108] But if no federal court has considered a particular issue of international custom, and assuming Congress and the president have likewise provided no guidance, state courts should themselves seek to determine the content of customary international law (as federal common law) and then apply it insofar as relevant under the Supremacy Clause.

State legislative enactments such as Massachusetts's therefore must comply with customary international law unless Congress says otherwise; the states may no more violate customary international law obligations than they may violate national treaty obligations. Even if neither Congress nor a federal court has spoken to a particular issue of customary international law, customary international law might turn out to be relevant and applicable to state legislation or the resolution of a state judicial proceeding. And of course, insofar as the states act internationally, their conduct, under international law, is attributable to the United States as a nation—every bit as much as conduct authorized or carried out by federal officials.

Yet at least for the foreseeable future, customary international law is unlikely to be an obstacle to state legislation on cybersecurity. At present, neither objective territorial jurisdiction nor passive personality jurisdiction can be said to limit cybersecurity laws, state or federal. Because of the comparative youth of the Internet and paucity of cyberlaw, as well as the substantial extent to which the Internet throws traditional jurisdictional principles for a loop, it would be difficult to argue that traditional indicia of custom—sufficiently dense, widespread, long-standing state practice and *opinio juris sive necessitatis*—have "ripened"[109]

---

106. *See* Bradley & Goldsmith, *supra* note 102, at 846.

107. 304 U.S. 64 (1938).

108. 28 U.S.C. § 1331 (2012).

109. *See* The Paquete Habana, 175 U.S. 677, 686 (1900).

into rules constraining the jurisdictional ambit of cyberlegislation of the sort enacted by Massachusetts.

In short, therefore, although customary international law on cyber-intrusions is not clear, at present no one can say authoritatively that the Massachusetts law violates it. Unless an international legal prohibition is clear, nations as well as subnational actors are deemed to have freedom to act. Under Massachusetts law, federal law, and current international law (custom as well as treaty), the data security act and its jurisdictional reach would survive legal scrutiny.

D. Federal Constitutional Concerns

But what of the United States Constitution? That the law is not clearly prohibited by international law does not mean that it is constitutionally permissible. Nothing in the Constitution prohibits the states from exercising extraterritorial jurisdiction. That jurisdiction might be exercised with respect to activities occurring within another state of the Union or within another nation. The Constitution does impose *limits* on the exercise of extraterritorial jurisdiction by states, but none of those limits prohibit state cybersecurity laws—unless and until the federal government says otherwise.

E. Due Process

The Constitution's limits are found in the Due Process Clause.[110] Due process requires reasonableness in the exercise of jurisdiction: a defendant should know whether she should expect to be hauled into court in another state.[111] This traditionally requires minimum contacts with the other state. The phrase "minimum contacts" has been taken to mean that a defendant must "purposefully avail itself of the privilege of conducting activities within the forum State, thus invoking the benefits and protections of its laws."[112] Requiring minimum contacts protects defendants against litigating in unfair and inconvenient forums and ensures that states do not exceed their jurisdictional limits.[113] But the Supreme Court noted in 1980 that the doctrine has been relaxed substantially in recent years because our

110. *See* U.S. CONST. amend. V; *id.* amend. XIV, § 1.

111. World-Wide Volkswagen Corp. v. Woodson, 444 U.S. 286, 296 (1980).

112. Hanson v. Denckla, 357 U.S. 235, 253 (1958).

113. *See World-Wide Volkswagen*, 444 U.S. at 291–92. *But see* Asahi Metal Industry Co. v. Superior Court, 480 U.S. 102, 114 (1987) (explaining that the minimum contacts standard was not met in this case because "the interests of the plaintiff and the forum in California's assertion of jurisdiction . . . [were] slight").

contemporary economy is characterized by the conduct of business transactions across both state and national borders without any physical presence.[114] Thus, the Court held four years later that the exercise of jurisdiction by California was proper in a defamation suit against a newspaper published outside the state but circulated within it.[115]

Cases concerning jurisdiction over Internet activities now arise more frequently, and due process questions loom large. In one of the more insightful judicial opinions on this issue, a federal district court suggested a useful way of categorizing websites. "When a defendant enters into contracts with residents of a foreign jurisdiction that involve the knowing and repeated transmission of computer files over the Internet," the court said, "personal jurisdiction is proper."[116] However, "[w]hen a defendant's [I]nternet use involves exchanging information with a host computer, the court must examine the level of interactivity and commercial nature of the exchange in order to determine the propriety of exercising personal jurisdiction."[117] The line between the two categories is, unfortunately, not altogether clear. Would Amazon's website, for example, involve the "knowing and repeated transmission" of computer files over the Internet, or merely "exchanging information"? Nor is it clear that it should matter that commercial responses to a web advertisement occur by telephone rather than email (or email embedded within the website). In any event, these are the sorts of considerations that would likely prove relevant in determining whether due process requirements are upheld in the enforcement of the Massachusetts law.

F. Preemption

Absent the knowing and repeated transmission of computer files, there would appear to be no insurmountable due process problem posed by the Massachusetts law. But what of the possibility of conflict with congressional enactments? If an unavoidable clash arises between state and federal law, or if federal law "occupies the field," then the state law is said to be preempted by virtue of the Supremacy Clause. Here, however, no comprehensive federal legislation on the issue of data privacy and data security currently exists, so Congress has certainly not occupied the field. Nor has it otherwise indicated an intention to preempt state law on cybersecurity. No

114. *World-Wide Volkswagen*, 444 U.S at 292–93.

115. *See* Calder v. Jones, 465 U.S. 783, 791 (1984).

116. Machulsky v. Hall, 210 F. Supp. 2d 531, 539 (D.N.J. 2002).

117. *Id.*

federal preemption issue arises.[118] Pending federal legislation may change this: the Massachusetts Assistant Attorney General warned in March 2015 that the House cybersecurity bill would preempt state action and leave Massachusetts citizens less protected than they would have been under that state's more stringent laws.[119]

G. The Dormant Foreign Affairs Power

That Congress has not preempted the states from acting in this realm does not, however, mean that the Constitution itself is also silent. In a handful of cases, as noted in Chapter 4, the Supreme Court has held that dormant foreign-affairs preemption precludes state conduct in an area even if the federal government has said nothing. Pursuant to this doctrine, the Court has struck down state statutes that intrude into that sphere of foreign affairs, which the Constitution is said to entrust exclusively to the president and Congress.[120] The indeterminate scope of the dormant foreign-affairs doctrine makes it difficult to apply, and for the reasons noted earlier, we doubt that it's a desirable (or intelligible) doctrine. But for present purposes, it suffices to note that it has been invoked rarely by the Supreme Court and only with respect to state statutes that represented individual, stand-alone initiatives rather than laws enacted by multiple states directed at vindicating common policy interests.[121]

H. The Dormant Foreign Commerce Clause

The constitutional gauntlet does not end here. The Court has also invalidated state laws under the so-called "dormant foreign commerce clause." The Constitution provides that the "Congress shall have Power . . . To regulate commerce with foreign Nations, and among the several States, and with the Indian tribes. . . ."[122] As explored in Chapter 5, the courts have held that this provision not only grants "positive" power to Congress but also imposes "negative" limits upon the states.[123]

118. *See generally* STEVENS, *supra* note 64 (analyzing extant federal information security and data breach law, and noting the absence of comprehensive federal legislation).

119. Shaun Zinck, *Massachusetts AG Slams House Data Breach Bill*, LEGALNEWSLINE.COM, Mar. 24, 2015, http://legalnewsline.com/news/federal-government/255531-mass-ag-slams-house-data-breach-bill.

120. *See* Am. Ins. Ass'n v. Garamendi, 539 U.S. 396, 428 (2003); Zschernig v. Miller, 389 U.S. 429, 432 (1968); see generally Chapter 4.

121. *See, e.g., Zschernig*, 389 U.S. at 432.

122. U.S. CONST. art. I, § 8, cl. 3.

123. *See* Japan Line, Ltd. v. County of Los Angeles, 441 U.S. 434, 449 (1979) ("The need for federal uniformity is . . . paramount in ascertaining the *negative* implications of Congress' power to 'regulate Commerce with foreign Nations' under the Commerce Clause." (emphasis added)).

Obviously the Foreign Commerce Clause does not prohibit every state law that has any effect on foreign commerce. But under Supreme Court jurisprudence, the states may not act simply because Congress has been silent on a particular issue of foreign commerce. Again, leaving aside reservations expressed earlier about current doctrine, under current law, a state statute such as Massachusetts's must pass two general hurdles: first, it must not discriminate against foreign commerce, and second, it must not impede the federal government's ability to speak with one voice in foreign affairs. Clearly the first hurdle is overcome. The statute treats foreign commerce no differently than it treats Massachusetts's own commerce: Business concerns within Massachusetts and those located abroad are equally burdened.

The conclusion is less clear with respect to the second hurdle, however. It's at least arguable that Congress, in choosing not to require businesses to adopt written security programs, considers it important that the United States speak with one voice. Meeting different program requirements from multiple states could discourage foreign businesses from dealing with Americans, which could easily become too burdensome. Multiple state voices mean multiple compliance requirements, which ultimately impede rather than promote commerce by making it too cumbersome for businesses to deal with persons protected by disparate regulatory schemes. Further, as discussed earlier, the danger of retaliation looms large; one reason for the "one voice" doctrine, the Supreme Court has suggested, is curbing the risk of retaliation against the United States for actions taken by a state. On the other hand, Congress hasn't spoken with *any* voice on the data protection question, let alone one voice, and its silence could be taken as approval of multifarious state regulatory schemes. After all, Congress could easily preempt those schemes if it wished to do so. Absent express or implied preemption,[124] however, there is no reason to assume that Congress would disapprove of state cybersecurity measures. To the contrary, there is every reason to believe those measures serve the national interest.

I. The Market Participant Doctrine

To whatever extent dormant foreign-commerce does preemption pose a problem for the states, states could overcome that hurdle by, as discussed below, moving more squarely into the business of cyber-protection—that is, by becoming what the Supreme Court has called "market participants."[125] The market-participant doctrine, so-called, has its roots in the actual words of the Commerce Clause,

124. *See, e.g.*, Crosby v. Nat'l Foreign Trade Council, 530 U.S. 363, 363 (2000).

125. *See, e.g.*, N. Carolina State Bd. of Dental Exam'rs. v. F.T.C., 135 S. Ct. 1101, 1110 (2015); Reeves, Inc. v. Stake, 447 U.S. 429, 436 (1980) (distinguishing between states as market-participants and as market-regulators).

which, again, empowers Congress "to regulate Commerce with foreign Nations, and among the several States . . . ." Under the market-participant doctrine, a state is not subject to the constraints of the Commerce Clause when it acts as a supplier or producer of goods or services rather than as a regulator. Thus far, the Court has applied the market-participant doctrine only to domestic, not foreign, commerce.[126] But it has strongly suggested that the market-participant exception applies equally in the context of foreign commerce.[127] That makes sense. In a globalized economy, interstate and foreign commerce are all but inseparable. The market-participant exception would be for naught if the two were evaluated under substantially different constitutional criteria. Lower federal courts have seemed to accept this view.[128]

All in all, then, although the matter is not free from doubt, it cannot be said that any clear legal prohibition or restriction from any relevant body of law clearly prevents a state from enacting a statute such as Massachusetts's data security law.

The apparently unobstructed path through this legal labyrinth has thus made it possible for a growing number of states to mitigate the effects of cyber-intrusions by requiring businesses to adopt data security programs and to notify customers when their personal information is accessed. Mitigation of this sort will also have a deterrent effect, as lower rewards for cyber-intruders diminish the intruders' incentives. Further, state legislation in this area may well be illustrative of one of the most frequently cited virtues of federalism: the ability of the states to serve as laboratories. State laws on cybersecurity provide examples that will inevitably be more or less effective, ideally yielding empirical data on the basis of which the federal government can craft effective national laws. At any rate, state

126. *See, e.g.*, South-Central Timber Dev., Inc. v. Wunnicke, 467 U.S. 82, 93 (1984); Hughes v. Alexandria Scrap Corp., 426 U.S. 794, 810 (1976). The Court declined to address the issue of the market-participant exception to the Foreign Commerce Clause in *Crosby v. National Foreign Trade Council*, instead relying on the Supremacy Clause to invalidate the state law in question. *See* 530 U.S. at 374.

127. *See* Wardair Canada Inc. v. Fla. Dept. of Revenue, 477 U.S. 1, 8 (1986) ("As in the context of cases alleging violations of the dormant Interstate Commerce Clause, the concern in these Foreign Commerce Clause cases is not with an actual conflict between state and federal law, but rather with the policy of uniformity, embodied in the Commerce Clause, which presumptively prevails when the Federal Government has remained silent."); *see also* Barclays Bank PLC v. Franchise Tax Bd., 512 U.S. 298, 311 (1994) ("In 'the unique context of foreign commerce,' a State's power is further constrained because of 'the special need for federal uniformity.' ") (citing *Wardair*, 477 U.S. at 8).

128. *See* Trojan Tech., Inc. v. Pennsylvania, 916 F.2d 903, 912 (3d Cir. 1990); K.S.B. Tech. Sales Corp. v. N. Jersey Dist. Water Supply Comm'n, 381 A.2d 774, 784–89 (N.J. 1977). If "states and localities ought to have greater power when acting in their proprietary capacity, then the market-participant doctrine might provide an analytic framework for introducing that principle into 'dormant foreign affairs clauses' jurisprudence." Lori A. Martin, Comment, *The Legality of Nuclear Free Zones*, 55 U. CHI. L. REV. 965, 1002 (1988).

legislation represents an important first step in filling a gaping hole in federal law. What more might the states do? Might it be possible to leverage their unique lawmaking powers to make money as cyber-defenders?

VI. An Opening for State Entrepreneurship?

The answer may be yes. A variety of possibilities present themselves. Begin with one of the most prevalent forms of cyber-intrusion—botnet attacks. Botnets are made up of vast numbers of compromised computers that have been "infected" with malicious code. Once they are infected, the botnet computers can be remotely controlled through commands from the "botmaster" to operate in concert to disrupt or block Internet traffic for targeted victims, to harvest information, or to distribute spam, viruses, or other malicious code.[129] Because of their versatility, botnets have been described as the "Swiss Army knives of the underground economy."[130] The attacks described above against Estonia and MasterCard, Visa, and PayPal were all botnet attacks. WikiLeaks itself has been the target of botnet attacks. Companies survive these attacks in part by successfully sequestering the malicious traffic and transferring it into "sinkholes,"[131] "honeypots,"[132] and "darknets."[133] Such techniques allow researchers to redirect the malicious traffic that comes from each client and place it in a "research box," where it can be analyzed and decoded.[134] Unfortunately, all this takes place after the fact; the sequestration capacity, in other words, is added, ad hoc, on the fly, in response to the attacks rather than beforehand, in anticipation of potential vulnerability. Affected companies must also collaborate with Internet service providers (ISPs) in order to

---

129. *See* CLAY WILSON, CONG. RESEARCH SERV., RL32114, BOTNETS, CYBERCRIME AND CYBERTERRORISM: VULNERABILITIES AND POLICY ISSUES FOR CONGRESS 5 (2008), *available at* https://www.fas.org/sgp/crs/terror/RL32114.pdf.

130. *Id.*

131. *See generally* David Sancho & Rainer Link, *Sinkholing Botnets* (Trend Micro, Research Paper, 2011), *available at* http://www.trendmicro.co.uk/media/misc/sinkholing-botnets-technical-paper-en.pdf (discussing the technique of "sinkholing" with regard to the "ZeuS" botnet from 2011).

132. *See generally* Cliff Zou & Ryan Cunningham, *Honeypot-Aware Advanced Botnet Construction and Maintenance*, 2006 Procedeeings of the International Conference on Dependable Systems and Networks 199, *available at* http://www.cs.ucf.edu/~czou/research/honeypot-DSN06.pdf (reviewing the use of honeypots for sequestering botnets).

133. *See generally* Michael Smith, *Darknets: Security's Bright Future*, INFO. SYS. SEC. (2007), *available at* http://www.infosectoday.com/Articles/Darknets.htm (addressing the use of darknets to increase computer security intelligence).

134. *See* Sancho & Link, *supra* note 131, at 1.

sequester the traffic. In some circumstances ISPs may be cooperative, while in others, they may not be as forthcoming.[135]

Here, then, is one place where the states might play a more forceful and potentially profitable role, by instituting, for example, a fee-for-service arrangement that could provide a number of benefits for voluntary subscribers. Subscribers could include almost anyone, including in-state and out-of-state businesses, other states, and potentially foreign businesses, and even foreign governments. "Vaccine" programs could be made available to subscribers (and computer "hygiene" made a condition of membership). An "early warning system" could be put in place to detect incipient botnet attacks on subscribers. Subscribers' servers and computers could be disinfected of "zombie" malware. Unwitting owners of infected computers joining in the attack could be identified and notified. ISPs could be mandatorily directed by the state to block or shut down compromised computers involved in a botnet attack. State forensic experts could work with private security firms to attempt to determine the object of the intrusion as well as the identity of the botmasters. States could even conduct "hack backs" against targets once identified, using software of their own design to destroy malicious networks.[136] Cooperative arrangements to protect subscribers could be entered into with other stakeholders. Knowing participants in a botnet, when identified, could be prosecuted and, if necessary, extradited. And by engaging in these entrepreneurial efforts the states should qualify constitutionally as market-participants, potentially exempting themselves from otherwise applicable limitations flowing from the dormant Foreign Commerce Clause, discussed above.

Botnets pose one form of cyberthreat; others would require different protective measures. Some will be amenable to state-sponsored remedies; others will not. The point is that a space exists for imaginative, entrepreneurial thinking about potentially profitable cyber-defense by the states. States need not resign themselves to being eighteenth-century relics in an age of globalized commerce. Opportunities are available for creative rejuvenation. Using traditional police and regulatory powers, states can leverage their assets to succeed where the federal government and the international community have not. The result

135. *See id.* at 6.

136. *See* Jeremy Kirk, *Irked by Cyberspying, Georgia Outs Russia-Based Hacker—with Photos*, IT WORLD, Oct. 30, 2012, http://www.itworld.com/308638/irked-cyberspying-georgia-outs-russia-based-hacker-photos (using software to identify a hacker through his own webcam); *see also* Donna Leinwand Leger & Kevin Johnson, *Federal Agents Knock Down Zeus Botnet, CryptoLocker*, USA TODAY, June 2, 2014, http://www.usatoday.com/story/news/nation/2014/06/02/global-cyber-fraud/9863977/ (describing a combined effort by federal law enforcement and the private sector to destroy a Russian botnet). For a state to avoid penalties under the Computer Fraud and Abuse Act of 1986, however, it would probably have to clear its action with federal authorities.

could be a "race to the top" as states compete with one another to provide top-notch cybersecurity to those willing to pay for it. This strategy has already played itself out within NATO. By capitalizing on its cyber expertise, the tiny nation of Estonia was able to mobilize international funding to create the Cooperative Cyber Defence Centre of Excellence, a NATO-accredited organization, in Talinn in 2008.[137] The Centre now provides NATO with a wide range of products and services related to cybersecurity, while also serving as an intellectual hub for confronting cyber threats worldwide.

Cyber-intrusions have caused and will continue to cause widespread harm. Their danger should not be underestimated. But with innovative thinking on the part of local policymakers, the states can, as indeed they already have, contribute substantially to mitigating the effect of those intrusions. States have led the way with data security laws. There is no reason to stop there. With the right combination of farsighted policymaking and technological prowess, the states might prove, even in a globalized twenty-first century, to be the effective dual sovereigns that the Framers considered essential to preserving and enhancing the security and well-being of the American people.

---

137. *Centre is the first International Military Organization hosted by Estonia*, COOP. CYBER DEF. CTR. OF EXCELLENCE, Oct. 28, 2008, https://ccdcoe.org/centre-first-international-military-organization-hosted-estonia.html

11

Conclusion

OUR AIM IN this book has been to describe what states and cities in fact do in the realm of foreign affairs, to explain the basic principles of the Constitution that authorize or limit those activities, to assess how well those principles reflect and conform to actual practice, and finally, to suggest how, if at all, those principles might usefully be modified. A summary follows.

I. Summary

The story of American federalism began, as outlined in Chapter 1, even before the adoption of America's first constitution, the Articles of Confederation. It began, of course, with the establishment of the thirteen colonies. Upon independence, each of these colonies became an independent, sovereign nation. When they later joined together in a single nation, they had existed as autonomous entities for many years. Citizen loyalty to them ran high—sometimes higher than the loyalty directed to the federal government. It would have been all but unthinkable, given suspicions about centralized authority, that these thirteen nations could have, in effect, agreed to abolish themselves upon forging a new nation. It is history more than logic, therefore, that explains the origins of American federalism. The policy justifications for states must be understood more as after-the-fact rationales than as motivating reasons that actually shaped the United States government's federal structure.

The Articles of Confederation were a product of that history. The Articles established a Union that was in many respects comparable to today's European Union. The states retained sovereignty. Thus they retained exclusive authority over taxation and full power to regulate commerce within their borders. No national courts were established. The federal government was given no power to enforce the Articles. Amendments to the Articles required unanimous approval by the states. As time went on, the Articles came to be regarded as aspirational guidelines rather than binding law. In this juridical vacuum, the states reigned supreme. Their broad powers were abused, so extensively, in fact, that it became clear that—unless the whole, grand experiment were to collapse—an entirely new constitutional structure was required.

Hence Philadelphia. The Framers addressed the paramount weakness of the Articles in the new Constitution's Supremacy Clause, making clear that the laws of the federal government are the supreme law of the land and trump any conflicting state law. Contrary to popular belief, however, the Constitution that emerged from Philadelphia did not confer all foreign affairs powers on the federal government (let alone on the president). The rights of states were preserved in the new Tenth Amendment, which said simply that the "powers not delegated to the United States by the Constitution, nor prohibited by it to the States, are reserved to the States respectively, or to the people."[1] Nothing decreed that those powers excluded all foreign affairs powers. What those powers might *include*, however, was not spelled out, and for 230 years the state and federal governments have struggled to define their concrete meaning.

One method of defining that meaning has been to examine the classic justifications for federalism. There are commonly thought to be three chief benefits to a federal system. First, states safeguard freedom by providing a check on potential federal autocracy. Second, efficiency is maximized by managing governmental programs at as low a level as possible. And third, the states provide laboratories for innovation and experimentation.

On examination, it turns out, as suggested in Chapter 1, that the first two values bear little relevance to foreign affairs. In fact, they undercut claims to national foreign-affairs exclusivity. State power to act internationally poses no self-evident restraint on the exercise of arbitrary or corrupted federal power. Whatever the benefits in traditional domestic matters, there is little reason to believe that geographic proximity of the government to the governed promotes efficiency in most realms of foreign relations. The third justification cuts both ways. Although it is true that experimentation generates innovation, experimentation can also produce Frankensteins. In the federalism context this can translate into parochialism and the proverbial race-to-the-bottom, an evil most effectively remedied not by diversity but by uniformity in approach. For this and other reasons, in well-defined circumstances it makes sense that the United States speak with "one voice"—a federal voice—in its foreign affairs. On the other hand, there is little

1. U.S. CONST. amend. X.

reason to insist that the United States *always* speak with one voice internationally. The United States today consists of different people of different ethnicities, different religions, and different politics, much more than in Madison's time. Foreign nations know that, and foreign policy—as well as domestic democratic processes—often are strengthened, not weakened, by permitting local participation in addressing foreign affairs issues. The nation is no longer the fragile, fledgling country that it was in the Framers' time, an era in which a single misstep could imperil the entire nation. Sometimes it makes sense to "let a thousand flowers bloom." Rather than insisting upon rigid federal exclusivity, therefore, it makes more sense for the courts to ask whether effective federal control is feasible, and, except in extraordinary circumstances, to permit the states to act unless Congress has clearly prohibited them from doing so. It is reasonable, in short, to begin by looking not to theory but to experience—by examining what, in the real world, states and cities have actually been doing.

Chapter 2 described what they are actually doing in some detail. As it shows, states and cities have emerged as major participants in U.S. foreign affairs. They have entered into compacts and agreements with foreign countries; adopted international standards on matters such as climate change, even when the federal government has declined to do so; established offices in foreign countries; sent representatives to foreign countries; offered economic incentives to attract businesses from those countries; barred purchases from those countries with "Buy American" statutes; established countless "sister-city" relationships with foreign cities; adopted statements of policy, often based on local referenda, about international issues; given teeth to some of those policies with, for example, economic sanctions and trade bans; enacted laws and adopted police practices to discourage illegal immigration; acted to protect their citizens' data and privacy on the Internet; and contributed to the effort to keep the country safe from national security threats.

At least three factors account for much of this new and reinvigorated "local internationalism." First, globalization: the same globalizing forces that perforate state and national boundaries, perhaps paradoxically, lead state and local officials to venture into an international arena that, until comparatively recently, they regarded as forbidden territory. Second, federal inaction or inertia: the federal government has been unable or unwilling to address many of the most serious problems caused by globalization, including, for example, those relating to immigration and cyber-intrusions (see Chapters 9 and 10). Third, state capacity: because of the size of their populations and economies relative to many foreign countries, states have an enormous stake in how those countries differentiate among them, and conversely, an ability to differentiate among those countries on issues such as the latter's human rights practices. Together, these drivers are fundamentally altering the nation's political and constitutional landscape, and their net effect is to nudge the nation back to federalism's early days—an era in which the states played a much larger role internationally.

Theory is not irrelevant, however, and in Chapter 3 we moved from practice to theory, laying out the central principles that structure this study. Chief among them are a rejection of the idea of any comprehensive "field" theory of constitutional interpretation, and acceptance of Chief Justice Marshall's insight that any constitution intended to endure for and adapt to the ages must be construed flexibly, with reference to what the United States has actually become. There are good reasons in a democracy to constrain judicial power, we suggest, but the fact that judges are unelected is not one of them. More powerful than objections relating to majoritarian legitimacy is the objection deriving from the indeterminacy of the decisional rules on which judges might rely, and from the related objection that the power to resolve such disputes is allocated, constitutionally, to some other decision-maker. It is neither provocative nor original to suggest, as we do, that judges ought to interpret and apply constitutional standards, not create them.

It is unfortunate, therefore, that the Supreme Court seems to have resurrected, without any textual basis, a doctrine that circumscribes the states' role. The so-called "dormant foreign-affairs doctrine" has it that even in the face of congressional and executive silence, and even if nothing in the constitutional text limits its action, a state is nonetheless precluded from acting in certain international matters in which it has at least some demonstrable interest. As Chapter 4 described, the Court in 1968 offered scant guidance as to when the doctrine applies. Local courts and officials were left to distinguish incidental effects on federal foreign policy from non-incidental effects, indirect effects from the direct effects, proper from improper legislative motives, routine review of foreign law from review that implies or expresses judgment on foreign laws or nations, and traditional from nontraditional exercises of state power. Few could figure it out, and seldom was it applied. Little wonder that many legal scholars came to see the doctrine as a dead letter—until 2003. In that year the dormant foreign-affairs doctrine was revived, but with virtually no additional warning to the states as to when the judicial ax might next fall.

We lament this state of the law. Three possible standards are available to address this confusion: (1) a rule of per se federal exclusivity, (2) some kind of balancing test that considers the effects of state activity on federal foreign-affairs policy, perhaps providing greater leeway for such state conduct in legal realms of traditional state competence, and (3) the hands-off, pre-1968 approach—judicial deference to the states absent affirmative preemption, with a possible exception for exigent circumstances. Each approach has potential advantages and disadvantages; the most sensible approach, however, is the third—judicial deference to the states in the absence of affirmative federal preemption under accepted doctrine or genuine exigency. Such exigencies, as we explained in Chapter 5, can be resolved more easily, predictably, and defensibly under the dormant Foreign Commerce Clause. Resolving cases under it holds greater promise of keeping the courts in their proper role. If the federal government is silent, there is no constitutional reason to permit courts to stop states from experimenting with solutions to problems that their electorates want addressed.

The Foreign Commerce Clause, discussed in Chapter 5, empowers Congress to regulate commerce with foreign nations. Until 1979, the Court applied the same doctrinal standards to evaluate foreign commerce that it had applied for nearly two centuries in evaluating domestic commerce. In 1979, relying in part on a supposed imperative that the nation "speak with one voice" in international trade and relations, the Court imposed a new, tighter standard on foreign commerce, exposing potentially vast stretches of state regulation to review, legal uncertainty, and possible invalidation. We suggest that this new one-voice theory is misguided. First, the Constitution does not presuppose national uniformity in foreign policy; to the contrary, it recognizes the inevitability of fractiousness. Second, the federal government is possessed of neither the desire nor the capacity to exercise plenary foreign affairs powers. Third, although the presumptively supreme "one voice" invoked is typically that of the executive, Congress, not the executive, is textually empowered to regulate foreign commerce. Fourth, judges' capacity to make the necessary findings of fact in identifying federal foreign policy is limited. Fifth, the risk of retaliation against the nation as a whole for actions undertaken by a single state is frequently overstated. Finally, judicial review of state regulation of foreign commerce should be less, not more restrictive, than review of interstate commerce with respect to its discriminatory effects. The Interstate Commerce Clause is aimed at preventing states from trying to get a leg up on other states by isolating themselves economically, but nothing in the Constitution prohibits states from attempting to gain an economic advantage over foreign countries or businesses; equal treatment of international trade historically has been a subject of negotiation and a matter regulated by agreement or federal statutory law, which is where it should remain.

Rethinking the reach of the dormant Foreign Commerce Clause, we point out in Chapter 5, must begin with the realization that it and the dormant foreign-affairs doctrine (discussed in Chapter 4) are virtually coextensive, that is, almost any factual scenario that could be seen as presenting a problem under one could also be seen as presenting a problem under the other. If the arguments we have made in Chapter 4 against a revitalized dormant foreign-affairs doctrine are correct, it would make little sense to breathe new life into the dormant Foreign Commerce Clause. Rather, a high presumption of validity ought to apply to state regulation reviewed under the clause, with the recognition that judicial intervention is always possible in extraordinary, unforeseeable cases. Grounding judicial review in the dormant Foreign Commerce Clause (rather than the dormant foreign-affairs doctrine) will not only provide a textual basis for otherwise untethered judicial intervention; it will also subject judicial judgment to revision or reversal by Congress—which is, after all, accorded express power over foreign commerce by the text of the Constitution.

Chapter 6 examined the treaty power as it relates to the states. It considered, specifically, a controversy that remained largely a matter of academic speculation for many years. But that has recently changed. The controversy centers on the power of the federal government to make a treaty that limits state authority in situations where a federal statute could not constitutionally do so. For decades it was thought that, acting under powers conferred upon it by the Commerce Clause, Congress could regulate virtually any state activity. In the 1980s, however, the Supreme Court initiated a series of cases in which it found that congressional power under the Commerce Clause was in fact subject to distinct limits. (The Tenth Amendment lay at the obverse side of these cases, because Commerce Clause limits on congressional power generally correspond closely to Tenth Amendment guarantees of state power.) These cases raised anew the dilemma of whether there exists a certain category of treaties—those arguably trenching upon powers that are constitutionally reserved to the states—that the federal government is effectively precluded from concluding. If such a category does exist, a number of modern treaties could become binding within the United States only through negotiation by foreign nations with the fifty states, one at a time. If it does not exist, however, the states might, at least hypothetically, be subject to federal authority that could be validly exercised through the treaty power but not by statute, raising the possibility that constitutional limits could be circumvented through contrivance. The dilemma had been resolved by a famous 1920 case in which the Court opted for the second horn of the dilemma, holding that treaties are not subject to the same Tenth Amendment hurdle faced by statutes.

The Supreme Court purported recently to sidestep the question whether it continued to stand behind that holding.[2] It did so by abandoning the assumption that the Tenth Amendment validity of implementing legislation depends upon the Tenth Amendment validity of the underlying treaty—and then by applying to the implementing legislation at issue a canon of constitutional avoidance based on what the Court characterized as (mandatory) federalism limits.[3] It thus suggested

---

2. *See* Bond v. United States, 134 S. Ct. 2077 (2014).

3. *Id.* at 2088-90.

that the hot-potato issue could be avoided by deciding the question on exclusively non-constitutional grounds of statutory interpretation. It could do so, the Court claimed, because of a "background principle" of statutory construction.[4] In particular, it insisted that "the statute—unlike the [treaty]—must be read consistent with principles of federalism inherent in our constitutional structure."[5] The common understanding of the Court's recent decision on this issue is that it therefore left the 1920 precedent essentially undisturbed.

We suggested in Chapter 6 that this reading is mistaken. The Court's new unwillingness to view the Tenth Amendment validity of the implementing legislation as dependent upon the Tenth Amendment validity of the treaty is inconsistent with the settled 1920 precedent. Further, the background principle that the Court recently proceeded to apply in fact assumes that that earlier precedent is not controlling—that the constitutional structure exists as it did before 1920. This result, we suggest, is inconsistent with recent, important Supreme Court case law and represents a lamentable step backward for the United States that will disable it from meeting important international obligations.

In Chapter 7 we moved to issues raised by federal common law, or judge-made law, specifically that which includes norms of customary international law. Federal common law consists of rules made by federal judges who effectively act in the stead of Congress, subject to legislative override. This represents an exception to the understanding that judges interpret rather than make law. The exception exists for certain practical reasons described in Chapter 7, and at any rate, Congress is aware of the practice and has the opportunity at any time to supplant judge-made rules with its own; its failure to do so generally implies consent. The Court long ago curbed the power of federal judges to make federal general common law. But pockets of federal specialized common law remain.

One of those pockets consists of clearly defined and widely accepted rules of customary international law. Customary international law results from a general and consistent practice of nations followed by them from a sense of legal obligation. English common law, adopted by the American colonies before independence, was regarded as including the "law of nations" (as international law was then called). When the colonies became independent nations, as described in Chapter 1, they continued to apply the same substantive principles of the law of nations as part of their own common law. That international law is part of our law was basically taken as so obvious at the time of the Philadelphia Convention that it was thought to be unnecessary to be spelled out in the Supremacy Clause,

---

4. *Id.* at 2088.

5. *Id.*

just as the Court on various occasions over the years has had no hesitation in reaffirming that proposition. Because the clause does make federal common law binding on the states, it effectively subjects them to customary international law. But, again, Congress can always in effect exempt the states from the operation of customary international law simply by permitting them to act in a manner contrary to its precepts.

Chapter 8 deals with the constitutional prohibition concerning states' agreements. The states are flatly forbidden from entering into "any Treaty, Alliance, or Confederation."[6] They may, however, with the approval of Congress, "enter into any Agreement or Compact with another State, or with a foreign Power."[7] The latter provision is referred to as the Compact Clause. At least six principles governing the Compact Clause have been widely accepted. First, Congress can consent to a compact either before or after it has been made. Second, Congress can consent explicitly or implicitly. Third, a state compact that receives Congress's consent thereby acquires the status of federal law—and consequently, presumably preempts state law to the contrary, although the case law on this issue is scarce to nonexistent. Fourth, by enacting a statute, Congress can preempt certain compacts in advance, obviating any need to consider consent later; in effect, the statute constitutes anticipatory refusal. Fifth, Congress can consent to a particular compact, but it can also, if it wishes, consent to a whole category of compacts on the same issue, such that states may later proceed without further legal hesitation. Sixth, Congress can withdraw its consent, explicitly or, under the last-in-time doctrine, implicitly—although if the compact is with a "foreign Power," it presumably remains binding upon the United States as a nation under international law, which could render the nation in violation of international obligations.

Although many other matters concerning these constitutional provisions remain clouded, historical practice plays a prominent role in providing guidance to state policymakers. Perhaps the most prominent lessons to be gleaned from history are that states have entered into a considerable number of agreements with foreign nations without securing congressional approval, and neither Congress (with one exception) nor the Supreme Court has ever disapproved of them. State policymakers looking for judicial guidance have thus focused on the case law governing interstate compacts, which some consider applicable by analogy. While that case law suggests that Congress may consent implicitly, its relevance to so-called foreign-state compacts is uncertain, though most jurists

6. U.S. Const. art. I, § 10, cl. 1.

7. *Id.* art. I, § 10, cl. 3.

have assumed that it controls. The default rule has thus been reversed, having begun with the presumption that agreements are invalid unless approved, and having ended up, today, with the presumption that they're valid unless Congress disapproves.

In Chapter 9 we looked at federal directives that prohibit the states from acting. Unlike circumstances of federal silence, in which any constitutional command is at best implicit, when the federal government has acted, an explicit constitutional command exists. That command, of course, is the Supremacy Clause. The clause makes the Constitution, treaties, and federal laws supreme over state law of any sort: valid federal measures trump state constitutional provisions, statutes, common law rules, ordinances, and any other form of state or local law. This assumes, of course, the constitutional *validity* of the federal measure; obviously, an unconstitutional federal measure trumps nothing. Disputes involving claims of federal disapproval of state conduct thus often raise threshold questions about the constitutionality of the federal measure at issue. Chapter 9 touched upon the uncertainty concerning federal power in a variety of respects, but for purposes of discussion largely assumed the validity of the federal measure in question. It then described the operation of different aspects of the doctrine of preemption, the principle that a federal law precludes and displaces any conflicting state law. Applicable federal law, we pointed out, can take the form of a treaty, statute, or executive agreement, with different issues surrounding the preemptive power of each.

Finally, in Chapter 10, we looked at how all this applies to a contemporary, nerve-center security and privacy problem—cyber-intrusions. As an illustrative case study, we examined state laws that protect their citizens' computer data from hackers. A number of states have enacted laws requiring companies to implement security procedures to protect personal information from unauthorized access, destruction, use, modification, or disclosure. These statutes, like the earlier, more basic data privacy and data breach notification laws, also apply to entities headquartered outside the state in question—including in foreign countries. This extraterritorial application, considered in the light of the applicable federal regulatory regime, raises many of the questions that have been discussed in this book. We concluded Chapter 10 by reflecting on how the states might play an even more active, indeed entrepreneurial role, in combatting cyber threats. States have led the way with data security laws, and, we suggested, there is no reason for them to stop there. With the right combination of farsighted policymaking and technological prowess, the states might develop important cyber-defense capabilities and prove, even in a globalized twenty-first century, to be the effective dual sovereigns that the Framers considered essential to preserving and enhancing the security and well-being of the American people.

II. *Foreign Affairs Federalism in Other Nations*

In concluding, a word is in order on what the reader may by this point believe to be an important topic that we have neglected—the foreign affairs practices of other federal countries.

Our focus has been almost exclusively on the United States and its constitutional system. This is not a work, and this conclusion is not a chapter, on comparative constitutional law, as useful as that might well be. Sound comparativism requires far more than merely an acontextual lining-up of analogous rules and cases. Comparative law scholarship, when well done, involves a multifaceted penetration of the legal culture of a nation, a thoroughgoing excursion into not only its formal legal rules and institutions but also into the history, tradition, politics, religion, and economics that have shaped those rules and institutions.[8] Even then it's often problematic to extrapolate from seemingly causative social data to concrete legalist results—to try to draw reliable inferences about what caused a given nation's law to take the shape that it does, to explain why one nation's approach to a particular issue is different from another's, and to assess why a particular rule works or doesn't work in one country as opposed to another. Such an inquiry, although no doubt fascinating, lies far beyond the bounds of this study.

It is appropriate, nonetheless, to survey briefly how a few other federal nations deal with a few of the same questions of foreign affairs federalism—for a simple reason. As Justice Breyer explained in his dissent in *Printz v. United States*,[9] other nations' experiences may "cast an empirical light on the consequences of different solutions to a common legal problem."[10] The purpose of reviewing another nation's experience is not to suggest that its constitution should affect the interpretation of our own. "[W]e are interpreting our own Constitution," Justice Breyer emphasized, "not those of other nations . . . ."[11] The point is simply that it is useful to know how different solutions to the same problem have actually worked in practice. The results of such an inquiry are empirical, not normative; they may—contingent on a host of factors—provide practical guidance.

Whether "the same problem" has in fact arisen in different countries is of course a vexing question. At one level, problems that different nations confront

---

8. For a fine comparativist study, see A GLOBAL DIALOGUE ON FEDERALISM: FOREIGN RELATIONS IN FEDERAL COUNTRIES (Hans Michelmann ed., 2009).

9. 521 U.S. 898 (1997).

10. *Id.* at 977 (Breyer, J., dissenting).

11. *Id.*

are never the same because nations' cultures and histories always differ. In this sense Justice Scalia, writing for the *Printz* majority, was correct: "The fact is that our federalism is not Europe's."[12] Switzerland's population, for example, is less than 2 percent the size of that of the United States. In Switzerland, the causes of internal conflict through the nineteenth century were much more religious than cultural.[13] Germany's twentieth-century history could hardly be more different than that of the United States. The United States occupied West Germany after World War II and continues today to station troops within German territory. Justice Breyer's rejoinder to Justice Scalia thus seems a bit of an understatement: "[T]here may be relevant political and structural differences between their systems and our own."[14] Comparisons and contrasts must be made with care, with considerable skepticism directed at claims that "what works for them can work for us." Why something works for one country is often complex, and submerged trade-offs in that country—trade-offs that the United States or another nation may be unwilling to make—may account for the success of a constitutional structure, law, or policy in another nation. Those trade-offs, in turn, may be possible only because its sociopolitical environment differs substantially from that of the United States. Like any other potential evidence, therefore, comparative data should be taken for what it's worth—no more, no less—in weighing, empirically, the effectiveness of one valid solution against another.

For what it's worth, we thus lay out below how foreign affairs powers are constitutionally allocated as between the federal government and local authorities in four different nations—Switzerland, Germany, Canada, and India. We select these four countries from among the two dozen federal nations[15] because they are prominent, well-established democracies whose political values are roughly similar to those of the United States, and because they seem reasonably representative of other federal systems in their treatment of foreign affairs questions. Although the nations themselves are in many ways very different from the United States, with the exception of India, their constitutions reveal one fact of overriding significance: as in the United States, local authorities play a considerable role in foreign affairs. For context, we begin with a bit of background on each.

---

12. *See id.* at 921.

13. *See* THOMAS FLEINER, RECENT DEVELOPMENTS IN SWISS FEDERALISM 4 (2000).

14. *See Printz*, 521 U.S. at 977 (Breyer, J., dissenting).

15. These are Argentina, Australia, Austria, Belgium, Bosnia and Herzegovina, Brazil, Canada, Comoros, Ethiopia, Germany, India, Malaysia, Mexico, the Federated States of Micronesia, Nigeria, Pakistan, Russia, St. Kitts and Nevis, Serbia, Montenegro, South Africa, Spain, Switzerland, UAE, United States, and Venezuela.

A. Switzerland

The Swiss Federation lies in the center of Europe, bounded by Germany, France, Italy, Austria, and Liechtenstein. It has four official languages: German, French, Italian, and Romansch.[16] The principal ethnic groups are German (65 percent), French (18 percent), Italian (10 percent), and Romansch (1 percent). Principal religious groups are Roman Catholic (38.2 percent), Protestant (26.9 percent), Muslim (4.9 percent), other Christian denominations (5.7 percent), and none (21.4 percent).[17] Its population is about 8 million, 74 percent of which lives in urban areas.[18] Its per capita GDP is $58,100, ranking it fifteenth in the world.[19] Its 2014 unemployment rate was 3.2 percent.[20]

Switzerland "was founded in 1291 as a defensive alliance among three cantons."[21] Today it is "similar in structure to a federal republic."[22] The federal government is bicameral: the Federal Assembly consists of the National Council (similar to the U.S. House of Representatives) and the Council of States (similar to the U.S. Senate).[23] The executive is unique. The Federal Assembly elects a seven-person body called the Federal Council, one of whom is annually chosen as president.[24] Below the federal government are twenty-six cantons, with governmental structures similar to the federal government except for three significant differences. "[T]he cantonal executives are elected directly by the people" rather than by members of the assembly.[25] Also, most cantonal governments are unicameral.[26] Finally, municipal citizenship is fundamental; cities exercise broader legal authority than in the United States.[27]

---

16. *See* CIA World Factbook: Switzerland, https://www.cia.gov/library/publications/resources/the-world-factbook/geos/sz.html (last visited Nov. 20, 2015).

17. *Id.*

18. *Id.*

19. *Id.*

20. *Id.*

21. *Id.*

22. *Id.*

23. *Id.*

24. *Id.*

25. Paul C. Bauer, Markus Freitag & Pascal Sciarini, Political Trust in Switzerland: Again a Special Case? 6 (Dec. 20, 2013), *available at* http://papers.ssrn.com/sol3/papers.cfm? abstract_id=2471152.

26. *Id.*

27. *Id.* at 4-6.

Article 3 of the Swiss constitution is rather like the U.S. Constitution's Tenth Amendment. It provides that the "Cantons are sovereign except to the extent that their sovereignty is limited by the Federal Constitution. They exercise all rights that are not vested in the Confederation."[28] The Swiss constitution then proceeds to spell out the powers of the federal government, but because residual powers subsist in the cantons, those powers are not detailed in the constitution. Switzerland's federal courts invalidate cantonal laws inconsistent with federal law, although judicial review does not extend to "[a]cts of the Federal Assembly or the Federal Council."[29] Its constitution, however, gives considerably more power to the cantons in the realm of foreign affairs than the U.S. Constitution gives to the states.[30]

Article 54 of the Federal Constitution of the Swiss Confederation, which concerns foreign relations, provides that "[f]oreign relations are the responsibility of the Confederation."[31] Article 184 makes the Federal Council "responsible for foreign relations, subject to the right of participation of the Federal Assembly; it represents Switzerland abroad."[32] "It signs and ratifies international treaties. It submits them to the Federal Assembly for approval."[33] Federal powers predominate in the realm of national defense. The Confederation is required under Article 54 to "ensure that the independence of Switzerland and its welfare is safeguarded . . . ,"[34] and Article 185 makes the Federal Council responsible for both external and internal security, subject to specified limits.[35]

The constitution also requires, however, that the Confederation "respect the powers of the Cantons and protect their interests."[36] Article 55 requires, specifically, that the cantons "be consulted on foreign policy decisions that affect their powers or their essential interests" and that they be informed "fully and in good time . . . ."[37] If their powers are affected in particular cases, "the Cantons shall

---

28. BUNDESVERFASSUNG DER SCHWEIZERISCHEN EIDGENOSSENSCHAFT [BV] [CONSTITUTION] Apr. 18, 1999, SR 101, art. 3 (Switz.).

29. *Id.* art. 189(4)

30. *See id.* art. 55; *id.* art. 56.

31. *Id.* art. 54.

32. *Id.* art. 184.

33. *Id.*

34. *Id.* art. 54.

35. *Id.* art. 185.

36. *Id.* art. 54.

37. *Id.* art. 55.

participate in international negotiations in an appropriate manner."[38] Article 56 permits a canton to "conclude treaties with foreign states on matters that lie within the scope of its powers."[39] Such treaties may not, however, "conflict with the law or the interests of the Confederation, or with the law of any other Cantons."[40] A canton "may deal directly with lower ranking foreign authorities; in other cases, the Confederation shall conduct relations with foreign states on behalf of a Canton."[41] And some treaties must be approved by a vote of both the cantons and the people, including those concerning "accession to organisations for collective security or to supranational communities."[42]

B. Canada

Canada is bounded only by the United States. It has two official languages, English and French. Principal ethnic groups are Canadian (32.2 percent), English (19.8 percent), French (15.5 percent), Scottish (14.4 percent), Irish (13.8 percent), German (9.8 percent), Italian (4.5 percent), Chinese (4.5 percent), North American Indian (4.2 percent), and other (50.9 percent).[43] Principal religious groups are Catholic (40.6 percent), Protestant (20.3 percent), and none (24 percent).[44] Its population is about 35 million, 81.8 percent of which lives in urban areas.[45] Its per capita GDP is $45,000, ranking it 29th in the world.[46] Its 2014 unemployment rate was 6.9 percent.[47]

Canada is a parliamentary democracy and member of the British Commonwealth.[48] The prime minister is chosen from among members of his or her party who sit in Parliament. Parliament is bicameral, with a Senate and House of Commons.[49] Canada comprises ten provinces and three territories.[50]

---

38. *Id.*

39. *Id.* art. 56.

40. *Id.*

41. *Id.*

42. *Id.* art. 140.

43. CIA World Factbook: Canada, https://www.cia.gov/library/publications/resources/the-world-factbook/geos/ca.html (last visited Nov. 20, 2015).

44. *Id.*

45. *Id.*

46. *Id.*

47. *Id.*

48. *Id.*

49. *Id.*

50. *Id.*

Rules governing the allocation of foreign affairs powers between the provinces and federal government cannot be neatly identified because the Canadian constitution is a mix of "unwritten and written acts, customs, judicial decisions, and traditions dating from 1763."[51] Nonetheless, it is clear that residual powers are left with the federal government.[52] Treaty-making is a federal executive prerogative and does not require parliamentary approval.[53] Only the provinces, however, may enact implementing legislation within their jurisdictions. Before signing a treaty involving one of the provinces, the federal government negotiates with that province in an effort to obtain its cooperation and approval.[54] And "[a]lthough provinces may not make full-fledged treaties, they have entered into international agreements in areas of provincial jurisdiction."[55]

C. Germany

The Federal Republic of Germany also lies in the center of Europe, bounded by the Netherlands, Poland, and Denmark and the North and Baltic Seas. German is the only official language. The principal ethnic group is German (91.5 percent).[56] Principal religious groups are Protestant (34 percent), Roman Catholic (34 percent), Muslim (3.7 percent), and none (28.3 percent).[57] Its population is about 81 million, 75 percent of which lives in urban areas.[58] Its per capita GDP is $46,200, ranking it 27th in the world.[59] Its 2014 unemployment rate was 5 percent.[60]

Germany, initially united in the nineteenth century under Chancellor Otto von Bismarck, was reunified in 1990 after forty-five years of division.[61] Today, it is a federal republic. The federal government is bicameral: the Parliament "consists

51. *See id.*

52. *See* Ronald Watts, Comparing Federal Systems (3d ed. 2008).

53. 1 A Global Dialogue on Federalism: Constitutional Origins, Structure, and Change in Federal Countries 126 (John Kincaid & Alan Tarr eds., 2005).

54. *Id.*

55. *Id.*

56. CIA World Factbook: Germany, https://www.cia.gov/library/publications/the-world-factbook/geos/gm.html (last visited Nov. 20, 2015).

57. *Id.*

58. *Id.*

59. *Id.*

60. *Id.*

61. *See id.*

of the Federal Council, or Bundesrat, . . . and the Federal Diet, or Bundestag."[62] The Bundestag is popularly elected; members of the Bundesrat are appointed by sixteen state governments, or landtags.[63] The Chancellor is head of government and is elected by a majority of the Parliament.[64] Below the federal government are the Länders.

The German constitution, or Basic Law, provides in Article 32 that "[r]elations with foreign states shall be conducted by the Federation."[65] Article 73 makes clear that that such power resides exclusively with the federal government: "The Federation shall have exclusive legislative power with respect to . . . foreign affairs and defence, including protection of the civilian population."[66] Article 59 specifies that "the Federal President shall represent the Federation for the purposes of international law. He shall conclude treaties with foreign states on behalf of the Federation. He shall accredit and receive envoys." Article 30, however, makes the authority of the Länder the default position: it provides that "[e]xcept as otherwise provided or permitted by this Basic Law, the exercise of state powers and the discharge of state functions is a matter for the Länder. Consultation with the Länder is required "[b]efore the conclusion of a treaty affecting the special circumstances of [one]. . . . "[67] The Länder may—insofar as it has power to legislate—"conclude treaties with foreign states with the consent of the Federal Government."[68] A special new provision, Article 23, governs the participation of the Länder in the European Union.[69]

D. India

India lies, on the north, between Burma and Pakistan, and is bordered on the south by the Arabian Sea and the Bay of Bengal. India has sixteen official languages.[70] The principal ethnic groups are Indo-Aryan (72 percent), Dravidian

62. *Id.*

63. *Id.*

64. *Id.*

65. GRUDGESETZ FÜR DIE BUNDESREPUBLIK DEUTSCHLAND [GRUDGESETZ] [CONSTITUTION] May 23, 1949, art. 32 (Ger.).

66. *See id.* art. 73.

67. *See id.* art. 32.

68. *Id.*

69. *Id.* art. 23.

70. CIA World Factbook: India, https://www.cia.gov/library/publications/resources/the-world-factbook/geos/in.html (last visited Nov. 20, 2015).

(25 percent), and other (3 percent).[71] Principal religious groups are Hindu (79.8 percent), Muslim (14.2 percent), and Christian (2.3 percent).[72] Its population is about 1.25 billion, 32.7 percent of which lives in urban areas.[73] Its per capita GDP is $5,800, ranking it 160th in the world.[74] Its 2014 unemployment rate was 7.3 percent.[75]

It is a federal republic.[76] The "bicameral Parliament[,] or Sansad[,] consists of [a] Council of States, or Rajya Sabha," with "12 members appointed by the president" and 233 "indirectly elected by state and territorial assemblies," as well as a "Peoples' Assembly[,] or Lok Sabha," which consists of two members appointed by the president and 543 directly elected from single-seat constituencies.[77] The head of government, the prime minister, is elected by members of the majority party in parliament.[78] India has twenty-nine states and seven union territories.[79]

As in Canada, another Commonwealth country, residual powers rest in the federal government.[80] India's 471-page constitution appears to give the federal government virtually exclusive control over foreign relations. The central government is not constitutionally bound to consult states on matters of foreign policy.[81] The states have no role in treaty negotiations. Even if a majority of states oppose the federal government, it is not required to take their opposition into account.[82] States require permission from the Union to conclude agreements.[83]

---

71. *Id.*

72. *Id.*

73. *Id.*

74. *Id.*

75. *Id.*

76. *Id.*

77. *Id.*

78. *Id.*

79. *Id.*

80. FEDERAL SYSTEMS OF THE WORLD: A HANDBOOK OF FEDERAL, CONFEDERAL, AND AUTONOMY ARRANGEMENTS (Daniel J. Elazar ed., 2d ed. 1994).

81. Amitabh Mattoo & Happymon Jacob, *Republic of India*, *in* FOREIGN RELATIONS IN FEDERAL COUNTRIES 166, 173 (Hans Michelmann ed., 2009).

82. *Id.*

83. *Id.*

III. Making Versus Interpreting a Constitution

This brief survey shows that the United States is not alone in according state and local governments a good deal of authority in the realm of foreign affairs. But, again, so cursory a review cannot begin to reveal how the federalism principles of the nations surveyed above actually operate in practice. It does not unmask conflicts that have arisen between local and national authorities, why such tensions have arisen, or how they have been resolved. It does not begin to consider how foreign affairs federalism has worked in actual practice. For answers to these and the many other questions that arise in assessing the efficacy of other nations' constitutional structures, careful and extensive research would be required. A textual provision in any nation's constitution can look very different than the rule that actually prevails in its workaday world. This is true even in the United States. The proverbial Martian emerging from a flying saucer might have no idea, reading only the Constitution's Reception Clause,[84] that from it has sprung the president's exclusive power of recognition,[85] or that a vast array of cases explain the meaning of the Commerce,[86] Due Process,[87] and Equal Protection Clauses[88]—but that virtually no cases illuminate the meaning of the Guarantee Clause,[89] or the Double Offices Clause,[90] or the Accounts Clause.[91] In fact, viewing the constitutional text by itself, the Martian might well have no inkling that the U.S. Constitution's greatest contribution to the jurisprudence of the rule of law in other nations has likely been the doctrine of judicial review—or that many of the most heated debates over its meaning have occurred in recent years over a word that appears nowhere in its text: "privacy." For all these reasons, a reader might doubt whether knowing the bare-bones constitutional provisions of other countries sheds much useful light on hard-and-fast, concrete foreign-affairs federalism controversies in the United States.

Why, then, consider other nations' experience *at all*? It is, after all, the interpretation of the U.S. Constitution that is at issue. Why not conclude, as the Supreme

84. U.S. CONST. art. II, § 3, cl. 4.

85. *See* Zivotofsky v. Kerry, 132 S. Ct. 2076 (2015).

86. U.S. CONST. art. I, § 8, cl. 3.

87. *Id.* amend. XIV, § 1.

88. *Id.*

89. *Id.* art. IV, § 4, cl. 1.

90. *Id.* art. I, § 6, cl. 2.

91. *Id.* art. I, § 9, cl. 7.

Court did in *Printz v. United States*, that the experience of other nations is irrelevant to constitutional interpretation? "We think such comparative analysis inappropriate to the task of interpreting a constitution," the Court said, "though it was of course quite relevant to the task of writing one."[92]

The reason is that, however attractive this view may be in theory, a hermetic distinction between writing and interpreting a constitution ultimately turns out to be untenable in practice. To interpret a constitution, one must inevitably consider many of the same sources that were considered by those who wrote it. Experience is one such source. The experience of the newly independent colonies under the Articles of Confederation, discussed in Chapter 1, weighed heavily on the minds of the Framers in curbing the powers of state governments. When the Supreme Court passes upon disputes concerning where power currently resides, it regularly takes into account how powers have divided in actual practice. Its decision in *Zivotofsky v. Kerry*[93] is but the most recent example.[94] The Court's practice of looking to custom as a reality test for resolving federalism cases evinces the same real-world pragmatism. Its frequent inquiry into whether a given activity falls within a realm of "traditional state competence"[95] provides a series of examples. In these and other realms, U.S. constitutional jurisprudence has in modern times been guided by one of the most important, and most accurate, insights into how law works: Holmes's famous dictum that "[t]he life of the law has not been logic: it has been experience."[96]

Why should interpreters of a constitution, in the United States or any other country, educate themselves to the benefits of a given practice in their own countries but blind themselves to the benefits of that practice in another country? Assuming two equally plausible interpretations of a given constitutional provision, why ought modern-day interpreters not take into account that one has met with abysmal failure everywhere it has been tried but that the other has been smashingly successful? The answer that the Constitution requires the interpreter to proceed in ignorance, without considering the empirical evidence available, can flow only from blinkered ideology, disconnected from experience and wedded to

---

92. *See* Printz v. United States, 521 U.S 898, 921 n.11 (1997).

93. *See* Zivotofsky v. Kerry, 132 S. Ct. 2076 (2015).

94. *See generally* MICHAEL J. GLENNON, CONSTITUTIONAL DIPLOMACY (1990); Curtis Bradley & Trevor Morrison, *Historical Gloss and the Separation of Powers*, 126 HARV. L. REV. 411 (2012); Alison L. LaCroix, *Historical Gloss: A Primer*, 126 HARV. L. REV. FORUM 75 (2013); Michael J. Glennon, *The Use of Custom in Resolving Separation of Powers Disputes*, 64 B.U. L. REV. 109 (1984).

95. *See* Hess v. United States, 361 U.S. 314, 328 (1960).

96. OLIVER WENDELL HOLMES, JR., THE COMMON LAW 1 (1881).

a misguided fidelity to abstract provisions frozen in time—provisions too general, in themselves, to resolve matters in controversy. The Framers, all know, were dazzlingly gifted in many respects, but as Robert Dahl has pointed out,[97] there were things that they simply could not know—the future and the lessons future experience would impart, at home and abroad. This book has proceeded on the premise that in interpreting the Constitution and assessing its operation, the contextual lessons of history and experience are indispensable.

97. Robert A. Dahl, How Democratic Is the American Constitution? 7–10 (2003).

Table of Cases

A

B

C

D

E

F

G

H

I

J

K

L

M

N

R

S

T

U

V

W

X

Y

Z

Index

www.ingramcontent.com/pod-product-compliance
Ingram Content Group UK Ltd.
Pitfield, Milton Keynes, MK11 3LW, UK
UKHW020843150926
475595UK00004B/132

9 780199 941490